MANAGEMENT OF NEW ENTERPRISES

MANAGEMENT OF NEW ENTERPRISES

A Casebook of
Problems on the Establishment and
Operation of New Businesses

LYNN L. BOLLINGER, D.C.S.
ASSOCIATE PROFESSOR OF BUSINESS ADMINISTRATION
GRADUATE SCHOOL OF BUSINESS ADMINISTRATION
HARVARD UNIVERSITY

JOHN S. DAY, M.B.A.
ASSISTANT PROFESSOR OF RESEARCH IN BUSINESS ADMINISTRATION
GRADUATE SCHOOL OF BUSINESS ADMINISTRATION
HARVARD UNIVERSITY

1954
RICHARD D. IRWIN, INC.
HOMEWOOD, ILLINOIS

First Printing, January, 1954

PRINTED IN THE UNITED STATES OF AMERICA

Acknowledgments

The cases in this book are based on material made available by a large number of independent businessmen. Without the confidential information and valuable time which they so generously contributed, this casebook could not have been written.

Professor Myles Mace was responsible for the original impetus which culminated in this book being prepared. A number of the older cases were either prepared under his direction or written by him. We appreciate his initial effort and permission to use some of the material for this book. Our appreciation is also extended to several other members of the Faculty of the Harvard Graduate School of Business Administration. Professor H. R. Tosdal and Assistant Professors T. J. Raymond and J. R. Surface each contributed a case for the book.

Mr. T. F. Bradshaw and Mr. Joseph Davis also prepared several of the cases. In particular, we wish to recognize the contribution of Messrs. D. R. Booz, F. G. Secrest, and C. D. Howell, who handled the field research and drafts for some of the cases.

We sincerely appreciate the work done by Miss Lois DeAndrade, who cheerfully and tirelessly performed the typing and innumerable other details necessary to the successful completion of a work of this kind.

The case entitled "The Von Hoff Research Company" is based on material originally prepared and copyrighted by Harbridge House, Inc. The "Yankee Assemblers, Inc." case was also prepared by Harbridge House, Inc., for use by the U.S. Air Force. Both cases are used by permission. Except for these two, the cases in this book are copyrighted by the President and Fellows of Harvard College and used with their permission.

Despite the assistance received in the preparation of the volume, all cases have been edited, revised, or written by the authors. Accordingly, we accept full responsibility for the contents of this volume.

LYNN L. BOLLINGER
JOHN S. DAY

GRADUATE SCHOOL OF BUSINESS ADMINISTRATION
HARVARD UNIVERSITY
November 1, 1953

Table of Contents

PART V. DEVELOPMENT OF THE NEW AND GROWING ORGANIZATION

INDEX OF CASES

What Is a New Enterprise Case?

The cases in this book have been selected to develop through classroom discussion the student's ability to evaluate new enterprise opportunities and to make intelligent management decisions. They are not designed to illustrate either correct or incorrect business procedures.

A prime purpose is to help the student attain perspective and judgment to determine whether any of the new enterprise opportunities he may later encounter realistically fit his own business aptitudes, objectives, and resources. Throughout, he is encouraged to take a highly subjective viewpoint. "How would I handle that problem? Is this a situation I could master—now, or later in my business career? Is this the kind of business life I want?" When the student asks himself these questions as applied to the specific case situations, he should gain some comprehension of the different way of life commonly faced by the individual who undertakes the risks and responsibilities of managing a new enterprise.

Cases involving inherent elements of failure, as well as of success, are presented to develop both an understanding of common pitfalls and a capacity to appraise probabilities of success. The objective is not to disillusion but to encourage those who have the requisite ability and ambition for new venture. Accordingly, the real rewards and satisfactions inherent in such activity should not be overlooked through analytical emphasis on the obvious difficulties.

Another objective of more than secondary importance is that of developing understanding and judgment on the part of those who may never participate directly in the management of a new enterprise but who will, in all probability, have frequent occasion to deal with new businesses. A capacity to determine the probability of success of a new venture is important to most businessmen as they are called upon to consider investment opportunities, credit risks, procurement policies, and evaluation of new companies as potential customers.

The approach to these cases, even for those students who do not contemplate active participation in a new enterprise, should not be that of a third party merely making an analytical critique. The objective, rather, is for the student to place himself realistically in the position of the top administrator and to develop a capacity to determine what can be done to produce successful results in situations where managerial action can be decisive.

The case material is presented under the following headings:

I. Starting a New Enterprise with a New Product
II. Starting a New Enterprise with an Existing Product
III. Acquisition and Development of Established Organizations
IV. New Enterprise Financing
V. Development of the New and Growing Organization

Five conditions distinguish the new enterprise case:

1. *The factor of innovation,* the untried element which makes the enterprise "new" relative to the experience of the individual, creates a challenge and risks beyond those normally faced in established companies. For example, the young war veteran who acquired an established soft-drink bottling plant in the Red Rock Bottling Company case was embarking upon an enterprise that involved for him a major element of innovation. If, however, he had already had many years of experience with the problems of setting up Red Rock Cola distribution in new communities or if he had continued with the same organization and old product line of the plant he bought, the lessened extent of his personal venture into the untried would have eliminated its consideration here.

2. *Reliance upon one key man* and his business judgment is characteristic. One or at most a few men carry the full responsibility and must handle individually—and often simultaneously—the full range of "departmental" problems. Moreover, limitations in experience, in available time, and in finances commonly create conditions in which crucial decisions must be made rapidly and without elaborate investigation. In general, when a business has become sufficiently well established so that experienced administrators have been assigned to each of the major departmental functions or when the company has evolved an experienced staff as well as a line organization, it may be considered beyond this entrepreneurial environment.

3. *Financial independence,* together with full responsibility for the adequancy and management of capital resources, is an essential part of the challenge. The problems include determination of financial requirements, the raising of funds and the maintenance of financial resilience in the face of organizational inexperience, and the inevitable uncertainties of new enterprise.

4. *The full gamut of administrative problems* must usually be considered even though the initial phases of the venture may involve only a few individuals. The long-range objective is usually the development of

a business of sufficient stature to require the building of an integrated organization. Questions of planning, timing, and human relationships are, therefore, important in these cases. Thousands of other new ventures and small businesses, ranging from candy stores to uranium prospecting, are of real importance to the national economy but may not involve the degree of administrative challenge or the scope of management responsibilities being considered here. The real consideration is, not so much the size of the initial venture, but rather the intent and objectives of the key individuals.

5. *Growth and rapid evolution* complicate the administrative environment. The conception and birth of the new enterprise mark but the beginning of the problems considered. Those problems particularly associated with new enterprise cover an adolescent period that may last for a number of years, during which rapid and basic changes must be anticipated. While the fundamental business administrative problems may be objectively identical to those encountered in long-established companies, they may at the same time be subjectively quite different to the new entrepreneur as the result of the interaction of untried elements and the pressure of uncertainty upon the entire organization. Whether the difference should be termed one of kind or one of degree is not so important as is the fact of emergence of a very real set of characteristic problems for the man who undertakes a new enterprise.

A word about the case system may prove helpful to the student accustomed primarily to lectures and textbooks. A typical case seldom presents all the facts the student might like to have to guide his decision. It frequently presents solely the presumed facts, opinions, and points of view held by one or more of the people involved, and hence leaves those discussing the case with only the information that the persons in the actual situation possessed at the time. The student must recognize that just such severe limitations as to factual data and as to the time available for the decision-making process commonly characterize the actions of businessmen in general—and of the new entrepreneur in particular.

These cases generally involve highly debatable alternative courses of action, as is true for the day-to-day business problems they typify. Indeed, experienced businessmen frequently demonstrate their ability to solve an identical problem successfully in different ways. The cases thus do not necessarily lead to a single "right" answer upon which the class and the instructor are expected to reach unanimous agreement. In fact, some of the discussions most conducive to the development of penetrating analysis and balanced judgment may at first leave the student with a feeling of frustration, since no uniformity of class opinion may have resulted. The purpose of the case has been served if it provokes intelligent discussion, independent thinking, and progress toward the ability to make sound, well-considered decisions.

PART I

STARTING A NEW ENTERPRISE WITH A NEW PRODUCT

Ski Bike

When William Sweeney was separated from the Army with the rank of major early in January, 1946, he was considering whether (1) to return to the Harvard Business School for one semester to complete the requirements for the M.B.A. degree, (2) to accept a position as head of the new business department in a bank in Minneapolis, Minnesota, or (3) to accept the proposal of Mr. Sam White and Mr. Ray Stone to assume responsibility for producing and selling a patented winter recreation device carrying the trade name "Ski Bike."

Mr. Sweeney was graduated from Davidson College in June, 1940, with the B.S. degree and a reserve commission as a second lieutenant in the United States Army. While in college, Mr. Sweeney played varsity tennis for three years and was cocaptain of the tennis team during his senior year. In addition, he was an active member of a national social fraternity, an honorary language fraternity, and an honorary military fraternity. In May, 1940, he was elected to Phi Beta Kappa. Upon graduation he applied for admission to the Harvard Business School, and in one of the letters of recommendation he was described as "personable, aggressive, gregarious, and an independent thinker." Mr. Sweeney's father, a minister, could not provide more than nominal financial assistance for his son's further education; but with the award of a regional alumni scholarship, Mr. Sweeney entered the Business School in the fall of 1940. Since the scholarship covered tuition expense only, it was necessary for him to borrow money and to work as a student waiter. He had completed three semesters of the four-semester course when in January, 1942, he was called to active duty with the United States Army. In June, 1942, he married a girl from his home town.

When Mr. Sweeney entered the service, he intended to return to Harvard, complete the work for his degree, and accept employment in some large, well-established business. This seemed to be the assured security he wanted. During the four years Mr. Sweeney served in the Army, however, he gave more and more thought to what he really wanted to do in life. Although he felt that his choice of alternatives was somewhat limited by the responsibilities of his wife and one child, he became convinced that his happiness, as well as his business success, depended upon "being his own boss."

Late in December, 1945, Mr. Sweeney received a telephone call from Mr. White, a Harvard Business School graduate with whom he had worked while in the service. Mr. White mentioned his relatively recent association with a Mr. Stone, who had designed and secured patents on the Ski Bike, and then described a situation which seemed to offer a very attractive opportunity. Although Mr. Sweeney had no experience in business, the description of the Ski Bike and an invitation to discuss the development of such a product appealed to him immediately.

During the middle thirties, Mr. Stone had owned and operated a trucking service in the Pittsburgh area; but a diverting interest in inventions, combined with strong local trucking competition, led to the failure of the business. Thereafter, and as the result of his service work in connecting gas heaters and gas stoves, Mr. Stone invented the Surelock gas connector. After securing patents on this device, he began production in a small way in a three-car garage. During this time Mr. Stone was assisted by his sister Helen, who handled the administrative details and shared profits on a partnership basis. The demand for the connectors increased, and Mr. Stone found it necessary to transfer the operations to a leased three-story building previously used as a pickle factory. In July, 1944, Mr. Stone exercised his option to purchase the building. By this time, 24 people were employed and the company had accumulated a moderate financial reserve. While he was happy to receive help from his sister, Mr. Stone felt that the business was growing to a size which required the services of an organizer and administrator, someone to relieve him of the management problems so that he could devote more time to his inventions and other necessary developmental work.

In July, 1945, Mr. Stone asked Mr. Sam White to become a copartner in the Stone Company and to devote full time to managing the business in return for a one-third interest in the partnership profits. Mr. White graduated from Pennsylvania State College in 1938 and from the Harvard Business School in 1940. He was called to active duty with the Air Force in June, 1940, and was discharged on points in July, 1945. Mr. White separated from the service as a lieutenant colonel and moved his family to Pittsburgh to commence work with the Stone Company.

Soon after starting to work, Mr. White discovered several patents and patent applications which seemed to him to have real merit. He was particularly impressed with the possibilities of the patent application for the Ski Bike (Exhibit 1). The Ski Bike consisted of a bicycle tubing frame mounted on two hickory skis each 5 inches wide. On the bottom of each ski was a steel keel 18 inches long, ½ inch deep, and ½ inch wide. This keel was attached to prevent skidding as the bike was steered by the rider. The Ski Bike was 36 inches long and weighed 12¾ pounds, including an 8-inch-wide marine plywood seat. A footrest was fastened on the opposite sides of the steering column. The Ski Bike combined the sports of skiing, sliding, and bike riding. Mr. White believed that the Ski Bike would be used by adults as well as by children old enough to ride bicycles.

Exhibit 1

PHOTOGRAPH OF SKI BIKE

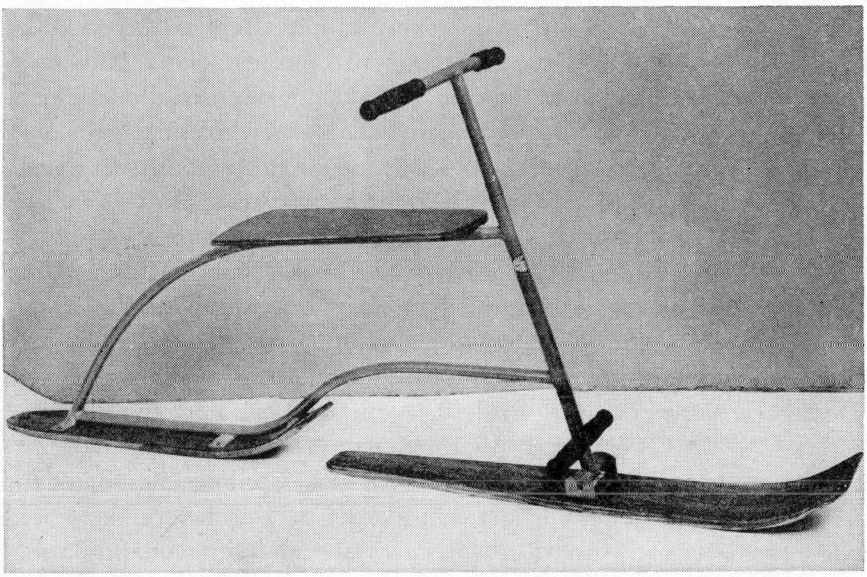

Although no patent had been granted covering the Ski Bike idea, applications had been filed in 1944–45 covering basic patentable concepts. Mr. Stone's primary search disclosed that no patent of this nature had ever been applied for in the United States but that an Austrian patent had been granted in 1889 on a similar device. The Austrian patent, however, provided for control of direction by means of a steel rudder fastened to the end of the rear ski. In the opinion of patent attorneys in Pittsburgh, this patent did not preclude the validity of Mr. Stone's idea.

After a brief discussion of the business prospects of the Ski Bike, Mr. Stone and Mr. White decided to produce a few Ski Bikes for the 1945 Christmas trade; and they agreed to hire 15 new employees to work on this project. Accordingly, in September, 1945, 10 men and 5 women employees began production of Ski Bikes. Because of existing production setups for the Surelock connector and for costume jewelry, the manufacture of the Ski Bike had to be divided between the second and third floors of the company's building.

Some procurement problems were encountered. Although steel tubing could be easily and quickly purchased from small companies in the area, rubber handle grips and hickory skis were difficult to find. The first order for 400 sets of formed but unbent and unfinished hickory skis cost $1.65 a set. The second order of 600 sets cost $1.50 a set, but a later order of 600 sets was obtained for $1.00 a set. Mr. Stone and Mr. White believed the $1.00 price to be fair and reasonable.

Requests for bids on handle-bar and footrest grips were sent to eight of the largest rubber molded-parts manufacturers. Replies offered sets of 2 grips at prices varying from 11 cents to 18 cents per set. This price did not satisfy the partners, who then phoned a small manufacturer of rubber products. This latter company offered a wholesale price of 5 cents per set, and a contract was made for 200,000 sets. At this time, identical bicycle handle-bar grips were being sold at retail in Pittsburgh bicycle sporting goods stores for 15 cents each, or 30 cents a pair.

Because of the importance of testing the market for Ski Bikes during the Christmas buying season, Mr. Stone and Mr. White decided to distribute the bikes through a few of the manufacturers' agents who sold the Surelock connector. As the bikes were produced in November and December, shipments were made to agents in New York, Detroit, and Hollywood. By Christmas, 1945, each of these agents had received 200 Ski Bikes. It was expected that retailers would sell the Ski Bikes for $19.95, thus providing a 40 per cent margin to the retailer, who would pay $11.97 for each bike. Rather than waste time in negotiating a special commission basis for the manufacturers agents, separate from that given on the connector product, Mr. Stone and Mr. White adopted the existing manufacturers-agents' margin of 15 per cent. On all deliveries the transportation costs were paid by the retailers, thus shading what they regarded as their customary 40 per cent margin on sporting goods. The manufacturers agents had no trouble in selling their quota of Ski Bikes. In New York, Abercrombie and Fitch and Macy's department stores bought as many bikes as they could get and asked for more. Shortly before Christmas, each store was receiving 6 Ski Bikes daily; and within a few hours after these were placed on the selling floor, all were sold.

Early in December, Mr. Giles, a resort owner in Canada, called Mr. Stone to say that he had heard about the Ski Bike and wished to request as many bikes as he could get. Mr. Stone agreed to send him 100, payment for which was received in Pittsburgh three days after the phone call. In a subsequent conversation, Mr. Giles requested 10 per cent of all Ski Bikes produced for the 1946–47 season, as well as an exclusive license for their sale in Canada.

Mr. Stone and Mr. White were surprised at the market reception to the Ski Bike and, after discussing plans for increased production, concluded that they should employ a full-time businessman to carry the entire responsibility for the Ski Bike venture. Mr. White suggested his Army acquaintance, Mr. Sweeney, for the job. During the past four months, Mr. Stone had spent most of his time directing the production of the Ski Bikes. However, he wanted to return to his primary interest in the development of new patentable products. Mr. White also felt that he could not handle the management responsibilities of the Stone Company satisfactorily if he devoted the time necessary to develop the Ski Bike business.

At the invitation of Mr. Stone and Mr. White, Mr. Sweeney went to Pittsburgh early in January, 1946, to discuss his interest in the project. The two partners proposed to Mr. Sweeney that he join their group and come to Pittsburgh immediately to direct and supervise all phases of the Ski Bike production and sales. It was tentatively agreed that Mr. Sweeney be paid 33⅓ per cent of net profits. Money necessary to finance the project would be provided by Mr. Stone and Mr. White. Mr. Sweeney was urged to make whatever investigations he desired and to come to a decision within two weeks so that other men could be considered for the job should Mr. Sweeney decline.

Mr. White took Mr. Sweeney through the existing production process and provided estimated cost figures per Ski Bike on a volume basis, as shown in Exhibit 2. Mr. White pointed out that these cost figures were merely estimates, inasmuch as the company had no cost accounting system, but he felt that the calculations were fairly accurate. Labor,

Exhibit 2

ESTIMATED TOTAL COST FOR ONE SKI BIKE

Labor	$2.00
Steel tubing at 5 cents per foot	1.00
Overhead	1.00
Rubber grips (set of 4)	0.10
Plywood seat	0.18
Hickory skis	1.00
Steel keels (2)	0.10
Name stamp	0.35
Brass rod	0.10
Cardboard packing box	0.35
Total	$6.18

for example, was paid $1.00 an hour for an 8-hour day. At the present time, approximately 60 Ski Bikes were produced daily. Fifteen employees, working 8 hours a day, represented a daily labor cost of $120.00. This amount divided by the number of Ski Bikes produced resulted in the estimated labor cost per bike of $2.00.

Several production problems which earlier had slowed down the output were now believed to be satisfactorily solved. The company had some difficulty during November with the ski bending processes. The formed but unbent skis, as purchased, were soaked or steamed in standard commercial solutions and then bent by placing a clamp over the ends and holding the clamp in place with a heavy timber. At first, 30 per cent of the skis thus processed broke under the strain, but further experimentation with soaking times and solutions reduced the breakage rate to 20 per cent. Finally, a suggestion by one of the workers that plain water be used as a soaking solution was adopted, and it was found that the breakage dropped to about 10 per cent. This rate appeared to be about as low as could be expected.

As Mr. Sweeney walked through the production process, he noticed several ways in which output could be increased without involving additional machines and personnel. For example, he believed that, by rearranging the manufacturing procedures of the Surelock connectors, all production of Ski Bikes could be accomplished on one floor of the building. Also, the simple spot welding and assembly required on Ski Bikes could be routed through an elementary production line.

Before Mr. Sweeney made any decision on whether to join this company, he wanted to check the potential market for an article of this kind. While in the Army, he had become acquainted with several purchasing agents representing large chains of automobile accessory stores; he believed that these people could appraise the market possibilities of the Ski Bike. Accordingly, he took one of the Ski Bikes to Akron, Ohio, for their inspection. Their immediate response was very encouraging. One purchasing agent said: "If you can sell this to us at a price so that we can retail it at $14.95, allowing a 35 per cent margin to the retailer and a 20 per cent margin to us, we will place an immediate order for at least 10,000 and possibly more." Another purchasing agent stated that he would buy 10,000 on the same terms and further suggested that he "take the bike to the large mail-order houses" if they really wanted sales volume.

Mr. Sweeney felt that he had made as much of an investigation as possible within the limited time available, and he returned to Pittsburgh to give his decision to Mr. Stone and Mr. White.

Ellings Company

The Ellings Company, established in a medium-size New England city, manufactured a 2-ounce bass and trout lure for light fishing tackle. The lure was marketed under the name "Blu-Oreno," and distribution was confined to the state in which the company was located. In February, 1953, the Ellings Company was considering an offer made by the Miracle Minnow Company, a national manufacturer of fishing lures and equipment, to purchase all rights to the Blu-Oreno for a price of $2,800.

Mr. Ellings, the senior partner of the firm, was a corporation lawyer by profession; but he made a hobby of fishing and spent much of his spare time experimenting with fishing equipment in his workshop, which contained a lathe and a tank in which the actions of various lures in water could be studied. Ninety-five per cent of the lures sold in the United States were made by Middle Western manufacturers, distributing on a national scale, and Mr. Ellings believed that their lures were not equally well adapted to all sections of the country in which they were sold. Consequently, he had been interested in designing a lure which would be particularly effective in local waters, and after two years of careful study and experimentation he developed the Blu-Oreno. It was made of hard pine wood, weighed about 2 ounces, and was fitted with a patented metal head which gave it a distinctive spinning and wiggling motion as it was pulled through the water.

Mr. Ellings had originally intended the lure for his own use. During the fishing season[1] in 1951, however, he constructed a number of lures in his workshop and gave them to his fishermen friends. These men found the lure to be unusually effective, and at their suggestion Mr. Ellings decided to place it on the market in the 1952 season.

At that time, there were about 14 national manufacturers selling bass and trout lures in the state. These firms sold to wholesalers, who, in turn, distributed the lures to retail, hardware, sporting goods, variety, and general stores. In addition, the manufacturers occasionally sold direct to variety chains and to mail-order houses such as Sears Roebuck

[1] Technically, the trout season was open from April 15 to July 31 and the bass season from July 1 to February 15. For commercial purposes, however, the season was usually regarded as extending from April 15 to the early fall.

and Montgomery Ward. As a general rule, the lures were sold in units of a dozen or more, mounted on a display card portraying strings of fish that had been caught with that particular type of lure. National advertising was carried on in magazines such as *Hunting and Fishing, Fur-Fish-Game, Field and Stream, National Sportsman, Fishing Annual, Outdoor Life, Collier's,* and the *Saturday Evening Post.* Retail prices ranged approximately from 69 cents to $1.25, with the majority of the lures being sold around the $1.00 figure. The retail stores were customarily allowed a discount of about 33⅓ per cent from the listed retail prices.

After making detailed cost calculations, Mr. Ellings decided to sell the Blu-Oreno direct to hardware, sporting goods, and general stores at a price of 26 cents per unit, to be retailed at 49 cents. His estimates indicated that the lure could be made in eight different color schemes in lots of 100 at a cost of about 12 cents per unit, as follows:

Treble hooks	$0.04
Tin head	0.01
Screws	0.01
Enamel	0.01
Wood	0.01
Material cost	$0.08
Labor	0.04
Total cost per unit	$0.12

Mr. Ellings was anxious to keep the price low, not only because it would give the Blu-Oreno a competitive advantage, but also because he felt that the national manufacturers were charging prices which forced the public to pay excessive sums for their products.

For advertising, Mr. Ellings decided to rely on point-of-sale display material. Accordingly, he mounted the lures on an attractive display card which held two lures of each color, or a total of 16. At the top of the card was the inscription "The Only Proven Lure for New England Fishermen," and space was provided for mounting pictures of well-known fishermen and the fish they had caught with the Blu-Oreno. The display cards and the pictures were printed independently, and for each local area a picture was attached which showed a fisherman well known to the sportsmen in that district. The retail price of 49 cents was also printed on the card. By virtue of a friendship with a local printer, Mr. Ellings was able to have the cards, including pictures, printed at a total cost of $7.80 per 1,000.

In anticipation of the 1952 fishing season, Mr. Ellings manufactured a number of the lures in his workshop in his spare time. In the summer of 1952 he took Mr. Luckenbill, a real estate agent, as a partner in the venture, and in July the two men spent two days in the field selling the Blu-Oreno. Their first move was to secure the interest and support of the buyer for the largest of a chain of hardware stores. At his suggestion and with his help, they were able in the subsequent two days to induce 26 other stores in the chain to handle the lures. In selling the Blu-Oreno, Mr. Luckenbill and Mr. Ellings emphasized the fact that the lure was especially designed for fishing in local waters. The 27 stores of the hardware chain were the only outlets secured in 1952, but in the few remaining months of the fishing season approximately 2,000 lures were sold. The store managers reported that the lures had sold exceptionally well and stated that many of their customers bought two or three of the Blu-Orenos, where previously they had bought only one of the more expensive lures.

After the close of the fishing season in 1952, Mr. Luckenbill made a study of the potential market for their artificial lures in their home state, to aid the Ellings Company in planning its activities for the coming year. From the State Division of Fisheries and Game he learned that approximately 254,000 fishing licenses had been issued in the state during 1951 and that the total number of licenses issued had increased about 10 per cent each year since 1945. Mr. Ellings stated that most of the fishermen of his acquaintance were unable to keep a lure for more than one season and usually had to replace their stock each year. Accordingly, Mr. Luckenbill estimated that every licensed fisherman in the state would constitute a potential customer for at least one artificial lure. In addition, the experience of fishermen during the 1952 fishing season had indicated that the Blu-Oreno was just as effective for salt-water as for fresh-water fishing. As a result, Mr. Luckenbill believed that there was a fairly large group of potential customers for Blu-Orenos which was not represented by the figure for total fishing licenses issued. Taking all these factors into consideration, he concluded that the potential market for Blu-Orenos in his home state was in excess of 100,000 per year. He was unable, however, to find any data which would indicate, directly or indirectly, the actual number of lures sold annually in the state.

In view of the large potential demand and their favorable experience in 1952, Mr. Ellings and Mr. Luckenbill decided to market the Blu-Oreno on a somewhat larger scale in 1953. At the same time, Mr. Ellings had no intention of neglecting his legal practice and Mr. Luckenbill intended to spend the majority of his time in his real estate office.

During the winter months Mr. Luckenbill spent about thirteen afternoons visiting retail hardware, sporting goods, and general stores in the state capital, taking advance orders for the 1953 season. He called on a total of 27 stores and obtained orders from 26 of them for a total of 78 display cards containing 16 Blu-Orenos apiece. Mr. Ellings called on about 40 stores in the surrounding area in his spare time and obtained orders from about 25 of them for a total of approximately 70 cards.

On January 1, 1953, a young trade-school graduate was employed to work full time manufacturing the lures for the coming season. At the same time, direct-mail pieces were sent to 1,173 hardware, sporting goods, and general stores in the state. Within six weeks, answers were received from 100 of the retail stores containing orders for 572 display cards, or a total of 9,152 lures. The cost of the direct-mail material, including return postage, was estimated to be about 7 cents per piece sent out.

In February, two months before the opening of the 1953 fishing season, Mr. Ellings and Mr. Luckenbill received an offer from the Miracle Minnow Company to purchase all rights to the Blu-Oreno for $2,800. The company was one of the largest manufacturers of artificial lures, and it had a greater distribution in the state than any of the other national manufacturers. The executives of the company had opened negotiations with Mr. Ellings after the close of the fishing season in 1952 by claiming that the Blu-Oreno infringed certain patents held by the Miracle Minnow Company. Mr. Ellings' knowledge of the law, however, enabled him to convince them that their claim was unfounded; and after the exchange of several letters, they finally made the offer to purchase the Blu-Oreno. Mr. Ellings made no definite reply to the offer, and subsequently he received a communication indicating that a representative of the company was coming to discuss the negotiation with him.

At that time, the Ellings Company had on hand a supply of finished lures sufficient to fill the advance orders that had already been secured. New sales were being made with little difficulty, and Mr. Ellings and Mr. Luckenbill felt that the outlook for the company was quite favorable. They saw no reason to believe that the large manufacturers would offer their products at lower prices during the 1953 season, but they had noted that the new spring catalogue of a large mail-order house listed a lure at a price of 49 cents.

Infant Menus

Infant Menus, after three months of organization and six weeks of sales promotion, faced in late September, 1946, both a discouraging lack of customers and a mounting deficit from equipment and operating costs. The three partners were deciding whether to increase promotional expenditures, continue operations at the same rate, or liquidate the venture as a failure.

Returning to Detroit from Okinawa in April, 1946, for release from active duty in the Navy, Lieutenant Thomas Narvik was met at the airport by his family and by Scott Randall, a former classmate at Oberlin College, who lived in a wealthy suburb of Detroit a few miles from Mr. Narvik's home. Mr. Randall, recently discharged from the Army and now a salesman for a well-known manufacturer, had an idea for a new service to prepare and deliver individual baby "formulas"; and he insisted that Mr. Narvik join him and Dr. Harry Summers, an intern at the neighborhood hospital, in a partnership to provide such a service to mothers.

The idea had occurred to Mr. Randall while he was preparing his own baby's feedings. Sterilizing nursing bottles, nipples, tongs, and other equipment, mixing and boiling the ingredients, and carefully filling and nippling the bottles had taken from forty-five minutes to an hour of his time daily. It seemed reasonable to him that a firm with proper equipment could do the work much more efficiently and with less chance of contamination from the air and unsterile objects. The "Evenflo" type bottles which he was using appeared to be ideal for delivery, since the wide flange of the nipple inverted in the mouth of the bottle under a threaded plastic closure sealed hermetically. To prepare for feeding the infant, the mother merely unscrewed the closure, turned the nipple right side up, and again screwed down the closure to hold the nipple in place.

Mr. Randall and Dr. Summers, another formula-making father, were convinced that the service would "sell like hot cakes with no selling problems at all" to the higher-income families around Detroit. Dr. Summers had made a survey of the mothers in his maternity ward and had found that they would all be willing to subscribe to such a service. The

Exhibit 1

INFANT MENUS

PARTNERSHIP AGREEMENT

Articles of Co-Partnership, made the first day of May, nineteen hundred and forty-six between Scott Randall, Harry Summers, M.D., and Thomas Narvik as follows:

The said parties above named have agreed to become co-partners in business to prepare, distribute, and sell baby foods and other infant supplies and, by these presents, do agree to be co-partners together, under and by the name or firm of "Infant Menus" in the city of Detroit, state of Michigan, and surrounding areas, their co-partnership to commence on the first day of May, nineteen hundred and forty-six, and to continue until one or all of the partners withdraws from the firm. To that end and purpose and to the mutual benefit and advantage of the partners, the funds and assets of the firm will be used and employed.

It is agreed that each of the partners shall contribute on the day the partnership commences, one thousand dollars to the firm; Scott Randall and Thomas Narvik contributing one thousand dollars in cash, and Harry Summers, M.D., a non-interest bearing note for one thousand dollars, payable on demand. And also that each of the partners shall give their best endeavors and the utmost of their skills in the direction of the firm for their joint interest, profit, benefit and advantage.

It is agreed that they shall allow as expenses of the firm all rents and other expenses that may be required for the support and management of the said business; and that all gain, profit, and increase that shall come, grow, or arise, from or by means of their said business, shall be divided between them in equal shares, except that all payments to Harry Summers, M.D., shall be applied by him toward the payment of his note to the firm until it is liquidated; and also that all loss that shall occur in their said joint business by commodities, bad debts, or otherwise, shall be borne and paid by them in equal portions.

It is agreed by and between the said parties that there shall be kept at all times during the continuance of their co-partnership perfect, just and true books of account, wherein shall be set down all money received, paid, and the expenses in and about the said business, which books shall be available at all times to the partners. And also, that at the beginning of each month an accounting of all incomes, costs, and profits shall be rendered; and at that time the just shares of the profits shall be computed and disposition of them made as mutually agreed herein.

The said parties mutually covenant and agree to and with each other, that during the continuance of the said co-partnership no indebtedness beyond the proper and reasonable operating expenses of the business shall be incurred without the full knowledge and consent of all partners. Minor decisions and the general management of the firm shall be delegated to a General Manager, who may be one of the partners and who shall operate

Exhibit 1—Continued

the firm in the spirit of this agreement with respect to all matters not including those decided by mutual agreement of the partners.

In the event of withdrawal of one of the partners, the remaining partners may purchase his share at such mutually agreed price as recognizes the value of the firm as a going business. At the end of this co-partnership, a true, just, and final accounting of all things relating to the business shall be made, and all the assets as well as the gains and increases thereof, which shall appear to be remaining, either in money, goods, wares, fixtures, debts, or otherwise, shall be divided equally between the partners or surviving partners in the event they have first purchased the rights to firm assets of a retiring partner.

In witness thereof we hereunto set our hand and seals, the day and year first above written.

/s/ *Scott Randall*
SCOTT RANDALL

/s/ *Thomas Narvik*
THOMAS NARVIK

/s/ *Harry Summers*
HARRY SUMMERS

Signed and sealed in the presence of

/s/ *John Lamb* — JOHN LAMB
/s/ *P. Swift* — P. SWIFT

reasons Mr. Randall and Dr. Summers were not going ahead with their plans alone were that each was then working full time and each had family responsibilities; they wanted to find someone with a wider business background to supervise operations. Mr. Randall had suggested Mr. Narvik, whom he had known at Oberlin. Mr. Narvik had spent a year at a graduate business school and had worked as an accountant in several corporations and with the War Production Board before entering the Navy.

During an evening's discussion in April an agreement was reached to establish such a partnership, with profits and losses to be shared equally by the three partners. Formal articles of copartnership were later drawn up by Mr. Narvik, following a textbook model (see Exhibit 1). For capital Mr. Randall and Mr. Narvik each contributed $1,000; Dr. Summers, living on an intern's income, signed a note for an equal amount. In addition, Mr. Randall was to contribute his sales-promotion ideas; Dr. Summers was to lend his name and title to add prestige to the business; and Mr. Narvik was to devote full time to the undertaking, receiving in return a fixed monthly salary of $200, in addition to his share of the earnings.

It was believed that $2,000 plus a bank loan of an equal amount would purchase all necessary equipment, and that one month from then, or by June 1, 1946, the business would be in operation. Exhibit 2 presents the estimate on which these hopes were based.

Exhibit 2

INFANT MENUS

ESTIMATED CAPITAL REQUIREMENTS, MAY 7, 1946

Nursing bottles and nipples (100 customers at 20 each at 20 cents each)	$ 400
Autoclave sterilizer (used or war surplus)	200
Water sterilizer (coffee urn)	100
Refrigerator (8 cubic feet) for milk storage	100
Bottle-washing tank	50
Shelves, tables, fixtures	200
Office supplies	100
Truck ($1,200 new, financed)	500
	$1,650
Working capital (two months):	
Rent ($50 per month)	$ 100
Salaries: Nurse (half time at $125 per month)	250
Delivery ($125 per month)	250
Manager ($200 per month)	400
Truck operation ($50 per month)	100
Milk and other ingredients (70 × 60 days × 15 cents)	650
	$1,750
Total	$3,400

At the same time, an estimate of monthly operating income and expense (see Exhibit 3) was made at operation rates of 100 and of 200

Exhibit 3

INFANT MENUS

Estimated Monthly Operating Statement, May 7, 1946

Income	*100 Customers*	*200 Customers*
Priced at $30 per month	$3,000	$6,000
Priced at $25 per month	2,500	5,000
Priced at $20 per month	2,000	4,000
Expenditures		
Milk and other raw materials (15 cents per formula)	$ 450	$ 900
Nurses' salaries	250	400
Laboratory assistant's salary	100	100
Driver's salary	150	300
Manager's salary	200	200
Truck expenses	200	400
Sales promotion	100	100
Rent	50	50
Utilities	50	50
	$1,550	$2,500

customers; the figures were based on the assumption that 10 per cent of the babies born at local hospitals in Detroit and adjoining suburbs would take the service for six months. Various prices for the service were suggested.

Dr. Summers explained that all formulas were made up of three ingredients: milk, water (to dilute the milk), and a carbohydrate. Milk used included the various brands of evaporated, fresh, homogenized, certified, lactic acid, and goat milk. The water was usually boiled tap water, but older babies needing more calories were sometimes given strained water in which oatmeal or farina had been boiled. The carbohydrates included sugar, Karo, Dextro-Maltose, Dexin, Casec, and a number of other trade-marked products. In addition, two rather expensive powders, Similac and SMA, which required water but no milk, were available for the youngest babies. Because of the great number of combinations and proportions possible, it was unlikely that any two formulas from different doctors would be alike. On returning home from the hospitals, babies were customarily given six bottles a day, at 2:00 A.M., 6:00 A.M., 10:00 A.M., 2:00 P.M., 6:00 P.M., and 10:00 P.M. After a few weeks the 2:00 A.M. feeding would be omitted, and after four or five months only four feedings daily would be given. The amount of the daily formulas ranged from 18 to 32 fluid ounces, depending on the infant's age, size, and appetite.

There are two methods of preparing the formulas: (1) the "sterile" method, universally used until recently and, of necessity, used in all homes; and (2) the "simplified" method, now being adopted by progressive hospitals. In the first procedure or technique, all pieces of equipment which come in contact with the formula, or which touch other pieces of equipment which might do so, are sterilized in boiling water for ten to twenty minutes. Water, dairy milk, and other ingredients which do not come in a sterile state (as do evaporated milk, Dextro-Maltose, and other powders) must all be boiled. Working on a sterilized surface, the ingredients are mixed in a sterile graduate, poured into bottles, and then nippled, all equipment being handled with tongs or rubber gloves. These precautions are not taken in the second procedure, where clean but not sterile equipment is used. The secret in the "simplified" method lies in the final sterilization of the filled nursing bottles in a steam autoclave, wherein any bacteria present in the formula, on the surfaces of the bottles and nipples, in the enclosed air above the formula, and under the nipples are killed by subjection to temperatures of 230° F. to 250° F. Besides being easier and faster, this procedure has the additional advantage of killing the air-borne bacilli which always enter during the preparation of "sterile"-procedure formulas.

Having decided to "give it a try," since only a small amount of capital and two or three months' time would be lost if the business did not succeed, the partners first decided to investigate government regulations. The State Department of Agriculture stated that no control would be exercised by that office so long as the local health department had jurisdiction. Several county offices approached said the same. The city health commissioner was very interested in the project as presented to him by Dr. Summers, and could see nothing against it so long as "proper sanitation standards were maintained."

Thus encouraged, Mr. Narvik found two business rooms which the partners leased for a year, one as an office and the other as the laboratory. Although small, the laboratory was well lighted from two large windows facing south. It was equipped with a hand sink and hot and cold water but needed linoleum, several coats of white paint, and electrical outlets.

Purchasing equipment proved to be much more of a problem than expected. New refrigerators were being delivered only to four-month reservations; cabinet sinks were also behind schedule. There were no used or surplus electrically powered autoclaves available. Used panel trucks, all over four years old, cost from $500 to $900; new ones required a year's reservation. The desired type of nursing bottle was on strict allocation to past customers, and a phone call to the manufacturer brought the statement that all capacity through October was already sold and booked.

It was apparent that the cost of equipping Infant Menus, as it now began to be known, would be much greater than had been anticipated and that the number of months' expenditures before beginning operations would also be increased. Furthermore, it was difficult to find a bank which would make a GI loan for a type of business in which the partners (or anyone else) had not previously worked. Finally the neighborhood bank where Mr. Randall's family had always kept deposits offered to make a GI loan of $2,000, secured by the truck and all the equipment.

The autoclave problem appeared to have no immediate solution; so a new custom-made model was ordered for four months' delivery from one of the three manufacturers in the industry. The price was $1,138.57, with a $200.00 deposit required. (Autoclaves were not under price control; before the war the price was about $600.00.) Several weeks later a seventeen-year-old autoclave, rebuilt by a hospital equipment repairman, was found and purchased for $438.98. The original order for a sterilizer was not canceled, because the partners felt that it was possible the Infant Menus might expand in a few months if successful; and at that time, prices would probably be higher and the delivery period longer. The refrigerator problem was temporarily solved by ordering a household-type refrigerator from a large mail-order house, which promised one-month delivery of its private brand at a very low price. A 54-inch linoleum-covered cabinet sink was finally located in a low-price department store for immediate delivery, priced at $99. Sinks in hardware and appliance shops had been priced from $175 to $275, with only the higher-priced ones immediately available. Used kitchen cabinet bases in good condition were found by answering classified ads in the local weekly newspaper.

Through another friend of Mr. Randall's, a Chevrolet truck dealer just opening an agency was found who gave hope of thirty-day delivery on one new panel truck priced at "about $1,000." A $50 deposit was made, and no further truck orders were placed because it was apparent by now that formula deliveries would not begin for several months and because, by ordering from only one dealer, the firm would show its dependence on his promise.

Since there seemed no possibility of buying large quantities of the Evenflo nursing bottles, prices of other types of nursers were investigated. The other types proved so inferior to the Evenflo bottle, in susceptibility to contamination during delivery, that it was decided to visit the Evenflo factory in Ravenna, Ohio, to try to buy enough to get started.

Meanwhile, after considerable search, an electrician and plumber were secured, who grudgingly installed a 220-volt line and the sink and autoclave plumbing. The respective bills were $116.51 and $41.85. All the rest of the carpentry, painting, and laying of linoleum was done by Mr. Narvik, with help on week ends by Mr. Randall. By the first week in June the installation was complete, except for refrigerator, delivery truck, the village license, and the nurses to operate it.

At this point, Mr. Narvik took a two weeks' vacation driving East. During the trip he stopped to visit the Evenflo bottle manufacturer, the U.S. Children's Bureau in Washington, D.C., and leading maternity hospitals in New York and Boston to observe techniques. He was successful in getting immediate delivery of enough nursing bottles for 45 customers.

On his return to Detroit, Mr. Narvik found that neither the refrigerator nor the truck had been delivered. The refrigerator was most important immediately because it would complete the laboratory equipment. As a result of his observations in eastern hospitals, Mr. Narvik decided to buy a large two-door box in which racks of completed formulas, as well as fresh milk, could be cooled and stored. He found a 20-cubic-foot one in a store window just across the street priced at $550 for immediate delivery.

Now ready for operation, an application for a license was made at the city hall. The immediate result almost put an end to the Infant Menus idea. The existence of a section in the state "Hospital Code" pertaining to formula rooms was forcibly brought to Mr. Randall's and Mr. Narvik's attention. (Dr. Summers had by that time left for active duty in the Army, pursuant to his ASTP agreement.) The health commissioner (who had not known earlier of the code), the city nurse, and the sanitation inspector made a thorough examination of the premises and asked for sweeping changes to bring the plant up to hospital standards. The main change was the construction of a partition across the already small laboratory room to divide the bottle-washing area from the filling area. Superfluous wooden trims and base moldings were removed and plastered. For this work Mr. Narvik and Mr. Randall became carpenters and later plumbers, because an additional sink in the filling room was required. To finish all these changes took over a month; bills of $20.82 (electrical), $48.55 (plumbing), $72.00 (lumber), and $23.00 (rubber base molding) were incurred.

With advice from the formula nurse at the local hospital, a "technique" was developed and submitted in writing to the health commissioner. After additions and alterations it was approved, and the city nurse came to observe the process in operation. One of the changes was the use of custom-made aluminum racks in which each customer's bottles were held "untouched by human hands" through processing and delivery in the white metal containers (surplus 0.50-caliber ammunition cases enameled and silk screened with the trade-mark).

The staff of Infant Menus at this time consisted of one nurse, who came for two hours each morning after her regular night shift at the hospital. With more changes, and after another month's delay in trying to get the application on the city council's agenda, the partners finally secured a license as a "milk bottler" on September 9, 1946. During this delay the partners risked the displeasure of the city fathers by operating without a license.

As Mr. Narvik had feared, the problems of production were "nothing" compared with the sales problems. Orthodox mediums of advertising would not be too satisfactory because babies under six months represented only 1 per cent of the population; it would be a waste of money to present more than an announcement to the bulk of the people. One specialized channel, however, was available and necessary: "detail" work to the physicians.

First, a multigraphed letter of announcement and technical description of the production technique was mailed to 200 local physicians, and two weeks later an eight-page booklet was sent as a follow-up. Visits to pediatricians (who care for babies) and to obstetricians (who care for expectant mothers and make the deliveries) were made by Mr. Narvik to explain Infant Menus procedures and answer questions. These doctors were extremely busy with the "bumper baby crop," and a great deal of time was spent waiting in outer offices. Unanimous approval was expressed by the doctors, but there was no way of translating this approval into an active recommendation of the service to new mothers. Financial inducements to these doctors were out of the question.

Simultaneously, four-column announcement advertisements were placed in six local suburban weeklies, illustrated with photographs of the product and of the laboratories. (To add prestige, Dr. Summers' name was included as "Director"; this was a mistake, for it displeased several established doctors as being "unethical advertising" for Dr. Summers.) After that, a 3-inch advertisement, topped by the Infant Menus trade-mark, was kept standing in each paper every week. Other advertising mediums included weekly direct-mail leaflets and booklets to all new mothers and window displays in two well-placed store fronts. Mr. Randall distributed over a thousand booklets to grocers on his route, to be distributed among their customers. Booklets were also distributed at baby-care lectures for new mothers by two local hospitals and by the infant welfare society. The results were discouraging. The display advertisements on August 9 (costing $190), for example, netted one mail inquiry, one phone inquiry, and no customers.

On August 15 there were 3 customers; on September 1, 3; on September 15, 3; and on October 1, 6. Seventy-five personal calls to homes where new babies had been reported in the press had brought only one sale. Although "the times" were prosperous and the potential large, the people having babies were, as expected, younger ones in the lower-income levels who had recently had to pay high medical and hospital fees. The price set was 70 cents per day ($21 per month) for six to eight bottles of almost any formula plus two bottles of sterile water. This price was determined after a discouraging return from a survey letter asking 80 cents and a study of returns from various prices (see Exhibit 3).

Needless to say, the prospects were discouraging. The monthly advertising bill alone was greater than the gross sales. Businessmen without exception gave encouragement to the partners, but mothers said they "couldn't afford it." The partners did not believe that anything short of a 50 per cent cut in prices (35 cents a day) would produce immediately an appreciable number of customers. From a statistical viewpoint, however, sales to only 2 per cent of the babies born among the local delivery area's 200,000 population for a six months' period would give a list of 40 customers and a small profit, and the partners refused to believe this potential impossible.

All advertising and printing were neat and professional in appearance. Mr. Narvik, who had edited several publications in college, wrote copy and made layouts; Dr. Summers' wife, a commercial artist, drew the trade-mark and did other art work. Laboratory standards were equivalent to or better than those at local hospitals. Each baby's bottles, nipples, and racks were used by him alone, assured by the use of a numbering system. Signed copies of the formulas were included in each box to give the mothers assurance as to the accuracy and purity of the product.

Late in September, 1946, the partners were still convinced that their product could be sold but were at their wit's end to find the correct sales "angle" or "gimmick." Because of the length of time required to become established and because the simplicity of the idea invited competition, they felt they should now be planning for expansion to other cities. Unfortunately, the cold budgetary figures showed a monthly income of only $100, against overhead expenditures of about $400 (including as salaries only $60 for the nurse; all other work was done by Mr. Narvik, who was drawing $100 monthly self-employment allowance under the GI Bill). In addition, there were frequent necessary purchases of additional capital equipment.

To date, $600 had been borrowed on the promised GI loan of $2,000. The balance, when borrowed, would cover several months' current expenditures, as well as finance the truck when it came. No other sources of money were in sight. If the firm incorporated to sell stock, the GI loan would have to be repaid immediately. A balance sheet as of September 30, 1946, is shown in Exhibit 4. On the basis of experience to date, it was estimated that a volume of 50 customers would net, over all expenses and salaries (but none for any of the partners), a profit of $100 per month; 100 customers, $555, and 200 customers, $1,570.

See also Exhibits 5 and 6 for additional data.

Exhibit 4

INFANT MENUS

Adjusted Balance Sheet, September 30, 1946

ASSETS		
Cash	$ 165.77	
Accounts Receivable	32.92	
Deposits on Equipment Ordered	358.57	
Raw Materials on Hand	63.65	
Plant and Office Equipment	1,406.82	
Autoclave	438.98	
Bottles and Nipples	104.77	
Containers and Racks	424.00	
Bottle Warmers	51.86	
Office Supplies	75.10	
Prepaid Insurance	200.00	$3,322.44
Organization (Operating) Costs to Date (see Exhibit 5)		1,155.06
Total Assets		$4,477.50
LIABILITIES AND PROPRIETORSHIP		
Accounts Payable	$ 227.50	
Notes Payable (Bank)	600.00	$ 827.50
Partners' Cash Investment		3,650.00
Total Liabilities and Proprietorship		$4,477.50

Exhibit 5

INFANT MENUS

Organization Costs* to September 30, 1946

Expenses:		
Rent	$225.00	
Telephone and electricity	93.72	
Advertising (itemized below)	674.41	
Raw materials used	21.29	
Delivery expenses (used own car)	7.87	
Insurance expense	40.00	
Bacteriological tests	25.50	
Paint and cleaning materials	55.62	
Labor: nurse	65.50	
Miscellaneous expenses	35.88	
Total expenses		$1,245.79
Less: Sales income during this period		90.73
Net organization costs		$1,155.06

Advertising:	
Newspaper space	$255.94
Booklets (5,000)	192.23
Printing; mimeographing	80.87
Postage direct mail	40.50
Art work	31.85
Photography	56.50
Rent of windows for displays	12.00
Miscellaneous	4.52
Total	$674.41

* Includes all expenses of the period less income from sales arising from these expenses.

Exhibit 6

INFANT MENUS

ABBREVIATED BUSINESS DIARY OF MR. THOMAS NARVIK, APRIL 27–JUNE 4, 1946

April 27	Returned to Chicago. Discharged from Navy. Heard about project.
April 28 (Sunday)	Wrote partnership agreement. Discussed budget.
April 29	Visited grandparents in Indiana.
April 30	Returned home. Conferred. Received Evenflo letter; bottles not available.
May 1	Phoned Evenflo; sales manager out. Searched for offices; none available.
May 2	Phoned Evenflo; bottles not available. Saw health commissioner. Says O.K. to go ahead. Building commissioner says manufacturing not O.K. in residential area. Investigated bottles and nipples at wholesale houses.
May 3	Wrote survey letter and had it mimeographed. Looked for rooms.
May 5 (Sunday)	Big partners' conference. Heard GI loan O.K.
May 6	Phoned Evenflo for other types of nipples. Found available office. Editor of local paper helped to have zoning approved.
May 7	Prepared new budget. Picked up mimeographed survey letters. Rented offices on one-year lease.
May 8	Signed up with WAA for surplus truck, autoclave, bottles, etc. Signed partnership agreement.
May 9	Saw hospital supply house on autoclave and equipment; sterilizer company agent; insurance agent.
May 10	Saw other sterilizer and insurance agents. Mailed survey letters to 300 new mothers listed in four months' file of local papers. Discussed techniques with nurses at hospital.
May 11	Got zoning O.K. Opened bank account. Interviewed sterilizer agents. Began buying nursing bottles in retail stores.
May 12 (Sunday)	Set up accounting system. Talked with friends on possible substitutes for electric autoclave.
May 13	Received lease and discussed telephone and electricity rates. Saw two milk companies for used trucks; none available.
May 14	Deposited $50.00 with truck dealer; $238.57 on a new autoclave. Received cheaper insurance rates.
May 15	Found used autoclave available. Revised estimated income statement. Returned lease. Conferred at hospital.
May 16	Interviewed an advertising executive; located ammunition cases for sale; answered ads for sink and refrigerators, but found already sold.
May 17	Saw nurses again.
May 18	Bought 1¼ gross bottles and nipples.
May 19 (Sunday)	Conference. Ordered linoleum.
May 20	Bought sink. Talked to electric company, local druggists, Karo agent, autoclave supplier, and building inspector.
May 21	Ordered paint. Bought autoclave for one-week delivery. Listed sales ideas. Dr. Summers' wife supplied finished drawing of trade-mark.
May 22	Ordered stationery printing. Saw electrician for estimates on 240-volt lead-in. Ammunition boxes not in yet. Took empty bottles to hospital for their experiment.
May 23	Bought two used base cabinets and a desk. Saw leading pediatrician.
May 24	Picked up linoleum, paint, fluorescent fixture. Washed walls.
May 25	Began painting room. Received promise of ultra-violet unit.
May 26 (Sunday)	Finished painting.

Exhibit 6—Continued

May 27	Electricians began. Took hospital bottles for bacteriological tests. Received plumber's estimate. Picked up desk and bases.
May 28	Electricians finished. More painting and plastering. Sink and bases received.
May 29	Began laying inlaid linoleum.
May 30 (Memorial Day)	More linoleum. Washed reception room.
May 31–June 2	Ill at home.
June 3	Bought bottles, waste can, shelf lumber. Ordered drawer handles, silk screen trademark for ammunition boxes. Was promised autoclave in three days, truck in three to four weeks.
June 4	Bought 200 ammunition boxes. Picked up stationery. Got withholding tax data.

Etc.

Roger Chase and Company

Mr. Roger Chase believed that 1952 would bring a major increase in the sales volume of his patented product. Although Mr. Chase had initially planned to handle sales and distribution in 1952 in about the same manner as during 1951, he had just received an interesting offer from a direct-sales organization with nation-wide distribution. As an alternate to this offer, he was giving serious thought to the establishment of his own direct sales group. In addition, he was experimenting with the possibility of a new sales approach developed by one of his regular distributors.

Roger Chase and Company was an old Philadelphia firm established in 1851. Prior to World War II the company acted as a sales agent for mill supplies and laundry equipment. In 1946 Mr. Chase decided to develop and sell his own product, rather than be dependent on the vagaries of several manufacturers.

Since he knew of no available product that fulfilled his specifications, Roger Chase hired an engineer to experiment and develop one. Time passed; and although both men advanced several ideas, a salable product seemed as far from fruition as ever. One day, while discussing his problem, a friend suggested that Mr. Chase try the consumer market. Mr. Chase had read the results of a survey conducted by the *Woman's Home Companion* magazine, on what the housewife wanted most in her post-war kitchen. The first three choices were all expensive electrical gadgets which required the mass-production facilities of a large corporation. The fourth choice was a good, inexpensive, easy-to-operate knife sharpener.

On a Friday afternoon, Mr. Chase told the engineer about his interest in developing a consumer, rather than an industrial, product. He asked the engineer if a knife sharpener could be designed that would be different from any currently on the market, cheap to produce, patentable, and so simple that any housewife could operate it without difficulty. The following Monday the engineer presented Roger Chase with a model that appeared to fulfill all the requirements.

The new knife sharpener was elemental in its simplicity. It consisted of two rubber-tired glass "wheels" with a circular grindstone mounted between them (Exhibit 1). The inside faces of the "wheels" were formed at an angle so that, when a knife blade was laid between the inside face of one of the "wheels" and the grindstone, the edge of the blade was forced against the grindstone at the correct angle for proper sharpening. To sharpen a knife blade, the sharpener was placed on a table top or counter and the knife laid in the slot against one side of the grinding wheel and then in the slot against the other side of the grinding wheel. Moving the knife back and forth rolled the grinding wheel against the knife blade and gave a razorlike edge to the knife.

Exhibit 1

ROTO-SHARP WITH KNIFE IN POSITION FOR SHARPENING

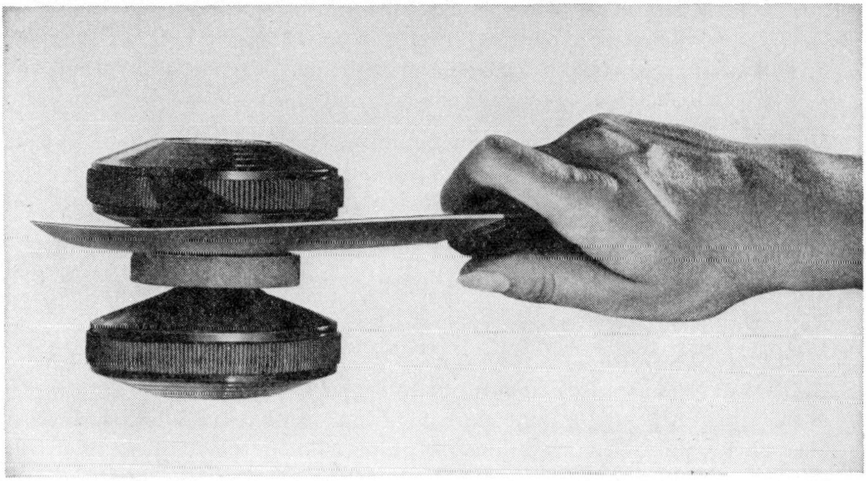

Mr. Chase's patent attorney assured him that he had a patentable item. Although it appeared to Roger Chase that he now controlled the basis for a new enterprise, he had been in business too long and seen too many ideas that appeared to be virtual gold mines disappear under the hard impact of the market to immediately invest in the tooling and dies necessary to produce the product.

Initial conversation with various manufacturers indicated that the probable retail sales price for the new knife sharpener would have to be around $1.49 in order for Mr. Chase to make a reasonable profit. Since he still had to carry on his old business, Roger Chase hired a market survey consultant to aid him in his appraisal of the product potential. The consultant's report is presented below:

Pursuant to arrangement with Roger Chase and Company, the following report is presented, based on 4 days' study in New York, during which 15 outlets were contacted. These outlets included department stores, department store chains and syndicates, variety store chains and syndicates, jobbers, and one buying organization for drug chains.

The results and opinions, together with the name of the organization and buyer contacted, are as follows:

McCorry Inc.
Mr. Myer, Merchandise Manager

The McCorry chain operates ten, \$0.10 to \$1.50 variety stores in large eastern seaboard cities.

Question: Does the item appeal to you?

Answer: It looks like an interesting item, but we feel it would require personal demonstration.

Question: What do you think the item should sell for in your chain?

Answer: An item of this type should sell for between 29 cents and 39 cents and would have to be extremely well packaged to sell for the latter figure. Don't think you could sell any at a price greater than \$1.00; we would not buy to sell at a price above 49 cents.

Question: What quantity would you buy if the above requirements were met?

Answer: Initial order of probably three dozen for our ten stores.

Question: Why do you think it would require "live" demonstration?

Answer: Because in my opinion it is a radically new design of knife sharpener, and it would have to be shown in actual use to facilitate its sale.

Knott Department Stores
Mr. Beyer, Buyer

A chain of 40 stores located principally in the middle west and eastern seaboard cities. All buying done through the main office in New York City. Sharpener requires demonstration. Probably would not sell as a counter article. A retail price of 49 cents would be high. In the last few days, Mr. Beyer rejected 4 new types of knife sharpeners. Our sharpener could not be "pushed" through the efforts of the regular store sales force. Would not be interested at any price.

Thurnauer, Inc.
Mr. Adler, Buyer

Largest jobber of household wares in the United States. Supplies a majority of all housewares sold to department stores. Mr. Adler liked rotary idea, but felt item needed considerable "dressing up." Objected strenuously to the residue which came from the grindstone. Definitely would be a deterrent to the housewife using item. Suggested a finer grain and harder stone to solve this. Item needs good packaging and should be sold by demonstration. Promote through national advertising in women's magazines, particularly *Good Housekeeping*. The keen edge obtained and the fact that the knife blade wears down evenly are good features. Emphatically stated he would not be interested in the item unless it was in the competitive price range. Suggested replacement of the glass wheels with plastic ones to cut cost. Might sell at 69 cents retail if sufficient promotion were put behind it.

BETTER HOUSEWARES, INC.

Housewares jobber. Our sharpener compared with six other models in stock. Buyer admitted our item better. Felt ours could be sold from 69 cents to 75 cents retail, but would be overpriced at $1.00. Would definitely not handle it at the $1.49 price.

NEW YORK MERCHANDISE CORPORATION
Mr. Schuman, Buyer

Third of the large housewares jobbers contacted. Sells exclusively to chains and department store syndicates. Was not interested in the present model of the sharpener. Felt any price over $1.00 was too high. Was the only jobber which believed demonstration unnecessary if good instruction sheets were included in the package. Felt only way to successfully merchandise was to give large advertising allowances to the trade which in turn could pass them on to the customer. Even with this aid, doubted that it would have large sales volume. This company has brought out the new "Super Edge" sharpener. Claims to have done an excellent job with it. Stated packaging most important. Admitted that "Super Edge" was not perfect, but that it was a better looking item than ours.

HARDWARE AIDS
Mr. A. M. Convachian

Contacted to get more information from the wholesale trade. Mr. Convachian in charge of houseware merchandising. Felt we had a new and novel type of sharpener. $1.49 would be chief deterrent to its sale. Did not understand why we needed to get such a high price. In production, plastic wheels should be substituted for glass ones, and a harder grindstone should be used. Particularly interested in the fact that our sharpener hit the edge of the knife at the correct angle, but even this good performance does not justify the high price. Thought it would sell in volume at a price between 49 cents and 79 cents. Demonstrators would pay for themselves.

ALLIED STORES CORPORATION
Mr. Borden, Buyer

Consists of 38 large department stores from coast to coast. Not particularly interested since he felt sharpener was not a big enough item for their stores. Felt it could best be sold by demonstration and should not retail for more than $1.00. Would require packaging in an attractive display box. Might recommend it to the stores, but would not place a central order at any price since "there are a million knife sharpeners on the market."

W. T. GRANT COMPANY
Mr. Orr

Operates 429 variety stores all carrying housewares. Definitely thought demonstrators should be used. Needs packaging with descriptive literature and illustrations. National advertising would be wasted. Money should be spent on store promotion. Rubber tires should be colored and glass wheels red or clear crystal. Mr. Orr stated: "At 49 cents we could not sell enough to put in your eye." Considered the $1.49 price as "ridiculous."

GIMBEL BROS.
Mr. Butler

Live wire buyer searching for new items to promote. Liked item but would have to sell it at 50 cents retail. Item requires demonstration, and should be packed with complete instructions and illustrations for use. National advertising would definitely help. Suggested *Colliers* and the *American Home* with the *Woman's Home Companion* as an alternate. Prestige of these magazines would contribute to both its consumer and outlet sales. Definitely could not sell many at $1.49, but probably could move a considerable number at 50 cents. Particularly liked the colored models.

MACY'S
Mr. Alexander

All knife sharpeners tested in their own lab, which takes 5 to 8 weeks. Negative reaction to glass wheels. Suggested plastic wheels to prevent breakage. Would not require demonstration or allot space for it. Display card best way to show the item. Maximum retail price should be 50 cents. Would not sell many since their sales people are trained to sell carborundum stones and steel sharpeners. Would not buy item to retail at $1.49 as he felt the sharpener did not give that much value.

ASSOCIATED CHAIN DRUG STORES
Mr. H. Lavac

Buying organization for most large drug chains. Represents about 2,700 stores including Liggett's, United, Whelan, Walgreens, etc. Already have a sharpener retailing for $1.00 which has a carborundum wheel turned by a handle. Felt their item looked like a greater value. Felt our sharpener would require demonstration to sell. Should use counter cards instead of packaging. Wheels should be plastic instead of glass. Price of 25 cents retail would be a fair one, although realized it probably could not be made to sell for that. Stated it did not have enough eye appeal or value to sell for $1.49.

B. ALTMAN
Mr. Walcott

Felt this type of sharpener spoils good cutlery and would not carry it. Item should be packaged in a box and retail for not more than 50 cents. It would not sell for $1.49.

G. C. MURPHY
Mr. Messner, Buyer

Represents 209 stores. Felt the price should be in the neighborhood of 25 cents to 49 cents retail. Would require demonstration to sell. If retailed above $1.00 would not be interested. Might possibly buy a gross per store if retail price kept under the 50 cents level.

ASSOCIATED MERCHANDISING CORPORATION
Messrs. Lyon and Reed, Houseware Department

Should not retail over 50 cents. Would require a demonstration to sell. Recommend that it be boxed with colorful and instructive illustrations. Need a foolproof method of holding knife in sharpener to insure the correct sharpening angle. Would not estimate number he could sell at 50 cents. Stated he would not buy it to retail at $1.00 or $1.49. Selling would basically be by some type of trick merchandising. Red is a good color and possibly clear crystal. Definitely do not use blue. Vehemently objected to the residue from the stone. Claimed stone was too soft and too coarse and that it would ruin good cutlery.

LEWIS & CONGER
Mr. W. C. Lewis
Largest exclusively retail housewares store in the United States. Definitely interested in a good knife sharpener. Did not object to the $1.49 price. Did say that he was unable to see $1.49 worth of value in the item. Stone we are using is too coarse. Would require a good steel sharpening after use. Visited the Sherry Netherlands Hotel where the head chef tried the sharpener on a number of his kitchen knives. He strongly objected to the coarseness of the grind. Stated it would be necessary to finish the edge with a fine stone or steel. If we refine the sharpener, Mr. Lewis may be interested in purchasing a considerable volume. Would require excellent packaging and display. Did not feel demonstration was necessary.

CONCLUSIONS:

As a result of our survey, we have come to the following conclusions:

1. The item is definitely overpriced. It should sell in the neighborhood of 50 cents at retail. Even at this price, the sales results would be highly problematical unless well packaged and backed by an extensive promotion campaign.
2. The sharpener has certain faults that would be objected to by the consumer and should be redesigned to include the following features:
   a) A finer and harder stone.
   b) Substitution of plastic for glass.
   c) Attractive package needed with well-illustrated instructions.
3. Most buyers feel the sharpener can best be sold through direct demonstration in stores. This is an expensive way of selling, but often in a household item proves extremely satisfactory.
4. Costs must be lowered if the sharpener is to be successfully sold. Therefore it appears to be a mass production item which must be manufactured and sold in volume if it is to be a profitable venture.

It is the opinion of the writer that there is a need for a new type of sharpener. Mr. Lewis of Lewis and Conger stated he felt that the power propelled, either by hand or motor, was the best answer.

Macy's also felt that the power type was the best kind as did Thurnauer and Murphy. Such a hand propelled sharpener is now made to sell at $3.00, the stores getting 50 per cent discount on same.

Mr. Chase spent considerable time analyzing the report. As a result, the product was reworked and redesigned. Colorful plastic wheels were substituted for the glass ones. A harder and finer grained grindstone was used in lieu of the one found unsatisfactory. A number of ideas to keep the production cost at the absolute minimum were studied and tried. A smaller model was developed. Although cheaper to manufacture, it left a slight mark on the knife blade, which raised strong objections from the cutlery experts.

Mr. Chase was not convinced, however, that the survey gave him all the answers to what the consumer wanted in the way of a knife sharpener or the best way to reach that market. He had read of the new product service offered by the Abraham & Straus department store in New York City (Exhibit 2). As soon as he had received his first production model and found that his actual retail price would have to be $2.50, he contacted the buyer handling knife sharpeners to give a demonstration of the new product. The buyer's advice was brief and to the point. He told Mr. Chase: "You have the best darn sharpener in the business, but we don't want it. First, your $2.50 retail price is way high. Second, the only way you will ever sell it regardless of price is by demonstration. Our girls are paid to wrap bundles and make change, not to show a customer how a product works. Third, people want something they can hang on the wall."

Offsetting the conclusions of the research report and the above comment of the Abraham & Straus buyer was the extreme ease of operation of the knife grinder. Almost everyone who tried it told Mr. Chase that it was the best home sharpener they had ever used. Based on the belief that he had what was essentially a "better mousetrap" kind of product, Roger Chase decided to discount the recommendations both for the lower price and for the need for demonstration. A small advertising agency was hired to develop a marketing plan and push the product, and in 1947 the first sales of the knife grinder were made through the use of sales agents.

For the first few months, sales were very satisfactory. "Roto-Sharp," as the knife grinder was called, was placed in about every key department store east of the Mississippi River. Then sales began to slacken, no repeat orders were received, and it became apparent that Roto-Sharp was not moving off the department store shelves.

The sales campaign was intensified, but no one seemed to be able to write copy that would sell the item. On the advice of one of the large East Coast department stores, Mr. Chase allowed that store to cut the retail price from $2.50 to $1.95 for a special sale. He sold no more grinders but did receive a number of complaints from other established outlets.

Different methods of marketing the product were given experimental runs. Mail-order selling was tried without success. An attempt was also made to hire demonstrators to sell Roto-Sharp in department and chain

*Exhibit 2**

DEPARTMENT STORE MERCHANDISING SERVICE FOR NEW PRODUCTS

ABRAHAM & STRAUS

It Starts a Division for Search for New Products for Promotion

Even a well established manufacturer may have the devil of a time persuading a department store to carry a new product. Perhaps he can't get an appointment with a busy buyer, or a buyer may be conservative about new wares. Naturally, the problems of the small, unknown manufacturer are multiplied many fold (*Tide*, December 6).

But at least one department store, Abraham & Straus (Brooklyn), a member of the powerful Associated Merchandising Corp., has scoured the market for new products and aggressively promoted them. To accelerate this activity, last June Sidney Solomon, A&S vice-president, established a Division of New Merchandise Projects under Peter Cogan. And last month Cogan sent a letter about the new project to manufacturers and advertising agencies.

A&S is interested in dealing with both the big firms (it has cooperated considerably, for instance, with Dow Chemical and U.S. Rubber) and also with the thousands of small manufacturers, many of which boomed during the war and have now reconverted. The newcomers particularly are in a tough spot; previously they sold to the government and they don't know much about civilian distribution problems.

How It Works

When a manufacturer brings a new product to Cogan, he makes an appointment for him with the appropriate buyer or merchandise manager and assists him with the presentation of the product. Both he and the buyer may suggest changes in the styling if the product is still in the development stage. Once the product is accepted, the manufacturer and store develop a promotional plan, which is likely to include an advertisement in a Sunday newspaper with national circulation.

For a new product, A&S sets up a special display in the store, uses both its own point-of-purchase signs and material supplied by the manufacturer. In some cases, the manufacturer may also supply his own demonstrator.

In short order A&S can tell the manufacturer whether the product is a dud or a hit from the sales figures. Additionally, the manufacturer can talk to salesgirls and find out why people bought his product.

The other, and equally important, advantage to the manufacturer of this promotion is the reaction of stores all over the U.S. All department stores watch the New York Sunday newspapers closely and if an item looks promising will quickly contact the store or local buying office to learn the manufacturer, price and initial consumer reaction. Other large stores may mail order a sample; small retailers and other distributors may make inquiries. Thus with comparatively small effort, a manufacturer can get national distribution in a relatively short time. The method is known as a radial advertising and distribution: the manufacturer obtains initial advertising and distribution in key cities and his product radiates from these points to the wholesalers and retailers in the surrounding areas.

To Agencies

Not only has Cogan written to manufacturers, but he has also urged advertising agencies to contact him when any clients develop new products. The agency response has been most enthusiastic. Some reasons: the A&S method is a quick way to test a product and build national distribution; and it is a refreshing change from some department stores' unfriendly or indifferent attitude. Agencies may be able to build small accounts into national advertisers.

Among the merchandise A&S claims it has introduced: a Dazor floating fluorescent lamp; the Dow magnesium wheelbarrow; an electric lawn mower; a pressure cooker divider (for cooking several foods at one time); the Plasticor, for molding plastic gadgets and toys; and U.S. Rubber Koylon Foam Cushioning.

* Reprinted from *Tide* for December 13, 1946.

variety stores. The demonstrators were offered $40 per week salary and a small commission. Although some people were obtained, the sales volume was unsatisfactory and this method was considered a failure.

In 1949 a smaller edition of the Roto-Sharp, called the "Roto-Hone," was introduced to retail at $1.00. This unit, although it resembled the larger edition, had an additional ingenious design feature. By giving the wheels a countertwist, they would close down around the grindstone to form a neat disk about 7/8 inches thick, slightly larger than a silver dollar in diameter. This was a convenient size to carry in the pocket, keep in the office, etc. The new Roto-Hone was introduced into one of the large chain variety stores. It, like the older, larger, and higher-priced Roto-Sharp, did not sell in adequate quantities. As an experiment, the retail price was cut to $0.69. The Roto-Hone still remained on the chain-store counters.

The years between 1946 and 1949 were not easy ones. Sales never reached the point where they provided a satisfactory income, and Mr. Chase was obliged to use his savings to help support both himself and the business. Throughout this period, however, he remained firm in his belief that both the Roto-Sharp and the Roto-Hone were salable products that filled a definite need. Actually, Roger Chase was faced with the peculiar fact that everyone seemed to believe that his product was like the "better mousetrap," but no one appeared to be beating a path to his door. Eventually he was forced to conclude that the houseware buyers with whom he had talked two years before were correct, and the only way he could sell either of his two sharpeners was by a personal demonstration for each and every sale that was made.

Once Mr. Chase made this decision, he revised his sales program to put emphasis on the types of selling that would allow for personal demonstration. By the end of 1951, nearly all selling effort was concentrated in the following sales channels:

1. Roto-Sharp and Roto-Hone were advertised in the various trade magazines read by house-to-house salesmen operating their own businesses. These men bought directly from Mr. Chase. Each man generally served his own small market of about 300 accounts. Normally they sold Roto-Sharp at the $2.50 price (sometimes at a higher price) like a "house-afire" for about ninety days. After that their relatively small markets became saturated and sales fell to the zero point.

2. Mr. Chase attempted to place his product with some of the big house-to-house selling companies such as Stanley Home Products. These firms often operated on the "party" method. For example, a housewife would be induced, by special gifts, to open her home of an evening so

that a company salesman could demonstrate his line of products to a group of the housewife's friends. At the party the salesman took orders, which were later delivered to the housewife for distribution. He also attempted to obtain a member of the group as a new sponsor for another "party." By early 1952, he had not been successful in selling his knife sharpener to the companies which dealt in a general line of products.

3. A large manufacturer of cooking utensils selling house-to-house used the Roto-Sharp free as part of its $19.95 knife-and-fork carving set. The customer received this set for $6.95 if she bought a set of aluminum worth about $125.00. This one account used about 2,000 Roto-Sharp units per month.

4. Two well-known cutlery manufacturers included the Roto-Hone as an integral unit in several of their carving sets. One of these companies selling house-to-house had initially tried the Roto-Hone in one set and then increased its use to two other sets.

5. Another well-known cutlery manufacturer sold its cutlery on a house-to-house basis on the argument that its products were the sharpest knives ever made. The salesman for this firm would demonstrate this by using the knife to reslice, without crumbling, a slice of precut fresh bread. Unfortunately for the salesman, the housewife could not maintain the keen edge using the ordinary types of household sharpeners. As complaints were received, the salesmen were forced to make regular return trips to resharpen the knives they had sold. Once Mr. Chase convinced the manufacturer that a Roto-Sharp should be given with each knife set, the service calls almost completely ceased.

6. Some sales were still being made through wholesale channels to department stores and hardware stores. One large New York department store was selling about 200 Roto-Sharp units per month.

In early 1952, Mr. Chase was planning his sales campaign for the forthcoming year. Two new factors were present. One was a new product called the "Roto-Sharp Jr." This was merely the small Roto-Hone made without the telescoping feature. The same retail price of $1.00 was set for the Roto-Sharp Jr. as for the Roto-Hone. Roto-Sharp Jr.'s only reason for existence was that it could be manufactured for a few cents less than the telescoping model. This slightly lower cost provided the extra margin necessary to sell the item successfully by large-scale demonstration in the novelty chains.

An offer had already been received from a direct-sales company, which had a large force of demonstrators working in the Woolworth stores and in the outlets of one other large chain. This company offered the following terms to market Roto-Sharp Jr. by demonstration. It guaranteed a purchase of 250,000 units per year from Roger Chase and Company on a yearly contract renewable at the discretion of the marketing firm. It agreed to sell Roto-Sharp Jr. at the $1.00 retail price and to pay 60 per cent off list for the item; that is, 40 cents to Mr. Chase. This was in accordance with the usual markup rate which gave the demonstrator 20 per cent off list and the chain store 40 per cent off list. The marketing company also agreed to pay any increase in cost to manufacture Roto-Sharp Jr. during the life of the contract but would not pay a corresponding percentage markup in profit. Both Mr. Chase and the market group expected sales during the first year to be about 500,000 units.

Mr. Chase wondered whether he could not perform the same function more profitably by setting up his own demonstrator force. He would probably train this force himself. Mr. Chase felt the best way to get demonstrators was to advertise in magazines such as *Bill Board.* Good demonstrators were expected to work for about four to six weeks in each store. At the end of that time, the store's market seemed to become saturated. However, if a demonstrator returned to the store in a few months, he usually could repeat about the same total sales volume. Wages were not considered a problem, for a good store demonstrator managed to make about $150 a week from his 20 per cent of the list price.

Mr. Chase cited a case that he overheard in Chicago. The demonstrator was selling a knife sharpener for $1.00 which ordinarily retailed for 50 cents. He had just told the store manager that he had sold only 588 sharpeners that week. He considered such a sales volume too small to keep him there any longer, and planned to move to a new location where he could make more money.

A second sales method which was being tested in early 1952 in the New York area had been developed by a "live-wire" distributor from New York City. He had made a two-hour wire recording of a program designed to sell Roto-Sharp and Roto-Hone. Interspersed with music were sales talks on both of the knife sharpeners and other products that an individual store might wish to push. The distributor intended that the program would be broadcast from a store to the people passing in the street by the use of an outside loudspeaker.

The first store tested was a small cutlery and gift shop with about a 12 × 36-foot floor area. It was located across from a large New York post office in upper Manhattan. Mr. Chase observed the store for a half hour before the recording was turned on. In that time, not one customer entered the store. After the broadcast started, customers began to flow into the store; and in two hours, $38 worth of Roto-Sharps and Roto-Hones were sold and at least double that dollar amount in other merchandise. The second test was run in a slightly larger store on 45th Street, between 5th and 6th Avenues. Unfortunately, the proprietor was not present at the store during the trial week and the clerks failed to cooperate. In addition, the weather was very poor. Consequently, sales of the two grinders amounted to only about $18 per day.

One of the best hardware stores in New York City, located on 6th Avenue, was selected for the third trial. The first day's sales of knife grinders were $150. Second day's sales were $100, although the weather was extremely cold. Chase had no report of sales for the third day, but he had received a telephone call requesting 6 gross of Roto-Hones be shipped immediately to the hardware store. He was convinced that this method would work for even a small store which had only a small volume of customer traffic.

The next question Mr. Chase wished answered was whether the idea would pull customers into a particular department within a large department store where the traffic was already heavy. A representative from Allied Purchasing had already asked him to set up a test broadcast as soon as possible in a Grand Rapids department store.

During 1951, Roger Chase, his son, and one part-time sales agent were able to do all the selling, either to distributors or to the various agencies mentioned above. All manufacturing was subcontracted, although Roger Chase and Company did the warehousing. The only other employees of the company were two girls, to handle the correspondence and bookkeeping. Mr. Chase expected to do a 50 per cent greater volume in 1952 than in 1951, although the latter year was a very satisfactory one. He believed that his experiment showed that direct selling was the best marketing method for the small businessman who wants to sell a new product in considerable volume.

Tab-Wash

A REPORT ON THE MARKET ANALYSIS AND BUSINESS ORGANIZATION OF TAB-WASH, A PATENTED SOAP PELLET

CONSUMER REACTION

The general reaction to Tab-Wash as a mechanics' hand cleaner was favorable. The features of convenience, individual use, and nonwastefulness are considered to be real assets with valuable sales appeal. Tab-Wash performs the cleaning job as effectively as other general-purpose mechanics' hand cleaners. The product has the potentiality of capturing a significant portion of the total market for industrial hand cleaners. To do this will require an active and aggressive sales campaign.

During the past two months' period, Tab-Wash was used by well over one hundred individuals. The majority of these were industrial workers—mechanics, machinists. Others included garagemen, farmers, persons working about the home, traveling repairmen, hardware store proprietors, sporting goods store buyers, industrial purchasing agents, and individuals experienced in evaluating new products. Most users were questioned and their reactions noted. In no case was the reaction to the idea of a hand-cleaning tablet unfavorable. There were important specific criticisms of the product. These are covered elsewhere in this report.

TEST AT UNIVERSAL

During the early part of October, 1950, a test was made on Tab-Wash at the Universal Chemical Co., plant. The purpose of the test was to collect firsthand information concerning the reaction of industrial workers to Tab-Wash. A dispenser was installed in the machine-shop washroom. It was filled on two occasions, following which users were questioned. Men using the tablets had greasy, grimy hands. In most cases the lower portion of the arms also needed cleaning. The cleaning agent normally employed is described elsewhere in this report.

Tab-Wash obviously had the appeal of newness. The tablets were used at a phenomenal rate. It was discovered that individuals from other departments made special trips to this washroom to try out the tablets.

Of those questioned, there were no complaints as to Tab-Wash's cleaning ability. The users would not admit to its superiority over the powdered agent but stated that it was just as good. Approximately one quarter of those questioned used two tablets for a thorough cleaning. Lathering was considered important. This is a drawback of the Nacconol tablets. In no case did individuals take advantage of the final nonabrasive wash. They would rather take a second tablet if more cleaning was needed. At least two persons had difficulty holding on to the tablets as they dropped out of the dispenser. If a tablet falls out of a worker's hands, he merely takes another.

The dispenser operated satisfactorily but is not so convenient to use as a powdered-soap dispenser.

On the worker's part, there were no objections to substituting Tab-Wash in their washroom.

Several management people tried and liked Tab-Wash.

PRODUCT

Over the past few months a considerable body of knowledge has been built up in the field of tableting detergent-filler compositions with the characteristics of dry mechanical strength and rapid wet disintegration. For the future this provides excellent background in the development of a variety of products for special applications. A few of the possibilities are:

a) The nonabrasive, scented tablet for use by women, to be carried in the pocketbook.
b) A tablet especially compounded for use in automatic washing machines at home or at laundramats, available from dispensers. This would eliminate the inconvenience of using dry powders.
c) A tablet for dishwashing in the home.

It is inadvisable to prosecute any of these until the current Tab-Wash project is well under way.

On the basis of information received from a large number of users of Tab-Wash, the product must be modified in the following respects:

Lather. It is imperative that the tablet lather profusely in use. Lather, of course, has no bearing on the detergent properties of a cleaning composition, but the psychological relation between lather and cleaning power has been so firmly fixed in the public mind by soap makers that it is deemed advisable to incorporate this feature in Tab-Wash.

Laboratory investigation has indicated that by using Santomerse D, a detergent of alkyl aryl sodium sulfonate class, in place of Nacconol NR as the active ingredient lathering may be substantially improved.

Size. The dimensions of the tablet are approximately correct for convenient use. However, when the tablet is used in hand cleaning, a number of individuals complained that there was not sufficient material "to work with." This has been overcome by substituting insoluble sawdust for the soluble sodium sulfate constituent of the previously used Nacconol NR.

Stickiness. The tablet now leaves barely any "stickiness" on the hands after use. In turn, the "final wash" is not so effective as previously. However, the "final wash" has been found to be utilized to a negligible degree by users. This is particularly true of industrial workers. This latter group tends to use another tablet if the hands are not sufficiently clean after the preliminary wash.

MARKET FOR MECHANICS' HAND CLEANER

Mechanics' hand cleaners as used in this report include all the materials which are marketed for the express purpose of cleaning greasy, grimy, or very dirty hands. Examples of these materials are: (1) mixtures of hand soap and an abrasive agent sold in powdered or granulated form (Boraxo and Pax are typical products), (2) bar soap containing an abrasive agent (Lava), (3) paste sand soaps (Gre-solvent), and (4) waterless cleaners consisting of an organic solvent and a detergent (Quickee). In addition, other "homemade" cleaners are used, such as kerosene, pine oil, and soft soap and sand.

Not included in mechanics' hand cleaners are powdered soaps (with no abrasive), liquid soap, and ordinary bar soap. These are marketed as general-purpose mediums and contain no attrition agent.

The total market for mechanics' hand cleaners may be conveniently divided into two segments: (1) the industrial market and (2) the retail market. The industrial market comprises bulk purchases by factories, plants, etc. Concerns employing more than 6 to 10 industrial workers generally purchase mechanics' hand cleaners through janitors' supply houses, or in a few cases directly from the manufacturer. The retail market comprises small-quantity purchases through hardware stores, grocery stores, and even drugstores. Individuals who work at home in the garage or workshop, small machine shops, etc., make up this purchasing group.

INDUSTRIAL MARKET FOR MECHANICS' HAND CLEANERS

The industrial market is, of course, the large volume market. The predominating hand cleaner in use for this market is powdered abrasive soap. The powdered form is used for several reasons: (1) bar abrasive soap is inconvenient and unhygienic when used by a large number of individuals; (2) paste sand soaps do not lend themselves to easy dispensing; and (3) the solvent type cleaners are expensive and inconvenient. Powdered soap cleaners are inexpensive and efficient.

Dispensers for powdered soaps have been developed to a rather high degree. They are rugged, attractive, and reliable. The dispensers are regulated to deliver a fixed quantity of soap each time the valve is hit by the hand. Normally the user takes several helpings from the dispenser. This may mean as much as 4 grams. In addition, it is not unusual for an individual to use more powder after a preliminary wash. The average total use per washing is roughly 3 to 4 grams. Thus, approximately 125 washings are obtained from a pound of cleaning agent. It must be realized that these are rough figures, since the washing compounds vary in density rather widely.

In most plants and factories, washroom facilities are provided both in the operating departments and in the locker rooms. In the departments the abrasive compound is provided, whereas in the locker room a nonabrasive soap is available. The nonabrasive product is used on the face and body.

Utilizing figures of the number of workers in heavy industry and estimating their daily hand-cleaning requirements, there is a probable industrial market of $5 million, or 100 million pounds of hand-cleaning compound a year. This is equivalent to 11 billion hand washings per year. At a use of one tablet per wash, the tremendous potential market for Tab-Wash is indicated. To be specific, if Tab-Wash were successfully introduced into an organization consisting of 15,000 industrial workers, the usage would be roughly 11 million tablets a year. Assuming a sales price of $2.00 per 1,000, this is $22,000 per year.

NATURE OF THE INDUSTRIAL COMPETITION

As indicated previously, the important industrial competition for Tab-Wash is from powdered or granulated abrasive hand soaps. In general, these soaps are made by a large number of rather small producers. Typically, they buy powdered hand soap from the large soap companies in bulk, mix it with an abrasive (sawdust, corn meal, sand, etc.) and package it in convenient sized containers. The large soap companies up to the present have not sold industrial hand cleaners. The one outstanding exception is Lava Soap, manufactured by Procter and Gamble. This cannot be considered strictly competitive with Tab-Wash in the industrial field, for reasons previously mentioned.

The powdered abrasive hand-soap producers normally sell through janitors' supply houses. In fact, it is not unusual for a janitors' supply house to mix its own product. This is then sold on a personal sales basis to factories and plants. Powdered soap dispensers are easily available and are either given to a customer or sold at a nominal price. Negligible advertising or sales promotion accompanies the product. There appears to be little differentiation between products.

Boraxo. There is a significant exception to the above composition of the industry. Boraxo, a product of the Pacific Coast Borax Co., is nationally sold and advertised. It is sold both in small handy metal containers in retail stores and in cardboard packages for use in industrial plant dispensers. The company has successfully created consumer demand for the product. Unquestionably, this has had its effect on the industrial purchasing agent. Boraxo is the single most widely used mechanics' hand cleaner. It has captured a significant fraction of the total industrial market.

Exhibit 1

PRICE SCHEDULE FOR BORAXO

Quantity Purchased	Price	Cents per Pound	Washings per Cent		
			2 Gm.	3 Gm.	4 Gm. per Wash.
5-lb. carton	$1.25	25	9.1	6.0	4.5
1 case, 30 lb.	6.95	23.3	9.8	6.5	4.9
2–4 cases	6.50	21.7	10.4	6.9	5.2
5–9 cases	6.10	20.4	11.2	7.4	5.5
10–24 cases	5.25	17.5	13.0	8.6	6.5
25–99 cases	5.10	17.0	13.4	8.9	6.7
100 up cases	4.60	15.4	14.8	9.8	7.3

Boraxo consists of a mixture of hand soap and finely divided borax as the abrasive agent. Boraxo does an effective cleaning job but has no marked superiority over numerous other products. It is a white powder and thus helps keep wash basins clean looking. Like all soap cleaners, it has decided disadvantages in hard-water areas.

It is worth while to keep Boraxo in mind as a standard for comparison. The price schedule of Boraxo is shown in Exhibit 1. Column 3 indicates the selling price of Boraxo per pound versus quantity purchased. The three columns to the right indicate the number of washings per penny, dependent on the quantity used per wash.

CLEANING AGENT USED AT UNIVERSAL CHEMICAL COMPANY

This product is typical of many industrial hand powders. It consists of a mixture of tall oil soap purchased from Swift and Company for 15 cents per pound and sawdust finer than 30 mesh. The ratio of ingredients is 1:1.

The selling price to industrial concerns is 19.25 cents per pound. There is a year end return to the purchaser, dependent on the quantity used.

Universal Chemical Co. uses this cleaner throughout the plant. The workers, when questioned, seemed satisfied with its effectiveness as a hand cleaner. Management, however, was not well satisfied. The area around each dispenser is usually messy due to spillage. The accompanying waste also bothered management even though the hand cleaner is a small item costwise.

PRICING THE INDUSTRIAL PRODUCT

Industrial purchasing agents are extremely price conscious. A product cannot be far out of line with other competitive products without this fact being obvious. More leeway is permitted in pricing a consumer product.

It is inadvisable to underprice new, superior products such as Tab-Wash. A long-range attempt should be made to bring the price down. It should eventually be possible to make Tab-Wash an industrial hand cleaner less costly than any of the powdered cleaners because of the no-waste feature.

The pricing of Tab-Wash must primarily consider: (*a*) the prices of competitive products and (*b*) production costs.

Industrially, Tab-Wash's major competition is powdered hand cleaners. These are sold on a per pound basis. It therefore is advisable to sell Tab-Wash on a per tablet basis because the price comparison is less obvious; and Tab-Wash tablets are extremely light compared to soap products, owing to the highly concentrated detergents used.

Indicated elsewhere in this report are these facts: The production costs of Tab-Wash are roughly 71 cents per 1,000, delivered in the Boston area. When using Boraxo, the cost to the user varies from 14.8 washings per cent to 4.5 washings per cent, dependent upon the quantities purchased and the amount used and wasted per washing.

At a price of $2.00 per 1,000 to the industrial consumer, Tab-Wash yields 5 washings per cent. This is approximately the same price as Boraxo if Boraxo is freely used. This price provides sufficient spread for jobber's discounts and is consistent with manufacturing costs. These costs can be decreased substantially when volume warrants. This would permit a price decrease and in turn an expansion of the market.

Quantity discounts may eventually be given. A rough guide would be the Boraxo price list.

TAB-WASH PRODUCTION FACILITIES

The production of Tab-Wash has been arranged for in the following manner:

An executive at Universal Chemical Co.'s plant has offered to make up a batch of granulation in equipment at his disposal. It would be possible to make up a batch sufficient for one million tablets. It is believed that this service from Universal would be regularly available either at no charge or at a nominal one if Universal detergents were used as a chief ingredient in Tab-Wash.

Tableting may be done by a local company at a charge of $0.30 per 1,000 in batches of one million tablets. It may be possible to reduce this charge eventually or justify purchase of a tableting machine.

Exhibit 2

TAB-WASH MANUFACTURING COST DATA

Basis: 1,000,000 tablets (bulk containers)
2,200 pounds at 1 gram per tablet

Materials: Santomerse S, 13 cents per pound, 1,760 pounds	$229.00
Freight	33.60
	$262.60
Sawdust, No. 2 Maple, 1,650 pounds, $35 per ton delivered	28.80
Camphor, powdered, 106 pounds, 50 cents per pound	53.00
	$344.40

$$\frac{344.40 \times 100}{1,000} = 34.5 \text{ cents per 1,000 tablets}$$

Make-up of granulation and shipment to tablet manufacturer:	
Barrels or drums, four round trips	$ 20.00
Fifth-class shipping rate, 1,000–6,000 pounds, $0.46 per 100 pounds	11.50
Tableting at manufacturer's:	
Bulk packing, tableting quotation $0.30 per 1,000	$300.00
Packing in smaller containers and packing for shipment, including container cost:	
3 cents per container of 1,000	30.00
Shipment to Boston area	20.00
	$381.50
Total manufacturing cost	$725.90

Or 73 cents per 1,000 tablets

Handling, storage, and shipment can be handled on a contract basis. The tablet manufacturer also offers a bottling, labeling, and packing service on a contract basis. Initially, the retail-market bottled product may be handled in this manner. Bottles of 50 ready for shipment would cost 10 cents per bottle in lots of 10,000 bottles. Thus the manufacturing end of Tab-Wash is extremely simple, requiring only occasional supervision. Costs of production are tabulated in Exhibit 2.

Manufacturing costs, therefore, are 73 cents per 1,000 tablets delivered in the Boston area. Changes in composition of the product or in packages might increase this somewhat. Also, an initial batch would probably be more costly than eventual routine batches.

DISPENSER FOR THE INDUSTRIAL PRODUCT

The importance of the dispenser program is obvious in any investigation of the industrial field. The dispenser which has been designed operates satisfactorily but is not so convenient to use as a powdered soap dispenser. None of the Tab-Wash dispensers have been continuously used for long periods.

It is simple to hand-make a dispenser. Materials cost about $3.50 for each dispenser, if made of Bakelite. Machinists' charges for quantity production would be approximately $2.00 each. It should be possible to make improvements as a result of operational experience.

The alternative to a machine-shop job is a stamped or molded dispenser. This necessitates investment in dies. This investment would amount to $2,000 to $3,000. The cost per dispenser would then be $1–$2 if ordered in lots of 10,000 or more. In all, at least $12,000 would be tied up initially in dispensers.

There are several possibilities as regards dispenser policy: (1) outright sale at a nominal price, (2) give free or loan with an initial order, or (3) sell at a nominal price to be returned to purchaser when total sales reach a given point.

From a sales promotional standpoint, policies 2 and 3 have much to recommend them. Boraxo uses policy 1 and does not seem to suffer by the policy. The firm which supplies hand cleaner to Universal Chemical Co., has adopted policy 2, but this policy can prove very costly if the dispensers were misused or laid idle. By adopting policy 3 and setting the total sales for rebate at, say $50 per dispenser, many of the advantages of the other approaches are secured. At a nominal sales price per dispenser of $3.50, out-of-pocket charges for the dispenser are covered.

DEVELOPMENT OF THE INDUSTRIAL MARKET

Conceivably, the industrial market could be reached by two means: (*a*) the normal channel of distribution—manufacturer to janitors' supply house to industrial consumer or (*b*) direct sale to the industrial consumer. There is much to be said for each method.

The dispenser situation as it stands presently necessitates the direct approach. For jobbers to handle the distribution, it would be necessary for them to stock dispensers. Supplying them in quantity would be a difficult job and per se would not result in Tab-Wash sales.

On the other hand, dispensers could be made as needed when using the direct approach. A plant normally would order a few dispensers on a trial basis. These could be readily supplied.

Using the direct approach, it would be feasible to approach individuals in large concerns only, since selling expense would be prohibitive in other cases. However, a large selling commission could be paid to a high-grade salesman capable of making a direct convincing approach to industrial purchasing agents.

Jobber salesmen often are mere order takers and deal with individuals at a much lower management level.

Thus, the procedure in making industrial sales would be to in turn establish Tab-Wash in several large plants (probably in the New England area) on a trial basis. The trial would probably consist of placing Tab-Wash in certain departments. On the basis of this, Tab-Wash might be introduced throughout the plant. Delivery of Tab-Wash would be direct from the tablet manufacturer, and stocking would be done by the purchaser in his storehouse. As distribution becomes a problem, jobbers could be called upon. At this point the dispenser problem conceivably would be solved.

OPERATIONAL PICTURE (INDUSTRIAL PRODUCT)

The accompanying analysis (see Exhibit 3) assumes direct sales of Tab-Wash in bulk to industrial concerns. Sales would be made through salesmen, who would receive a 25 per cent commission on all sales made.

Tab-Wash sales price is assumed to be $2.00 per 1,000. Out-of-pocket manufacturing cost is $0.75 per 1,000. The item in Exhibit 3

Exhibit 3

CONTRIBUTION AT $2.00 SALES PRICE

PER THOUSAND BASIS

Selling price	$2.00	
Sales commission	0.50	
Net to Tab-Wash		$1.50
Less manufacturing cost (from Exhibit 2)		0.75
Contribution		$0.75

MONTHLY BASIS

Total Sales	No. of Tablets in 1,000's	No. of Users	No.* of Plants	Sales Comm.	Net to Tab-Wash	Contribution
$ 200	100	1,340	13.4	$ 50	$ 150	$ 75.00
500	250	3,340	33.4	125	375	187.50
1,000	500	6,700	67.0	250	750	375.00
2,000	1,000	13,400	134.0	500	1,500	750.00
5,000	2,500	33,500	335.0	1,250	3,750	1,875.00

* 100 workers each.

entitled "Contribution" is the amount remaining after commission and manufacturing costs are deducted from the selling price. Administration and overhead must be paid and profit earned from "Contribution."

It is useful to remember that there are 1,200,000 industrial workers in New England alone. The "No. of Users" column in Exhibit 3 is derived from the "No. of Tablets" column on the basis of hand-washing requirements per month. The "No. of Plants" column indicates the number of industrial customers (of 100 industrial-worker size) which would have to be sold and serviced each month.

Organization. There are obviously several ways in which Tab-Wash as a business venture can be prosecuted. But for the purpose of estimating operating expenses, it is assumed that a small company would be formed to produce and sell Tab-Wash to large industrial concerns. A small business in the bottled product could also be developed without substantially increasing expenses.

Up to a total sales volume of nearly $5,000 per month, the business management of the enterprise could be handled by one individual, working full time with the aid of part-time office help and commission salesmen.

At a volume in excess of $5,000 per month, basic changes would have to be made in policy. No attempt is made at present to estimate expenses under this mode of operation.

Estimated monthly administration and overhead at a sales volume of $5,000 or less per month will be:

Manager's salary	$417.00
Office help	100.00
Telephone	25.00
Rent	25.00
Supplies, postage	30.00
Selling	100.00
	$697.00

Thus, administration and overhead would be in the neighborhood of $700 per month. Fixed expenses of this amount indicate a gross sales break-even figure of $1,870. Therefore, a sales volume of near $2,000 per month is needed before operations can be taken out of the red. Reference to the previous chart indicates that Tab-Wash would have to be introduced to 134 plants of 100 workers each.

To execute a sales goal of this magnitude would require several months' sales effort—say six. During this period the average loss by the company would be, say, $400 per month. The total loss, therefore, might be around $2,400 before the concern found itself on a paying basis.

CAPITAL REQUIREMENTS

In order to establish Tab-Wash as a business, funds will be required for the following purposes:

Production of one million tablets	$ 750.00
Organization expenses, including incorporation	350.00
Working capital to cover initial operating expenses and losses	2,500.00
Contingency	1,000.00
	$4,600.00

Entering upon production and marketing of the bottled product would necessitate an additional initial capital expenditure of approximately $1,500. This would be largely for production and promotional purposes.

RETAIL MARKET FOR MECHANICS' HAND CLEANERS

Mechanics' hand cleaners sold in the retail market are of many different kinds. Some products enjoy preference merely because they are a new approach to the hand-cleaning problem. Lava soap, Boraxo in metal cans, and, to a far lesser extent, Gre-solvent are the dominating products in the field. In addition, there is an almost endless list of powders, pastes, solvent cleaners, etc. These latter products are typically marketed in local areas and are sold on a point-of-sale basis. The store proprietor recommends the item which gives him the largest discount and has, in addition, some interesting features.

Lava soap and Boraxo are seldom "pushed," as is the case with other low-margin, nationally advertised products. These products, however, are sold through chain grocery stores, variety stores, and drugstores. A product not nationally advertised has little opportunity to be so distributed.

The total national retail market for mechanics' hand cleaners is estimated to be about $1 million per year. The channels of distribution are from manufacturer to hardware store jobbers to retailers. Except for Lava and Boraxo, almost all of the mechanics' hand cleaners are sold through hardware stores. The sale of mechanics' hand cleaners by mail, for example, conflicts with the normal buying habits of individuals. Sales promotion and advertising of cleaners are almost nonexistent. Manufacturers rely on large discounts to "push" the products through. Hardware-store jobber salesmen act as mere order takers. Manufacturers of the hand cleaners usually can obtain formulas for them from trade publications such as *Soap and Sanitary Chemicals.* This leads to little differentiation among products of a given type except in unimportant aspects such as color and odor.

In general, these products do a good job in hand cleaning. Certain products are designed specifically for such cleaning jobs as removal of paint, dye, and printing ink.

The prices of these hand cleaners run from 15 cents to about 65 cents per jar, tube, or can. The solvent-type cleaners are most costly; the sand soaps, least expensive. The cost per wash runs from about ⅓ cent to 2 cents. The public certainly does not buy the cleaners on a cost-per-wash basis. A large can at a low price has more appeal than a small can at a high price, even though the latter may be the better buy.

Unless a special merchandising and marketing effort accompanied Tab-Wash as it was introduced to the retail trade, the product would be relegated to the dealers' shelves and would enjoy only limited sale. To promote a product costs money. Large dealer discounts have ceased to be a sales incentive in this field. A survey of about 20 hardware stores in the Boston area indicated that only one mechanics' hand cleaner had even so much as a counter display to attract sales.

A carefully worked-out campaign consisting of counter displays, free samples, limited advertising, pamphlets, and missionary calls on dealers would place Tab-Wash far ahead of other hand cleaners from a promotional standpoint.

There undoubtedly is a market for Tab-Wash among sportsmen, fishermen, yachtsmen, and campers. Buyers at Abercrombie and Fitch in New York City and Brine's in Boston were enthusiastic about Tab-Wash. They particularly liked Tab-Wash's salt-water possibilities. At Brine's, however, a number of camper accessory items were on sale. These included an insect repellent, windshield cleaners, brass cleaners for boats, etc. The buyer stated that these sales were very small and were not "pushed" by the store because of the small unit profit. The same situation would exist for Tab-Wash.

In the sportsman field, Tab-Wash is a specialty item. It is a convenience, not a necessity. The sales volume would be roughly proportional to sales-promotion effort. In all, the total volume of sales through sporting-goods outlets would be small. An estimate of the total volume in the Boston area is $2,000 per year.

MAIL-ORDER BUSINESS

On October 31, 1948 a 1-inch advertisement was placed in the *New York Times* magazine section, offering an introductory container of

30 tablets for 10 cents. Within ten days after appearance of the advertisement, approximately 50 responses were received. A few inquiries from dealers were received.

The *New York Times* has a Sunday circulation of 1.1 million, with over 3 million readers. It has good coverage in all income brackets, with a concentration in the higher ones. The cost of the ad was $35.70. The magazine section is used as an effective mail-order medium for certain items.

Experience with the *New York Times* is not conclusive as to mail-order prospects for Tab-Wash. It does indicate that a large mail-order volume is unlikely. For example, assume that a profit of 10 cents per bottle of tablets, sold through the mail, is possible.

One hundred responses per $10 of advertising expenditure would have to be realized to break even. This is unlikely. Higher unit margin items better lend themselves to mail-order business.

CONTAINER: SIZE AND PRICE

An investigation of the various types of containers, such as cardboard tubes, cans, bottles, etc., has indicated that bottles are the most suitable for present needs. The size bottle selected and the consumer selling price are intimately tied together. The logical quantities of tablets to consider for sale in bottles are 25, 50, and 100.

The sample bottle of 30 tablets shows the following cost picture:

Bottle	2.34 cents
Cap	0.49
Label	0.25
Tablets	2.25
Filling and packing	1.00
Shipping containers	1.00
	7.33 cents

An estimate from the tablet manufacturer has not been obtained for packaging this size bottle. It would probably work out to be a total of 9 cents. This indicates a mimimum retail selling price of 25 cents per bottle.

An estimate has been received for tableting the granulation and for packaging bottles of 50 tablets, labeled, capped, packed 1 dozen bottles to a chipboard box, 1 gross of chipboard boxes to a shipping container. The cost picture per bottle is:

Granulation	2.25 cents
Tablet manufacturer's charge	10.00
	12.25 cents

A retail selling price minimum of 35 cents is indicated in this case.

The bottle of 100 tablets would come to about 17 cents. This would mean a selling price of about 50 cents per bottle.

Ideally, the 25-cent and 50-cent bottles would appeal to the convenience market, consisting of sportsmen and motorists and also to the home and garage market. The 35-cent size is a good initial compromise. It simplifies the marketing program and decreases the capital outlay.

The cost per tablet to the purchaser is 35 cents per 50, or 0.7 cent a piece. This is about twice as expensive as Boraxo when purchased in 8-ounce tins for 19 cents. It is in line with the other types of mechanics' hand cleaners.

CHANNELS OF DISTRIBUTION

There is no alternative to the distribution of Tab-Wash through jobbers. Certain large accounts might eventually be sold direct. The normal outlets for Tab-Wash are hardware stores, filling stations, and sporting-goods stores. They are serviced by jobbers in the respective fields.

For distribution to filling stations, there is the possibility of using gasoline-company distributing organizations. These organizations are operated as divisions of the major oil companies. In general, they handle company-branded products. They sometimes will use the manufacturer's trade name in a distinctive package conforming to the general appearance of the remainder of the line. Typically, these distributors exact a large discount. They offer immediate wide coverage and some sales-promotional work. These services will introduce a product to the public, following which a manufacturer can put out the same product under his own trade name without an initial sales promotional expenditure.

DISCOUNT SCHEDULE

A new product such as Tab-Wash would be sold to wholesalers at approximately half of the price to ultimate consumers. The retail store's discount is up to 40 per cent on the retail price.

Thus, for the 35-cent Tab-Wash product the discount schedule would be approximately as follows:

			Percentage of Retail Price
Retail sales price	35 cents		100
Retailer's discount	13 cents		37.2
Wholesaler's discount	5 cents		14.3
Tab-Wash sales price		17 cents	

OPERATIONAL PICTURE

The following table indicates the relation of retail sales volume to the operations of the Tab-Wash enterprise. "Contribution" has the same meaning as when previously used.

MONTHLY BASIS

Retail Sales	No. of Bottles	Retail Comm.	Jobber's Comm.	Tab-Wash Company Sales Volume	Contribution
$ 350	1,000	$ 130	$ 50	$ 170	$ 47.50
1,750	5,000	650	250	850	237.50
3,500	10,000	1,300	500	1,700	475.00

A retail sales volume of $1,750 could be handled without expanding the previous outlined organization. Initially, time would have to be spent in lining up distributors for the retail trade.

Expenditures would mainly be in the line of promotional literature, displays, and salesmen's aids. These would amount to approximately $100 per month.

Capital requirements to prosecute the marketing of the bottled product are as follows:

Material for 500,000 tablets	$ 225.00
Tableting charge (10,000 bottles of 50 at 10 cents each)	1,000.00
Counter display cards	300.00
Miscellaneous	200.00
	$1,725.00

To have the tablet manufacturer package a smaller quantity of bottles would not be economical.

The alternative to subcontracting the bottling would be to have the Tab-Wash company itself purchase materials for packaging a portion of the one million bulk tablets and package them. This would permit only a token sales effort. Even for this, at least $400 would be required.

In summation, the total monthly expenses and capital required to establish a company based on the patented product described in Exhibit 4 and to develop an industrial and retail market with a total sales volume up to $7,000 per month are:

Capital	$6,300.00
Monthly expenses	800.00

Exhibit 4

TAB-WASH PATENT

Patented July 10, 1951 **2,560,097**

UNITED STATES PATENT OFFICE

2,560,097

HAND CLEANING TABLET

Cherry L. Emerson, Jr., Newton Highlands, and William R. Cuming, Boston, Mass., assignors to Lawrie L. Witter, as trustee

No Drawing. Application January 25, 1949, Serial No. 72,756

2 Claims. (Cl. 252—89)

This invention relates to a new one-use hand cleaning tablet for individual use and particularly adapted to give a thorough cleaning to soiled or grimy hands. The invention aims to provide a tablet so regulated in composition, structure and method of fabrication that the tablet will be effective in cleaning the hands through attrition and emulsification, will have sufficient strength prior to use so that it will not disintegrate in handling and transportation and yet will readily disintegrate in use when in contact with water and when gently crushed in the hands of the user. Throughout the remainder of this application these two latter characteristics are referred to as "dry strength" and "wet disintegration" respectively.

We are aware that individual cleaning tablets including small pellets or bars of soap, have been heretofore known but these have not been satisfactory products. Further, we are aware that tablets, primarily in the pharmaceutical field, have been adapted to disintegrate rapidly in water, but the techniques used are not feasible in producing a rapidly disintegrable hand cleaning tablet.

Small bars or pellets of soap or non-soap detergents are not satisfactory for individual use because in the normal manufacturing process the product is so dense that the surface exposed to water for effecting solution of the detergent is small, necessitating prolonged rubbing by the user. Penetration of water into the interior of the bar is negligible. During the rubbing the bar is likely to slip from the hands of the user and become lost; moreover, the central portion of the bar is wasted should the user be able to extract sufficient detergent for his hand cleaning requirements. To decrease the density of the bar to the point where rapid disintegration in use occurs is impractical as the product then becomes too fragile prior to use.

In tableting pharmaceutical products the technique used for effecting rapid disintegration consists of compressing in a mold a granulation to which has been added a small quantity (3 to 5% by weight) of dry starch or similar substance. Upon contact with water the starch swells, breaking apart the tablet granules. Effervescence is also occasionally employed, the escaping gas serving the disintegrating function. To maintain the integrity of pharmaceutical tablets when in the dry state a bonding agent is also added in small quantities (under 10% by weight). The bonding agent is normally of a plastic nature. Bonding agents include gelatin, gum tragacanth, concentrated glycerin or sugar syrups. The quantity of bonding agent is purposely kept as low as possible for reasons which will presently become clear.

In fabricating a rapidly disintegrating hand cleaning tablet the techniques employed in the tableting art are not applicable. The detergents which we have found suitable with regard to their cleaning and emulsifying properties are of a plastic nature, that is, they undergo considerable plastic flow when subjected to the pressures normally used by us in the process of our invention. Moisture content increases the degree of plastic flow during compression. We normally use a granulation which contains approximately 2% moisture. Typical satisfactory detergents used by us are alkyl aryl sodium sulphonates, and cocoanut oil soap.

To produce an effective hand cleaning tablet it is necessary that a significant portion of the composition be a detergent which as previously indicated is of a plastic (flowable under pressure) nature. To produce a hand cleaning tablet in which the active detergent ingredient is less than approximately 10% of the tablet weight, the remainder being a pressure non-flowable and water insoluble filler, is feasible by utilizing established pharmaceutical tableting methods as previously outlined. Such a tablet however is impractical since the active ingredient is diluted to such a degree that the tablet is cumbersome and ineffective.

We have invented a new and improved one-use hand cleaning tablet and the method of making same in which the proportions of active detergent may be as high as 75% of the weight of the tablet while still maintaining the desirable properties of dry integrity and rapid disintegration in use. The actual percentage of detergent which we use depends primarily upon its activity as a cleaning agent. In general, the non-soap detergents are used in smaller proportions than soap. We have used soap and non-soap detergents together in several formulations. In preparing a granulation for tableting, we may either mix together the tablet ingredients in the dry state or in the presence of water. In the latter case the material must be dried prior to tableting.

The following is a preferred composition. The ingredients as listed will produce approximately 100 grams of dry composition:

25 grams sawdust
25 grams alkyl aryl sodium sulphonate
50 grams sodium sulfate
0.8 cc. 1% methylene blue solution
1.0 cc. ortho cresol in a mixture of 5 cc. ethyl alcohol and 5 cc. water

The alkyl aryl sodium sulphonate and the sodium sulfate are dissolved in 250 cc. of water and the solution is brought to a boil. The methylene blue is then added. When the solution is clear the sawdust is added and boiling is continued to drive off a part of the water and leave the material in the form of a thick slurry. This is placed

Exhibit 4—Continued

2,560,097

3

in a shallow pan in a drying oven maintained at a temperature of 110° C. The material is stirred from time to time to prevent caking and the formation of a detergent film on the surface. When the material is dry it is wetted with the ortho cresol solution and again dried. The material is then broken up, and passed through a 10 mesh per inch sieve. The moisture content of the material is brought to approximately 2% by spraying with water and mixing thoroughly. The granulation is then ready for tableting.

Approximately 1.3 grams of material is introduced to a die which is ⅝" in diameter with dome faced plungers. The granulation is compressed to 6,500 pounds per square inch. The resulting tablets have a void volume to solid constituent volume ratio of roughly 0.5. These tablets have excellent dry strength, disintegrate readily in use and are extremely effective as hand cleaning agents.

We have used a variety of detergents as the active ingredient in the hand cleaning tablet of our invention. Specifically, the following detergents have been used and are illustrative:

The alkali salts of palmitic, stearic, oleic and linoleic acid. These soaps are present in the wool soap manufactured by Swift & Co.

Sodium lauryl sulfate, an organic alcohol sulfate manufactured by Dupont and sold as Duponol M E Dry.

An alkyl aryl sodium sulphonate manufactured by Monsanto Chemical Co. and sold as Santomerse D.

An alkyl sodium sulphonate manufactured by Dupont and sold as M P 189. Sodium sulfate is incorporated in this product as a diluent.

A sulphonated glyceride ester manufactured by Colgate Palmolive Peet Co. and sold as Arctic Syntex M.

A protein derived detergent manufactured by Kalide Corp. and sold as Lamepon 4C.

Obviously other detergents, for example sulfated or sulfonated amides, sulfated or sulforated amines and quaternary ammonium compounds may be incorporated in the hand cleaning tablet of our invention to achieve desired characteristics.

In the process of our invention we combine one or more pressure non-flowable and water insoluble solids with the detergent used as active ingredient. This solids material is referred to as the filler. It is desirable that the filler act as an attrition agent when the tablet is in use. Other ingredients are added in relatively small quantities for imparting color, odor, lathering ability and maintenance of moisture content. For purposes of description herein, we have considered as "pressure flowable" a material which coalesces into a homogeneous mass when subjected to a pressure of 6,000 pounds per square inch and as "non-pressure flowable" a material which does not coalesce into or resemble a homogeneous mass when subjected to a pressure of 12,000 pounds per square inch.

As fillers we have used organic and inorganic materials and combinations thereof.

The organic materials used include maple wood sawdust, pine wood sawdust, wood flour, arrowroot starch, corn meal, wheat hulls, ground leather, comminuted paper, cane sugar and sorbitol. Inorganic materials include silica gel, alumina gel, sand, pumice, kieselguhr, sodium carbonate, sodium sulfate and trisodium phosphate. Obviously, other materials may be used for imparting specific features to the final prod-

4

uct. For example, sodium silicate may be used as a water softening agent.

We prefer to use as a filler a porous hydrophilic solid with a water permeable structure of the ultimate particle. Among the organic fillers, those high in cellulose and/or starch content have particular merit. We have found the following to be highly satisfactory: wood sawdust, wood flour, corn meal, silica gel and alumina gel. Sodium sulfate is a preferred non-porous filler when using sulfated or sulphonated detergents as it is often incorporated as a diluent in commercially available products.

The particle size distribution of the filler is selected in accordance with the degree of attrition desired in the final product. We have found that wood sawdust of screen analysis through 40 and on 48 mesh per inch is satisfactory when mild scrubbing is desired. If gentle action is desired a more finely divided filler is used.

We have discovered the tablet structural conditions which must be fulfilled in order to produce satisfactory hand cleaning tablets in which the percentage of detergent constituent is high. We have also discovered the mathematical expression which relates the percentage plastic constituent in the granulation to the maximum permissible pressure to which the granulation may be subjected in the tableting operation. Higher pressures than those given by the expression will produce tablets which are unsatisfactory as regards wet disintegration in use.

The expression is:

$$P_{max}=35{,}000e^{-2D}$$

where—

P_{max}=the maximum permissible compression pressure in pounds per square inch to produce a satisfactory hand cleaning tablet.

D=the fraction by weight of plastic constituent in the tablet. The plastic constituent is normally a detergent.

e is the base of the natural logarithms and has the value 2.72.

We prefer to produce tablets in which the amount of detergent is roughly 0.35 of the tablet weight. We find that the expression holds exceedingly well over the range of plastic constituent fractions from 0.125 to 0.75. Tablets containing less than 0.125 detergent are ineffective hand cleaners, while those containing more than 0.75 detergent have the undesirable characteristics of a solid bar or pellet.

In developing the mathematical expression referred to a large number of tablets were produced from granulations containing various percentages of plastic constituent. The granulations were prepared by either mixing together the ingredients in finely divided dry form or by preparing a water slurry of the constituents, drying and screening.

Each granulation prepared was compressed in a die at various pressures to produce several tablets. Each tablet so prepared was tested by actually using it for hand washing. The characteristic of wet disintegration was particularly noted. Each tablet was rated as excellent, good, poor and unsatisfactory. The results were plotted and curves drawn for each rating The plotted results approximate a logarithmic function. The equation was developed for the unsatisfactory tablet data, since pressures higher than those given by that equation will not be used. The equation developed agrees closely with the experimental results when plotted on semi-log

Exhibit 4—Continued

graph paper. Compression pressures which are greater than those given by the equation yield tablets which do not disintegrate readily. The equation holds over the range from 0.125 to 0.75 detergent. Below 0.125 plastic constituent tablets may be subjected to pressures considerably higher than those given by the equation. For example, tablets containing 0.05 plastic constituent with wood flour as the filler have been compressed to over 50,000 pounds per square inch and were very satisfactory as regards wet disintegration. Compression pressure is not critical at low percentages of plastic constituent and may be varied over wide ranges, while still producing satisfactory tablets. This accounts for the low percentage of plastic constituent normally used in tableting.

In addition, we have discovered the structure of a hand cleaning tablet which must be realized so that the tablet will have the desirable properties of dry strength and rapid wet disintegration. We have discovered that the voids within the tablet must bear a definite relationship to the volume occupied by solid constituents. We have discovered that the void volume to solid constituent volume ratio cannot be below 0.12 nor greater than 1.8. We prefer to use in our tablets a ratio of roughly 0.5. By void volume we mean that volume of a tablet prior to use not occupied by a solid or liquid constituent. Normally the voids are filled with air which is quickly displaced by water and causes rapid disintegration when the tablet is used.

Experimental data was obtained by preparing a number of granulations and tablets therefrom. The tablets were compressed at various pressures. Flat faced plungers were used in the die. The dimensions of each tablet were measured; and each tablet was weighed. The total volume of the tablet was obtained by calculation. Tablets for each pressure used were subjected to "dry strength" tests and "wet disintegration" tests in use. In these two respects tablets were rated as excellent, good, poor and unsatisfactory. It is to be noted that a tablet rated as unsatisfactory in either respect is not suitable as a hand cleaning tablet. Tablets designated at unsatisfactory as regards "wet disintegration" were, in general, produced at pressures higher than those given by the previously referred to mathematical expression, whereas those rated excellent, good and poor were produced at pressures below that given by the expression.

The determination of voids was accomplished in the following manner. Dependent upon the materials used in a specific tablet composition, a low viscosity liquid was selected in which all constituents were sparingly soluble. For example, it was determined that tablets containing only maple sawdust and Santomerse D, an alkyl aryl sodium sulfonate detergent manufactured by Monsanto Chemical Co., were sparingly soluble in acetone. Prior to use the selected liquid was saturated with the constituents of the tablet. This was accomplished by allowing a large quantity of the constituents to stand in the liquid for several days with occasional stirring. Tablets of each granulation and of each pressure used were then immersed in the selected saturated liquid as prepared above. The liquid was contained in a graduated cylinder. The change in the liquid level in the cylinder then was interpreted as the solid constituent volume of the tablets. In the case of very dense tablets several hours were allowed for penetration of the liquid throughout the tablet. The void volume and the "ratio" of void volume to solid constituent volume was then obtained by calculation. In cerain cases it was possible to check the void volume obtained in the above manner by calculation, utilizing as basic information the densities of constituents obtained from either published sources or our own experimental data.

The following examples indicate the structural characteristics of a few of the many tablets of various compositions which were prepared.

Example 1

Composition:
- 1 part (by weight)—alkyl aryl sodium sulphonate
- 2 parts—sodium sulfate
- 1 part—pine sawdust

The granulation was prepared essentially in accord with the previously outlined procedure. The particle size distribution in the granulation was "through 10 and on 60 mesh."

Dry Strength	Wet Disintegration	Ratio
Excellent	Excellent	0.502
Do	Poor	0.167
Do	Unsatisfactory	0.099
Poor	Excellent	0.748
Unsatisfactory	do	1.820

Example 2

Composition:
- 2 parts—alkyl aryl sodium sulphonate
- 4 parts—sodium sulphate
- 3 parts—calcium carbonate

The granulation was prepared in accord with the outlined procedure. The particle size distribution was "through 10 mesh (0.065" screen opening) and on 60 mesh."

Dry Strength	Wet Disintegration	Ratio
Excellent	Good	0.433
Do	Unsatisfactory	0.118
Poor	Excellent	0.748
Unsatisfactory	do	1.87

Example 3

Composition:
- 2 parts—alkyl aryl sodium sulphonate
- 4 parts—sodium sulfate
- 3 parts—silica gel

The granulation was prepared in accord with the outlined procedure. The particles in the granulation passed through a 10 mesh sieve.

Dry Strength	Wet Disintegration	Ratio
Good	Good	0.550
Do	Poor	0.294

Example 4

Composition:
- 1 part—alkyl aryl sodium sulphonate
- 1 part—cocoanut oil soap
- 2 parts—sodium sulfate
- 4 parts—maple sawdust

The granulation was prepared in accord with the outlined procedure. The particles in the granulation passed through 10 mesh screening.

Dry Strength	Wet Disintegration	Ratio
Excellent	Excellent	0.557

Exhibit 4—Continued

2,560,097

7

Having thus disclosed our invention and described in detail illustrative embodiments thereof, we claim as new and desire to secure by Letters Patent:

1. A dry one-use cleaning tablet having a dry strength sufficient to sustain it against breakage in transit and storage and a void content sufficient to cause it readily to absorb water and rapidly disintegrate in the presence of moisture, consisting essentially of a solid ionic organic detergent and a substantially water insoluble solids filler mixed together and compressed at a pressure of about that given by the expression $P=35{,}000e^{-2D}$ in which D is the weight fraction of detergent in the tablet and e is the base of the natural logarithms and has the value of 2.72, the detergent being not less than 0.125 and not greater than 0.75 of the tablet weight and the tablet having a gas void volume to solid volume in a ratio of not less than 0.24 and not greater than 0.76, the tablet being readily crushed and disintegrated in the palm of a hand when brought into contact with water.

2. The hand cleaning tablet defined in claim 1

8

in which the weight of the detergent is between .25 and .50 of the weight of the tablet and the filler comprises a granular cellulose.

CHERRY L. EMERSON, Jr.
WILLIAM R. CUMING.

REFERENCES CITED

The following references are of record in the file of this patent:

UNITED STATES PATENTS

Number	Name	Date
2,175,285	Duncan	Oct. 10, 1939
2,407,647	Bodman	Sept. 17, 1946
2,422,128	Percy	June 10, 1947

FOREIGN PATENTS

Number	Name	Date
5,698	Great Britain	1881

OTHER REFERENCES

Publication: U. S. Dept. of Commerce, National Bureau of Standards Circular C424—"Washing, Cleaning and Polishing Materials," p. 17.

Fluid-Lock Distributors, Inc.

Shortly after the outbreak of armed conflict in Korea, the management of Fluid-Lock Distributors, Inc., found itself unable to obtain an adequate supply of the patented product which it sold. Mr. James Trainor, the major stockholder and president of the company, was considering either the liquidation of the firm or the continuation of its operations on a limited basis.

Exhibit 1

FILLING A GLASS WITH THE FLUID-LOCK

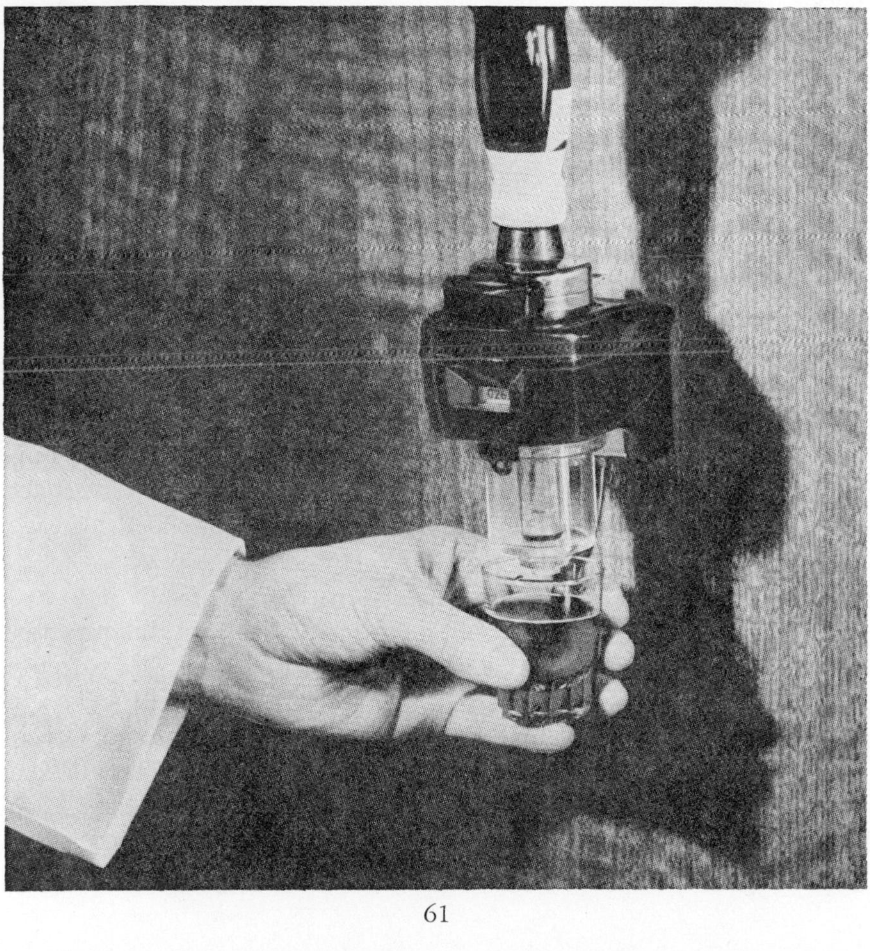

The Fluid-Lock (Exhibit 1) was an inventory control device for restaurants, bars, and other places in which liquor was dispensed by the individual serving. Specifically, it automatically registered and metered a set amount of liquor each time the bartender poured a drink. Fluid-Lock Distributors, Inc., had the exclusive right to sell and service the unit in the New England territory and in the various armed services officers' clubs within the continental United States.

THE PRODUCT

Mr. Wilder, the inventor of the Fluid-Lock, had, at one time, worked as a hotel clerk. He had been impressed by the fact that the hotel management did not consider it unusual to be able to account for only 80 to 90 per cent of the liquor issued to the bartender. Mr. Wilder believed that this wastage could be adequately controlled by some sort of mechanical means. His answer to the problem was the invention of Fluid-Lock.

The device consisted of two major units—the neck lock and the automatic dispenser (Exhibit 2). The neck lock comprised an internal expanding metal wedge affixed to a gate-valve and lock assembly with a rubber stopper which slid over the wedge and rested on the base of the lock assembly. This stopper replaced the original bottle stopper. To engage the device, a special wrench was used to reach down through the stopper and expand the metal wedge, which forced the sides of the stopper tightly against the inside walls of the bottle neck. Since a bottle neck is usually tapered with the small end at the pouring point, this effectually prevented removal of the bottle contents without unlocking the stopper or breaking the neck of the bottle. The opening was locked shut by pulling the slider of the gate-valve assembly across the opening into the closed position, whereupon concealed, spring-actuated pins snapped into matching slots in the slider and locked it firmly. The slider could be released only by using a circular key (two provided for each complete installation), which properly repositioned the pins.

Mounting the locked bottle on the dispenser automatically unlocked the opening. A locked bottle could not be removed from the dispenser unless the slider was in the closed position, so that, even if a partially full bottle were taken off a dispenser, its contents were still locked in and could not be tampered with by the bartenders. The bartender operated the unit by pulling a small lever once for each drink. This allowed the liquor to flow into a metering cup and thence into the glass. Each operation of the lever registered on an easily read meter, sealed in the dispensing unit. It was impossible for anyone to change the meter read-

Exhibit 2

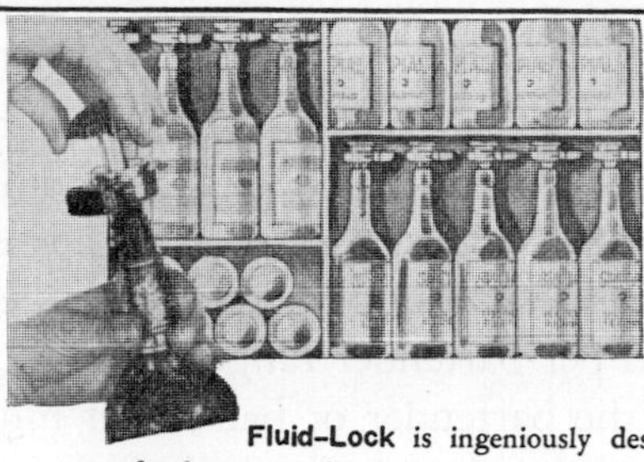

Fluid-Lock is ingeniously designed bar equipment, engineered to guarantee full profits from every bottle in your stockroom and to provide faster and more attractive service at your bar. Each bottle leaving the stockroom is sealed with a neck lock which interlocks at the bar with a separate dispenser for each brand. All liquor served at the bar flows through these dispensers where each drink is accurately measured and automatically recorded on a meter.

1. Bottles Sealed at Stockroom

A neck lock is inserted by the steward or owner into all bottles leaving the stockroom. Locking up is usually done once a day and sufficient bottles are locked up at one time and sent to the bar to last throughout the day (or throughout the shifts, etc.)

2. Locked Bottle Interlocks with Dispenser

A series of distinctive **Fluid-Lock** dispensers — one for each brand—attractively equip your bar. Having placed a locked bottle on its dispenser, the bartender presses the gate valve, thereby permitting liquor to flow into the transparent measuring cup ready for serving. Replacing empty bottles on the dispenser with full locked standby bottles is a much faster operation than the conventional uncorking procedure.

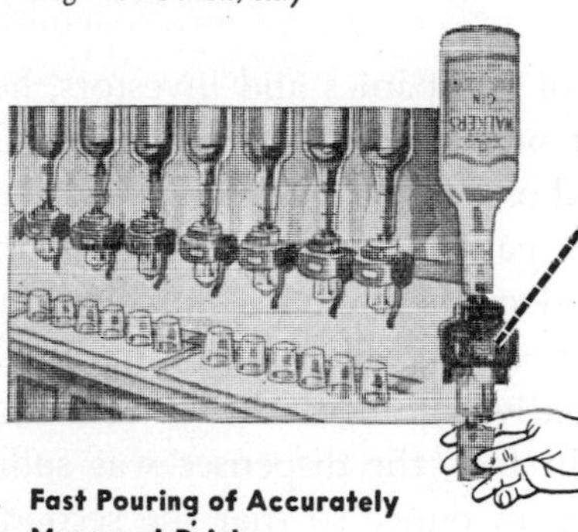

3. Fast Pouring of Accurately Measured Drink

With the glass held under the cup, the flick of a finger trips the trigger lever and an accurately measured drink is delivered — without a drop being spilled or wasted. (Two drinks may be pulled simultaneously using both hands.) The clear-vision measuring cup automatically refills to await the next serving.

As each drink is dispensed it is recorded on a counting meter.

4. Complete Control of Inventory and Cash

A rapid check of the counting gauges on a simple tally form at the end of each day or shift, etc., quickly indicates by brands the number of drinks dispensed and total sales. Cash in the cash register should correspond with sales totals on the tally sheets. A simple up-to-the-minute office record can also be maintained of inventory on hand and rate of sales of each brand.

ings without breaking the seal or otherwise rendering the unit inoperable.

One dispenser was required for each brand in use (Exhibit 2). Usually two neck locks were sold with each dispenser, so that a "stand-by" bottle was available while an empty was returned to the stockroom to have its lock removed and placed on a full bottle, which was then issued to the bar and became the next "stand-by." Depending upon the type of bar, the number of dispensers needed per bartender ranged from 12 to 20. Since, for a number of reasons, the bartender or bar owner might wish to give a free drink to a customer or visitor, a simple form, similar to a petty-cash receipt, was made available to record these noncash transactions. Thus, at the end of the day, the reading of the meter multiplied by the sales price per drink should equal the cash in the register plus the chits signed by the bartender.

The first models of the device were manufactured by the inventor's son-in-law. The idea proved to be patentable, and "good" patents were obtained. The inventor had no desire to manufacture Fluid-Lock. Rather, he wished to sell the patent rights for a cash payment plus a royalty.

After showing it to a number of companies and investors, he eventually interested the management of a large corporation, the General Precision Apparatus Company, whose subordinate divisions manufactured such things as machine tools, gauges, air-conditioning equipment, and test equipment. Mr. Wilder demonstrated his models before the executives of General Precision Apparatus. They were impressed when he showed that his dispenser actually obtained 25 and $\frac{6}{10}$ one-ounce drinks from a $\frac{1}{5}$ gallon bottle. In fact, the dispenser was sufficiently accurate to accumulate the $\frac{6}{10}$ of an ounce so that the second bottle placed on the dispenser gave 26 one-ounce drinks with $\frac{2}{10}$ of an ounce left over. Mr. Wilder explained to the executives of General Precision Apparatus that most bar owners were obtaining, on the average, only 20 to 22 one-ounce drinks per bottle.

After some investigation of both the patent and the probable market, General Precision Apparatus purchased the invention. It was a number of months before the product was ready for the market. The inventor was initially hired to handle sales of the item, but for several reasons his progress in marketing Fluid-Lock did not satisfy the company. The sales manager, who replaced Mr. Wilder, was also discharged after a few months, since he, too, had little success pushing the Fluid-Lock sales.

FORMING THE NEW COMPANY

About this time, Mr. Trainor became interested in the product. James Trainor was in his early thirties and had graduated as a chemical engineer from one of the leading engineering colleges in the country. He had worked for seven years in a medium-size chemical company, eventually becoming plant manager of a branch plant. He then left the chemical company to become assistant to the president of a new enterprise established to manufacture sonic measuring apparatus. After a year and a half, he resigned from this company to devote full time to managing a family trust fund. Although this position required nearly full-time attention, Mr. Trainor did have some free time that he could devote to other enterprises. On the other hand, his trust work provided him with sufficient income to live reasonably well.

Mr. Trainor first learned of Fluid-Lock from a lawyer friend. One of the lawyer's clients, a Mr. Stanley Payton, had seen the product at a hotel show and had discovered that General Precision Apparatus was without a New England distributor. Mr. Payton, a salesman with considerable industrial experience, had convinced General Precision Apparatus that he should be appointed the New England distributor. Although General Precision Apparatus was interested in Mr. Payton's proposition, they refused to assign him the franchise until he had formed a sales organization with a working capital of at least $100,000. Although Mr. Payton personally had no such amount, he did discover a man who claimed that he was willing to back the company for the required $100,000. When Mr. Payton attempted to follow up this initial contact, he found the man had left town without leaving a forwarding address.

John Stanford, the lawyer, believed the distributorship offered an excellent new-enterprise possibility. He suggested that a corporation be formed to market Fluid-Lock in New England. Since neither he nor Mr. Payton had any money to invest, they would accept the minority interest in the company. Mr. Payton would devote full time to the selling effort. John Stanford would handle any legal problems that might arise, and give all possible aid in any area. James Trainor would handle all the financial details.

Mr. Trainor made a thorough check of Fluid-Lock. He found that the product was extremely well made. There had never been a complaint about quality from the few people who had already purchased the item. He also found that the statements made by Mr. Payton and

Mr. Stanford checked in every detail with the information he obtained from present users and the General Precision Apparatus Company. Although he realized that Fluid-Lock was an item that at some distant date might find its market saturated, he estimated the potential sales for Massachusetts alone at about 240,000 units. He arrived at this amount by multiplying total state liquor licenses by an average number of machines per license. Furthermore, an item which made possible a complete financial control by semimechanical means intrigued both his engineering and financial interest.

Mr. Trainor offered to invest $10,000 for 100 per cent of the preferred stock and 65 per cent of the voting stock. Several days were spent in convincing General Precision Apparatus that $10,000 would be sufficient capitalization for the new venture. Eventually a franchise was granted, and the new company opened its office early in 1949. Under the terms of the franchise, Fluid-Lock Distributors, Inc., was given exclusive selling rights for all of New England. It was required to maintain at all times an inventory of at least $5,000 worth of machines. James Trainor was able partially to offset the effect this had on the capital structure of the business by obtaining from the General Precision Apparatus' credit manager an $8,000 line of credit.

General Precision Apparatus Company recommended that the retail sales price per unit be set for $40. A unit consisted of two bottle locks and one dispenser. Fluid-Lock purchased the unit from the manufacturer for $26. All accessories were extra.

SELLING THE PRODUCT

As soon as the company was formed, Mr. Payton started his sales campaign. He made no attempt to concentrate on any particular area within the territory, but rather sold to those outlets which he thought would offer the least sales resistance. If after a few days he believed a particular city was not going to produce a sale, he would move on and try another location. As the only salesman covering all of New England, he had a wide area in which to work. At the end of the first four months, he had sold 200 units. At the $40 retail price, this gave the firm a gross profit of only $2,800, an amount insufficient to cover the actual expenses of operating the company.

Mr. Trainor believed that the selling price was entirely too low and that sales could be made just as easily at a price of $55 on a cash basis, or $62.50 for a time sale. He also wished to charge $3 per unit installation fee. General Precision Apparatus Company at first refused to go along with the recommended price increases; but after some discussion,

Mr. Trainor was able to convince the company that he would not be able to continue operation under the old $40 ceiling. As a further means of cutting the cost of sales, Mr. Trainor attempted to convince Mr. Payton of the necessity of confining sales effort to one area, so that a number of installations could be made at once. This would reduce both the sales and the installation cost per unit. Although Mr. Payton made some attempt to follow this advice, he still tended to sell in the areas and places where he believed his personal selling job would be easiest.

Mr. Trainor described Mr. Payton as an excellent salesman for the product but as a man "who had little administrative ability." Mr. Trainor admitted that selling Fluid-Lock was not an easy task. The class of businessmen who were the logical customers—namely, small cafe owners, bartenders, restaurateurs, and hotel managers—were generally suspicious of a new innovation and somewhat doubtful that it ever could supplant or add to the control offered by their $2,000 or $3,000 cash register. In addition, most selling effort had to be concentrated in the early morning hours from 12:00 A.M. to 2:30 A.M., the only period many owners and managers had time to talk. Mr. Trainor further characterized Mr. Payton as "being the only man outside of the inventor who was ever able to close a sale on Fluid-Lock."

FINANCING THE SALES

In his search for customers, Mr. Payton found a number of small bars and grills, as well as several large roadside taverns and night clubs, which were willing to purchase the product if some type of credit could be granted. At first Mr. Trainor arranged for the financing of the customer notes by a large city bank. The terms were one third of the sales price, payable in cash with the remainder on a six to eighteen months' note. The balance bore an interest charge of 10 per cent, and the notes were made out to the Fluid-Lock Company. Mr. Trainor in turn endorsed these notes to the bank, which discounted them at 6 per cent.

The company soon found that this financing did not answer the needs of some of their less prosperous customers. These could not afford the one-third down payment and, in addition, wished to pay by some method which varied directly with their sales volume. Eventually, Mr. Trainor offered a plan which called for a down payment of an installation fee of $3.00 per unit in addition to a purchase price at $62.50 per unit to be paid at the rate of 2½ cents per drink drawn from the dispensers, billed biweekly or monthly. Such a system required capital far in excess of the original $10,000. As manager of a trust fund, Mr.

Trainor had developed several financial contacts in New York City which he believed would be interested in loaning money for this purpose. He was able to obtain a sufficient amount at an interest rate of 2⅞ per cent from a New York financial group. In turn, he charged the customer 10 per cent for the use of this money. From the known volume of drinks being dispensed through units already installed, Trainor estimated that it would take, at 2½ cents per drink, about eighteen to thirty-six months for a customer to pay both interest and principal on the cost of a Fluid-Lock installation.

CUSTOMER REACTION TO FLUID-LOCK

Although Mr. Payton was able to estimate closely the number of machines a bar owner would require for his current volume of business, a number of the customers preferred to estimate their own requirements. In general, the company was perfectly willing to go along with their estimates and install the number of machines that the bar owner believed necessary. If, after a reasonable period of time, the proprietor found that he had procured too many machines, Fluid-Lock Distributors would accept the return of the extra machines and credit his account accordingly. For example, one tavern owner estimated his needs at 87 machines. Three months later, he was convinced that 55 machines could handle even his peak requirements. Fluid-Lock Distributors took the 32 machines back without question. The owner of this particular establishment estimated that his Fluid-Lock installation had allowed him to reduce his inventory by $7,000.

Another small bar was owned by a man who did most of the bartending himself. His only employee was an elderly man who, as a result of age and a strenuous life, suffered from a form of palsy. When the owner took his day off, he turned the operation of his bar over to this employee. Each time the owner returned, he received many and bitter complaints from the patrons of the establishment, who pointed out that the old man's hand shook so much while filling the glass that he spilled most of the drink. Furthermore, the owner was not sure that his old friend and employee was always completely honest about the day's receipts.

Mr. Payton sold this bar a Fluid-Lock installation. This solved the honesty question; and, since Fluid-Lock automatically poured the drink, it did away with the problem of wasted liquor and customer complaint. To prevent spillage while the drink was being carried to the customer, Mr. Payton advised a 3-ounce glass for a 1-ounce drink with a line etched around it to indicate the 1-ounce level. This innovation became popular for a number of Fluid-Lock installations, and the company was able to sell about 3,000 dozen of these glasses. Some of the establishments requested that the 1-ounce etched line be lowered so that it actually represented ⅞ ounce. Since a full 1-ounce was still metered into the glass, the customer believed that the bar was giving him a generous drink.

EXPANDING THE MARKET

In February, 1950, Mr. Stanford, the lawyer, conceived the idea of selling the Fluid-Lock to military officers' clubs. He was sure that, with the probable Congressional ban to be placed on slot machines, club stewards and club managers would be interested in cutting down their operating expenses. A large Air Force base in New York was selected for the trial sale. Sixteen machines were sold and placed in operation despite the resistance of the civilian steward and bartender. Mr. Trainor found that this club had previously averaged only about $100 monthly profit on its bar sales.

About ten months later, Mr. Trainor visited the same officers' club to show some possible investors the machines in operation. He was surprised and chagrined to find no sign of the installation. Both the club manager and the civilian steward were new. Upon inquiry he found that the new steward had convinced the club manager that the Fluid-Lock machines were not worth using; the steward claimed they slowed down bar service and caused other inefficiencies.

Mr. Trainor pointed out to the club manager that his predecessor, after a thorough investigation, had paid over $1,000 for the machines because he believed they would result in savings. Even if the present manager never intended to use them again, he suggested that he be allowed to set them up and at least show the manager how they were supposed to work. The manager granted permission to place the units back on the bar for a demonstration.

After the machines were operating satisfactorily and Captain Jones, the club manager, had learned exactly what they were supposed to do, Mr. Trainor suggested a meeting with the civilian club steward. As soon as they had all been seated, Mr. Trainor asked the club manager: "Captain, what is the present monthly profit on bar sales?"

"Well, Mr. Trainor, it varies between $100 and $200 per month."

"What has been your sales volume over the last year?"

"That also has been relatively constant. I don't think it has varied more than $100 or $200 per month."

"Now Captain Jones, will you do me the favor of getting out your books and looking up the bar profit for the four months, March through June? That is the period during which our machines were in operation."

"Certainly, Mr. Trainor. Let's see now. Profit in March was $1,200; April, $2,000; May, $2,200; June, $1,800. Well, I'll be —— —— ——!"

At this point Mr. Trainor excused himself, since he believed it would be embarrassing to hear what was going to be said to the steward.

This sale had been made outside of the Fluid-Lock Distributors, Inc., territory. However, the military-club market seemed so promising that Mr. Trainor and his friends requested the General Precision Apparatus Company to give them a national franchise for all military posts and stations in the United States. After some discussion, the franchise was granted to them.

THE SALES CRISES

By the spring of 1950, Fluid-Lock had 76 accounts outstanding, representing about $70,000 worth of sales. These were almost entirely from the smaller-type establishments. At this time, Mr. Payton unfortunately suffered a complete nervous breakdown. He announced that he felt he would be of no further use to the company, and accordingly retired to a farm in New Hampshire.

Payton's retirement pointed up a question which had been gradually forming in Mr. Trainor's mind, that is, whether the company should continue with its present small capitalization. He was sure that it would take some time to find a salesman to replace Mr. Payton. Mr. Trainor was disappointed in the amount of help received from the General Precision Apparatus Company and the fact that the parent company seemed to have no over-all plan for selling Fluid-Lock. Never had the parent company developed, either through the use of its own accounting talent or by employing professional hotel accountants, the corollary accounting system which Mr. Trainor believed to be absolutely essential to installations in large restaurants, hotels, and similar locations operated by top-grade, cost-conscious managements. Nothing had been done in the way of large-scale advertising. He believed that another distributor would soon be set up to cover the New York territory and that General Precision Apparatus Company had already established its own sales office to sell Fluid-Lock in the Philadelphia area. On the other hand, experience had shown that Fluid-Lock was, in all respects, a quality product and so well made that, to date, no major complaint had ever been received from a customer. Some of the first machines installed had readings on their meters indicating they had served 25,000 to 30,000 drinks.

With his retirement, Mr. Payton gave up all claim that he might have had against the company and turned over his stock to the corporation. This left Mr. Trainor and the lawyer, Mr. Stanford, as the only two stockholders. The longer they looked at their capital position, the more convinced they were that additional capital was needed. In addition, they believed that more sales talent was required than either of the two men possessed.

In May, 1950, Mr. Trainor visited a venture-capital firm in New York City. He talked with one of the senior partners and at the completion of their conversation had convinced the partner that Fluid-Lock Distributors, Inc., was an opportunity in which the venture-capital company might be interested. The partner assigned one of his research men to investigate the possibilities of Mr. Trainor's company. This turned out to be a very thorough investigation. The research man visited every one of the 76 installations to query the proprietors about the product, the saving that could be made by its use, and how they liked it.

The resulting research report was favorable; but before any action could be taken by the venture-capital firm, the Korean war intervened. Within a few weeks, three of the partners of the venture-capital firm were called to active duty. The remaining management members decided that they would not increase the number of enterprises in their present group until they were able to obtain some estimate of future conditions.

A few days after Mr. Trainor was notified of this decision, the General Precision Apparatus Company forwarded a letter to Fluid-Lock Distributors, Inc., which stated that, because of the Korean situation and the resulting material shortages, General Precision was discontinuing the manufacture of the Fluid-Lock machines. All metal parts in the Fluid-Lock which came in contact with the liquor were manufactured from nickel or nickel alloy. Nickel was the only known metal that could stand constant immersion in an alcoholic beverage without contaminating the liquor. With this scarce metal restricted to crucial items, General Precision saw little hope of supplying Fluid-Lock Distributors with new machines until the present emergency was over. However, the General Precision Apparatus Company did have about 2,000 complete units in stock which would be made available to Trainor should he decide to continue with the business.

Mev Control Company

In March, 1947, the Mev Control Company of Boston, Massachusetts, was attempting to interest investors in supplying $35,000 to finance expansion of its operations. The company had one year's experience in research and development in the fields of electronics, mechanics, and optics and hoped to become profitable by meeting part of the great demand for research in these fields. The following excerpts from the then current literature indicated the growing interest in research in these fields:

A large publishing firm sent thousands of questionnaires on the utilization of electronic equipment to its subscribers in 1944. Nearly 17,000 electronic devices were reported in operation by 796 companies in eleven industries. The metalworking industry made use of nearly 8,500 devices, or more than 50% of the total, while metal producing, chemical processing, electrical utilities and miscellaneous nonmanufacturing industries utilized about 1,500 to 2,000 devices each. The total for the six other industries amounted to slightly more than 1,500. Users classified their electronic devices according to the following functions: (1) heating; (2) control; (3) regulation; (4) power conversion; (5) counting, sorting, weighting and inspecting; (6) molecular vibration; (7) measurement and analysis; (8) safety. By far the most important headings were control, and measurement and analysis, each of the two accounting for almost 6,000 devices.[1]

Army appropriation for 1947 basic research in all fields is $70,000,000. Navy has earmarked $45,000,000. About 14% of the Navy nut will apparently be spent with the electronics industry. Army telleth not.[2]

Mev Control Company was formed in December, 1945. Initially, five men participated equally; four contributed $2,000 each, in return for 200 shares of $1 par value common stock and 18 shares of $100 par value preferred stock. The fifth man, Mr. Louis C. Ott, contributed $20 and signed a note for $1,980 for his share of the stock.

The president was Mr. Don Ashby, an electronics engineer. Dr. Fred Sommer of the Laboratory of Ophthalmology, a private research foundation, was head of the research department on a part-time basis. Mr. Ott was business manager and chief contract negotiator. The manage-

[1] "Electronics from War to Peace," in National Industrial Conference Board, *The Conference Board Industry Record,* Vol. V, No. 3 (April 30, 1946), p. 7.

[2] *Electronics* (New York: McGraw-Hill Publishing Co., Inc., January, 1947), p. 69.

ment believed that it was well equipped to fulfill any contract it might secure.

In May, 1946, a difference of opinion on policy between the stockholders resulted in a reorganization of the company. One stockholder withdrew; and his stock was purchased by the company, funded by a $2,000 note advanced by Mr. Ashby. At about the same time, another partner-director resigned, for personal reasons, but retained his preferred stockholdings. Subsequently, Mr. George Barnes, a Boston investment analyst, invested $1,500 in the company. At the time of the reorganization, Mr. Ott redeemed his note to the company with funds raised through a GI loan. In February, 1947, the capital structure was as follows:

	Common Stock*	Preferred Stock†	5 Per Cent Notes
Mr. Ashby	$200	$1,800	$3,500
Dr. Sommer	200	1,800	1,800
Mr. Ott	200	1,800	....
Mr. Southard	...	1,800	....
Mr. Barnes	...	....	1,500
	$600	$7,200	$6,800

* 50,000 shares authorized $1 par value common stock.
† 500 shares authorized $100 par value preferred stock.

Mr. Ashby, forty-four years old, held engineering degrees from Harvard University and the Massachusetts Institute of Technology. He had worked for the General Electric Company for eight years, five years of which he had been with the research laboratory. Later he became a research associate at the University of Syracuse. When the head of the Psychology Department at Syracuse became president of a college near Boston, he invited Mr. Ashby to come with him as assistant director of the Research Laboratory of Sensory Psychology and Physiology. After further research work on electronic instruments for this laboratory, Mr. Ashby spent over two years in an industrial electronic concern; and during the war he was an independent consulting engineer. He retained his connection with the college as a research associate. Mr. Ashby's primary interest in Mev Control Company was in research and development; he delegated all sales and promotion responsibilities to Mr. Ott.

Dr. Fred Sommer, thirty-seven years old, was well known for his work in optics and ophthalmology. During the war he had performed research work for the United States Navy and made many contacts which the Mev Control management hoped would facilitate its securing Navy contracts during the postwar period.

Mr. Ashby and Dr. Sommer had met during the war and became interested in forming their own research and consulting firm. Mr. Ashby desired to become president of his own company, while Dr. Sommer wanted to supplement his income.

Because neither Mr. Ashby nor Dr. Sommer had interest or experience in business matters, they secured the services of Mr. Ott, thirty-two years old, who had had a varied business experience. Mr. Ott had studied business administration at Boston University night school. He had worked for a loan company, had sold insurance, and had been general manager of an estate. At one time he managed his own leather-trading company, until his principal financial backer sold out to a rival firm. During the war he served in the Merchant Marine except for a short period of service in the U.S. Marine Corps, from which he received a medical discharge.

In October, 1945, Mr. Ott opened a sales office in Boston with the idea of securing franchises for household products. While awaiting franchises, he was able to secure a reasonable income by offering his services to insurance agents as customer representative, explaining insurance terms to prospective policyholders. In November he learned of the opportunity of joining Mr. Ashby and Dr. Sommer and, after investigating the market for control devices, decided to join them as vice-president and business manager. Although he had had no previous knowledge of the electronics field, he believed he could handle the business problems and would easily acquire sufficient technical knowledge for sales work. His sales work, the management believed, would be very important because he was the only company officer with sales experience or with an interest in selling.

Mr. Ott became chairman of the board of directors, composed of Mr. Ashby, Dr. Sommer, Mr. Barnes, and himself. Salaries paid during 1946 were $10,400 to Mr. Ashby, $8,800 to Mr. Ott, and $4,800 to Dr. Sommer for half-time services.

The original plan of the management was to obtain sufficient consulting work from industrial firms to pay current expenses while developing products on which they later hoped to make profits. The first project was the development of a stimulator, a device for use in student laboratory experiments. The Mev Electronic Stimulator would replace the biological laboratory induction coils used in measuring muscular reactions of frogs to electric shock. This stimulator, sold by direct mail, was the only commercial product manufactured in quantity during the first year of operation.

Other items had been developed on individual orders; but, because of their special nature, repeat sales had not been secured. Repeat sales were very important to the company's success, since the initial cost of developing and constructing the devices was extremely high. For example, the cost of the first pulse generator developed for Tufts laboratory was about $1,200, including all development costs; the second machine could be sold for $485 after a 100 per cent markup. All sales were handled by company officers, who followed up on inquiries from direct-mail campaigns or displays at scientific exhibitions.

The officials of the company decided in early 1946 to make strenuous efforts to secure government research contracts because such contracts would insure good salaries for the management and the company would be allowed to retain commercial rights to its research developments. Some of the difficulties experienced in attempting to secure a government contract are illustrated in the report on the status of the Guided Missiles Systems Tester (Exhibit 1).

Exhibit 1

MEV CONTROL COMPANY

CONSOLIDATED REPORT ON THE STATUS OF THE GUIDED MISSILES SYSTEMS TESTER

When it was decided to reopen the question of the Guided Missiles Systems Tester, the following things were done:

1. Letters were sent to the Bureau of Aeronautics, Bureau of Ordnance and Special Devices, requesting them to reconsider the procurement of this device.
2. Colonel Starch of Army Ordnance was approached. He stated that in his opinion the proposal had merit and he sent me to Colonel White of the Guided Missiles Section, AAF and General Wolfe of Personnel Training, Guided Missiles Section AAF. General Wolf then—
   a) asked for a complete file on the subject which was provided;
   b) assured me personally and by letter of his continuing interest in the project;
   c) through channels requested that Wright Field personnel make a technical appraisal of the proposal;
   d) had me go over the matter with his junior officers, particularly Colonel Black, Colonel Morgan, and Lieutenant Colonel Young.

Colonel White was not in my first visit there and Lieutenant Colonel Capp suggested we send a copy of the proposal to the Joint Research and Development Board, attention L. V. Nash, for transmittal to the Guided Missiles Committee. Later, Colonel White and Colonel Smith went over

Exhibit 1—Continued

our proposal with me and said that in their opinion the proposal had merit. They suggested that I bring it to the attention of Wright Field personnel. I, in turn, suggested that they write a letter to Wright Field, sending me a copy, at which time I would make the trip.

Colonel Starch had also suggested that I see Dr. Jenkins of General Electric at Schenectady and Dr. Lewis of Bell Telephone Laboratories. Dr. Jenkins said that the proposal had merit but that it did not fit in with their immediate plans. However, he volunteered the following statements:

1. The principal point in favor of the proposal was that the equipment was in existence.
2. When the system was worked out, it would make a wonderful trainer.

I then brought the matter up with Mr. Ammon of Naval Research Laboratory and he said the proposal had merit, but did not fit in with their plans.

I then brought it up with Dr. Smiddy and Dr. Olson of the Applied Physics Laboratory. Dr. Olson made the following comments:

1. It was a thing for ONR to do.
2. He would be interested in using it by putting their stimulator in series with it.
3. We should propose to develop our own system in its entirety.

I then talked to Mr. H. L. Pope of the Bureau of Ordnance and with Mr. H. F. Roberts in Bureau of Ordnance. They were interested and Mr. Roberts was extremely interested in the Mark III and the possibility of the Bureau of Ordnance procuring a Mark III for use with their Guided Missiles projects.

They sent me to Commander O. K. Bache of the Bureau of Aeronautics, who went over the matter and turned me over to Mr. C. R. Frye who was extremely interested in the airplot feature and suggested that the matter be taken up with ONR.

Accordingly, I brought the matter to the attention of Captain Joseph, Captain Eller and Commander Loomis. I went over the proposal with Commander Loomis in great detail several times. This finally resulted in his becoming seriously interested and requesting an instruction book for the Mark III, which was provided him.

I then informed Mr. Ralph Jones, at his request, of the status of the proposal. He called in a Dr. S. D. Colgate (formerly Commander). Their attitude was that the proposal had a great deal of merit, and they strongly urged that I take it up with Mr. Pringle at Special Devices and Dr. Lewis of Bell Telephone Laboratories. They assured me of their continuing interest.

Mr. Pringle's initial attitude was that the solution of the equation of motion was the first job and it should take several years. His opinion was that the tools developed for the solution of the mathematics of the problem would then be available, in whatever form they might take, to do the test-

Exhibit 1—Continued

ing and training required. I pointed out that our proposal could be used as a tool immediately and that there was positive assurance that it would meet the other requirements. He said that it would not serve as a tool. I said, "Why not?" In attempting to answer me he convinced himself that it could serve as a tool to the extent that he would like to reopen the whole matter and go into it with Dr. Sommer.

I then went down to see Dr. Lewis of Bell Telephone Laboratories, who brought in a Mr. Michael Wells and Dr. W. A. Lewis. They were extremely interested—said that it has distinct merit, that there is a possibility, even a likelihood, that they will want to go ahead and procure the device or some modification of it. I left with them a copy of the schematic and proposal and also a copy of our proposal on the SX Radar Trainer, as giving a little additional information on the method of placing the antenna patterns on photographic wedges. I am to telephone them next Monday, December 2.

In going over the proposal at Wright Field, I talked to Mr. Vancott of the Guided Missiles Section, Lieutenant Colonel Ruggles, who is Colonel Waters' assistant, and a conference was arranged at which the Equipment Laboratory was represented by Mr. M. H. Marsh and Mr. A. C. Whiteside; the Armament Laboratory was represented by Captain R. N. Brown, Dr. J. E. Potter and Mr. B. B. Parker.

Lieutenant Colonel P. E. Johnson sat in on the conference. He is interested in Air to Surface Guided Missiles so I gave him a copy of the Hendricks Corrector outline as prepared by Major Hendricks. The Electronic Subdivision was represented by Mr. P. E. French. The proposal was outlined and discussed. In my opinion it was thoroughly understood by most of the people present. Captain Brown grasped the idea immediately and defended it strongly against the criticism of his colleagues.

The result of the conference can best be summed up by repeating the statement made by Dr. Potter. He said, "Thank you for coming out. You have given us a great deal to think about. This is a highly novel and apparently quite worth-while proposal, and we feel sure that we have enough knowledge, after further study of the papers you have left us, to render an adequate report."

LOUIS C. OTT

By the spring of 1947, the Mev Control Company had not secured any substantial government contracts; and although the "internal" research work in progress was developing to the management's satisfaction, the lack of income was endangering the company's future. A list of the projects in process or completed in January, 1947, are given in Exhibit 2.

Current expenses in early 1947 amounted to $1,400 weekly, and the officers estimated that approximately $35,000 in additional funds would

Exhibit 2

MEV CONTROL COMPANY

Project List as of January 28, 1947

No.	Name	Status	No.	Name	Status
1	Stimulator	Completed	36	Vibration Apparatus	Inactive
2	Low Frequency Source	Inactive	37	Servo Mechanisms	Sales
3	DDT Project	Completed	38	Servicing and Repairs	Active
4	Special Devices Project	Active	39	Range Indication for RTAP	Completed
5	Radar Trainer, Mark III	Promotional	40	Memory Wheel Improvement	Completed
6	Radar Trainer, OCZ	Completed	41	Continuous Rate Indicator	Completed
7	Frequency Converter	Completed	42	Portable Automatic Awakener	Active
8	Guided Missiles Tester	Sales	43	Wilman Laboratory Proposals	Sales
9	Mathematical Problem	Dropped	43A	Data Projector	Sales
10	Power Supply	Inactive	44	Guide Buoy	Inactive
11	Counting Device	Completed	45	Replacement of 200 Condensers—Memory Wheel	Completed
12	D.C. Amplifier Report	Completed	46	Valve Operating Mechanism	Sales
13	RTAP Coordinator	Active	47	Laboratory Precipitator—Godfrey Carter, Inc.	Dropped
14	Precipitation—Godfrey Carter, Inc.	Completed	48	Refractory Period Stimulator	Inactive
15	Logarithmic Response Circuit	Inactive	49	Oscilloscope Recording Camera and Enlargers	Active
16	Stimulator—Demonstration Models	Completed	50	Exhibit at AAA's Meeting	Completed
17	Stimulator—Production	Active	51	Two Magazines and Roller for 35 Mm. Camera	Completed
18	Small Power Supplies	Inactive	52	Electromagnetic Clutch	Inactive
19	Improved Electronic Counting Device	Inactive	53	Industrial Counting Device (Packaging)	Sales
20	Wedge Production for OCZ	Completed	54	Grinding Machine Control	Sales
21	Impulse Rate Indicator	Completed	55	Power Amplifier for Exciter Units, MB Manufacturing Co.	Sales
22	Bio-assay	Active	56	Test of Inventive Ability	Inactive
23	Research Stimulator	Completed	57	Precision Shutter	Inactive
23A	Pulse Generator	Active	58	Railroad Electronics	Dropped
23B	Research Stimulator	Active	59	Ten Pulse Marker R. L. S. P. & P.	Completed
24	Discriminator	Completed	60	Captain Vollney's Problems (Stethoscope, Ultra-Violet, CO_2)	Sales
25	Razor Blade Counting	Dropped	61	Traffic Timer	Active
26	Fish Weighing Device	Dropped	62	Oscillating Grinder Tolerance Control	Inactive
27	Device 15-M-7c Direction Radio Sono-Buoy Modification Kit	Sales	63	Popular Games	Inactive
28	Traffic Signal Control, portable	Inactive	64	Portable Room Cooler	Sales
29	Hendricks Corrector	Active	65	Research on Accuracy of Gearing	Sales
30	High Speed Paper Making	Dropped	66	Research on Derivative Sense	Sales
31	Trainer for SX Radar	Sales	67	Cardiotachometer	Inactive
32	Device for Recording Airplane Reservations	Inactive	68	Low Voltage D.C. Source	Active
33	Navigation	Inactive	69	Photo Electric Amplifier	Completed
34	Stimulator Pre-production	Completed	70	Impact Testing	Sales

Exhibit 3

MEV CONTROL COMPANY

PROSPECTUS: PURPOSES FOR WHICH CAPITAL IS REQUIRED

1. *Purchase of Additional Tools*

Additional electrical test equipment and furniture and office equipment will be required for expansion. In addition to the research and development work we are presently engaged in, it is our intention to manufacture products in the electrical field which are now in extremely short supply. At present it is our intention to engage in the production of fractional horsepower electrical motors. The amount of tooling necessary would be determined by the production we hope to achieve.

2. *Manufacture of the Mev Electronic Stimulator Model 461*

This device is described in the booklet prepared for the exhibition of the American Association for the Advancement of Science. We have received sample orders from the following schools:

University of Pennsylvania
Ohio State University
University of Oregon
Temple University
Western Reserve University
Long Island College of Medicine

The stimulators are also in classroom use at the following schools:

8 stimulators at Harvard University
12 stimulators at Tufts College

We anticipate that we should sell 2,000 stimulators over the next two years. We are now in production on this item.

3. *Hendricks Fire Adjustment Corrector*

This device has been brought to the demonstration stage and a model has been built at our expense that is going to require the expenditure of additional sums for demonstration and promotion. The amount required will be in the order of hundreds rather than thousands of dollars.

4. *Instrumentation for the Nuclear Fission Laboratory at the Massachusetts Institute of Technology*

We are informed by the Director of this Laboratory that they are at some pains to find a manufacturer who has experience in D.C. amplification of a very high order so that they may secure safety devices for the Laboratory. These devices will be essentially a Geiger counter or other device very sensitive to radio activity, the output of which will be amplified by an electronic circuit and caused either to sound an alarm or shut off a machine or process.

They inform us that work on nuclear fission, particularly as it applies to its use as an industrial power source, is being expanded throughout the

Exhibit 3—Continued

country and that, while they want safety devices numbering in the hundreds themselves, if we develop reliable instruments we will have an expanding market throughout the country as these other Laboratories are set up. Just as soon as nuclear fission becomes commercially justifiable as a power source, safety devices will be a necessity in each commercial installation. Accordingly, it is my opinion that, inasmuch as we have a very definite know-how in this field already, we should expend whatever sum is necessary to develop the required safety devices. My estimate of the sum required for internal research and development is at the most $10,000.

5. *Automatic Awakener*

This is a device which will be battery operated and use miniature tubes, but will be small enough to carry in a man's pocket and have electrodes which will clip on a man's ear. If the man wearing it should fall asleep or his attention level fall below a certain amount, the device would give him a shock and sound an alarm at some remote point if desired. The uses of such a device are legion. It is apparent that such a device would be required equipment for airplane pilots, locomotive engineers, watch keeping officers on steamboats, etc. At the present time this device is under development by the Mev Control Company in cooperation with Laboratory of Sensory Psychology and Physiology. The project is out of the research stage and when the device is perfected, the arrangement is that the Laboratory shall patent it and the Mev Control Company be given the exclusive license to manufacture it.

6. *Frequency Modulation Broadcasting*

The situation in the FM receiver field is in a very confused state and there are a number of FM broadcasting stations that are very anxious to place an order for FM home receivers. We have been approached as to the possibility of our building 30,000 FM receivers at $60 apiece. Whether it would be desirable to enter this field at all is a question which would require further study; however, it is a distinct possibility.

7. *Patents*

Up to the present time we have developed about twenty ideas which are distinctly patentable and which we have not patented because of lack of capital.

8. *Advertising*

It is desirable to engage in a certain amount of advertising in trade papers as well as a considerable quantity of direct mail advertising. We propose to build up a mailing list of college and Government laboratories which would be a market for our biological and psychological research instruments. In the event that we brought out some device of a consumer goods nature, an advertising project for that particular item would be set up. On our regular research business I think that $3,000 should be expended during the next year.

be required to enable the company to be profitable. A prospectus (Exhibit 3) was written to interest prospective investors, and Mr. Ott spent considerable time calling on wealthy individuals with the hope of interesting them in the company and its future.

Mr. Ott believed that potential investors would secure a 15 to 20 per cent return on their investment if the company was able to meet only a small part of the current demand for electronic devices and that, at worst, investors would not suffer more than a 20 to 40 per cent loss if the company proved unsuccessful and was forced to liquidate.

In spite of the keen interest in electronics and the outstanding reputation of the company's scientific officers, the imperative need for funds prompted one of the officers to remark: "If this company fails, it will be for reasons which will defy analysis."

Exhibit 4 lists some of the services and products which the company

Exhibit 4

MEV CONTROL COMPANY

SERVICES AND PRODUCTS

The following material was prepared for visitors to the International Science Exhibition, Boston, Massachusetts, December 26–31, 1946.

Mev Control Products

Mev Control products include instruments embodying electronic, mechanical and optical principles for use in industrial and college laboratories, also devices for use in controlling industrial processes and machinery.

At present, we are in quantity production only on the Stimulator Model 461. As we go into production on other devices we will send announcements to those leaving their names on the registration cards at the Mev booth, or who will indicate by letter that they wish to be placed on our mailing list.

Any of the equipment described in this booklet may be ordered for prompt delivery. Prices will be furnished on request. The equipment will be guaranteed to meet specifications.

Mev Control Services

The technical personnel of the Mev Control Company is at present composed of faculty members or former faculty members of Massachusetts Institute of Technology, Harvard University, Tufts College and the University of Alabama. This personnel is qualified by training and experience to undertake research and development problems involving a knowledge of the following fields:

1. Instrumentation of Bio-chemical Research
2. Instrumentation of Bio-physical Research

Exhibit 4—Continued

3. Cathode Ray Tubes
4. D.C. Amplification
5. Electrical Mathematical Computation
6. Extreme Low Frequency Circuits
7. High Impedance Circuits
8. Magnetrons
9. Mechanical Mathematical Computation
10. Ophthalmic Mathematical Computation
11. Optical Mathematical Computation
12. Oscilloscopy
13. Instrumentation of Physiological Research
14. Instrumentation of Psychological Research
15. Psychology
16. Pulse Circuits
17. Radio Link Communication Methods
18. Radio Teletype Communication Methods
19. Servo-mechanisms
20. Synchronizers
21. Thyratron Circuits
22. Ultra High Frequency Techniques
23. Video Amplification
24. Low Voltage Control Circuits
25. Visible and Ultra-violet Spectrophotometry
26. Visual Education, Training and Instrumentation
27. Electron Microscopy

Following is a list of projects in the field of biological and psychological instrumentation which have been completed since the formation of the Mev Control Company, or on which we are presently engaged.

1. *RTAP Coordinator* (Scoring System)

This system is designed to receive electrical signals which are D.C. voltages or currents proportional to errors in azimuth and elevation, and to combine these signals in such a way that a score of radial errors may be obtained. Also radial, azimuth, and elevation errors as functions of time are recorded on a moving chart.

The score of radial error is provided by combining the azimuth and elevation errors to produce a signal proportional to the square root of the sums of the squares of the two errors. In order not to penalize operators unduly for azimuth errors at high elevations, the voltage in the device which is proportional to the error in azimuth angle is modified by a voltage divider which is varied to give an output proportional to the azimuth error angle multiplied by the cosine of the angle of elevation.

The signals representing azimuth, elevation, and radial errors are suitably amplified and fed to the recorder, and to the excess error detector and indicator. The recorder provides a continuous graphic record of the three

Exhibit 4—Continued

errors. The excess error detector and indicator will indicate when any of the errors exceed desired limits, and will actuate times which will provide indications after each course of the total time during which each error had exceeded its limit.

2. *Impulse Rate Indicator*

This device is designed to indicate the number of spontaneous electric impulses given out by a section of cockroach nerve. It is used in the investigation of the effects of DDT on the central nervous system of the cockroach. . . .

desired to offer. The balance sheet and profit and loss statement for the first year of operations are given in Exhibits 5 and 6. The company's independent auditor, Mr. John Jay Jackson, submitted a letter to the com-

Exhibit 5

MEV CONTROL COMPANY
BALANCE SHEET AS OF DECEMBER 31, 1946

ASSETS

Current Assets:		
Cash:		
In Bank	$ 989.24	
On Hand	100.00	
Deposit	145.00	$ 1,234.24
Accounts Receivable:		
Clients	$ 1,589.04	
Other	134.35	1,723.39
Inventories:		
Raw Materials	$ 2,751.09	
Work in Process	1,029.92	3,781.01
Total Current Assets		$ 6,738.64
Deferred Items:		
Advances to Employees		311.68
Insurance Premiums Prepaid		689.16
Internal Research and Development		8,537.70
Organization Expenses		2,430.30
Total Deferred Items		$ 11,968.84
Fixed Assets:		
Office Equipment		$ 895.75
Laboratory Equipment		499.63
Total Fixed Assets		$ 1,395.38
Treasury Stock:		
Preferred	$ 1,800.00	
Common	200.00	$ 2,000.00
Capital Stock Preferred (Unissued)	$41,000.00	
Capital Stock Common (Unissued)	49,200.00	$ 90,200.00
Total Assets		$112,302.86

(Continued on next page)

LIABILITIES AND CAPITAL

Current Liabilities:		
Accounts Payable		$ 3,954.41
Notes Payable		6,800.00
Taxes Accrued		1,360.17
Payroll Accrued		2,814.81
Interest Accrued		149.33
Total Current Liabilities		$ 15,078.72
Capital:		
Capital Stock Preferred (Authorized)	$50,000.00	
Capital Stock Common (Authorized)	50,000.00	$100,000.00
Surplus Account—Deficit		2,775.86[d]
Total Capital and Surplus		$ 97,224.14
Total Liabilities and Capital		$112,302.86

[d] Deficit.

Exhibit 6

MEV CONTROL COMPANY

PROFIT AND LOSS STATEMENT FOR THE FISCAL YEAR ENDING DECEMBER 31, 1946

Sales		$54,386.56
Cost of goods sold:		
Raw materials	$ 3,964.80	
Salaries and wages	21,145.12	
Manufacturing expenses	4,331.72	29,441.64
		$24,944.92
Less: Selling expenses		5,893.06
		$19,051.86
Less: Administrative and general:		
Taxes paid	$ 1,220.12	
Accounting and legal	630.50	
Rent	1,101.50	
Sundry expenses	3,590.64	
Office salaries	3,979.54	
Officers' salaries	10,926.90	
Interest	156.04	21,605.24
		$ 2,553.38[d]
Less: Discount allowed		237.68
		$ 2,791.06[d]
Add: Discount earned		15.20
Net loss		$ 2,775.86[d]

[d] Deficit.

pany with the year-end statements, included as Exhibit 7, with Mr. Ott's reply to Mr. Jackson, shown as Exhibit 8.

Exhibit 7

MEV CONTROL COMPANY

AUDITOR'S APPRAISAL OF YEAR-END STATEMENTS

February 10, 1947

MEV CONTROL COMPANY
BOSTON, MASSACHUSETTS

GENTLEMEN:

Financial statements in duplicate consisting of balance sheet as of December 31, 1946, and profit and loss statement for the year ended that date were delivered to your representative last week together with closing journal entries to be made by your office accountant.

I particularly call your attention to certain factors which are a part of these statements:

1. No part of Organization Expenses has been charged off during 1946.
2. There has been no provision for depreciation on either Office or Laboratory Equipment.
3. The majority of your inventory items were actually counted and priced by your employees; part of it, however, located at Washington Machine Company is based on an estimate only and that portion is valued at $300.
4. Internal Research and Development expense is carried at a total of $8,537.70. Of this amount $5,458.04 covers the period from August 1, 1946 to December 31, 1946, and can be accounted for by Projects and under projects in the classifications of Labor, Material, and Manufacturing Expenses.

   The balance of $3,079.66 represents charges to this account prior to August 1, 1946, *and cannot be itemized or specifically allocated.* So long as it remains in the account it will have to be arbitrarily allocated to certain projects and later absorbed on the basis of such allocation.

   This account is out of proportion to volume of business. From a conservative accounting standpoint it should be reduced as rapidly as conditions will permit.

In reviewing the past year, results are, in my opinion, disappointing. It is my belief that your future would be much more secure if more attention had been given to conserving cash, keeping down expenses, restricting Research, and devoting more time and effort to obtaining sure-income business from clients available rather than to have devoted so much time and money to what may be termed long-range planning.

Various elements, all a part of the above, were brought to your attention in my letters of February 11, March 6, April 5, May 9, and August 21. In these letters I pointed out the necessity of controlling officers' time, the

Exhibit 7—Continued

heavy fixed expenses you were burdened with, the increasing inventory, the fact that you could not afford heavy expenditures for Research, etc., etc.

Applying the above to the present situation we find the following:

Inventory—Raw Material $2,751.09

Too high. Sales volume to date, taking into consideration the relative unimportance of material in your costs, provides no justification for this amount. The funds could be put to better use.

Internal Research and Development $8,537.70

Absolutely no justification for expenditures in any such amount as this. This represents 110% of your invested capital; approximately 60% of invested capital plus capital on loan; and about 16% of your total sales for the year!

Rent . . . . $ 415.00 per mo.

Out of proportion. True, you have not paid this each month the full year, and also you have had some offset; nevertheless, the liability is there ($5,000 per year) and nothing to date has warranted the use of this volume of space.

Telephone and Travel . . . . Approx. $ 500.00 per mo.

No doubt it has seemed necessary in each instance but you cannot spend 12% of your sales volume for these two items alone.

Salaries

Executive salaries (Messrs. Ashby, Sommer, and Ott) are $28,000 per year and as Mr. Sommer is on a half-time basis this is really at a rate of $34,000 per year. The administrative and selling portion of these salaries can only be paid if maximum use is made of the technical ability of the trained executives on income-producing activities, leaving Research until you can afford it and leaving Selling and Administration to Mr. Ott with him devoting his time to getting the business that brings in cash. Even then you would have been, and still would be, better off if salaries were set more conservatively in line with potential earnings. The Government took about $4,000 of these salaries which benefited neither the company nor the officers!

If there had been more conservative salaries in effect, tighter control over other expenses, sharply reduced Research expenditures, you could have ended the year with a clean balance sheet, no deficit, and in all probability a real tangible surplus, all of which would have been of tremendous assistance to you in your present efforts to raise additional capital.

As one interested in your success, I offer this in all sincerity as a basis for operations during the present year.

Yours very truly,

(*Signed*) John Jay Jackson

Exhibit 8

MEV CONTROL COMPANY

COMPANY'S REPLY TO AUDITOR'S APPRAISAL OF YEAR-END STATEMENTS

February 11, 1947

MR. JOHN JAY JACKSON
BOSTON, MASSACHUSETTS

DEAR JOHN:

In going over the confidential letter which you sent to me I feel that a formal answer is in order, because you are at some time in the near future going to be talking to Mr. Barnes (who is apparently deferring a reply to my letter until he talks with you) and also because I wish to have my answer to these points on record.

Inventory—Raw Material $2,751.09

I agree that this is too high. The purchase of raw material in this amount was contrary to the policy of the company and it occurred in a relatively short time. However, your statement that materials are relatively unimportant in our costs is not justified by the facts as they exist at the present time. The bulk of these materials are going into our stimulators, orders on which are coming in continually. They total 47 at the present time and the parts cost for each of these stimulators is approximately $25.

Internal Research and Development $8,537.70

You say that there is absolutely no justification for expenditures in any such amount. I disagree. We would have been entirely unjustified not to spend this amount, inasmuch as this work was never done at a time when we had work of a chargeable nature which we could do. Accordingly, what this figure represents is not money which was expended as a policy of the company but rather represents time which was put to useful work which would otherwise have been lost. Furthermore, it provides a basis for future work of this nature which can be charged as a cost against Government contracts, according to the settled policy of the Government to encourage research to the extent that any contractor has been previously engaged in research.

Rent . . . . $ 415.00 per mo.

We actually paid $1,101.50 in rent. This is definitely not out of proportion; as far as our incurring the liability of this space, we have done so on the basis of an explicit promise made to Dr. Sommer and me by the Navy that we would secure the SX Radar contract for $50,000. We will need this space to do it—not only the amount of space, but the degree of security which can be maintained for top secret work is important. Accordingly, we gambled on this. It is a calculated risk, and in any event the choice is forced on us. We had, and have, no alternative.

Exhibit 8—Continued

Telephone and Travel . . . . Approx. $ 500.00 per mo.

These items within the next few weeks will have secured us business totaling over $60,000. There is a distinct possibility that we will secure an additional contract on the Guided Missiles program, totaling between $250,000 and $500,000. If we do not take this risk, we will surely go out of business.

Salaries

If our customers were industrial concerns or people who had no desire to and no right to look at our books, I would concur with your idea on executive salaries. However, on three different occasions in the past year, we have had to justify our charges to the Navy. On one occasion we stopped work for three days while the matter was being adjudicated, and if we had been taking smaller salaries and making our usual time charges to the Navy, we would have had to reduce our charges or lose the business, inasmuch as they would have taken the position that our profits were extortionate and they would not pay them.

Incidentally, my decision to go along with these salaries was taken after a conference with friends at the First National Bank who agreed that the ordinary rules of business did not apply in this particular case. Actually, we received less from the business for the entire year than our yearly rate.

I will take point by point your paragraph summarizing your letter.

1. "if there had been more conservative salaries in effect"—In my opinion it would have made very little difference in our operating picture, because we would not have been able to charge for our time as we did.
2. "tighter control over other expenses"—This business was formed by men who had very little or no experience in business. At various times, particularly during the first six months of operation, they did things which were definitely in the realm of the incredible, viewed from the business standpoint. The personnel of the company is made up of men who are scientific giants, but who simply had to receive an education in the things which can and cannot be done. I do not imply by this statement that they were being educated by me. I wish to state explicitly that they are being educated by events. That was an inherent hazard in the formation of this business. The first year's operation has resulted in this hazard being eliminated for the future. It has resulted in my condoning actions done in the past which I considered to be not merely ill advised but extremely harmful. In other words we have bought and paid for experience.
3. "sharply reduced research expenditures"—This has amply been covered above in paragraph three. If we get enough business to keep us busy, the research expenditures will automatically be reduced. If we get enough work to keep us going but not enough to keep us

Exhibit 8—Continued

busy, then the difference will be expended on internal research and development and entered on our books at the usual time charges.

I question seriously if we could have ended the year with a tangible surplus. By tangible I mean cash in the bank that we could take out and distribute. Also, I question very seriously the statement that a surplus figure on our financial statements would have enhanced our possibilities of getting working capital, because we have been making a serious effort to interest capital for some five or six months, of which time we could almost always show a profit for operations to date.

I am grateful to you for your expression of opinion, even though, as is apparent from the foregoing, I am in complete disagreement with you. There is one point on which I concur and that is that the basis of operations which you have outlined will be an excellent one for us to follow just as soon as we are actually embarked on a substantial Government contract or get any capital in the business. Lest you should think this statement shows fuzzy thinking on my part, I wish to point out that because I think it is a good basis to follow for next year, it does not follow that it would have been a good basis for last year. In fact I am convinced it would have resulted in our dissolution by reason of personality differences.

Sincerely yours,

LOUIS C. OTT
Vice President

Jonathan Black

In the summer of 1953, Mr. Jonathan Black approached Mr. James MacDonald, a recent business-college graduate, to ask the latter's advice about an idea for a new product. Several years before, Jim MacDonald had inherited a moderate amount of money. While in school, he and two of his classmates, Thomas O'Brien and Jackson White, both with similar financial means, had discussed the desirability of investing a portion of their capital in new ventures. The three men agreed that, after graduation, they would meet periodically to keep each other informed of possible opportunities for joint participation in venture financing.

Mr. Black had heard of James MacDonald and his friends. Through a mutual acquaintance he asked that he might tell them of his new device. At this stage, Mr. Black had no plans for exploitation of his product. He thought he would like to form his own company and wanted advice as to what he should do next.

Mr. Jonathan Black had invented what he called the "Nowork Waxer." This device consisted of three major parts: a simple stamped metal plate, a cheap cotton pad, and a small plastic bottle filled with a common type of self-polishing liquid wax.

In use, the bottle was uncapped and screwed into the place provided for it on the back of the metal plate. The cotton pad was fastened to the other side of the metal plate with the convenient clips provided. The liquid wax steadily dripped onto the pad as long as a light pressure was applied to the unit. Provision was made for the attachment of a long handle when doing floors. The unit was conveniently shaped so that it also might be used without the handle for waxing counter and table tops.

The amount of wax contained in the bottle was sufficient to do one large-size floor. When the contents of the plastic bottle were exhausted, Mr. Black intended that the entire unit, with the exception of the handle, be thrown away.

The three men decided to talk with Mr. Black when they held their first meeting to discuss new investment ventures. Since all were relatively inexperienced, James MacDonald suggested that, after listening to Mr. Black, they should each allow themselves an hour to set forth a plan of action in outline form sufficiently specific to guide Mr. Black in determining whether he really wanted to form his own company to exploit the product.

Their recommendations, Mr. MacDonald suggested, should provide a complete-enough coverage so that Mr. Black would, after carrying out their instructions, be able to determine within reasonable bounds whether his item justified formation of an independent new enterprise. Since Mr. Black was not asking for a specific answer to the potential of the product, they decided not to make any decision themselves on this point. Rather, they hoped to show Mr. Black how he could obtain sufficient knowledge to be his own judge of the value of his product.

The outlines drawn up by the three men at the end of the hour were as follows:

James MacDonald's Outline

A. Mr. Black should thoroughly examine his product, asking such questions as—

1. Will it work well enough for its intended purpose?

   Make a few of them, use them himself, try on friends, neighbors, persons unknown. Then follow up to determine possible improvements, price a person would pay for it, defects, opinions on end worth, etc.

2. Can it be improved?

   Use data from 1, check with friends, possibly wax sellers or manufacturers, other inventors, etc.

3. Does it last long enough to do job? Too long? Is it as cheap as I can make it? Are best materials used? Available? Source of supply? Steady? Subject to price change? How much wax is used for this purpose? How often would this waxer be used? Are other materials better? Substitutable?

   See library data, check defense needs, critical metals, etc. See friends in business if possible.

4. Will it sell?

   Get bank appraisal, advice of friends, storekeepers, department stores, wax salesmen. If money available for research, see marketing experts. Talk to professors in schools, housewives, floor-waxing concerns, etc.

5. Can it be protected? How can it be protected?

   Patentable? Know how? Trade-mark? Catch name? Product quality? Is it a new product, or are others on market? Is it most efficiently designed, or will other designs outsell it? What other designs? See lawyers, manufacturers, marketing experts.

6. Depending on Black's present occupation, financial condition, station in life, personal desires, belief in invention, and other pertinent considerations, he might attack one or all of the first five questions in any order—but he should be well satisfied with the answer he obtains on all points before he goes to next group.

B. Mr. Black might now ask himself some personal questions, assuming he is satisfied that he has a product:
   1. What do I want out of the product?
      Money?
      Hobby or vocational interest?
      Own business?
      Challenge of a new enterprise?
      Pay back for work put in? Etc.
   2. How badly do I want what I want? Do I have to have money, for example?
   3. What are my own abilities? Likes and dislikes?
   4. What do I have to lose? Can I afford it? Is it risky or not?
   5. Does what I want "fit" me? Station? Age? Ambitions? Willingness to work?
   6. Are other ways open to me of satisfying these desires?
   7. Who can I hurt or help by going on? Family? Self? Friends?

C. Assuming now that Mr. Black is satisfied he has a salable product and wants to exploit it, a number of avenues are open:
   1. Manufacture himself, sell rights, buy parts and sell it himself. His course will depend on many things:
      a) His own occupation, financial condition, contacts, desires, etc.
      b) Estimation of cost to make or buy, in various lot sizes, using various materials.
      See product manufacturers, consult engineers, get bids, estimates from manufacturers, see marketing firms, etc.
      c) Availability of a buyer for product, to produce it on royalty basis.
      See wax manufacturers, household-item manufacturers, Sears or dime-store chains, novelty manufacturers, hardware makers, mop or broom makers, etc.
      d) Market estimates.
      Try appropriate retail outlets for estimates, see a marketing firm, try chains for orders, set up own distribution system to wholesalers.
      e) Nature of product selling.
      Long-term sales or one-shot affair? High promotion rate, or "shelf" item? Is the Nowork Waxer to become a part of the inventor's "line" or only a single item?
      f) Will it sell when all margins are taken into account? What are the channels?

D. Mr. Black, having now decided on a method of exploiting the venture, must examine the financial and managerial aspects—these tend to go together.
   1. Size of enterprise foreseen versus short- and long-term cash demands, personnel and equipment demands—housing.
   2. Availability of funds—sources, quantity, use, etc.
      See banks, investors, financial houses, etc., for opinions on probable costs, cushions required, rate of expenditure, and rate of return. Set up *pro forma*

statements based on realistic estimates, material and inventory needs, payrolls, expenses, distribution, etc.

3. Risks involved, return desired or required, alternate sources of capital, short-term and long-run needs.
4. Allow for exigencies and unforeseen emergencies (use perhaps a capitalization factor up to 2, as a maximum and, if possible, decide how much you are willing to risk).
5. Even at this relative late stage of the development, keep one's ears and eyes open to all previous decisions and considerations.

E. Mr. Black might also remember some generalizations that can be usefully applied at various stages of the search.

1. At any stage of the plan of action, a single consideration may either kill the project or direct it into certain channels.

   For example, his present occupation might have bearing on his decision whether to make or buy the item.
2. Luck may play an important part in the whole venture.
3. There are many sources for advice and information, perhaps even real aid, at each stage of the process.

   Schools: marketing, new-enterprise, and small-business courses.
   Communities, development groups.
   Small business organizations.
   Other small businessmen.
   Stores and merchants.
   Libraries and books.
   Banks and insurance companies.
   Appropriate friends.
   Persons or groups in similar businesses.
   Potential customers.
   Potential investors.
   Potential manufacturers.
   Potential retailers.
   Armed services advice to small businessmen.
   Public forums.
   Chambers of commerce.
   Newspapers and their research staffs.
   Small-business financing groups.

Thomas O'Brien's Outline

I. Product and market

   A. Has the Nowork Waxer created a need? Will housewives or others find it useful?

   B. Is it different? Has it got selling claims and appeal? Will it be acceptable?

   C. If there is a demand for this waxer, will it be lasting?

   D. What does competition offer in the way of waxers?

E. Is it covered by patent? If so, can others easily infringe upon your idea? Have you sufficient time and money to defend the patent if it is patentable?

F. Will you depend on others for production, or will you produce it yourself? Capacity?

G. Will it comprise your sole product line?

H. Will it have a brand name?

I. What research and preparation have you made to market this waxer?

J. Have you any sales contacts or potential outlets?

K. How will you time the marketing of this waxer?

L. How limited and specialized is your market?

M. Who will buy this product, and why will they buy it? Where? When? How often?

N. Will it provide repeat sales? Are sales frequent?

II. Working team

A. Personnel of organization must have experience and eagerness to promote a new concern.

B. Should have production know-how.

C. Should be compatible.

D. Should not risk their current careers.

E. Incorporation or partnership? Any legal agreement should:

1. Stipulate profit distribution plans.
2. Liability, limited or unlimited.
3. Investment required of each associate in the enterprise.

F. Evaluation of time required to devote to the company. Therefore, are personnel interested in opportunity for a job or investment, etc.?

G. Number of personnel required, sales organization?

III. Capital requirements and financing

A. Starting costs:

1. Do not underestimate.
2. Include minimum and maximum estimates.
3. Reserve for contingencies.
4. Costs of production, organization, legal fees, taxes, etc.

B. Need for good financial records and cost-control systems.

C. Risks on capital and production, consumer credit.

D. Method of financing.

1. Loan from bank, RFC, investment house.
2. Small investment house.
3. Large investment house.
4. Industrial capitalist.
5. Equity stock.
6. Raw-material inventories, once established.
7. Customer deposits, once established.

E. Costs of construction, working capital requirements, minimum cash requirements, must all be determined.

F. Control: What degree of control do you wish to enjoy? Must reconcile sources and amount of funds available with control desired.

IV. Costs

A. Marketing costs.

B. Purchasing costs.

C. Production costs.

D. Advertising and promotional costs.

E. Research costs.

These are but a few of the costs to consider in addition to general administrative and overhead expenses. In addition, are cost estimates and break-even points (fixed costs divided by gross margin) realistic?

V. Other factors

A. Labor supply near at hand.

B. Site for plant, if you decide to produce product.

C. Accessible to materials.

D. Accessible to markets, transportation.

E. Good place to live?

F. Personally acquainted with the area?

VI. Availability of friends

A. Current contacts or need to solicit friends.

VII. Availability of counsel and guidance

A. Have you any business support or source of counsel from business acquaintances?

B. Need to give careful thought to preliminary plans and organization and possibility of help from experienced men in the industry to eliminate risk of ignorance in starting the business.

VIII. What is your object in forming an enterprise?

IX. What are the principle risks?

X. Reminder that (1) Poor management,
(2) Lack of funds,
(3) Lack of experience and know-how,
(4) Poor financial records,
(5) Lack of preparation
constitute the main reasons for failure in small business.

I recommend that Mr. Black ask himself these pertinent questions before proceeding to organize an enterprise to market these waxers. If he can answer all of these questions and meet the requirements mentioned in each area, we should be in a position to consider his plan of forming a new company.

JACKSON WHITE'S OUTLINE

A. Product

1. Is this thing really useful, new, and an improvement?
2. Does it work well; have all the bugs been worked out of it?
3. Get housewives' reaction to it. Let them try it, and ask them if they would buy it? At what price?
4. Check U.S. Patent Office. Has anything like this been patented? Is it patentable?
5. If patentable, how easy would it be to get around it by competition?
6. Make decision to patent or not from this information, but wait until you get sales and cost estimates before going ahead with the expense of getting a patent.

B. Costs

1. How much is the thing going to cost to make? Check metal shops for metal piece, cotton supplier, bottle supplier (or surplus stores, etc.).
2. Get prices for component parts according to quantity ordered.
3. Get estimate from box manufacturers as to the costs of packages.
4. Assume you assemble and package these things yourself.
5. Assemble total cost figures and prepare a statement of what the total costs will be at various volumes.
6. Add in any transportation costs involved in getting the parts, etc.

C. Sales

1. Contact buyers in—
   a) Department stores.
   b) Chain grocery stores.
   c) Buying concerns for affiliated stores.
   d) Variety chains.
   e) Drug chains.
   f) Premium merchandise houses.
   g) Door-to-door wholesalers.
   h) Wholesalers to independent drugstores.
   i) Wholesalers to independent variety stores.
   j) Wholesalers to independent housewares stores.
   k) Wholesalers to hardware stores.

   See, first, if they would sell your item; and, secondly, how much they would be willing to pay for it.
2. What other arrangements would they want—exclusives, etc.?
3. What price would they sell them for?
4. What minimum quantities would they order?
5. Would any one of these channels object to your selling through other channels? At a different price?
6. Determine if they would insist on a consignment basis? (Don't recommend, of course.)

7. It might be necessary to have some samples of the waxer made up so that you can mail it and a letter asking the above questions to buyers who are outside of this town. The item probably doesn't warrant excessive traveling to secure information.
8. Try to get figures of sales of waxers (items that are roughly competing) in an attempt to get some idea of the magnitude of the market and the share you could conservatively expect to get.

D. Evaluation
1. Now that information has been gotten on sales possibilities, costs, etc., figure out what profits could you conservatively make.
2. After doing this, the question to ask yourself is: Is it worth it?
3. Explore opportunities for sale of the patent (if obtainable) to a company now selling waxes for home use (Johnson's, etc.).
4. Explore possibilities for leasing the idea out on a royalty basis to those companies.
5. Check with someone who can make an impartial appraisal of the facts that you have gathered, plus getting any new thoughts that you may have on the subject before you make your final decision.

Before drawing up the consolidated report to guide Mr. Black in his investigation, the three men decided to review the adequacy of the individual outlines they had prepared. Mr. MacDonald was asked to extract the best points of each and to prepare a single report. They hoped thus to develop a basic document which, with appropriate modification, could also be given to other inventors to show them in general the kind of investigations they should make before expecting MacDonald and his associates to decide on investing.

PART II

STARTING A NEW ENTERPRISE WITH AN EXISTING PRODUCT

John Valos

On Monday morning, April 17, 1950, Mr. John Valos, a second-year student at the Harvard Business School, was faced with deciding by 9:00 P.M. that night whether he wanted to lease and operate the fruit and vegetable store at Brookside Acres, a new housing development in a suburb of New York City. Mr. Peter Smith, the rental agent for the Brookside Development Company which owned Brookside Acres, had told John Valos and his father, Mr. George Valos, that they had first chance at the lease but that, if they did not accept by 9:00 P.M. that evening, he would offer it to some other interested party.

BROOKSIDE ACRES

Brookside Acres consisted of about 1,000 rental housing units and a shopping center which had parking space for 550 cars. Construction of the project had been started in 1946 by the Brookside Development Company, a group of investors headed by Mr. William Bessey, president of a New York City bank. The first families had moved into the units in 1947, and by the middle of 1948 all housing units were occupied. The first tenants of the shopping center's stores had moved in during the fall of 1948; and the fruit and vegetable store, which was the last store to be leased, began operation in August, 1949.

The housing units were one-, two-, and three-bedroom apartments, the rents for which ranged from $100 to $170 per month. All apartments had been occupied since their completion. About 2,500 people lived in the 1,000 apartments.

The shopping center was on a main highway which linked the New York City business district and many suburban residential areas. In addition to a motion picture theater, it contained the stores shown in Exhibit 1 (p. 102). Except for these stores, the nearest shopping center was a new and larger one under construction on a site which was about two miles north of Brookside.

THE FRUIT AND VEGETABLE STORE'S HISTORY

John Valos had first heard about the opportunity to lease the fruit and vegetable store from his father. Mr. Bessey had for many years been a customer of George Valos' fruit and vegetable store, The Valos Market. On April 14, when Mr. Bessey learned that the Brookside fruit and vegetable store lease was available, he notified George Valos, suggesting that Mr. Valos see Mr. Smith if he was interested in leasing the store. The senior Mr. Valos did not wish to undertake the operation of a second store himself. However, he thought his son, John, might wish to consider it, and so he telephoned John, asking him to come to New

Exhibit 1

BROOKSIDE ACRES

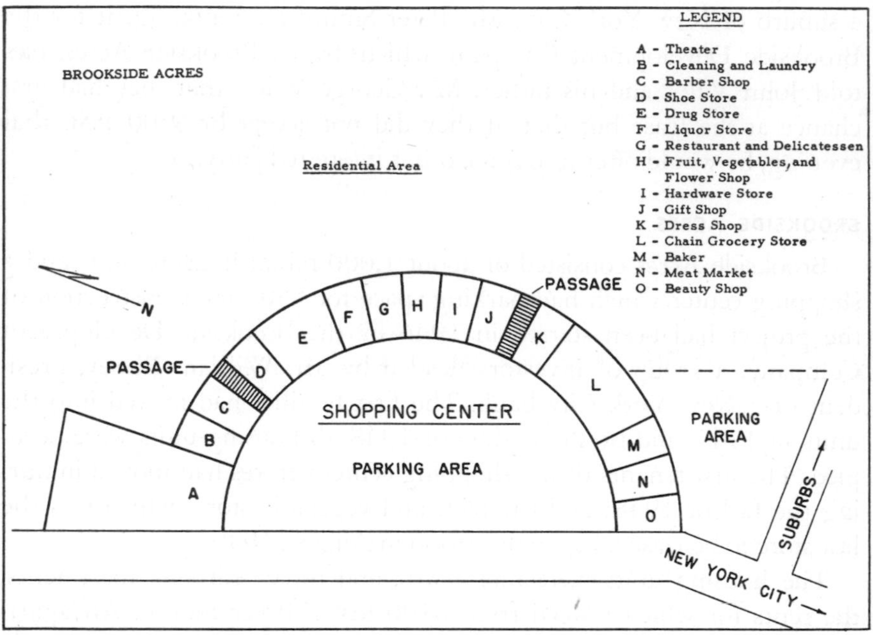

York City to investigate the matter. John arrived in New York on Saturday and made an appointment to see Mr. Smith on Monday morning, April 17.

Meanwhile John tried to find out what he could about the Brookside store. He learned that on April 12, 1950, the development company had canceled Mr. Al Chaldis' lease on the store because on the previous day the police had visited the place and found a dice game in progress in the rear of the store. Chaldis had purchased the lease for the store in November, 1949, from three brothers who had been the original operators.

John Valos and his father learned from wholesalers at the markets where the Valoses bought produce for the store that the three brothers had sold their Brookside lease to Chaldis because their operation of the store had not been successful. The market men seemed to think that the three brothers had not been experienced operators. On the other hand, some of them believed that Chaldis had been successful at the Brookside store. He had the reputation of being an excellent fruit and vegetable man, and it was believed at the market that he would have liked to retain the Brookside store lease. The market men who knew Chaldis estimated that his sales were between $5,000 and $6,000 per month. During his operation of the Brookside store, Chaldis had also managed a second fruit and vegetable store. John and his father also learned that Tom Bolte, who was considered a successful fruit and vegetable retailer, was interested in securing the Brookside lease.

ON-THE-SPOT INVESTIGATION

John next visited Brookside Acres. As he looked over the shopping center, he noted that the traffic volume, both pedestrian and automobile, which passed the store was less than that at his father's store. At the same time, he noted that parking facilities were much better than those available in the area around his father's store. He found part of the fruit and vegetable store occupied by a florist. The florist told John that he had become a subtenant of Chaldis on April 1, 1950. He added that, when officials of the development company evicted Chaldis, they had given him permission to keep the store open as a flower shop. The florist said that he, too, hoped to lease the entire store from the development company and that, if he did secure the lease, he would sublet the part of the store which Chaldis had used to a fruit and vegetable dealer. However, the florist was willing to remain as a subtenant if he were not successful in securing the lease. The florist said that, although he had been in operation only two weeks, one of which was Easter week, he expected to realize flower sales of at least $2,000 a month throughout the year. He told John that he believed Chaldis' sales had been between $5,000 and $6,000 a month and that the chain grocery was selling about $3,000 worth of fruits and vegetables each week.

John was impressed with the beauty of the store and was convinced that there was ample space for the combination of fruits and vegetables and flowers. Mr. Chaldis' equipment (display bins, counters, and so forth) was in the store; and after inspecting it, John decided that it would be adequate for his needs. He estimated that, in the light of pre-

Exhibit 2

DIAGRAM OF FRUIT, VEGETABLE, AND FLOWER STORE AT BROOKSIDE ACRES SHOPPING CENTER

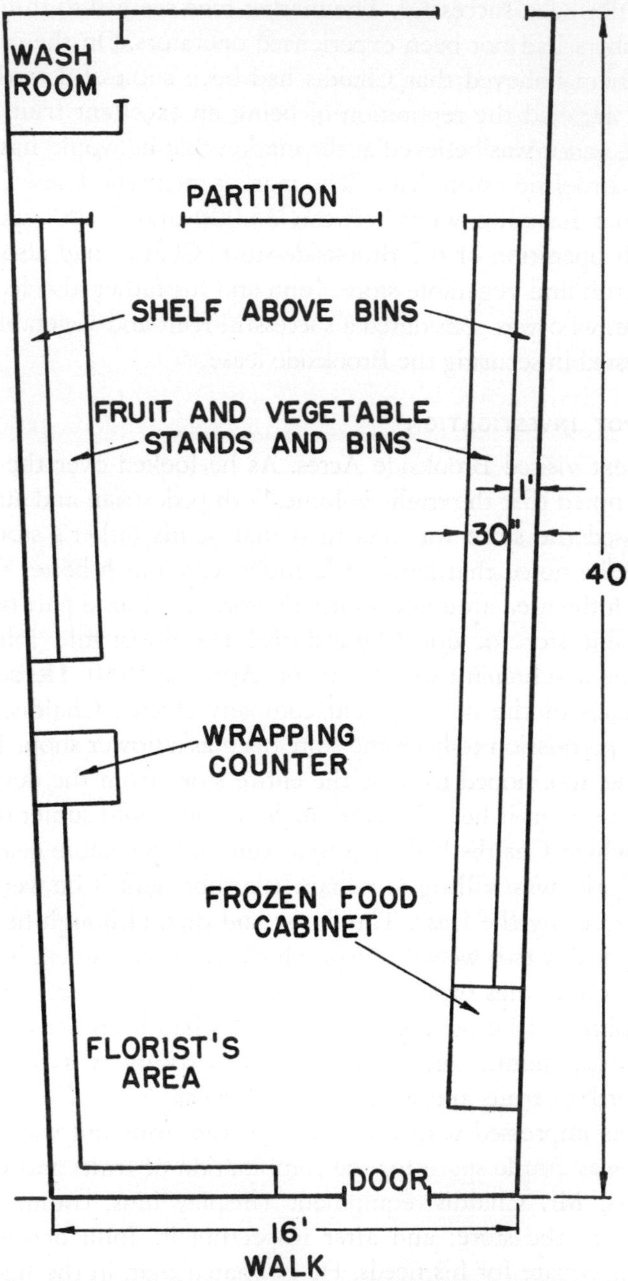

vailing prices for similar equipment, he could buy this equipment from Chaldis for not more than $3,000 (see Exhibit 2).

JOHN VALOS' BACKGROUND

Because he had worked in his father's store since he was twelve, John Valos was confident of his ability to operate the Brookside store. Having finished high school in 1942, John entered Yale in the class of 1946. He joined the Air Force before finishing the four-year college program and served as an electronics officer for three years. Returning to Yale after the war, he received an A.B. in the spring of 1948 and entered the Harvard Business School that fall. He was not married and had no brothers or sisters. Throughout his high-school career John had worked in his father's store during evenings, week ends, and vacations. He also spent his college and business-school vacations working in the store. John felt that buying fruits and vegetables was the only phase of the business which he could not perform as well as his father. He had remarked to one of the wholesalers that, although his father had let him do a lot of buying and he felt some confidence in his ability to buy, he knew that he was not so good as his father. To this the wholesaler had replied that, in his opinion, very few buyers were as good as George Valos.

John and his father decided that the new store would not require any increased buying activity or buying expense. George Valos went to the market every morning, except Sunday, and bought for his store. If John took over the new store, his father would merely increase his own orders by the amount of merchandise that John wanted.

TERMS OF THE LEASE

John and his father met with Mr. Smith at 9:00 A.M. on Monday, April 17. Mr. Smith outlined the terms of the lease as follows: (1) the store was to sell only fruits and vegetables, fresh and frozen; (2) because the development company needed the basement for storage, the lease would not include use of the basement; (3) the new tenant could continue Mr. Chaldis' arrangements with the florist—viz., he could sublet part of the store to the florist, charging him 25 per cent of his flower sales. The fruit and vegetable tenant, in turn, would have to pay the development company 12 per cent of the flower sales, retaining 13 per cent for himself; (4) the development company was to provide heat and water, the tenant paying for his electricity and furnishing his own store equipment; (5) each month the tenant was to pay rent of $350 or 6 per cent of that month's fruit and vegetable sales, whichever was greater. At the end of each year the development company would make an adjustment so that the tenant's rent for the year would equal either $4,200 or 6 per cent of that year's sales, whichever amount was larger; (6) the lease would run for five years, at the end of which it could be renewed for another five years on the same terms at the tenant's option.

John asked Mr. Smith if he could carry fresh eggs, coffee, and a line of jelly and preserves. He explained that his father had built a good reputation on the quality of the eggs he sold and that a special brand of coffee and a line of jelly and preserves carried by his father had proved very popular. John explained that he intended to name his store "Valos Market" and, therefore, that customers would expect to find the same items in the new store as they found in his father's store. John also said that he would like to carry a line of bottled soft drinks because it would attract customers into the store. Mr. Smith replied that it would not be possible to allow the fruit and vegetable store to carry these items, which would compete with products already sold at the chain grocery and the delicatessen. He explained that the development company granted its tenants exclusive rights to sell certain products. The delicatessen and the chain grocery had the right to sell eggs, coffee, and bottled soft drinks. The chain grocery had the exclusive rights to sell preserves and jellies.

John pointed out to Mr. Smith that Christmas trees had always been a profitable item at his father's store. He knew that his father realized a gross margin of about $1,000 each year on Christmas trees. Therefore, he asked whether he would be allowed to sell them at Brookside. Mr. Smith suggested that they wait until Christmas time to make that decision, but John told him that he would insist on a definite agreement on the matter before he signed the lease. Mr. Smith then said that, although the lease with Mr. Chaldis had contained no mention of Christmas trees, the development company had allowed him to sell them, had provided him with display space for the trees in front of the store, and had charged him 6 per cent on Christmas-tree sales. He added, however, that in the future the tenant would probably be given Christmas-tree display space in a parking lot about 100 yards from the store and that the tenant would have to pay 14 per cent on Christmas tree sales.

Mr. Smith told the Valoses that recent surveys had shown that 25,000 people lived within one mile of the shopping center, including the 2,500 people living in the project, and that there were 65,000 people living within two miles of the shopping center. He stated that, when the housing units were first opened, government regulations required the company to offer them first to veterans. He said that gradually, however, most of the veterans had moved out because the rents were too high for them, and that he would estimate that the majority of the families now living in the project had annual earnings of $4,000 or more. He added that many of the present residents were couples who had sold their homes and moved into Brookside Acres because their children had grown to adulthood and had left to make their own homes.

Mr. Smith explained an advertising program which was being planned jointly by the shopping-center merchants and the development company. Each store proprietor had agreed to pay $15 per week for thirteen weeks; the total was to be used to purchase one-minute spot radio advertisements which would urge people to do all their shopping at the Brookside shopping center. The appeal was to be aimed primarily at people living outside the Brookside area, and the advertisements were to emphasize the ample parking space at Brookside and the variety of stores operating at the center. The parties had agreed to extend the program for a second thirteen weeks if a majority of the merchants thought that the results of the first effort seemed to justify doing so.

At the end of their discussion, John Valos asked Mr. Smith if he could have some time to think the matter over and perhaps to make a counterproposal. Mr. Smith said that several persons wanted the lease on the terms being offered to John and his father. He added that, because of Mr. Bessey's interest, he was offering the Valoses the first opportunity to lease the store but that, since several others wanted the lease on the explained terms, there would not be room for bargaining or counterproposals. Mr. Smith ended the conversation by saying that the company was eager to get the vacancy filled quickly and that, if he did not hear from John by 9:00 P.M. that day, he would offer the lease to one of the other interested parties.

COMPARISON OF THE BROOKSIDE STORE AND THE VALOS MARKET

After leaving Mr. Smith's office, John and his father went to their store, where they compared the expected performance of the Brookside store with that of The Valos Market. Exhibit 3 (p. 108) shows the operating statement for Mr. George Valos' store for a typical three-month period. Exhibit 4 (p. 108) contains the expenses, except rent, which John and his father estimated would be incurred at the Brookside store.

The men decided that the Brookside store would have an advantage over the present Valos store in that no merchandise would be displayed on outside stands. An outside display required at least one full-time man to handle sales. They also decided that the Brookside store would require relatively smaller window displays. Less display produce meant

Exhibit 3

OPERATING STATEMENT OF THE VALOS MARKET FOR A RECENT TYPICAL THREE-MONTH PERIOD

Sales*		$37,295
Cost of goods sold		27,495
Gross margin		$ 9,800
Operating expenses:		
Payroll†	$2,800	
Rent, light, heat	1,200	
Truck expense	300	
Maintenance expense	300	
Paper and twine	250	
Linen and laundry	50	
Legal and auditing	120	
Licenses and fees	150	
Insurance	150	
Telephone	50	
Depreciation	430	
Advertising	0	
Total		5,800
Net profit before income tax		$ 4,000

* Includes all items except Christmas trees.
† George and John Valos' withdrawals and/or salary not included in payroll figure.
Source: Compiled by John Valos from The Valos Market records.

less spoilage. By operating two stores, the Valoses believed that higher turnovers with closer inventory control were possible. In addition, the Valoses could purchase certain slower-moving items, such as mushrooms and string beans, in larger quantities and at prices lower than those obtainable at the Valos' present volume of purchasing. These op-

Exhibit 4

ESTIMATED MONTHLY EXPENSES AT BROOKSIDE STORE AT VOLUME OF $5,000 TO $6,000 OF SALES

Item	*Amount*	*Comment*
Payroll	$ 600	Three men at $200 per month
Auto expense	40	Owner's car used for short deliveries
Lights	40	
Paper and twine	60	
Linen and laundry	10	
Insurance	50	
Telephone	15	
Legal and auditing	30	
Licenses and fees	50	
Depreciation	30	On-store equipment
Advertising	65	The shopping-center agreement
Delivery charge for purchases*	80	
Miscellaneous	50	
Total	$1,120	

* Trucking expense from markets to Brookside store.
Source: Estimates by John Valos, April 17, 1950.

portunities for savings plus the fact that the Valos family would not be taking vegetables and fruits for their own table from the Brookside store, as they did from the Valos market, led John to believe that he could probably realize a 2 per cent greater gross margin than his father was presently averaging on fruits and vegetables.

John and his father believed that the Valos name had come to mean high-quality fruits and vegetables to many people in the general area surrounding The Valos Market, including Brookside Acres. Several of George Valos' customers who lived at Brookside had suggested to him that he open a store there.

John and his father had always purchased their produce at markets frequented by the buyers who represented chain stores, jobbers, and large independent retailers. They believed that on some items, such as potatoes and onions, there was little noticeable qualitative difference. They paid about the same price for those items and sold them for about the same price as did the chain stores. However, they believed that customers easily recognized differences in the quality of certain fruits and vegetables, such as grapes and tomatoes. Consequently, the Valoses bought more-expensive, higher-quality produce of this type, selling it for a higher price. For this reason, the Valoses did not consider chain groceries as direct competitors. They thought of fruit and vegetable retail establishments as being divided into two groups: (1) chain stores and (2) "quality" stores.

The Valos Market was about five miles from Brookside Acres. Although the men did not know the exact figure, they were certain that the numbers of people living within one and two miles of The Valos Market were much higher than the comparable figures for Brookside. They also believed that those who resided near The Valos Market enjoyed incomes equal to those living in the Brookside area. The shopping district of which The Valos Market was a part contained at least one of each type of store represented at Brookside. There were two chain stores and two other independent fruit and vegetable stores located near The Valos Market, whereas at Brookside the only other store which sold fruit and vegetables was the chain grocery. The Valoses regarded one of the independent stores as their main competitor.

The following information regarding sales of items other than fruits and vegetables was available from George Valos' records. The Valos Market sold about 120 dozen eggs per week. The price of eggs fluctuated throughout the year; recently it had averaged 75 cents a dozen. Whatever the price, the market's margin on egg sales was about 20 cents a dozen. The market sold about 25 pounds of coffee each week, the price averaging between 90 and 95 cents per pound and the margin about 20 cents per pound. Sales of preserves and jelly totaled about $1,000 per year, and the margin was 50 per cent of selling price. The Valos Market sold about $45 worth of bottled soft drinks each week, and the margin was 33⅓ per cent of selling price.

John planned to have the Brookside store open on Saturday from 8:00 A.M. to 11:00 P.M.; and on the other six days of the week he planned to be open from 8:00 A.M. until 9:00 P.M., the same hours that his father's store observed and that Mr. Chaldis had observed. The chain grocery was closed on Sunday but was open from 8:00 A.M. to 9:00 P.M. on Friday and from 8:00 A.M. until 6:00 P.M. on the other five days. John believed that staying open in the evenings and on Sundays would be more profitable if he could sell eggs, coffee, and beverages. Having observed that the nighttime traffic by Brookside was smaller than that by his father's store to a greater degree than was the case of daytime traffic, John was even more desirous of carrying items which would attract customers at night. John felt that the restrictions on what could be sold at the Brookside store were also undesirable from a psychological point of view. He felt that an energetic merchant should be constantly trying to discover new merchandise which would appeal to his present customers and attract new customers. As he saw it, the Brookside lease stifled such activity.

John saw no need for the use of the store's basement, since he considered the store space adequate for his purposes. He planned to employ three clerks to help him in the store.

John and his father believed that house deliveries would present a problem at the new store. Approximately 10 per cent of sales at The Valos Market were received by telephone and delivered to the customers' homes. The Valos Market owned one truck and hired a driver to make these deliveries. John planned to make some deliveries within Brookside Acres in his own car, but he believed that these trips would be to take purchases to the homes of customers who had walked into the store to make their own selections. He hoped that telephone customers would phone his father's store for deliveries because the truck would be dispatched from there. He believed, also, that to pay 6 per cent to the development company on telephone delivery sales would render those sales almost profitless. John also hoped to make the Brookside store a cash market; however, he felt that he could carry charge accounts which amounted to 8 per cent to 10 per cent of total sales, since this was about the proportion of his father's sales which were made on monthly charge accounts. The charge-account customers spent between $15 to $60 per month at The Valos Market.

John and his father felt that the lease provisions which required the tenant to pay 6 per cent of his sales had certain disadvantages. The major reason that John disliked this provision was that it reduced his incentive to increase sales. He told his father that he would prefer to pay a flat $400 per month rental because then he would not have to share sales increases with anyone. John also believed that the rent provisions made the tenant less flexible in his pricing. He felt that he would not be able to cut prices to cost if he should wish to do so to meet competition or to dispose of slow-moving perishable produce because the 6 per cent rental charge would mean that he was actually selling below cost. Also, the lease made it less desirable for him to cut prices in order to obtain a higher volume of sales.

Although his father agreed with John that these disadvantages were significant, both men were certain that the development company would not alter its offer. George Valos had previously been assured by Mr. Bessey that the rental provisions offered them were the same as those offered other fruit and vegetable dealers interested in leasing the store. The men thought that the rental was high but also that it would be reduced considerably by payments from the florist to the fruit and vegetable store tenant.

JOHN'S ASPIRATIONS

After discussing these matters with his son, George Valos told John that he wanted him to make the decision. The father pointed out that the family had ample funds to purchase the equipment needed at the store, that he would be able to buy for the store without extra effort, and that the family's credit standing at the wholesale market was such that no other funds would be needed.

At this same time, John was also considering a job offer which a large Providence department store had made him. John's major interest at the business school had been retailing, and he had made an excellent scholastic record. The Providence store managers had seemed eager to secure his services. They had offered John $70 per week to join their staff and had emphasized that they were hiring him in the hope that he would move rapidly into an important executive position.

John had a strong desire to operate his own business. He did not feel, however, that he would be content to operate a store like the Brookside one for the remainder of his life. He aspired to reach eventually a more important managerial position. He also realized that, if he undertook the operation of the Brookside store, he would have to work twelve hours a day, seven days a week. His father had worked such a schedule almost all his life; and although John was not unwilling to do the same, he felt that the financial reward for such effort should be substantially more than that paid for a forty- or forty-eight-hour week.

John would have preferred to have the Brookside proposition appear after his graduation from the business school. However, his father had assured him that, if he wanted the store, he, George, would start it into operation and thereby enable John to finish his studies at Harvard.

Popcorn Vending Machine

In the summer of 1952 a group of four businessmen met in Boston with Mr. Harry Spence, a promoter, to discuss the possibility of entering the vending-machine business. This group of four men met regularly to consider making small investments in promising businesses. In the past they had made several investments which had turned out reasonably well. The policy of the group was to put their funds in companies which would require some directional supervision but no operating service, since each member of the group was involved in his own business or profession.

At dinner, Mr. Spence unfolded his proposition. He began with the story of a California inventor who had developed a machine for dispensing popcorn about twelve years before. The completed machine (Exhibit 1, p. 114) was simple in design and operation. It consisted of a white-enameled box, 17 × 17 × 60 inches, with a rounded plexiglass dome. Already-popped popcorn was placed under the Plexiglass cover and was warmed by means of a small heating element. The only other parts to the machine consisted of the dispensing mechanism and a small pocket for bags. By inserting a dime and pulling down a lever, the customer could fill a bag with hot, crispy popcorn. The main features of this machine were its attractive appearance and its simple construction.

Prior to World War II, the inventor, with the aid of a group of West Coast businessmen, had distributed a number of the machines throughout California. Although this company was known to be successful, no operating statistics were available. Shortly after the war, a Texas businessman of considerable means had obtained manufacturing and distributing rights for the machine. A Texas corporation, called the Texmac Company, was formed in 1949 to manufacture and sell the units. The Texmac Company vigorously set about to obtain national distribution for the machines. Within two years, distributing franchises had been issued to cover all states. In some instances, a group of states comprised a distributing area. New England had been considered a single distributing area.

A distributing company had been formed under the name of Harley, Inc., by a group of Boston businessmen, and the franchise for all the

New England states had been secured. The terms of the franchise were that Harley, Inc., would buy from the Texmac Company a specific number of machines each year for two years. In case Harley, Inc., did not buy

Exhibit 1

the stipulated number of machines, the franchise would be lost. Harley, Inc., had been financed on a very thin margin of capital, and it had soon become apparent to the officers of Harley, Inc., that the New England territory was too big for them to cover with their insufficient capital.

Harley, Inc.'s solution to the difficulty had been to divide the New England area into subareas, generally on the basis of state boundaries, and to appoint subfranchise holders for each of the new subareas. Most of Massachusetts was to be reserved for Harley, Inc. The subfranchise for the state of Maine had been let out to a Coca Cola distributor in Maine. The subfranchise for the state of Connecticut had been sold to a newly formed corporation, of which Mr. Spence was a director. The subfranchise for the state of Rhode Island and Cape Cod was open, and Mr. Spence hoped to secure it for a group of his own choosing. Inasmuch as

Exhibit 2

POPCORN VENDING MACHINE
OPERATING STATEMENT

Income:		
100 machines at $1.50 per day for 30 days (100 × 1½ × 30)...	$4,500.00 per month	
Less: Location cost, 25 per cent of monthly sales.............	1,125.00	
Net sales income........................		$3,375.00
Operating Cost:		
Labor:		
It is calculated that a serviceman is required for every 50 machines. Men to be paid $200 per month plus 3 per cent of sales.		
100 machines required two men at $200 per month..........	$ 400.00	
Men to receive 3 per cent of sales........................	135.00	$ 535.00
Material:		
Popcorn—1 peck = 10 bags		
15 bags per machine per day − 1½ pecks per machine per day		
Popcorn cost—32 cents per peck		
Monthly cost of popcorn per 100 machines, 1½ pecks × 32 cents × 100 machines × 30 days....................	$1,440.00	
Bags—1,000 bags cost $1.75		
33⅓ per cent wastage should be expected		
100 machines × 30 days × 15 bags × 1⅓ = 60,000 bags		
60,000 bags at $1.75 per 1,000..........................	105.00	$1,545.00
Deduct total labor and material costs.....................		$2,050.00
Gross operating profit..................................		$1,295.00

Mr. Spence owned a small share of Harley, Inc., and since he had been the driving force behind the organization of the Connecticut company, there seemed little reason to doubt that the subfranchise for the state of Rhode Island and Cape Cod was his for the asking.

The terms of the Rhode Island subfranchise were these: (1) that 600 machines be bought from Harley, Inc., the first year and 600 machines the second year at a price of $225 each; (2) that all popcorn be bought from Harley, Inc., unless another company offered a cheaper price; and (3) that the penalty for failure to observe either of the above two conditions would be loss of the exclusive franchise.

Mr. Spence next discussed the profit potentialities of the machines.

From his experience in Connecticut, he stated that each machine averaged $1.50 (gross) a day. Most contracts with locations (drugstores, theaters, taverns and bars, bowling alleys, supermarkets, bus and railway stations, amusement centers, dance halls, etc.) provided for payment of 25 per cent of the gross take of the machines to the location owners. Mr. Spence estimated a monthly gross operating profit of $1,295 from each 100 machines. To support his claim he drew up a *pro forma* operating statement on a napkin (see Exhibit 2, p. 115).

In addition to the direct operating costs which Mr. Spence listed, there would, of course, be certain items of overhead expense. For instance, a manager would be required at a salary estimated by Mr. Spence to be $300 a month. The installation costs would run about $5 per machine. Office and storage rental expense would run about $100 a month for any number of machines up to 600; thereafter, office and storage rental would probably increase to $200 a month. Telephone expense was estimated at $50; travel expense at $50 a month as long as there were 400 machines or less in the field; when more than 400 machines had been distributed, the travel expense would increase to about $100, which would include the travel expense of a maintenance man whose wages of $250 per month would also be added at that point. Costs of trucking machines to location and from one location to another might run $125 a month; repair parts, $25 a month for 600 machines or less; $50 a month for more than 600 machines. Office personnel expense would be nothing for the first 300 machines; $150 a month for 400 to 700 machines; and $300 a month for anything above 700 machines. Miscellaneous expenses were estimated at $200 for 600 machines or less and $400 for 600 machines or more.

Mr. Spence had already investigated terms of financing. The Bartwell Acceptance Corporation, a finance company specializing in coin machine financing, had informally agreed to finance 75 per cent of the cost of the machines at a yearly interest rate of 5.75 per cent. The loans were to be repaid in eighteen monthly installments, beginning one month from the date of purchase of each machine. The 5.75 per cent interest would be included in each payment and would be figured on the entire outstanding balance of the loan.

The remaining 25 per cent was to be financed by Harley, Inc., at no cost under the condition that payment for each machine would be made in six equal installments beginning six months from the date of installation.

The stockholders of the proposed Rhode Island company were to furnish working capital. Mr. Spence estimated that about $8,000 would be

Exhibit 3

VENDING MACHINE ADVERTISEMENT

IF YOU'VE ALWAYS WANTED YOUR OWN SOUND, RESPECTABLE BUSINESS, BUT THOUGHT IT WOULD TAKE TOO MUCH MONEY, OR WOULD REQUIRE SPECIALIZED KNOWLEDGE OR SKILL, OR WOULD DEPEND ON SELLING, OR WOULD BE TOO GREAT A RISK . . . THEN HERE IS THE OPPORTUNITY YOU SHOULD INVESTIGATE . . .

A SMALL INVESTMENT PUTS YOU INTO THE MOST PROFITABLE END OF THE FABULOUS DEPRESSION-PROOF SOFT DRINK BUSINESS!

It used to take many thousands of dollars to get started in the soft drink business. But amazing things have been happening . . . and now it takes less than you ever imagined.

What is it?

The fastest growing business in the U.S. today is automatic merchandising. Particularly in the soft drink business, automatic cup drink dispensers have been grabbing an ever increasing share of the total dollar volume. In 1951, for example, cup drink dispensers accounted for a healthy 25% of soft drink vending sales, although they comprised only a small 5% of the total vending equipment in use!

Who is it?

The world's largest manufacturer and developer of cup drink dispensers is the Cole Products Corporation, producers of the most advanced, most successful cup drink dispenser ever made, the three flavored Cole-Spa. Cole-Spa operations are owned today by hundreds of prosperous, prominent businessmen—most of whom knew nothing about the business when they started.

What does it take?

A minimum investment of $2000 (which can be financed) puts you in business full or part-time. You may attend the three-day Cole School to learn the simple fundamentals of successful operation. In setting up and running your business, you are helped in every detail by Cole factory experts and by Cole's international, travelling field staff which has offices in most principal cities. The Cole products Corporation even helps you sign up profitable locations.

How much can you make?

A reasonably small investment can return up to $15,000 income the first year. Cole-Spa Three Flavor Cup Drink Dispensers not only sell more drinks per dispenser than old-fashioned, one-flavor bottle machines, but do it at tremendous profit margins for both owner and location. The reason there is more profit in selling a cup drink is that, over and above savings in delivery, space, handling, and breakage, there is actually a manufacturing profit. The Cole-Spa not only sells the drink . . . it also makes it fresh on the spot, for almost half the cost of a bottle drink. The truth of the matter is that full return on your investment is likely within one year.

What's the potential?

Frankly, it's staggering! Just imagine . . . there are less than 50,000 cup dispensers in operation today . . . yet, there are conservative business forecasters who estimate that about 2,500,000 additional locations are available. You need only look around you for many potential locations, not to mention thousands upon thousands of busy areas now serviced the old fashioned way—by bottle dispensers. In addition, new locations continue to develop from day to day as populations and industries grow and change. Within a few years the industry will be in the billion dollar class!

How does it work?

Your Cole-Spa Three Flavor Cup Drink Dispenser serves any three nationally famous ice-cold drinks, such as Coca-Cola, Canada Dry, Hires, Cole-Spa Beverages, etc. With a slight adjustment, a hot drink can also be served, along with two other cold drinks. Each drink is freshly cooled, carbonated, mixed, and served . . . in about five seconds . . . after a coin has been inserted. There's an automatic changemaker for dimes and quarters.

Interested?

Without doubt, Cole Products Corporation, on this page, offers one of the outstanding opportunities in the United States. If you are thinking about getting into a highly profitable business, with stability and prestige, even on a part-time basis, this merits your most earnest investigation. It costs you absolutely nothing to write away for more details . . . more facts and figures. Why not drop us a line today, while the matter is fresh in your mind?

Write Dept. B

The famous Cole-Spa Three Flavor Cup Drink Dispenser with AUTOMATIC Coin Changer and HOT DRINK attachment.

Cole Spa HERMETIC

COLE PRODUCTS CORPORATION

World's Largest Manufacturer of Cup Drink Dispensers

Executive Offices: 39 South LaSalle St., Chicago 3, Ill.

Offices in all principal cities. In Canada: Cole Products Canada Ltd., Toronto.

needed, of which he proposed to supply $2,000, in return for 49 per cent of the stock.

The investing group was intrigued by the profit possibilities but dubious about the slender working-capital requirements outlined by Mr.

Spence. One of the men pointed out that he had just seen an advertisement in a national magazine (Exhibit 3, p. 117) for a soft-drink vending machine. The advertisement seemed to further carry out the thought that a profitable business could be built with a reasonably small investment. The members of the group agreed to individually think over the specific popcorn machine venture as well as the general area of vending machine operation. They intended to meet the following night to discuss the whole problem further.

Summit Manufacturing Company

By November, 1947, the Summit Manufacturing Company had been operating for four months as a producer of residential woodwork. Having attained a profitable production rate, the company's executives were considering long-range measures to put their firm on a sound permanent basis.

The Summit Manufacturing Company was incorporated in Ohio in May, 1946, by four veterans of World War II. The incorporators expected to go into the manufacture of door frames and window sashes for the construction industry. Since the capital requirements for entering this field were beyond their immediate means, they decided to begin by making wooden toy and novelty products. The company's original paid-in capital consisted of $8,000, representing investments of $2,000 each by the four organizers.

The president of the Summit Manufacturing Company, and the motivating force behind its organization, was Mr. George G. Collins, twenty-eight years old, of Brecksville, Ohio, a small community twenty miles south of Cleveland. Mr. Collins had graduated from Ohio Wesleyan University, where he majored in business administration. His father was a prominent real estate broker. George had spent several summers working for contractors and architects and in 1941 had built his own home. While in college and for two years after graduation, he had worked for a large advertising agency as salesman and copywriter. He had also had experience on the business staff of a small newspaper.

Mr. Collins joined the U.S. Navy in 1942 and rose to the rank of lieutenant in the Naval Supply Corps. He served as disbursing officer at a large naval air base and later was supply officer for a fleet repair ship, where his responsibilities included inventory control, auditing, and budget planning. After the close of hostilities in 1945, he was assigned to the Cleveland area as an inspector of naval payrolls and accounts. In the course of this work he became well acquainted with Mr. Richard Peterson, twenty-seven years old, another naval lieutenant engaged in inventorying surplus equipment. Mr. Peterson's home was in Cleveland; he had taken a prelaw course before the war at Western Reserve University. Mr. Peterson had spent one summer as personnel director of a New England camp and had achieved a chief purser's rating by summer work on United Fruit Company ships. Upon his release from the Navy in the spring of 1946, he entered law school at Western Reserve.

Mr. Neil Benson, a classmate of Mr. Collins at Ohio Wesleyan and a resident of Brecksville, joined Mr. Collins and Mr. Peterson in organizing the Summit company. Mr. Benson, who had held various selling jobs while in college, became vice-president in charge of sales, while Mr. Peterson took over the position of secretary. A Cleveland law firm whose senior partner was a friend of Mr. Peterson's father handled the legal details of incorporation and stock issue. On the recommendation of the attorney, the young entrepreneurs also secured the services of a small firm of public accountants. These accountants set up a bookkeeping system; aided in the preparation of a cash budget; and recommended, as another potential stockholder, Mr. Edward J. Dean, thirty-three years old, another Cleveland war veteran. Mr. Dean was a graduate of a well-known eastern business school; his commercial experience had consisted of managing a family-owned farm and other real estate in the Cleveland area. After talking with the Summit company organizers, Mr. Dean agreed to come in as treasurer and to invest $2,000 in common stock.

Mr. John Crowill, another neighbor of Mr. Collins, had also planned to purchase an interest in the Summit company but had withdrawn before incorporation. Mr. Crowill, forty years old, was chief engineer of a Cleveland radio station and had spent several years as works manager of a small textile mill. He had expected to become production superintendent for the Summit company but finally decided that his family responsibilities would not permit him to leave his radio position to join an admittedly speculative venture.

In setting up the Summit company, the owners decided that they needed the benefit of continuing advice and guidance from mature businessmen. Accordingly, they invited four leading citizens to serve as directors. These "elder statesmen" included Mr. Peterson's father, the Ohio sales representative for a nationally distributed line of brick and tile; Mr. Benson's father, a paper-company executive; the Midwestern sales manager of a leading appliance manufacturer; and a feed-and-grain dealer. The other members of the board were Messrs. Collins, Peterson, Dean, and Benson.

The period between May and August, 1946, was devoted to getting the company ready for the production of wooden toys and novelties. The selection of the company's initial product had been based on the advice of a large toy distributor in New York City whom Mr. Collins had visited in early June. This distributor pointed out that the demand for toys during the 1946 Christmas season was expected to reach a new peak, and he therefore recommended that the Summit company produce a pine toy chest to retail at $12 to $15. The design of the chest was worked out jointly by Mr. Collins and the distributor and was later modified to fit the company's machinery. The final product was 36 inches long, 15 inches wide, and 17 inches deep and weighed 28 pounds packed for shipment. It was made of ¾-inch kiln-dried western pine, had a hinged lid, and was available in pink, blue, or ivory finish or in a knotty-pine stain. A wooden toy cabinet was to be added in a few weeks if demand and production facilities warranted it. The New York firm, given exclusive distribution rights on the chest, estimated that more than 4,000 units could be sold by Christmas at a price of $7.50 to wholesalers and $8.50 to department stores. Mr. Collins estimated that these selling prices would bring the company a unit profit of between 10 and 20 per cent.

Mr. Peterson, as a naval officer assigned to surplus disposal, was prohibited from buying surplus goods for two years after release from active duty. The Summit company, however, could legally purchase excess military and naval equipment. While Mr. Peterson could not reveal confidential information to his associates, he was able to point out to them the tremendous amount of usable machinery being offered at public auction. In the spring of 1946 the executives of the company purchased a surplus planer, sanding machines, several saws, and miscellaneous jigs and fixtures. Mr. Collins found these machines to be in excellent condition and estimated that they could be resold for $8,000 on the open market; the Summit company had paid a total of $5,700 for them.

Factory space in the basement of a Brecksville furniture factory was rented at $25 a month. The company spent $2,000 during June and July on the purchase and installation of heating and plumbing equipment for this building. Through one of the older directors, Mr. Collins arranged to purchase pine lumber from the operators of several portable sawmills in northern New York.

Since none of the Summit company's organizers felt qualified to take charge of production in a woodworking plant, an advertisement for a production foreman was placed in a Cleveland newspaper. In the latter part of June, Mr. William Galvin, thirty-eight years old, was hired for this position. Mr. Galvin had had ten years of experience as a time-study engineer with an electric utility. During the war he had been a lieutenant commander in the Navy and had been assistant production superintendent of an eastern naval yard. Mr. Galvin agreed to invest $2,000 in the company to become the fifth stockholder. In August an additional $4,000 for working capital was raised by the sale of 6 per cent cumulative nonvoting preferred stock to eight friends and relatives of the original investors. The preferred stock was sold at $100 a share and was callable at $110. The buyers understood that preferred dividends probably would be allowed to cumulate during the first two or three years of operations.

Production of toy chests reached a total of 3,000 units by December 1, 1946. As of that date the company had accumulated a deficit of $7,000. The selling price of the chests had been lowered in October to $6.50 to wholesalers and $7.50 to department stores. Pressure from customers was the determining factor in this change, but Mr. Collins was willing to lower prices because the company's increased production had reduced unit costs.

The Summit company encountered considerable difficulty in shipping chests to customers. The New York distributor notified the company to ship a given number of chests to a certain retail store or wholesaler. Shipments were made on a C.O.D. basis and often were not accepted by the customer because of claimed damage to the merchandise in transit. Customers receiving damaged chests would notify the distributor as well as the Summit company; consequently, they often got conflicting instructions regarding disposition of the shipments. Some chests were returned to the factory in unopened cartons, and the Summit executives believed that these returns were made, not because of damage in transit, but because the customers did not want to be overstocked. Since the customers were scattered from Boston to St. Louis and included several hundred different wholesalers and retailers of all sizes, it was difficult for Mr. Dean, who was in charge of shipments and billings, to make accurate decisions about the disposition of the various returned shipments.

Another difficulty in the manufacture of toy chests stemmed from the uncertain quality and delivery of lumber. Shipments of pine were received from several portable sawmills, each of which moved from one stand of timber to another in New York and Vermont. Consequently, the quality of the shipments was not uniform, and many chests had to be discarded because of improperly dried lumber which showed signs of warping or cracking near the end of the production process. In the fall of 1946, Mr. Dean began to buy western pine in carload lots through a Cleveland distributor. Since good-quality western pine was still in extremely short supply, the Summit company continued to supplement these purchases with lumber from the portable sawmills.

Additional production difficulties were encountered because Mr. Galvin was relying on semiskilled trade-school graduates for the bulk of his labor force, which consisted of ten men. These workers were ex-service men eligible for "on-the-job-training" benefits, whereby the federal government paid the difference between their apprenticeship salaries of about $150 a month and $200 a month. It became apparent, however, that skilled cabinetmakers, who commanded wages of at least $1.70 an hour, were needed to replace the trainees. Unfortunately, there was an acute shortage of skilled woodworkers, and Mr. Galvin was able to add only two or three to his working force.

Because of labor difficulties and the impending drop in the market for toys which both Mr. Collins and the distributor anticipated after Christmas, the Summit company executives decided in December to discontinue the manufacture of toy chests. At the same time, they abandoned plans for the introduction of other finished wooden products, such as toy wheelbarrows, cupboards, kitchen cabinets, and bed tables.

A free-lance furniture designer had been urging Mr. Collins to produce a line of modern-interior furniture based on production methods which he stated would result in lower costs than those of competing factories. This idea was definitely discarded in December because it was found that at least six months' time and several thousand dollars for additional capital would be required to get into production as a furniture factory. The production of window sashes and door frames, which had been the company's original goal, was also rejected because of the prohibitive cost of skilled technicians and of additional complex machinery required. During November and December the Summit plant turned out over a thousand unpainted wooden chests, which were sold to a Cleveland department store. This product, however, met with limited commercial acceptance, and its quality standards were difficult to maintain.

In December, 1946, Mr. Collins bought a surplus molding machine for $800, and on January 1, 1947, the Summit company began to produce oak flooring. Flooring was in extremely high demand; and although the unit profit margin was small, the company could sell all that it could produce. Production operations were relatively simple. The accumulated deficit rose to $11,000 as of January 31, 1947, but during February the company finally earned a profit of $300 and in March added another $500 to profit.

Flooring did not appear to be the answer to the search for a permanent product line. New molding machines, costing about $2,500 each, would be required to equip the firm for large-scale production of flooring. The Summit executives believed that such a fixed investment would not be practicable, since its facilities would then be too inflexible.

In the spring of 1947 the owners of the Summit company decided to produce inside-finish work for residential construction. "Inside finish" included baseboards, moldings, railings, stairways, mantelpieces, built-in cabinets and bookcases, and related home interior woodwork. The decision to enter this field had been made after long consultation with local contractors and was based on the following factors:

1. The tremendous demand for new housing in the area immediately south of Cleveland. New industrial development in Brecksville alone indicated a need for more than 3,000 new homes before the end of 1948.
2. Limited competition. Only four other finish mills were located in the Cleveland area, and none of these was within ten miles of Brecksville. Mr. Collins believed these mills to be in the hands of extremely conservative managers.
3. The company's present machinery could be utilized without expensive additions.
4. The profit margin on inside finish was higher than on flooring. Inside finish generally accounted for about 8 per cent of the total cost of a house.
5. The supply of high-quality western pine lumber which the company could obtain was increasing. The Cleveland lumber distributor with whom Mr. Collins dealt had become convinced that the Summit company would be a good customer for many years.

Having decided on a product line, Mr. Collins and his associates started in March, 1947, to build a new factory. Working conditions and storage space were extremely inadequate in the furniture factory basement. By performing the bulk of the work with their own plant labor, the Summit personnel completed a one-story, 10,000-square foot building by July. The structure was built of cement blocks with wooden interior work and was located on a rail spur at the southern edge of Brecksville. A drying kiln was attached to the plant, which Mr. Collins believed would not only assure the company of a steady supply of properly dried lumber but would contribute a monthly profit of $400 by rental of drying space to other lumber dealers and users. The floor layout of the building was designed specifically for production of inside finish.

The new building cost the Summit company about $26,000, plus $1,100 for the land; it was partially financed by a twenty-year bank mortgage for $15,000. The bank's appraisers estimated the building's fair market value at $38,000. Additional capital had been raised from four sources: (1) A small local bank extended a $5,000 line of credit, in the form of 4 per cent 60-day notes, to be used for buying lumber by the carload. (2) One of the Summit directors loaned the company $15,000, to be repaid by 1949. (3) Each of the five stockholders invested an additional $3,000 in common stock. (4) Another $5,500 in common stock was sold to friends of the owners' families.

Mr. Galvin concluded in April, 1947, that he did not have sufficient woodworking experience to manage the Summit plant efficiently. Accordingly he resigned, although he retained his stock interest in the company. He was replaced by Mr. Owen Dunn, fifty-five years old, who had made his career as superintendent of various small woodworking shops. Mr. Dunn had taken an active part in the planning and construction of the new plant. His salary was $100 a week.

In April, 1947, Mr. Collins hired a salesman to call on contractors, make cost estimates, and draw up job specifications. He proved unsatisfactory because his cost estimates were not always accurate. He continued to work for the Summit company until August, 1947, since Mr. Collins had been unable to locate a replacement. Mr. Oscar Noggle was then hired as company salesman, and the first man was released.

Mr. Noggle, who had been an inside-finish salesman for twenty years, had retired in 1941 when the mill which had employed him switched to war production. He had then taught woodworking at a trade school. He agreed to join the Summit company for the remainder of 1947, with the provision that, if the company could establish a permanent position in the industry, he would become a permanent employee. Mr. Noggle proved to be a thoroughly competent salesman and an expert at developing friendly relations with contractors. He received factory cost estimates for various products and was allowed to draw up his own job bids.

In September, Mr. Benson, who had been working as a laborer in the Summit plant, began to accompany Mr. Noggle on selling tours. Within a few weeks he was able to take over sales to builders of standard low-price homes which were being erected in large numbers on suburban real estate developments.

In August, Mr. Dean resigned from his position as treasurer of the Summit company. The pressure of family obligations had interfered to some extent with the effective discharge of his company duties, and the directors felt that a change would be beneficial to all concerned. Mr. Dean retained his stock interest and directorship. Mr. Collins took over the treasurer's job in addition to his duties as president. He drew a salary of $100 weekly and had complete charge of all company activities.

Mr. Peterson spent a minimum of one day a week at the Summit office during 1947. He participated in all major policy decisions, approved contracts and other company commitments, prepared minutes of board meetings, and determined when the advice of legal counsel should be sought. He planned to enter a Cleveland law firm in June, 1948, retaining his present responsibilities with the company. The older members of the board of directors regarded Mr. Peterson as a conservative and steadying influence in the Summit management.

Regular board meetings were held quarterly, and all members of the board were frequently called on for advice. One of the outside directors, the appliance sales manager, resigned in August, 1947, because of the requirements of his own business. He was replaced by a professor of business administration from a Cleveland university. At the same time, Mr. Lloyd Johnson, a partner in the Summit company's accounting firm, was added to the board.

In September, Mr. Collins hired a young male graduate of a commercial school as bookkeeper and secretary at $35 a week, replacing a girl who had been paid a similar salary. The young man proved energetic and capable and was learning to operate the company's cost accounting system under Mr. Johnson's supervision.

The executives of the Summit company believed that the success of their business depended on quality, prompt delivery, and accurate cost estimates. Contractors were generally willing to pay a few dollars more to a finish mill with a reputation for uniformly high-quality work rather than award all contracts to the lowest bidder. The location of the Summit plant and the fact that its owners were veterans and well liked in their home community gave the firm an initial advantage in securing trial orders from contractors. Mr. Collins hoped to concentrate sales efforts on those builders who were producing good-value homes and who would therefore be most likely to remain active after the immediate housing boom had leveled off. He planned to inaugurate a direct-mail advertising campaign in November, 1947, to speed up the penetration of this market and to attempt to counteract the expected winter business slump.

A plant-opening celebration was scheduled for the latter part of 1947. This ceremony had originally been planned for August. Mr. Collins had received a promise from the regional correspondent for *Life* magazine to cover the event. A prefabricated toolshed was to be built in the Summit plant and raffled off among the townsfolk. The plant opening had been postponed because of the pressure of getting into production.

No further major expansion of plant facilities was envisioned for several years. The incorporators were reluctant to dilute their equities by

Exhibit 1

SUMMIT MANUFACTURING COMPANY

Balance Sheet as of October 31, 1947

ASSETS			
Current Assets:			
Cash on Hand and in Bank			$ 1,188.45
Accounts Receivable—Customers			6,958.30
Inventories:			
Raw Materials		$ 7,604.08	
Goods in Process		500.00	
Finished Goods		4,265.53	
Factory Supplies		700.00	13,069.61
Fixed Assets:			
Land at Cost		$ 1,100.00	
Building—Appraised Value		37,827.50	
Equipment and Machinery—Appraised Value		24,107.69	
Office Furniture and Equipment at Cost		453.10	
		$63,488.29	
Less: Depreciation		1,160.05	62,328.24
Other Assets:			
Prepaid Insurance		$ 662.70	
Deposits		75.00	
Organization Expense		474.87	1,212.57
			$84,757.17
LIABILITIES AND CAPITAL			
Current Liabilities:			
Notes Payable—Banks		$ 4,433.74	
—Others		2,118.85	$ 6,552.59
Accounts Payable—Trade			5,593.09
Employees' Withholding Taxes			398.13
Accrued Items:			
Federal and State Taxes		$ 194.57	
Interest on Notes Payable		26.13	
Wages		142.56	
Light, Heat, and Power		150.00	513.26
Portion of Mortgage Note Payable Currently Due			1,320.00
Fixed Liabilities:			
Due to Officers and Stockholders			16,997.00
Mortgage Note Payable less First Installment			13,250.00
Capital Stock and Surplus:			
Capital Stock—Preferred		$ 4,100.00	
—Common		30,500.00	34,600.00
Surplus—Capital		$ 1,076.00	
—Revaluation		22,338.08	
—Earned:			
Balance, April 1, 1947	$11,092.91[d]		
Loss, Old Plant (April 1, 1947, to July 31, 1947)	8,952.78[d]		
Profit, New Plant (August 1, 1947, to October 31, 1947)	2,164.71		
Balance, October 31, 1947		17,880.98[d]	5,933.10
			$84,757.17

[d] Deficit.

Source: Company records.

selling additional common stock, nor could they afford any further personal investments. Mr. Johnson had prepared a cash budget for the second half of 1947 to which Mr. Collins was determined to adhere. In October, 1947, the new drying kiln was being used solely as a lumber storeroom, and the company was renting space in other kilns to dry its

Exhibit 2

SUMMIT MANUFACTURING COMPANY

PROFIT AND LOSS STATEMENT FOR THREE MONTHS ENDING OCTOBER 31, 1947

Sales (net)		$26,719.12
Cost of sales (see Exhibit 3)		19,157.42
Gross profit on sales		$ 7,561.70
Expenses:		
Selling:		
Advertising	$ 49.35	
Commissions	235.25	
Salesmen's salaries	1,309.00	
Shipping supplies	153.78	
Sundry	72.70	
Travel	301.07	
Trucking	387.05	2,508.20
Administrative:		
Depreciation on office furniture and fixtures	$ 12.48	
Executive and clerical salaries	1,776.00	
Office supplies	109.45	
Sundry	83.87	
Telephone	199.96	
Postage	18.49	2,200.25
		$ 2,853.25
Other income:		
Discount on purchases	$ 38.66	
Interest	0.26	
Sale of shavings	31.25	70.17
		$ 2,923.42
Other charges:		
Discount on sales	$ 374.15	
Interest expense	394.36	
Sundry	9.80*	758.71
Net profit		$ 2,164.71

* Credit.

Source: Company records.

green lumber. The cost of building a new storage shed was estimated at $2,200; no provision for such an expenditure had been included in the budget.

Deliveries of finished products were made in station wagons belonging to Mr. Dean and Mr. Noggle. Since new orders were being booked rapidly during September, it became obvious that a truck would be needed. With no funds for buying a truck provided by the budget, Mr. Collins himself was considering the purchase of a truck, charging the company for its use on the basis of actual operating cost plus depreciation. The truck would be sold to the firm at its depreciated value whenever the budget would permit it.

The budget for the six-month period beginning July 1, 1947, estimated sales at $45,000 and cost of goods sold at $29,831. Materials

Exhibit 3

SUMMIT MANUFACTURING COMPANY

COST OF SALES FOR THREE MONTHS ENDING OCTOBER 31, 1947

Finished goods purchased		$ 4.66
Materials used		14,492.32
Factory wages		6,540.65
Manufacturing expenses:		
Real estate taxes	$ 33.72*	
Rent	35.00	
Insurance	450.56	
Equipment repairs	60.44	
Social security taxes	373.22	
Factory supplies	205.72	
Depreciation:		
Building	162.19	
Machinery and equipment	247.98	
Heating and lighting equipment	54.06	
Heat, light, and power	441.87	1,997.32
Cost to manufacture		$23,034.95
Goods-in-process inventory:		
Beginning of period	$ 250.00	
End of period	500.00	250.00
		$22,784.95
Finished goods inventory:		
Beginning of period	$ 638.00	
End of period	4,265.53	3,627.53
Total cost of sales		$19,157.42

* Credit.

Source: Company records.

were expected to comprise 30 per cent, and factory wages 25 per cent, of selling prices. Other cost estimates included: selling expense, $4,050 (including $3,600 for commissions to Mr. Noggle); and administrative expense, $3,670 (including $1,560 for officers' salaries). Net profit before taxes was estimated at $6,638. The informal financial committee (Mr. Collins, Mr. Richard Peterson, and Mr. Johnson) agreed that this figure was a reasonable and conservative minimum and that for the first year of inside-finish production the company might well achieve a volume of $150,000.

Sales during July totaled about $1,000; during August, $5,000; in September, $10,000; and in October $12,000. Exhibits 1, 2, and 3 give the company's balance sheet as of October 31, 1947, and the August-October income and cost of sales statements.

On November 1, 1947, Mr. Collins planned to ask the board of directors for authority to obtain immediately at least $10,000 to augment working capital. The funds would be used for the following purposes:

1. *To increase inventory.* During September and October, Mr. Collins had not been able to take full advantage of discounts on lumber purchases and had been forced to forego opportunities to buy additional carloads of lumber under favorable terms.
2. *To expand plant labor force.* Mr. Collins felt that a monthly sales level of $18,000 to $20,000 would represent optimum utilization of the company's existing machinery. To attain this volume, several new employees would be needed.
3. *To carry increased receivables.* Since large builders normally received thirty-day payment terms from their suppliers, the Summit company had to sell most of its products on a similar basis.

Mr. Johnson prepared a budget for the five-month period beginning November 1, 1947, estimating sales at $70,000 and net profit at $4,000. Mr. Collins believed, however, that after capacity production was attained, profits would average 15 per cent of sales. Orders on hand as of November 1 totaled about $30,000, chiefly for cabinet work which could be installed in homes during the winter months.

The management of the Summit company believed that, in order to support a $20,000 monthly sales volume, working capital would have to be increased by about $20,000. Mr. Collins hesitated to ask the board to approve so large an expansion at once. There appeared to be no possibility of further loans from any of the directors, and the company's local bank could not increase the $5,000 line of credit already outstanding. Among the sources of funds which the officers were considering were: sale of additional preferred stock; sale of preferred and common on a "package" basis; chattel mortgage on machinery; RFC loan; and loans from private individuals. Mr. Collins also planned to ask the board for permission to install an automatic sprinkler system in the factory, buy another molding machine, and complete construction of a lumber storage shed. These fixed-asset projects would cost about $13,500. Mr. Collins thought that they might be financed through either installment purchases or an RFC loan.

The Summit company's financial committee was studying several other problems in November, 1947, but did not plan to present suggestions to the board until after working capital expansion had been considered. Among these less urgent matters were the establishment of a profit-sharing plan for the nonstockholding employees and of a sinking fund to retire the director's loan and the outstanding preferred stock.

Carbury Tractor Corporation

The Carbury Tractor Corporation, established in the fall of 1944 at Carbury, Pennsylvania, produced a 1½-horsepower garden tractor and a line of attachments marketed under the trade name "Carbury." Between January 1, 1945, and July 1, 1947, the company produced and sold 14,579 tractors, of which 2,600 were assembled in a second plant, at Danville, Oregon.

Mr. J. J. Mentzer was the president and principal stockholder of the Carbury Tractor Corporation. From 1929 to 1939 he had been an auditor and appraiser for the executive committee of a national investment company. His duties had included examination of the methods and policies of manufacturers throughout the United States who were applicants for loans in excess of $250,000. When his firm granted a substantial loan to the Chicago Tractor Company, Mr. Mentzer assumed the position of assistant treasurer with the Chicago corporation. In 1939 he resigned from the investment firm and became treasurer of the Chicago Tractor Company.

Early in 1944 Mr. Mentzer learned that the Chicago Tractor Company would be merged with the Farm Machinery Corporation, one of the dominant national manufacturers of farm equipment. Reappraising his own business future in view of this consolidation, he faced three alternatives:

1. Remaining as chief financial officer of the Chicago factory, which would become a manufacturing plant of the Farm Machinery Corporation.
2. Accepting a vice-presidency in a metropolitan bank.
3. Organizing a company of his own.

The Farm Machinery Corporation operated six factories in large Midwestern cities. Mr. Mentzer felt that, when earnings and working hours were reduced at the end of the war, labor unrest in these areas would become acute. Because the company's executive organization had been functioning well for many years, Mr. Mentzer believed the chances for personal advancement were limited. He was fifty years of age and was not willing to accept his present position as the upper limit. Furthermore, as treasurer at the Chicago branch he would no longer have complete authority over the plant's financial policies, since he would have to report to Farm Machinery's central finance officers as well as to the general manager of the Chicago unit.

In the position with the bank, Mr. Mentzer would be responsible for establishing and directing a consumer-credit and installment finance department. Although his salary would be quite satisfactory, he doubted whether he should exercise full control over his department if his ideas conflicted with those of the senior vice-presidents and bank directors. He further discovered that he and his family would have to live far out at the edge of the metropolitan area because of crowded housing conditions in the city where the bank was located.

To determine the feasibility of establishing his own business, Mr. Mentzer began in the spring of 1944 a survey of the farm-equipment industry, with which he was naturally most familiar. He talked and corresponded with makers of farm implements, four-wheeled tractors, and garden tractors; farm-equipment distributors; bankers; and business associates throughout the country. He also studied statistics which showed prewar sales of various types of tractors, the distribution of farm population, the size of farms in the United States, and the trends in farm incomes.

As a result of this survey, Mr. Mentzer concluded that the garden-tractor field was particularly promising for a new business venture. The early garden-tractor models had been heavy and cumbersome and had developed a reputation as "mankillers." Consequently, the larger manufacturers had never concentrated on mass production of garden models. Mr. Mentzer believed that he could produce a garden tractor more efficiently than a large corporation because he would be able to devote all his procurement, engineering, production, and sales efforts toward the development of a single product. He also expected the postwar demand for large tractors and earth-moving equipment to be sufficient to keep the larger firms busy for several years.

In 1944 a small Illinois firm, the Schroder Company, was producing a garden tractor which had been marketed locally for twenty years. The Schroder tractor was powered by a 1½-horsepower gasoline engine; it was one of the lightest, simplest, and lowest-priced machines on the market and embodied certain features enabling it to compete in performance with many heavier units. The machine weighed 225 pounds, could be turned within its own length, and was particularly well adapted to use on farms of five acres or less. Mr. Mentzer believed that it could also be used on larger farms as an economical auxiliary unit and by railroads, power companies, bus lines, and municipalities as a small snowplow. Another potential market was the "gentleman's" farm, on which a retired executive might dabble in truck gardening, fruit growing, or poultry raising.

To avoid the time and expense involved in developing his own garden tractor, Mr. Mentzer secured the exclusive right to manufacture a machine based on the Schroder model and to sell it in Pennsylvania, New York, and New England, as well as the eleven western states, and the export market. He agreed to pay the Schroder Company a 3 per cent royalty on every tractor he sold in return for the use of the Schroder engineering and design information. Since the Schroder tractor had never been sold nationally, Mr. Mentzer was not interested in using the Schroder trade-name or in committing himself to making an exact duplicate of the Schroder machine.

Mr. Mentzer selected Carbury, Pennsylvania, a city of 30,000 located on the Delaware River 80 miles north of Philadelphia, as the site for his new enterprise. His choice had been based on the following factors:

1. *Labor Surplus.* Between 1870 and 1910, Carbury had flourished as a river port, railroad junction, and trading center for a Pennsylvania mountain resort area. The development of the automobile, however, had resulted in rerouting tourist traffic directly to the mountains, by-passing Carbury. In 1940, Carbury's industrial activity was concentrated in shirt factories, employing predominantly female labor. The town possessed a reservoir of male workers of Dutch and German stock whom Mr. Mentzer believed temperamentally suited for training as metalworkers and machine-tool operators.
2. *Less Severe Postwar Adjustment.* Mr. Mentzer did not expect that postwar economic reaction in Carbury would be as severe as in larger cities. Carbury had not experienced any sizable wartime expansion, and the cessation of war business would therefore have little effect on the workers' gross earnings.
3. *Accessibility to Materials.* Carbury was favorably located for bringing in steel from Pennsylvania, gears and bushings from New England, and tires and motors from Ohio and Michigan. It was served by the Pennsylvania Railroad and by several scheduled truck lines.
4. *Market Area.* Carbury was within easy reach of the farming areas in New England, upstate New York, and the East Central states, where small farms predominated. Direct mail, highway, and barge connections with eastern seaports favored development of an export market from Carbury.
5. *A Good Place to Live.* Carbury had a high percentage of home owners, a low tax rate, and was close to excellent hunting, fishing, and winter sports areas. It offered a lower cost of living and a healthier, less smoky climate than most cities.
6. *Personal Knowledge.* Mr. Mentzer was familiar with the Carbury vicinity, and his brother had been a public relations consultant there for twenty-five years.

In December, 1944, the Carbury Tractor Corporation was incorporated under the laws of Pennsylvania with an authorized capitalization of 4,000 shares of 6 per cent cumulative $50-par preferred stock callable at $55 and 6,000 shares of no-par common stock. Preferred stockholders would obtain voting rights whenever one year's preferred dividends were in arrears.

A group of twenty friends and business associates of Mr. Mentzer participated in the organization of the Carbury Tractor Corporation. They invested a total of $35,000, receiving in return 700 shares of each class of stock. The smallest individual investment was $100. Mr. Mentzer contributed $20,000 personally and received an extra 2,000 shares of common stock for his research and organizing efforts. Other investors included: Mr. W. H. Bradley, twenty-nine years old, who had been in charge of government contract termination and dealer financing for the Chicago Tractor Company; Mr. C. P. Krause, thirty-one, who had also worked under Mr. Mentzer at the Chicago plant and who had had ten years of purchasing and accounting experience with auto-parts manufacturers; and Miss Jane Wright, forty-five, who had been secretary to top executives of Chicago Tractor for fifteen years.

A building previously occupied by an automobile agency near the center of Carbury was purchased, and an AA-5 priority was obtained from the War Production Board. This priority entitled the new concern to obtain steel, tires, and gasoline motors for the manufacture of farm equipment. Mr. Mentzer considered the priority as "just a hunting license," since it was not high enough to enable him to compete with the armed forces and munitions plants in procuring materials. Consequently, the management's primary efforts were directed toward obtaining steel and machinery. Fortunately, the early 1945 breakthrough by American forces in the Rhineland brought about a cutback in military needs and had the indirect effect of bringing some secondhand machine tools into the market. The Carbury Tractor executives scoured northeastern United States and were able to find a turret lathe, a forge, some drill presses, a steel shearing machine, and other metalworking equipment. The difficulties which they incurred were indicated by the company's long-distance telephone bills, which averaged about $400 a week during the first few months of 1945. Most of the machinery was rebuilt from top to bottom by a concern in Watervliet, New York, whose guarantee Mr. Mentzer had found to be entirely reliable. The name "Carbury" was selected for the company's product, and application was made for a federal copyright.

Mr. Krause became treasurer of the Carbury Tractor Corporation and assumed personal direction of the task of locating tools and machinery. Dealer solicitation, advertising, and sales promotion were placed under Mr. Bradley, who was appointed sales manager. Miss Wright became secretary of the company and was responsible for office management and accounting. The works manager was Mr. E. T. Varner, a thirty-four-year-old native of Carbury for whom Mr. Mentzer had obtained a position in 1942 in the engineering department of the Chicago Tractor Company.

In January, 1945, Mr. Varner hired 25 employees and put them to work cleaning up and renovating the factory building. All production operations were concentrated on the first floor, which had previously been used as a showroom and garage. The second floor was partitioned into offices for the management and clerical staff. The entire building was insulated. Half of an adjoining garage was rented a few months later for a tractor assembly department, and a warehouse was leased for receiving, shipping, and storage. Total floor space occupied by the end of 1945 was 25,000 square feet.

The Carbury Tractor Corporation executives established a production goal of 1,800 machines for the first nine months of 1946. By June, 400 tractors had been produced and sold. A shortage of gasoline motors during the next two months brought a halt to production. After V-J Day the Carbury staff located 1,100 surplus Army gasoline engines in a Columbus, Ohio, warehouse, and Mr. Mentzer immediately offered to buy these motors at the same price the Army had paid. To finance this purchase he obtained a $25,000 line of credit from each of two local banks ($25,000 was the legal limit for each bank). Another production bottleneck resulted from the shortage of rubber tires. After unsuccessful experiments with tires used by midget auto racers, the Carbury company purchased its own tire molds and persuaded a manufacturer to produce 5.00 × 12 tires with an agricultural tread and carrying the Carbury name. As a result of these procurement achievements, 853 Carbury tractors were assembled during the last four months of 1945.

Early in 1946, several stockholders of the Carbury Tractor Corporation formed another company, Carbury Tractor Co., Inc., to assemble and distribute the Carbury tractor west of the Rocky Mountains. All the stock of this firm was owned directly by individual investors and not by the Pennsylvania corporation. The new affiliate had a total paid-in capital of $25,000. A small plant was leased in Danville, Oregon, a city somewhat smaller than Carbury; the factory was equipped with the necessary machinery to assemble the tractor, but all heavy fabricating operations were carried on at Carbury and the manufactured parts shipped to Danville. The Oregon affiliate purchased motors, tires, and other purchased-finished parts direct from suppliers. For parts shipped from Carbury it paid the Pennsylvania company a price equal to cost plus a normal profit. Mr. Mentzer became president of the Oregon company but continued to spend most of his time at Carbury. Miss Wright moved to Danville and took over active direction of Carbury Tractor Co., Inc. Her brother Frank, who had worked in the Carbury Tractor Corporation sales department during 1945, became sales manager of the Oregon affiliate.

In January, 1947, Mr. Mentzer canceled the Carbury company's royalty agreement with the Schroder Company and prepared to distribute Carbury equipment throughout the entire country. Because of design improvements worked out by Carbury engineers during 1946, the Carbury tractor no longer bore a particularly close resemblance to the Schroder machine. Mr. Mentzer felt that the Schroder Company had been well paid for its engineering information, since it had already received about $40,000 in royalties from the Carbury companies. Although the Schroder Company held certain patents on its garden-tractor model, Mr. Mentzer was sure that the Carbury tractor did not infringe on any of these patents in 1947. No objection was raised by the Schroder firm to the termination of the royalty agreement.

The Carbury Tractor Corporation also distributed a line of Carbury attachments for use with its tractor. Originally, a plow and a disk harrow had been offered; by June, 1947, the line also included a cultivator, a spike-tooth harrow, a snowplow-grader, and two sizes of field cutters. In September, 1947, a lawn-mower attachment was added. The Carbury Tractor Corporation built some of these attachments and purchased others from plow manufacturers, depending on the availability of materials and the relative costs of the alternatives.

Carbury tractors and implements were sold to dealers and distributors throughout the country. The majority of the dealers were engaged in a general farm-equipment business; many handled competing lines of garden tractors, since the limited number of Carbury attachments did not meet the needs of every small farmer. Eleven salesmen, working under Mr. Bradley and Mr. Wright, called on dealers and distributors. The salesmen were compensated on a commission basis, receiving 5 per cent of factory price on all Carbury products shipped into their territories and paying their own expenses. One star salesman earned $1,180 during June, 1947.

All Carbury sales to dealers were on a C.O.D. basis, although most competing manufacturers offered thirty-day credit terms. The Carbury

Exhibit 1

CARBURY TRACTOR CORPORATION

EXCERPT FROM SALES BULLETIN, NOVEMBER 4, 1947*

On November 1, 1947, the following discount scale shall become effective for all distributors and dealers.

If a dealer or distributor buys from us in any quarter as follows:

1st quarter	November	—December	—January
2nd quarter	February	—March	—April
3rd quarter	May	—June	—July
4th quarter	August	—September	—October

From one to four tractors, discounts shall be 25 per cent.

When a dealer or distributor has bought the fifth tractor, an extra 1 per cent credit memorandum will be issued to him on all five tractors.

The distributor or dealer will receive 25 per cent discount on the sixth, seventh, eighth, and ninth tractor which he purchases from us.

When a dealer or distributor has bought his tenth tractor from us, he will receive an additional credit memorandum of 1 per cent on the first five tractors sold and 2 per cent on the second five tractors sold. In other words, this gives him 27 per cent on all ten tractors.

Twenty-five per cent discount will apply on the eleventh, twelfth, thirteenth, or fourteenth tractor purchased from us.

When a distributor or dealer purchases his fifteenth tractor from us, he will receive a credit memorandum for 1 per cent on the first ten tractors and 3 per cent on the next five. This will give the dealer 28 per cent discount on the entire fifteen tractors.

Twenty-eight per cent discount applies on the sixteenth through the twenty-fourth tractor purchased from us in any quarter.

Quarterly discounts apply to "less truckload" and "less carload" shipments only.

The word "tractor" above has been used for demonstrative purposes only, as the same scale of discounts applies to implements in their specific category.

When a distributor or dealer purchases from twenty-five to forty-nine tractors with related implements in one load, he will receive 30 per cent discount on all of the equipment.

When a distributor or dealer purchases from fifty to one hundred nineteen tractors and related implements in one load, he will receive 25 per cent and 10 per cent discount.

When a distributor or dealer purchases a carload of 120 tractors and related implements, [he will receive a chain discount of 25 per cent—10 per cent—5 per cent].

Our regular cash discount of 2 per cent applies in addition to the foregoing scale of discounts.

The cash discount is a financial discount by us and is based upon our receiving payment for shipments to you within five days of the date of the invoice. This means that on a S/D basis, it will be necessary that S/D be paid within five days of the date of our invoice. On any C.O.D. shipments picked up at our plant, or any cash-with-order shipments, dealers and distributors will receive the 2 per cent cash discount. On any shipments made by our contract carrier, the dealers and distributors will receive the 2 per cent cash discount. Because of the delays in obtaining payments on C.O.D. shipment from common carrier, we cannot allow cash discount on common carrier shipments by C.O.D. If you desire shipments by motor freight and the 2 per cent cash discount, send your check with your order.

Source: Company records.

Corporation issued a discount schedule (Exhibit 1, p. 137) in October, 1947, which had the effect of placing all customers on an equal basis and granting dealer or distributor discounts in accordance with the number of tractors ordered by each buyer. Each dealer was granted the exclusive right to sell Carbury equipment in a given territory and could sell directly to users, to other farm equipment retailers, or to both. Mr. Mentzer and Mr. Bradley were convinced that dealers' territories should be kept small and that the great majority of Carbury tractors should be sold directly to the retailer.

Export sales accounted for about 5 per cent of the company's volume in 1947. Carbury tractors were in use in Mexico, Colombia, Venezuela, Brazil, Uraguay, Argentina, France, Holland, Belgium, Sweden, South Africa, India, and China. All exports were handled through a company sales office in Washington, D.C. Mr. Mentzer had set up this office in 1945 to expedite the securing of priorities and to keep abreast of government procurement and production regulations. At that time, Mr. Joseph M. Robertson, one of the original Carbury stockholders and a banker of long experience, was placed in charge of this liaison office. After the end of the war, it became obvious that all United States exports would have to be approved or licensed by some branch of the federal government until conditions became more settled. Consequently, Mr. Robertson remained in Washington and supervised both exports and southeastern domestic sales.

Mr. Mentzer did not place much reliance on the further expansion of the export market, although he considered the Carbury tractor ideally suited for use on the small farms of Europe and Asia. He cited the fact that a dealer in India had ordered 500 tractors in March, 1947, but that in November this order had not yet been filled because of the refusal of the Indian government to release dollar balances for payment.

Mr. Henry Dwyer of Detroit, Michigan, joined the Carbury Tractor Corporation staff in 1946. He maintained an office in Detroit and was given the responsibility of co-ordinating and expediting the purchase of materials in the Midwestern industrial area. His purchases accounted for about sixty per cent of the total dollar value of materials bought by the Pennsylvania and Oregon corporations. Mr. Mentzer's brother James became executive assistant to the president at Carbury in 1946. He co-ordinated research and production activities, and it was under his direction that design changes were made which eliminated the need for royalty payments to the Schroder Company. The 1947 model Carbury garden tractor was lighter than its predecessor, and attachments could be changed more rapidly.

The working force at Carbury numbered 80 men in 1947 and included die and tool makers, welders, drill-press and punch-press operators, painters, assemblymen, and receiving and shipping employees. Their average hourly wage had risen from 70 cents in January, 1945, to $1 in June, 1947. In addition, the company allowed six paid holidays and one day's vacation for each two months of service, with a maximum vacation period of two weeks. The management also placed on the bulletin board semiannually a report on the past six months' business and on the outlook for the immediate future. A Christmas bonus was paid to the workers; the amounts were determined by the directors and distributed on the basis of length of service, total yearly earnings, job responsibility, spirit, and special achievements.

On several occasions Mr. Mentzer had authorized loans by the corporation to employees who were in temporary financial distress. He was proud of the fact that his workers came to him, rather than to bankers or civic aid groups, for personal advice and assistance. During 1946, union organizers had approached Mr. Mentzer at various times claiming to represent a majority of the plant workers. Since no agent had ever requested a NLRB election, Mr. Mentzer believed that organizing efforts had been unsuccessful. No union representatives had visited him since October, 1946. Mr. Mentzer paid his junior executives, as well as his plant workers, on a profit-sharing basis.

Normally, Mr. Mentzer worked a nine-hour day and a five-day week, but on many occasions he and the entire executive and clerical staffs returned to the office at 7:00 P.M. and worked until 10:00 P.M. A night shift was occasionally operated at Carbury, but Mr. Mentzer did not plan to set up a permanent night shift until the supply of gasoline motors showed substantial improvement. He believed that by the end of 1947 the backlog of orders would be filled; in July, 1947, therefore, he launched a large-scale sales-promotional campaign. The company's advertising budget was increased from 1 to 2 per cent of sales; advertisements were placed in national magazines which circulated among higher-income farm families. Previous advertising had been confined to farm-equipment trade journals. The Oregon company contributed 2 per cent of each sales dollar to the advertising fund.

Since the organization of the company, the original group of shareholders had made additional investments totaling $22,370, receiving in return 433 shares of $50-par preferred stock and 391 shares of no-par common stock. In July, 1947, the common and preferred stocks of the Carbury Tractor Corporation were split on a ten-for-one basis. Stock ownership after the split was as follows:

	No. of Shares	
	Common (No Par)	6 Per Cent Preferred ($5 Par)
Mr. J. J. Mentzer	25,000	5,000
Other executives	5,500	5,500
Outside stockholders	410	830
Unissued	29,090	18,670
Total authorized	60,000	40,000

Preferred dividends had been paid regularly since the company's inception. An initial common dividend of $1.00 a share was declared before the stock split in 1947.

Although Mr. Mentzer planned to continue aggressive research on the Carbury tractor, he did not foresee a broad extension of the product line or a substantial increase in manufacturing facilities. By the fall of 1947 the Carbury Tractor Corporation had established four open-credit lines, permitting total loans of $200,000, from banks in Philadelphia and Carbury. The Carbury management utilized these credit lines for short-term working-capital loans, paying from 4 to 6 per cent interest. The company's outstanding bank debt had never risen above $125,000. Mr. Mentzer believed that full utilization of existing bank credit would enable the company to produce at capacity without further outside investment. He estimated that the Carbury plant could turn out 3,000 tractors monthly, if operated on a three-shift basis. Under capacity operation Mr. Mentzer planned to assemble about 75 per cent of the tractors at Carbury and ship the remaining 25 per cent to Danville. His distribution goal called for the expansion of the dealer organization to 3,000 firms throughout the world.

In September, 1947, the Carbury Tractor Corporation acquired a controlling interest in the Lawn-Till Company of Pittsburgh, Pennsylvania, which had manufactured a power lawn mower for many years. The Lawn-Till Company had been unable to purchase gasoline motors or to build an effective dealer organization because of lack of working capital. It was equipped to produce about 5,000 power mowers a year. In exchange for a 20 per cent stock interest in the Lawn-Till Company, Carbury Tractor agreed:

1. To guide and advise the present management of the Lawn-Till plant.
2. To loan $3,500 to the Lawn-Till Company to provide for essential plant retooling, the loan to be repaid through a $1 reduction in the price of finished mowers delivered to Carbury.
3. To purchase all mowers produced by the Lawn-Till Company and resell them under the Carbury name and through Carbury dealers.

4. To purchase 400 motors for Lawn-Till mowers by pledging these motors as partial collateral for a purchase loan.

The Lawn-Till Company agreed to manufacture a mowing attachment for use with the Carbury garden tractor, as well as to continue production of the Lawn-Till power mower.

Approximately fifty companies, including divisions of Graham-Paige, Sears-Roebuck, and Food Machinery, were building garden tractors in 1947. Several of these firms manufactured an extremely wide range of sizes, models, and attachments. Power lawn mowers were produced and sold by more than forty companies.

Exhibit 2

CARBURY TRACTOR CORPORATION

U.S. MANUFACTURERS' GARDEN-TRACTOR UNIT SALES

	Industry Total	Carbury		Industry Total	Carbury
1929	5,895	....	1944	16,852	....
1939	9,777	....	1945	27,962	1,253
1941	16,896	....	1946	109,189	7,226
1942	12,963	....	1947	Not available	8,600*
1943	9,610	....			

* Estimated.

Source: Company records and *Facts and Figures*, Series M35A-C6, U.S. Department of Commerce, May 9, 1947

Exhibit 2 shows the production of Carbury tractors from 1945 to 1947, compared with prewar and postwar national garden-tractor production. Exhibit 3 indicates list prices of Carbury equipment F.O.B.

Exhibit 3

CARBURY TRACTOR CORPORATION

CONSUMER'S PRICE LIST EFFECTIVE OCTOBER 15, 1947

1½-horsepower Carbury Tractor with 5.00 × 12 pneumatic rubber tires	$225.00
2.4-horsepower Carbury Tractor with 5.00 × 12 pneumatic rubber tires	275.00
7-inch plow with rolling colter	20.00
Disk harrow (eight 12-inch disks—two gangs)	32.00
Spike-tooth harrow (12 teeth)	20.00
Cultivator (6 teeth and two gauge wheels)	29.00
48-inch snowplow	45.00
32-inch field mower (cutter bar)	70.00
48-inch field mower (cutter bar)	90.00
25-inch Trac-Mower	90.00
21-inch Carbury 1½-horsepower Lawn-Till	165.00

Prices F.O.B. Carbury, Pennsylvania, subject to change without notice and to payment by the buyer (in addition to purchase price) of any tax now or hereafter levied and of any extraordinary charges due to government legislation. A charge for boxing or crating is made when shipment is by common carrier and crating is required.

Source: Company records.

Exhibit 4

CARBURY TRACTOR CORPORATION

BALANCE SHEETS

ASSETS

	September 30, 1947	September 30, 1946
Current Assets:		
Cash on Hand and in Banks	$ 4,836	$ 22,290
U.S. Treasury Certificates of Indebtedness (7/8 per cent, Series E, due June 1, 1948)	35,000	
Note Receivable—Customer	31,000	
Accounts Receivable—Customers	43,966*	15,480
—Others	5,402	11,706
Inventories of Finished Goods, Work in Process, and Raw and Processed Materials (at cost not in excess of market)	384,950†	218,708†
Purchase Advances	9,620	
Due from Affiliate (Carbury Tractor Co., Inc.)	69,612	44,521
Total Current Assets	$584,386	$312,705
Due from Officers and Stockholders	......	4,378
Land, Building, Machinery, and Equipment (Note 1)	92,744‡	56,382‡
Prepaid Expenses and Deferred Charges	16,800	9,389
Total Assets	$693,930	$382,854

LIABILITIES AND CAPITAL

	September 30, 1947	September 30, 1946
Current Liabilities:		
Notes Payable to Banks—Material as Collateral	$ 64,700	$102,844
—Equipment as Collateral	.....	3,567
—Other	9,000	6,000
Accounts Payable	79,405	44,709
Customers' Deposits on Purchases	121	8,088
Real Estate Purchase Contract (portion due in year)	500	750
Taxes—Federal Income (estimated)	138,500	45,000
—State Franchise and Other	22,321	6,468
Salaries, Wages, and Bonuses	46,711	45,848
Interest, Insurance, Royalties, etc. (Note 2)	7,517	9,399
Total Current Liabilities	$368,775	$272,673
Real Estate Purchase Contract (portion due after year)	5,250	5,750
Reserves for Contingencies, Product Development, and Advertising	50,394	10,000
Capital Stock (Note 3):		
Preferred 6 per cent Cumulative (Par Value $5 a Share, Callable at $5.50—Authorized 40,000 Shares)	56,650	56,650
Common (No-Par Value—Authorized 60,000 Shares, Issued Consisting of 29,280 Shares at No Stated Value and 1,630 Shares Stated at $720)	720	720
Earned Surplus	212,141	37,061
Total Liabilities and Capital	$693,930	$382,854

* Net after reserve for $500.
† Includes materials pledged as collateral to loans: 1947, $64,700; 1946, $87,930.
‡ Includes $5,237 pledged as collateral to equipment loans. Figures are net after reserves for depreciation: 1947, $12,490; 1946, $4,160.

Note 1: Land and building were acquired through assignment of a contract for the purchase thereof for $9,000, of which $5,750 was unpaid at September 30, 1947. A purchase-money mortgage would be executed when payments under the contract amount to $4,000. Since acquisition of this property, the corporation has expended $8,424 for building improvements.

Note 2: Patent issued in October, 1934, and under which the corporation had operated, was terminated by the corporation as of January 16, 1947. Royalties have not been paid or accrued in the books of the corporation with respect to sales made subsequently to that date because, in the opinion of the management, the specifications covered by the patent have not been used in tractors or tractor parts produced by it after January 16, 1947.

Note 3: On July 24, 1947, the certificate of incorporation was amended by the corporation, increasing tenfold the authorized number of shares of each class of capital stock. Accordingly, the number of shares issued and outstanding was likewise increased without change in the aggregate stated values for each class of stock.

Source: Company records.

Carbury, Pennsylvania. A 2.4-horsepower Carbury tractor had been added to the line in August, 1947; it was identical with the smaller machine except for the motor. In October, 1947, about one third of new orders for Carbury tractors were for the larger model. Balance sheets and income statements for the fiscal years 1946 and 1947 are given in Exhibits 4 and 5.

Exhibit 5

CARBURY TRACTOR CORPORATION

SUMMARY OF INCOME AND EARNED SURPLUS

	Year Ended September 30 1947	1946
Net sales*	$1,901,707	$783,933
Cost of goods sold	1,325,771	560,440
Gross profit on sales	$ 575,936	$223,493
Less: Selling and administrative and general expenses	208,021	126,127
Profit from operation	$ 367,915	$ 97,366
Other income	5,839	4,131
Gross income	$ 373,754	$101,497
Other charges	11,205	4,098
Net income before provision for federal income tax	$ 362,549	$ 97,399
Provision for federal income tax	138,381†	45,000
Net income for year	$ 224,168	$ 52,399
Appropriations:		
To reserve for contingencies	$ 10,000	$ 10,000
To reserve for product development	22,206	......
To reserve for advertising	8,188	......
	$ 40,394	$ 10,000
Remainder	$ 183,774	$ 42,399
Earned surplus at beginning of year	37,061	3,973[d]
	$ 220,835	$ 38,426
Dividends paid in cash:		
Preferred stock	$ 5,603	$ 1,365
Common stock	3,091	......
	8,694	1,365
Earned surplus at end of year	$ 212,141	$ 37,061

[d] Deficit.

* Includes sales to Carbury Tractor Co., Inc., in 1947, $201,268; in 1946, $77,091.

† $138,500 less unused portion of 1946 provision ($119).

Note: Accumulated unpaid dividends on the 6 per cent preferred stock amounted to $850 at September 30, 1947.

Source: Company records.

Mr. Mentzer planned to retire in 1950. He felt that the Carbury Tractor Corporation had achieved a satisfactory niche as an important producer of a badly needed farm tool. The company was considered one of the three most important firms in Carbury from the standpoint of payroll and value of products. Mr. Mentzer cited the following arguments, which he felt weighed against the expansion of the Carbury Tractor Corporation beyond its present physical and financial capacity:

1. Expansion would probably require a public sale of stock, with consequent dilution of the present owners' equity and possible loss of control.
2. Even if additional capital were raised, it would be many years before Carbury could compete with the large equipment manufacturers in engineering, research, and mass-production techniques.
3. Expansion would necessitate more key executives, all of whom would have to be consulted before major decisions could be made.
4. An increase in the plant labor force beyond about 150 employees would diminish the personal contact and friendliness between management and workers.
5. Overexpansion would render the corporation more vulnerable to changes in the business cycle. Mr. Mentzer believed that 1948 might conceivably bring a slight reduction in Carbury unit sales, owing to the much tighter export market and to increasing competition. He felt, however, that dollar volume would not be adversely affected because the broader line of Carbury attachments would tend to increase the average "package sale" to consumers. The average Carbury retail sale in 1947 was $254; Mr. Mentzer estimated that this figure would be close to $300 in 1948.

Dorrance Chemical Corporation

A REPORT ON THE FORMATION OF THE DORRANCE CHEMICAL CORPORATION, A NEW COMPANY FOR THE MANUFACTURE AND SALE OF SODIUM ALUMINATE AND OTHER INDUSTRIAL CHEMICALS

1.0 INTRODUCTION

On July 15, 1951, the Universal Chemical Company ceased production of sodium aluminate, an industrial chemical used largely for water treatment and as a chemical agent in the manufacture of paper.

The management of Universal had decided that it was uneconomic for them to produce sodium aluminate, since a proportionate share of overhead could not be carried by their sodium-aluminate plant. In addition, the company wanted to use the building for the expansion of a more profitable department.

Shortly thereafter, Chemton Associates became aware of Universal Chemical's decision. Mr. L. J. Bostwick, plant superintendent for Universal Chemical, was asked his opinion of the feasibility of organizing a company to manufacture sodium aluminate, using Universal's process and equipment and selling to Universal's old customers. Both Mr. Bostwick and Mr. John Campbell of the Universal Chemical Company's sales department were enthusiastic and thought this could be done with the good will and blessing of the Universal's management, which would sell the existing plant at a low figure and supply a list of customers as well.

The sodium-aluminate plant was one of the activities under Mr. Bostwick's jurisdiction, and from his intimate knowledge of the facts he could see possibilities in a profitable operation for a small specialty company. It was his opinion that such a company could even manufacture sodium aluminate at the same manufacturing cost as Universal and make a larger profit because of much lower overhead.

He cited the example of the Marshall Company of New Britain, Connecticut, which had arranged with Universal to take over the distribution of acids in packages. Marshall Company was receiving full co-operation from Universal Chemical. It bought Universal's bulk chemicals and then repackaged them in drums and carboys for sale to small users. At Mr. Bostwick's suggestion a survey was made of the opportunity to set up a small company for the manufacture and sale of sodium aluminate. This report is a result of that survey. The survey was unusual in that practically all necessary facts concerning sales, engineering, production, and finance were made available from the records of the Universal Chemical Company.

2.0 SODIUM ALUMINATE—IT'S USE AND APPLICATION[1]

2.1 Paper Industry

Sodium aluminate is used in the paper industry together with sulphate of alumina.

The advantage of using a combination of sodium aluminate and sulphate of alumina is that it allows better sizing and lower acidities. This leads to a number of important advantages, such as more permanent paper, elimination of foam in the paper-making process, better use of dyes in making colored papers, better machine conditions, somewhat shorter process, increase in sheet weight, and the prevention of discoloration.

2.2 Water Purification

Sodium aluminate is widely used in the water-purification industry. It has the distinct advantage of acting as both a coagulating agent and a softening agent in water treatment.

2.2.1 *Sodium Aluminate in Internal Treatment of Boiler Feed Water*

The internal chemical treatment of boiler feed water is intended to accomplish two purposes: (*a*) to change soluble scale-forming materials, such as silicate, magnesium, and calcium sulphate, to insoluble nonscaling compounds; and (*b*) to coagulate the insoluble compounds formed so that they will be readily removed as sludge during slowdowns. To accomplish these ends, the usual procedure is to add sodium phosphate and soda ash, plus a supplementary dosage of sodium aluminate, to the water.

2.1.2 *Sodium Aluminate in External Treatment of Boiler Feed Water*

In either hot or cold external softening of boiler feed water by the lime-soda process, the same principle applies as in the internal treatment, namely, the addition of chemicals to react with water hardness to

[1] Considerable technical information has been omitted from this section of the report.

form easily removable insoluble compounds. It is, of course, desirable to complete the reaction before the water leaves the sedimentation tank, and also to remove as much of the precipitated matter as possible to prevent clogging of pipe lines and too frequent backwashing of filters. A properly coagulated water will clarify more quickly and completely than an uncoagulated water.

The use of sodium aluminate offers distinct advantages and assures a more positive control in this type of feed-water treatment.

2.1.3 *Sodium Aluminate as a Coagulant of Water for Municipal and Other Industrial Uses*

Sodium aluminate is an alkaline salt of high alumina content. This property renders it especially valuable for the sodium aluminate-alum treatment of certain classes of water used by municipalities and industries.

2.3 Chemical Industry

In addition to the above uses, sodium aluminate is used in the chemical industry as an alkaline source of alumina in the manufacture of certain pigments, catalysts, and (casein) paints, in processing glycerin, and in cleaning solutions.

2.4 Textile Industry

Sodium aluminate is used in the textile industry to improve strength and water resistance of synthetic wool and also to whiten wool.

2.5 Paint Industry

Sodium aluminate is used in the paint industry to improve paint-drying qualities.

3.0 THE SODIUM ALUMINATE INDUSTRY

The statistical abstract of the Bureau of Census lists the total United States production of sodium aluminate in 1947 to be 8,774 tons. More recent census information is not available; however, according to Universal Chemical industrial reports, United States production for 1950 was in the neighborhood of 17,500 tons—a growth rate of over 100 per cent. These quantities were based on a composition of 73 per cent sodium aluminate.[2]

[2] One pound of the Universal Chemical Company's 90 per cent sodium aluminate is theoretically equal in price and use to 1.233 pounds of 73 per cent sodium aluminate. List price of 73 per cent sodium aluminate was $9.50 per hundredweight F.O.B. plant.

The major producers in 1947 were the Columbia Light Weight Metals Corporation, Fort Worth, Texas; the North American Reaction Company, Paterson, New Jersey; and the Universal Chemical Company, New Haven, Connecticut. North American Reaction has not been in production since 1947, and Universal Chemical ceased manufacture of this material on July 15, 1951.

The Columbia Light Weight Metals Corporation has always been the major producer and now accounts for all known production. This company produces sodium aluminate on a 73 per cent maximum strength basis only and has catered primarily to the water-conditioning industry.

The Universal Chemical Company sold 2,354,645 pounds in 1947, which accounted for 14 per cent of the production in that year. Universal Chemical's volume had remained fairly constant since that time, and in 1950 it produced approximately 2,500,000 pounds.

Universal Chemical produced a concentrated product of great purity that assayed 90 per cent sodium aluminate. Because of its quality, it enjoyed a constant demand for many purposes and was preferred over sodium aluminate, obtainable from other sources. Since Universal Chemical's abandonment of this market, their former customers have reluctantly resorted to utilization of Columbia Light Weight Metals' product, since it is the only material now available.

There are certain other factors that indicate a favorable situation for the establishment of an additional producer of sodium aluminate. Since Columbia Light Weight Metals Corporation is located in Fort Worth, Texas, a producer located in New England would have an advantage in lower transportation charges. Added is the fact that the Universal Chemical product is approximately 20 per cent lighter in weight (90 per cent assay, as compared with 73 per cent). One should also not be unmindful of the fact that Columbia Light Weight Metals Corporation now has a monopoly in sodium-aluminate production and, in view of the present attitude of government, would probably welcome the entrance of another producer into the field. In any event, it is extremely doubtful that they would engage in any severe price cutting; they would most likely allow the eastern market to be taken by default.

4.0 ESTIMATE OF SALES BY THE NEW COMPANY

Since the new company will be the only producer of white soluble sodium aluminate of 90 per cent assay, it is probable that the great majority of the former customers of the Universal Chemical Company will purchase from the new company. As was previously stated, the largest proportion of white soluble 90 per cent sodium aluminate is purchased by the paper industry. The breakdown of Universal Chemical's sales in various industries is as follows:

	Per Cent
Paper industry	44.3
Chemical wholesalers	34.9
Chemical process industry	10.4
Machinery manufacturers	9.1
Water treatment	1.3
Total	100.0

Major customers are listed below:

	Percentage of Total Sales (Pounds)
Cranton and Hartford	4.2
Glenford Paper Company	4.0
Stevenson and Lehigh	5.2
Universal Pulp Products	4.0
Jorgenson Chemical Co.	24.5
Production Items Co.	4.3
Tassar Co., Inc.	4.1
Total	50.3

As can be seen from the foregoing, the sales situation is simplified because of the concentration of the market. It can be appreciated that the purchasers of industrial chemicals are rational and expert buyers and will purchase sodium aluminate from the new company if it meets the quality standards and price required for their operations.

Difficulty is not expected in obtaining Universal Chemical's former customers. The Universal Chemical Company has provided a complete list of their former customers, together with their yearly requirements. Several of these customers were interviewed by telephone, and in every case the purchasing agent expressed a desire to purchase from the new company. The following are the results of these interviews:

Company	*Are You Interested in New Supplier?*	*Yearly Requirements in Pounds per Year*
Stevenson & Lehigh Co.		
Mr. Daniels	Yes	100,100
Old Country Paper Co.		
Mr. Skidmore	Yes	44,000
Algonquin Wrapping Co.		
Mr. Glotnick	Yes	12,000
Blackston Paper Products Co.		
Mr. Blackston	Yes	71,000

An interesting development has been the receipt of an inquiry by the Universal Chemical Company from the Williams Chemical Co. Williams Chemical buys about 650,000 pounds of sodium aluminate from National Aluminate. Universal Chemical advised Williams that they were out of the sodium-aluminate business for good but advised them of the possibility of purchasing their requirements from a new company that was being formed.

It is conservatively estimated that by approaching Universal Chemical's old customers, advising them that the new company has taken over the Universal Chemical process and plant and can supply their requirements for the same quality material, at least 80 per cent of the business can be regained. Present indications are that the Universal Chemical Company will also be willing to recommend the new company as a supplier.

It is thus estimated that annual sales of at least 2,000,000 pounds of sodium aluminate will be obtained. There seems to be an excellent possibility that this business can be expanded through aggressive sales methods.

5.0 RAW MATERIALS

The raw materials used in the manufacture of sodium aluminate are hydrated alumina (Al_2O_3), caustic soda solution ($NaOH$), dextrine, and silicate of soda.

Caustic

The 50 per cent caustic soda solution is a standard industrial chemical that can be obtained from many chemical manufacturers. Some of these companies are: Diamond Alkali Co., Dow Chemical Co., Allied Chemical and Dye Co., and Wyandotte Chemical Corporation.

The Dow Chemical Co. has provided the following quotation on their current price schedule:

Dow Chemical Quotation

Price:

Tank cars:

Solution 48%–50% .... $2.55 per cwt. (100% basis)

Deliveries: F.O.B. Midland, Michigan, or Velasco, Texas, freight equalized with Syracuse, New York, in New England

Terms of Payment:

Net 30 days to firms of approved credit

Containers: Size and type

Solution 48%–50%

	Net
Tank cars—8,000 gals.	52,000 lbs.
Tank cars—10,000 gals.	64,000 lbs.

The freight charge to New Haven, Connecticut, amounts to 0.3595 per hundredweight on the 50 per cent solution. The net cost, including freight, is therefore $3.269 per hundredweight on the 100 per cent caustic soda (NaOH) delivered basis.

Alumina Hydrate

Hydrate of alumina can be obtained from Kaiser, Reynolds Metal, and the Aluminum Company of America. The Aluminum Company of America has provided the following quotation in their current price schedule:

Alcoa Quotation

Price:
Carload:* (40,000 lbs. minimum) 100-lb. paper bags....................$3.00 cwt.
Deliveries: F.O.B. Plant, East St. Louis, Illinois
Terms of Payment: Net 30 days from date of invoice

* The freight charges to New Haven, Connecticut, are $0.53 cwt. shipped in 40,000-lb. lots. This rate is reduced to 0.46 cwt. when shipped in 80,000-lb. lots.

The net cost including freight, therefore, is $3.46 per hundredweight.

Stabilizing Agents

The stabilizing agents used are dextrine and silicate of soda. These materials are used in relatively small amounts and can be purchased in 100-pound lots from practically any chemical wholesale house. The prices quoted are as follows:

Prices of Stabilizing Agents

Dextrine	$7.84 cwt.
Silicate of soda	1.65 cwt.

Shipping Containers and Miscellaneous Shipping Costs

The usual shipping containers used are standard paper bags holding 100 pounds. An estimated price of $1.00 per bag is made, which includes the cost of printing and incidental shipping costs.

Availability of Raw Materials

The raw materials used in the manufacture of sodium aluminate are presently available in almost any quantity. The various suppliers contacted did not see any possibility of shortages in the foreseeable future.

6.0 PRODUCTION PROCESS[3] (see Exhibit 1, p. 152)

Sodium aluminate is made from hydrate of alumina and 50 per cent sodium hydroxide solution, with small amounts of stabilizing agents, at

[3] This is a highly summarized version of the process.

Exhibit 1

SODIUM ALUMINATE PRODUCTION

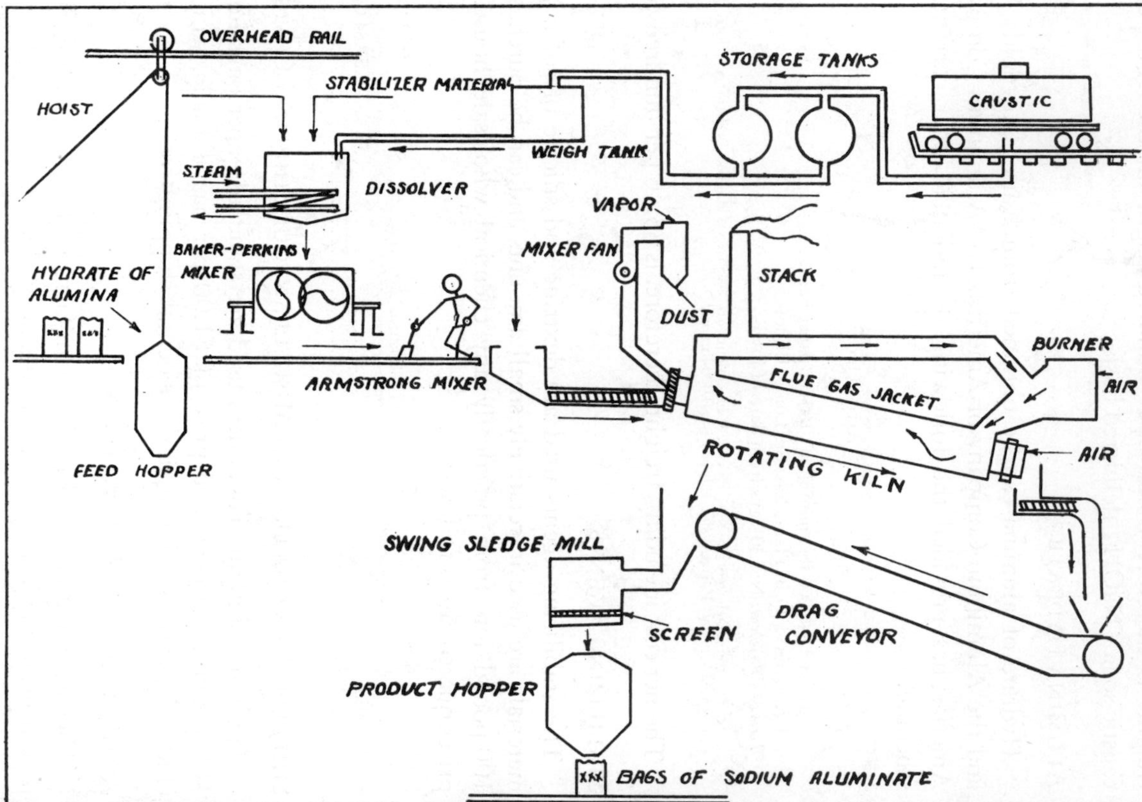

a maximum rate of 12 × 1,000-pound batches per day, or 6 tons for 3 eight-hour shifts. Each batch requires 900 pounds of hydrate and 1,035 pounds of caustic (50 per cent basis).

The hydrate of alumina is dumped from bags into a feed hopper, which is hoisted to the dissolver. The caustic is blown from tank cars to a storage tank from which the batch weigh tank may be filled as required for each dissolver charge. In the dissolver the mixture is heated by a nickel steam coil.

The solution is boiled and then dumped into the Baker-Perkins mixer. This is a steam-jacketed dough-mixing machine; and the batch is further concentrated, while being kneaded mechanically, until it nearly reaches the maximum power load of the machine. The mixer is revolved on a shaft to dump the doughy material onto the floor of the "Armstrong" mixer before it gets too thick. "Armstrong" is a facetious name invented by the men who work the batch on the floor with shovels to prevent its setting to a solid mass. The resulting lumpy material is shoveled into a feed hopper, from which a short screw conveyor carries it to the dryer. In this inclined cylinder, the sodium aluminate tumbles downward, surrounded by a jacket containing hot (above 600° F.) flue gases from a furnace. The flue gases are recirculated in order to conserve as much heat as possible, although some of the gas must be vented to allow for the fresh air required for fuel combustion.

A stream of air through the dryer carries the moisture from the drying product to a steam-heated cyclone separator for recovery of any dust in the stream, in order to prevent a nuisance in the area where these gases are discharged into the atmosphere.

The lump product drops from the dryer to a screw conveyor, which discharges into a drag conveyor. At the top of the drag conveyor a mixture composed of another stabilizing agent and some of the finished product from previous batches is added. The conveyor delivers the material to a swing sledge mill. Here the lumps are pulverized and passed through a perforated screen to a product hopper for bagging.

Composite samples from the bagged sodium aluminate are tested at the laboratory for stability by dissolving in water and examining, after twenty-four hours, for any separation of solids. Other analyses are performed on a composite of the several batches comprising one lot to determine the assay and the amount of excess caustic. The ratio of combined alumina to sodium oxide is calculated as an indication to the department supervision that the proper quantities of raw materials are being used.

7.0 DIRECT LABOR COSTS

In the operation of the sodium aluminate plant of the Universal Chemical Company, two direct labor employees were utilized on each working unit. These men have ample time to load and unload the raw materials and finished product and to run the plant as well as take care of the general housekeeping.

The general pay rate for workers of the type required would approximate $1.50 per hour. This is on the high side, and a better class of worker should be obtained at this scale. The total labor charges for an eight-hour shift would amount to $24. On the basis of a production of 2 tons per eight-hour shift, the direct labor charges will amount to $12 per ton. This is not a realistic value, since one cannot run 100 per cent on schedule. There are repairs, breakdowns, sickness, and other interruptions. To allow for these contingencies, an estimate of 50 per cent additional is made, which raises the direct labor cost to $18 a ton; and a 10 per cent allowance for social security, taxes, and compensation insurance amounts to an additional $1.80 per ton.

8.0 DIRECT MANUFACTURING BURDEN

In the production of sodium aluminate, quantities of steam, electricity, water, and fuel oil are consumed.

Accurate consumption figures are available, which were obtained from the Universal Chemical Company. These are actual budgeted figures based on the production of 1 ton of sodium aluminate. These values are shown in Exhibit 2.

Exhibit 2

UNIT QUANTITIES AND UNIT VALUE FOR 1 TON OF ALUMINATE

	Material Unit	*Std. Quantity Used*	*Std. Unit Price*
Material:			
$NaOH$ 100% caustic soda	lbs.	1,072	0.03269
$Al(OH)_3$ hydrate alumina	lbs.	1,810	0.0346
Dextrine	lbs.	12	0.0784
Silicate of soda	lbs.	43	0.0165
Bags, paper, including shipping cost	100-lb. size	20	1.000
Utilities:			
Steam	M lbs.	4.7	1.00
Electricity	kw-hr	100	0.015
Water	cu. ft.	50	0.0015
Fuel oil	gal.	75	0.07

9.0 BUDGET

Exhibits 2 and 3 accumulate all cost information previously outlined in Sections 5, 6, 7, and 8.

Exhibit 3

PRODUCTION COSTS PER TON SODIUM ALUMINATE

	Budget Cost	
Material:		
Caustic soda	$35.04	
Alumina hydrate	62.62	
Dextrine	0.94	
Silicate soda	0.71	
Bags (paper), including shipping cost	20.00	
Total material cost		$119.31
Direct conversion cost:		
Steam	4.70	
Electricity	1.50	
Water	0.08	
Fuel oil	5.25	
Labor manufacturing	18.00	
Social security tax and compensation insurance	1.80	
Repairs, major	10.00	
Supplies	0.50	
Total direct conversion expense		41.83
		$161.14

10.0 PRODUCTION EQUIPMENT

The production equipment necessary for the manufacture of sodium aluminate will be obtained from the Universal Chemical Company.

A complete listing of the equipment is shown below. All the machinery listed can be purchased from Universal Chemical for $10,000, provided it is removed by the purchaser.

Plant Equipment Purchased from Universal Chemical

Hydrate hoist	Finished-product storage hopper
Caustic storage tank	Caustic weight tank
Boiling-down tank	Valve Pac bag filling and stretching machine
Boiling-down nickel coil	Dryer exhaust fan
Dryer feed hopper and screw	Flue-gas circulating and exhaust fan
Dryer	Caustic pump
Starch feeder	Calciner
Hammer mill	Baker Perkins mixer
Motors	

Cost $10,000

In addition to the items listed above, a steam generator and heating plant will be required. The following lists the approximate cost of these items together with other capital costs to be entailed:

Plant Expense Summary

1. Purchased from Universal Chemical	$10,000
2. Removal from present site	5,000
3. Installation at new site	10,000
4. Purchase and installation of steam generator	10,000
5. Contingency	5,000
Total plant expense	$40,000

11.0 BUILDING AND SPACE REQUIREMENTS

The building required for the manufacturing plant must meet the following specifications:

1. 3,000 square feet of area for production area
2. 1,000 square feet of area for raw-material storage
3. 1,000 square feet of area for finished inventory
4. Railroad siding
5. Facilities for truck loading
6. Ceiling height of at least 30 feet
7. Location within 30-mile radius of New Haven, Connecticut
8. Must have utilities available—water, electricity

A very suitable plant site has been located at the plant of the Marshall Company at New Britain, Connecticut. The plant has all of the outlined requirements together with certain other intangible advantages that might be discussed.

The Marshall Company is a firm engaged in the wholesaling and retailing of industrial chemicals. It buys chemicals in carload and tank-car lots, and resells in smaller quantities to industrial users.

The plant includes facilities for loading and unloading from truck and rail transportation, and these facilities would be available to the new concern.

Advantages would also accrue to the sodium-aluminate plant, in that caustic could be piped directly from the Marshall storage tank, thus eliminating the need for storage, pumping, and heating equipment necessary to keep the caustic in a fluid state.

Additional storage space would be available, if necessary, at the standard storage rates.

Since Marshall is a distributing company, it would be to the mutual advantage of both concerns to have a distributing and a manufacturing concern in close proximity.

12.0 OFFICE EQUIPMENT

The office equipment expense will be nominal. The only items required are listed as follows:

Office Equipment

1 Executive-type desk	$ 100
1 Secretarial desk	100
3 Filing cabinets	200
1 Cardex file	50
1 Stationery cabinet	200
1 Typewriter	150
1 Adding machine	250
Books, stationery, and supplies	400
Miscellaneous	300
Total	$1,750

13.0 BURDEN CHARGES

13.1 Rent and Building Charges

A verbal agreement has been worked with the owners of the Marshall Company to rent the space outlined in Section 11 at a rate of $150 a month for approximately 5,000 square feet of space. This is a very reasonable figure, since current rates are approximately 75 cents per square foot per year. This will include use of terminal facilities for rail and truck transportation.

Suitable office space can be obtained in New Britain at approximately $40 per month. Thus the total rental charges would be $190 per month, or $2,280 per year.

13.2 Power Expense

The power expense has been allocated directly to the cost of manufacture of sodium aluminate. An additional charge of $25 per month is estimated for the cost of fuel oil for heating the plant for the comfort of operating personnel.

13.3 Depreciation Expense

The depreciation expense is charged at the rate of 10 per cent of the assets listed below, or $4,375 per year, or $365 per month.

Engineering design expense (Section 14.0)	$ 2,000
Office equipment	1,750
Plant equipment	40,000
Total	$43,750

13.4 Interest Expense

The amount of charges for interest depends upon the amount of outside financing required. It is not expected that outside financing will be necessary, since sufficient funds will be obtained from invested capital.

13.5 Indirect Labor and Miscellaneous Expense

All services, such as maintenance, janitor, etc., will be performed by direct labor personnel, and there will be no other service expenses incurred.

13.6 Insurance Expense

A provision of $50 a month, or $600 per year, is made for fire and liability insurance.

13.7 Burden Summary

The following table gives a summary of all the estimated burden expense:

BURDEN SUMMARY

	Month	Year
Rent (13.1)	$190	$2,280
Heat expense (13.2)	25	300
Depreciation expense (13.3)	365	4,375
Interest expense (13.4)	0	0
Indirect labor and miscellaneous expense (13.5)	0	0
Insurance expense (13.6)	50	600
Total	$630	$7,555

14.0 ENGINEERING EXPENSE

The engineering expense will be incurred in two general categories: The first includes the cost of plant layout, supervision of installation, and getting production under way. The second includes the solution of general engineering problems that occur during the plant operation. It is intended that the new corporation utilize the service of the Chemton Associates, a firm of consulting chemical engineers who have intimate knowledge of the problems involved, to perform this work.

The charge for the service in the first category will be $2,000 in cash and $5,000 in capital stock, to be disbursed as outlined in Sections 18 and 19. The fee for the services in the second category will be charged on a retainer basis at the rate of $150 per month.

15.0 ORGANIZATIONAL EXPENSE

This expense is made up of the cost of making the initial survey and organizing the formation and operation of the company. The costs include: completion of a survey, control of operations, accounting expense, and legal fees.

15.1 Survey and Control of Operation

This cost includes: collection and consolidation of facts, analysis of these facts to determine the feasibility of setting up the company, completion of this report, and responsibility for getting the organization in operation once funds are obtained.

The total cost of this is $10,000, which will be paid by common stock in the company. The method and terms of distribution will be as outlined in Section 19.

15.2 Accounting Expenses

This expense will be incurred to defray the costs of setting up the books of account and retaining advice as required. It is intended that a reputable accounting firm will be retained. This expense is estimated to be $1,000 and will be paid in cash.

15.3 Legal Expense

This expense will be incurred to defray the costs of preparing the articles of incorporation and the other necessary legal work to form the corporation. It is intended that a reputable legal firm will be retained. This expense is estimated to be $1,500 and will be paid in cash.

15.4 Summary of Organizational Expense to Be Paid

Paid in common stock—Survey and control of operation		$10,000.00
Paid in cash (to be capitalized):		
Accounting expense	$1,000	
Legal expense	1,500	
Total cash		2,500.00
Total organizational expense		$12,500.00

16.0 SELLING AND ADMINISTRATIVE EXPENSE

Selling and administrative expenses as listed include the salaries of the president and general manager, the production foreman, the wages of a secretary, together with advertising, selling, and telephone expense. An estimate of these administrative expenses is given in a table below:

Administrative and Selling Expenses

	Month	*Year*
President and general manager	$ 700	$ 8,400
Plant foreman	400	4,800
Secretary	225	2,505
Selling expense	300	3,600
Telephone expense	100	1,200
Advertising (catalogues, brochures)	250	3,000
Miscellaneous	100	1,200
Total	$2,075	$24,705

17.0 BREAK-EVEN CHART

Exhibit 4 (p. 160) is a break-even chart which shows the relative picture for varying production rates. If the maximum plant capacity of 120 tons per month is reached, it would seem that a very favorable profit picture will be obtained. Of course, this will not be an exact picture because it is expected that fixed costs will increase to some extent as the business expands.

18.0 CAPITAL REQUIREMENTS

The capital requirements must be sufficient to purchase the necessary production equipment as well as to allow for all necessary expenditure to get the enterprise under way. Exhibit 5 (p. 161) outlines these requirements.

Exhibit 4

BREAK-EVEN CHART: SODIUM ALUMINATE

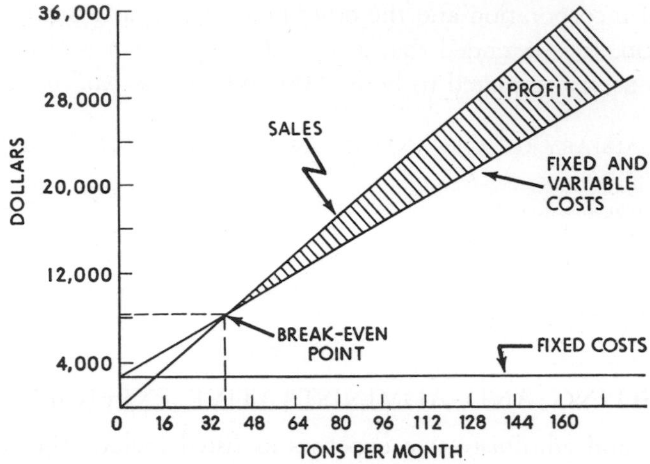

19.0 COMPANY STRUCTURE

19.1 Proposed Organization

In the light of ascertainable facts, it is seen that approximately $70,000 will be required to get this enterprise under way. It is expected that these funds will be obtained from the issue of common stock.

It is proposed that this new enterprise be a corporation with a simple capital structure consisting entirely of common stock.

A capitalization of $110,000 is thought adequate. This will consist of 1,100 shares of $100 par common shares.

Of these shares, 700 shares will be issued to investors to raise the $70,000 in additional funds now required.

One hundred and fifty shares will be held in escrow, to be ultimately distributed in payment for the $15,000 equity now present in the proposed venture. This $15,000 represents the valuation placed on services already performed (see Section 14, "Engineering Expense," and Section 15.1, "Survey and Control of Operation"), as well as obligations that will be fulfilled before this stock is dispersed. These obligations involve assuming complete responsibility for getting the organization under way and in operation. Seventy-five of these shares will be distributed when sales of sodium aluminate average 40 tons per month for three consecutive months. The remaining 75 shares will be distributed when sodium aluminate sales average 80 tons or more a month for three consecutive months. The two hundred and fifty shares of common remaining will be held as treasury stock. Options to purchase this stock

Exhibit 5

CASH REQUIREMENTS

1. *One month's raw material based on 80 tons per month production:*	
See Section 9: Caustic soda (80 tons × 135.04)	$ 2,803.20
Alumina hydrate (80 tons × 62.62)	5,009.60
Paper bags (80 × 20)	1,600.00
Other chemicals	132.00
2. *One month's direct conversion cost:*	
See Section 9 (80 × $41.83)	3,346.40
3. *Two months' burden cost:*	
See Section 13.7 (2 × $630.00)	1,260.00
4. *Two months' engineering expense and design cost:*	
See Section 14 (2 × $150 + $2,000.00)	2,300.00
5. *Accounting and legal expense:*	
See Section 15.4	2,500.00
6. *Two months' selling and administrative expense:*	
See Section 16 (2 × $2,075.00)	4,150.00
7. *Production equipment and plant:*	
See Section 10	40,000.00
8. *Office equipment:*	
See Section 12	1,750.00
9. *Cash reserve for contingencies*	5,000.00
Total capital required	$69,851.20

at $100 per share will be given to the holders of the $15,000 equity now present in the proposed venture.

19.2 Principals Involved

The principals presently concerned with this venture and the amount of their present interest are as follows:

Paul R. Humphrey	$2,500	Engineering expense
Mark Peterson	2,500	
Clarkson P. Dorrance	5,000	Survey and control of operation
L. J. Bostwick	2,500	
John Campbell	2,500	

Messrs. Humphrey and Peterson are associated with Chemton Associates. Messrs. Bostwick and Campbell are associated with the Universal Chemical Company. Mr. Dorrance, the author of this report, is expected to be president and general manager of the new company.

Clarkson P. Dorrance

M.E., M.B.A., Stevens Institute of Technology, Harvard University Graduate School of Business Administration.

Inspector, Jamison Instrument Co.; Production Expediter, Union Engineering Co.; Ordnance Officer—Lieutenant, U.S.N.R.; Staff Member, Mechanical Engineering Department, Stevens Institute of Technology; Assistant to the President, Pico Instrument Co.; Sales Engineer, Retail Apparatus Inc.;

Plant Manager, Retail Apparatus Laboratories, Inc.; Mechanical Engineer, Chemton Associates.

Member of faculty, Babson Institute of Business Administration.

Mr. Dorrance has had broad and varied experience in the instrument manufacturing field. He has been engaged in engineering aspects of medical equipment manufacture. He has had over four years' service in the U.S. Navy.

PAUL R. HUMPHREY

M.E., M.B.A., Stevens Institute of Technology, Harvard University Graduate School of Business Administration.

Design Engineer, Universal Chemical Co.; Staff Member, Electrical Engineering Department, Massachusetts Institute of Technology.

Electronic Project Engineer, Naval Research Laboratory.

Electronics Officer—Lieutenant, U.S.N.R.

Treasurer and Chief Engineer, Chemton Associates.

Mr. Humphrey has been engaged in engineering administration in the mechanical, chemical, and electronic fields. He served for four years in various engineering capacities with the U.S. Navy and is familiar with many of the technical problems peculiar to the services.

MARK PETERSON

A.B., M.A., M.S., Emory University, Massachusetts Institute of Technology.

Chemical Engineer, Universal Chemical Co.; Plant Manager, Universal Chemical Co.; President, Chemton Associates.

Registered Engineer, State of Massachusetts; Active member, American National Society of Professional Engineers.

Mr. Peterson has done advanced research work in the field of organic chemistry. He has administered the operations of a major chemical plant. With the Chemton Associates he has supervised the activities of many engineers and technical personnel.

LAWRENCE J. BOSTWICK

B.S., Colby College.

Chemical Engineer, Universal Chemical Co.; Plant Manager, Universal Chemical Co.; Department Superintendent, Universal Chemical Co.; Plant Superintendent, Universal Chemical Co.

It is recommended that these men be elected to the board of directors, since it is felt that their advice and counsel, as well as their contacts in the chemical industry, will be a valuable contribution to the progress of the new company.

It is proposed that Clarkson P. Dorrance be appointed president and general manager of the new company. He has had past experience in the formation and management of a new enterprise. He recently participated in the organization and management of Retail Instrument Laboratories, Inc., a company incorporated on February 1, 1950, and now enjoying considerable success.

Exhibit 6

PRO FORMA OPERATING STATEMENTS

		Production per Month		
		80 Tons	120 Tons	160 Tons
Sales $225 per ton		$18,000.00	$27,000.00	$36,000.00
Cost of manufacture:				
Material, labor, packaging, and direct factory burden at $161.14 per ton (see Section 9)		12,891.20	19,336.80	25,782.40
Gross margin		$ 5,108.80	$ 7,663.20	$10,217.60
Expense:				
Burden cost (Sec. 13.7)	$ 630			
Engineering (Sec. 14)	150			
Selling and administration (Sec. 16)	2,075			
		2,855.00	2,855.00	2,855.00
Net profit before taxes		$ 2,253.80	$ 4,808.20	$ 7,362.60

20.0 FUTURE PROSPECTS

Although this company is to be organized to produce sodium aluminate, there are excellent possibilities to produce and sell other chemicals.

There are many chemicals that the Universal Chemical Company would like to stop producing. Although profitable and enjoying a consistent demand, these items are not sold in sufficient quantities to warrant their continued interest. It is expected that, as soon as their customers can obtain a new source of supply, the production of these small-volume items will be terminated. Because of close contacts with the Universal organization, it is expected that the new company can obtain some of these, along with a portion of Universal's plant facilities and good will at a very low cost.

The proximity of the Marshall Company, a distributor of these items for Universal, will simplify the marketing problems.

21.0 CONCLUSION

It is not often that an opportunity arises to initiate a business venture where as many ingredients for success are available as this instance. We present: (1) an existing and profitable business with known customers and a constant demand for a product not available from another manufacturer; (2) an established production process with the option to purchase existing plant facilities at an extremely low figure; (3) a packaged program provided with persons experienced in the art and the good will of a large chemical company who are anxious for its success; and (4) a situation that provides profit possibilities that will more than repay the original investment in two years.

Red Rock Bottling Company of Boston

In February, 1947, Mr. James T. Stern, thirty-two years old, was negotiating for additional bottling plants and personnel to expand sales in the Boston area for Red Rock Cola. Since his discharge from the Army in May, 1946, he had formed and financed the Red Rock Bottling Company of Boston and had secured a franchise, a plant, and the nucleus of personnel experienced in the bottling business. The franchise, which Mr. Stern secured without charge, had a potential value of $1,500,000 exclusive of other assets.

After graduating from college and before entering the service, Mr. Stern had been a newspaper reporter, an assistant sales manager, and an account executive for a Boston advertising agency. With the beginning of the war, the War Production Board requested that Mr. Stern be given a year's leave of absence from the advertising agency to head the salvage program for New England. Upon completion of that campaign Mr. Stern was commissioned by the Army and served as an instructor in the Public Relations School. His final service was as a special service officer on a troop transport ship.

Although he was invited to return to the advertising agency upon discharge, Mr. Stern decided to own his own business; and he believed that the only way to make substantial income and to create a personal estate was through equity ownership. The State Development Commission of his home state of New Hampshire supplied him with a list of New Hampshire businesses for sale. After considerable investigation of all these possibilities, he rejected them one by one because they were either "war babies," which had no peacetime potential, or high-priced, old-time concerns staffed by old management who wished to sell for cash in the boom market. Mr. Stern had only a few thousand dollars to invest and did not consider either type of available business desirable. Through a friend, Mr. Thomas P. Brown, in a Boston brokerage house, Mr. Stern learned that several studies of the soft-drink industry indicated that this industry was a rapidly expanding field. Between 1927 and 1941 the following increases in sales had taken place:

Candy	15 per cent
Ice cream	22
Soft drinks	257

Further study convinced Mr. Stern that it was ideal for him to enter this industry at this time, although he had had no previous experience with soft-drink bottling. During the first two years of the war, the mortality of soft-drink businesses was never over 9 per cent per year, while the mortality in other small-business lines was over 30 per cent annually. In volume of sales, soft drinks outranked cereal, confectionery, and ice cream. It had climbed to eighth place in the food-processing trades, with only baking and meat packing greatly exceeding it. The soft-drink industry maintained a fleet of 50,000 trucks and spent $15,000,000 annually on new machinery. Sales expanded from 129,000,000 cases in 1933 to 740,000,000 cases in 1941, the last year before sugar rationing. For all major franchise companies, net profit before income taxes was 64 per cent of net worth. During the sugar shortage, soft-drink companies could not fill the demand, with the result that there was a ready market for new brands of soft drinks. The *Wall Street Journal* of September 3, 1946, estimated that only 60 per cent of the current soft-drink demand was being met.

After deciding to enter the soft-drink industry, the first problem Mr. Stern faced was that of deciding whether to bottle a franchised or a non-franchised drink. National bottling companies sold to small independent bottlers franchise rights to produce their brands of drink in the local markets. The alternative was to develop a drink himself and popularize it. If he chose to secure a franchise, he would be marketing a tested product and would have national advertising, a large laboratory, and experienced advisers assisting him. Also, Mr. Stern believed that fund raising for his company would be easier with a franchise. These advantages convinced him that it was essential to secure a franchise.

Between 60 and 80 per cent of all soft drinks sold were cola drinks. The leading cola drinks, in order of sales, were: Coca-Cola, Pepsi-Cola, Royal Crown, Spur, and Red Rock. The first four drinks were then well established in the Boston area. Red Rock was attempting to expand its distribution into this area but had so far issued no franchise.

At this point Mr. Stern considered that he had four major problems: securing a franchise, financing the company, renting a plant, and hiring necessary personnel. He proceeded to work on these problems simultaneously.

Mr. Brown, through his investment connections, was able to secure the franchise for the Boston area from the Red Rock company. To raise

Exhibit 1

RED ROCK BOTTLING COMPANY OF BOSTON

MEMORANDUM TO PROSPECTIVE INVESTORS, OCTOBER, 1946

INDUSTRY

Carbonated beverage bottling, since its inception some sixty years ago, has exhibited a steady growth. However, it is only in the last twenty years that the development of the industry has been of a spectacular nature.

In 1933, gross sales of the soft-drink industry in the United States totaled $111,297,000. In 1941, gross sales for the industry had risen to $525,000,000. It is of interest to note that the total number of cases of carbonated beverages sold in Massachusetts in 1941 was approximately 17,000,000, and considerably more than half of that total was "cola" sales.

An article in the *Wall Street Journal* of September 3, 1946, states: "The market for soft drinks during the first year in which ample sugar supplies are available will be *at least* 20% above the highest pre-war yearly rate of consumption. . . . Part of this increase will result from increased consumption of soft drinks in industrial plants. The remainder will come from higher home consumption."

An interview with the President of the Nehi Corporation (Royal Crown Cola), Columbus, Georgia, on September 15, 1946, by a principal of the Red Rock Bottling Company of Boston produced the following observation: "Sugar will probably remain in short supply for another two years. It will likely be the second quarter of next year [1947] before the allotment quota for bottlers (based on consumption of sugar in 1941) will be increased." During the year 1946, bottlers operated on a 58 per cent quota of the 1941 consumption.

RED ROCK COMPANY

The Red Rock Company, Atlanta, Georgia, was organized sixty-one years ago and has successfully marketed various flavors of soft drinks during that period.

In May, 1938, shortly after the courts of the United States and Canada decreed that any company was privileged to use the name "cola," the Red Rock Bottlers, Inc., was incorporated to distribute the concentrate for Red Rock Cola on a national basis.

In Atlanta, where Pepsi-Cola and Royal Crown Cola have not been outstandingly successful in competing with Coca Cola in its home territory, *it is of more than passing importance to note that the Red Rock Bottling Company of Atlanta sold 1,000,000 cases of Red Rock Cola in 1941, compared with total Coca Cola sales of approximately 3,000,000 cases.* Red Rock bottling operations of comparable size are being currently carried on in Cleveland, Pittsburgh, Youngstown, Athens, Georgia, etc.

With 242 franchises granted as of September 1, 1946, it is estimated that well over 300 franchises will be granted by the end of this year. In

Exhibit 1—Continued

New England, four recent franchises have been granted in Connecticut—one in Providence, one in Lowell, one in Worcester, one in Portland—and a number of others are in the process of negotiation. Twenty-two Red Rock plants are located in Canada, four in Venezuela, one in Cuba, and one in Mexico.

The following is an excerpt from the annual report for 1945 of the Red Rock Bottlers, Inc., Atlanta, Georgia:

"Your Company's gross profit on sales for the fiscal year ended December 31, 1945, showed an increase of approximately 11½% in spite of the fact that your bottlers operated throughout the year on a sugar quota of 58¾%, as compared with 77½% during the fiscal year of 1944.

"For the first quarter of 1946, your bottlers have operated on a sugar allotment of 50% which is below the allotment for the first quarter of 1945. In spite of this reduction in available materials, your Company's sales for the first quarter of this year show a most satisfactory increase over the same period last year."

Due to the fact that Red Rock Cola has only recently approached national distribution, it has been considered inadvisable to initiate a national advertising program. Conversations between Roy Durstine & Co., 730 Fifth Avenue, New York City, and James T. Stern reveal that a national consumer advertising program will be initiated around September, 1947. It is the justifiable belief of the parent Company and the advertising agency that the creation of a demand for the product through advertising at a time when no bottler is able to meet present demands would react unfavorably against the Company.

RED ROCK BOTTLING COMPANY OF BOSTON

The franchise area being granted to this company covers a radius of approximately 25 miles from the center of Boston, plus an option on the entire Cape area. In general, this area extends to Salem and Beverly on the northeast, to Billerica on the north, Acton and Maynard on the northwest, Framingham on the west, and extending, with option, to the end of the Cape on the south. A map of this area is available for inspection.

Initial plant facilities will be located in East Boston (near Logan Airport). This plant has sufficient sugar, based on current OPA quotas, to produce 150,000 cases of Red Rock Cola per year. Bottling machinery is modern and is adequate to produce the above quantity. The Company further has a priority with Crown Cork and Seal Co., Cambridge, Massachusetts, for a 28-spout bottler, capable of producing 375,000 cases per year. Delivery is expected in March, and purchase of this equipment ($13,000) will be effected through a bank loan.

It is the intention of the management of the Company to obtain additional plant facilities and warehousing facilities at points throughout the enfranchised area as soon as feasible. With such a large area, as well as large population, it will be impossible to achieve adequate distribution un-

Exhibit 1—Continued

til additional facilities are acquired. The present East Boston plant will serve, for the time being, only a portion of the franchise's territory.

Since the success of the operation of the Red Rock Bottling Company of Boston will depend very largely upon effective merchandising and distribution, the Company is fortunate in securing Mr. A. B. Thomson, former sales manager of the Coca Cola Bottling Company of Boston, to direct sales.

Mr. Thomson has been with the Coca Cola Company until very recently. He was, in 1929, appointed sales manager for the Boston area, and in that year Coca Cola sales totaled 94,956 cases. In 1941, when Mr. Thomson was still sales manager, Coca Cola sales were 2,385,000 cases. Mr. Thomson had made plans for the distribution of 5,000,000 cases in 1942, a goal that was not realized due to drastic sugar reductions. Mr. Thomson's reason for accepting a position with the Red Rock Company of Boston lies in the fact that he foresees the potential in Red Rock sales and will further participate in the Company's stock incentive plan. (Details are outlined in capital plan.)

It is the intention of the management of the Red Rock Bottling Company of Boston to compete with other cola companies in this area on a basis comparable with that of the Red Rock Company of Atlanta and other successful Red Rock bottlers.

On such a basis, gross sales of Red Rock in Boston would eventually reach 1,500,000 cases, with no allowance for a general increase in per capita consumption of soft drinks. Based on the industry-wide accepted method of evaluating any given franchise on $1 per case sold per year, the ultimate value of the Red Rock franchise exclusive of other assets, would be $1,500,000.

In anticipating future sales in the Boston market, it must be realized that growth will come from participation in increased per capita consumption, as well as from sales gained competitively.

In commencing operation now, the Red Rock Bottling Company of Boston enjoys the following favorable factors:

1. A franchise territory embracing approximately 3,500,000 people.
2. Demonstrated competitively successful operations of Red Rock bottlers elsewhere.
3. An existing market where maximum production can be sold. Considerable consumer acceptability and dealer co-operation for the product will be achieved during the two-year period that this market is expected to exist.
4. Sales and distribution directed by a man of Mr. Thomson's demonstrated ability.

Included in the following pages is a *pro forma* investment schedule, a *pro forma* operating statement, and an outline of the capital structure of the Corporation.

Exhibit 1—Continued

PRO FORMA INVESTMENT SCHEDULE

Cash	$10,000
Plant, equipment, two trucks	42,500
Bottles, cases, crowns	11,000
Rent on four trucks	8,000
Sugar and concentrate	1,000
Insurance	1,000
Plant improvements	1,500
Reserve	5,000
Total	$80,000

PRO FORMA OPERATING STATEMENT FOR FIRST TWELVE MONTHS

Maximum gross sales (150,000 cases)—Anticipated gross sales (125,000 cases)

		Per Case	*125,000 Cases*
Sales		0.80	100,000
Cost of goods:			
Concentrate and sugar-syrup		0.20	25,000
Advertising (point of purchase)		0.05	6,250
Operating expenses:			
Plant labor		0.06	7,600
Soaker feeder	$ 1,800		
Filling-machine operator	2,400		
Caser	1,800		
Floorman	1,600		
Total	$ 7,600		
Sales labor		$0.19	$ 24,000
Sales manager	$ 5,000		
Route supervisor	3,000		
Route salesman	16,000		
Total	$24,000		
Administrative labor		0.06	7,000
Manager	$ 5,000		
Bookkeeper	2,000		
Total	$ 7,000		
Crowns		0.03	3,125
Carbon dioxide and water		0.01	1,250
Rent, power, telephone, and heat		0.03	3,750
Depreciation		0.03	3,750
Gasoline and oil		0.02	2,500
Insurance		0.01	1,250
Incidentals		0.02	2,500
Total costs		$0.71	$ 87,975

It has been possible to have the above *pro forma* operating statement reviewed and checked by the operating management of disinterested bottling companies. In the two cases where this has been done, it has been pointed out that the above figures are conservative and that, after initial distribution is effected, noticeable decreases in operating costs could be expected.

In estimating operating costs based on increased sales, certain expenses will increase proportionately. However, substantial reductions in the per

Exhibit 1—Continued

case operating cost will be effected in the following items: selling and delivery cost, administrative labor, plant labor, rent, power, gas, and heat. Such items represent almost 50 per cent of operating cost.

It should be noted that the cost of sugar is based on the price of sugar following the OPA increase of September 16, 1946, and that an additional ½ cent is allowed for any possible fluctuation.

CAPITAL STRUCTURE

The Red Rock Bottling Company of Boston is being incorporated as a Massachusetts corporation by Jones, Smith, and White, Boston, Massachusetts.

The company is being capitalized for $80,000 on the following basis:

800 shares, 5 per cent cumulative, convertible, callable, preferred stock, par value $100.00 . . . . $80,000

When called for redemption, holders of preferred stock will have the privilege of subscribing to two (2) shares of Class A common stock at twenty-five dollars ($25.00) per share. Preferred stockholders have the right to convert preferred stock to common stock at any time after purchase on the basis of two (2) shares of common stock for each share of preferred stock converted. Preferred stock votes equally with common stock.

3,200 shares, Class A common stock, no-par value:

Reserved for conversion of preferred stock	1,600 shares
Issued to James T. Stern, President of Corporation, for services in organizing enterprise. Services include negotiation of purchase of plant, formation of Corporation, securing of key personnel, and travel and time devoted thereto.	300 shares
Issued to Thomas P. Brown, Boston, Massachusetts, for obtaining franchise and handling all related details with Red Rock Bottlers, Inc., Atlanta, Georgia.	300 shares
Reserved for purchase by James T. Stern and Thomas P. Brown. Messrs. Stern and Brown will have the privilege of subscribing to one and one-quarter (1¼) shares at twenty-five dollars ($25.00) per share for each share of preferred stock called or converted.	1,000 shares
	3,200 shares

No dividends will be paid on common stock until all preferred stock is converted or called for redemption.

400 shares, Class B common stock, no-par value, nonvoting.

Reserved for issuance to employees of Company for incentive purposes. This stock will be issued by directors of Company, upon recommendation of management. Method of issuance and basis to be determined by directors of the Company. No stock to be issued until end of first fiscal year. The President will not participate.

Directors of the Corporation will come from preferred stockholders. In organizing the Corporation it is the intention to have each preferred stockholder either on the board of directors or personally represented by another preferred stockholder, selected with his approval.

the necessary funds Mr. Stern "rang doorbells." Through his acquaintances in the Boston area he was able to secure interviews with potential investors. At the close of an interview with a prospective investor, Mr. Stern left a memorandum outlining his project and its possibilities (see Exhibit 1). In a short time he was able to raise $80,000, his goal, and refused offers of an additional $70,000. Twenty-eight people supplied the funds, no onc backer putting up more than $10,000. Mr. Brown and Mr. Stern together furnished $3,000. Exhibit 1 outlines the financial arrangements. Until all preferred stock was retired, no dividends were to be paid on common stock and the preferred stockholders would control the company. If the company approached its sales goals, however, the preferred stock would be called in and the 3,200 shares of Class A common stock, no-par value, would control the company. Messrs. Stern and Brown's $3,000 in preferred stock would then be converted into 60 shares of class A common stock. These 60 shares, together with the 1,600 shares of common which Messrs. Stern and Brown already had, would give them control of the company, with 1,660 shares out of 3,200 outstanding.

Mr. Stern located an independent bottler operating in a rented building, 200 × 100 feet; the business was for sale for $42,500. This business had a yearly sugar quota of 185,000 pounds, sufficient to make 150,000 cases of Red Rock Cola. Mr. Stern estimated that the machinery in the plant was worth $30,000 and that the sugar quota and remainder of the business were worth $12,500. All sugar was purchased from the American Sugar Refinery Corporation. Shortly after Mr. Stern purchased the business, dealers who had purchased bottled drinks from Mr. Stern's predecessor phoned the plant desiring refunds on the bottles in their possession. Mr. Stern informed them that he no longer supplied that brand of soft drink but that he would refund their deposit price on all bottles and cases. Dealers were refunded 70 cents for each case of bottles, and Mr. Stern subsequently sold these cases to another bottler for $1.05 each. This transaction netted a profit around $6,000, which might be considered a reduction on the purchase price.

Because Mr. Stern knew nothing about the soft-drink industry, he considered it essential that he secure personnel who were well qualified in that field. Consequently, he hired Mr. A. B. Thomson, the former sales manager of the Coca-Cola Bottling Company of Boston, as sales manager for Red Rock. Mr. Thomson consented to join the Red Rock company at a substantial salary reduction because of an opportunity to earn, on a performance basis, 200 shares of Class B common stock, no-par value, which, if the company succeeded, would be worth, he believed, at least $100,000. The production manager was secured from a small Coca-Cola bottling plant. Mr. Thomson and the production manager were able to bring with them other skilled personnel from the local Coca-Cola company. Two of the three men in the production section of the company had formerly been foremen of the Coca-Cola company. Mr. Stern remarked that his plant was known as the East Boston Alumni Association of the Coca-Cola company.

All employees of the firm had an opportunity to examine all the books of the new company. The Red Rock company paid Blue Cross and Blue Shield insurance on all personnel. Mr. Stern believed that his personnel relations were excellent and cited the fact that frequently his men voluntarily came to work at 7:15 in the morning and worked until 5:30 and 6 o'clock at night without overtime pay.

The company was incorporated on the first of October, 1946. The equipment was purchased on October 16, 1946. A three-year lease was signed on the building with an option for an additional three years. Mr. Stern said that the previous proprietor had kept a very dirty plant and had manufactured a cheap drink sold at a high markup. The plant was soon cleaned up, and $19,000 worth of new machinery, bottles, and cases were ordered.

The production of Red Rock Cola was essentially simple. Concentrate was purchased in gallon jugs from the Red Rock company of Atlanta, Georgia. The concentrate was mixed with sugar, water, and a few minor ingredients in large stainless steel vats on the second floor. The solution then flowed in tubes to the first floor, where it was mixed with chemically purified water that had been carbonated. This final mixture was then piped across the room to a bottling machine. Bottles were sterilized, filled and capped automatically, and hand loaded into cases. During the week of November 25, 1946, the first 208 cases were sold to 23 dealers. During the week of January 31, 1947, 894 cases were sold to 336 dealers of the area's approximately 5,000 dealers. In early February the company was losing approximately $200 a week because of small distribution but expected to be making a profit by the end of the month. Current expenses were approximately $1,100 a week. "Because of the low volume we haven't watched pennies so far," said Mr. Stern. Mr. Stern believed it was a sound idea to expand his sales during the slack winter season when dealers had sufficient time to talk to his four salesmen. Despite the intended winter sales effort, Mr. Stern's estimate of cash flow (Exhibit 2) showed the cash balance continuing to drop until June, 1947. There were sufficient bottles and sugar to make the company profitable as soon as increased sales had been obtained. No effort would be made to place Red Rock syrup in soda fountains for counter sale.

Mr. Stern decided not to purchase all the trucks necessary for delivery, which would cost about $10,000. He adopted the policy of buying one out of every four trucks needed and hiring the remainder from a trucking company. This policy, he felt, would make him fairly independent of the trucking concerns and would give him protection in the event of fluctuation in sales.

Exhibit 2

RED ROCK BOTTLING COMPANY OF BOSTON
PROJECTED CASH FLOW, FEBRUARY, 1947—JULY, 1947

Based on Estimated Sales as Indicated (Sales at 80 Cents per Case with Sugar at 8 Cents per Pound), Assuming That Collections Are Current, i.e., That February Sales Produce February Income

(Cents Omitted)

	February	March	April	May	June	July
Sales, cases	4,600	6,800	9,200	12,000	1,500	1,500
Cash balance beginning 2/17/47	$19,871	$19,051	$ 9,191	$ 3,175	$ 2,375	$ 3,625
Income	3,680	5,240	7,360	9,600	12,000	12,000
Total	$23,551	$24,291	$16,551	$12,775	$14,375	$15,625
Disbursements:						
Factory cost, general and administrative, and sales cost	$ 2,000	$ 6,100	$ 7,176	$ 8,400	$ 9,750	$ 9,750
Machinery	......	2,500	1,600	......	......	......
Legal fee	......	......	......	1,000	......	......
Bottles	......	5,500	......	......	......	......
Cases	1,500	......	3,600	......	......	......
Contingencies	1,000	1,000	1,000	1,000	1,000	
Total	$ 4,500	$15,100	$13,376	$10,400	$10,750	$ 9,750
Cash balance closing	$19,051	$ 9,191	$ 3,175	$ 2,375	$ 3,625	$ 5,875

The board of directors was composed of four preferred stockholders, including Mr. Stern, Mr. Brown, and a man of independent means who acted as unpaid treasurer of the company. At Mr. Stern's suggestion he and the treasurer were bonded for $25,000 as additional protection to the investors. The company maintained fire, theft, business interruption, and casualty insurance, as well as insurance on goods in transit. Both state and municipal licenses had been obtained, and board of health inspections were made monthly. While the company was starting, representatives of the national Red Rock company visited the plant on the average of every two weeks to give help and advice. Once a week, four bottles were sent to Atlanta, Georgia, for laboratory analysis. Reports were returned on the quantity in the bottle, the gas volume, sugar content, taste and odor, and the acidity. Mr. Stern on occasions had used the Red Rock laboratory to test possible sugar substitutes which had been offered to him locally. The national Red Rock company also supplied a manufacturing manual to aid the Boston plant. For every case of Red Rock Cola sold, the Boston company received 5 cents' credit toward advertising material prepared by the national Red Rock company. For example, the sale of 100 cases of Red Rock Cola would give Mr. Stern's company a credit of $5. Mr. Stern could then order without charge $5 worth of signs, display cards, or other advertising media listed in a catalogue issued by the national Red Rock company. Mr. Stern stated that this arrangement had been devised to force local bottlers to use adequate and standardized advertising materials.

Exhibit 3

RED ROCK BOTTLING COMPANY OF BOSTON

Estimated Sales by Cases, Assuming Unlimited Production	
1 February	4,600
1 March	6,800
1 April	9,200
1 May	12,000
1 June	15,000
1 July	15,000
1 August	22,200

Percentage of Annual Sales by Month for Soft Drinks in Boston Area	
January	4.03
February	4.06
March	5.34
April	6.34
May	9.47
June	12.15
July	14.84
August	18.22

Maximum Capacity by Cases per Month as of February, 1947, Capacity	
Capping and bottling machine	13,500
Trucks	15,500
Sugar (approximate)	18,000

Mr. Stern secured the services of a legal firm at a cost of approximately $1,000 to handle the incorporation and the purchase of the plant and equipment, to review the franchise, and to secure necessary licenses.

An accountant was hired to set up a bookkeeping system, using as a basis the forms of a rival bottling company and those supplied by the American Bottlers of Carbonated Beverages Association.

Bottles were in short supply, but this was no limitation to his current production. Mr. Stern thought bottles would be available as his sales increased (see Exhibit 3). Bottles were contracted for by the national Red Rock company. The Boston company was then allowed to draw on the quotas set by the national Red Rock company as it required new bottles.

Mr. Stern stated that the immediate future success of his business depended on the maintenance of sugar rationing. Decontrol of sugar would raise prices and make it extremely difficult for small producers, such as himself, to secure the necessary sugar. Further, if a sufficient supply of better-known brands of soft drink was available before Red Rock had opportunity to get established, dealers might be reluctant to stock Red Rock Cola.

In the late spring of 1947, Mr. Stern hoped to introduce Hep, a Red Rock drink comparable with 7-Up. The green bottles for Hep could not be secured until that time because they required a large portion of soda ash, which was in very short supply. Mr. Stern believed that Hep was a desirable drink to produce because it used reasonable amounts of dextrose, which was available, rather than the pure sugar required by cola drinks.

Mr. Stern had plans to establish four additional plants in his New England franchise area. He believed this expansion would enable him to reduce distribution costs and would permit efficient production at lower cost should his sales decline. To help finance additional plants, the treasurer of the company had offered personally to buy plants and sell them to the Red Rock Bottling Company of Boston as the company was able to purchase them.

If sugar rationing was maintained, Mr. Stern further hoped to exercise his options to purchase the Red Rock franchise for the Worcester, Massachusetts, and Washington, D.C., areas. His major difficulty in expanding, as he saw it, was in securing adequate personnel.

PART III

ACQUISITION AND DEVELOPMENT OF ESTABLISHED ORGANIZATIONS

Pelley and Hanover Company

During the winter of 1947 a community Industrial Development Corporation became interested in the Pelley and Hanover Company. The Development Corporation decided that, with the addition of new management and capital, the old firm might provide a good opportunity for long-term growth. Mr. Jackson LeGrande, a recent business-school graduate who had just accepted a position with the Development Corporation, was asked to study the company and present his analysis of the following points:

1. What specific financial plan, including price and terms, should be offered the present management group for equity control?
2. What, if any, additional incentive provisions should be offered either the old or new management?
3. What experience and qualifications should be set for selection of new management?
4. What changes in company policies and practices are recommended?

Mr. LeGrande was assured that the Development Corporation could raise sufficient funds to finance acquisition of the Pelley and Hanover Company at any reasonable price. Its objective was, however, to tie up as little capital as possible and only for so long as might be required to re-establish the company successfully in the hands of a strong aggressive management. A fair profit commensurate with risks was expected by the Development Corporation so long as it participated financially, but the prime purpose for its existence was the furtherance of community industrial progress and development.

Jackson LeGrande spent several days at the plant of the Pelley and Hanover Company. He found that the firm's history could be traced back to the year 1855, when Mr. Pelley came to this country from England. He soon set himself up in business, distributing sheet music and musical instruments. In 1893 Mr. William Hanover, with $17 as his total fortune, came to America from England and joined Mr. Pelley's firm. In addition, he accepted an engagement as clarinetist for Mr. James Bowen, at that time an eminent orchestral leader. During the succeeding three years Mr. Hanover performed with the best musical organizations in Philadelphia as player and director, but in 1896 he discontinued playing the clarinet in order to devote full time to the Pelley and Hanover Company. After Mr. Pelley's death early in the 1900's, Mr. Hanover took over the company, and from then until November, 1946, continued as the active head of the wholly owned enterprise.

Prior to 1910, most of the musical instruments sold by the company were imported from European countries, principally France. In that year, however, believing that clarinets could be made equally as well in America as in Europe, Mr. Hanover visited several European factories and studied the manufacturing techniques and methods. Upon his return he, with a few workmen, began manufacturing high-grade wood instruments to compete with the best products imported from abroad. The company prospered; and in 1925, after considerable experimentation with metals, a metal clarinet was developed which could be sold for approximately half the price of the previously accepted granadilla wood instruments. The greatly reduced price for the metal clarinets enabled the company to obtain much higher volume, and by 1935 the company was supplying over half the United States sales of clarinets, piccolos, and flutes. The development of metal clarinets contributed greatly to the school music program, which began to expand rapidly in the middle 1920's. The trade association of musical-instrument manufacturers contributed substantial sums of money to assist in the establishment of musical interest at the school level. The company continued to publish sheet music, but these sales constituted a continuously decreasing percentage of total sales.

In November, 1946, Mr. Hanover was seventy-eight years old and, although almost completely deaf, served as the company's president, chairman of its board of directors, and treasurer. Because of his hearing difficulties, he seldom talked with employees other than his daughter and the production manager, or with visitors to the plant, but managed the company through his daughter, Mrs. Helen Hanover Smith. Mrs. Smith graduated from a well-known women's college in 1927 and immediately thereafter went to work with her father. During the two following years she attended night-school classes in order to learn advertising and accounting. Her primary interest was in handling the company's advertising; but after several years of this work, and owing to the press of enlarged management responsibilities as general manager and assistant treasurer, she concluded that the advertising program could be handled much better by a commercial advertising agency. Mrs. Smith was married in 1930 to a Philadelphia bank employee, who in 1946 was manager of a large suburban branch bank. George Hanover, Mrs. Smith's brother, worked at the Pelley and Hanover Company after graduating from Haverford College in 1920. However, George found it rather difficult to get along with his father and in 1942 left the company. In November, 1946, George, not having attempted to seek employment with other business firms, was unemployed and lived with his father and mother. When George worked at the company's plant, he usually devoted much of his time to sales work. He had never held an official position with the company.

Miss Riley, sixty-eight years old, was secretary of the company and in charge of the office staff, which consisted of five girls: one stenographer, one general bookkeeper, one order clerk, one file clerk, and one payroll clerk. Mr. Boehm became production superintendent in 1944. He had worked for the company for twenty-five years, first as a workman and later as foreman, room foreman, and assistant production superintendent. Mr. Boehm was a musician and, as a result of his experience in the plant, knew the technical aspects of manufacturing clarinets, piccolos, and flutes so as to assure proper tone and pitch characteristics. In June, 1944, the production superintendent had been overwhelmed with the task of supervising the work of 250 employees and resigned from the company. Mr. Boehm succeeded him; and although completely familiar with the production methods of the plant, he had no previous experience in supervising women employees, typically 75 per cent of all workers.

The company's board of directors was comprised of Mr. William Hanover, chairman of the board, Mrs. Hanover, Mrs. Smith, and Mr. George Hanover. They met once a year to comply with the corporation law of the state and performed no functions other than those required by the law.

Sales volume of the company grew steadily throughout the years of direction by Mr. Hanover and was particularly high in the years 1939 through 1941 because the war cut off imports from Europe. After the reciprocal trade agreements were established in 1937 and prior to 1939, a large number of flutes and clarinets were imported from Czechoslovakia and France. These imports constituted keen competition for the company's low-priced instruments. As a result of the removal of foreign competition in 1939, combined with the high level of national income in 1939, 1940, and 1941, the demand for instruments exceeded the productive capacity of the company. In May, 1942, however, the government prohibited the manufacture of musical instruments; and except for a few instruments produced for the armed forces, the normal business of the company was discontinued. In the summer of 1942 Mr. Hanover, after considerable investigation, accepted an experimental contract for radar mounts. This order proved to be successful, and the company concentrated on the production of radar mounts for the duration of the war. The work on these mounts was similar to peacetime work because it involved soldering and assembling small parts of metal. The wartime business was profitable, and the company's contracts for 1942 were renegotiated. Thereafter an amendment was passed to the renegotiation act whereby all companies with annual sales of less than $500,000 were exempt. For the war period the sales of the Pelley and Hanover Company never exceeded this amount. The net worth of the company increased from about $101,700 in 1937 to $282,500 in 1944.

In November, 1946, the company was gradually resuming its peacetime business. The number of employees had increased to 100, and efforts were being made to employ more workers. Price ceilings on musical instruments, an early postwar obstacle to full production, were removed in the spring of 1946. Shortages of materials prevented rapid resumption of peacetime production schedules, but the company hoped to attain full utilization of their plant sometime in 1947.

The Pelley and Hanover Company sold "name" instruments and "stencil" instruments. The former were instruments which bore one of the company's several brand names. These were all sold to jobbers, each of whom had an exclusive territory. The stencil instruments were sold to other jobbers for their own private brands. In addition, substantial sales were made to Sears, Roebuck & Company. The stencil instruments sold to jobbers for a few dollars less than the corresponding grade of name instruments. Sales of stencil instruments exceeded 50 per cent of total instrument sales.

The company sold four brands of clarinets. The highest priced was made of granadilla wood, and the top retail price was $225. The next two lower-quality models sold for $175 and $130, respectively. The fourth model, which was made of metal, retailed for $100. The lowest-price brand was intended particularly for school musicians. There were three brands of piccolos and flutes. The most expensive were made of sterling silver. There was also a medium-price brand and a low-price one primarily for school work. Prices ranged from $65 to $280.

There were a number of different models of the more expensive brands. For example, the clarinets were sold with 17 keys, 6 rings; 17 keys, 7 rings; and 20 keys, 7 rings. The more expensive clarinets were available in the keys of B flat, A, and E flat. Piccolos and flutes were sold in either the key of C or D flat. During the years of peak sales, clarinets were produced at the rate of about 100 a day, flutes at 25 to 30 a day, and piccolos at 8 to 10 a day.

Mrs. Smith stated that there were about 50 reliable jobbers of musical instruments in the United States, and of these the Pelley and Hanover Company sold to 25 or 30. Before the war, jobbers were given a 66⅔ per cent discount from the retail price on all instruments, and the jobbers in turn sold to retail stores at a 50 per cent discount from the retail price. In June, 1946, this price schedule was revised to allow jobbers a 50 per cent discount and retailers a 35 to 40 per cent discount. It was believed that jobbers and retailers could prosper on reduced discounts because of the large backlog of demand for musical instruments. Furthermore, manufacturers had never been satisfied with the previous discounts, inasmuch as the large allowances to jobbers and dealers had led to price cutting and to the offering of unwarranted allowances on trade-ins. Mrs. Smith had hoped that jobbers and dealers would "go along" with the reduced discounts, but she had heard that the old margins were being maintained by the simple expedient of raising prices. During the fall of 1946 a convention of musical-instrument manufacturers was held in Chicago, and Mrs. Smith discovered that other manufacturers had raised their prices substantially. When she returned, she discussed the price situation with her father and they agreed that the retail price listing of each instrument should be raised $3 to $5.

Before the war, one salesman was employed on a commission basis, and until 1939 he traveled all over the country making calls on jobbers. After 1939, however, he settled in San Francisco and personally traveled only in the territory west of the Mississippi. Jobbers east of the Mississippi were handled directly from the home office by mail. In 1943 the salesman's contract with the company expired, and he was not interested in renewing it immediately, since he had acquired a small factory producing brass musical instruments on the West Coast. Mrs. Smith believed that, with the present demand and with the necessity of rationing their growing production to jobbers, no salesman was required for some time. Copies of orders from the various jobbers before the war had been retained; and in November, 1946, the office girls used these to compile lists showing the volume of each instrument which had gone to each jobber. These ratios were used to prorate the sales of new instruments as they were produced.

The advertising agency retained by the company prepared fliers from time to time for each of the three major products. These were sent to the jobbers in the industry. In addition, the agency prepared and inserted quarter-page ads in music and musicians' trade magazines, such as the *Music Educators Journal* and *International Musician.* These ads included not only the musical instruments but also sheet music and music folios.

A small amount of sales was made up of accessory equipment such as pads, music holders, and reels. Also, the company did some repair work on name instruments. Users of name instruments were urged to return the instruments to the company whenever repair work was necessary. Usually, repair charges were nominal; the price for a complete overhaul of the company's most expensive clarinet was $20. In November, 1946, the company received 500 instruments to be repaired for the government.

In November, 1946, Mr. Boehm supervised about 100 employees in the production department. This number included two girls who worked in the production superintendent's office and 20 foremen, each of whom supervised a separate department. The company manufactured all parts of each instrument except clarinet mouthpieces (which were molded rubber materials) and reeds and pads (which were imported from a company in France).

Clarinets, consisting of about 125 different parts, were the company's most complicated instruments. Some of the 125 parts were used as many as 12 times in each instrument. Flutes contained 77 different parts. The majority of parts of any clarinet were interchangeable with the same parts for other models of clarinets in the same price market. Nevertheless, each model of clarinet contained some parts which were unique to that model. The basic design of the company's musical instruments had changed little through the years. The only major change had been the substitution of nickel silver for brass, although the dimensions of the affected parts remained the same. Because of the stable design policy, the company felt safe in carrying substantial inventories of finished and semifinished parts from year to year.

The former superintendent had worked out production schedules in his own mind. Having worked in that capacity for twenty-five years, he felt he knew what quantities to make. Accordingly, when an order for instruments was received, he would check the stock of parts available. If the number seemed inadequate, he would make out production orders for the parts.

Mr. Boehm relied largely upon two types of records: "production records" and "instrument schedules." The production record for each part consisted of a card, on the face of which were detailed the operations used in making that part. On the back were recorded each production run of that part together with information on the quantity produced, hours required, the labor cost, the pounds or ounces of material, and the amount of scrap. (It was necessary to be very careful in keeping track of the scrap for sterling-silver parts.) Some cards picked at random showed that there were production runs in 1937 and no other production runs of that part until 1941.

The instrument schedules showed each part of an instrument and the number of times that it was used. Such schedules had been mimeographed for each instrument and for certain accessories, such as music holders. Whenever Mr. Boehm wished to produce a given quantity of instruments, he sent a copy of the schedule to the stock room. The girls in the stock room would record the number on hand for each part. Then he would make out production orders for those parts of which insufficient numbers were on hand.

Before the war, instruments being assembled were accompanied by large I.B.M. tags, which were made of a number of smaller tags separated by perforations. As each worker finished the operation on that instrument, he tore off the corresponding portion of the tag. At the end of the day the worker turned in the tags and was credited with that number of pieces during the day. Most of the workers, at least in the assembly operation, were on piecework. The small tags which they tore off showed the code number of the operation and the price which had been assigned thereto. These tags were numbered so that it was possible to trace which operator was responsible when defects were found in the final inspection. These I.B.M. tags had been abandoned during the war because they were not applicable to wartime processes. In November, 1946, the system had not been resumed, since Mr. Boehm felt that production was still too low to warrant its use.

The Pelley and Hanover Company produced the plush-lined boxes in which all new instruments were sold. Mr. Boehm believed that these boxes could be manufactured more cheaply than they could be purchased from regular box manufacturers. He indicated that all the company's costs were included in the comparison, inasmuch as the company added 130 per cent overhead to the direct labor and materials used. In November, 1946, however, considerable difficulty was encountered in securing suitable wood for these boxes. Typically made of basswood, pine boards were being experimented with to find an adequate substitute. In December, 1946, the company learned of a stock of surplus boxes used during the war for shipping stockings abroad. This inventory was purchased, and the boxes were modified for use as instrument cases.

Mr. Boehm interviewed and hired all applicants for employment by the company but had considerable difficulty in the fall of 1946 in securing capable and steady employees. He believed the wage scale offered was competitive for the area and nature of the work but concluded that most potential workers had been spoiled by the wartime overtime wages. Not only were fewer people applying for work, but also the turnover rate was rising. Of the production employees in November, 1946, 20 per cent had been employed five years, 20 per cent had been employed less than five years but more than one year, and 60 per cent had been employed from one to six months. In December, 1946, Mrs. Smith stated that the employees were not members of a union. In August, 1938, a union had attempted to organize the employees. The decline in demand for musical instruments in the fall of 1938 led to considerable laying-off of workers. When work was resumed early in 1939, no further word was heard from the union representatives.

When production of musical instruments was stopped in 1942, it was found that there were sufficient numbers of some parts to make over 7,000 clarinets, while other parts were sufficient for less than 200 clarinets. Some parts were completely out of stock. Also, a substantial stock of obsolete semifinished brass parts was discovered.

Typically, the inventory consisted of about 3,500 different items. This was a rough estimate, inasmuch as the annual physical inventory check usually disclosed various lots of supplies previously overlooked, and it was not always possible to find materials listed on the inventory cards. Four stock rooms were used: one for raw materials, one for semifinished parts, one for completed goods, and one for sheet music. A separate group of inventory cards was used to control each of the four general types of inventory. On one side, the inventory card showed receipts, vendor, date, quantity, and cost. On the other side, issues of stock were shown in black ink and receipts in red ink. Whenever stock was issued, a stock girl entered the date, quantity, department to which issued, and the balance on hand.

Mrs. Smith believed she should learn more about production control and inventory control. She indicated that, while Mr. Boehm knew the production processes very well, he had never had any experience in control work. Mrs. Smith hoped that she could find a book which outlined simple systems for inventory and production control, but for the present she believed it was more important to get production going.

Until musical-instrument production stopped in 1942, the company used a cost accounting system. Mrs. Smith said that it never was effective to control costs because it was acknowledged to be inaccurate. Also, since prices were based on competition, information on cost was not regarded as necessary. During the war, however, some cost accounting was required on government contract work, with the result that fairly accurate data were collected on direct labor and material costs. Mrs. Smith had discussed the installation of a cost accounting system with several public accounting firms, but their estimates of the cost of such a system were so high that action was deferred. Once a year a well-known public accounting firm came to the company and prepared the federal and state tax returns. The company bookkeeper prepared quarterly profit and loss statements and balance sheets.

The Pelley and Hanover Company maintained the following books of account: general ledger, sales ledger (accounts receivable), purchase ledger (accounts payable), purchase journal, and cashbook. The latter showed receipts on the left-hand pages and disbursements on the right-hand side. A separate checkbook was used for wages. The stub of each check had columns for the tax and insurance deduction from wages, and the check had corresponding columns. After payroll checks were written, the check stubs were used to post the individual employee's weekly pay and deductions to a government-required form.

Invoices were sent out with every shipment of instruments, accessories, or sheet music. These were kept in two separate binders: one for instruments and accessories and one for sheet music. Since instruments were sold to jobbers, the average amounts of invoices in the first binder were large. Sheet music was sold to individuals and retailers as well as jobbers, with the result that many sales were for 80 cents or $1. Forty to fifty invoices a day for sheet music were quite common.

All purchase requisitions were prepared by Mr. Boehm. Using the inventory cards, he prepared a requisition whenever he believed the raw-material inventory was below what he regarded as reasonable at the time. The requisitions were then sent to Mr. Hanover, or in his absence to Mrs. Smith, for approval. On several occasions, purchase requisitions were canceled or returned to Mr. Boehm because too large quantities were to be ordered, because the requisitions were to be sent to the wrong supplier, and for many other reasons.

In November, 1946, 90 per cent of the company's common stock was owned by Mr. William Hanover. The balance was held by Mrs. Hanover, Mrs. Smith, and Mr. George Hanover. Since all the stock was held by the family, Mr. William Hanover stated that he did not have to worry about keeping the stockholders happy. He attributed his good health to this lack of worry. Each day Mr. Hanover spent most of his time in the office. Mr. Boehm came to see him seven to eight times a day, and in this way Mr. Hanover participated very closely in the day-to-day running of the plant. Mr. Boehm, for example, estimated the weekly production of each department as a basis for setting production schedules. Mr. Hanover went over the estimates in order to see whether all the production department plans meshed. He stated that Mr. Boehm could make good estimates for each department, but his planning fre-

Exhibit 1

PELLEY AND HANOVER COMPANY

BALANCE SHEETS AS OF DECEMBER 31

	1938	*1939*	*1940*	*1941*	*1942*	*1945*
ASSETS						
Cash	$ 2,828	$ 3,379	$ 7,567	$ 10,819	$ 50,993	$ 12,787
Accounts Receivable (net)	60,395	64,666	56,202	85,220	47,336	22,266
Officers and Others	30,419	29,345	9,488	20,242	1,850	11,254
Notes Receivable	412	2,259	3,541	1,150	34,500	......
Government Bonds	......	......	......	......	34,528	66,310
Inventory	42,848	42,569	43,197	46,716	59,809	51,068
Industrial Stocks and Bonds	......	......	......	......	......	250,559
Cash Deposits with U.S. Army and Navy	......	......	1,357	1,518	......	......
Accrued Interest	......	......	......	......	......	675
Total Current Assets	$136,902	$142,218	$121,352	$165,665	$229,016	$414,919
Building	......	......	......	15,050	15,050 }	50,074
Equipment (net)	18,966	24,026	26,512	26,434	21,673 }	
Prepaid Interest	30	......	......	......	......	......
Copyrights	98	137	187	267	285	337
Cash in French and German Banks	......	274	......	......	......	......
Investment in Restaurant	278	315	......	434	437	......
Postwar Refund of Excess Profits	......	......	......	......	7,475	......
Total Assets	$156,274	$166,970	$148,051	$207,850	$273,936	$465,330
LIABILITIES						
Notes Payable	$ 31,050	$ 18,400	......	......	......	......
Accounts Payable	11,079	20,875	$ 13,369	$ 2,316	$ 5,313	$ 5,160
Salaries and Wages Accrued	2,290	2,290	5,132	1,266	978	2,895
Employees' Deposits—War Bonds	......	......	......	......	173	129
Provision for State and Federal Taxes	4,494	7,449	6,600	49,031	93,974	123,739
Withholding and Payroll Taxes	......	......	......	......	......	1,642
Payroll Tax Accrued	......	40	......	......	......	......
Interest Accrued	......	......	......	......	......	9,959
Dividends Payable	......	......	......	......	......	5,750
Total Current Liabilities	$ 48,913	$ 49,054	$ 25,101	$ 52,613	$100,438	$140,274
Common Stock	106,462	106,462	106,462	106,462	106,462	106,462
Surplus	899	11,454	16,488	48,775	67,036	218,594
Total Liabilities	$156,274	$166,970	$148,051	$207,850	$273,936	$465,330

quently did not combine into a logical schedule for the whole factory. When this conflict occurred, Mr. Hanover amended the plans.

During the past ten years Mr. Hanover took a long vacation in the summer. During these absences the company was managed by Mrs. Smith, assisted by Miss Riley and Mr. Boehm. Whenever important questions came up, Mrs. Smith would get in touch with Mr. Hanover at his summer camp. Mr. Hanover was proud of his company and of its steady growth throughout the years. He liked to keep on working because his hearing interfered with ordinary social activities.

Balance sheets and operating statements of the Pelley and Hanover Company are shown in Exhibits 1 and 2.

Exhibit 2

PELLEY AND HANOVER COMPANY

PROFIT AND LOSS STATEMENTS AS OF DECEMBER 31

	1938	*1939*	*1940*	*1941*	*1942*	*1945*
Gross sales:						
Merchandise	$306,055	$456,240	$397,386	$664,015	$539,654	$376,545
Music	17,279	16,522	17,106	21,400	22,850	20,542
	$323,334	$472,762	$414,492	$685,415	$562,504	$397,088
Less: Discount on sales	4,775	7,711	7,204	11,885	9,670	507
Net sales	$318,579	$465,051	$407,288	$673,530	$552,834	$396,581
Less: Cost of goods sold:						
Beginning inventory	$ 59,918	$ 42,850	$ 42,570	$ 43,197	$ 46,716	$ 45,255
Purchases—merchandise	16,902	16,370	12,279	28,979	29,261	1,450
Purchases—music	1,304	942	1,538	2,300	4,931	187
Supplies—merchandise	60,357	85,098	63,690	98,259	40,329	23,368
Supplies—music	2,775	6,177	2,988	6,142	6,147	1,751
Freight-in	2,233	1,784	1,401	1,984	1,994	361
Wages	137,230	237,375	224,180	354,273	272,877	130,840
	$280,719	$390,596	$348,646	$535,134	$402,255	$203,212
Less: Ending inventory	42,848	42,569	43,197	46,716	59,808	51,068
Total cost of goods sold	$237,871	$348,027	$305,449	$488,418	$342,447	$152,144
Gross profit or loss	$ 80,708	$117,024	$101,839	$185,112	$210,387	$244,437
Less: Operating expenses	82,005	108,791	99,100	155,923	192,587	209,155
Profit or loss from trading	($ 1,297)	$ 8,233	$ 2,739	$ 29,189	$ 18,700	$ 35,282
Add: Other income:						
Purchase discount	$ 1,447	$ 1,451	$ 1,352	$ 2,210	$ 1,079	$ 346
Interest received	143	248	117	98	75	2,216
Royalties received	116	48	......	229	585	573
Bad debts collected	31	20	85	55	47	44
Income from restaurant	228	1,799	1,887	2,819	1,543	598
Profit on machinery sold	......	......	......	......	1,457	......
Gain on sale of securities	......	......	......	......	......	4,982
Dividends received	......	......	......	......	......	10,170
	$ 1,965	$ 3,566	$ 3,441	$ 5,411	$ 4,786	$ 18,929
Less: Other expenses:						
Rental of machines	$ 214	......	$ 442	$ 444	$ 301	$ 76
Interest paid	759	$ 1,000	673	144	......	453
Royalties paid	......	244	31	......	......	......
	$ 973	$ 1,244	$ 1,146	$ 588	$ 301	$ 529
Net profit or loss from trading	($ 305)	$ 10,555	$ 5,034	$ 34,012	$ 22,285	$ 53,682

Note: Figures in parentheses are losses.

Martin Oliver

On October 13, 1952, Mr. Martin Oliver, at the age of thirty-five, started to work on a project that had been planned fourteen years earlier while he was a student at the Harvard Graduate School of Business Administration. On Thanksgiving Day in 1938, Martin Oliver was visiting at a classmate's home. Also present as a guest that day was an older man nationally known for his success in the financing and reorganizing of business enterprises.

After listening to the experience and advice of the older man, the two younger men had a long discussion about their own career objectives. They decided that their goal would be to join forces and seek to take over the ownership and management of a small manufacturing company when they had reached an age of about thirty-five. They agreed with the older man's advice regarding the desirability of having ten to fifteen years' business experience before endeavoring to take over such top-management responsibilities.

Upon receiving his degree, Mr. Oliver worked for three years in the industrial credit department of a large city bank. His work included surveys and on-site investigations of small- and medium-size industrial plants.

In mid-1942, Oliver joined the Army Air Forces. His activities while in service are described in detail in Exhibit 1. In March, 1947, he was re-employed by his former employer, the Algonquin National Bank in Philadelphia. His work was essentially the same as before, and is also described in Exhibit 1.

Exhibit 1

MARTIN OLIVER

PERSONAL RÉSUMÉ

PROFILE DATA:

Name:	Martin Thomas Oliver.
Permanent Address:	Omaha, Nebraska.
Vital Statistics:	Age—35. Born March 23, 1917, at Lincoln, Nebraska. Height 5′7½″. Weight 148 lbs.
Marital Status:	Single.
Ancestry:	Swedish, Scotch, English.

Exhibit 1—Continued

Outside Interests:	Photography, meteorology, reading, fishing, golf, travel and exploration, development of new business ventures.
Organizations:	American Institute of Management; Sigma Xi; Harvard Club of New York City; Western University Club of New York City; Sigma Nu Fraternity.
OBJECTIVE:	Share ownership and management of manufacturing enterprise.
EDUCATION:	
College:	Graduate School of Business Administration, Harvard University, two years, 1937–39. Major: Manufacturing, Industrial Management and Finance. Held service scholarship. Degree: Master of Business Administration, June, 1939.
	North Dakota State College, Fargo, North Dakota, one year, 1932–33.
	University of Nebraska, Lincoln, Nebraska, three years, 1933–36. Major: Geography, Geology and Meteorology. Minor: Economics and Finance. All college expenses earned. Class standing—upper fifth. Degree: Bachelor of Arts, August, 1936.
High School:	Lincoln High School, Lincoln, Nebraska, three years, 1929–32. Graduated June, 1932—Valedictorian.
BUSINESS EXPERIENCE:	
March, 1951—March, 1952	Manager—Administration Department, Defense Production Operations, Refrigerator Division, Electric Appliance Corporation, Chicago, Illinois. Responsible for assisting top management in seeking and evaluating defense business, launching defense projects in new and existing plants. Specific responsibility for organization, procedures, special studies and reports, and administrative services. Operations transferred to St. Louis Aircraft Plant in July, 1951, were served in the same capacity. Assigned to Defense Production Manager's staff in Chicago in January, 1952. Resigned in March, 1952, to establish own business.

Exhibit 1—Continued

BUSINESS EXPERIENCE—*Cont.*

April, 1949—March, 1951	Administrative Assistant to the Manager—Production Programming and Control, Refrigerator Division, Electric Appliance Corporation, who directs a department of 560 people and exercises functional supervision over 4,600 additional Production Control personnel in 16 assembly plants. (Control of approximately 5,000 end items, with an average daily inventory of over $50,000,000 is required to support average daily production of over 60,000 units.) Responsible for assisting the manager in administration of the activities of the department, recommending plans and policies, co-ordinating general operating plans and procedures, measuring effectiveness of current operations, performing special studies and providing operational control.
October, 1947—April, 1949	Financial Analyst—Planning Office, Central Staff, Electric Appliance Corporation. Made special financial studies and recommendations to management, and responsible for staff supervision and evaluation of budgets for the Purchasing, Sales, and Industrial Relations departments.
March, 1947—October, 1947	Assistant Credit Manager and New Business Representative—Algonquin National Bank, Philadelphia. Responsible for investigation of industrial and commercial enterprises which requested bank loans, preparation of financial analyses and recommendations for bank officers, making industry-wide surveys, and soliciting new industrial and commercial business.
April, 1942—March, 1947	Officer—United States Army Air Forces. See description below.
September, 1939—March, 1942	Credit investigator and Analyst—Algonquin National Bank, Philadelphia. Responsibilities were essentially the same as above.

Exhibit 1—Continued

MILITARY EXPERIENCE:

March, 1947—November, 1952	Reserve Officer, U.S. Air Force. Active in reserve affairs. Appointed to Roster of Special Air Force Personnel, Headquarters, U.S. Air Force, July, 1952. Member of Personnel Policy Board, 10th Air Force, 1950–51. Represented Refrigerator Division of Electric Appliance Corp. in 1951 and 1950 at two-week Field Economic Mobilization Course presented in Chicago by Industrial College of Armed Forces. Served 1948 and 1947 as Production Consultant to Headquarters, U.S. Air Force, Washington, D.C.
September, 1946—March, 1947	Special Assignments—Headquarters, Army Air Forces. Planned and initiated a system for transferring weather equipment to foreign governments. Completed a three-month supply mission to Europe. Attained rank of Lieutenant Colonel and was offered a permanent commission.
June, 1943—September, 1946	Production Liaison Officer between the Army Air Force, the Signal Corps, and Industry. Responsible for co-ordinating the procurement, production, and shipment of over $300,000,000 of electronic equipment required by the Air Force Weather Service. Received Legion of Merit Award and Letter of Commendation.
April, 1943—June, 1943	Student—Weather Equipment Technician School. Graduated first in class of forty-three. Qualified as a Weather Equipment Engineer.
November, 1942—April, 1943	Personnel Procurement Officer—Headquarters, Army Air Forces. Planned, organized, and directed a nation-wide campaign to obtain 7,500 candidates for weather officer training.
April, 1942—November, 1942	Staff Plans and Projects Officer—Headquarters, Army Air Forces. Helped prepare basic plans for personnel, equipment, and operation of world-wide Air Force weather network.

Exhibit 1—Continued

COLLEGE EXPERIENCE:	
September, 1932—September, 1939	Held a series of full-time and part-time jobs throughout college years, including meteorological observer, assistant instructor at University of Nebraska, and supervisor of thirty people engaged in a Water Supplies Survey for National Resources Board.
REFERENCES:	Will be furnished on request.

In October, 1947, Mr. Oliver accepted an offer at a substantially more attractive salary from the Electric Appliance Corporation. This large company was going through extensive reorganization under its new management and was hiring a number of men who combined graduate business training with military experience. His responsibilities with that organization during the following four years are also described in the personal résumé, Exhibit 1.

In the meantime, Oliver's classmate had spent three years in a family wholesale business before going into the armed services. After the war he joined one of the country's larger manufacturing companies as a management engineer. He was assigned to the headquarters organization in a staff capacity and during 1952 was made acting general manager of a small branch plant. His basic salary by 1953 was $15,000, and his annual bonus was estimated as approximately $10,000. Oliver's own promotion opportunities and offers were such that he felt confident he could return to the Electric Appliance Corporation or to another large manufacturing company at an income level comparable to that being earned by his classmate.

By early 1952, Oliver's classmate had accumulated sufficient funds through his share of profits in the sale of the wholesale business so that he was prepared to put as much as $100,000 into a mutual venture. Oliver himself had received no inheritances, nor had he been able to save enough to make any appreciable equity investment. He had, however, won the confidence of a former employer who had substantial funds. This man was willing to invest up to a maximum of $200,000 in a new enterprise, provided the two younger men could establish such a venture through acquisition of a going concern on an attractive basis.

After resigning from the Electric Appliance Corporation in March, 1952, Oliver spent the summer with his family. During this time he was in frequent communication with his two prospective business partners. Through correspondence and conferences, they developed a mutually satisfactory plan of action. This plan involved Oliver's devoting a minimum of one year and a maximum of three years' full time to a systematic search for the kind of business opportunity desired. During this period, Oliver would pay one third of his expenses and the other two men would each contribute a third.

If they could acquire control of a good business on attractive terms, Oliver expected to take over top-management responsibility and would receive one third of the common stock acquired by the group. His third of the purchase price would be advanced by the older man, who would then receive repayment out of Oliver's share of the profits of the business. Accordingly, the other two men agreed to provide an initial down payment of $150,000 for any business that might be acquired. Each of them would also receive one third of the stock so acquired. The balance of their available funds, they decided, should be held as a reserve either to meet unusual expansion opportunities or to forestall difficulties.

Oliver and his classmate decided that as a matter of personal preference they would like to live in the New England area. Accordingly, Oliver mapped out a program which involved dividing his time between New York and Boston, with the greater part being spent in and around Boston.

He then prepared the "Specifications for Purchase of a Business" shown in Exhibit 2. He had 500 copies made and left one with each business acquaintance and friend in the two cities that he thought might be helpful to his search.

Exhibit 2

MARTIN OLIVER

SPECIFICATIONS FOR PURCHASE OF A BUSINESS

GENERAL: Established manufacturing concern engaged in production of industrial goods. Also will consider staple consumers' products.

Capitalization: $25,000 to $1,000,000. Preferably in $50,000 to $300,000 category.

Financial condition: Working capital position adequate to maintain existing operations.

Will purchase company outright or buy controlling interest, and will provide management.

LOCATION: Preferably in New England area but will consider locations east of Rocky Mountains.

PRODUCT: Basic, essential product with established usage.

Relatively high-unit volume with a broad market.

Product which lends itself to continuous technical improvement.

Exhibit 2—Continued

Typical examples—but not confined to following:
- Precision instruments
- Control systems and equipment
- Gauges, dial indicators, meters, and thermometers
- Hand tools and small machine tools
- Roller and ball bearings
- Grinding machines and wheels
- Light specialty machinery
- Electronic equipment
- Powdered metal products
- Plastic molding, machining and extruding operations
- Fluorescent lighting fixtures
- Industrial fasteners
- Containers, paper cups, and office supplies
- Food processing and packaging operations
- Drugs, cleaning and polishing agents
- Metals processing and fabricating operations

REFERENCES: Will be furnished upon request.

Through his previous employment with the Algonquin National Bank in Philadelphia, Oliver had a number of acquaintances in the New York, as well as the Philadelphia, financial community. Proceeding entirely on the basis of personal introductions, he first presented his objective to executives in the industrial departments of a number of New York banks, to numerous investment bankers, law firms, accounting firms, and to several management consulting firms in the New York area. He also called on a number of business brokers, insurance agencies and insurance companies.

After a month in New York, he spent another month "laying his lines" in Boston in a similar manner prior to making any effort to initiate purchase negotiations. During this initial period, he amassed a list of over a hundred New England manufacturing companies that might be acquired from present owners. At the end of nine months, his prospect list of companies for sale in New England had mounted to over three hundred. Fifty of these had appeared sufficiently attractive to merit careful personal investigation. In three instances tentative proposals had been submitted. None of these had been accepted to date.

Mr. Oliver's negotiations were described by a friend, who was trying to assist him in the Boston financial community, as being "characteristic of the more aggressive young Midwesterner, free of the diffidence and reserve that marks many of my New England business associates. If we New Englanders have as much confidence in our plans and in ourselves as Mr. Oliver evidences, most of us hesitate to express ourselves as forcibly and directly as he does. Perhaps these more unrestrained attitudes that we associate with younger businessmen from the Midwest and Southwest may explain why more new businesses get started in those areas."

In general, Mr. Oliver's friends who were endeavoring to help him in New England concurred that he seemed unusually quick, direct, and forceful in formulating and expressing his ideas. Being analytical both by training and temperament, Mr. Oliver also showed more than usual interest in communicating the full background and pertinent details of his own plans and, in turn, asked equal frankness and detail from those with whom he was negotiating. One associate described Oliver's conference methods by saying: "He puts all his cards on the table at a speed which surprises some people, but at the same time I think this also convinces them of his sincerity and determination."

In June, 1953, Oliver's classmate was considering taking a leave from his job to spend a few months making a similar investigation in the Midwest. He believed that conditions in the Midwestern states might prove more conducive to location of an attractive opportunity. Accordingly, Oliver prepared the following report to summarize his experience to date:

REPORT BY OLIVER

June 1, 1953

This is to summarize my experience and to give you some suggestions as to how to proceed if you decide to make investigations in the Midwest along the lines I have been following here in New England.

First, I want to stress the importance of always working on the basis of personal introductions. The man you talk to will want to know not only why you are there, but who sent you. The degree of personal friendship and confidence between the man you are calling on and the individual who sent you can have a big influence on your reception. Usually the man you are seeing will telephone the mutual acquaintance immediately afterward to find out how much he knows about you.

All my contacts to date have stemmed originally from family friends, classmates, former professors, former employers, and business associates. The number of leads I have been able to develop from these people and from their friends in turn seems almost inexhaustible.

Relatively few interesting leads, however, have come out of first-hand introductions from these personal friends. The effective pattern has been for them to introduce me in turn to friends of theirs who are top executives in financial and professional organizations. In particular, I have received my best leads from (1) *commercial bankers* (but not trust department officers, who generally will not talk); (2) *investment underwriting firms;* (3) *law firms* and individual lawyers having substantial estate or corporate practices. Altogether almost three quarters of my good leads have come from these sources. The fact that roughly an equal number have been obtained from each source probably reflects my own distribution of effort as much as anything else.

I shall continue numbering these general sources of leads here in rough order of their usefulness to me to date: (4) *Certified public accounting* firms and individual CPA's have not been used as extensively as the preceding three sources, but to date they have been equally productive when tried. (5) *Management consultants* have been very generous with advice, but have afforded only a few interesting leads. (6) *Insurance brokers and agents* who handle both estate and corporate policies do not have so many suggestions numerically, but are likely to know when estate-planning objectives make a business owner especially eager to sell. Incidentally, the insurance underwriting companies themselves unquestionably have their files loaded with good leads, but to date I have not found any way to crack this source.

The seventh source, in order of usefulness to date, has been the professional *business broker* who deals in the purchase and sale of established companies. The lack of results from these brokers may surprise you, as it did me. I had expected them to be far more fruitful. At least in this part of the country it looks to me as though the owner of a business does not list it with a broker until he has tried to peddle it quietly and found no takers. There was, however, one exception to this rule. One well-established firm in New York that concentrates on the purchase and sale of businesses did have a number of good leads.

At the bottom of my list in terms of specific leads, I put the *risk-capital firms.* They gave me a lot of good advice on how to evaluate a business, but the few prospects they turned over to me proved to be ones they had dropped from their active list, and for good reason. None of them looked worth following up. In fact, I turned over many more leads to them than I received in return.

You will find no problem in picking up more suggestions than you could explore in a life time. I am finding that more and more of these prospects can be culled simply by keeping our own requirements and abilities clearly in mind. Too many times I have spent a full day exploring a situation only to find that some basic fact, which I could have determined by three minutes' more discussion at the source of the suggestion, made the situation one we should not consider.

In particular, I would say we should stay away from companies having an annual sales volume much less than a million dollars. They generally cannot support much of a top-management organization. Moreover, I am convinced that it takes just as much brains to make a 10 per cent profit on a half million dollars' volume as it does to make the same profit margin in a comany with five million sales. If anything, the smaller company is harder work for the top man who has to be Jack-of-all-trades.

I also think we would be smart to stay away from industries that are stagnant or that are moving out of a particular area. I have in mind a number of companies that are for sale in the textile, paper, and shoe industries in New England. Lots of plant and equipment can be bought cheap, and for a good reason. Often they are in distress and can be purchased accordingly.

At the same time, I think we might get burned even worse if we follow the crowd and try to buy into one of the currently popular glamour industries. Apparently chemistry is being superseded by electronics as the magic word. If the word "electronics" can be stretched so that it in any way fits the product line of a small business for sale in the New England area now, you can be sure that the owner is asking 10 to 30 times earnings—if there, indeed, are any earnings. Tangible asset values are also generally small in relation to the asking price.

I have also seen a number of companies that we should shy away from because of personality problems. Most easily spotted are those companies that have been dominated by one or a few families whose relatives are packed throughout the organization. At first, it looks simple just to cut out the dead wood and thus build up the profits. If we do that, however, we are probably fooling ourselves about buying a going concern.

Another pitfall in the personality area is the small company with good earnings and a good financial record that depends excessively on the abilities and contacts of one top man. Too many times I have seen an opportunity to buy earning power which would prove an illusion once the former owner retired.

All in all, you may be surprised and possibly discouraged at the number of interesting prospects that will blow up when you apply these tests. During the past nine months, I have had approximately 300 companies called to my attention. In each case, my adviser had reason to believe that the company could be acquired and thought that it might meet our requirements. Simply by applying the general standards I have developed, about 250 were quickly eliminated.

Fifty of the companies seemed sufficiently attractive to merit my making more careful personal investigation. In each case, I visited the plant and had a conference with one or more of the officers. As you know, in three instances we later submitted tentative proposals. However, two of these situations were of sufficiently questionable value to us so that our proposed price was very low—so low, in fact, that we could have liquidated the operation without losing money if it didn't pan out well after a year or two. The owners of these two companies could probably do better liquidating their companies themselves now. The third, Judson Precision Products, is still under consideration.

It would be misleading to imply that only one company out of 300 leads looked like a good business opportunity for us. In fact, the majority of the 50 companies that I selected for personal investigation were inherently attractive. In most instances, however, the owners' ideas of terms and prices seemed so totally unrealistic to me that there was no use wasting further time.

This inability to reach even a reasonable negotiating range is evidently not peculiar to us. In fact, I find that the venture-capital firms who have large organizations constantly combing the woods and whose reputation brings in hordes of would-be sellers still locate very few they can buy.

Most commercial bankers seem to agree with our judgment and with the advice I have received from investment firms about not offering more than five times earnings for a well-established company together with all the assets necessary to produce those earnings. At the same time, the owners of established businesses are apparently being advised by their financial advisers that it does not make any sense for them to consider selling at less than ten times earnings. This amount is usually greater than book value. I am sure the bankers and the financial advisers are not giving out double-talk, but sincerely believe in this apparently conflicting advice—depending upon the point of view and interests of the man they are advising. The pattern seems to be that most owners are holding out for about twice what most buyers will pay.

During the last nine months, I have been maintaining a record on close to 100 companies being offered for sale in New England. During this period, only

Exhibit 3

MARTIN OLIVER

32 STOCKS CHEAP ON WORKING-CAPITAL BASIS*

	Net Working Capital per Share†	Recent Price	1952 Earnings	Dividends Past 12 Months	Percentage of Yield
Air-way Elec. Appliance	$15.60	13‡	$2.47	$1.10	8.5
American Distilling	57.56	35	2.81	2.00	5.7
Barker Brothers	19.52	16	1.63	1.50	9.4
Blumenthal (S.)	14.76	10‡	1.45	1.00	10.0
Brunswick-Balke-Coll.	27.15	18	1.32	1.00	5.6
Century Ribbon Mills	11.61	8	0.78	0.70	8.8
Dejay Stores	8.49	7‡	1.15[i]	0.50+	7.1
DeVilbiss Co.	26.56	19	3.01	1.40	7.4
Devoe & Raynolds A.	23.03	21	2.49[h]	2.00	9.5
Endicott Johnson	37.59	28	2.82[h]	1.60	5.7
Goodall-Sanford	24.99	17	3.02[a]	1.50	8.8
Hart, Schaffner & Marx	36.33	24	2.96[h]	1.60	6.7
Lee Rubber & Tire	60.95	50	6.66[g]	3.50+	7.0
Magic Chef	9.78	9	1.26	0.60§	6.7
Manhattan Shirt	39.36	25	2.78[a]	1.40	5.6
Marion Power Shovel	24.26	23‡	4.26	Nil	Nil
McQuay-Norris Mfg.	16.88	14	1.51	1.00	7.2
Mergenthaler Linotype	41.49	28	3.41[f]	2.50	8.9
Montgomery Ward	81.97	61	7.41[i]	3.00	4.9
Munsingwear, Inc.	16.05	14	2.42	1.00	7.1
Murray Corp. of Am.	25.83	22	3.87[e]	2.00	9.1
National Dept. Stores	26.40	15	1.05[i]	1.50	10.0
Nesco, Inc.	15.05	15	1.27	Nil	Nil
Oliver Corp.	18.45	13	2.71[g]	1.20	9.2
Pacific Mills	37.66	26	2.11[i]	0.85	3.3
Pullman, Inc.	49.26	41	4.51	3.00	7.3
Reliable Stores	40.40	29	4.38	2.10	7.2
Reliance Mfg.	15.46	11	1.33	0.60	5.5
Schenley Industries	37.70	25	2.76[e]	2.00	8.0
Starret (L. S.) Co.	48.59	44	6.13[a]	3.00	6.8
Waukesha Motor	21.43	17	3.22[b]	1.00	5.9
White (S.S.) Dental	28.03	26	2.31	1.50+	5.8

* Taken from *United Investment Report*, United Business Service, June 1, 1953. Reproduced by permission.

† Based on latest balance sheet.
‡ American Stock Exchange.
§ Indicated rate.
+ Plus stock.
[a] Year ended June.
[b] Year ended July.
[e] Year ended August.
[f] Year ended September.
[g] Year ended October.
[h] Year ended November.
[i] Year ended January 1953.

five of these owners were able to dispose of their businesses. Three liquidated their companies voluntarily, with facilities and equipment being sold at public auction. One was merged into a larger company in the same industry, and the fifth was acquired by its own largest customer. I do not know whether this was accomplished simply by an exchange of securities—as I suspect—or whether it was an actual cash buy-out. None have been sold to investors or to new investor-managers like us.

This is, indeed, a puzzling siuation. There is no lack of capital seeking investment. On the contrary, there seem to be even more people and groups with capital looking for businesses to buy than there are companies available. Many prospective investor-managers are also in evidence. In fact, the competition from other prospective buyers is terrific. I would say there are 5 to 10 potential buyers for every business for sale. Why then are there so few sales?

I should like to swap ideas with you on this problem in the near future. Is something wrong with our timing, or have I been looking in the wrong part of the country? Please give this a lot of thought because I think the three of us should get together very soon to decide whether our present objectives are realistic.

P.S. The attached report (Exhibit 3) just came to my attention and throws interesting light on the inability of investors to pay corporate owners even as much as liquidating value in many situations.

Judson Precision Products Company

Early in 1953, Mr. Martin Oliver was preparing a proposal for the purchase of the Judson Precision Products Company, a manufacturer of jewelers' supplies located in the vicinity of Boston, Massachusetts. Mr. Oliver, age thirty-six, had resigned his position in the production department of a large household-appliance manufacturer and had been spending full time for over six months seeking an attractive enterprise opportunity.

Mr. Oliver had for many years been planning to acquire control and top-management responsibility of a small company as soon as he felt he had sufficient business experience and adequate financial backing. Since he was planning to spend a minimum of one year and a maximum of three years selecting such an opportunity, he was not under pressure. The Judson Company was, however, the most interesting situation among approximately forty that Oliver had investigated up to this time. It was, in fact, one of the very few he considered sufficiently attractive to merit a firm offer.

Two men associated with Mr. Oliver were willing to invest $150,000 if a demonstrably good purchase could be arranged. Oliver's own contribution was limited to his experience and to his willingness to assume the risks of spending from one to three years searching for an enterprise opportunity. The other two partners were paying two thirds of the expenses of the search. Oliver expected to assume the position of president in whatever company might be acquired.

One of his associates, a former classmate in a graduate school of business administration, expected to join the new firm as executive vice-president or in some equivalent capacity. This man would be contributing approximately one third of the new capital. The third participant in this project would contribute two thirds of the new capital. He was an older man who had no expectation of participating in the management other than as a director. Oliver would also receive one third of the stock thus acquired, for which he would repay the older man over a period of years.

The president of a commercial bank in Boston first brought the Judson Company to Oliver's attention. The banker pointed out that sale of the company by its present owner was of such obvious logic that Oliver might be well advised to approach the owner, Mr. Carl Judson, even though the company was not ostensibly for sale. The banker warned that Mr. Judson might be difficult to approach on the subject: "Just last week, I understand that Judson virtually threw a smart young promoter from New York out of his office, when the subject of selling the company was raised." Further discussion of the violent reaction encountered by the promoter from New York indicated that his proposal had apparently anticipated either liquidation or resale of the company for a quick profit. The banker believed that an offer from a young man such as Oliver who wished to come into the business and to make it his life work would engender a totally different reaction.

The banker then telephoned Mr. Judson and explained briefly the nature of Oliver's interest, with emphasis upon the fact that Oliver was interested in joining a company in the near future upon some basis whereby later he might be able to buy control. The question of immediate sale of the company was not discussed on the telephone. On the basis of this introduction, Judson said he would be willing to give young Oliver a few minutes of his time.

Upon arrival in Judson's office, Oliver found that an initial cool and brusque attitude quickly dissipated when the long-term nature of Oliver's interests were made apparent. Mr. Judson, at the age of seventy-six, was a widower and had a niece, who managed his household, but had no male heirs. Neither did he have any individuals within his organization who had been prepared to take over top management. The bulk of his personal estate was represented by the equity ownership of the Judson Precision Products Company. Accordingly, he was quite aware of the fact that he should be making plans for continuation of the company after his retirement or death.

The management organization under Mr. Judson consisted of a sales manager, who had in recent years taken over most of the responsibilities for customer relations, and a production manager, who carried complete responsibility for day-to-day factory operations. "The production processes are well organized and are now so routine," Mr. Judson explained, "that we have had no troubles and have had to make no changes for over ten years. My production manager has been with the company almost twenty years and knows the business inside-out."

Mr. Burke, the sales manager, had joined the company when it was started in 1927. He supervised the work of three resident salesmen, who handled approximately 700 accounts with jewelry wholesalers throughout the country. Two of these men, ages fifty-eight and sixty-two, had been with the company for over fifteen years. The third, a veteran of World War II who had been employed in 1946, was the son-in-law of one of the older salesmen.

Most of the selling activity during recent years had been confined to correspondence and to distribution of catalogues by mail. The company had attained a strong position in the trade during its first ten years after being founded by Mr. Judson in 1927. During the last fifteen years it had maintained this position, but without further growth. Mr. Judson seemed confident that sales volume could easily be tripled if the company wanted to exert an effort to enter the market with lower-cost items. His policy, however, had been to adhere to the production of only high-precision, high-quality tools and accessories for jewelers. He had been content, he explained, to hold a leading position in the high-price segment of the market.

All questions dealing with finances and business policy had always been handled by Mr. Judson. Neither the sales manager nor the production manager were considered by Judson to be candidates for the long-range financial management of his business. Judson was, however, very proud of his organization, which consisted of approximately 100 employees, and was most desirous that the personnel have an opportunity to continue with a successful company.

The Judson Company had been stable and prosperous for a long number of years. Except for a slight inflation of sales volume during the war, when shortages of material forced the company to accept a few government contracts for surgical instruments and other items which utilized the company's precision machinery, volume had held fairly constant between $800,000 to a million dollars annual sales. During the last few years, Mr. Judson had been working shorter hours and had not made any effort to continue the development of new items to replace those which gradually lost competitive appeal. The sales volume for 1952 had been $803,000.

Earnings since the war had been remarkably stable, ranging from $51,000 to $68,000 per year. The company had had no losses since it had incurred a $10,000 deficit during the 1938 recession.

Mr. Oliver was particularly interested in the possibilities of utilizing the excess plant capacity and surplus working capital on other products. He estimated that current production could be handled with not more than half the available floor space and that it required not over one third the capacity of the key pieces of the precision machinery. Oliver believed that in many ways he was better equipped and more interested in dealing with industrial markets than in catering to retail organizations. Accordingly, he saw in the Judson Company a possible opportunity to develop a line of general industrial instruments utilizing the precision machine tools and other equipment on hand.

The company's excess of working capital evidently reflected the fact that Mr. Judson preferred to retain his earnings in the business he understood instead of investing in the securities of other companies. Oliver estimated that current assets included at least $200,000 in excess of the

Exhibit 1

JUDSON PRECISION PRODUCTS COMPANY

INCOME STATEMENT

(In Thousands)

	Five-Year Average, Incl. 1951	*1951*	*Nine Months Sept. 30, 1952*
Net sales	$942	$855	$586
Cost of goods sold	601	541	359
Gross profit	$341	$314	$227
Administration and sales expense	192	175	136
Operating profit	$149	$139	$ 91
Federal taxes	75	83	52
Net income	$ 64	$ 56	$ 39

Exhibit 2

JUDSON PRECISION PRODUCTS COMPANY

BALANCE SHEET SUMMARY, DECEMBER 31, 1952

(In Thousands)

ASSETS			LIABILITIES		
Cash	$231		Accounts Payable	$42	
Accounts Receivable	104		Payroll Taxes	9	
Inventories	250		Federal Taxes	83	
Current Assets		$585	Miscellaneous	4	
Plant and Equipment	$122		Current Liabilities		$138
Reserve for Depreciating	64		Capital Stock		97
Plant and Equipment, Net		58	Earned Surplus		414
Miscellaneous Deferred Charges		6			
Total Assets		$649	Total Liabilities		$649

amount required to conduct the business. An inventory of $150,000 appeared quite adequate to carry the current operations comfortably. The $100,000 excess above this amount had been invested in highly marketable precious metals, which Judson stated he considered a method of investing his savings. The cash balance was also at least $100,000 higher than the business required. Moreover, rigid adherence to good credit practices might, Oliver believed, permit reduction of accounts receivable by as much as $50,000.

The plant and equipment were carried at very conservative figures and had apparently been depreciated at the maximum rate allowed by the Bureau of Internal Revenue. The plant itself was a relatively modern, well-maintained two-story building containing 15,000 square feet of floor space. A recent appraisal by experienced industrial appraisers had resulted in the estimate that the plant and equipment could be readily sold on the current market for at least $160,000.

Mr. Oliver considered the Judson Company a likely prospect for acquisition, provided he could set a price, a method of payment, and a procedure for acquiring control which would be attractive to his associates and acceptable to Mr. Judson.

Kitchen Housewares Company, Incorporated (B)

Tom Heath, treasurer and production manager of Kitchen Housewares Company, Incorporated, was optimistic in June, 1953, as he sat down to discuss the current situation with George Iverson, the company's president. He was, at the same time, fully aware that the company still faced a number of immediate problems. Foremost among these problems, he reported that several of the older workers had expressed dissatisfaction with the hourly wage rates, that the work-in-process inventory appeared to be much too large, that floor space was so limited that it interfered with material handling, that any additional new machinery would require a rewiring of the plant, and that poor scheduling was causing inefficiencies in the production flow.

Despite these problems and a balance sheet which at the end of 1952 had shown a deficit of over $7,000, both men were proud of the progress they had made, and they confidently expected to wipe out the deficit by the end of 1953.

Tom Heath graduated from college at the beginning of World War II and had immediately entered the Navy. At the end of the war he accepted a position as time-study trainee with a large New England textile manufacturer. A few months later he was offered the opportunity to establish and operate a small sewing plant to manufacture ladies' lingerie for the parent corporation. During the early months of struggle to organize the new operation, Heath found that he enjoyed managing a small plant.

At the end of six months, the sewing plant was employing 100 girls and was operating smoothly. The parent company then promoted Heath to the position of director of industrial relations for a division consisting of several plants. Although he had found the task of managing and operating a small enterprise with all the personnel problems inherent in a group of 100 workers a very satisfying experience, his new staff personnel position soon began to irk him. Within a few months he requested a transfer to a production activity and was made assistant to the division production manager.

Although he found his new work interesting, he still looked back fondly on his experiences in the small plant. Believing that he needed additional business training to operate his own company, he left the textile manufacturer to take a graduate course in business. His ultimate aim was to buy a company or to work in a small firm with the opportunity to buy into ownership.

During his two years at the business school and for about six months after graduation, Heath investigated a number of new business ideas. By December, 1950, he was beginning to lose hope of ever finding a good opportunity. Just as he was about to accept a job, a banker friend told him about an interesting opportunity to purchase the Iverson & Fox Company.

The machinery and equipment of this old and at one time profitable company was to be sold at auction in a nearby city. Iverson & Fox had once been a leading manufacturer of kitchen wire goods. The banker attributed its decline and failure to mismanagement and the refusal of the president to keep in step with the times. One of the founders, the banker pointed out, had remained as operating head until the company failed; he was ninety-six years old at the time and had steadfastly resisted all change for more than twenty-five years. Consultants, brought in by others who held an interest in the company, had been met at the front door by the president, who invariably asked: "Young man, what do you know about wire goods? Have you ever worked in this business? No? Then go away; don't bother me; you can't tell me anything about my business."

The banker's brief description convinced Heath that this might well be the kind of opportunity he was seeking—an old, successful family business, run to the ground by poor management. His investigation confirmed this initial impression.

Heath learned that the company had been founded over fifty years before and had at one time employed 300 people. In 1947, sales were \$170,000, with a resultant profit of \$8,000; in 1948, sales were \$140,000, and a \$5,000 loss resulted. By 1949, sales had dropped to \$110,000, and the year's loss reached \$15,000. Shortly thereafter the company failed.

Heath made a quick trip to the plant. He found that, although the company had originally occupied four floors of an old wooden factory building, at the time of its failure it had used only certain areas on each floor. He could not judge the quality of the machinery. Talks with some of the former employees reaffirmed his belief that the company had suffered from inadequate management.

Heath also went to see the manufacturer's agent in New York City through whom the major portion of Iverson & Fox sales had been made. Mr. Montague, the sales agent, stated that Iverson & Fox had made good products but had priced them lower than necessary to compete. He did not think the company had known its costs. Mr. Montague estimated that he had lost about $40,000 in sales from the time the company failed (September, 1950) to the time Heath visited him (December, 1950).

Competition in the wire kitchenware field was keen; but, Mr. Montague pointed out, Iverson & Fox had competed successfully for many years. The largest competitor, Household Products, Inc., had its main plant only a few miles from the Iverson & Fox plant. In addition, Household Products operated two other plants in the United States and one in Canada. There were three other major competitors and a large number of small companies which sold only in local markets.

THE PARTNERSHIP

While investigating the company, Heath had become acquainted with George Iverson, son of one of the founders of the business. Iverson was a few years older than Heath and had been working for the company for about five years. Although he had had little to do with policy decisions, he had acquired an intimate knowledge of the machinery and manufacturing operations. Since both men were interested in restarting the business and since both had limited capital, they decided to pool resources and form a partnership. Heath considered Iverson's knowledge of the manufacturing process a valuable asset.

A third partner was found to take a third interest, but he was able to devote only part of his time to the company. Mr. Jacob Stein had built a prosperous business wholesaling a complete line of notions to independent novelty stores and small variety chains. In addition to his partnership participation, Mr. Stein also agreed to lend the company funds. His name was highly respected in local business and financial circles.

BUYING THE MACHINERY

As a first step toward deciding upon the machinery to buy, the partners compiled a list of products to manufacture (Exhibit 1, p. 210). They then visited the plant and selected the machinery they would need. Since each piece of machinery had been tagged and labeled by the auctioneers, it was an easy matter to make up a list. Iverson then put a price on each piece. The total came to $5,750. Because this entire sum would have to be paid in cash on the day of the auction, the partners felt that

Exhibit 1

KITCHEN HOUSEWARES COMPANY, INC.
HOUSEHOLD WIRE GOODS

Factory No.	Description	Wholesale Cost per Dozen	Minimum Order	Suggested Retail
348	*Diamond egg whip	$0.80	12 doz.	$0.15
331	Egg whip	1.08	12 doz.	0.19
8343	*Egg whip (natural-lacquered handle)	1.44	6 doz.	0.29
9343	*Egg whip (red-enameled handle)	1.44	6 doz.	0.29
8555T	Masher (natural-lacquered handle)	1.65	6 doz.	0.29
9555T	Masher (red-enameled handle)	1.65	6 doz.	0.29
8444	*Masher (natural-lacquered handle)	2.00	6 doz.	0.39
9444	*Masher (red-enameled handle)	2.00	6 doz.	0.39
90B	Roasting rack (with box)	5.25	2 doz.	0.98
918	Cake tester	7.20 gr.	12 doz.	0.10
452	Little Devil lobster fork (6 to card)	3.24	6 doz. cards	0.59
325T	Fry basket	3.00	6 doz.	0.59
751T	Cake cooler 10″ × 10″ without center bar	1.30	6 doz.	0.25
762T	*Cake cooler 10″ × 10″ with center bar	1.44	6 doz.	0.29
791T	*Cake cooler 9″ × 11¾″	1.80	6 doz.	0.35
792T	*Cake cooler 10″ × 14″	2.25	6 doz.	0.45
309T	*Cake cooler 9″ diam.	1.50	6 doz.	0.29
310T	*Cake cooler 10″ diam.	1.75	6 doz.	0.35
407	*3-ring cake cooler 7½″ diam.	1.35	6 doz.	0.25
409	*3-ring cake cooler 9″ diam.	1.53	6 doz.	0.29
410	*3-ring cake cooler 10″ diam.	1.76	6 doz.	0.35
505T	Broiler 8″ × 8″	2.15	6 doz.	0.39
86T	Checker broiler 9″ × 6½″	2.75	6 doz.	0.59
87T	Checker broiler 9″ × 8½″	3.25	6 doz.	0.69
88T	Checker broiler 8″ × 8″	4.70	3 doz.	0.85
100T	Simulated checker broiler 10″ × 10″	6.50	3 doz.	1.20
424T	Hot-dog roaster	1.50	2 doz.	0.29
1415	Dish drainer	4.00	2 doz.	0.59
3	Napkin holder	1.00	6 doz.	0.19
1229	Sterilizing rack	4.00	3 doz.	0.79
1388	Stroller shopping basket (painted)	8.64	3 doz.	1.59
1388P	Stroller shopping basket (plated)	10.00	3 doz.	1.89
801	12″ suction towel bar	1.88	2 doz.	0.35
802	18″ suction towel bar	2.60	2 doz.	0.49
510	Pie-plate tray	4.50	1 doz.	0.85
510B	Pie-plate tray, braided	7.00	1 doz.	1.29

Terms: 2% 10 days, net 30 F.O.B.

On orders weighing 200 lbs. or more, freight allowed up to $1.80 per 100 lbs. On orders less than 200 lbs. but more than 100 lbs., freight allowed 50 cents per 100 lbs.

* First products made by the company.

their limited working capital could not stand the strain.

Mr. Stein suggested they approach the auctioneers prior to the day of the sale and offer them a lump sum for the machinery and equipment they wanted. Accordingly, they met one afternoon with the auctioneers at the plant to try to arrange such a purchase. The three men stated their needs, explained that they intended to resurrect only a part of the business, and then presented their list of equipment, along with an offer of $2,500 cash. One of the auctioneers took the list, started at the top floor, and walked rapidly from machine to machine, from cart loads of in-process materials to items piled on benches and from floor to floor. Approximately an hour later he turned to the men and said: "Your price is too low. This stuff you have listed is worth over $5,000."

Heath pointed out that the partners did not have that much cash available but might be interested in giving a note to make up the difference between $2,500 cash and whatever price could be agreed upon. The partners were told they would be notified sometime before the sale as to whether the auction firm was interested in the offer. On the day before the auction, the partners were told that the auctioneers had a counteroffer.

The auctioneers agreed to sell the entire list of equipment for $5,250, with a down payment of $2,500 in cash and the remainder on a 4 per cent note, with payments of $135 a month plus interest. The partners accepted. Heath was instructed to be prepared to bid on every item on the list at the public auction the next day and to bid any amount necessary to get such an item. The auctioneer would bid up the listed items so as to protect the partners' interest. Although the partners would have been able to buy most of the equipment more cheaply on the auction block, there were five or six major pieces of machinery which would have gone at much higher prices than they had paid for them. In addition, before the auction, the auctioneers had allowed them to pick up whatever hand tools they felt they needed.

GETTING THE BUSINESS UNDER WAY

Since most of the machines which the partners had bought were located on the top floor of the building, the partners decided that this would be the home of the new business. For the first three weeks after the sale, Heath, Iverson, and a foreman, a former Iverson & Fox foreman, were engaged in moving the remaining machinery to the top floor and rearranging the machinery on the floor to give some semblance of production flow. Conditions of work were not of the best during this time. The building was not yet heated. Heavy machines had to be pushed and hauled. Heath went home at night, after a twelve-hour day, his hands blackened with grease and his fingernails broken. At the end of three weeks, four girls were hired and the partners looked with some pride and awe at Kitchen Housewares' first product.

During this initial period Iverson and Heath were aided by the guidance of the third partner, Stein. It had been understood that Stein would give all of his available time without drawing a salary until the business gathered momentum. As a matter of fact, Stein had told the other two: "I intend to help you all I can; but until you really get your business running and sales and profits are at a point where it will not handicap the business to pay me a salary, my contribution will be on a part-time basis. Until the business reaches that point, you boys will have to do a good deal of the sales work with whatever advice and guidance I can give you." Actually, there were times during the early days of the company when Stein devoted more time to Kitchen Housewares than he did to his own firm. The other two men looked to Stein especially for guidance on marketing problems.

THE PRODUCT LINE

During the first twenty-five months of operation, a number of new products were added to the firm's basic line of household wire goods (Exhibit 1). New product ideas for the housewares line came primarily from the three owners. Heath, for instance, had contributed the idea for a fry basket (Exhibit 2); and Mr. Stein had pointed out the need for a wire insert to use in a roasting pan (Exhibit 3).

Since the dies for a dish drainer had been included in the original material purchased from the auctioneers, this item was added to the line. Unfortunately, none of these new household products were outstanding sales successes. In fact, some of them never went beyond the preliminary model. With the exception of the cake tester, sales volume on these new items was mediocre to nonexistent. A new, simply constructed, and lower-priced potato masher was, for instance, offered to the trade to retail at 29 cents. It was functionally equal, if not superior, to the old model. Customers, however, still seemed to prefer the old-style masher, retailing for 39 cents, which had remained unchanged for forty years.

This kind of experience was costly, but both men were satisfied that they had learned valuable lessons. Originally they had thought that inquiries among their sales personnel and customers, together with Mr. Stein's advice and their own intuitive judgment, would allow them to make a reasonable estimate of a new product's sales potential. "We learned the hard way," said Tom Heath. "We bought 30,000 boxes for our new roaster about two years ago. Most of them are still up in the loft. Saving a few dollars on a quantity purchase sure didn't make up for the $700 we now have tied up in special cardboard."

While scouting around for business, Heath had visited a firm in Boston which specialized in the production and sale of colorful counter dis-

Exhibit 2

3 New Kitchen Housewares Items

FRENCH-FRY BASKET

No. 320

WITH EASY-GRIP AIR COOLED HANDLE

This new K-H French Fry basket, with air cooled handle that fits the hand, is of welded construction throughout. Easy cleaning, with rest for sauce or fry pan. Size: 7" diameter, 4" deep. Hot tin dipped finish. Weight per doz. 6¾ lbs.

No. 325

WITH CONVENTIONAL HANDLE

The same lasting quality is also found in the conventional handle French Fry basket. Easy cleaning, welded construction throughout, with rest for sauce or fry pan. Size: 7" diameter, 4" deep. Hot tin dipped finish. Weight per doz. 6 lbs.

"Pierre" CAKE TESTER

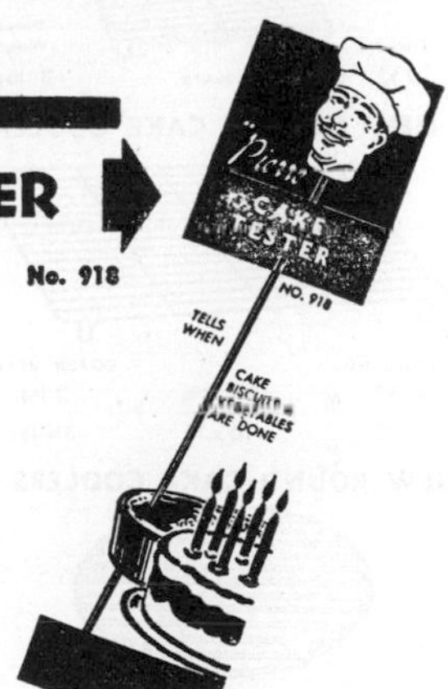

No. 918

K-H presents this brand new "Pierre" Cake Tester of novelty design. White plastic head, highlighted in red, with hole for hanging up in kitchen. A must for every housewife for telling when cakes, biscuits and vegetables are done. Mounted on a striking red, white and blue card for faster sales. Weight per doz. 2 lbs.

play racks made of wire. The apparent potentialities of the wire-rack business led Heath to seek advice from the management of another firm, the largest in the household wire-goods business, Household Products, Inc. Heath and Iverson were received cordially by the officers of Household Products Inc., and a helpful discussion of the problems of the new company took place. When Heath asked about the wire-rack business, the president of Household Products pointed out that his company had produced such items about twenty years ago but was

Exhibit 3

KITCHEN HOUSEWARES COMPANY, INC.

PART OF THE PRODUCT LINE

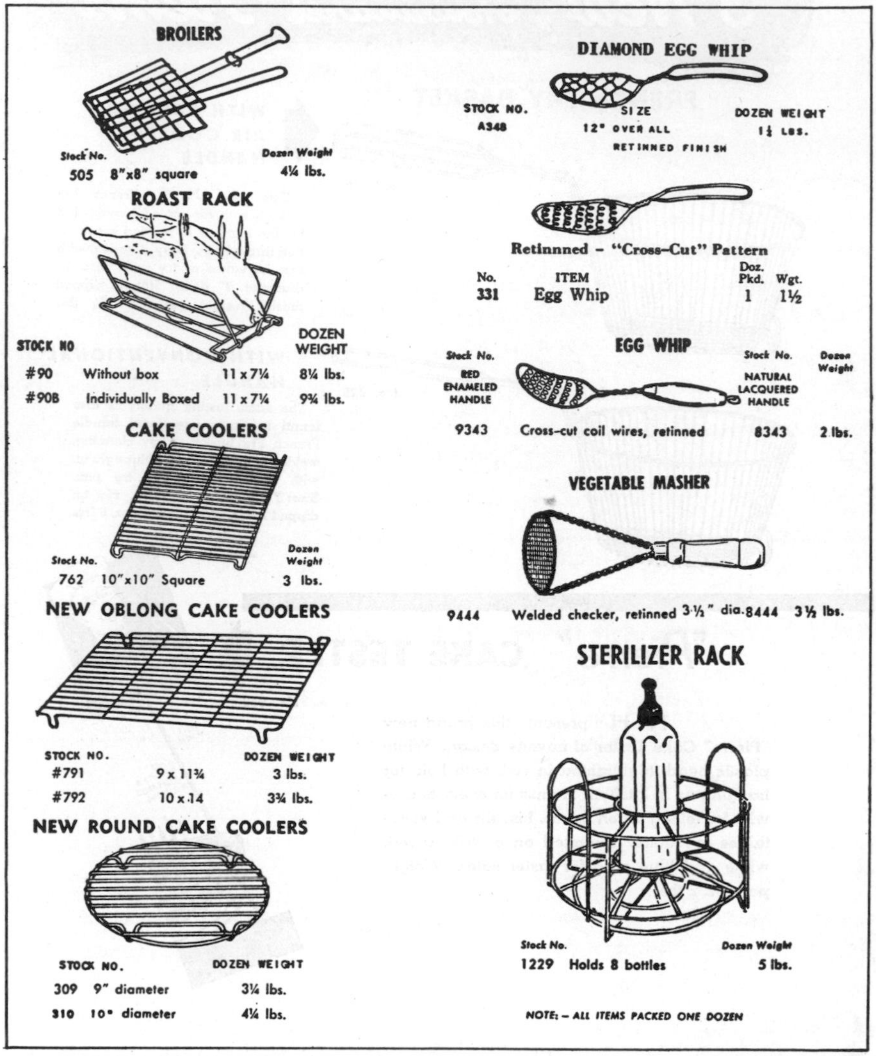

no longer interested. He promised to refer all requests for bids on that type of work to Kitchen Housewares. By the spring of 1953, Heath had bid on several jobs referred to him by Household Products, the last of which had resulted in a sizable order to modify some counter display racks for cigars.

Although the wire-rack business had been responsible for about one third of the gross sales in 1952, Tom Heath believed it offered little future promise. The advertising-display-rack company which had been responsible for the bulk of their orders to date was beginning to produce its own wire racks. Moreover, the ultimate users of such racks seldom purchased more than a few hundred units at a time. The only known exceptions to this small-lot procurement procedure were among the very large tobacco and soap companies. Without an order for at least 1,000 units, Heath found it difficult to make a profit and still bid competitively.

During a classroom discussion about his sales problems with graduate students at a nearby business school, one of the students suggested that the company consider consulting an industrial designer for new product ideas. Heath acted on the suggestion and by June of 1953 had received orders totaling about $30,000 from ideas presented by one industrial designer. These products included attractive wire handles, "Susans" (a circular device to hold a wicker basket and six glasses), and component parts for special-purpose trays.

Although these new orders were relatively large, not everything went smoothly. In one case, the designer supplied a glass for which Kitchen Housewares was to make 100,000 holders. The entire order was completed and shipped before Heath and Iverson discovered that the designer had substituted another glass with slightly different measurements. The original fit, however, had been so close that the substitute was too large for the holder. Although both men felt that the designer was at fault, they decided to accept a portion of the cost of making new holders. Fortunately, they discovered a way of permanently springing the wire holders so they would fit the new glass without requiring return of the goods to the plant.

During 1952 the company had received about $10,000 worth of miscellaneous industrial business. In the first five months of 1953, this volume had jumped to $15,000. Heath expected that Kitchen Housewares would obtain its greatest growth from miscellaneous industrial orders of that type. Past industrial orders consisted of such products as TV aerials, electric heater guards, footrests for baby carriages, etc. Heath was particularly impressed with the size of these orders. A current order for 25,000 ultra-high-frequency television aerials, for instance, provided for automatic renewal when the order was 80 per cent completed unless the customer notified otherwise. The changing character of the company's product line during the first part of 1953 was illustrated by the following sales figures:

Approximate Allocation of Gross Sales

	1952	First Five Months of 1953
Housewares line	$40,000	$15,000
Wire display racks	25,000	5,000
Miscellaneous industrial orders	10,000	15,000
Government orders	....	10,000
Industrial designer products		15,000
Total	$75,000	$60,000

SALES

The impetus to sales volume caused by the Korean war continued through January, 1951. Thus, during their first month of operation, January, 1951, the month's sales of $918 were better than expected and close to the amount they had estimated for their second month of operation (see Exhibit 4). The second month's sales were $3,800, $800 over the $3,000 figure estimated for the third month of operation.

Exhibit 4

KITCHEN HOUSEWARES COMPANY, INC.

Pro Forma Estimate in Dollars of Sales and Expense for First Nine Months of Operation and Actual Figures for First Two Months

Item	Pro Forma Estimate 1st mo.	2nd mo.	3d mo.	6th mo.	9th mo.	Actual 1st mo.	2nd mo.
Sales	....	1,000	3,000	6,000	9,000	918	3,803
Inventory		1,600	2,600	3,100	3,600	....	
Material purchased	1,000	2,000	2,000	3,000	3,000	730	
Wages	500	1,500	2,000	3,000	3,000	430	5,443
Rent and power	150	200	250	300	300	135	
Miscellaneous	500	700	900	1,800	1,800	3,241	
Totals	2,150	4,400	5,150	8,100	8,100	4,536	5,443
Cumulative expense	2,150	6,550	11,000	31,300	56,100	4,536	9,479
Receipts	....	....	1,000	6,000	9,000	352	1,012
Cumulative receipts	....	....	1,000	16,000	40,000	....	1,364
Net expense	2,150	6,550	10,000	15,300	16,100	4,184	8,695
Loans (70% of accounts receivable)	....	700	2,100	4,200	6,300	....	....
Net cash required	2,150	5,850	7,900	9,000	9,800	4,184	8,675

During the third month, sales rose to $4,500. With the fourth month came a drastic reduction to only $2,500. Two factors explained this sudden decline: first, the boom in customer demand for metal goods of almost all kinds caused by the Korean war dropped sharply; second, and perhaps more important, Mr. Montague, the sales agent, became sick. His business suffered considerably during the spring, and in June he entered a hospital.

In the latter part of the summer, Mr. Montague left the hospital but was not yet ready to assume his business activities. In September, Heath and Iverson went to New York to review the sales problem. They found that manufacturers of three other lines which Mr. Montague handled had already placed their business with the Crowden Associates, a large firm of manufacturers agents. Heath and Iverson also decided to place their business with Crowden Associates; Crowden in turn offered Mr. Montague a position as soon as he was able to work.

The arrangement with Crowden Associates provided Kitchen Housewares with sales coverage from Maine to Maryland and as far west as Pennsylvania. Commission rates with Crowden were the same as they had been with Montague: 5 per cent for sales to chains, 7½ per cent for sales to jobbers, and 10 per cent for sales to independent stores.

During these first few months, the three owners tried in a number of ways to increase sales. A salesman who sold a line of expensive aluminumware had complained during one of his regular visits to Mr. Stein that, because of aluminum quotas, he was not getting enough of his product to maintain a satisfactory income. Mr. Stein suggested that he handle the Kitchen Housewares' line, since the same customer bought both types of items. The salesman thought it a good idea and requested permission from his sales manager to carry Kitchen Housewares' products. The sales manager, who knew his men were not getting enough aluminumware to sell, was most enthusiastic about the idea. He wrote to Kitchen Housewares and offered to supply the partners with a list of all his sales personnel so that a similar offer could be made to each salesman. Three new salesmen were obtained in this way—one covering New Jersey, another New York, and the third, New England.

For the first two months, June and July, 1951, the three new men reported almost no sales. Furthermore, they gave no indication to the company as to the reason for this lack of sales volume. At the end of the second month, Heath and Iverson wrote to the three salesmen terminating the agreement. Their letter apparently passed a letter of resignation from the New Jersey salesman in which he explained that, since his aluminum allowance was so low that he could sell it easily, the additional income from sales of Kitchen Houseware line was not worth the many extra calls.

Undaunted, the three men continued to advertise for salesmen in trade journals and contacted manufacturers' representatives whom they felt would be interested in carrying their line. Heath was anxious for representation in the Chicago area. One man did handle the line for a while in Chicago and then dropped it after having contributed no sales.

In the South, two representatives had been obtained, one covering Texas and Arkansas and the other selling in Georgia and the surrounding states. Although these two men, along with Mr. Stein, contributed only about 20 per cent of the sales volume for the household goods, they were consistent sellers. The remaining 80 per cent of the household line was sold by Crowden Associates, the New York agents.

Mr. Stein continually emphasized to his two associates that an adequate sales organization was essential to the growth of the company. Neither of the two active partners was, however, particularly interested in handling the sales responsibilities. Tom Heath described his feeling when he said: "Of course I could probably take over the selling job—in fact, we've all had to lend a hand on the selling end at various times. But, whenever there is a difficult selling problem and an equally difficult production problem existing at the same time, I always seem to rationalize myself into straightening out the production bottleneck first."

In the spring of 1952, Tom Heath talked to the placement personnel at a nearby business school, hoping to interest a young graduate in taking the job of sales manager. He soon found that Kitchen Housewares' inability to offer anything but a small drawing account precluded reasonable hope of obtaining a man from this source.

Heath and Iverson had several times remarked upon the effective manner in which Clifford Walsh, a salesman for a special type of wire, approached their company. For example, when Walsh found that Kitchen Housewares seldom used his type of wire, he set about discovering new uses for it within the framework of their product line.

Shortly after April, 1953, Walsh resigned his position with the wire company to become an independent manufacturers' agent. He had previously asked to handle the Kitchen Housewares industrial business with the expressed hope that, should he greatly increase sales, he would be able to buy an interest in the company.

Two months after Walsh started to sell for Kitchen Housewares, he had increased sales by $20,000 and declared that he expected to account for a minimum of $100,000 new sales by December 31, 1953. He was paid a straight commission and was given a small drawing account after the first month.

PRODUCTION COST

Kitchen Housewares' old and often inadequate machinery sometimes inflated production costs to a point where Heath found it difficult to quote a competitive price. For example, the french-fry basket sold for $3.75 per dozen against a competitor's price of $3.20 per dozen. By using a conventional handle, the price was reduced to $3.50 per dozen, only to be offset by a competitor's price of $3.00 per dozen. Although most buyers admitted that Kitchen Housewares' item was superior in quality and appearance, the cheaper competitive items seemed to satisfy the housewife on both these points.

At first, Heath did not believe he could reduce the manufacturing cost of Kitchen Housewares' french-fry basket without investing in a large and expensive press. French-fry baskets were ordinarily made from wire mesh which was stamped to basket shape in one operation. In the

Exhibit 5

KITCHEN HOUSEWARES COMPANY, INC.
MANUFACTURING COST SHEET, NOVEMBER 17, 1951
100 FRENCH-FRY BASKETS, DELUXE MODEL NO. 320

41 pounds wire at 7 cents	$ 2.87
5% waste, 2 pounds at 7 cents	0.14
Material cost	$ 3.01
Straighten and cut wire, 43 pounds at 2½ cents	1.07
Piece rates	6.38
5% make-up and repair (5% × 6.38)	0.32
Direct labor	$ 7.77
Material	3.01
Labor	7.77
Overhead*	7.77
Tinning 41 pounds of finished goods at 20 cents	8.20
Cartons	1.34
Cost to manufacture	$28.09
Profit at 10% of selling price	3.13
	$31.22
Sales price per dozen 31.32/100 × 12	$ 3.75

* Overhead is computed at 100% of direct labor on all stock items.
Overhead is computed on the following sliding scale for all special orders and job lots:

5,000 pieces	170% of direct labor
10,000 pieces	140% of direct labor
15,000 pieces	120% of direct labor

Kitchen Housewares' plant, however, the fry basket was made by welding lengths of straight wire to form the bottom grille and then shaping the sides with a hand press operated with a 5-foot wooden lever.

Since the manufacturing processes could not be changed without a large capital investment, Heath tried experimenting with different materials and finishes. Normally the various products were tinned after the shaping and welding processes. Tinning was performed by an outside manufacturer and was a significant cost, ranging between 25 and 30 per cent of total manufacturing cost (Exhibit 5). Heath's first effort to reduce costs was through use of nickel-plated wire to eliminate the tinning process. The difficulty with nickel-plated wire, however, was that the cut ends of the wire tended to rust. Heath then discovered that tin-plated wire could be purchased much more cheaply than the nickel-plated wire and was equally satisfactory for most work.

These experiments with preplated wire failed initially because Kitchen Housewares' electric welders discolored the wire. Various alternatives were considered. New controls for the old machines would cost $200. To install an adequate secondhand welder would have cost about $300, as against the $800 cost of a new machine. At the same time, need developed for an electric paint-baking oven. A number of orders had been received for display racks with a baked-enamel finish. The installed cost of such an oven was about $1,000.

By June, 1953, both the new $800 welder and the baking oven had been purchased. Four additional small new welders had also been installed at a cost of several hundred dollars each. The purchase of such new equipment was generally made on the basis of either of the following two reasons: (1) A specific pending order could not be completed without the new equipment, and the contribution to overhead and profit anticipated from this order would at least equal the cost of the new machinery. (2) The increase in contribution to overhead and profit gained by processing existing shop orders on a new machine, as compared to doing the work on an old machine, would be at least equal to the cost of the new machine. Actually, the first of the foregoing rules was far more persuasive, and most of the new machinery was procured for that reason. If an old piece of equipment could be used to produce an item, their limited capital was ordinarily not employed to buy a new machine. In fact, most of the new equipment was purchased with borrowed money.

Even with the five new welders, Tom Heath found it necessary to operate a second shift in June, 1953. Much of the available floor space was employed to store work in process. Still more space was occupied by some of the original machinery purchased at the auction. Much of this original equipment was special-purpose machinery. Heath was seriously considering selling this equipment even though it might mean cutting several of the standard items from his kitchenware line.

The new machinery had so loaded the ancient electrical circuits that the addition of any more equipment would necessitate the expenditure of at least $1,000 for new main electrical lines. The main line-shaft motor had broken down, and inspection proved that it also had been heavily overloaded. This breakdown necessitated the addition of another motor and division of the main electrical line into two sections at the cost of about $300. "The simple fact," said Tom Heath, "is that we've just about reached our capacity in these two shops." Iverson and Heath had already made some inquiries about renting the first floor of the building.

THE WORK FORCE

Personnel in November, 1951, consisted of the 2 active partners, a foreman, an elderly shipper, a young man, and 9 girls working in the plant. Three of the girls, the foreman, and the shipper had worked for the old company, the latter two for more than thirty years. Labor turnover was high. During September and October, Heath had hired 21 girls, 14 of whom had lasted less than two weeks. Many of these had worked only one day. The girls seldom announced that they were leaving; they merely did not appear for work.

Heath followed the practice of taking each new candidate through the plant and pointing out the nature of the work. He stressed that it was often dirty and laborious. There was no need to emphasize the fact that the plant was also very noisy and likely to be chilly during the winter months. Heath also took care to point out to each applicant that he could not afford to pay for holidays, vacations, or fringe benefits such as hospital insurance. He usually wound up his talk by saying: "Basically, Miss Jones, the only pay in any form that you receive is for the actual time you put in the shop producing goods." In spite of this, new girls continued to accept employment and turnover continued to be high.

In the hope of finding out how to improve labor turnover, Heath contacted the state employment office from which most of the applicants were sent. The director assured him that the labor market for factory girls was very tight in his area and that all employers were receiving "bottom of the barrel" workers. In particular, Kitchen Housewares Company, as a very small company, was getting "drifters and girls who wanted to work just long enough to collect employment insurance."

The usual seasonal drop in sales appeared in the late spring of 1952. As an offset, Tom Heath had secured a $10,000 government order, but the steel strike prevented him from processing it during the summer months. Fortunately, he was not forced to discharge any of his work force, since the majority of the women who left did so voluntarily to take care of their children during the summer vacation. When the steel for the government order finally arrived, Kitchen Housewares had only 6 women on its payroll. A newspaper advertisement provided 35 applicants. By June, 1953, the work force consisted of the senior foreman, the night foreman, a straightening-machine operator, a move boy, a working forelady, and 19 girls.

As business increased, Heath and Iverson granted a week's paid vacation to all employees who had been with the company a year. A soft-drink dispensing machine was added, which the employees were free to use at any time.

Some labor problems were already beginning to appear. The 6 girls who had been with the company during the summer of 1952 considered themselves "old hands." When it became necessary to operate a night shift, one of these "old" girls complained bitterly that the night operator left her welding machine in improper condition. Eventually she demanded that either the foreman schedule the night work onto some other welder or she would resign. The company refused to acquiesce, and the woman angrily left.

Hours of work were from 7:00 A.M. to 4:00 P.M. Heath had initially tried several times to get the workers to accept an 8:00 to 5:00 work period. But his best workers, the older girls, objected; so he continued to rise at dawn to be on the job with them. With the advent of the second 4:00 to 11:00 P.M. shift, Tom Heath usually arrived at the plant around 9:00 A.M. and left at 6:00 P.M. He was, in general, satisfied with the friendly atmosphere that existed in the company. Relationships between the partners and the workers were very informal; in some cases they were on a first-name basis.

WAGE PAYMENTS

New girls were started at 75 cents an hour. At the end of the first month, the rate was raised to 80 cents per hour, and at the end of the second month to 85 cents per hour. This was the top hourly wage rate. However, nearly all the jobs had an assigned piece rate. At the end of a week a worker's piece-rate earnings were totaled and compared with her earnings computed on an hourly basis; she was paid the higher of the two. It was expected that at the end of three months an average worker would be earning about 85 cents per hour and a good worker would be averaging about $1.10 per hour.

Each worker submitted a daily job card, which she filled out herself. On it she listed the job numbers, number of pieces, and the time spent for each batch. From these cards, Heath made up a weekly earnings analysis for each worker, as at the top of page 223.

Although nothing definite had been said, Tom Heath had heard rumors that the "old hands" wanted some monetary recognition for their loyalty and seniority. They felt that it was unfair to be dropped from a piece rate which was averaging $1.10 to $1.25 per hour to the regular hourly rate of 85 cents per hour at the start of a new job while waiting

JANE JONES

Date	*Total Earned under Piece Rate for Day*	*Total Earned on Hourly Rate*
November 19	3.61	$6.00
November 20	2.88	6.00
November 21	No piece-rate report	6.00
November 23	3.17	6.00
November 24	2.40	6.00

Time spent waiting for work 1 hour 20 minutes at 75 cents per hour cost the company $1.00.

for a new piece rate to be set or when poor scheduling caused them to go onto work which did not bear a piece rate.

Tom Heath disputed their claim that there was no loss in efficiency when working under the hourly rate. He did agree that the gap was perhaps too wide in the case of the experienced girls, and he was considering a basic 95 cents hourly rate for those employees who had been with him for at least a year.

Heath recognized that a girl could easily falsify her card for minor amounts. But since he and Iverson were familiar with the lots being processed and the number of items in each lot, he did not consider it a problem. He intended to spend the vacation week, while the plant was shut down, in developing a ticket with detachable stubs which would accompany each order through the plant.

More important to him was the difference between the piece rate and the hourly rates paid while learning. If a girl did not surpass her hourly rate by the end of the third month, she was dismissed. Most of the indifferent and inefficient workers resigned before the third month was up. However, the first three months could be costly. Heath considered the "wait for work" periods to be another problem. These could be traced back to poor scheduling of the work flow.

ACCOUNTING AND PRODUCTION CONTROL

Kitchen Housewares Company boasted no office. In one corner of the shop, Iverson's desk was piled high with samples, papers, and other odds and ends. Nearby, Heath used a stand-up foreman's-type desk for his work place. The books of account were at first kept on a part-time basis by Mr. Stein's secretary. By the late spring, 1953, she was devoting full time to Kitchen Housewares Company and had been placed on its payroll. The accounting records were audited once annually by a CPA who prepared the year-end statements (Exhibits 6 and 7, pp. 224 and 225).

Most of the company's control records were kept on a series of spring

Exhibit 6

KITCHEN HOUSEWARES COMPANY, INC.
COMPARATIVE BALANCE SHEETS AS OF DECEMBER 31

	*1951**	*1952*
ASSETS		
Cash in Bank and on Hand	$ 948.77	$ 523.95
Accounts Receivable, Trade	1,349.66	12,707.27
Inventories of Raw Materials, Work in Process, and Finished Goods at Estimated Cost	15,253.82	19,854.00
Total Current Assets	$17,552.25	$33,085.22
Machinery and Equipment (net)	4,292.00	4,439.74
Prepaid Insurance	188.97	.....
Deposits	75.00	325.00
Total Assets	$22,033.22	$37,849.96
LIABILITIES AND NET WORTH		
Accounts Payable, Trade	$ 2,605.45	$ 3,892.72
Notes Payable Bank, Unsecured	....	2,145.00
Loans Payable	....	5,070.00
Machinery Notes Payable (Note 1)	2,765.00	....
Notes Payable Officers (Note 2)	16,350.00	26,704.06
Accrued Taxes	424.77	763.59
Accrued Wages	431.08	946.95
Accrued Interest	346.17	873.00
Taxes Withheld from Employees' Wages	718.98	1,799.07
Total Current Liabilities	$23,641.45	$42,194.39
Capital Stock:		
Authorized 900 Shares of No-Par Value; Outstanding and Issued 300 Shares	3,000.00	3,000.00
Deficit from Operations	(4,608.23)	(7,344.43)
Total Liabilities and Net Worth	$22,033.22	$37,849.96

Note 1: The machinery notes payable are secured by the personal endorsements of the three officers of the company.

Note 2: Notes payable to officers are subordinated to other notes payable, accounts payable, and all other indebtedness of the company.

* Company commenced operations, January 26, 1951.

clips hanging from nails over Heath's desk. Initially, the accounts-payable file was also handled in that manner, but more recently it had been given to the secretary to keep.

The finished-goods inventory cards were held on one of these clips. Entries were made on these cards weekly, and each card contained the following information:

NAME AND STOCK NUMBER OF ITEM

Orders on hand
Finished in stock
Number of units waiting to be tinned
Number of units in process

The inventory record was used by Heath during the first year of the company's existence as a basis for production planning. At the end of every week, he examined the cards and from them estimated the stock

Exhibit 7

KITCHEN HOUSEWARES COMPANY, INC.
Comparative Profit and Loss Statements

	January 26, 1951 to December 31, 1951		*January 1, 1952 to December 31, 1952*	
Sales		$32,441.08		$74,263.47
Beginning inventory	$ 1,221.00		$15,253.82	
Purchases	13,938.49		14,628.17	
Freight-in	689.22		3,593.30	
Direct labor	8,521.45		21,728.25	
Indirect labor	3,972.49		8,464.89	
Light, heat, and power	270.00		802.04	
Tool expense	661.05		2,655.58	
Rent	1,864.00		2,616.00	
Machinery depreciation	1,057.50		1,123.74	
Taxes	952.09		1,676.58	
Supplies	1,901.48		2,777.68	
Outside work	8,683.55		7,476.24	
Insurance expense	198.93		836.31	
Repairs	421.08		467.49	
Total charge to manufacturing	$44,352.33		$84,100.09	
Less inventories of raw material, work in process, finished goods, and finding as December 31, 1951	15,253.82		19,854.00	
Cost of sales		29,098.51		64,246.09
Gross profit		$ 3,342.57		$10,017.38
Officers' salaries	$ 4,520.00		$ 5,275.00	
Commissions	1,125.63		2,013.40	
Price lists	269.65		1,268.67	
Miscellaneous selling expense	533.96		1,293.12	
Office expense	268.50		163.43	
Telephone expense	157.79		421.81	
Legal and accounting	......		323.77	
Miscellaneous expense	286.68		155.86	
Total selling and administrative expense		7,162.21		10,915.06
Net loss on operations		($ 3,819.64)		($ 897.68)
Other charges:				
Interest expense	$ 391.25		$ 1,059.89	
Sales discounts	490.73		904.89	
	$ 881.98		$ 1,964.78	
Less purchase discounts	93.39		126.26	
Other charges (net)		788.59		1,838.52
Net loss		($ 4,608.23)		($ 2,736.20)

levels for each item four weeks hence. He used a four-week period because that was the average time it took for an order to be processed through the shop from raw wire to packaged goods. Heath then wrote out a cutting order for any items which would be out of stock or at a dangerously low inventory level at the end of the four-week period.

Heath's judgment and experience determined the size of individual cutting orders. Priority was given to those items most nearly out of stock or to special orders with delivery dates in the near future. The actual amount of work scheduled for any one week was computed from the estimated direct labor of the planned work. The allowances for direct labor were obtained from the cost sheets for stock items (Exhibit 5) or from a direct-labor estimate in the case of a special job.

For example, Heath knew that the girls were paid an average of $35 per week, or a total of $280 for the 8 girls employed during the first year. Regardless of the number of different jobs, this $280 was the probable maximum he would spend for direct labor in any one week. He then added up the estimated direct-labor charges for cutting orders, taking the top priority cutting-order first, until the direct-labor cost of the orders approximated a total of $280. His work-sheet computation then would appear as below:

Priority 1 2,000	Units of #90B	at labor cost	$4.00/100	$ 80.00
Priority 2 5,000	Units of #1444	at labor cost	3.50/100	175.00
Priority 3 1,000	Units #762	at labor cost	2.40/100	24.00
Total labor cost for one week's cutting work				$279.00

Heath realized that this system left much to be desired and that it probably would break down under a flow of rush orders. As the proportion of time spent on job orders, such as display racks and industrial goods, increased, Heath stopped scheduling the cutting process and continued to schedule only the bottleneck operation, the welding process.

The welding process was usually one of the middle operations on a unit; it was ordinarily preceded by the cutting and bending operations and followed by trimming and finishing. Heath had expected his senior foreman to use the assigned welding schedules as a basis for developing a cutting schedule and for preparation of a machine-load chart which would feed the required work to the welders. This plan was, however, not operating successfully.

Many of the larger orders called for interim deliveries of smaller lots. The senior foreman, however, would frequently schedule completion of certain operations for the entire order, even though the welding operation was scheduled to process only one fifth or less of the total order. This practice tremendously increased the work-in-process inventory and tended to create bottlenecks and storage problems all along the line.

The senior foreman also frequently preferred to use some of the older machines with which he was more familiar but which required use of the highest-skilled workers to produce work of satisfactory quality. Heath and Iverson hoped to be able to solve this problem by transferring the night foreman to the day shift and then to promote the straightening-machine operator to the position of night foreman. They

Exhibit 8

KITCHEN HOUSEWARES COMPANY, INC.

TIME-STUDY SHEET

Weld Thayer Basket
Operator: Mary M.
Study by: T. H.

Operation	*Reading*	*Adjusted Operations Time*
1. Load bench with long filler (6 pcs) / 2. Load bench with short filler (14 pcs)	20 pcs at 0.002*	0.040
3. Load jig	0.48—80†	
	0.48—80	
	0.50—80	
	(0.48—85)‡	0.680
4. Weld and away	0.35—90	
	0.34—90	
	(0.35—90)‡	0.525
5. Count and put in truck (47 pcs)	(1.80—80)§	0.051
		1.296
Personal and fatigue 11%		0.143
		1.439

$$\frac{1.44}{80} \times 1.10 = 0.0198 = 2 \text{ cents per pc}$$

Cycle checks for operations 3 and 4:

No.	*Continuous Reading*	*Actual time for Operations 3 and 4*	*No.*	*Continuous Reading*	*Actual time for Operations 3 and 4*
1	0.65	0.81	6	0.02	0.92
2	0.58	0.93	7	0.90	0.88
3	0.38	0.80	8	0.70	0.80
4	0.26	0.88	9	0.60	0.90
5	0.10	0.84			

Piece rate set $2.00 per 100 pcs., 3/18/53

* Time computed from previous studies.

† 0.48 is the actual time in minutes.

0.80 indicates this worker was $\frac{80}{60}$, or 30% more efficient on this operation than could be expected of the normal worker.

‡ Bracketed figures are averages used as the basis for adjusted times, i.e.,

$$148 \times \frac{85}{60} = 0.68 \quad \text{and} \quad 0.35 \times \frac{90}{60} = 0.525$$

§ $\frac{1.80}{0.47} \times \frac{80}{60} = 0.051$

hoped that the night foreman could be developed into a good assistant for Heath and eventually might be able to take over the time-study work and operate a detailed scheduling system.

Heath endeavored to make time studies on all operations. This was done with the full co-operation of the employees, most of whom were able to improve their total pay under the piece-rate system. Heath had watched output carefully under both methods and had found that it increased considerably when piece rates were substituted. In one case, output had been about 300 pieces an hour at the day rate of 85 cents per hour; when a piece rate was substituted, the operator increased her output to about 500 pieces an hour and her wages to about $1.10 per hour.

Heath followed the policy of never lowering a rate once it had been set. Depending on the size of the job, he might spend anywhere from a half hour to a full morning setting the piece rate and developing better methods for performing the operation. For example, as a result of Tom Heath's experiments, a job had recently been tooled with new-type Formica jigs which appreciably cut the time for loading operation. Heath described his time-study work (Exhibit 8, p. 227) as "something that would cause a professional time-study man to throw up his hands. I know my workers, however, and they know me; so a few readings on a small job seem to work out pretty well. Furthermore, I usually only record every other reading. Anyway, I don't have time to do the more thorough job I would like to do."

MATERIALS CONTROL

The materials inventory was maintained on 4 × 6-inch cards. Each time the foreman drew wire from stock, he dropped a slip showing the size and number of pounds used into a small wooden box. These amounts were later entered on the inventory cards. Although Heath had originally performed most of the bookkeeping on these control records, he was gradually shifting the written work to his new secretary.

Control of materials inventory was complicated by the Controlled Materials Program (CMP) in the spring of 1950. Since Kitchen Housewares Company had no history of production for 1950 or 1949, it was forced to base its request for an allotment of steel on estimated sales. Its first application for 40 tons of steel wire per quarter was promptly denied. The partners appealed the decision to the appeal board set up for that purpose; and since their products did not appear on the official list, they were refused once again. The board recommended that they procure their steel on the "free market"—that is, the portion of steel production that was not covered by allotments. Apparently, this did not exist, or at least the partners could not find it.

After a few months, CMP set up field offices to handle directly the problems of the smaller manufacturers. Through one of these field offices the company was able to obtain an allotment of 40 tons per quarter. Sales, however, did not come up to expectations, and only about 20 tons of the fourth-quarter allotment were fabricated. This necessitated a heavy investment in unused inventory. After the difficulties of finding steel before the allotment was granted, neither partner wanted to return any sizable amount of the unused portion, although they planned to cut back on their first quarter of 1952 requirements. Increased business in 1952 solved this difficulty.

WORKING CAPITAL

The shortage of working capital was a continuing problem during the first ten months of the company's existence. At times the cash balance fell to a dangerously low point, once even reaching 46 cents. Initially, each of the three men—Heath, Iverson, and Stein—contributed $1,000. Most of this was used for the cash payment on the machinery. As more cash was needed, the officer who at the moment was best able to supply it loaned it to the company on an indefinite repayment basis. This was done deliberately, since the officers wished to keep the ownership interest equal. By December 31, 1952, $26,704 in notes to officers was outstanding.

During the summer of 1951, Heath and Iverson had approached a local banker for a working-capital loan. The banker had looked over their statements and had stated that he would lend the money, but only by discounting their receivables. They had discussed the matter with Mr. Stein, who had said, "I may be old fashioned, boys; but whenever I hear about a firm that is discounting its receivables, I begin to wonder whether it is a good credit risk."

Heath and Iverson decided that their situation did not warrant discounting receivables. Much of their inventory was in unfinished steel, a very salable item. They had over $2,000 in receivables. The following day they returned to the bank and told the loan officer they would be very happy to borrow the money on a short-term unsecured note. After a few minutes' conversation they emerged with the loan. Thereafter, they had no difficulty obtaining small unsecured bank loans whenever they wished.

Initially, the company's steel suppliers were reluctant to advance credit. As Heath paid for each order promptly and forwarded the company's latest financial reports whenever asked, the amount of credit available to it steadily increased. Eventually, the combined line of credit from these raw-material suppliers was over $2,000.

The first two years in business had left the men little time for planning much beyond tomorrow. Kitchen Housewares was, however, still in business, and the sales volume was expanding. Heath considered survival in such a highly competitive industry during the first few years in itself an accomplishment.

Both active partners were drawing only $50 per week in salary. In

Heath's case, his wife had gone to work to aid the family finances. Despite the hard work and continuing struggle, Heath felt he had made a good choice. "We should get into the black for at least $8,000 this year," Tom Heath said; "of course we still have to do something about a more efficient production setup, particularly if sales continue to increase."

Hobart Instrument Company

In the spring of 1953 Henry Baker, aged twenty-six, was looking for a business which he could manage personally upon graduation from a business school. He was considering requesting his father to purchase the Hobart Instrument Company; he believed that his father would guide him in the initial phases of the business. The Hobart Instrument Company, located in Chicago, Illinois, manufactured liquid-level gauges, well and U-tube manometers, absolute pressure manometers, constant-feed lubricators, electronic-level controls, electronic pressure gauges, and dynamic measuring equipment.

Mr. Baker had entered the armed services directly after receiving a mechanical engineering degree and had served for two years as an officer in the U.S. Corps of Engineers. Since his high-school days Mr. Baker had been keenly interested in mechanical and electrical experiments. He had built radios and phonograph players and at one time had constructed an improvised air-conditioning system for his college fraternity house.

Concerning the possibility of managing a small family-owned business, Mr. Baker said: "I believe I will work harder, get more experience, and have more fun if I work for myself than if I work for a large corporation." Mr. Baker believed that his educational background and Army experience qualified him to manage a small-instrument business.

A lawyer who handled the legal affairs of the Hobart Instrument Company had introduced Mr. Baker to Mr. J. L. Hobart, aged fifty-three, president of the company. Mr. Hobart gave Mr. Baker all the information about the Hobart company which was readily available.

HISTORY OF THE HOBART COMPANY

In 1935, Mr. Hobart, who had been in the instrument business since 1928, and Mr. Haddock formed the Hobart Instrument Company to manufacture Foto-Flo meters and steam recording flo-meters. As a result of a disagreement on company policies, Mr. Hobart sold his share in the company to Mr. Haddock in 1937. In October, 1939, Mr. Hobart repurchased the company from Mr. Haddock.

In December, 1947, the Hobart Instrument Company purchased the equipment and assets of the Allen Potter Company (not incorporated), which had been engaged in the manufacture of manometers[1] exclusively for the Hobart Instrument Company. The total cost of purchasing the Allen Potter Company was $8,900, of which $900 was paid in cash and liabilities totaling $8,000 were assumed.

An electronics division of the Hobart company was started in 1950 with the hiring of an electronics engineer and the purchase of electronics equipment.

CURRENT STATUS

The Hobart Instrument Company was owned and operated by Mr. Hobart and Mr. E. E. Cummings, thirty-two years of age, who served as vice-president in charge of operations. Common-stock ownership was divided as follows:

Authorized shares		10,000
Total outstanding shares		7,500
Mr. Hobart	5,700	
Mr. Cummings	1,600	
Miscellaneous outstanding	200	

In 1953, Mr. Hobart and Mr. Cummings wanted to sell their stock in the company, since they preferred to set up a sales-engineering firm which would have no manufacturing activities. Both men, however, were willing to render general management aid and service to help the new owners become established in the business.

Mr. Hobart stated that the assets of the company, including 100 per cent of the stock, could be delivered to a buyer for $53,000, plus the cost of purchasing the 200 miscellaneous shares from the various holders at a price between $5 and $10 a share. Mr. Hobart and Mr. Cummings, however, desired to retain a distributorship for Hobart products in the surrounding area.

The results of operations from 1948 to 1951 are given in Exhibits 1, 2, and 3.

Mr. Hobart told Mr. Baker that the company had developed several items which were leaders in their respective fields:

1. An electronic level tank control, used extensively in dairies and chemical plants where foamy liquids are encountered. The electronic control was insensitive to foam and therefore was claimed to measure the true liquid level.
2. An oil-tank gauge for domestic heating installations. Mr. Hobart stated that the three other United States manufacturers of this

[1] A manometer is an instrument for measuring the pressure of gases and vapors by balancing the gas force against a column of mercury, a spring, or an elastic diaphragm.

Exhibit 1

HOBART INSTRUMENT COMPANY

PROFIT AND LOSS STATEMENTS, 1948–51

	1948		1949		1950		1951	
Net sales	$108,439	100.0%	$226,994	100.0%	$291,461	100.0%	$265,249	100.0%
Cost of goods sold	70,320	64.9	138,870	61.8	191,924	65.8	152,087	57.3
Gross profit	$ 38,119	35.1	$ 88,124	38.2	$ 99,537	34.2	$113,162	42.7
Selling and administrative and general expense*	38,009	35.0	82,830	36.5	85,266	29.3	100,400	37.9
Net operating profit	$ 110	0.1	$ 5,294	2.3	$ 14,271	4.9	$ 12,761	4.8
Other income	1,138	1.1	937	0.4	1,084	0.4	2,373	0.9
	$ 1,248		$ 6,231		$ 15,355		$ 15,134	
Other expenses	909	0.8	5,540	2.4	3,553	1.2	3,196	1.2
Net profit before taxes	$ 339	0.3	$ 691	0.3	$ 11,802	4.1	$ 11,938	4.5
Federal income and excess profits tax	100	0.1	325	0.1	3,200	1.1	3,150	1.2
Net profit	$ 239	0.2	$ 366	0.2	$ 8,602	3.0	$ 8,788	3.3

* Includes executive salaries of Messrs. Hobart and Cummings at $14,900 a year.

Source: Company records.

Exhibit 2

HOBART INSTRUMENT COMPANY

PROFIT AND LOSS STATEMENT, FISCAL YEAR 1951

			Percentage of Net Sales
Gross sales	$266,747		
Less: Returns and allowances	1,498		
Net sales		$265,249	100.0%
Cost of sales		54,756	20.7
		$210,493	
Manufacturing expense:			
Direct labor	$ 70,568		
Indirect labor	10,203		
Insurance	499		
Light, power, and maintenance	3,153		
Miscellaneous tool and shop expenses	6,617		
Depreciation	2,691		
Rent	3,600	97,331	36.6
Gross profit		$113,162	42.7
Selling expense:			
Advertising	$ 13,664		
Auto expense	1,145		
Sales expenses	5,187		
Sales salaries and commissions	40,038		
Bad debt	1,573		
Freight and miscellaneous	859	$ 62,466	23.6
Administrative and general expense:			
Administrative salaries	$ 13,900		
Office salaries	7,029		
Legal and professional	1,300		
Office supplies and expenses	2,758		
Taxes	4,126		
Telephone and telegraph	3,393		
Traveling expenses	1,836		
Other miscellaneous expenses	3,592	$ 37,934	14.3
Other income:			
Interest, discounts, and miscellaneous	$ 1,861		
Freight and sales tax invoiced to customers	512	$ 2,373	0.9
Other expense:			
Discounts and interest paid	$ 2,911		
Patent expense	285	$ 3,196	1.2
Net profit before taxes		$ 11,939	4.5
Taxes, 1951		3,150	1.2
Net profit		$ 8,789	3.3

Source: Company records.

type gauge had been unable to keep up with their orders because of material shortages and increased demand.

3. A new simplified pressure switch development. In addition, Mr. Hobart stated that the Hobart company's electronic research was already at the point where a capable specialist could develop it into a highly profitable business.

Exhibit 3

HOBART INSTRUMENT COMPANY

BALANCE SHEET AS OF OCTOBER 31, 1952

ASSETS

American Air Lines Deposit		$ 425.00
Automobile	$ 833.00	
Equipment—Electronics Department	767.30	
Equipment—Other	19,926.40	
Furniture and Fixtures	1,920.70	
	$23,447.40	
Less: Reserve for Depreciation	10,078.52	13,368.88
Bank Account—Regular		255.17
—Payroll		595.02
—Bonds		30.06
Consigned Stock		815.25
Advance to Employees		150.62
Employee Hospital Insurance		13.60
Prepaid Insurance		411.07
Inventory		27,842.19
Hobart and Cummings (Miscellaneous Accounts)		1,605.19
Office Cash		21.29
Accounts Receivable		41,621.70
Prepaid Rent		1,000.00
St. Anne Foundry—Receivable		4,767.77
Shop Petty Cash		4.84
Midwest Crusher Instrument		20.01
Total Assets		$92,947.66

LIABILITIES AND NET WORTH

Reserve for Bad Debts		$ 1,000.00
Accrued Commissions		12,399.68
Accrued Interest		1,619.68
Mr. Cummings—Personal Account		322.10
Mr. Hobart—Miscellaneous Account		617.77
Hobart and Cummings—Notes Payable		19,064.32
Accounts Payable		5,774.00
Accrued Royalties		165.00
Accrued Salaries and Wages		1,679.18
Accrued Taxes		798.00
Old Age Benefits—Reserve		115.27
Accrued Taxes—State Unemployment		28.81
—Federal Unemployment		200.42
Withholding Tax Reserve		777.63
Bond Reserve		30.06
Loan (Cummings)		1,000.00
Loan (Hobart)		4,544.10
Loan (Treasurer of United States)		2,865.07
Total Liabilities		$53,001.09
Capital Stock		17,900.00
Surplus Account	$21,371.37	
Profit for Year	675.20	22,046.57
Total Liabilities and Net Worth		$92,947.66

Note: Ratio of current assets to current liabilities = 3.1 to 1.

Source: Company records.

The Hobart Instrument Company had obtained a patent on a certain type of manometer in 1943. The company also had a patent on an absolute pressure gauge. Four patents were pending in the electronics field.

The 1952 edition of *Thomas' Register* lists 34 manufacturers of manometers in the United States. Seven of these companies were located in Chicago.

Sales for the first ten months of 1952 were approximately as follows:

Manometers	$ 66,000
Electronic equipment	64,000
Gauges	18,000
Miscellaneous sales	3,500
Total	$151,500

In December, 1952, Mr. Hobart reported that the company's backlog of orders amounted to $71,000. By 1953 the electronics division accounted for 42 per cent of sales.

Orders were secured from manufacturers' agents in Boston, New York, Pittsburgh, Detroit, Chicago, Houston, San Francisco, and Los Angeles. These agents had exclusive territories and collected commissions on all sales, varying from 10 per cent on repair orders to 20 per cent to 30 per cent on product sales. Automobile companies, aircraft companies, and soap and chemical companies were among the users of Hobart instruments.

The Hobart plant contained 7,500 square feet of floor space in a one-story building and was rented for $250 a month. The lease on the plant space expired in May of 1953. Mr. Hobart believed that after May the rent on the plant would be increased more than $50 a month, and he recommended to Mr. Baker that the shop be moved to a lower rent area. The administrative office was located one block north of the plant, nearer the commercial section of town.

Job-shop methods of manufacturing were employed. Production runs were made on subassembly, but final assembly was made out of stock. Manufactured products often required extensive engineering and design services. These services were charged separately. Exhibit 4 lists the machine tools and electronics equipment owned by the Hobart Instrument Company.

Mr. Donald Keller, thirty-nine years old, was the electronics engineer of the company. He had been with the Hobart Instrument Company since 1948 and was formerly a field engineer with the Otis Elevator Company. Mr. Keller held both electrical engineering and mechanical engineering degrees and had also completed several courses in elec-

Exhibit 4

HOBART INSTRUMENT COMPANY

LIST OF EQUIPMENT ON HAND

1	48″ shear
1	48″ brake
1	marker, Aeromark
1	spray booth, 10′ × 4′ × 6′
1	bake oven, 5′ × 10′ × 6′
1	¾″ drill press, floor type
1	12-gauge nibbler
3	½″ drill presses, Craftsman bench type
1	½″ drill press, 4-spindle multiple, floor model with one pecunior tapper unit
1	power grinder, heavy duty, replaceable belt type
1	milling machine, #2 Brown & Sharp
1	milling machine, Cincinnati
1	shaper
1	Barden & Oliver #2 turret lathe with air chuck
1	turret lathe, heavy duty, 2″ capacity
1	turret lathe, ⅞″ capacity, complete with sheaves for variable drive
2	lathes, South Bend, 9″ swing, 36″ bed, floor model
1	lathe, 13″ swing, South Bend, 5′ bed
1	lathe, Logan, 9″ swing, floor model
2	drill presses, Duro-floor mounted
1	engraving machine, micro
1	electric welder, 150 amp. Craftsman, with complete gas-welding equipment
1	spot welder for 14 gauge
2	kick presses, 1″ capacity
1	kick press for eyelets, etc., floor mounting
1	drill press, small bench model
1	drill press, Cannady-Otto, floor mounted, 1″ capacity
1	power wood saw
1	saw, metal cutting, Wells
1	saw, vertical metal cutting, Delta type
1	sanding machine, vertical belt, Delta type
2	grinders, Craftsman for drills
Electronic Test Instruments:	
1	electronic volt ohmmeter
1	type 185A electronic switch
1	generator, audio signal
1	cathode-ray oscillograph
1	ohmmeter, micro
1	Brown recorder, circular chart
1	Brown recorder, strip chart
1	voltmeter, ohmmeter, electronic
1	special coil winding machine
1	special Hi-Pressure test unit
1	special test flow bench

Source: Company records.

tronics. Mr. James Carter, twenty-six, a former captain in the U.S. Air Corps, was in charge of shipments and purchases of standard items. Mr. William Ernst, forty-eight, was shop foreman, directly responsible for production under Mr. Cummings. Mr. Ernst was reported to have a vast background of supervisory machinist's experience; he had been with the Hobart Instrument Company since 1942. Fifteen shop machinists worked under Mr. Ernst. Miss Harriet Bell handled the company's bookkeeping and financial affairs. Except for Mr. Hobart and Mr. Cummings, the personnel would be willing to remain with the company in the event of its sale.

The Hobart Instrument Company had branched out into a number of diversified fields. Mr. Hobart believed that any new purchaser would want to curtail certain activities and expand others to achieve better operating efficiency. He suggested further that all experimental and developmental work be discontinued except that paid for by purchasers of Hobart products. Mr. Hobart estimated that, since the company had been started, $100,000 had been put into nonproductive research. Mr. Hobart and Mr. Cummings believed that one good mechanical engineer could easily take over their joint duties and develop the company into a highly profitable business.

After receiving the above information, Mr. Baker was anxious to interest his father in purchasing the company for him.

Sun Candy Company

In March, 1947, two middle-aged brothers, John and Fred Ruhl, of St. Louis, Missouri, were faced with the problem of building up business careers for themselves. They were considering the purchase of the Sun Candy Company of Chicago, which was for sale at a price of $200,000.

Mr. August Ruhl, father of Fred and John Ruhl, had emigrated from Germany to St. Louis in 1910, where he had built up a very successful business in the manufacture and sale of flour-milling machinery. Later he had acquired the Lanning Milling Company, one of the largest flour mills in the St. Louis area. He continued active management of both firms until 1946. In 1929 his eldest son, John, after graduating from Massachusetts Institute of Technology and Harvard Business School, joined the Lanning Milling Company as vice-president and treasurer. A younger son, Fred, had also graduated from Massachusetts Institute of Technology and Harvard Business School and had then spent six years at Northwestern University doing research work in flour engineering and product development. He was considered one of the best-qualified men in the country in this field. In 1940 he assumed the position of chief engineer and research director for the Lanning Milling Company.

In early 1947 Mr. August Ruhl decided that the mill industry was approaching the status of a public utility, with costs, prices, and profits depending more on government regulations than on individual initiative. Consequently, without consulting his sons, he sold the Lanning Milling Company to outside interests. John and Fred Ruhl had not anticipated this sale; and although they were left in comfortable financial circumstances, they no longer had definite business futures. Both men were qualified for high-salaried positions in the flour industry, but they wanted an enterprise of their own—one which they would not only finance but also manage and direct. They were not interested in joining another flour-milling company because they shared their father's skepticism regarding the difficulty of obtaining a satisfactory reward for individual initiative in this industry. Furthermore, their father's machinery company still occupied a predominant spot among flour-mill suppliers, and the brothers did not want to be dependent in any way on his reputation or backing. Accordingly, the brothers wanted either to sponsor a completely new venture or to buy and assume active management of an existing company in some field within range of their talents.

On March 1, 1947, John Ruhl received a letter from Mr. Jerome Meyers, a Chicago investment banker and acquaintance. Mr. Meyers wrote that he had learned from Mr. Allison Clark of Chicago that the Sun Candy Company in that area was up for sale at a price of about $200,000. This company had earned $80,000 before taxes during 1946 and $67,000 before taxes during the first two months of 1947. Mr. Clark was engaged in business brokerage, i.e., the expediting of transactions involving the sale, purchase, or reorganization of small business concerns, and the Ruhl brothers knew him to be a man with a reputation for reliability and integrity.

John Ruhl immediately telephoned both Mr. Clark and Mr. Meyers and stated that he and his brother would like to find out more about the proposal. Mr. Clark explained that he had learned of the opportunity through a "finder" who was an agent of the Sun company's present owners. The finder had first gone to a large investment banking house but had found that this firm, engaged in underwriting and distributing new security issues, was not interested in trying to refinance new businesses with assets of less than $500,000. Mr. Clark invited the Ruhl brothers to come to Chicago on March 10 to look over the plant and books of the Sun Candy Company. They agreed and also accepted Mr. Clark's offer to secure for them a thirty-day purchase option on the company.

In Chicago the Ruhl brothers talked with Mr. Clark, visited the Sun company's plant, and examined the firm's history and current position. The Sun Candy Company, established in 1921, produced a 2-ounce chocolate caramel candy roll, known as the "Sun Roll." This item sold for 5 cents until November, 1946, when the price was raised to 10 cents. The company leased a three-story, 60-foot by 100-foot building in Chicago. With its existing machinery about 10 million rolls could be produced yearly. Sales in 1946 amounted to about $500,000.

Before the war, Sun Rolls had been sold through independent salesmen and candy brokers, who received commissions amounting to 5 per cent of the manufacturers' selling price. These men received exclusive Sun Roll franchises for their territories but also handled many other nickel candy products for other small manufacturers. They sold to candy wholesalers throughout the country. Large candy makers generally maintained their own sales staffs rather than utilizing brokers and commission agents.

The production process for Sun Rolls was as follows: Sugar, condensed milk, and other ingredients were cooked in kettles for thirty minutes; cocoa and vegetable oil were added; and the mixture was placed in trays and allowed to cool. A special machine then stretched and pulled the candy to give it resiliency and chewiness; this quality was further developed by heating the compound in ovens for half an hour. The candy was next put through a chopping or grinding machine, which cut it into small particles; finally it was rolled, cut into segments, wrapped, and packed.

Sixty workers were employed in the plant under the supervision of Mr. Marowitz, the plant manager. He was thoroughly familiar with the candy industry; and although he owned no stock in the Sun Candy Company, he was willing to remain with the firm in the event of a change of ownership. Mr. Marowitz indicated that he would be able to reduce the labor force substantially if additional automatic packaging machines could be purchased.

Mr. J. J. Krell, president of the Sun Candy Company, owned one third of its stock; the remaining two thirds was divided between the estates of the two founders, both of whom had died in 1941. Mr. Krell, one of the largest candy brokers in the Chicago area, had joined the company in 1939, when it was suffering from severe declines in sales and profits. During the war years he had improved the company's financial condition and profits by selling 80 per cent of its products through his own brokerage agency to Chicago wholesalers. Previously, the Chicago market area had accounted for only one third of Sun Roll sales. Because Mr. Krell had not charged the Sun company any commission on these sales, selling expense had been reduced to 0.8 per cent of sales in 1945–46, as compared with an average prewar figure of 5 per cent. Mr. Krell's distribution policy had resulted, however, in a drastic slash in the quantity of Sun Rolls available to salesmen and dealers outside the Chicago area. Mr. Krell, as a broker, continued to distribute the products of other small candy manufacturers.

After price controls expired in the fall of 1946, the price of cocoa and condensed milk rose by about 300 per cent. Candy manufacturers generally met this condition by reducing the size of their 5-cent bars or by bringing out new bars to sell at 10 cents. Because of Sun Roll's cylindrical shape, the Sun company found that any change in the diameter of its product would render its automatic rolling and wrapping machinery useless and thus would greatly curtail production. The quality of the Sun Roll could be lowered somewhat, but the variations between different formulas were not sufficiently great to enable the company to make substantial cost savings without completely altering the characteristics of the product. Exhibit 1 shows the costs as of March 1, 1947, for three alternate Sun Roll formulas.

Exhibit 1

SUN CANDY COMPANY

COST OF INGREDIENTS FOR SUN ROLL CANDY AS OF MARCH 1, 1947

*Formula No. 1**

9 oz.	vegetable oil	$ 1.25 per lb.	$ 0.72
65 lbs.	sugar	8.20 per cwt.	5.33
125 lbs.	corn syrup	4.50 per cwt.	5.63
2 lbs.	salt	1.19 per cwt.	0.03
120 lbs.	sweetened condensed milk	12.50 per cwt.	15.00
30 lbs.	cocoa mix	23.92 per cwt.	7.18
10 lbs.	shortening	35.75 per cwt.	3.57
352 lbs.	(335 lbs. of candy after processing)		$37.46 or 11.2 cents per lb.

* This formula was being used for current production on March 1, 1947.

Formula No. 2

Substitute in Formula No. 1: 55 lbs. sugar, 135 lbs. corn syrup, and 20 lbs. cocoa mix for like items. Cost per pound of candy is 10.35 cents.

Formula No. 3

Substitute in Formula No. 1: 55 lbs. sugar, 140 lbs. corn syrup, 100 lbs. sweetened condensed milk, and 20 lbs. cocoa mix for like items, and 30 lbs. soya mix for 10 lbs. shortening. Cost per pound of candy is 10.30 cents.

In November, 1946, Mr. Krell decided to raise the price of the Sun Roll to 10 cents while maintaining its original weight of 2 ounces. After this policy was instituted, Chicago candy wholesalers no longer ordered Sun Roll. Mr. Krell therefore distributed the 10-cent Sun Roll solely through independent commission salesmen. In early 1947, twenty salesmen were handling the new Sun Roll bars; their combined territory included almost all the United States except Chicago. These salesmen did not buy the candy themselves but merely solicited orders from wholesalers and notified the Sun company, which then shipped the desired lots directly to customers.

Orders for the 10-cent bar poured in during January and February of 1947; gross sales during these months totaled $160,471, while sales expenses reverted to 5 per cent of sales. Net profits before taxes for January and February, 1947, totaled $67,000. These results had confirmed Mr. Krell's belief that the Sun Roll would sell well at 10 cents in the current market and that the company's unit profits on the 10-cent bar would be sizably increased. Mr. Krell had recognized, however, that a return to normal competitive conditions would force the Sun company to re-enter the 5-cent field, particularly since its major competitor was already selling for 5 cents a chocolate roll weighing 1⅞ ounces. Consequently, Mr. Krell had ordered $10,000 worth of new rolling and wrapping machinery and planned to change over to a 5-cent 1¼-ounce bar. This machinery was to be delivered in May, 1947.

In view of the company's current earnings, the Ruhl brothers questioned the present owners' reason for selling. Mr. Krell was in Florida; but it was explained that, as a broker, he had been under considerable pressure from his other candy-manufacturing clients to disassociate himself from the Sun company. Mr. Clark indicated Mr. Krell's position as follows: Mr. Krell had only taken a hand in the firm originally in order to help the Sun company out of a very tight spot; he had not intended to remain as long as he had, and he now felt that he had to give up either the manufacturing or the brokerage business. The Ruhl brothers surmised that Mr. Krell's stock in the Sun company had been given him either as a bonus for efficient performance or as an inducement for him to take over the management. They were told by Chicago business associates that large candy brokers such as Mr. Krell had been known to earn as much as $200,000 in some years. The heirs of the two original founders had never taken any active part in the management of the Sun company and were anxious to convert their share of the business into cash and divide the proceeds. During the war, dividend payments had totaled only $3,600 yearly; earnings had been allowed to accumulate in the business so that future management would be able to utilize the funds as it saw fit.

Mr. Clark stated that the sale price of the business represented the book value of the assets as of February 28, 1947, plus the value of the company's sugar quota and an additional $10,000 for estimated March profits. No attempt was being made to base the price on the unusually high profits of the past few months. The Ruhl brothers inspected the audited financial statements of the company (see Exhibits 2 and 3) and found the net worth of the concern as of February 28, 1947, to be $140,849.16. The balance sheet did not include any valuation on the company's annual sugar quota of 600,000 pounds. This figure had been fixed by Mr. Krell at $50,000, the amount being determined by multiplying the current price of sugar (8.2 cents per pound) by the company's annual quota. Although there was a possibility that sugar rationing might end before 1948, this was outweighed by the greater likelihood that the value of this quota would be increased because of retention of rationing coupled with an increase in the poundage allotment to each producer.

After spending two days in Chicago with the company, the Ruhl

Exhibit 2

SUN CANDY COMPANY

BALANCE SHEET AS OF FEBRUARY 28, 1947

ASSETS

Cash on Hand			$ 100.00
Cash in Bank			77,936.76
Accounts Receivable		$56,652.97	
Less: Discounts	$ 1,133.06		
Freight Reserve	2,266.12	3,394.18	53,253.79
Merchandise Inventory			61,619.10
Total Current Assets			$192,909.65
Unexpired Insurance			1,856.25
Deposits			415.00
Notes Receivable—Employee			1,475.00
Installation of Machinery		$ 4,153.51	
Less: Amortization		2,145.98	2,007.53
Machinery		$56,385.32	
Less: Depreciation		45,206.04	11,179.28
Total Assets			$209,842.71

LIABILITIES AND NET WORTH

Accounts Payable			$ 1,175.00
Due to Salesmen			3,157.38
Auditing Accrued			400.00
Payroll Accrued			797.10
Taxes Accrued:			
Federal Income Taxes:			
1947 (January and February Estimated)	$25,492.95		
1946 (balance)	24,579.31		
1944 (additional)	2,440.98		
1943 (additional)	1,692.98	$54,205.70	
State Franchise Taxes:			
1947	$ 2,973.81		
1946 (balance)	3,975.77		
1945 (balance)	687.10		
1944 (additional)	212.83	7,849.51	
Federal Old Age Tax		314.62	
State Unemployment Tax		424.74	
Federal Unemployment Taxes		47.20	
Withholding Taxes		622.30	63,464.07
Total Liabilities			$ 68,993.55
Common Stock (360 shares)			$ 360.00
Donated Surplus			4,000.00
Capital Surplus			34,596.12
Earned Surplus			101,893.04
Total Net Worth			$140,849.16
Total Liabilities and Net Worth			$209,842.71

Source: Company records.

brothers decided to make a brief investigation of the candy business in general and the reputation of the Sun Roll in particular. Accordingly, they secured from Mr. Marowitz the names of several Midwestern wholesalers who had purchased Sun Rolls during the past few months.

Exhibit 3

SUN CANDY COMPANY

OPERATING STATEMENT, JANUARY–FEBRUARY, 1947

Sales			$163,113.81
Less: Returns and allowances			2,642.90
Net sales			$160,470.91
Less: Discounts allowed and reserved			3,153.26
Net amount to be realized			$157,317.65
Cost of sales:			
Inventory (January 2, 1947)		$ 50,165.67	
Purchases		66,145.96	
Labor		11,627.26	
Payroll taxes		442.66	
Freight-in		101.26	
		$128,482.81	
Less: Inventory (February 28, 1947)	$61,619.10		
Discount on purchases	596.76	62,215.86	66,266.95
Gross profit			$ 91,050.70
Inside expenses:			
Supervision	$ 1,369.20		
Rent	1,250.00		
Light, heat, and power	806.54		
Factory supplies and expenses	262.39		
Uniforms	196.90		
Depreciation—installation	69.23		
Depreciation—machinery	384.22		
Repairs and maintenance	69.68	$ 4,408.16	
Selling expenses:			
Salesmen's commissions	$ 6,317.31		
Advertising	208.50		
Traveling expense	357.00	6,882.81	
Officers' salaries:			
J. J. Krell, president	$ 1,260.00		
I. H. Marowitz, plant manager	1,050.00	2,310.00	
General business expenses:			
Office salaries	$ 714.00		
Freight, parcel post, and express	4,242.70		
Shipping materials	226.31		
Insurance	400.00		
Stationery, printing, and postage	221.65		
Shipping salaries	507.72		
Bank charges	2.49		
General expenses	49.50		
Telephone and telegraph	75.42		
Payroll taxes	189.09		
Auditing and legal fees	650.00		
Storage and freezer charges	180.73		
State franchise tax accrual	2,973.81	10,433.42	24,034.39
Net operating income			$ 67,016.31
Add: Sales of shipping materials			70.39
Net profit			$ 67,086.70

The first interview was with a large St. Louis wholesale dealer who had a rather scornful opinion of the Sun Roll and of the company's policies. He said that the Sun Candy Company had not done as well as other manufacturers in keeping up deliveries to wholesalers during the war. Although he recognized the fact that all manufacturers had been forced to curtail shipments, he maintained that the Sun company, because of its policy of selling primarily through Mr. Krell in Chicago, had gone much further than its competitors in reducing his supplies. He further stated that, while he carried the Sun Roll before the war and was now carrying it again, he probably would not continue to stock Sun Rolls when the market picture shifted a little more. The Ruhl brothers checked the Sun company sales records and found that in 1945–46 this wholesaler had received three shipments from the company, which was more than most of its prewar customers had been able to obtain.

The St. Louis wholesaler also said that the 10-cent roll was not selling well and would be the first item he would drop when demand lessened. He pointed out to the Ruhl brothers that the labels had not been changed with the price increase; a 10-cent sticker had merely been pasted over the old 5-cent label. He denied that the quality of the candy was noticeably better, although Mr. Marowitz had maintained that the company was now using the most expensive of the three basic Sun Roll formulas, whereas previously they had shifted from one to another according to the cost and availability of the different materials.

The Ruhl brothers then called on Mr. Alvin Carter, sales manager of the Carter Candy Company in Milwaukee, Wisconsin. The Carter company was a relatively new entrant in the nickel candy field but had already established three or four different bars that were nationally advertised items; it had a much larger sales volume than the Sun Candy Company. Mr. Carter predicted that only five or six manufacturers of nationally distributed candy bars would survive the coming scramble. He believed that, when sugar rationing was discontinued, all the larger plants would greatly increase production in order to reduce unit costs and to secure as large a share of the market as possible. To be ready for this competitive situation, the Carter company had invested its wartime earnings in new machinery and was prepared to strive for extremely efficient high-volume production. The Carter company had also spent large sums on advertising to build up consumer demand for its candy, whereas the Sun Candy Company had carried only a nominal amount of advertising in trade journals.

Mr. Carter said that any really new developments in candy bars were immediately copied by all the big manufacturers and that large producers could shift from one type of bar to another as consumer preferences changed; however, the manufacturers generally tried to keep the number of bars being offered at any one time as low as possible. Mr.

Carter nevertheless felt that an individual could enter the candy industry on a small capital investment and occasionally could score a success with a regional or highly specialized business. As a general rule, however, he believed that only high-volume producers would be able to achieve a satisfactory profit margin.

Exhibit 4

SALES AND PROFITS OF FOUR MAJOR CANDY MANUFACTURERS, 1936–45

Year	Sales (000's Omitted)	Net Profit (000's Omitted)	Percentage of Sales	Year	Sales (000's Omitted)	Net Profit (000's Omitted)	Percentage of Sales
			HERSHEY CHOCOLATE CORPORATION (Hershey Bars, Chocolate, and Cocoa Products)				
1936.....	$37,393	$3,730	10.0	1941.....	55,505	5,944	10.7
1937.....	38,267	932	2.4	1942.....	60,370	5,012	8.3
1938.....	34,764	4,126	11.9	1943.....	65,915	5,403	8.2
1939.....	39,846	6,233	15.6	1944.....	79,190	5,272	6.7
1940.....	44,180	5,908	13.4	1945.....	71,241	5,017	7.0
			SWEETS COMPANY OF AMERICA, INC. ("Tootsie Rolls," Caramels, etc.)				
1936.....	$ 1,542	$ 68	4.4	1941.....	3,586	113	3.2
1937.....	2,045	63	3.1	1942.....	4,372	129	3.0
1938.....	2,099	100	4.8	1943.....	5,620	175	3.1
1939.....	1,882	32	1.7	1944.....	6,591	191	2.9
1940.....	2,463	34	1.4	1945.....	6,567	174	2.6
			D. L. CLARK COMPANY (Clark Bars, "Zig-Zags," etc.)				
1936.....	$ 2,606	$ 10	0.4	1941.....	4,787	309	6.5
1937.....	3,014	224	7.4	1942.....	6,439	413	6.4
1938.....	3,202	348	10.9	1943.....	8,307	475	5.7
1939.....	3,236	285	8.8	1944.....	10,441	391	3.7
1940.....	3,681	194	5.3	1945.....	8,192	314	3.8
			GENERAL CANDY CORPORATION ("Oh Henry" Bars, etc.)				
1936.....	$ 4,962	$ 275	5.5	1941.....	5,028	224	4.5
1937.....	5,758	185	3.2	1942.....	5,818	177	3.0
1938.....	4,364	145	3.3	1943.....	6,995	173	2.5
1939.....	3,730	171	4.6	1944.....	8,560	182	2.1
1940.....	3,986	134	3.4	1945.....	7,637	170	2.2

Source: *Survey of Listed Corporations* (Securities and Exchange Commission), data for 1936–42 in 1943 issue, pp. 68–73; for 1943–44 in 1945 issue, pp. 30–32; for 1944–45 in 1946 issue, pp. 36–37.

Mr. Carter gave the Ruhl brothers a breakdown of the sales dollar which he claimed a candy company must attain in order to be successful:

Cost of materials (including wrappers)	60.0 cents
Labor	10.0
Selling expenses	5.0
Freight	7.5
Discounts to wholesalers	2.0
Overhead and administration	10.5
Profit	5.0
Sales dollar	100.0 cents

Mr. Carter said that the only way to increase the profit margin was to reduce unit labor and overhead costs through increased production; one of the largest candy producers had been able to reduce its labor costs to 5 per cent.

Exhibit 5

PRODUCTION OF CANDY IN UNITED STATES, 1927–45

Year	Volume in Pounds (000's Omitted)	Pounds per Capita	Value (000's Omitted)	Per Capita Production in Dollars
1927	1,733,255	14.7	$401,398	$3.40
1928	1,756,079	14.7	403,131	3.36
1929	1,902,196	15.7	413,134	3.40
1930	1,789,360	14.5	367,533	2.99
1931	1,621,403	13.1	299,295	2.41
1932	1,625,186	13.0	237,634	1.90
1933	1,631,124	13.0	226,086	1.80
1934	1,815,770	14.3	259,979	2.05
1935	1,897,651	14.9	281,218	2.21
1936	2,048,721	16.0	308,383	2.41
1937	2,009,651	15.5	320,628	2.47
1938	1,955,000	15.0	298,000	2.29
1939	2,050,000	15.7	308,000	2.36
1940	2,225,000	16.9	336,000	2.55
1941	2,536,000	19.0	403,224	3.05
1942	2,519,000	18.7	490,000	3.64
1943	2,561,000	19.1	575,000	4.26
1944	2,804,000	20.5	658,000	4.81
1945	2,562,000	18.5	620,000	4.47

Source: *Industry Surveys* (New York: Standard & Poor's Corporation, November 15, 1946), p. B3–3.

The Ruhl brothers then visited investment houses and libraries to obtain professional analyses of the candy industry and its future. The general tenor of these forecasts indicated that as of January 1, 1947, the national demand for candy greatly exceeded the supply and that the short-run prospects for the leading candy producers were excellent. The increased costs of raw materials had brought about a temporary pricing problem which would be greatly aggravated if sugar rationing were abandoned while supplies of sugar were still scarce. Industry analysts nevertheless felt that consumers would be willing to bear these higher costs either by paying more for the same bars or by paying the same amount for a smaller bar. Additional information about the industry which the Ruhl brothers obtained is summarized in Exhibits 4, 5, and 6.

On their return to Chicago on March 17, the Ruhl brothers began to analyze the Sun company's financial statements in order to determine unit costs. They found that profits during January and February, 1947, amounted to 41 per cent of sales. Since the company's price to whole-

Exhibit 6

DISTRIBUTION OF CANDY IN UNITED STATES, 1927–44

Year	Percentage of Total Distributed Through—					
	Jobbers	Direct to Retailers		Direct to Consumers		U.S. Govt.
		Chain Stores	Independents	Own Stores	Mail Order	
1927	53.0	10.0	27.5	9.3	0.2	
1930	55.9	15.9	19.6	8.4	0.2	
1933	56.7	18.7	15.1	9.4	0.1	
1936	59.5	20.5	11.8	8.1	0.1	
1937	60.9	19.2	11.6	8.2	0.1	
1938	59.1	19.3	12.7	8.7	0.2	
1939	58.6	20.0	12.6	8.7	0.1	
1940	58.8	20.8	12.0	8.3	0.1	
1941	58.0	21.4	11.7	8.8	0.1	
1942	49.9	18.3	16.2	7.2	0.1	8.3
1943	48.6	17.3	15.9	6.5	0.1	11.6
1944	40.0	14.6	18.0	4.1	0.2	23.1

Source: *Industry Surveys* (New York: Standard & Poor's Corporation, November 15, 1946), B3–3.

salers was $1.36 per box, they deduced that the cost of a box of twenty-four 2-ounce rolls must be about 80 cents. Mr. Marowitz showed the brothers the following data which he had calculated for the 5-cent, 1¼-ounce bar which was to be produced in May:

Estimated Cost of Box of Twenty-four 1¼-Ounce Rolls
(Mr. Marowitz)

Candy (9 cents per pound)	18.00 cents
Labels	3.75
Box	4.00
Proportionate cost of shipping carton (holding 16 boxes)	1.00
Freight (1 cent per pound)	2.00
Selling cost (5 per cent of selling price)	3.40
Discounts (2 per cent of selling price)	1.36
Labor (2½ cents per pound)	5.00
Overhead (15 per cent of selling price)	10.20
Total cost	48.71 cents

This box would be sold to wholesalers for 68 cents. Unit profits would therefore amount to 19.29 cents, or about 28 per cent of sales. Mr. Marowitz explained that, although the candy in a box of twenty-four $1\frac{1}{4}$-ounce rolls would weigh only 30 ounces, candy costs were figured on a basis of 32 ounces to allow for shrinkage during processing.

The Ruhl brothers noted that the cost of materials in the formula currently being used in Sun Rolls was 11.2 cents per pound, while that of the cheapest acceptable substitute formula was 10.3 cents per pound (see Exhibit 1). Mr. Marowitz explained that his estimate of 9 cents per pound for materials was based on the belief that prices for cocoa and milk would decrease by May. He also stated that his figures for labels, boxes, and shipping containers had been set slightly higher than the present costs of these items because he felt that these prices would rise between March and May.

Mr. John Ruhl observed that Mr. Marowitz was calculating labor costs at 5 cents per box, or about 7 per cent of selling price, a figure considerably lower than Mr. Carter's estimate of what a relatively large and efficient manufacturer could expect to pay at full volume. Mr. Ruhl believed that 10 cents per box, or about 15 per cent of selling price, would be a more realistic labor cost for the Sun company. To check the validity of this assumption, he projected Mr. Marowitz's estimated cost figures for the $1\frac{1}{4}$-ounce bar to the current production of the 2-ounce bar. Using current material prices and a labor cost of 10 cents per box, he calculated the total cost of making and selling a box of twenty-four 2-ounce rolls in March, 1947, at 77 cents. This figure was close enough to the actual cost of 80 cents to convince Mr. Ruhl that 10 cents per box was a fair estimate of labor costs. He revised Mr. Marowitz's cost estimate for the $1\frac{1}{4}$-ounce roll accordingly, substituting the current prices of all materials and using a labor cost figure of 10 cents per box. The Ruhl brothers believed that their revised estimate reflected the minimum cost for a box of twenty-four $1\frac{1}{4}$-ounce rolls attainable with the company's present capacity:

Estimated Cost of Box of Twenty-four $1\frac{1}{4}$-Ounce Rolls
(Mr. Ruhl)

Candy (11.2 cents per pound)	22.40 cents
Box	3.50
Labels	3.00
Proportionate cost of shipping carton (holding 16 boxes)	0.75
Freight (1 cent per pound)	2.00
Selling expense (5 per cent of selling price)	3.40
Discount (2 per cent of selling price)	1.36
Labor (5 cents per pound)	10.00
Overhead (15 per cent of selling price)	10.20
Total	56.61 cents

This box would be sold to wholesalers at 68 cents, leaving a profit for the Sun company of 11.39 cents per box, or 16.75 per cent of sales.

(Mr. Ruhl's figures allowed the same margin as Mr. Marowitz's for shrinkage of candy during processing.)

Looking over the sales records of the Sun company since November, 1946, when the 10-cent price was introduced, the Ruhl brothers noticed that only about one order in ten represented repeat sales. Mr. Marowitz explained that most of the salesmen covered large geographical areas and generally had not yet made a second visit to the wholesalers in their territory. Furthermore, entries in the sales records covered only sales made on credit. Mr. Marowitz stated that many of the large wholesalers paid cash in advance for shipments and that these orders were consequently not reflected in the books. He also showed the brothers the following statistics to establish that the ratio of collection on accounts to total sales was improving:

	Monthly Sales	Monthly Collections	Balance
November, 1946	$ 58,000	$ 45,000	$13,000
December, 1946	63,000	59,000	17,000
January, 1947	89,000	57,000	49,000
February, 1947	73,000	73,000	49,000
Total	$283,000	$234,000	

The option to purchase the Sun Candy Company would expire unless a notice of acceptance was mailed to Mr. Krell by April 3, 1947. If the option were taken up, the Ruhl brothers would buy all the common stock of the company, giving 45 per cent of the shares to Mr. Clark, who would, in turn, compensate Mr. Meyers and the original finder and pay the legal and auditing fees and any other costs of transferring ownership. A new issue of preferred stock or debentures would then be created in the amount of $200,000. The Ruhl brothers would be given all these new shares. Before any dividends could be paid on the common stock, the entire senior issue was to be repurchased at par by the company. In this way, the Ruhl brothers would be assured of getting their initial investment returned before having to divide company earnings with Mr. Clark.

The Ruhl brothers returned to St. Louis on March 20 to consider the proposition and seek the advice of friends and business associates. On March 22, Mr. Clark telephoned Fred Ruhl and advised him that the Sun company's independent auditors had estimated profits before taxes for the month of March at $30,000. This profit figure, of course, did not change the sale price of the company as stated in the option.

Queen Metal Corporation

Early in 1947, after a month's operation, the Queen Metal Corporation was for sale because the strains of organizing the enterprise had impaired the health of the president. Mr. Lewis Stow, president and organizer of Queen Metal Corporation, had been advised by his physician to dispose of the business and retire. He was, therefore, faced with the problem of establishing a selling price for his business and of making arrangements to sell the entire enterprise.

Queen Metal was organized in May, 1946, to manufacture and sell light metal products, primarily of aluminum and magnesium. The specific product selected for initial operations was a cast aluminum roaster developed by Mr. Stow. A sample of the roaster was produced early in 1946 and submitted to four sales agents whom Mr. Stow knew personally through earlier business connections. In only a few days these agents had obtained firm orders for over 30,000 units for shipment "when and as" produced.

From May to December the company was occupied with constructing a building and obtaining the necessary machinery and equipment to produce the Queen roaster. Production was started early in December, and approximately 2,700 units were shipped on orders during the month. No additional orders were solicited since the first sample was shown; nor was the roaster released for sale to other sales agents, because the first objective of the company was to get production moving.

The company was incorporated on July 5, 1946, under the laws of the state of Illinois and was chartered to engage in general manufacturing and to buy and sell materials of all kinds. Prior to the date of incorporation, the business had been conducted as a proprietorship.

The company was capitalized for 200 shares of no-par-value common stock, of which 50 shares were issued and outstanding. All 50 shares were held by Mr. Stow and his wife. In addition to Mr. Stow and his wife, Mr. Clarence Bascom, Mr. Stow's brother-in-law, was an officer of the corporation. The business was financed by the personal resources of the president. The land and buildings were owned by Mr. Stow's daughter.

A balance sheet which reflects organization expense is shown in Ex-

Exhibit 1

QUEEN METAL CORPORATION

BALANCE SHEET AS OF DECEMBER 31, 1946

ASSETS

Current:			
Cash on Hand		$ 50.00	
Cash in Bank		599.52	
Accounts Receivable (pledged $3,389.28 per contra)		5,814.20	
Inventory (estimated)		3,663.00	
Advances to Building Account		29,628.40	
Total Current Assets			$39,755.12
Fixed:			
Patterns and Molds		$ 5,211.22	
Furniture and Fixtures		1,302.90	
Machinery and Equipment		11,898.16	
		$18,412.18	
Less: Reserve for Depreciation		1,168.49	
Total Fixed Assets			17,243.79
Prepaid and Other Assets:			
Prepaid Insurance		$ 298.72	
Prepaid Advertising		1,300.00	
Prepaid Supplies		1,000.00	
Employees' Loans		32.00	2,630.72
Total Assets			$59,629.63

LIABILITIES AND NET WORTH

Current:			
Notes Payable—Bank		$25,000.00	
Notes Payable—Bank (Accounts Receivable assigned per contra)		2,700.00	
Notes Payable—Other		10,000.00	
Accounts Payable:			
Trade	$10,589.08		
Rentals	1,350.00	11,939.08	$49,639.08
Accruals:			
Reserve for Old Age Benefits Tax		$ 171.96	
Reserve for Illinois Unemployment		235.97	
Reserve for Withholding Tax		937.95	
Reserve for Personal Property		397.00	1,742.88
Other:			
Officers' Accounts			16,567.18
Net Worth:			
Capital Stock	$25,000.00		
Unissued Stock	20,000.00	$ 5,000.00	
Surplus Deficit		13,319.51[d]	
Net Worth Deficit			8,319.51[d]
Total Liabilities and Net Worth			$59,629.63

[d] Deficit.

Source: Company records.

hibit 1. Since production was not started until December, 1946, no profit and loss statement is presented. The short time the company was in production did not permit an accumulation of receivables or cash.

The objective of the company was to develop products from lighter metals that could be sold under a brand name. The company had several opportunities to engage in job-shop or subcontract work but refused these offers in order to concentrate on getting production on its own

Exhibit 2

ILLUSTRATION OF THE MAJOR PRODUCT

products. The only product currently produced was the cast aluminum roaster shown in Exhibit 2. This item had been selected because of the excellent acceptance of the sample submitted to prospective purchasers. Mr. Stow had planned to introduce other products as soon as roaster production was in smooth operation.

Two products in the developmental stage were a cast aluminum shovel and a cast aluminum teakettle. The cast aluminum shovel had been designed for use in the packing industry. There appeared to be a substantial demand in the industry for a metal shovel that was noncorrosive and that would not contaminate food products. A company sales agent had submitted samples to several packers. Tentative orders for 250 shovels per week were obtained, subject to final approval of the sample. This product was to be manufactured by a sandcasting foundry and distributed by the Queen company.

A model of a cast aluminum teakettle was being developed and would be submitted to the company's four sales agents shortly. The management believed that a substantial volume of business could be obtained on the teakettle. If the sample was well received, molds would be ordered and the teakettle put into production. Prospective purchasers were reported to be enthusiastic about the product.

Exhibit 3

QUEEN METAL CORPORATION
FACTORY EQUIPMENT AND TOOLS* AS OF
JANUARY 31, 1947

	Net Cost†
Factory machinery, equipment, and tools	$ 7,100
Foundry equipment	2,158
Polishing, buffing, and grinding equipment	5,121
Electrical equipment	1,168
Office and shipping furniture and fixtures	1,188
Total	$16,735

* Principal equipment and tools included: 2 aluminum melting furnaces, 2 temperature holding furnaces, 3 bandsaws, 8 drill presses, 1 grease removing tank (automatic degreaser), 1 shot-blast machine, and 5 grinding and buffing machines.

† Figures are based on depreciated cost and do not include moving and installation costs of approximately $7,000. Small tools, jigs, and fixtures are not included.

Source: Company records.

Queen Metal Corporation was located on a corner plot of land 125 feet by 200 feet, in a manufacturing district of Chicago, Illinois. The main street was macadam, paved in the center; and the alley on the south side of the property was also paved. Both bus and streetcar transportation were available within two blocks from the plant.

When the company was started, plans and specifications were drawn up by Mr. Stow for a building of about 17,500 square feet of factory and office space. Owing to the difficulty of construction at that time and the limited scope of the initial operations, only 5,000 square feet were used for the building. It was erected at the rear of the lot, leaving ample room for expansion. Brick and concrete construction provided a completely fireproof factory. Fluorescent lighting and other modern developments in factory construction were incorporated in the building. Water, electricity, and other facilities were provided to service the completed land area. The present building was appraised at $28,750. The land, including underground utilities, had been appraised at $20,950 by independent real estate appraisers.

All equipment in the plant was new; it had been purchased as the foundation for a general light-metal manufacturing business. Net cost figures for the equipment purchased are shown in Exhibit 3 (p. 255).

The manufacturing process was simple. The roaster consisted of three separate castings—the bottom, top, and handles—all made by the permanent-mold process. The top was trimmed, polished, and drilled for a handle. The handle, after being trimmed, drilled, and tapped for screws, was fastened to the cover by two Phillips screws. The interior of both bottom and cover were degreased and shot-blasted. The manufacturing operation was then completed, and the roasters were packed and shipped in individual cartons.

In the few weeks that the Queen Metal Corporation was in operation, a production volume of 1,200 roasters a week had been achieved. A total of twenty-four employees worked a forty-eight-hour week. Production was limited by the capacity of the bottom mold. Mr. Stow found that the addition of a second bottom mold would materially increase production at only a small rise in labor costs. An additional set of molds was therefore being machined. Minor changes in layout and materials handling which would contribute to greater production volume also appeared to be possible with little expense.

Cost estimates per unit based on the third week of production were as follows:

Aluminum type 95–5 at 17 cents a lb. (8.4 lbs.)	$1.428
Two Phillips oval-head screws 3/8″ × 1/32″ at $16.30 M	0.032
Brand label	0.007
Individual carton	0.089
Shipping carton (proportionate cost)	0.005
Total materials cost	$1.561
Direct labor cost (estimate based on a week's payroll of $1,062 and production of 1,059 units)	1.000
Indirect expenses (estimated at $500 a week)	0.500
Total cost per unit	$3.061

At an average sales price of $4.60, a gross margin of $1.54 per unit was realized. Mr. Stow believed that improvements in the manufacturing process and the addition of a second shift would reduce unit costs in the future.

In early 1947 the company was purchasing aluminum ingot from smelters at 17 cents a pound in 25,000-pound quantities delivered to the plant. The Aluminum Company of America quoted a price of 15 cents per pound in 100,000-pound quantities; and as soon as an allocation could be obtained from this company, raw-material costs could be reduced correspondingly.

Mr. Bascom drew a modest salary, but Mr. Stow drew none. Mr. Bascom handled all administrative work, under the direction of Mr. Stow. Two additional people were needed at once for administrative work: an office girl for general office work and correspondence, and a night foreman to enable the company to enter two-shift operation. This new help would add from $125 to $150 to weekly expenses. Records and accounts were kept by an outside accountant. Because of the short period of operation, standard methods of distributing burden, depreciation, and other expenses had not been established.

Sales were handled by four manufacturers' agents, who received a commission of 5 per cent on sales to wholesalers and 7½ per cent on sales to retailers. An additional discount of 2 per cent for cash was also allowed. A special price of $4.50 net had been made to one agent who had secured the bulk of sales.

The company had a backlog of orders on hand for approximately 30,000 units. In the few weeks of operation, orders received from the agents had substantially equaled production of about 3,000 roasters. Prices for the Queen roaster were as follows:

Trade Class	*Discount*	*Price*
List	....	$9.95
Jobber	50%	4.975
Chains	40	5.95
Retail	53⅓	6.64
Sales agent	5%–7% commission	

A special discount of $1 per unit had been granted to a large New York department store with the understanding that full-page ads on the roaster would be run in local newspapers.

Thomas' *Register* listed 31 manufacturers of aluminum cooking ware in the United States, ranging from large corporations to small job-shops. Six of these manufacturers were in the Chicago area. Mr. Stow stated that the nearest comparable competitive roaster retailed for $13.95.

Queen Metal Corporation was nonunion, and the employees appeared to be loyal to the company and the owner, owing partly to the close personal relationship that had been established and partly to the fact that several key employees had been associated with Mr. Stow in his previous ventures.

The company was founded, financed, and put into operation solely through the efforts of Mr. Lewis Stow, who wanted to retire at the earliest possible date. Mr. Bascom would stay with the company or leave, depending on the circumstances of the sale. The company had engaged the part-time consulting services of a competent metallurgist who was familiar with light metals and permanent mold-casting techniques. He was interested in full-time work with the company as soon as the volume of business made it possible. Another metallurgist and a mold-design consultant, who had been employed part time, were also interested in joining the Queen Metal organization on a permanent basis.

Mr. Stow believed that the future success of the company depended on its three products:

1. *Roaster King.* The backlog of orders for roasters amounted to between 30,000 and 40,000 units; this number had remained constant during the first weeks of operation. Because these sales had been restricted to the four sales agents, there was reason to believe that additional accounts could be secured if other agents were allowed to handle the roaster. Based on past sales and reports from agents, the potential profits for 1947, with a production of 150,000 units, appeared as follows:

Net sales ($4.97 less 5%)	$708,000	100%
Direct costs ($3.06 per unit)	459,000	65%
Operating profit	$249,000	35%

This operating profit would be ample to cover all additional expenses and leave a fair profit.

2. *Aluminum Shovel.* On the basis of prices submitted to the subcontractor and tentative orders on hand, it was estimated that a profit of $2,000 a month would be realized on the shovel.

3. *Cast Aluminum Teakettle.* Samples of the proposed teakettle were to be submitted to sales agents shortly. Mr. Stow was going ahead with this item and anticipated sales of about $250,000 during the first year. Mr. Stow believed the company would enjoy a profitable future because of the sustained demand for light metals of all sorts arising from wartime improvements in metallurgy and production. The demand for cast aluminum cooking utensils appeared very strong, and additional products could be developed if markets for them were discovered.

Mr. Stow regretted that his health did not permit him to continue in this profitable venture. He therefore desired to realize a maximum return for his efforts to date. He believed the value of a going business was greater than the cost of the items which had gone into its formation.

PART IV

NEW ENTERPRISE FINANCING

Huron National Bank

On February 2, 1950, Mr. Scott, the loan officer of the Huron National Bank, was considering whether he should recommend, at the board of directors' meeting scheduled for the next day, that the bank grant a GI loan of $6,000 to Mr. John Bolin. Mr. Bolin planned to purchase the capital stock of the Acme Distributors, Inc., local wholesalers of carbonated beverages, for $42,000. He already had $36,000, which he had inherited, and needed to borrow the remaining $6,000.

The Huron National Bank was located in an Ohio industrial city, the population of which exceeded 250,000. At the time this loan was under consideration, the bank's resources totaled approximately 15 million dollars and it had outstanding loans of about 2.5 million dollars. Like most banks at the time, the Huron was seeking good loans. Acme Distributors had held a checking account at the bank since 1935 and had negotiated a small loan there in 1941 to enable it to take advantage of a special quantity price. This loan has been paid off on schedule.

Acme Distributors sold the carbonated beverages of two bottlers—Waldorf Club, a nationally advertised brand, and Silver Springs, a locally produced and advertised brand. For the most part, sales were made to small retail outlets such as drugstores and grocery stores; however, the company sold some stores of the two largest chain groceries in the area. Approximately 20 per cent of sales were made to hospitals and other institutions. The company operated five trucks in delivering its merchandise.

In the fall of 1949, Mr. Terry, owner of Acme, decided to sell the company and to move to the Southwest. He later told Mr. Scott that he had expanded the company's operations about as much as he could and that he was eager to enter some other company whose problems promised to be more challenging and interesting than those which he anticipated in continuing to operate Acme. In November, 1949, Mr. Terry asked a local small business broker to seek a buyer for the company. After Mr. Bolin, a teller in a local savings and loan company, had become interested, he and Mr. Terry arrived at a price of about $42,000 which Mr. Bolin was to pay for the company's capital stock. Mr. Terry also agreed to stay on for several weeks to introduce Mr. Bolin to the company's customers and to help him get started.

Exhibit 1

HURON NATIONAL BANK LOAN APPLICATION

APPLICATION FOR PERSONAL LOAN

City, Jan. 10, 19 50

I hereby apply for a loan of $ 6,000 The purpose of this loan is as follows:

to provide working capital to buy Acme Distributors, Inc.

This statement is furnished for the purpose of procuring credit, and is to be regarded as continuous until another shall be substituted for it. If the undersigned, or any endorser or guarantor of the obligations of the undersigned, at any time becomes insolvent, or commits an act of bankruptcy, or if any deposit account of the undersigned with you be attempted to be held by writ of garnishment, or otherwise, or if any of the representations made below prove to be untrue, or if the undersigned fails to notify you of any material change in financial condition as given below, then and in either such case, all of the obligations of the undersigned to or held by you, either as borrower or guarantor, shall immediately become due and payable without demand or notice. In consideration of the granting or renewing of any credit to the undersigned hereafter, the undersigned hereby waives the pleading of the statute of limitations as a defense to any obligation of the undersigned to you.

PLEASE ANSWER ALL QUESTIONS

Print Name in Full	Age	Married	Residence Address	How Long There
John Alden Bolin	33 1/2	Yes	17 Chestnut St.	8 yrs.

Full Name of Wife or Husband	Number of Dependents	City	Phone
Sally Jones Bolin		City	Wy-6-1234

Employed by (If self give Trade Name)	Business Address	Phone
City Savings and Loan	121 Main St.	LA-3-4798

How Long There	Position Held	Kind of Business	Name — Title of Superior
10 1/2 yrs.	Teller		J. R. Sams, Treas.

		Source of Other Income
Salary or Wages Per Month	$ 200	
Other Monthly Income	$ 50	Stocks, Bank interest, etc.
Total	$ 250	

Monthly Expenses		Bank Reference	Checking Savings No.
Rent	$		
Living	$ 120	City Savings and Loan	C-43985
Miscl.	$ 140		
Total	$ 260		

Amount of Life Insurance and Beneficiary	Cash Value	Name of Company
$ 23,000	new ins. 1 yr. $ old	Ohio Mutual Ins. Co. G.I. Term Ins.

Amount borrowed, if any, on life insurance $ None

Name of Former Employer	Position Held	How Long There
Midwest Electrical Mfrs.	Stock Clerk	2 yrs.

Do you own an Automobile Yes ? Give make and year Plymouth '39

The bank's credit file on the proposed loan contained the information given in Exhibits 1 through 8. Mr. Scott, in examining the latest balance sheet (Exhibit 2), kept in mind that Mr. Terry had agreed to tear up the Notes Payable—Officer, totaling $4,000, which he held. Concurrently, the asset item, Accounts Due from Officer, was to be surrendered by the company. In studying the profitably of the company

Exhibit 1—Continued

HURON NATIONAL BANK LOAN APPLICATION—*Continued*

Location of Real Estate Owned	Title in Whose Name	Purchase Price $
17 Chestnut St. City	Husband & Wife	Assessed Value $5,500 Built by owner in '41 for Date acquired $7,000

Amount of First Mortgage	Held by	When Due
Pending with Homestead Savings & Loan		

Amount of Second Mortgage	Held by	When Due
None		

(LIST IN DETAIL)

Are Any Taxes and/or Assessments Unpaid? All paid

(LIST IN DETAIL)

Are You the Owner of Any Securities, including U. S. Gov't. Savings Bonds?
None now
Cashed all in to go into business

LIST OF DEBTS OR INSTALLMENT PAYMENTS, INCLUDING BANK LOANS AND MONTHLY CHARGE ACCOUNTS

To whom Owed and Address	Present Amount of Debt	Original Amount	Amt. pay. ea. Mo.
None			

(EXPLAIN IN DETAIL)

Have you ever gone through Bankruptcy? No

Have you now or ever had Any Judgments, Garnishments of Other Legal Proceedings Against You? No

Are you an Endorser or Guarantor for Others? No

Personal References Donald Wilson 21 Hillside Ave.
Thomas O. Terry 2150 Western St.

UNLESS STATED ABOVE TO THE CONTRARY, all Real Estate and Stocks and Bonds are carried in the name of the undersigned alone (not in the name of relative, trustee or others); no homestead or other encumbrance affects the Real Estate; Stocks and Bonds are not pledged.

I authorize you to obtain such information as you may require concerning the statements made in this application and agree the application shall remain your property whether or not the loan is granted.

I hereby certify that I have carefully read the foregoing statement, and that it is a complete, true and correct statement of the undersigned on Jan. 10, 1950, to the best of my knowledge and belief.

/s/ John A. Bolin
Signature

Date Signed Jan. 10, 1950

(Exhibit 3), Mr. Scott recalled that Mr. Terry had personally drawn all of the Officer's Salary item and about $2,000 of the Sales and Administrative Salaries item.

The officers of the Huron National had decided among themselves that the bank had a responsibility to help veterans establish themselves in business. Mr. Scott realized that the Veteran's Administration would require that a non-real estate loan, such as the one being considered, be

Exhibit 2

HURON NATIONAL BANK

BALANCE SHEET OF ACME DISTRIBUTORS, INC.,
YEAR ENDING DECEMBER 31, 1949

ASSETS	*1948*	*1949*
Current Assets:		
Cash	$10,442	$10,256
Accounts Receivable	10,664	8,190
Inventory	3,171	3,709
Total Current Assets	$24,277	$22,155
Fixed Assets:		
Office Equipment	375	375
Trucks and Delivery Equipment	13,859	15,052
Total Fixed Assets	$14,234	$15,427
Deposits	40	40
Prepaid Auto Expense	136	156
Accounts Due from Officer	....	2,502
Total Assets	$38,687	$40,280

LIABILITIES		
Current Liabilities:		
Accounts Payable	$ 8,739	$ 8,109
Notes Payable—Officer	4,000	4,000
Accrued Expense	821	551
Withholding Taxes	701	1,084
Reserve for Federal Tax	263	223
Health and Accident Advances from Employees	399	125
Total Current Liabilities	....	4
	$14,923	$14,096
Reserves:		
Reserves for Bad Debts	300	300
Reserves for Depreciation	6,675	8,538
Reserves for State Excise Tax	....	100
Capital Account:		
Capital Stock	4,700	4,700
Surplus	12,089	12,546
Total	$16,789	$17,246
Total Liabilities	$38,687	$40,280

Acme Distributors, Inc.

/*s*/ Thomas O. Terry, Treas.

discounted at 3 per cent, whereas the bank's usual discount on similar loans was 5 per cent. He also knew that the Veteran's Administration would guarantee one half of any such loan up to a maximum guarantee of $2,000. As the loan was repaid, however, the amount guaranteed by the government was also reduced, so that the ratio between the unpaid balance and the guaranteed portion always remained the same. Thus, in this case, the Veteran's Administration would guarantee $2,000 of the original $6,000 note. By the time the outstanding balance had been reduced to $3,000, the guaranteed amount would stand at only $1,000. Mr. Scott recalled one situation where a local bank had failed to collect

Exhibit 3

OPERATING STATEMENT OF ACME DISTRIBUTORS, INC.,
YEAR ENDING DECEMBER 31

	1948	*1949*
Gross sales	$158,891	$156,899
Less: Discounts, returns, and allowances	113	149
Net sales	$158,778	$156,750
Cost of goods sold	109,091	104,022
Gross profit	$ 49,678	$ 52,728
Operating expenses:		
Advertising	66	52
Truck and delivery	3,304	3,294
Depreciation	2,546	2,294
Bad debt	.....	114
Heat and light	136	79
Insurance	1,075	1,643
Miscellaneous	109	222
Drivers' and helpers' salaries	15,739	17,441
Officer's salary	9,000	11,300
Sales and administrative salaries	11,270	9,940
Rent	1,500	1,550
Sales and travel	1,193	1,756
Stationery and office expense	552	460
Taxes and excises	1,038	1,077
Telephone	261	239
Total	$ 47,789	$ 52,146
Miscellaneous income	1	.....
Net profit before taxes	1,899	582
Less: Reserve for federal tax	399	125
	$ 1,500	$ 457

Acme Distributors, Inc.
/*s*/ Thomas O. Terry, Treas.

the insured portion from the Veteran's Administration because the latter had found a technical error in the date of the chattel mortgage securing the loan. As he put it, "Now that bank won't make any GI loans."

The Huron National had made about twenty-five GI mortgage loans averaging about $10,000 each, and in Mr. Scott's opinion its experience with them had been highly satisfactory. The bank had made about thirty non-real estate, or "business," GI loans, averaging about $1,500 each. Three of these had, in Mr. Scott's words, "gone sour," resulting in moderate losses to the bank. Although they had not defaulted, another ten of the latter group of loans had engendered such a quantity of correspondence and negotiation between the bank and the Veteran's Administration that Mr. Scott believed the bank had not covered expenses on them.

Mr. Scott had expressed confidence in Mr. Terry's business ability. He

Exhibit 4—VA APPRAISAL FORM

APPRAISAL
(Non Real Estate Business Loans)

VA LOAN NO. L-8

DATE OF APPRAISAL

The undersigned appraiser submits the following information for consideration of the lender in connection with the business loan being negotiated by:

NAME OF VETERAN: BOLIN, JOHN A.	ADDRESS *(Street Number, City and State)*: 17 Chestnut St.
NAME OF LENDER: Huron National Bank	ADDRESS *(Street Number, City and State)*

PURPOSE OF LOAN *(Explain in detail)*
In order that the veteran may purchase all of the capital stock of the Acme Distributors, Inc., 6 Wilson St., City

I AS THE RESULT OF YOUR INQUIRY REGARDING THE PERSONAL RESPONSIBILITY OF THE VETERAN, WHAT IS YOUR CONCLUSION?
After consulting with the former employers of the veteran, it is our opinion that he is of the highest moral character, and lives an exemplary life, and that they were sorry to lose his services.

II AS THE RESULT OF YOUR INQUIRY REGARDING THE BUSINESS ABILITY OF THE VETERAN, WHAT IS YOUR CONCLUSION?
Our inquiry leads us to believe that from his former work, he has a fine aptitude for business life.

III PAST RECORD AND/OR FUTURE PROSPECTS, IF APPLICABLE:		YES	NO
1 DO PAST RECORDS INDICATE THAT THE BUSINESS HAS OPERATED AT A PROFIT		X	
2 IS THE LOCATION DESIRABLE FOR THIS TYPE OF BUSINESS		X	
3 WILL EXISTING BUSINESSES AFFORD KEEN COMPETITION			
4 WHAT CLASS OF PEOPLE WILL THIS BUSINESS SERVE	middle class thru drug stores, groceries, etc.		
5 ARE PREMISES AND DISPLAYS NEAT AND ATTRACTIVE		X	
6 WILL ANY MAJOR REMODELING OR ALTERATIONS BE NECESSARY			X
7 ARE THERE ANY BUILT-IN FIXTURES OR EQUIPMENT			X
8 ARE THE TERMS OF THE LEASE SATISFACTORY		X	
a DOES IT PROVIDE FOR CANCELLATION	– only for nonpayment of rent	X	
b FOR SUBLEASING			X
c FOR RENEWAL		X	
9 IS THE RENT A FIXED DOLLAR AMOUNT		X	
a AMOUNT	$125.00 monthly		
b IF A PERCENTAGE OF SALES, STATE PERCENT AND HOW COMPUTED			
10 WHAT IS YOUR ESTIMATE OF GROSS SALES PER MONTH	$3,000		
a EXPENSE	2,000 to 2,200		
b NET	800 to 1,000		
c ARE SALES FOR CASH OR CREDIT	both		
d IF CREDIT, SHOW THE USUAL TERMS	ten and thirty day terms, open account		
11 DOES THE BUSINESS HAVE SUFFICIENT WORKING CAPITAL		X	

IV ASSETS TO BE ACQUIRED, TANGIBLE OR INTANGIBLE *(State whether new or used and identify with Serial Number if pledged)*

DESCRIPTION	ORIGINAL PURCHASE PRICE	ESTIMATED CASH OR RESALE VALUE
Veteran is acquiring capital stock of corporation which owns among other assets the following:		
'48 Chevrolet Truck		$1,200
'47 White Truck	$2,000	1,500
'46 White Truck	5,490	1,000
'40 White Truck	4,325	300
'40 Chevrolet Truck	1,100	200
TOTAL		

V IN YOUR OPINION DOES THE PURCHASE PRICE STATED HEREIN REPRESENT A REASONABLE VALUE AS SO DEFINED YES [X] NO [ ]

COMMENTS *(For additional space use reverse side)*

The answers to the foregoing questions and the statements made above are true and complete to the best of my information and belief. I have no financial interest in the subject matter of the transaction contemplated except as fully disclosed in application for approval as designated appraiser.

APPRAISER'S EMPLOYER *(Name, Title, Address)*	SIGNATURE OF PERSON FUNCTIONING AS APPRAISER: /s/ Daniel Rodman (only as to trucks)
/s/ Lawrence E. Scott Huron National Bank	TYPE OR PRINT APPRAISER'S NAME AND ADDRESS

Exhibit 5

GREAT LAKES COMMERCIAL CREDIT CO.
CREDIT REPORT, JULY 13, 1949

Acme Distributors, Inc., Wholesalers
Evelyn N. Terry, Pres. Thomas O. Terry, Treas. and Clerk
DIRECTORS: The officers with Donald Wilson, Ella Jones
RATING: 6-C*

SYNOPSIS

BACKGROUND: Corporation formed under others in 1928. Present interests purchased control in 1940
NET WORTH: $16,789 (12/31/48) SALES: $150,000 yearly est.
PAYMENTS: Discount, prompt and cash
CONDITION AND TREND: Financial condition somewhat heavy. Annual increases in net worth noted.

HISTORY

Incorporated under Ohio laws June 21, 1928, with an authorized capital of 290 shares common stock with $100 par value. Statement of Dec. 31, 1948, showed 47 shares issued and outstanding, and a surplus of $12,089.

The business here was established by Harold German in 1928. The present officers purchased control in 1940. The stock interest was acquired by the Terrys in April, 1940. The purchase price was $9,000 cash and chattel mortgage, reported to have since been paid.

Thomas Terry was born in Michigan in 1914 and is married. For several years prior to starting here he was employed by the Zenith Mutual Insurance Co. He served in the Army from 1944 to 1946 and was discharged with the rank of First Lieutenant. He spends most of his time on the road in a sales capacity. Wilson and the other officers who are members of the principal's family are not active. Ella Jones is the mother of the principal.

OPERATION—LOCATION

Wholesales carbonated beverages and is a local distributor for the Waldorf Club and Silver Springs beverages. Sales are to about 100 regular accounts, principally retailers in the metropolitan area. Terms are cash and 30-day, and charge accounts represent the majority of the sales. The company maintains pickup and delivery service in its own trucks. Company occupies about 2,000 square feet of floor space just off a principal artery in a middle-class residential section. Three are employed. The shop is located on the first floor of a three-story frame building which is in normal repair.

FINANCIAL INFORMATION

	Dec. 31, 1946	*Dec. 31, 1947*	*Dec. 31, 1948*
Current Assets	$17,540	$17,466	$23,977
Current Liabilities	9,105	12,458	14,923
Other Assets	4,636	10,281	7,735
Tangible Net Worth	13,071	15,289	16,789

* 6 = Financial strength between $10,000 and $20,000. The numbers following this category indicate the credit strength: A = High; B = Good; C = Fair; D = Limited.

Exhibit 5—Continued

BALANCE SHEET DECEMBER 31, 1948

ASSETS		LIABILITIES	
Cash	$10,442	Accounts Payable	$ 8,739
Accounts Receivable	10,363	Notes Payable—Officers	4,000
Merchandise	3,172	Accrued Expenses	2,184
Total Current Assets	$23,977	Total Current Liabilities	$14,923
Motor Vehicle	7,559	Capital Stock	4,700
Auto Expenses	136		
Depreciation	40	Surplus	12,089
Total Assets	$31,712	Total Liabilities	$31,712

No contingent liabilities not reported above. No assets pledged. No investment in or indebtedness from or to company closely affiliated.

Recent attempts to interview the principals have been unsuccessful, and on July 11, 1949, person in charge of the office declined all information. In comparing latest figures with those of Dec. 31, 1947, it is noted that notes payable due officers have been reduced from $5,000 to $4,000. This money was advanced by the principal to enable the company to purchase new motor vehicles during 1947. Actual schedule for reduction of this debt has not been learned.

Bank balances average in low five-figure amounts and the account is nonborrowing. Statements in recent years have shown a somewhat heavy financial condition, and it is known at this time that there is at least $10,000 in current trade payables outstanding. Figures have shown small but regular annual increases in net worth.

Sales for 1948 were reported about 10 per cent over those of the previous year and during 1948 the company was grossing between $13,000 and $14,000 per month. It is estimated on that basis that annual sales approximate $150,000.

PAYMENTS

HC	*Owe*	*P. Due*	*Terms*	*July 13, 1949*	
10,000	10,000	......	n 30	Ppt.	Sold sev. years to 7/49
100			2/10 cash	Ppt.-Disc.	Sold years to date

GREAT LAKES COMMERCIAL CREDIT CO. CREDIT REPORT, JANUARY 26, 1950

Acme Distributors, Inc.
Supplement to Report of 7/13/49
RATING: 6-B*

TREND

Calls on January 25, 1950, failed to obtain an interview with the principals or with anyone in authority to give out information. The party in charge of the office claimed inability to discuss any part of the affairs of the company. Other sources have indicated that the company is handling a good sized volume of business and currently experiencing some seasonal effects.

CONDITION

A current check has failed to reveal a certificate of condition later than that of Dec. 31, 1948. It is believed that there are no material changes in the general financial condition of the company from the satisfactory position shown at the end of the fiscal year.

Bank balances are averaging in low five-figure amounts and the account is a

Exhibit 5—Continued

nonborrowing one. It appears that there are adequate funds to reture trade obligations as agreed and to finance operations under the present scale.

PAYMENTS

HC	*Owe*	*P. Due*	*Terms*	*Sept. 15, 1949*	
65			10th	Ppt.	Sold sev. years
				Ppt.	
6,000	6,000	0	n 30 cash	Ppt.	Sold sev. years to 6/1949

* See note on first page of this exhibit.

Exhibit 6

LETTER TO MR. SCOTT FROM MR. BOLIN*

My dear Mr. Scott:

Enclosed find my Certificate of Eligibility from the V.A. I trust that my loan of $6,000 at 4% for the longest term of years possible can be processed soon.

Please acknowledge and keep me advised.

I did not receive a binder for my checks. Please send me one.

Also, do you not have one's name printed in green ink and not on a typewriter stencil? My wife said the checks were not as the sample.

Thank you for your courtesy.

Very truly yours,

John Bolin

* This letter, written in longhand, was received by the bank January 24, 1950.

Exhibit 7

LETTER TO MR. BOLIN FROM MR. SCOTT

January 24, 1950

Mr. John Bolin
17 Chestnut St.
City

DEAR MR. BOLIN:

Mr. Terry has given me the information which I originally requested.

In connection with the possible G.I. Loan, I have spoken to him on the telephone this morning about having a list of his accounts payable with the

Exhibit 7—Continued

names and addresses involved and also a list of his best customers. He tells me by telephone that about 80% of the business relates to retailers.

Will you please write me a letter stating the amount which you are planning to offer for the capital stock of the company? It is my understanding that you intend to buy the business through purchase of all of the outstanding capital stock and not through purchase of any of the individual assets.

Please also give me a list of your present investments or cash so that we shall have a formal record of the amount of money you have available for your part of the proposed purchase. It would also be helpful for the information of the V.A. to have the details on the new mortgage loan.

Very truly yours,

LAWRENCE E. SCOTT
Vice-President

Exhibit 8

MR. SCOTT'S NOTES OF MEETING WITH MR. AND MRS. BOLIN

G.I.

JOHN A. AND SALLY J. BOLIN

After discussion yesterday with Mr. Sanders, bank president, I have discussed with the Bolins a G.I. Loan of $6,000, running over a three-year period. The note would be signed by Mr. and Mrs. Bolin and secured by capital stock which he wants to buy in Acme Distributors. It would also be secured by a chattel mortgage on trucks owned by the corporation. Because of the complications of the corporation's setup and the various trucks, I have told Mr. Bolin that if we went ahead, we would start with Mr. William Phelps as our attorney from the very beginning. Mr. Bolin's lawyer is Gerald Elliott of 31 Merchants Street, City. Telephone No. Ar 6–2798.

Mr. Bolin, as his application shows, has been a teller in the City Savings and Loan. He seems to feel that other fields are greener and is, therefore, hoping to buy the Acme business for a gross of approximately $42,000, using for that purpose money inherited. In the absence of his superior, Mr. Swensen, I talked with the assistant treasurer, a Mr. Abel who spoke very highly of his ability and integrity. The company has told him that if he does not like the new business they would like to have him return.

The business, details of which are given in the file, distributes soft drinks in this area dealing entirely with products of Waldorf Club and Silver Springs. A satisfactory account has been kept here for some years and several years ago we made a small loan to the company. We think well of the proprietor, Mr. Terry, who introduced Bolin to us. Mr. Bolin has decided to keep the company account here if the deal goes through and has opened a personal checking account.

One good aspect offsetting Mr. Bolin's lack of experience is that Mr. Terry will

Exhibit 8—Continued

stand by for a period of some weeks and will introduce Mr. Bolin to the trade and in general supervise his activities. Furthermore, Mr. Terry has full confidence in an employee who acts as general office manager and is also experienced in selling. The office secretary is competent, and the five truck drivers, according to Mr. Terry, are reliable.

Terry is a tenant at will and the landlord has agreed to a three-year lease with an option to renew. Bolin would, apparently, keep, at least for the time being, the setup whereby the trucks are garaged and serviced by an independent garage.

Mr. Terry has given us 1948–1949 figures, including operating figures, balance sheet, and details of the accounts receivable as of December 31, 1949. He remarked that one of his suppliers had felt he was not taking sufficient credit risks based on the small amount of past due items. About 80% of the business is with retail outlets and about 20% with hospitals and other institutional buyers. The accounts payable as of 12/31/49 are Waldorf Club $7,022.25 and Silver Springs $1,086.27. Mr. Terry tells me they have since been paid.

It so happens that a representative of Great Lakes, whose current report is in the file, called recently to check the name. He told me that they had just completed a trade checking which was most favorable with all bills paid promptly or discounted and very little outstanding. One company in the trade is willing to go up as high as $6,000.

L. E. SCOTT

1/27/50

Exhibit 9

MR. SCOTT'S NOTES ON ACME DISTRIBUTOR'S ACCOUNTS RECEIVABLE AS OF DECEMBER 31, 1949

No. of accounts, 300
45 accounts have credit balances = $205
255 accounts show AR totaling $8,395
Average AR = approximately $32.53

ACCOUNTS RECEIVABLE BY SIZE

$345	Chain store #1
$312	Chain store #2
$199 to $100	10 accounts
$ 99 to $ 50	39 accounts
$ 49 to $ 10	134 accounts
Under $ 10	70 accounts
Total	255 accounts

ACCOUNTS RECEIVABLE BY AGE

Due in December, 1949	75.0%
Due in November, 1949	14.6
Due prior to November, 1949	10.4
	100.0

felt that it would help Mr. Bolin if Mr. Terry remained with the company to introduce the new owner to the company's customers and to give advice on company problems and procedures. Mr. Terry had told Mr. Scott that his office manager, who would be retained by Mr. Bolin, was dependable and capable of managing the business.

When discussing the loan with Mr. Sanders, president of Huron National, Mr. Scott described Mr. Bolin as "a typical bank teller—the type you see in the movies." He added: "He doesn't have the personality that Terry has." Mr. Scott expressed sympathy for Mr. Bolin's desire to get out of "his rut." Information from the officials of City Savings and Loan led Mr. Scott to believe that, if he remained there, Mr. Bolin would eventually be made assistant treasurer.

Mr. Scott knew that the profitability of the loan from the bank's viewpoint would be reduced because of the special legal work involved. Often on similar loans which were not GI loans the bank drew its own chattel mortgages. However, because some banks had been denied protection by the Veteran's Administration because of technical error in the legal documents they submitted, Huron officials had decided to have all details for GI loans handled by Mr. Phelps, a lawyer who was a specialist in these matters. Normally the borrower paid these expenses, but the Veteran's Administration specified a minimum charge which could be assessed against the veteran. This maximum, according to Mr. Scott, lacked about $120 of being sufficient to cover what he expected Mr. Phelps to charge. Mr. Scott realized the bank would have to pay this difference. He felt that Mr. Phelps deserved the larger fee because of his experience and the work involved in the transaction.

Mr. Terry had sent Mr. Scott a list of Acme's accounts receivables, as of December 31, 1949. Exhibit 9 (p. 271) contains Mr. Scott's notes on them. Mr. Scott had also computed the face amount of the GI loan as being $6,377.18. It would be amortized in equal payments at the rate of $177.16 per month for 36 months.

H. & H. Development Company

In March, 1950, the developers of a new semiautomatic conveyor system for specialized industrial applications were seeking sufficient capital to get their design from the experimental stage into production. An estimated minimum of $150,000 was required.

The entrepreneurs in the H. & H. Development Company were Mr. Alan Hammond, an engineer, and Mr. George Holden, a salesman.

Mr. Alan Hammond, age fifty, had long been recognized as one of the outstanding engineers in the conveyor industry. For the past twelve years he had been an independent consulting engineer and was frequently retained by manufacturers of such equipment to help solve technical problems. He had been successful in this work; and although the expenses of a large family had precluded the amassing of any personal fortune, he was financially independent. His resources were adequate for essential family needs and ultimate personal retirement.

His business partner, Mr. George Holden, age thirty-six, had, upon graduating from a large eastern college, spent several years as an analyst in the business loan department of a large New York bank. For the past ten years, he had been connected with the installation and operation of special-purpose conveyors, first in direct selling of such equipment for a leading manufacturer, then more recently as a specialist on installations for an industrial engineering firm. Holden had a comfortable income, but with a family of three school-age children had not been able to accumulate appreciable savings.

During January, 1948, Hammond and Holden had been working on the operational problems of a large and particularly difficult conveyor installation. During an informal dinner conference one evening they began comparing experiences with such problems during the past decade. Each had come to the conclusion that no manufacturer was producing a really satisfactory design.

Their ideas as to the operational requirements of such equipment were in close agreement. Both believed that the industry had failed to take advantage of many recent technical developments, ranging from advances in metallurgy to improvements in automatic controls and electronic devices. Apart from minor refinements, the basic characteristics of the particular kinds of semiautomatic conveyor systems with which these men were concerned had changed little during the past fifteen years.

Operation of the interrelated components of these conveyor systems required careful co-ordination and timing. In the types of industrial operations for which these specialized conveyer systems were designed, the characteristic requirement was for a flow of materials and heavy parts moving at varying rates into a continuous master assembly. The speed of component sections of such conveyer systems often had to be varied during different phases of the production sequence, and the proper co-ordination of these changes depended upon the skill and judgment of a highly trained man who operated the master control system. Minor mistakes in co-ordination of the control system could result in costly damage to the entire conveyer mechanism, in addition to disruption of the production flow. Not infrequently, errors in the control booth led to serious injuries and sometimes fatalities to workers.

The hazard factor alone had been responsible for a number of companies refusing to install equipment of this type or else removing it after it had been installed. Industrial insurance and workman compensation rates for employees who had to work on these conveyers, surrounded by heavy moving pieces, was excessively high. Annual costs for maintenance and repairs for such equipment commonly ran over 20 per cent of the original cost. Since the smallest of such installations cost over $20,000 and investments in excess of $100,000 per unit were not uncommon, the high and unpredictable repair costs were a major deterrent.

Another production disadvantage was that the frequent breakdowns and interruptions of service destroyed many of the economies being sought through the higher speed and more direct flow of work in process. Additional objections arose from the fact that the installations tended to be large and cumbersome and that they required too much valuable factory space. As a result, such equipment was employed in only a small proportion of those factories which might theoretically use the systems to advantage. Holden estimated that not over 10 per cent of those plants that needed and could afford the equipment had been willing to accept these shortcomings.

Both Hammond and Holden had been convinced by their observations that many of the more serious difficulties with present equipment could be overcome by better design and by incorporation of recent technological developments. Existing manufacturers, however, had heavy capital investments in the expensive dies, molds, fixtures, and other tooling required to fabricate such equipment. Moreover, the complexity of such equipment made the cost of new design work very high and the outcome uncertain. Both men had repeatedly tried to interest the established manufacturers in the need for improved designs, but without success.

In the course of his engineering work with various conveyer installations during the preceding ten years, Alan Hammond had accumulated a number of design ideas which he felt would increase in both reliability and safety. He also believed that, by incorporating more automatic control equipment and by employing more modern alloys in carefully redesigned parts, the amount of plant area required to house such equipment could be drastically reduced.

George Holden was impressed by the potential sales volume which he believed could result from the design improvements that Hammond had outlined. He was convinced from his own selling and consulting experience that, for each factory that had installed the integrated semiautomatic conveyer system, at least two others had declined solely because of objections to operational problems. He believed, therefore, that the current annual market of about $40,000,000 for total industry sales of such units would, with these improvements, exceed $100 million.

Based on his own experience in training operators for such equipment, Holden was convinced that the automatic control and safety features proposed by Hammond not only would reduce the skill required but would eliminate most of the costly consequences of inevitable mistakes on the part of operators. Moreover, the saving of factory space through the simplified and more compact design held promise of producing over-all factory economies substantially greater than the small increase in initial equipment cost that would be required.

Hammond's own estimate was that the increase in manufacturing costs for his new design features would add not less than 7 per cent, and possibly as much as 12 per cent, to the price of equipment of the same capacity as that currently being produced. Hammond had a background of technical experience and a reputation for conservatism such as to lead Holden to consider these estimates reliable.

In Holden's opinion, it was this conservative nature of Hammond's, in addition to his preoccupation with purely engineering problems, which had led him to work for a number of years on important design improvements without successful effort to interest the top management of the leading manufacturing firms. During the years, Hammond had in fact become a bit cynical about the ability of nonengineering personnel in top-management positions to evaluate the technical requirements of the product they were manufacturing. He had resigned himself to the fact that he would probably have to go on trying to make minor improvements in equipment which was technologically obsolete and to which major improvements could not be made because of the inertia and resistance to change on the part of those who exercised control.

The enthusiasm and optimism of the younger sales-minded man built up Hammond's interest in doing something with the design ideas he had long nurtured. Thus began a series of frequent lunch and evening conferences. Using Hammond's basic design ideas, tempered with the financial and operational requirements that Holden set forth, the two men developed a complete set of design specifications for a radically improved type of conveyer which would have all of the load and flow capacity of the older more cumbersome models.

Their new model was designed to be operated by less highly skilled men, and with almost complete elimination of the risks of those control errors which had in the past led to breakage of equipment and injury to personnel. Savings in equipment damage alone within a year's time could, they believed, easily make up the difference between the cost of the older crude mechanisms and the somewhat more expensive advanced design.

Before trying to interest others in the development, the two men decided to test the new mechanism at their own expense. During 1948 they began a series of experiments, and by the end of the year they had constructed a full-scale test model. Most of the work was done in a nearby machine shop, and the experimental tests were performed in a section of an adjacent garage rented for the purpose.

Hammond and Holden shared equally in the expenses and formalized their working arrangement only to the extent of signing a simple one-paragraph letter which stated that each man, or his heirs in case of death, were to have a 50 per cent interest in any proceeds which might result from the work.

After Hammond and Holden had spent approximately $7,000 of their personal funds successfully testing various components of the new design, Mr. H. R. Stephenson, who had formerly been Holden's employer, contributed $15,000 to the project in exchange for a 10 per cent interest. Mr. Stephenson had retired a few years previously from the presidency of an organization which sold industrial equipment including conveyers. He had been successful in this business.

Stephenson asked no specific assurances or guarantees from Hammond and Holden other than simple written evidence of his 10 per cent participation in the results. He explained to them that he was investing in their integrity and ability and that, if he was wrong, all the contracts and legal formalities in the world would do no good. If he was right in his judgment of the two men, he stated, legal formalities at that stage were superfluous.

With the added funds, Hammond and Holden soon completed the full-scale working model. It fully met Hammond's engineering claims. Holden and Stephenson were satisfied that the model had fully proved the sales and operational advantages for which they hoped. The test model had, however, been hand-built without the careful engineering, blueprints, specifications, and tooling required for the manufacture of salable equipment.

Hammond, Holden, and Stephenson decided to form a company which would hold the design and sales rights together with the drawings and special tooling required to produce the component parts. They planned to have all manufacturing operations performed outside on a contract basis. Although production of the component parts required considerable amounts of specialized machinery, there were several companies in the country which did contract manufacturing of this type. Two such companies were found to have available capacity, and they submitted satisfactory bids for manufacture of the component parts.

The cost of producing a completely engineered sample model, together with the basic tooling and engineering data needed to permit contract manufacturing by others, was estimated as requiring approximately $150,000. To allow an adequate margin for unforeseen contingencies, a total of $250,000 was set as the amount of capital to be sought.

Hammond, Holden, and Stephenson then had the H. & H. Development Company incorporated under the laws of Delaware. Hammond and Holden each took 45 per cent of the stock, with the remaining 10 per cent going to Stephenson.

Each of the three men served as a director; Hammond was elected president; Holden vice-president and treasurer. Both Hammond and Holden agreed to drop their other work and devote full time to the new company just as soon as adequate funds were in hand to pay them the minimum salary each required. They established this minimum figure for themselves at approximately 60 per cent of the amount earned during the preceding year. Each of the original participants had at this point invested as much cash and made as much personal contribution as he prudently could.

Holden's previous experience in banking had not included raising equity funds to finance new ventures. His familiarity with investment practices, however, led him to believe that established investment banking firms were not likely to be interested in such a small amount of financing or in underwriting an unproved product in the hands of a new company. Inquiry among numerous acquaintances in the investment banking business led to confirmation of this assumption.

A number of investment firms were, however, found to be keenly interested in having information about the product and asked to be kept closely informed of the company's progress. Several investment firms stated that they would like to participate in the financing when the company had reached a stage where it was ready to employ investmen-banking channels. Frequent reference was made by these bankers to their policy of waiting until a company was "seasoned."

Specifically, very few of the investment firms evidenced much interest in a financing operation until the company could justify at least a million-dollar issue. Justification for public financing would, moreover, apparently require that the company have concrete evidence as to the production costs and profit margins on its product, gained by actually producing and selling an appreciable quantity. None of the directors of the H. & H. Development Company were either surprised or disappointed to find that their financial needs could not be met through the public sale of stock. They had anticipated that, if funds could be raised at all, they would have to come from private sources.

While exploring possible sources of such funds, Holden was introduced to several individuals who controlled large aggregates of investment capital and who indicated a possible willingness to supply the entire amount required, provided they could thus acquire financial control of the corporation.

The directors of the H. & H. Development Company decided that, if it was necessary to sell more than a majority of the stock to outsiders in order to raise the required funds, they would be willing to do so. They preferred, however, to avoid, if possible, having any one individual or group dominate the company. Accordingly, they decided to seek not over $25,000 from any one investor. They also concluded that the best investor candidates would be found among executives of large manufacturing companies who were potential users of these specialized conveyers.

Shortly after the H. & H. Development Company was incorporated, Holden left his former position and devoted full time to the new venture. He spent the first thirty days calling on approximately fifty top executives of manufacturing concerns whose fabrication processes involved heavy flow of closely co-ordinated components. Many of these manufacturers already used the type of conveyer systems with which Hammond and Holden were concerned; others recognized the inherent advantages of such equipment but did not have installations in their own plants because of the very operational difficulties that Hammond's new design sought to eliminate.

These executives were found to be more than willing to discuss the new conveyer design. Repeatedly, busy top executives with whom Holden had expected to spend only a few minutes would spend several hours going over the photographs, designs, and specifications. Holden explained in advance of each conference that his purpose was to determine the possibilities of private financing for this project and that the company was not ready to accept orders. Despite this fact, Holden ended his first month with numerous offers for purchase of installations but with very few indications of willingness of these executives to invest personally.

Many of the executives expressed their confidence in the product and in the individuals behind it by offering to sign purchase contracts and to make substantial cash deposits in advance. Several of them pointed out that a number of new companies in the past had succeeded in financing their developmental work and production through the use of just such advance customer deposits. Both Hammond and Holden were, however, adamant in their refusal to even consider using customer deposits to fianance product development and tooling.

The most common reason given by executives for declining to invest personally, despite their apparent interest in the product, was the impact of federal taxes upon their personal saving and investment patterns. A number of executives whom Holden believed had sufficient personal funds to invest if they had been so disposed were firm and quite evidently sincere in their insistance that they would not, under today's conditions, invest in any new venture regardless of how attractive the product or how sound the management might be.

Holden also encountered a widespread belief among these experienced executives that a new manufacturing venture in the country's current heavily regulated and taxed economy was at a serious competitive disadvantage in relation to large and well-established competitors. The inability of a small company to finance its own expansion out of retained earnings was also frequently mentioned as an objection to new enterprise investing.

After a month of interviews which appeared fruitless, Holden discussed the financial problem with a number of acquaintances in the investment banking business. He was told by most of these men that the financing of a project of the size and type of the H. & H. Development Company was, in their opinion, a virtual impossibility.

Several of them did mention a few smaller investment firms that were sometimes willing to try to place highly speculative new issues—but on a "best-efforts" basis rather than with a guaranteed underwriting. Distribution costs of such financing would be at least 10 per cent and possibly as high as 20 per cent. Moreover, the probability of raising the required amount within a reasonable period of time was not believed to be good.

After careful consideration of the uncertainties facing their venture, both Hammond and Holden concluded that, regardless of the probabilities of success with the financing, they did not want to assume the responsibility of proceeding with funds which a small investment firm might possibly succeed in raising by public solicitation. Such an assortment of investors might not, they believed, understand the peculiarities of the company's product and might all too easily be oversold on the expectation of quick profits.

The time required for production engineering, tooling, and service testing of such a large complex machine was expected to take several years. Hammond and Holden themselves anticipated that from three to five years might elapse before any revenues of consequence could be expected from production and sales.

Holden was also introduced to several organizations established for the sole purpose of investing in new enterprise. In no instances, however, did he find that the policies of these groups fitted the objectives of the H. & H. Development Company. The amount being sought was relatively large in relation to the sum that most of these groups were interested in putting into any one company during the developmental stage.

In the one instance, where the amount was within the size the investing group would consider, there was a conflict on the point of financial control and management policies. Both Hammond and Holden felt that the degree of control over management policy which this investment group would desire was inconsistent with the group's understanding of either the technical requirements of the product or its market.

During the latter part of February, 1950, the three directors of the H. & H. Developmental Company had a conference on the financing problem and decided that, unless they could raise the funds from individual investors of their own selection, they would endeavor to sell or to license their design rights to an established manufacturer.

Holden entered into negotiations with two of the larger manufacturers in this industry. Both were interested in a license on a straight royalty basis but would not pay more than a few thousand dollars in advance or give minimum guarantees of any consequence. These offers to license were based on know-how and were not contingent upon the U.S. Patent Office's granting Hammond's claims.

By this time, news of the promising test results with the company's full-scale model had circulated rather widely through the industry and numerous inquiries from prospective users were being received. Sufficient facts were being circulated privately so that Hammond and Holden decided to release photographs and operational characteristics of their scale model. These were published in the trade journals with highly favorable commentaries. Interest among potential industrial users continued to mount.

Early in March, 1950, Mr. Holden received a telephone call from Mr. R. D. Fulbright, president of a large Midwestern manufacturing company. During January, Mr. Fulbright had attended a trade conference at which Mr. Holden had described the H. & H. conveyer design and its objectives. Mr. Fulbright explained in his telephone call that he and several business acquaintances in the area had been discussing the matter recently and had concluded that, since each of them was so eager to have the new conveyer design for his own factory, it must have an excellent market. As a result, they were interested in participating in the financing.

Fulbright stated that his interest in investing was in part in expectation of an ultimate capital gain but perhaps reflected even more his own eagerness to have such radically improved equipment available for his own plant. His company was wholly owned by the Fulbright family.

A lunch conference was arranged by Fulbright for Holden and the presidents of several other Midwestern manufacturing companies located in the same Midwestern city. Fulbright and Holden met prior to the lunch conference to discuss the basis for the proposed financial participation. Fulbright took the position that he and his associates were far too busy with their own responsibilities to exercise financial control. Moreover, during the early developmental phases of the corporation he believed it was important for those who conceived and understood the product to exercise majority control. Therefore, unless he and his associates had sufficient confidence in the product and in the management to take a minority position, he believed they should not consider the investment.

Fulbright was emphatic on the point of avoiding any complicated capital structure with different classes of voting and nonvoting stock. His idea of a sound financial plan was an all-common-stock capital structure with the management group retaining at least 51 per cent. This coincided with Holden's views.

The only remaining problem then appeared to be that of determining whether a fair price for an interest of 49 per cent or less would be adequate to finance the operation. Holden proposed $300,000 as the amount which should be subscribed by the outside group for a 49 per cent stock interest. This, he explained, allowed a 100 per cent margin of safety over the estimated $150,000 minimum budget required for additional product development and tooling.

Fulbright countered with the proposal that the new investors be offered 49 per cent in exchange for the $150,000 estimated minimum-capital requirement and that, if the expenses ran higher, the company might with that much equity base be able to borrow the difference. Holden maintained that a higher equity margin to allow for unforeseen contingencies would be sounder for all concerned. He suggested that an investment of less than about $250,000 might increase the risk disproportionately from the standpoint of the investors' own best interests.

The proposal seemed not unreasonable to Fulbright, and he promised to have a final decision for Holden by the time of the luncheon conference a few hours later. Fulbright spent the remainder of the morning conferring by telephone with the other interested executives and checking with several manufacturers of related kinds of equipment to determine their cost experience on similar types of engineering and developmental work.

At the luncheon, Fulbright acted as spokesman for the local group. He stated that, in his opinion, the H. & H. Developmental Company needed about $200,000 of equity capital to do the proposed job and that this amount appeared adequate. He had, moreover, made up his mind that a fair value for the engineering and developmental work on the test model which Hammond and Holden had produced at their own expense was at least $200,000. He attached no value at this time to Hammond's pending patent claims, and he agreed with the company's policy of proceeding on the assumption that know-how and a head start might be all they really had.

Fulbright told the group he was convinced that no other manufacturer could quickly catch up with the H. & H. development even if they could match Hammond's rather unique engineering accomplishment. He also believed that any effort by a large company to duplicate the design would require developmental expenditures in excess of $200,000. The low overhead of the small H. & H. shop and the individual services of the two key men appeared difficult for a competitor to duplicate. It would, moreover, take any other company starting at this time several years to develop a successful full-scale test model. For this reason he was prepared to accept $210,000 as a reasonable appraisal of the "tangible" value of the H. & H. company's present assets and was willing to participate in the purchase of a 49 per cent interest at a price of $200,000.

Fulbright then told Holden that he and several others present at the luncheon had already decided that morning that they would put up at least $60,000 of the new capital immediately and would undertake the responsibility for raising this to a total of at least $100,000 among their business associates.

In Holden's judgment, the time to negotiate had passed. He considered Fulbright's offer to be a firm and final proposal. Holden replied that he himself considered the offer fair and was sure that, subject to the necessary formality of a directors' and stockholders' meeting, his associates in the H. & H. Development Company would also accept.

Word of the offer of financial support by this Midwestern group quickly spread among other interested corporate executives in the area who knew and respected the judgment of Fulbright and his business associates. Among perhaps seventy-five or so executives who had discussed the H. & H. company's product and plans with Holden during past months it soon became apparent that some fifteen to twenty of these individuals were now willing to participate in the financing. The company's goal of raising at least $200,000 from carefully selected individual investors at last appeared attainable.

At this point the law firm that had handled incorporation proceedings for the H. & H. Development Company advised that it was legally impossible for the company to issue a total of $410,000 of securities to approximately twenty-five different investors located in four or five states without encountering prohibitive legal costs and delays.

In the first place, public sale of new securities for amounts in excess of $300,000 would require registration with the Securities and Exchange Commission.[1] The company's legal counsel and a partner of a

[1] The law is not specific as to definition of "public sale"; but in this instance, counsel advised that solicitation of over twenty individuals would probably be so construed. On the other hand, private placement of the entire issue with four or five individuals would clearly be exempt.

large public accounting firm conferred with Hammond and Holden on the problems of SEC registration. They estimated that it might be possible to accomplish the so-called "long-form" registration within about two months' time and for a cost that might not exceed $20,000. The company was advised, however, that an allowance of four months' time and $30,000 might be more realistic. This was considered prohibitive.

Necessity for the SEC long-form registration could be eliminated, however, by the simple matter of holding the total authorization of securities to be sold to new investors below $300,000.[2] The $210,000

Exhibit 1

H. & H. DEVELOPMENT COMPANY

PRO FORMA BALANCE SHEET

(Giving Effect to Proposed New Stock Sales)

ASSETS		LIABILITIES	
Cash (new)	$200,000	Accounts Payable	$1,200
Raw Materials	2,815		
Current Assets	$202,815	Current Liabilities	$ 1,200
Experimental Prototype	204,600	Common Stock:	
Patent Applications	685	Original Investors (51%)	210,000
Deferred Organizational Expense	3,100	New Investors (49%)	200,000
Total Assets	$411,200	Total Liabilities	$411,200

of stock issued to the three original investors did not have to be counted in that total. This meant that the $200,000 of immediate financing would be possible but that the company would be precluded from raising the larger sums which all concerned recognized might become desirable within less than a year's time.

For the next month, Holden spent full time working with the company's lawyer, prospective backers, and SEC officials in an effort to meet the requirements under the "simplified" short-form procedure. Although SEC officials theoretically do not "approve" such material, they were found to exercise considerable editorial and veto function.[3]

The first conflict between the SEC requirements and the desires of

[2] The Securities and Exchange Act of 1938 provides that companies selling not more than $300,000 of securities in any one year may be exempt from the full registration requirement and can submit, instead, a greatly simplified short form, plus filing in advance all data distributed or used in the solicitation of investment. After filing such materials with the SEC and waiting for five days, if no objections are raised by the SEC, the data can be used for purposes of solicitation.

[3] Any such prospectus filed with the SEC is required to carry a legend as follows: "Because these securities are believed to be exempt from registration, they have not been registered with the Securities and Exchange Commission; but such exemption, if available, does not indicate that the securities have been either approved or disapproved by the Commission or that the Commission has considered the accuracy or completeness of the statements in this communication."

potential investors arose from the request by Fulbright and his associates for inclusion in the prospectus of anticipated revenues and expenses during the critical first two years. They also requested a simple *pro forma* balance sheet showing the total assets and the allocation of stock between the new and old investors, as shown in Exhibit 1.

The SEC, however, would not accept the prospectus as filed by the H. & H. company with the projection of financial operations and the *pro forma* balance sheet included. The officials of the SEC explained it was contrary to their policies to permit such *pro forma* financial statements. Since the figures were based upon conjecture, they explained, investors might be misled. Even the simple *pro forma* balance sheet might, they maintained, mislead an investor into believing that the funds which are shown as coming from new investors would definitely be raised, when in fact such might not be the case.[4]

When Fulbright and his group were advised that the company could not circulate in its prospectus the desired financial projections, they requested, instead, that Hammond and Holden at least set forth their best estimate as to when production would start and the rate at which management might reasonably expect to fill sales orders thereafter. Accordingly, the two men prepared their own estimates of present and future sales for the industry as a whole, and the portion thereof which the H. & H. company might reasonably seek to obtain. This data was also vetoed by the local SEC officials as being the type of conjecture which could not be permitted in a prospectus.

During this period, the company's legal counsel was insistent that Holden not circulate through correspondence or in other form any statement about the company which had not been filed and cleared in advance with the SEC. After the company's prospectus had been subjected to the deletions and additions required to obtain clearance with the local SEC office, it was sent to Washington for final check by the SEC there.

In the meantime, Holden reviewed the tentative revised prospectus with Fulbright and several of his associates to determine its adequacy from their point of view. Fulbright stated that, so far as he was concerned, any copies which were sent to him for possible distribution to other prospective investors would wind up in his wastebasket. He described it as an overly detailed collection of excessive historical data which neither he nor any of his associates cared about. It was totally

---

[4] Legal counsel advised the company that such *pro forma* balance sheets would, however, probably be permitted if a responsible investment banking firm guaranteed the new funds by underwriting the issue.

lacking in the kind of management plans and projections which he would like to review and measure against his own experience.

Fulbright expressed annoyance that the company felt bound by what he considered purely arbitrary opinions of SEC officials and that the company therefore could not provide him with the kind of financial projections he felt he needed to interest his business acquaintances in the project. The delay "with all this red tape," he stated, was cooling his interest in making personal efforts in behalf of the project.

When the prospectus, as passed by the local SEC office, finally came back from Washington, an opinion was attached which condemned the presentation for "omission of material fact." Since the required waiting period after initial filing of this data had elapsed, the company had in the meantime distributed some of the material, as it was entitled to do. This ex post facto condemnation by the Washington SEC office was considered by the company's legal counsel to be a source of embarrassment and possible legal action at a later date, especially if any of the investors or their heirs should ever become dissatisfied and investigate with a critical point of view.

The "omission of material fact" for which the prospectus was condemned was its failure to define the company's relative status in its industry. Holden inquired at the local SEC office for advice as to how his company should define its relative position in the industry when it had no sales volume, no productive capacity, or any other relative yardstick. The local office had no suggestions whatsoever as to what the company could add to its prospectus to remedy the alleged omission. They suggested simply forgetting the objection by the Washington office in view of the fact that the company had not received the complaint prior to the time it was authorized to begin distribution of material.

The company's lawyers advised, however, that they did not want to have their client continue with the financing under an implication of bad faith in the record. After a series of conferences and telephone calls, the local SEC office assured the company and its legal counsel that the charge had been investigated to their satisfaction, found unjustified, and was being eliminated from the record.

The final form of the prospectus evidently satisfied SEC officials but appeared to be of little significance to the prospective investors. When questioned by Holden, most of them admitted that they had not bothered to read any of it. Others stated that they had skimmed through parts of it briefly and found nothing of particular interest. None of the prospective investors were found to have read completely through this document on which the company's lawyers, management, and SEC officials had struggled so long.

With the SEC filing out of the way, Holden then found that he faced a far more difficult and imposing hurdle in the form of the various conflicting state "blue-sky" laws.[5] In most of the East Coast states, such as the one in which the H. & H. Development Company was located, where important centers of business and finance had long been established, the state security laws were found to be less involved. The company could register and comply with the laws of states such as New York, Massachusetts, and Delaware without undue delay or expense.

Unfortunately, however, the Midwestern business group that was prepared to put up the bulk of the funds at this time was made up of executives who, despite being in effect members of the same industrial fraternity, had their plants and residences located in five different states.

One of these states, for example, required as the first step the filing of answers on ninety-two involved questions, some of which called for extensive data that would require costly accounting and legal work. Legal counsel estimated that his firm's minimum legal fees for simply preparing the first application in that state would run to several thousand dollars and would require that Holden be in the lawyer's offices for several days to assist in the preparation of data. The company was advised, moreover, that after the initial submission of this data the continuing requests for deletions, additions, and changes by officials of this state often became far more involved and more difficult to anticipate than the company's recent experience with the federal SEC.

In another of the Midwestern states in which several of the prospective investors resided, the statute required that, whenever the company had patents, design rights, or developmental items carried as assets on its balance sheet, an equivalent proportion of the securities held by the entrepreneurs had to be placed in custodianship with state officials.

In several of the states, the local officials not only exercised wide administrative prerogatives with respect to the filing of information but could—and sometimes did—reject a company's registration solely because in their judgment the issue represented an unsound business risk. The company's counsel advised that such rulings were utterly unpredictable by any known business or legal yardsticks, and sometimes appeared arbitrarily based on an official's personal opinion.

Holden consulted a number of his investment banking acquaintances

[5] The term "blue sky" is alleged to have been derived from a statement by a Kansas legislator that promoters would sell shares "in the blue sky itself."

regarding the problems of multiple state registration and found that his legal adviser had evidently not exaggerated the complexity of the problem. He was advised that, in some states, local investment houses had found that the only way to expedite registration of an issue without excessive costs and delays was by the discreet application of favors and gratuities to the right officials at the right time. This was a procedure that the officers of the H. & H. Development Company did not know how to use if they had wanted to.

Legal counsel also advised the H. & H. company that the punitive features for violating the various "blue-sky" laws were quite severe. In several states an individual soliciting the sale of unapproved securities could be subject to heavy personal fines as well as imprisonment. Likewise, investors could, at some later date, take legal action directly against the individuals concerned, as well as against the company, to recover any losses that might be involved.

The enforcement of "blue-sky" provisions in various states varied appreciably, counsel advised, according to the attitude of state officials at the time and the nature of the situation. Sometimes punitive actions appeared capricious and arbitrary. At other times, counsel reported, wholesale by-passing of the laws seemed to be ignored by state officials. His law firm was therefore unable to advise what the penalties for failing to comply with the "blue-sky" provisions might be, but stated that the risk was high and urged great care.

Legal counsel then reviewed the negotiations which Holden had been conducting and advised him that sale of H. & H. securities to any of the executives with whom he had had recent discussions might be construed as violation of the "blue-sky" laws in their respective states. If these individuals were now to purchase H. & H. stock, the previous discussions could be considered solicitations to purchase unregistered securities. Obviously, Holden had not been aware of this fact.

The company immediately proceeded to register its securities in those Eastern Seaboard states where the regulations could be met at reasonable cost. Counsel advised that, once the securities were properly registered with the SEC and in the company's home state, investors from other states could then, at their own initiative, purchase securities directly from the company. This could be done either through personal visit or by letter or telephone, provided the company itself engaged in no solicitation and did not send any descriptive materials to the investors in advance of their purchase.

Unfortunately, however, the nature of recent negotiations, as well as the fact that considerable descriptive materials and correspondence was now in the files of those executives with whom Holden had previously discussed the financing, precluded sale of the stock to any of these individuals without serious risk of violation.

The best advice that Hammond and Holden could get thus indicated that both the financial costs and the many months of delays required for compliance with the registration requirements of the "blue-sky" laws of the various Midwestern states greatly exceeded the maximum their project could endure. The legal and financial risks involved in proceeding with the offer from Fulbright and his group likewise appeared prohibitive. Hammond and Holden concluded that the financing either had to be accomplished within a relatively few weeks on the basis of existing investor interest or else the entire project would have to be abandoned.

Hydraulic Attachments Company

In March, 1950, Henry Clausson, president, and Douglas Winslow, treasurer, of the Hydraulic Attachments Company faced a marketing decision which might have considerable effect on the future of their young company. The Hydraulic Attachments Company had been formed in April, 1948, by the happy meeting of an inventor, Henry Clausson, and a budding businessman, Douglas Winslow, at that time a student in a business school.

The company's principal product was a hydraulic digger attachment, designed to be mounted on the rear of a Ford farm tractor (Exhibit 1). It had been evolved out of an older item, a farm loader attachment (Exhibit 2), which was no longer in production. The company had no sales force. Its products were sold by the Clement Equipment Company, a large tractor accessory distributor and manufacturer. In March, 1950, Mr. Clement, president of the distributor company, approached Clausson and Winslow with a proposition which would alter their relationship considerably.

HENRY CLAUSSON

Henry Clausson was one of those relatively rare people who seemed always to be buzzing with new and better ways of doing a particular job. Son of a farmer, he had been impressed in his youth with the large amount of unnecessary manual labor employed in agriculture. He had experimented with various farm devices and, while still in his twenties, had developed a hydraulic farm loader. Believing that his loader had significant advantages over others on the market, he had formed a small company with four employees to make and sell loaders. The company met with little success.

The Clausson loader, unlike competitive products, was designed to be attached to the rear end of a tractor. This was both a strength and a weakness. His product was superior to other loaders because it put all the weight on the rear wheels, an important factor on muddy or icy ground. On the other hand, the tractor operator had to turn around to operate the Clausson loader. Other manufacturers in the field stressed

Exhibit 1

HYDRAULIC DIGGER UNIT

the natural position of the tractor operator, who sat looking forward while operating the machine. Clausson attempted to counteract this sales appeal by stressing that, regardless of where the loader was attached to the tractor, a loading operation consisted of moving to and back from a pile of material. It made little difference whether the backing operation was performed first or last. Although Clausson's selling efforts met with reasonable initial success, the tractor manufacturer soon developed his own front-end loader, a fact which made the tractor distributors and dealers reluctant to handle the Clausson product.

Clausson also made a simple digger conversion unit, which generally performed well (Exhibit 3). However, the bucket could not be swung to the side to unload, a fact which necessitated movement of the tractor away from the ditch each time the bucket was loaded. This constant movement was fatiguing to the operator and limited the digger's sales

Exhibit 2

FARM LOADER ATTACHMENT

appeal. Another item was a special fork-type bucket for lifting brush, pea vines, and other light-weight material (Exhibit 3). All Clausson's products were sold through four Ford farm machinery distributors in New York and New England.

Henry Clausson found it extremely difficult to find enough time in the day to supervise the four employees in the production process and still handle sales. Occasionally he would advertise in the *New England Homestead* magazine. Almost invariably he would receive requests for further information about the products. He seldom found time to follow up these leads before it became necessary to devote his time to pro-

Exhibit 3

EARLY CLAUSSON HYDRAULIC ATTACHMENTS

Fork-Type bucket for use in loading manure mixed with straw, pea vines, brush and similar materials. Tines of heavy, high carbon steel are rugged and electrically welded for strength. The fork is 44 inches wide, 26 inches high and 30 inches deep. Tine points specially designed for easy penetration.

Prong-type bucket for use in handling hard-packed manure, manure mixed with straw or hay or conditions in which the material to be handled varies in consistency. The prongs, which provide excellent penetration in hard-packed material, are 20 inches long. Overall depth is 35 inches, width is 30 inches and height is 24 inches.

Conversion unit for hydraulic scoop utilizes the standard loader bucket to make a useful power tool. Can be used for preparing grassed waterways, water holes, grading, terracing and excavating. Reaches three feet below ground level of rear wheels and three feet behind rear wheels.

ducing another unit. Consequently, the sales volume remained small, approximately $20,000 per year.

The contacts he did manage to make convinced him that his farm loader was facing far too much competition to become a really profitable item. On the other hand, he was equally sure that there was a large market for a hydraulically operated digger with greater capacity and mobility than the present simple attachment he was producing. The dealers generally agreed that such an item held real possibilities providing it could be priced to sell for about $500.

By January, 1948, it was clear that the company could not continue without some drastic changes. Sales had remained at $20,000 or below. Losses had eaten into working capital and had forced Clausson to borrow until his notes payable were greater than his current assets. In this plight, he asked the advice of Mr. James Standard, a successful local businessman, who had extended a helping hand to several small businessmen.

Mr. Standard was impressed by Clausson's products and by his obvious talent for invention. He felt that most of the company's problems could be solved by bringing someone into the organization capable of assuming the burden of sales and administrative work, leaving Clausson free to devote his entire time to the technical and development side of the business. Mr. Standard suggested that the right kind of man could be attracted if the firm were incorporated and the new man given a stock interest as well as a salary. In fact, Mr. Standard had just the right man in mind—Mr. Douglas Winslow, a second-year student at the Harvard Business School. Clausson agreed that this sounded like a good idea "provided that I keep more than 50 per cent of the controlling stock."

DOUGLAS WINSLOW, BUSINESSMAN

James Standard had learned of Douglas Winslow's interest in establishing himself in a small business when Winslow had worked for his company during summer vacations. Since Winslow lived in the same town as Mr. Standard, the latter called him and suggested to Winslow that he investigate the possibility of becoming a stockholder and operating member of Clausson's Farm Equipment Company. Douglas Winslow was twenty-five years old and had been married for three years at the time he received the call from Mr. Standard. He had served as a naval officer on a patrol craft during World War II and, except for his summer work as a stock clerk, had had no business experience.

At first glance, Clausson's Farm Equipment Company did not seem to be what Winslow had in mind. Henry Clausson had borrowed heavily to keep his company in operation (Exhibit 4). He owed nearly $12,000 in notes payable, most of which had been endorsed by his friends: $5,000 of the notes were held by a local Ford tractor dealer, and the remainder by the local bank. The company's inventory consisted mostly of parts and finished assemblies for the farm loader, which had sold in relatively small quantities.

"Plant facilities" consisted of a large shed, an 8-foot by 10-foot shed which served as an office, and a former chicken coop, used for material storage. These buildings were owned by Clausson and were located adjacent to his home, about 20 miles from a large city. Heat was supplied by a potbellied stove, and there was no running water. Since the buildings were part of Clausson's farm property, he did not intend to include them as assets of the proposed corporation but would rent them to the new company.

Exhibit 4

CLAUSSON'S FARM EQUIPMENT COMPANY

BALANCE SHEET, APRIL 1, 1948

ASSETS			
Current:			
Miscellaneous—Finished and in Process			$ 8,975.58
Fixed:			
Machinery	$ 3,338.99		
Less: Reserve for Depreciation	570.44		
		$2,768.55	
Equipment and Tools	$ 3,217.68		
Less: Reserve for Depreciation	552.13		
		2,665.55	
Trucks and Tractor	$ 1,500.00		
Less: Reserve for Depreciation	300.00		
		1,200.00	
Furniture and Fixtures	$ 125.00		
Less: Reserve for Depreciation	14.06		
		110.94	
Total Fixed Assets			6,745.04
Total Assets			$15,720.62
LIABILITIES AND NET WORTH			
Liabilities:			
Current:			
Accounts Payable		$ 1,310.25	
Notes Payable		11,765.54	
Withheld Taxes		149.48	
Accrued Payroll Taxes		43.95	
Total Current Liabilities			$13,269.22
Net Worth:			
Investment:			
Henry Clausson			2,451.40
Total Liabilities and Net Worth			$15,720.62

Winslow, however, was much impressed with the thirty-one-year-old Clausson. He was convinced of his sincerity, his belief in his products, and his practical inventive capabilities. The preliminary work that Clausson had done on the hydraulic digger, in particular, seemed to show great promise. Most important to Winslow, he saw that he and

Clausson seemed to complement each other's interests and background and that they seemed to get along well with each other.

After adding up the pros and cons, Winslow decided to throw in his lot with Henry Clausson. He realized that the company had to be successful in a hurry or it would no longer be a company. Since Winslow was still in school and since the situation demanded immediate action, he decided to spend all available time, including several evenings a week as well as week ends, working for the new company.

FORMING HYDRAULIC ATTACHMENTS COMPANY

After some discussion, Clausson and Winslow incorporated the new firm, with Mr. Standard and several other prominent local businessmen as the board of directors. The capital structure consisted of 500 shares of $100 par value 6 per cent noncallable preferred stock and 2,000 shares of no-par common stock. Dividends on the preferred were cumulative. If dividends were passed for three consecutive semiannual periods, the preferred stockholders were to have voting rights as a group equal to those of the common stockholders. Dividends could only be paid from earnings. The preferred would be sold as a package—one share of preferred and one share of common for $100. Clausson was to receive 1,001 shares of common stock and one share of preferred for his interest in the assets of Clausson's Farm Equipment Company. Two hundred shares of common were to be given to Winslow for his "best-efforts" work in selling the preferred stock. The remaining 300 shares of common were to be set aside as treasury stock to be issued to Winslow when, in the opinion of the outside members on the board of directors, he had accomplished his task of successfully reorganizing the company and setting up its activities on a sound financial basis.

The new corporation, Hydraulic Attachments Company, was organized on April 1, 1948. The assets and liabilities of the Clausson's Farm Equipment Company (see Exhibit 4) were transferred to the new company.

SELLING THE PREFERRED STOCK

Winslow immediately started his search for possible customers for the preferred stock. He reasoned that the only class of people who could afford to invest in an enterprise as speculative as the Hydraulic Attachments Company were those who were relatively wealthy. Rather than work through such groups as the local chamber of commerce and other civic organizations, he tried to develop his own list of prospects. This was extremely difficult because he had few contacts in the part of the country where the plant was located. Bit by bit, he built up a list. For example, he included as prospective customers all members of a family known to be prominent in financial circles. Another promising group was composed of all the bank directors in the area.

Initially he attempted to contact his prospects at their offices by telephoning for an appointment. He quickly found that it was impossible to break through efficient secretarial barriers by telephone. Personal calls at the prospect's place of business were no more successful, and he spent many unprofitable hours sitting outside closed doors. As a result of these experiences, Winslow decided to concentrate on visiting his prospects in their homes.

Each week end he made a number of calls on prospective customers at their home addresses. Although the response was often very cool, in many cases the businessman would end the initial conversation by saying: "Oh well, you are here now. I suppose I might as well listen to what you have to say." By the end of July, Winslow had sold about $12,000 of the preferred stock, the smallest single sale amounting to $500 and the largest to several thousand dollars.

Although this sum satisfied only minimum capital needs of the company, both men believed that current operating problems during the summer of 1948 were of more pressing importance than raising additional capital. Accordingly, Winslow, who had started on a full-time basis with the company in June, 1948, spent the major part of his working hours on sales and production activities. He still spent evenings and week ends pressing the sale of the preferred stock, so that by the end of 1948 he had disposed of almost $20,000 worth. It was not until the summer of 1949 that the last of the $50,000 issue was sold, when an elderly gentleman with a long history of organizing and investing in new companies purchased a block of 150 shares.

OPERATING PROBLEMS

During this first summer of operation, Winslow answered the telephone, kept the books, made sales trips to the field, and helped Clausson and the four men as they worked to produce the first model of the hydraulic ditch digger. Some units of the farm loader were produced, and a small number were sold each month. In general, however, the major efforts of all concerned were devoted to developing the hydraulic digger.

The lack of ready cash was an ever-present problem. Seldom was there enough money in the checking account at the end of one week to meet the following week's payroll. Winslow was able to arrange several short-term loans from the bank for $1,000 and $2,000. These were personal loans, however, signed by Clausson and Winslow, for the banks refused to lend money directly to the new corporation. The cash strain on the business was reduced somewhat by an action of one of the creditors, a Ford tractor dealer, who agreed to accept some of the company's products and some stock in lieu of cash for repayment of his note.

In these difficult days, outside members of the board of directors were a great help to the two struggling managers. One of the board members advanced money at two different times. Although they were all busy men, they willingly devoted an afternoon each month to the directors' meeting. Clausson and Winslow often called individual directors to get their advice or help on some problem. Board meetings were held in the company "office building," very inadequately heated by a small electric heater. As cold weather came on, the directors wore overcoats at the board meetings.

PRODUCING THE HYDRAULIC DIGGER

By October, the first of the new hydraulic diggers was completed. While still on the drawing board, it had been sold to a large utilities company; and as the delivery date approached, the men worked day and night to assemble and test it. Winslow remarked: "If we hadn't been so strapped for money, we would have kept the experimental model for further test and redesign. As it was, we spent hours fitting the parts by hand so that the completed unit would operate smoothly." Although earlier dealer recommendations had suggested that the digger sell for about $500, the two men knew that the list price would have to be much higher. The list price of $1,090 was set by adding to the estimated cost of labor, material, overhead, and profit desired, an amount to cover a distributor's discount of 35 per cent of list. Some months later the actual cost of producing the digger was found to vary from the estimate by less than $5.

At the same time that the experimental model was being rushed to completion, parts were also being manufactured for the first production lot of 25 diggers. By the end of 1948, sales had reached nearly $26,000, of which 12 diggers at approximately $708 apiece formed an appreciable portion. Although prospects for the future were getting brighter, the first nine months of operation showed a loss of $449.68 (Exhibit 5).

Both Clausson and Winslow were determined that they would produce a quality product. Improvements were made as diggers were tested in the field. The hydraulic digger was the first to fill the gap between digging by hand and digging with a large expensive truck or crawler-mounted power shovel. Although Clausson and Winslow had the market to themselves for the moment, they realized that it was only a question of time before other firms were attracted to it. Patents were

Exhibit 5

HYDRAULIC ATTACHMENTS COMPANY
PROFIT AND LOSS STATEMENT FOR THE PERIOD
APRIL 1, 1948—DECEMBER 31, 1948

Gross sales		$25,862.62
Cost of goods:		
Inventory April 1, 1948	$ 8,975.58	
Supplies purchased	14,585.80	
Labor	7,520.73	
Heat, light, and power	586.97	
	$31,669.08	
Less: Inventory December 31, 1948	16,182.54	
		15,486.54
Gross profit		$10,376.08
Operating expense:		
Officers' salaries	$ 4,190.00	
Rent	590.82	
Advertising	497.80	
Telephone	518.51	
Office supplies and expense	162.37	
Employment taxes	433.05	
Repairs and maintenance	398.43	
Depreciation	626.44	
Insurance	752.13	
Interest paid	186.29	
Freight and express	115.68	
Legal and accounting	258.45	
Sales promotional expense	1,434.45	
Dues	31.00	
Truck and tractor maintenance	81.32	
Taxes and licenses	63.81	
Sales discounts	214.24	
Miscellaneous supplies and expense	52.30	
Insurance premiums—officers' life	232.60	
		$10,839.69
		$ (463.61)
Other income:		
Purchase discounts		13.93
Net loss		$ (449.68)

pending on the unit as a whole. Both men realized that these were only temporary advantages and that survival after competitive items appeared on the market would depend upon their reputation for reliability and quality.

Clausson and Winslow did not attempt to manufacture those parts which could be purchased more cheaply than they could make them. The hydraulic pistons, valves, cylinders, and pumps were bought from companies specializing in those products. Even with this subcontracting arrangement, production of a lot of 50 diggers more than filled the limited manufacturing space, and the company was forced to move the assembly operation to an abandoned chicken coop. In March of 1949, Clausson and Winslow found that four workmen could not handle the entire production load, and the first new employee was hired.

SELLING ARRANGEMENTS

Until this time—March, 1949—all sales had been made through four Ford tractor distributors. Although the sales volume was still relatively small, the first lot of 25 diggers had been completely sold except for 2 units retained as demonstrators. Sales on the lot of 50 were encouraging. Although vigorously pushing the product, the dealers knew little about what the digger could actually do. The majority of them lacked the necessary knowledge of hydraulic machinery to instruct the buyer in the proper maintenance and use of the new digger. Neither Clausson nor Winslow had time to do an adequate job of teaching the dealers how to service their equipment.

The two men had accepted the normal price structure used in the tractor and tractor-equipment industry. This called for a discount of 35 per cent off list for the distributor, who in turn sold to the dealer at 20 per cent off list. It soon became apparent that Hydraulic Attachment's price of $708 was not going to allow them pay for any educational program for the dealers. Accordingly, the list price was raised to $1,137, with Hydraulic Attachments taking all of the price increase.

In March, 1949, Clausson and Winslow received an offer which changed their entire approach to the sales problem. Mr. John Clement, one of the four Ford tractor dealers through whom the digger was sold, died suddenly. His brother, Tom Clement, owner of the Clement Equipment Company, in Chicago, Illinois, flew to Syracuse, New York, to handle the details of his late brother's estate. He learned from the acting manager of the distributorship the details of the new hydraulic digger made by Hydraulic Attachments Company.

The Clement Equipment Company was a substantial distributor and manufacturer of tractor attachments and accessories. Mr. Clement, enthusiastic about the market possibilities of the hydraulic digger, sent a telegram to the Hydraulic Attachments Company asking to meet a representative of the firm at the airfield in New York City to discuss the possibility of adding the hydraulic digger to the Clement line of equipment.

The telegram arrived at a time when the company's checking account was at a low point and the cost of a round-trip ticket to New York had the appearance of a relatively large cash expenditure. More important, during the previous three months the two men had been contacted by several firms, one of them a large mail-order house, with tentative offers to buy their entire output of diggers. In each case, after considerable time and money had been spent by Clausson and Winslow in investigat-

Exhibit 6

HYDRAULIC ATTACHMENTS COMPANY
PROFIT AND LOSS STATEMENT, CALENDAR YEAR 1949

Net sales		$223,527.86
Less: Cost of goods sold:		
Material	$121,654.72	
Provision for liability on defective parts	5,000.00	
Direct labor	25,718.27	
Manufacturing expense	14,727.64	167,100.63
Gross profit		$ 56,427.23
Less: Operating expenses		17,592.80
Net operating profit		$ 38,834.43
Add: Discounts received		227.31
		$ 39,061.74
Less: Other expense and losses:		
Interest paid	$ 676.55	
Bad debts	1,441.19	
Life insurance premium	201.10	2,318.84
Net profit before taxes		$ 36,742.90
Provision for income and excise taxes		15,236.12
Net profit		21,506.78
Analyses of surplus:		
Net profit for year		21,506.78
Deficit January 1, 1949	$ 449.68	
Tax adjustment	251.06	700.74
Available		$ 20,806.04
Preferred dividends	$ 1,280.50	
Common dividends	3,000.00	4,280.50
Balance December 31, 1949		$ 16,525.54

ing the proposal, the other company either withdrew its offer or the offer was found to be one in which Hydraulic Attachments Company was not interested.

Although the sales volume was still small, it was increasing at a slow but steady rate. Clausson and Winslow foresaw that a sudden increase in sales would bring with it a need for additional capital and plant expansion, steps which they were not sure could be taken at that time. After several hours of discussion, the two men decided that Winslow would go to New York and at least hear Mr. Clement's proposition.

Mr. Clement offered to undertake all responsibility for sales in return for an exclusive sales franchise. The Clement company would be able to provide national and Canadian distribution. Basically this meant that the digger would be sold by several hundred Ford tractor agencies in this country. The Clement Equipment Company salesmen were used to selling this general type of product and would be able to do the type of pioneering work which Clausson and Winslow had been unable to do in any large extent.

Exhibit 7

HYDRAULIC ATTACHMENTS COMPANY
BALANCE SHEET, DECEMBER 31, 1949

ASSETS			
Current Assets:			
Cash		$33,410.44	
Accounts Receivable—Trade	$19,337.39		
Accounts Receivable—Advances	49.61	19,387.00	
Inventories:			
Finished Goods	$ 6,820.93		
Process Goods	10,301.39		
Raw Material and Supplies	14,394.11	31,516.43	$ 84,313.87
Fixed Assets:		*Net Value*	
Building on Leased Land		$18,712.63	
Machinery and Equipment		5,813.78	
Furniture and Fixtures		902.10	
Trucks and Tractors		3,539.17	28,967.68
Deferred Assets:			
Unexpired Insurance		$ 1,242.93	
Prepaid Rent		57.50	
Organization Expenses		443.47	1,743.90
Total Assets			$115,025.45
LIABILITIES			
Current Liabilities:			
Notes Payable		$ 1,500.00	
Accounts Payable		26,789.58	
Accrued Income and Excise Taxes		10,935.67	
Other Accrued Expenses		1,609.39	
Provision for Liability on Defective Parts		5,000.00	$ 45,834.64
Net Worth:			
Preferred Stock (500 shares—$100 par value)		$50,000.00	
Common Stock (2,000 shares—no-par value)		2,665.27	
Surplus		16,525.54	69,190.81
Total Liabilities			$115,025.45

The price to the Clement Equipment Company would be the initial price at which sales had been made to the four distributors—$708. The difference between $708 and a new increased list price of $1,370 would cover the various markups. Although some thought was given to the effect the increase might have on sales, it was generally agreed by both companies that the extra sales effort and increased amounts to the dealer and distributor would probably offset any adverse tendencies which might develop. The resulting price structure still allowed the distributor 35 per cent off list, the dealer 20 per cent off list, and the difference between $708 and the distributor's price was to be the markup received by Clement. The hydraulic digger would be sold under the Clement Equipment Company trade name, although all advertising would indicate that the unit was manufactured by the Hydraulic Attachments Company. Diggers would be shipped directly from the Hydraulic Attachments plant to dealers.

The longer Clausson and Winslow discussed the offer, the more they were inclined to accept it. They both believed that their own time could be more efficiently employed in the financial, production, and research end of the business. It had become apparent that many new improvements could be incorporated into the digger. More capital had to be raised by the sale of the remaining preferred stock. Certainly, the company could not set up a sales force and obtain the complete coverage that Clement offered. Accordingly, they decided to give Mr. Clement the exclusive sales right for the hydraulic digger.

In a few months' time, Clausson and Winslow were fully convinced of the wisdom of their move. The Clement Equipment Company immediately sold the remaining units from the first production lot of 50. By the end of the year, 269 diggers had been sold. (In the fall of 1949, the company's original product, the farm loader, had been dropped from the line.)

The year 1949 closed with a profit before taxes of $32,442 on sales of $219,226 (Exhibits 6 and 7). Dividends were paid on the preferred stock, as well as $1.50 per share on the common stock.

PROGRESS DURING 1950

A small addition to the plant had been built in 1949 for a cost of about $18,000; additional tools and equipment had been added. Office space was still inadequate, and it appeared certain that more manufacturing space would be required, should the 1949 sales trend continue into 1950.

In the first two months of 1950 it became apparent that the market developed by the Clement Equipment Company could readily absorb 200 units a month. Hydraulic Attachments Company had already made plans for additional manufacturing space which would increase total capacity in excess of 100 units a month.

Henry Clausson and the Clement engineer had been engaged for several months in completely redesigning the digger. The resultant model had over two dozen major engineering changes. This new Model B, with its larger hydraulic ram, would undoubtedly find increased work application in industry, particularly since it could be used to load directly into a medium-sized truck. Most of the Ford tractor distributors realized by now the sales potential of the digger and were aggressively pushing sales. Several of the distributors were beginning to buy in lots of 10 or more at a time.

Reports from the field indicated that the hydraulic digger had opened up what was essentially a new market for the farm-type tractor. A major portion of the sales were being made to industrial users, an area which previously had accounted for only a very small volume of farm-tractor sales. Mr. Clement estimated that, in an excess of 75 per cent of the digger sales, the purchaser bought the digger first and then the tractor, because the tractor was a necessary power unit. Once possessing the tractor, the buyer was quite likely to purchase other standard accessories, such as a bulldozer blade, lights, etc.

COMPETITION

There had been no competition from similar products up to this time. There were well-founded rumors, however, that within the next few months a machine-tool manufacturer would place a hydraulic digger on the market. In appearance and price it was expected to be almost the exact duplicate of the Hydraulic Attachments product, even to the extent of being designed to fasten to the rear of the Ford tractor. There were also reports that at least two other equipment manufacturers were tooling up to produce a similar item.

The two men did not consider that the hydraulic digger competed directly with small power shovels, although there was evidence that some contractors were buying the hydraulic digger to perform work for which they would have ordinarily used a small power shovel. Contractors could buy the digger and tractor complete with some accessories for about $3,500, as compared to about three times that amount for a small power shovel. In fact, Winslow knew of a number of men who had gone into business for themselves by buying a hydraulic digger unit and renting it with operator for $5.50 an hour for various types of excavation work.

THE PROPOSAL FOR A NEW SALES ARRANGEMENT

Both Clausson and Winslow were well satisfied with the present progress of sales. It was their eventual plan to have no more than from 30 to 40 per cent of the company's total income from any one product.

Henry Clausson, with that in mind, had already started to work on new ideas, at least one of which seemed to have promise as a profitable new item. Both men felt that any major expansion should be based on a new product rather than on increased sales of the present digger.

It was against this background that in March, 1950, Mr. Clement made Hydraulic Attachments Company a new offer. Although he appreciated the fact that the two men did not wish an immediate large expansion, he thought that more effort should be made to satisfy the market which his salesmen had developed. He had watched with real concern the growing activity of possible competitors and believed that, if he and the Hydraulic Attachments Company did not soon move to satisfy the demand he had developed, other companies would.

Mr. Clement offered to set up a renewable contract which would guarantee the purchase of at least 50 units per month from Hydraulic Attachments Company, provided that the Clement Equipment Company could sell the units. Hydraulic Attachments Company would grant the Clement Equipment Company a manufacturing franchise for the new Model B unit. For each unit sold, whether manufactured by Hydraulic Attachments Company or by Clement, the Clement Equipment Company would pay a flat royalty of $35 per unit. Of course, the first 50 units sold in any one month would have to be purchased from Hydraulic Atachments Company. The next 50 units would be supplied by Clement. After the first 100 units sold in any one month, the production would be divided—60 per cent to Clement and 40 per cent to Hydraulic Attachments—providing Clausson and Winslow wished to produce that quantity. Mr. Clement planned to produce approximately 100 units per month. He estimated that the market for the remainder of 1950 and 1951 could readily absorb about 200 units per month.

The new Model B unit weighed over 300 pounds more than the Model 49. It used a larger pump and contained more hydraulic valves and cylinders than did the older unit. The costs that Clement and Hydraulic Attachments had developed for the Model B were based on the experimental model and standard times for certain operations. This, coupled with the steadily rising cost of materials, made it difficult to arrive at an estimated price in which the two men placed any trust, at least so far as signing a year's contract was concerned.

To solve this difficulty, Mr. Clement offered to place a $75 "cushion" on their estimated base manufacturing cost. Hydraulic Attachments already employed a competent accountant and had set up a simple cost accounting system. Mr. Clement requested that an audited inventory be taken twice a year and suggested that the Clement and Hydraulic Attachments' books of account be open to both parties. Clement would pay twice monthly the base manufacturing cost plus an amount for profit and administrative cost plus the full "cushion" amount for all diggers shipped by Hydraulic Attachments Company. The royalty would be paid quarterly. Semiannually the manufacturing cost would be reviewed. That portion of the "cushion" which had not been used for increases in manufacturing cost would be divided equally between Clement and Hydraulic Attachments. Mr. Clement also pointed out that Clement Equipment could immediately start the most difficult part of the tooling for the Model B while Clausson concentrated on finishing up production of the current model.

Sale of spare parts had already reached about $12,000 in 1949. Both Clement and Hydraulic Attachments had maintained stocks of parts for the digger. The two companies had divided the responsibility for supplying distributors by area. Mr. Clement proposed that the same division of territory remain under the new agreement. However, he would manufacture his own parts for the new Model B but would continue to purchase Model 49 parts from Hydraulic Attachments Company at a price which allowed the two men a profit.

To make sure that both companies, which were located 1,000 miles apart, produced a standard item, he suggested that they use the same blueprints for the Model B. Changes in construction would have to be approved in writing by both parties.

Portland Enameling Company

The Portland Enameling Company in Portland, Maine, performed porcelain enameling work on sheet-metal and cast-iron products. In 1945, Mr. R. A. Black, Jr., purchased a half-interest in the Portland company. He assumed the positions of vice-president and sales manager. Differences of opinion between Mr. Black and Mr. D. R. Scott, the other principal stockholder, culminated in Mr. Scott's offer in June, 1947, to resign from the firm and sell his stock. Mr. Black had to decide whether to purchase this stock and, if so, how much to pay for it.

HISTORY OF THE COMPANY, 1919–45

Mr. A. R. Clark, founder of the Portland Enameling Company, started out in the job-enameling business on funds advanced by relatives in 1919. During the early years of the business Mr. Clark did much of the shop work himself and evidenced little interest in expansion. From time to time he sold small financial interests in the company to friends to obtain capital for installation of new machinery. Mr. D. R. Scott, with financial backing from his father, had acquired a substantial interest in the Portland company in 1931. Mr. Scott, in his forties, was a lifelong resident of Maine and, while not a trained engineer, had had some experience in metal-trades fields.

Financial difficulties continued to trouble the Portland company, and in 1933 Mr. Clark resigned, leaving Mr. Scott in complete control. Since the company was on the verge of bankruptcy, Mr. Scott gave a half-interest to Frank Grady, a retired naval officer, who became general manager. Mr. Grady pursued an aggressive sales policy, secured the services of an independent accountant, and gradually brought the firm back to solvency. Liberal executive salaries and dividends, however, prevented the accumulation of any reserves for rehabilitation of plant and equipment. Mr. Grady's sudden death in 1937 again placed Mr. Scott in the position of sole operating executive, since the heirs, although retaining seats on the board of directors, had no desire to participate in the management.

During the war the national volume of porcelain enameling was drastically curtailed, although many enameling shops were able to bid successfully on war contracts involving annealing, heat-treating, or fabricating of steel products. Mr. Scott was reluctant to solicit war orders because he did not believe that his small organization possessed sufficient flexibility and know-how. Furthermore, he was so discouraged by delays and red tape involved in bidding for war contracts that he found it more desirable to accept only those orders which could be obtained with a minimum of traveling and selling effort.

The Portland labor force was not unionized, and Mr. Scott was not anxious to enter into contracts which might necessitate the hiring of large numbers of new employees.

Exhibit 1 lists selected operating statistics from 1935 through 1945.

Exhibit 1

PORTLAND ENAMELING COMPANY

ANNUAL OPERATING STATISTICS, 1935–47

(In Thousands)

Year	Sales	Net Income*	Executive Salaries	Net Working Capital
1935	$200	$ 1	$16	$ 5
1936	220	5	24	28
1937	224	16	12	29
1938	157	13[d]	6	16
1939	152	..	6	16
1940	181	5	6	20
1941	198	2[d]	7	17
1942	154	1[d]	7	18
1943	157	10	7	22
1944	163	6[d]	8	19
1945	132	30[d]	10	6
1946	326	19	17	22
1947 (6 mos.)	227	26	22	14

* Before income taxes but after profit sharing.
[d] Deficit.
Source: Company records.

MR. BLACK'S BACKGROUND

Mr. R. A. ("Bob") Black was born in Wisconsin in 1918. His father, who came from a poor family, had risen to the position of president of a prosperous Midwestern company engaged in the manufacture and sale of enamel materials and enameling equipment. It was an established family policy that none of the Black children would enter the management of this company. In line with this resolution, Bob had never worked in the family business. He had held a variety of part-time and summer jobs as filling-station attendant, counselor on an Arizona dude ranch, and time-study clerk in a small Canadian job-enameling plant. In the latter position, Bob had had the opportunity to make porcelain ash trays, signs, and gift trinkets and thus to learn something about the manufacturing processes of porcelain enameling. Bob also had accompanied his father on trips to several American enameling factories which were customers of the Black firm. Since he was naturally inquisitive, he continually asked questions about enameling practices.

Bob graduated from a small western college in 1941. His scholastic record was above average, but academic achievements were not easy for him. He had particularly enjoyed serving as business manager on the campus literary magazine. The next year, after being married, he enrolled in the Canadian Army as a private. During his three and a half years of war service he earned a commission and served in both the European and Pacific theaters as secretary to a committee which allocated Canadian war matériel to the various allied forces. Meanwhile the problem of a postwar career was foremost in his mind.

BUYING INTO THE BUSINESS

In 1944, while serving in Europe, Bob received a letter about the Portland company from his father. One of the Black firm's eastern salesmen had reported that Mr. Scott was experiencing a difficult time with his business and was looking for some young man to come in and give him some help. Bob's father pointed out that the company seemed to have been in constant financial difficulties but that, as far as he knew, it was the only porcelain enameling plant in New England and had possibilities of offering a decent living. Bob immediately wrote to Mr. Scott expressing interest in working for the Portland company and enclosing a personal résumé. Mr. Scott answered cordially and invited Bob to come to Maine to talk the situation over when he returned to the States.

Early in 1945, Bob came home on a ninety-day leave before being sent to the Pacific area. He got in touch with Mr. Scott, who, although he did not sound particularly encouraging, invited him to visit the plant. After going through the factory, Bob felt that the business had a definite future. The plant was located on three acres of land and had access to a railroad spur track and adequate water, gas, and electric facilities. The one-story wooden building was shabby and in poor repair but contained several metalworking machines and two large enameling furnaces. There were about fifteen employees, several of whom appeared to have little or nothing to do, although a considerable amount of work in process was evident in the shop.

When Bob mentioned joining the firm, he was surprised to learn that there was an immediate opportunity to buy a half-interest. Bob felt that this proposal was beyond his financial means but countered with the suggestion that he might purchase a small stock interest with an option to increase it as he built up savings. Mr. Scott was unable to furnish any concrete information as to his own future plans or the eventual disposition of his stock, but Bob believed that his reticence was due to native Yankee taciturnity rather than to any personal antagonism. Finally it was decided that Mr. Scott's lawyer should determine the terms under which the Grady heirs would be willing to sell their half-interest to Mr. Black.

Before going overseas again, Bob gave his father power of attorney and asked him to keep an eye on the purchase negotiations. Within a few weeks the lawyer wrote Bob a detailed letter, explaining that the Grady heirs would sell their stock for $14,000. The purchase included 71 shares of preferred stock for $7,100 and 264 common stock shares for $6,900. Mr. Scott held 279 preferred and 264 common shares, while Mr. George Bone, a former employee, owned 45 shares of common. The price asked for the common stock was based on the June 30, 1945, balance sheet, plus a slight increment for going-concern value.

Control of the Portland company resided in a "voting trust," established in 1935 by Mr. Grady and Mr. Scott to preclude the possibility of either shareholder combining with Mr. Bone to outvote the other. Each of the two principal owners placed 200 shares of his common stock in the trust, which therefore controlled 400 of the 573 outstanding shares of common. The trustee, a local attorney, was authorized to vote these shares as a unit upon receipt of instructions from the owners. The voting trust arrangement would remain in force if the Grady stock were sold to Mr. Black.

Although Bob had not seen any 1945 income statements, he and his father agreed that the price seemed ridiculously low. The elder Black was extremely busy with war work and could not take time to visit Portland and investigate the situation further. Bob therefore accepted the offer and arranged to finance the purchase from a personal trust fund. Mr. Scott invited Bob to become president of the Portland company upon his release from war service, but Bob decided that the position of vice-president would be more in keeping with his age and experience.

PRODUCTION PROCESSES

The Portland company was exclusively a subcontractor, producing no finished goods. Its manufacturing facilities included a metal shop, pickling tanks, four rotary mills for grinding enamel, spraying and dipping equipment, and two 300-cubic-foot firing ovens. In the metal shop a special grade of enameling steel was formed into desired shapes by cutting, pressing, and welding. The fabricated parts were then pickled in acid, degreased, rinsed, dried, and sent to spraying or dipping booths. The metal shop's capacity was about 40 per cent of that of the firing ovens. The remaining 60 per cent of the company's production consisted of "enamel-only" work, that is, fabricated parts shipped by customers to the Portland plant for porcelaining. The company performed both fabrication and enameling on signs, store-front panels, and refrigerator case parts; in the "enamel-only" category the chief products were steel stove panels, cast-iron stove legs and burners, and miscellaneous metal items such as chemical tanks.

While ordinary commercial paints and enamels consisted primarily of organic pigments and oils, porcelain enamel was made from "frit," a gravel-like glass which could be mixed with clay, fluxes, colored metallic oxides, and water to make a liquid enamel. In the mill room of the Portland plant, these raw materials were mixed and ground for four to six hours in rotary mills. Formulas for various mixes were supplied by the frit manufacturers, one of whom was the elder Black's firm. Fabricated metal parts were sprayed or dipped in enamel and then dried, leaving a hard-caked, finely ground coat of porcelain enamel. The coated pieces were baked at about 1,500 degrees in box-type, oil-fired ovens. At this temperature the enamel became cherry-red and was fused to the metal to produce a smooth glasslike surface. After each firing, the parts were allowed to cool before being resprayed and refired. The number of firings varied from two to six, depending on the variety of colors required for a given job.

The extremely high temperature required for fusing porcelain enamel tended to warp carelessly shaped parts. Breaks in the enamel coating and carbon deposits from careless welds resulted in scaly surfaces and poor fusing in the finished product. Consequently, great care had to be exercised over each step in the production process.

ORGANIZATION, DECEMBER, 1945

Mr. Black was released from active duty in October, 1945, and arrived with his wife in Maine about the first of December. They bought a house and prepared to settle in the area. Mr. Black spent the first several days talking with Mr. Scott and key employees. Mr. Scott indicated that he was tired, overworked, and discouraged and consequently wanted Mr. Black to take charge and have a free hand in making all operating decisions.

Mr. William Kellher, chief bookkeeper, was the oldest employee in terms of length of service, having been with the company since its inception. Besides handling the financial records under the general supervision of an outside accountant, he helped out in the plant by cutting stencils for enamel signs and occasionally writing shop orders. Clear, complete shop orders were particularly important because each job was different and it was essential for the shop workers to understand the exact requirements of each customer. Mr. Scott stated that Mr. Kellher had at one time requested a stock interest in the company and that, since then, co-operation between them had not been particularly effective.

Mr. George Martin, maintenance engineer and metal-shop foreman, had been working with the company for more than ten years. He was Mr. Scott's brother-in-law. Although not a graduate engineer or a journeyman plumber or electrician, he was familiar with the Portland equipment and possessed considerable mechanical aptitude. Mr. Black believed that the poor condition of the plant resulted, not from incompetence on Mr. Martin's part, but from a lack of funds for repair work and particularly from the fact that Mr. Martin had to serve as metal-shop foreman, mill-room operator, and sand blaster, in addition to his primary maintenance job. Mr. Martin seemed affable and pleasant but was not popular with the shop workers.

Mr. George Martin's wife was chief clerk and secretary. She was a strong-minded and efficient woman who had come to work for Mr. Scott during the war. She handled all confidential cost quotations and correspondence, as well as payrolls, invoices, and personnel records.

Mr. Robert Peterson was the plant superintendent. A quiet middle-aged man, he had joined the company in 1943 after thirty-five years with a stove manufacturing concern with which he had risen to the post of enameling foreman. He was conscientious and capable, although sensitive to criticism and easily disturbed by plant gossip. He appeared to have complete responsibility for managing the production end of the business. Approximately fifteen men were employed in the shop under Mr. Peterson and Mr. Martin.

Mr. Albert Shultz, architectural panel salesman, received fifteen per cent of the factory price on all sales, which consisted chiefly of retail store fronts. He wrote his own shop orders and made very few costly mistakes. He brought potential customers' specifications to Mr. Scott or Mr. Kellher, who would subsequently quote prices to the customers by telephone.

Mr. Max Meyer, a young war veteran, solicited orders from sign companies, which in turn sold the enameled signs to end users. Mr. Black found Mr. Meyer extremely personable and willing to work hard.

Miss Betty Towner, a very efficient bookkeeper, had worked in the

Portland shop for several years and was acquainted with most of the employees. She now worked under Mr. Kellher on a part-time basis, coming in at irregular intervals, and was paid $1.00 an hour. Miss Towner and Mrs. Martin were mutually antagonistic and generally were not on speaking terms. Neither of the two women had had any formal secretarial schooling. Mr. Black occasionally found his own secretarial-school training useful because it enabled him to improve the physical appearance of the company's letters. He believed that neat, clear correspondence exerted an important influence on the reputation of a small firm.

Mr. Black realized that the personnel were not working as an effective team. There was a suspicious atmosphere of formality about the plant, with everyone addressing each other as "Mr." or "Mrs." No one seemed to have a clear conception of his own responsibility and authority, and it appeared to Mr. Black that some employees were deliberately holding back information which should have been made available to the entire management group. Mr. Black learned from the outside accountant that the company was technically bankrupt. He then explained this condition to each key employee and succeeded in winning pledges of full co-operation. He tried to define responsibilities in such a way that no one would continue to infringe on anyone else's territory. Mr. Martin was directed to draw up a list of needed repairs, classified in order of urgency, and to give an estimate of the cost of each. Mr. Peterson compiled a similar list of gaps in the plant labor force.

Although Mr. Black was not fully satisfied with the work of some of his supervisory personnel, he made no major changes in the staff during 1946. He realized that his own lack of experience would make him dependent on his assistants for information and guidance. Furthermore, he did not want to dismiss anyone until he was sure that the employee was incompetent or was not acting in the best interests of the company.

INITIAL MANAGEMENT STEPS

During the month of November the Portland company lost about $6,000 on a sales volume of $11,500. Mr. Black felt that two things had to be done immediately to stave off bankruptcy: (1) increase the company's prices and (2) eliminate all unprofitable business. The plant had no cost system, but it was obvious to Mr. Black that many of the current orders were unprofitable. For instance, the company was processing every month an average of five "well screens," perforated steel plates used in lieu of concrete for well linings. These plates were 18 feet long, 3 feet wide, and ½ inch thick; moving them around the plant required the physical aid of all men in the factory. The quoted price was $18 per screen, based on the standard charge per pound for work requiring similar grades of enamel and number of firings. Mr. Black thought that $200 per screen would more accurately reflect the company's costs. In addition, a number of single-item jobs which carried no promise of repeat orders and took an inordinate amount of time and labor were being handled at the same prices as large-volume orders.

At about this same time, Mr. Black paid a visit to a friend who owned a porcelain enameling plant in the Midwest. He examined the cost system in this plant but did not feel that he could install a similar system in the Portland Enameling Company by himself; nor did he believe that setting up such a system would solve his problems fast enough. Upon returning to Maine, he decided to approach authorities in the regional Office of Price Administration to secure permission to increase the Portland company's prices. He wrote several briefs pointing out that during the base period used by the OPA for establishing price ceilings his company had lost money on its operations and that therefore these base prices were unfair. He estimated that a 20 to 30 per cent increase was necessary to permit a fair profit and, furthermore, was justified by prices in comparable Midwestern plants. The officials of the OPA, however, stated that a 20 per cent increase was out of the question and that there was small likelihood of any immediate price relief.

After three weeks of filling out forms and talking with government officials, Mr. Black went directly to the regional administrator and announced that he must increase his prices 28 per cent or go out of business and that, if the board would not authorize this increase, he would rather be jailed for violating an unfair regulation than for being unable to pay his creditors. He mentioned that, if he were denied the price boost, he would take his story to the newspapers; and he thought that as a veteran he would get a receptive response. The administrator was more co-operative, and within a few days Mr. Black was authorized by the OPA to increase prices by an average of 28 per cent. He put his new price schedule into effect at once, receiving several complaints but losing orders from only two small customers. At the same time, he directed the salesmen to refuse any more orders for certain unprofitable job-order products, such as the well screens.

To meet current payrolls in January, 1946, Mr. Black and Mr. Scott personally loaned the company approximately $27,000, receiving in return notes bearing 6 per cent interest. These funds were raised from the partners' own savings and by borrowings from personal friends. During the same month, Mr. Black called on the president of a local bank and

Exhibit 2

PORTLAND ENAMELING COMPANY

Balance Sheets as of December 31, 1944—December 31, 1946

ASSETS

	1944	1945	1946
Current Assets:			
Cash	$11,924	$ 6,158	$ 15,592
Accounts Receivable—Trade	9,626	12,138	29,659
—Employees	772	2,323	58
Notes Receivable	.....	.....	6,000
Federal Tax Refund Claim	.....	.....	2,770
Inventories	9,671	18,739	45,657
	$31,993	$39,358	$ 99,736
Deferred Charges	1,446	1,583	2,033
Fixed Assets:			
Land	19,072	19,072	19,072
Buildings (cost)	24,745	27,744	69,335
Less: Reserve for Depreciation	17,149	18,149	14,621
Buildings (net)	$ 7,596	$ 9,595	$ 54,714
Machinery and Equipment (cost)	75,876	76,616	96,922
Less: Reserve for Depreciation	63,757	66,013	64,618
Machinery and Equipment (net)	$12,119	$10,603	$ 32,304
Furniture and Fixtures (net)	949	1,082	1,285
	$39,736	$40,352	$107,375
Preferred Stock Held in Treasury (3 shares)	300	300	300
Total Assets	$73,475	$81,595	$209,444

LIABILITIES

	1944	1945	1946
Current Liabilities:			
Accounts Payable—Trade	$ 6,954	$19,583	$ 57,672
—Officers	1,846	2,468	3,692
Notes Payable	295	5,636	586
Accrued Taxes	2,492	2,825	4,571
Mortgage Payable	.....	240	.....
Commissions Payable	.....	.....	1,924
Accrued Payroll and Bonus	.....	.....	5,836
Advances from Customers	.....	.....	2,044
Other Accruals	1,177	2,080	1,712
	$12,764	$32,832	$ 78,037
Other Liabilities:			
Notes Payable—Bank	.....	.....	36,000
—Officers	.....	17,280	28,080
Mortgage Payable	3,348	2,868	.....
Deferred Commissions	.....	.....	876
Equipment Replacement Reserve (fire)	.....	.....	6,814
Provision for Vacation Pay	.....	.....	1,260
	$ 3,348	$20,148	$ 73,030
Total Liabilities	$16,112	$52,980	$151,067
Capital and Surplus:			
Preferred Stock ($100 par)	35,000	35,000	35,000
Common Stock (no par)	12,580*	12,580*	21,364†
Capital Surplus	13,671	13,671	14,175
Earned Surplus	3,888[d]	32,636[d]	12,162[d]
Total Capital and Surplus	$57,363	$28,615	$ 58,377
Total Liabilities, Capital, and Surplus	$73,475	$81,595	$209,444

* 573 shares outstanding.
† 720 shares outstanding.
[d] Deficit.

Source: Company records.

explained in detail the financial position of the company. He brought along a 1945 income statement and the balance sheet for December 31, 1945 (Exhibit 2, p. 315). He pointed out that he had recently obtained authority from the OPA to increase prices and was inaugurating a new sales program aimed at securing larger and more profitable orders. He also showed that, with the exception of two shops which processed only very small articles, such as thermometers, the Portland company operated the only plant in New England equipped to perform porcelain enameling work. Many New England manufacturers were shipping fabricated metal parts to Midwestern plants for enameling. Mr. Black was sure that he could obtain much of this business for his company, since freight costs and the danger of enameled parts being chipped while in transit would tend to give a New England processor an advantage. As a result of these negotiations, the bank agreed to loan the Portland company $36,000, in the form of a six-year note at 4 per cent interest, secured only by the signatures of Mr. Black and Mr. Scott. No payments on principal were to be made in the first year; thereafter the principal was to be repaid at the rate of $1,000 yearly, with the balance due in 1950. Presumably, the note could be extended at that time. If at any time the company's current ratio should fall below 2:1, the bank could call the entire note.

Although machinery was difficult to procure in the spring of 1946, Mr. Black placed orders for a production multistation punch press, a new power shear, welding equipment, another rotary enamel mill, and a third firing furnace. Deliveries came through slowly, but by October, 1946, most of the new equipment had been installed. A fire in March, 1946, completely destroyed the metal shop. While the loss was not fully covered by insurance, Mr. Black was able to build a larger and more modern concrete metal shop by using the insurance proceeds and part of the bank loan. Within two weeks after the fire the metal shop was operating at 60 per cent of its former capacity in an outside area next to the factory. Some equipment had been salvaged from the burned plant, and the heavy shearing and bending operations were subcontracted to other metal shops.

NEW PERSONNEL

In January, 1946, the Portland company had vacancies in several important skilled labor positions. Working conditions in the plant were bad; heat was inadequate; and rest rooms in a shameful condition. Wages were below the going rate; yet the company could not afford to grant a wage increase. Mr. Scott advertised in newspapers for employees and occasionally telephoned the U.S. Employment Office. These methods had resulted in securing only a few men, and the caliber of these newcomers was generally unsatisfactory. In a conference with the chief Maine official of the U.S. Employment Service, Mr. Black was told that the plant's reputation was poor and that, in a time of acute labor shortage, workers were unwilling to accept employment at what they considered substandard rates. Mr. Black concluded that he would have to secure certain key employees through personal solicitation.

The manufacture of porcelain enamel signs required a stencil cutter skilled in the porcelain technique. In addition to his role as bookkeeper, Mr. Kellher was trying to handle this work and had gradually attained some success in teaching the job to other employees. In April, 1946, after his discharge from the U.S. Marines, Mr. John McManus, a stencil cutter for the Portland company before the war, agreed to return to his previous job at a substantial wage increase. Mr. Black also rehired two former employees to fill the positions of shop-order man and metal-shop foreman. Since both of these men had been earning more money elsewhere than the Portland company could offer them, Mr. Black had to visit their homes several times to convince them that his company was being reorganized and had a bright future.

The shipping department, operating without a foreman, had created confusion and ill will by mixing shipments and failing to respect delivery priorities. Mr. Black learned from a waitress in a local restaurant that her husband, who had worked for Portland in 1940 at 40 cents an hour, was just being discharged from the Army and would be looking for a job in Portland, Maine. Mr. Black met the young man at the railroad station and offered him 85 cents an hour to take over the shipping department. He accepted and proved to be a competent worker.

Although Mr. Martin had been relieved of his duties as metal-shop foreman, he was still serving as mill-room operator as well as maintenance man. Several employees were tried out in the mill room, but Mr. Martin did not regard any of them as satisfactory. When Frank Peterson, son of the plant superintendent, was released from the Army, he was placed under Mr. Martin in the mill room and demonstrated considerable aptitude there. Within a few weeks he was made mill-room operator, and Mr. Martin was given the title of plant engineer and was assigned full time to maintenance.

SALES DEVELOPMENT

Sales to a single stove manufacturer had averaged more than half of the Portland company's dollar volume during the past ten years. This proportion rose to 80 per cent in late 1945, when the company was concentrating on stove parts and other "enamel-only" jobs. The stove manufacturer protested sharply when the new Portland price schedule was announced. Mr. Black discovered, however, that his price for stove enameling was about 10 per cent less than the cost assigned to similar work by those manufacturers who enameled panels in their own factories. Furthermore, the Portland company had to meet exceptionally close inspection standards and applied an extra coat of enamel to stove parts. The stove company's representatives had often come to the plant to ask Mr. Peterson to advance delivery dates. Mr. Black decided that, although he could not yet afford to drop all business with this customer, he would gradually reduce stove-panel sales to 20 per cent of total volume.

In May, 1946, Mr. Black secured a substantial order from a New England company which was starting production on a high-quality combination oil range. This firm proved to be a satisfactory and reliable customer. A few months later, Mr. Black informed the original stove manufacturer that Portland would no longer be able to handle its business, although several months' grace would be extended to facilitate new supplier arrangements.

In keeping with his diversification policy, Mr. Black made strenuous efforts to develop new customers. Mr. Meyer increased repeat-order sign customers from one to six, including a chain store and a large brewery. Elaborate tailor-made signs and smaller multicolored signs (made by a screening process rather than by stencils) were added to the company's line of signs, which Mr. Black hoped would account for 25 to 40 per cent of total sales. He expected that store-front panels would account for another 20 per cent. Enameling of cast-iron parts (chiefly stove legs and burners) was to comprise 10 to 20 per cent of the volume, while the remainder would be made up of miscellaneous specialties, such as refrigeration cases, coal chutes, aviation markers, and reflectors. Some of these items carried relatively low profit margins, but Mr. Black believed that they would become more lucrative; in the meantime they helped to absorb overhead expenses. The development of export sales to Canada and Latin America would also be stressed.

In March, 1946, the Portland company began to earn a profit. Exhibits 2, 3, and 4 show balance sheets, income statements, and departmental cost breakdowns for 1944, 1945, and 1946; Exhibit 5 lists monthly sales and profits from November, 1945, through June, 1947.

Mr. Black was convinced that his company's best long-run opportunities lay in processing highly specialized industrial and architectural products for established companies which could be depended on for repeat orders. In the fall of 1946 an Ohio engineering contractor, whose business was world-wide in scope, awarded Portland a contract to man-

Exhibit 3

PORTLAND ENAMELING COMPANY

COMPARATIVE PROFIT AND LOSS STATEMENT, 1944–46

	1944	*1945*	*1946*
Sales (net)	$163,396	$131,612	$325,605
Less: Cost of goods sold	143,587	131,649	252,499
Gross profit on sales	$ 19,809	$ 37[d]	$ 73,106
Selling and administrative expenses:			
Executive salaries	7,694	10,006	16,560
Clerical expense	7,669	8,080	9,951
Salesmen's salaries	......	1,326	4,009
Subscriptions and dues	1,258	636	1,103
Sales expense	1,116	1,834	2,115
Traveling expense	667	860	1,069
Legal and auditing	2,617	2,496	1,958
Stationery and printing	534	65	746
Telephone	739	785	1,740
Postage	89	104	164
Unemployment tax	90	113	172
Old age tax	113	141	215
Liability insurance	8	8	20
Delivery expense	......	17	343
Depreciation on furniture	197	106	139
Employees' vacation pay	......	......	509
Miscellaneous expense	748	788	1,895
	$ 23,539	$ 27,365	$ 42,708
Profit from operations	3,730[d]	27,402[d]	30,398
Add: Discounts on purchases	37	30	166
	$ 3,693[d]	$ 27,372[d]	$ 30,564
Deduct: Other charges:			
Interest on mortgage	208	193	46
Interest on notes payable	......	......	2,807
Other interest paid	34	235	......
Loss on bad accounts	72	238	402
Cash discounts on sales	1,635	2,180	3,764
Fire loss	......	......	1,101
	$ 1,949	$ 2,846	$ 8,120
Profit or loss (before income tax and bonus)	5,642[d]	30,218[d]	22,444
Deduct: Employee bonus	......	......	3,329
Profit before income tax	$ 5,642[d]	$ 30,218[d]	$ 19,115

[d] Loss.
Source: Company records.

ufacture porcelain-enamel steel cover panels for ten new gasoline stations being erected in Indiana and Ohio. Mr. Black realized that, under normal circumstances, his company could not meet competitive bids on Midwestern orders. He obtained this contract chiefly because the engineering firm's prewar enamel supplier had been unable to maintain pro-

***Exhibit* 4**

PORTLAND ENAMELING COMPANY

DEPARTMENTAL OPERATING STATISTICS, 1944–46

Department	Accounts	1944	1945	1946
Cast iron	Sales (net)	$ 27,258	$ 29,796	$ 81,085
	Less: Cost of goods sold	18,229	27,273	45,155
	Gross profit	$ 9,029	$ 2,523	$ 35,930
	Less: Selling expense	400	541	1,525
	Administrative expense	3,577	5,997	9,109
	Net profit from operations	$ 5,052	$ 4,015[d]	$ 25,296
Steel	Sales (net)	40,481	66,961	239,864
	Less: Cost of goods sold	50,862	74,196	205,073
	Gross profit	$ 10,381[d]	$ 7,235[d]	$ 34,791
	Less: Selling expense	716	1,211	4,511
	Administrative expense	6,103	13,453	26,953
	Net profit from operations	$ 17,200[d]	$ 21,899[d]	$ 3,327
Sandblast	Sales (net)	25,601	20,221	4,381
	Less: Cost of goods sold	12,907	12,557	1,453
	Gross profit	$ 12,694	$ 7,664	$ 2,928
	Less: Selling expense	......	54	83
	Administrative expense	3,992	3,563	493
	Net profit from operations	$ 8,702	$ 4,047	$ 2,352
Pickling and annealing	Sales (net)	7,074	5,786	......
	Less: Cost of goods sold	3,005	5,353	......
	Gross profit	$ 4,069	$ 433	......
	Less: Selling expense	......	14	......
	Administrative expense	1,157	898	......
	Net profit from operations	$ 2,912	$ 479[d]	......
Army contracts	Sales (net)	20,112	1,714	......
	Less: Cost of goods sold	20,914	1,354	......
	Gross profit	$ 802[d]	$ 360	......
	Less: Selling expense	......	6	......
	Administrative expense	2,066	362	......
	Net profit from operations	$ 2,868[d]	$ 8[d]	......
Miscellaneous paint	Sales (net)	42,870	7,134	$ 275
	Less: Cost of goods sold	37,670	10,916	818
	Gross profit	$ 5,200	$ 3,782[d]	$ 543[d]
	Less: Selling expense	......	8	5
	Administrative expense	5,528	1,258	29
	Net profit from operations	$ 328[d]	$ 5,048[d]	$ 577[d]
Total	Sales (net)	163,396	131,612	325,605
	Less: Cost of goods sold	143,587	131,649	252,499
	Gross profit	$ 19,809	$ 37[d]	$ 73,106
	Less: Selling expense	1,116	1,834	6,124
	Administrative expense	22,423	25,531	36,584
	Net profit from operations	$ 3,730[d]	$ 27,402[d]	$ 30,398

[d] Loss.

Source: Company records.

duction facilities during the war. The Portland company's performance on this contract was highly satisfactory, and Mr. Black entered bids to supply panels for ten more filling stations being built in New England by the same contractor.

Another new contract involved the construction of metal cab panels for a large New York City elevator manufacturer. The initial order

Exhibit 5

PORTLAND ENAMELING COMPANY

MONTHLY SALES AND PROFITS,
NOVEMBER, 1945—JUNE, 1947

Year	Month	Sales	Profit*
1945	November	$11,141	$6,738[d]
	December	13,116	1,164[d]
1946	January	17,915	1,566[d]
	February	22,771	378[d]
	March	26,663	2,483
	April	22,986†	4,994
	May	30,756	4,043
	June	29,272	1,038‡
	July	22,637§	905[d]
	August	36,226	3,918
	September	24,222	1,235
	October	32,857	2,720
	November	29,874	2,858
	December	29,449	1,309
1947	January	40,894	6,707
	February	36,494	5,449
	March	38,053	5,172
	April	48,809	7,405
	May	27,204	316[d]
	June	35,482	1,152

[d] Loss.
* Before federal income taxes and profit sharing.
† Metal shop burned April 5, 1946.
‡ Includes $1,600 total charges for employee vacation pay for year beginning July 1, 1946.
§ Plant shut down two weeks for vacation.
Source: Company records.

called for monthly delivery of sufficient sections to complete two elevator cabs, with the understanding that, if the work was satisfactory, subsequent monthly orders would call for ten or more cabs. The cab panels were both fabricated and enameled by the Portland company. The completed elevators were to be installed in metropolitan housing projects.

A third new customer was a manufacturer of commercial baking ovens. The Portland company's price for enameling these ovens was less than the cost to the manufacturer of performing the work in his own plant. The oven panels were of such complex construction and irregular shapes that special care was required in spraying them. Another large order had been obtained from an ice-cream firm for enameling porcelain signs on side panels of its delivery trucks.

Before these contracts had been successfully negotiated, inspectors, engineers, and auditors from the prospective customers had toured the Portland plant, examined product samples, talked with the executives, and investigated the firm's credit rating. The company's reputation with its bank and with suppliers had been bolstered by the presence of well-known firm names on its accounts receivable list.

Mr. Black continued to perform some work for small customers, using his judgment in extending credit. He obtained the services of a capable sales representative in New York City for a local entrepreneur who had developed a porcelain-enamel kitchen barbecue machine. In the spring of 1947 the demand for cast-iron enameling slumped severely, but Mr. Black was able to utilize his sandblasting equipment on jobs requiring only sanding and oiling.

In April, 1946, Mr. Black established a profit-sharing plan in which all nonsupervisory employees participated. Payments were distributed quarterly on the basis of individual gross earnings. The total distribution was set at 10 per cent of net profits before federal income taxes. Mr. Black felt that this percentage could be increased if profits declined during any given quarter for reasons beyond the workers' control. He had originally planned to distribute the bonus to the men in proportion to their basic hourly wage rates. The Wages and Hours Division of the U.S. Department of Labor, however, advised him that profit-sharing payments must be based on the workers' gross earnings, including overtime. Mr. Black accordingly made a few supplemental payments to those men whose share, under the original plan, had been less than they would have received under the government-approved program. He also inaugurated a group life, accident, and hospitalization insurance plan covering all company employees.

PLANS FOR EXPANSION

In the summer of 1946 Mr. Black considered the possibility of raising additional permanent capital and expanding the Portland company's production facilities. He estimated that New England manufacturers were then sending more than $150,000 a month in porcelain enameling work to shops in other parts of the country. Furthermore, the New York area, with an almost unlimited potential volume of enameling business, was well within the Portland company's competitive range; Mr. Black had obtained a New York sales agent to represent his firm there. He was also eager to bring to the production stage a number of new enamel specialty items on which the company's staff had been working. Among the most promising was a fluorescent enamel for signs developed in January, 1946. Other products in the development stage included prefabricated porcelain-enamel homes, grave vaults, shingles, enameled tubular steel chimneys, and aircraft exhaust stacks.

In connection with new financing plans, Mr. Black insisted on two requirements: (1) voting control must remain with himself and Mr. Scott, and (2) new capital must be supplied on a basis which did not involve giving executive positions to inexperienced or unqualified persons. Mr. Black thought that about $180,000 would be needed to increase plant facilities and working capital to a point where the company could realize its full sales potential. He planned to raise about $90,000 initially, and he expected that after a year or two of experience in expanded operations the additional sum might be obtained. Mr. Scott expressed complete agreement with these thoughts.

One source of funds which Mr. Black investigated was Business Ideas, Inc., a Boston investment syndicate. This organization had been established by a small group of New England businessmen and financiers who believed that the careful selection and promotion of new enterprises would prove more remunerative for venture capital than regular investment channels. Two full-time executives managed the syndicate, investigating various business enterprises and recommending to the stockholder-directors specific offers which the group might make for equity interests in promising ventures. After a few years, individual stockholders would take over these investments from the syndicate, releasing organization funds for reinvestment.

Although Business Ideas, Inc., was primarily interested in new scientific or technical processes which might be the forerunners of entire new industries, its managers were greatly impressed by the Portland company's competitive position and alert management. Its investigation confirmed Mr. Black's estimate of the potential New England enameling market. In November, 1946, the syndicate's directors voted to make the following offer to Mr. Black and Mr. Scott:

1. All outstanding stock, both preferred and common, should be replaced by Class A common stock, issued on a basis which would give the present owners a total of 1,000 shares.
2. Business Ideas, Inc., would purchase for $90,000:
   a) 750 shares of 3 per cent $100-par cumulative nonvoting preferred

stock, dividends to be waived for one or two years and the issue to be called if further financing became necessary;

b) 400 shares of Class A common stock;

c) A three-year option to purchase 800 shares of nonvoting Class B common for $180,000.

3. The sponsors of Business Ideas, Inc., would have two seats out of five on the board of directors.
4. The Portland company could issue additional stock only with the unanimous consent of the board.
5. Mr. Black would agree to a five-year employment contract.
6. The Portland company would take out $90,000 in life insurance on Mr. Black for repurchase of Business Ideas stock in the event of his death.

After careful deliberation, Mr. Black and Mr. Scott rejected the syndicate's offer, concluding that they would prefer to expand more slowly through plowed-back earnings rather than surrender so large a portion of their equity.

During the latter half of 1946, Mr. Black bought 147 previously unissued shares of Portland common stock, at an average price of $60 per share, and also purchased Mr. Bone's 45 shares at this figure. He financed these stock purchases by borrowing from his family and from friends. Mr. Scott did not increase his stock holdings, since his personal financial condition would not warrant any further investment at present. Majority control of the company remained with the 400 shares of common stock deposited in the Black-Scott voting trust.

SPLIT IN MANAGEMENT

As the Portland company's sales volume expanded, Mr. Black felt the need of energetic management assistance, particularly in the fields of production and finance. In January, 1947, he hired Mr. Fred Hannon as general manager. Mr. Hannon, forty years old, had been vice-president of a New England stove manufacturing concern and was thoroughly familiar with porcelain enameling processes. The closely owned nature of the stove company had precluded his obtaining a stock interest, and he joined Portland when he was offered an option to buy a 20 per cent common-stock interest in the firm.

In February, 1947, Mr. Black's health broke under the strain of his seven-day work week, and he was ordered to Florida for a rest. After two weeks, Mr. Scott telephoned him to say that Mr. Hannon would have to be released. Since the charges against Mr. Hannon were rather vague, Mr. Black refused to consent to his dismissal until he could make a personal investigation.

When he returned to New England in March, Mr. Black concluded that Mr. Hannon was carrying out his duties in an exemplary manner. The difficulty seemed to stem from a feeling on the part of Mr. Martin, the maintenance engineer, that the new executive had been given too much authority and that he was interfering with his own functions. Mr. Martin had also implied that, if and when Mr. Hannon should exercise his stock option, Mr. Scott might be outvoted by Mr. Hannon and Mr. Black. Furthermore, Mr. Scott stated that he was not in sympathy with any plans for expansion and that the company had been getting along all right before Mr. Hannon had been appointed. Mr. Black would not agree to dismiss Mr. Hannon, and Mr. Scott refused to accept the offered resignation of Mr. Martin.

As this impasse developed, Mr. Black discovered that the Portland preferred shares possessed equal voting rights with the common stock, even when preferred dividends were not in arrears. He had not been aware of this fact when he bought into the firm in 1945. Although Mr. Scott held 80 per cent of the outstanding preferred shares, the existence of the voting trust precluded any management decisions without the mutual consent of both stockholders. Combined common and preferred stockholdings totaled 527 shares for Mr. Black and 543 shares for Mr. Scott. The latter indicated in March, 1947, that he did not think the company needed any more funds and that no additional stock should be issued.

Sales of the Portland company had reached $48,000 in April but declined to $28,000 in May. Mr. Scott would no longer accept Mr. Black's decisions on daily operating problems or future company commitments, and Mr. Hannon was unable to secure the full co-operation of the work force so long as Mr. Martin openly challenged his position.

Mr. Black realized that everyone was spending so much time wrangling that the business was being grossly neglected. By the end of May the company's current ratio had fallen below 2:1, and the bank loan was technically in default. The strain on working capital resulted from the fact that Mr. Black had planned to step up plant capacity during the summer and had ordered equipment and materials to handle increased business. Furthermore, Mr. Hannon had been unable to invest in the company so long as the disagreement between the principal officers persisted.

After lengthy discussions Mr. Scott stated that he could not and would not buy out Mr. Black but that he might be willing to dispose of his holdings on the following terms:

1. A down payment of $25,000 in cash.
2. Receipt of a yearly salary of $2,500 for the next five years.

3. Repayment over a five-year period of the $12,000 loan which he had made in 1946.
4. Payment over a seven-year period of an additional $85,000 with an annual interest rate of 5 per cent on the unpaid balance. The Portland company would issue notes to Mr. Scott to cover this obligation.
5. No plant building, expansion, or other major capital expenditures to be made in the next seven years without Mr. Scott's consent.
6. No further borrowings or sale of stock to be undertaken during this time without Mr. Scott's approval.

Mr. Black was in a position to borrow the $25,000 for the down payment. If Mr. Scott's proposal were accepted, Mr. Hannon would remain with the company and invest from $5,000 to $10,000 in Portland stock. A young executive in the export division of a Midwestern industrial company, Mr. Arthur Farley, was considering the purchase for $20,000 of another minority interest in the Portland company; he would take over the firm's financial management as treasurer. He held a Master's degree in business administration and had at one time been assistant controller of a Canadian enameling firm.

In June, 1947, Mr. Black came to the conclusion that the Portland Enameling Company did not have a chance of survival so long as the present impasse continued. He was considering three possible alternatives:

1. He could reject Mr. Scott's proposal and let the company drift toward liquidation, hoping that at some point along the way Mr. Scott would be willing to sell out at a lower figure.
2. He could accept Mr. Scott's offer and operate the company with Mr. Farley and Mr. Hannon. He believed that under this management the company could earn enough money to conform with the terms of Mr. Scott's proposal.
3. He could attempt to raise enough money to buy out Mr. Scott immediately for cash. Mr. Black thought that, if cash were offered, Mr. Scott might accept $80,000 to $90,000 in full payment for his interests. To get funds, Mr. Black was contemplating an issue of preferred stock at a dividend rate of 7 or 8 per cent, callable at 110 per cent of issue price. If necessary, a minority common-stock interest could be given to preferred investors.

T. F. Manton Company, Inc.

The T. F. Manton Company, Inc., was founded in the summer of 1946 to develop and market some of Mr. Manton's ideas in electronic instrumentation. It was organized as a Rhode Island corporation in July of 1948. Since that time a profitable business has been built up through the sale of the company's own products and the performing of engineering and manufacturing services for outside firms, a business which is steadily expanding and which amounted to just under $75,000 in the fiscal year ending September 30, 1951.

In 1947 the company made an investigation of the principles of digital computers for a large petroleum company with a view to solving a plant balance problem in one of its refineries. The work done served to interest Mr. Manton in the commercial possibilities of electronic computation. He began to consider entering the business-machine field with a small, compact device based on the principles involved in the large computers. After efforts to arouse investor interest in the project had produced no results, largely because of skepticism as to the company's ability to produce a workable device, Mr. Manton raised a $10,000 private loan and set to work in the winter of 1948 to build an elementary machine to show the practicability of his ideas.

The result of this effort was the original Autocount (see in Exhibits 1 and 2, p. 328 and 329), which was completed in about a year and was demonstrated to representatives of companies in various fields. Of these, the department-store people showed the most active interest, and Mr. Manton was asked to show the machine to the Systems Committee of the Associated Merchandising Corporation in New York. The immediate result of a successful demonstration before this body was the placing by a member store of an order for an inventory-keeping machine as a pilot installation to precede a large-scale adoption of electronic accounting methods.

Since that time the company has received many evidences of a lively and general interest in its new product, ranging from requests for information to actual orders for Autocounts, amounting to more than $120,000. This interest has arisen in spite of the fact that the company has carefully avoided publicity, fearing to arouse a demand that it was not yet able to supply. In view of this acceptance, the company realizes that

Exhibit 1

DESCRIPTION OF THE AUTOCOUNT

The new

AUTOCOUNT

A REVOLUTIONARY BUSINESS MACHINE FOR ACCOUNTING, STATISTICS, CONTROL

Combines Electronic Calculation and Magnetic Memory To Maintain Running Records on 1,000 Items

Controlled by a simple keyboard, Autocount automatically tabulates and remembers up to 1,000 4-digit numbers. It adds to, or subtracts from, any of these numbers and automatically remembers the new balance. It produces a printed record of each transaction for checking purposes and, when required, produces a printed record of any or all balances held in the machine.

FAST--In one second Autocount will print the balance of any item--no time wasted looking up information and calculating balances by conventional methods.

ACCURATE--Complete accuracy is assured because operations are fully automatic. Keyboard use is readily checked by the printed record.

ECONOMICAL--Extensive personnel and equipment now used in slow manual operations (counting, posting, punching cards, filing, etc.), are eliminated.

PRINCIPAL COMPONENTS

Centralized Keyboard--Clearly indexed keys are divided into three banks--bank (1) for item designation, bank (2) for registering quantities, bank (3) for control of operation.

Electronic Calculator--Vacuum tubes perform additions or subtractions and automatically transmit results, in the form of electric impulses, to the Magnetic Memory.

Magnetic Memory--A cylinder 3" in diameter and 6" long magnetically stores electric impulses representing 1,000 4-digit numbers and retransmits these impulses to the Automatic Printer.

Automatic Printer--A conventional electric typewriter converts electric impulses into a printed record for information or checking.

SERVICE

Trained technicians are available to instruct personnel or service equipment whenever required.

SPECIFICATIONS

Operating current--any standard 110-volt AC outlet.
Dimensions--20" x 27" x 46".
Weight--75 lbs.

GUARANTEE

Autocount is fully guaranteed by the manufacturer. Any part or parts found defective due to faulty material or workmanship will be replaced without charge.

PRICE

Autocount as described, F.O.B. Providence, R. I., $3,500.00
Supplementary equipment to adapt Autocount for specialized applications, such as designating department as well as item, registering both physical quantities and dollar values, and summarizing physical quantities or dollar values by department or item.

Prices on Request

Manufactured by

T.F. MANTON CO., Inc.

33 MAPLE ROAD PROVIDENCE, R. I.

the time has come to secure additional financing to enable it to turn out a rapidly increasing volume of business.

THE PRODUCT

Imagine ten thousand adding machines compressed into a space less than that occupied by an ordinary office desk and all operated from a single keyboard. Essentially, that is what is shown in the photograph of the Autocount. Other models vary somewhat in capacity and in the manner of handling data, but the fundamental functions of all models are the same. Several thousand different totals are developed by keyboard entries and stored in the machine for any desired length of

Exhibit 2

HOW THE AUTOCOUNT WORKS

OPERATION OF THE AUTOCOUNT

1. To record the amount of an item--Depress appropriate keys for item, quantity to be recorded, and "add" key. Autocount automatically adds the quantity to previous balance of 0, records the result in magnetic memory, and produces printed record as shown.

001 0000 0111 0111

2. To add to an item--Depress appropriate keys for item, quantity to be added, and "add" key. Autocount automatically adds the new quantity to previous balance, records the new balance in magnetic memory, and produces printed records as shown.

001 0111 1000 1111

3. To subtract from an item--Depress appropriate keys for item, quantity to be subtracted, and "subtract" key. Autocount automatically subtracts the new quantity from the previous balance, records the new balance in magnetic memory, and produces printed record as shown.

001 1111 1000 0111

4. To obtain the balance of an individual item--Depress appropriate keys for item and "read" key. Autocount automatically produces a printed record as shown.

001 0111

5. To obtain the balances of several items--Depress appropriate keys for first item on which information is desired and "list" key. Autocount automatically produces a printed record as shown.

001 0111
002 9999
etc.
until "stop" key despressed

Note that the "read" and "list" operations mentioned in 4 and 5 above can be carried out any desired number of times without altering in any way information stored in the machine.

6. To cancel balance of an item--Depress appropriate keys for item and "cancel" key. Autocount automatically cancels the existing balance and produces a printed record as shown.

001 0111 C0000

7. To cancel balances of several items--Depress appropriate keys for first item to be cancelled and "erase" key which is so located as to make inadvertent use impossible. Autocount automatically cancels balances, beginning with item designated, and produces a printed record as shown.

001 0111 E0000
002 9999 E 0000
etc.
until "stop" key depressed

time, with each of them available at the touch of a key in a matter of five seconds or less. The Autocount is not dependent on punched cards or other such media for storage of data. It does, however, print a record of each transaction as it is made, which gives a means of observing an incorrect entry and provides a record that may be preserved for permanent reference. Lists can be made automatically of the whole or any part of the contents of the machine. Entries can be accumulated to a number of different totals, if desired; and subtotals may be provided. If remote operation is necessary, the machine can be made to function using standard teletype code for input and output.

The Autocount provides such great savings in time and clerical effort that it makes practical inventory and statistical controls now obtainable only at high cost and with considerable time lag, if they are obtainable at all. For instance, by substituting an Autocount for the cash register in a retail store, it is possible to maintain inventory control by recording sales as they are made, and also to distribute money receipts for internal accounting and statistical purposes. All this is accomplished with little more clerical effort than is now expended in the simple ringing-up of sales; and the Autocount for this use will sell for a price comparable to that of a large cash register, allowing for a profitable advance over manufacturing costs.

The company's line of instruments are in the field of electronic measurement and control. They include a radiation counter far more sensitive than the Geiger tube, which is meeting with increasing acceptance for use in the detection and treatment of cancer. Sales of all the instruments are increasing satisfactorily as a result of sales effort and adequate performance in the field. Sales of electronic components for the products of Klein Associates is a continuing source of business. At present the company is working on two small contracts for the Army, totaling some $40,000 and consisting of development work of a nature similar to its usual operations.

THE MARKET

An indication of the size of the market for electronic accounting may be given by the fact that one group of department stores has made plans to spend $80 million in this field. This group, while large, represents only a small fraction of the retail trade, and a complete coverage of retailers would still leave untouched the market afforded by the industrial, banking, and insurance firms, not to mention the various branches of the government. The Autocount offers rapid and inexpensive inventory control to industry and its service businesses, such as warehouses and industrial supply houses. It presents an easy method of distributing costs to the proper accounts or for keeping track of payroll deductions. It lends itself to statistical uses, as it automatically sorts random entries into their proper categories. The status of accounts receivable can be kept for immediate availability to the credit department. These are a few of the uses to which the Autocount can be put; others will undoubtedly suggest themselves to the reader.

PROBLEMS

In any discussion of the company's future, certain difficulties are frequently mentioned. The following is the thinking of management on some of the more important questions:

Reliability. The question is often raised: "Will such a complicated business-machine work and continue working under service conditions?" Actually, the Autocount is far simpler structurally than many existing business machines, for it substitutes rugged and well-proved electronic components for the many moving parts in mechanical equipment. Compared to the large-scale computers, the so-called "giant brains," the Autocount performs a trifling number of elementary calculations. The accuracy obtainable in even the big machines may best be shown by an analogy drawn by the engineers on the staff of the MIT computer. They point out that, if the telephone service were as accurate as their machine, the entire United States would receive but one wrong number in two years. The mildest conclusion to be drawn is that there is no drastic inaccuracy inherent in electronic computation. A regular program of preventive maintenance will be set up to detect any diminution in the effectiveness of each component before it can affect the operation of the machine. The magnetic storage itself is not affected by power failures or electrical difficulties of any sort, since the information in storage is in as permanent a form as is the field of an ordinary horseshoe magnet and can be changed or erased only by deliberate action of the machine operator.

Service. A sufficient organization is planned to assure regular routine service on a frequent basis and to answer immediately any emergency calls. The concentrated nature of Autocount installation makes this problem far less difficult than might ordinarily be expected. A single large store or other major user would have enough machines to justify a resident serviceman, and some stores have indicated that they prefer to maintain their own service operation. When sales are made to smaller users, they would be concentrated in the larger cities to permit their handling by one area serviceman. Thus it may be seen that a careful sales policy eliminates a great deal of service difficulty. Once the guarantee period is passed on each installation, service will be made to carry itself on a contract basis.

Patents. A patent program is now under way to cover certain novel details of the Autocount with application already made on some points, which should give the company adequate relative patent strength within the field of its activities. In electronic computation, few of the principles are covered by patents. Magnetic drum memory was devised around the turn of the century in connection with telegraphy and is, of course, no longer covered; and most of the other developments were made during work on government projects and are in the public domain. There is, therefore, little chance of infringement by the company of existing patents.

Competition. The overriding answer to the question of competition is the fact that the market for electronic business machinery is so vast that there is room for all comers. A small organization, particularly in a technical field, has advantages just as real, although often less obvious, than the disadvantages which are so frequently adduced. The quality of development work seldom varies directly with the number of workers; and a small, well-integrated group can move faster than a large engineering staff, has fewer internal strains, and is in more intimate contact with the thinking of the man at the top.

The Autocount is designed for the rapid handling of relatively simple numerical information. It is not competitive with the punched-card installations, which are concerned with much more complicated data and operate on a much slower cycle. In fact, an Autocount installation may well be used to increase the value of the card machines by gathering fast-moving information and putting it into a form that they can handle. So far as it has been possible to ascertain, none of the large business-machine firms of this type is currently working toward a small, simple electronic computer independent of punched cards, which gives this company at least a lead on possible competitors. The number of experienced computer engineers is limited, and at present their activity is directed more toward devices for calculating ballistics for rockets and other complicated matter than in the prosaic direction of business.

Materials. To date, all material requirements have been filled by the company's very adequate purchasing agent, at reasonable prices. The nature of the company's products and government contract work has provided sufficient priority assistance so far and will continue to do so unless complete mobilization were to stop all production for civilian uses. In such an event, the company will extend its present program of development work for the armed forces, which even now represents a fair share of its activities. Also, it is anticipated that the services will eventually become customers for the Autocount, since a good deal of preliminary work has already been done to acquaint them with the machine.

PRESENT FINANCES

The company is a closely held corporation with 5,000 shares of no-par common stock authorized, of which 964 are issued, 484 held by Mr. Manton, and the remainder by Klein Associates. Stock in Klein Associates is one of the holdings of a large venture-capital corporation. As may be seen from the enclosed statements, the company is currently operating at a profit. The September 30 statements are year-end reports prepared by an auditor, and the December 31 statements are included to show the progress made in the first quarter of fiscal 1952 (Exhibits 3 and 4). The most notable items are the increase in orders on the books by over $60,000 and the paying-off of two thirds of the bank debt. Of the notes payable shown on the balance sheet, those not labeled bank notes are held either by Klein Associates or by Mr. Manton's family.

Exhibit 3

T. F. MANTON COMPANY, INC.
COMPARATIVE BALANCE SHEET

ASSETS

	As of Sept. 30, 1951	*As of Dec. 31, 1951*
Cash in Banks and on Hand	$ 739.88	$ 4,342.33
Accounts Receivable	12,186.67	13,962.32
Work in Process (at lower of cost or market)	46,245.94	52,853.01
Total Current Assets	$59,172.49	$ 71,157.66
Machinery and Equipment (at cost)	4,748.32	4,860.43
Less: Reserve for Depreciation	1,732.71	1,732.71
Total Fixed Assets	$ 3,015.61	$ 3,127.72
Development and Engineering Costs Deferred	16,443.26	20,484.80
Prepaid Charges	105.47	....
Good Will, Patents, etc.	12,427.30	12,427.30
Total Assets	$91,164.13	$107,197.48

LIABILITIES AND CAPITAL

Notes Payable—Bank	$15,000.00	$ 5,000.00
Notes Payable—Others	20,000.00	20,000.00
Accounts Payable	6,218.38	7,198.35
Customers' Advance Deposits	14,000.00	36,500.00
Accrued Liabilities	1,919.72	1,470.15
Total Current Liabilities	$56,138.10	$ 70,168.50
Note Payable Due March 28, 1954	10,000.00	10,000.00
Capital Stock:		
No-par value—Authorized 5,000 shares		
Issued and outstanding 964 shares	24,000.00	24,000.00
Earned Surplus	26.03	3,028.98
Total Liabilities and Capital	$91,164.13	$107,197.48

The presentation of deferred development and engineering costs as an asset shows a reasonable picture of a development business, particularly in the electronic field, in which plant and equipment require (and will require) relatively little outlay; and the costs of developing a product and training an organization with which to do business are a burden to be borne by capital, just as it would bear the cost of machinery to begin the manufacture of a product that was already developed. It may be noted from the balance sheet (Exhibit 3) that the amount of paid-in capital about equals the total of machinery and equipment plus deferred engineering costs. Almost all engineering is now being charged to spe-

Exhibit 4

T. F. MANTON COMPANY, INC.

STATEMENT OF INCOME AND EXPENSE

	For the Year Ending September 30, 1951		*For the Three Months Ending December 31, 1951*	
Sales		$73,346.96		$26,853.40
Cost of sales:				
Material purchased	$21,531.21		$ 7,194.71	
Direct labor	31,779.33		9,493.48	
Labor on development and engineering projects	1,514.83		1,252.57	
Subcontracting	8,624.73		5,470.30	
Royalty expense	1,805.03		323.50	
Indirect labor	9,165.57		1,685.38	
Manufacturing supplies	1,789.32		616.07	
Sickness, holidays, and vacations	2,974.90		1,317.64	
Rent	1,539.00		384.75	
Taxes	2,879.87		264.93	
Insurance	139.70		96.28	
Depreciation	448.14		....	
Total cost of manufacturing	$84,191.63		$28,439.61	
Development and engineering expenditures deferred in previous periods charged off	3,137.13		....	
	$87,328.76		$28,439.61	
Less: Increase in inventory	42,498.52		6,607.07	
Less: Increase in deferred engineering	....		4,041.54	
Cost of sales		44,830.24		17,791.00
Gross profit on sales		$28,516.72		$ 9,062.40
General and administrative expenses:				
Office and administrative salaries	$12,289.92		$ 2,909.98	
Miscellaneous	....		407.71	
Travel	2,143.52		87.05	
Office expense	3,032.69		547.71	
Advertising	1,016.32		400.00	
Professional services	....		200.00	
Commissions	375.80		1,112.02	
Total		18,858.25		5,665.25
Net profit from operations		$ 9,658.47		$ 3,397.15
Other charges:				
Interest expense	$ 1,777.97		$ 237.20	
Bad debts	1,271.26		....	
Insurance premium on life of officer	157.00		157.00	
Total		3,206.23		394.20
Net profit before provision for federal income taxes		$ 6,452.24		$ 3,002.95
Provision for federal income taxes		250.00		....
Net profit		$ 6,202.24		$ 3,002.95
Deficit, October 1, 1950		6,176.21		
Earned surplus September 30, 1951		$ 26.03		

cific sales, and the deferred development figure was written down by over $3,000 in the past year. Good will in a technical business of this type is a highly important asset, for it is a reflection of the professional standing of the personnel, which is as important to the success of the organization as the reputation of the partners to a law office.

Of the inventory of work in process, nearly all is being produced against orders, while the remainder consists of items in steady demand being turned out for stock on a schedule made for greatest productive

Exhibit 5

T. F. MANTON COMPANY, INC.

LIST OF OUTSTANDING ORDERS

	October 19, 1951	January 18, 1952
Klein Associates, Inc.	$ 6,400	$ 7,570
The J. L. Hudson Co., Detroit, Mich	16,000	16,000
The John Shillito Co., Ohio	13,000	.....
Textron, Nashua, N.H.	18,000	18,000
B. Altman & Co., New York, N.Y.	.....	30,000
Iowa State College	555	.....
Associated Merchandising Corporation, New York, N.Y.	.....	60,000
Emory University, Ga.	1,450	.....
Massachusetts General Hospital, Boston, Mass.	1,140	1,175
Fort Belvoir, Va.	19,000	13,000
Dennison Mfg. Company	2,000	.....
Watertown Arsenal, Watertown, Mass.	14,000	8,750
G. W. Associates, El Segundo, Calif.	1,250	500
Harvard University, Cambridge, Mass.	.....	1,936
Iowa State University	280	.....
General Electric Co., Oak Ridge, Tenn.	.....	525
Ohio State University	125	.....
V.A. Administration Hospital, Long Beach, Calif.	.....	75
Central Scientific Co., Chicago, Ill.	280	.....
Sprague Electric Co., North Adams, Mass.	.....	410
San Francisco Naval Shipyard	600	.....
Dr. J. C. Roucayrol, Paris, France	2,050	2,050
Tracerlab, Inc., Boston, Mass.	280	.....
Massachusetts Institute of Technology, Cambridge, Mass.	.....	629
National Naval Medical Center, Bethesda, Md.	515	.....
Naval Research Laboratory, Washington, D.C.	.....	465
Brooklyn Navy Yard, New York, N.Y.	285	.....
Amherst College, Amherst, Mass.	.....	30
Globe-Union, Inc., Milwaukee, Wis.	1,230	.....
Midwest Research Institute, Kansas City, Mo.	.....	790
State of Maryland	285	.....
Stockholm, Sweden	.....	285
Total	$98,645	$162,190

efficiency. Since the computers are large items, requiring some months to construct and the outlay of a considerable sum for materials, doing business in the present undercapitalized state has at times required bank borrowing. However, the company's relations with the banks are good, and progress payments from customers have done a lot to relieve the situation. Payables are on a current basis, and the company is suffering no acute discomfort; but even at the present level of operations, additional capital would be justified and welcomed.

PLANS AND REQUIREMENTS

An estimate of future sales is all too often an exercise in wishful thinking, but some such projection must be made if any planning is to be done, and the following schedule can easily be justified on the basis of orders on hand and negotiations now in progress (Exhibit 5, p. 335). For the calendar year 1952:

Work for Klein Associates	$ 40,000
Instrument sales	40,000
Government contracts	75,000
Autocounts	100,000
Total	$225,000

Work for Klein and government contract work are shown continuing at their present level, while instrument sales show a small anticipated increase. Autocount orders now on the books, less progress payments, amount to some $90,000. In view of the demand for the company's products, the above sales total is shown more as the amount that the company can produce without excessive expansion than as the amount that could be sold to the existing market.

These sales should show a reasonable profit and stand on their own feet, as it were. However, expansion of personnel and equipment has already begun and must be accelerated to cope with the work on hand and be ready for the sharply increased volume foreseen for the near future. Therefore, certain expenditures beyond what can be carried by current operations are necessary for the year 1952 and may be outlined as follows:

New equipment	$ 20,000
Tooling costs	10,000
Moving expense and excess rent	10,000
Setting-up service organization	20,000
Training engineers and technicians	15,000
Allowance for forward buying	5,000
Reserve for contingencies	20,000
Total	$100,000

In addition, the $30,000 of notes payable should be retired, and the holders have expressed their willingness to accept a conversion plan that would put them on the same basis as other investors. Since even more rapid expansion is expected after 1952, when pilot machines will be proved, a substantial reserve should be on hand at the end of the year, even though orders can undoubtedly be financed on a short-term basis.

Taking the figure of $70,000 somewhat arbitrarily as the reserve for the beginning of 1953, the company needs to raise $200,000. A number of ways of doing this have been considered, and management has an open mind as to the best method. One financing that seems reasonable is the offering of debentures in a sufficient amount to raise the net sum required. Each $1,000 debenture will be accompanied by a stock bonus which in the aggregate will represent 20 per cent of the authorized common. A convertible issue might be equally effective. This type of security seems to offer a number of advantages. It gives the investor an immediate return, which is paid by the company before taxes, a feature which leads the company to prefer it to a preferred stock issue. After the company develops sufficient earning power, an equity financing may be made which will provide for the retirement of debentures that are not converted.

MANAGEMENT AND PERSONNEL

Thomas Manton, the president and treasurer of the Corporation, was born in 1907 in Montclair, New Jersey, and received his early education there in the public schools. Since that time, his experience has been as follows:

1925–27	American Machine and Foundry Company Assisted in the development of a machine for sorting cigars by color, the first machine successfully to use photoelectric cells.
1928–30	Western Electric Co., New York Worked in the inspection department on electronic amplifiers and associated telephone equipment.
1930–33	University of Virginia and Massachusetts Institute of Technology Special student.
1933–34	Raytheon Manufacturing Co. Worked on development of mercury rectifier tubes.
1934–37	Foxboro Company, Foxboro, Massachusetts Development engineer on electronic recording and control instruments.
1937–38	Massachusetts Institute of Technology Worked on a classified project.
1938–41	Champlain Corporation Assistant to the president and general manager, supervising a large plant manufacturing photoengraving and printing machinery.
1941–45	Naval Ordnance Laboratory In charge of development of an influence fuse for depth charges, which was completed in time for successful use by the Navy.
1946—to the present	The Manton Company President and Treasurer.

Dr. John T. Klein, vice-president and clerk of the corporation, received his A.B. from St. John's College in Annapolis in 1930 and his Ph.D. from Johns Hopkins in 1936. He was employed as a physicist at the Arsenal in Watertown, Massachusetts, in 1935 and 1936, and since that time has been president of Klein Associates, an industrial physics group. His services to the company are largely advisory and are most valuable in view of his wide experience and many contacts.

The foregoing are the only officers and, with Mrs. Manton, the sole directors of the corporation. Other members of the organization include:

Steven A. Bruce, A.B. Harvard 1938, assistant to the president, acquired his basic manufacturing experience with Bruce Thornton, Inc., and was then treasurer of the Cambridge Machine and Valve Company of Cambridge, Massachusetts, until joining the Navy in 1942. In the service he received considerable administrative experience, serving as executive officer and in command. Since the war and until coming to this company in the fall of 1950, he was active in the financing and direction of a number of small new businesses, gaining experience in the problems of growing enterprises.

Jackson P. Smith, A.B. Harvard 1942, engineer in charge of instrument sales, was a mechanical engineer at the Naval Ordnance Laboratory in Washington from 1942 to 1945. He was then connected with the Sulfied Ore Process Company in South Stafford, Vermont, and the Metals Research Laboratory in Burlington, Vermont, as a research assistant until joining the Manton organization in January, 1950.

Alan D. Sears, B.S. MIT 1938, computer engineer, had ten years of electrical and electronic manufacturing background as an engineer with the Colonial Radio Corporation and Sylvania Products, Inc., when he joined the company in 1948. He is in charge, under Mr. Manton, of the computer project.

David M. Schmidt, Jr., B.S. Tufts 1943, electronic production engineer, gained considerable manufacturing experience as a naval officer in charge of electronic assembly work at an ordnance depot and in development engineering at the Naval Ordnance Laboratory. Since leaving the service, he has been with this company, specializing in production.

Ira R. Stevenson, B.S. MIT 1947, computer engineer, is experienced in the techniques of digital computation, having been associated with MIT's "Whirlwind" project and with computer development at the Cambridge Research Laboratory. Besides, his experience as a communication and radar officer with the Air Corps during the war serves to give him a wide background in electronics.

In addition, the company employs several other electrical and mechanical engineers and has a strong nucleus of supervisory help and an office staff that can be expanded as required. Working conditions are pleasant, and employees' relations with the company have been excellent.

Emmons-Dane Company

The Emmons-Dane Company of San Francisco, California, was founded in March, 1940, by Mr. J. Walter Dane and Mr. Claude B. Emmons, both in their early forties. The company functioned as a merchandise brokerage service, buying durable consumer goods and electrical appliances on direct orders of customers and selling them at a discount from retail price.

Mr. Emmons had been a salesman of gas ranges and heating equipment for a leading San Francisco wholesaler. In 1938 he left this firm and became a salesman on the staff of Edward Gregg, a retail appliance dealer who also bought merchandise for certain customers on individual orders and gave them discounts. The Gregg Company was highly successful, with a substantial part of its volume coming from these discount sales.

In 1938 Mr. Dane, a member of the sales research staff of a national refrigerator manufacturer, came to spend several months with the Gregg organization to find out why that company was compiling such an excellent record on refrigerator sales. After a few months he resigned his position with the refrigerator company to accept a position with Mr. Gregg as a buyer.

In March, 1940, Mr. Emmons and Mr. Dane decided to set up their own business. Because their available capital was limited to a few thousand dollars, they could not open a retail store, with the attendant costs of a large display showroom, inventory, advertising, and sales promotion. They felt, however, that by virtue of their selling experience and contacts with manufacturers and with a minimum of capital outlay they could operate a successful merchandise brokerage service. Accordingly, they consulted an attorney and incorporated as the Emmons-Dane Company with an authorized no-par-value capital stock of 1,000 shares. Each of the partners received 251 shares; the remaining 498 were not issued. Mr. Emmons became president; and Mr. Dane, vice-president and treasurer.

Nonexclusive retail franchises were secured from twenty-five well-known wholesale appliance companies. At this time, manufacturers were willing to grant selling rights to anyone who could increase their sales in a metropolitan area. No charge was made for these franchises. The friendships and reputations which the two men had acquired in their previous positions were particularly helpful in obtaining franchises. Assets of the Emmons-Dane Company were listed at $10,000, of which $7,500 consisted of franchises and goodwill and the remainder of office equipment and samples, both on credit and for cash. Merchandise samples were obtained on credit from several manufacturers.

Announcements of the firm's opening and of the products it was set up to supply were sent to 400 potential customers. The customer list was drawn from personal friends of the partners and from persons whose trade they had developed while with the Gregg Company. The company had leased a 10-foot by 50-foot store in a relatively low-rent district. It was centrally located but not on a main shopping street. The store was clean and attractively furnished but had no neon signs, fancy showrooms, or glib salesmen.

Sales in 1940 amounted to $60,000 and in 1941 to $100,000. By the end of 1941 the customer list had grown to about 6,000. A complete file was maintained on each customer, and through this means the firm was able to expand the scope of the purchasing service beyond the household appliance field. For instance, if a customer wanted to buy a half-ton of paper, Mr. Emmons would try to obtain it at less than the usual retail price from another customer who sold paper. The savings thus effected were split between the buyer and the Emmons-Dane Company. Mr. Emmons believed that the company's fees on such transactions averaged about 10 per cent of retail price. Customers were willing to give discounts to Mr. Emmons because he had been effective in filling their own needs at lower prices.

Franchised goods were sold to customers at prices ranging from wholesale cost plus 10 per cent to retail price to normal retail price less 10 per cent. The price depended on the competitive situation and the over-all sales volume of the Emmons-Dane Company. When merchandise was plentiful and slow moving, retailers often slashed prices; and the Emmons-Dane Company was then forced to offer larger discounts in order to maintain its price differentials. Furthermore, as the company increased its sales, unit profits rose rapidly, and a share of these savings could be passed on in the form of better discounts to customers. During 1941 the larger discounts usually prevailed; for example, an article which cost the Emmons-Dane Company $50 and which retailed at $100 would be sold to customers for $60.

The Emmons-Dane Company collected in advance on all sales. This policy enabled the firm to settle all accounts with suppliers promptly

Exhibit 1

EMMONS-DANE COMPANY

INVITATION TO CUSTOMERS TO PURCHASE STOCK

DEAR FRIEND:

We have been engaged in a unique co-operative experiment with some of our clients, and we have all benefited by it so much that we have decided to advise others in the event that they might wish to participate.

It enables our clients to obtain additional savings on their individual purchases and, by doing us a small service, to receive a payment or merchandise credit in proportion to the number of their friends whom we are able to serve as a result of their recommendation. This is a great aid to us, as it helps to expand our clientele.

It all began with the hope that we could decrease the distance between producer and consumer. With the success that we have enjoyed along this line, several of our clients have become enthusiastic about our merchandising plan to the point of inquiring about the possibilities of helping us and in turn helping themselves by financially participating in the corporation.

Originally we had made no provision for this additional group of participants, but more recently we have been able to allow a few to become a part of our program, on an experimental basis, through the authorization of an additional block of stock.

The results have been so gratifying that we are adding a limited number of new associates to replace those who have been obliged to drop out and to strengthen the balance of the organization.

How the plan works:

1. As one of our clients, you may purchase from five to twenty shares of fully paid, nonassessable stock in the corporation at fifty dollars each share. We would prefer to have them purchased in groups of five; how, ever, that is optional. Unfortunately, there are not enough shares available to include our entire clientele, and thus we must limit this offer for acceptance to thirty days; yet payment may be scheduled beyond that time.

2. As a stockholder, you will be able to purchase through us anything in the field of general merchandise available from our normal sources of supply at a saving even greater than is customary. Thus, dependent on the volume of purchases, you can save or earn an amount equal to or greater than the initial investment within a relatively short time.

3. As an associate, you automatically become a source of new business for the corporation through the voluntary recommendation of our services to others. For any business resulting from your recommendations you will receive either a cash or merchandise credit representing a sales commission on the transactions. In this manner, depending only on the number of successful contacts, you may be credited, as earned, an amount greater than the original purchase price of the shares.

Exhibit 1—(Continued)

4. The third method of additional income for you is made possible through the earning power of the shares themselves.

5. In your interest, as well as ours, we are including a repurchase agreement which makes it necessary for you to first offer your shares for sale to the corporation, should you ever be obliged to dispose of the stock.

Your participation helps us too, as it makes it possible to:

1. Expand our clientele and in turn our sources of supply, thus increasing our immediate value to those we serve.

2. Take advantage of the many opportunities surrounding us relative to unexpected merchandise offers that present themselves almost daily and which in many cases require immediate cash purchases, previously unnecessary, in order to assure those additional values for our clients.

3. Increase our present value in securing more supplies for war plants. This is an additional service which is exceptionally worth while at this time. We have already entered this field, yet find that our present scope of operation is somewhat limited.

4. Plan for the distribution of new products as current conditions improve, the groundwork for which is now being laid.

5. Plan for further expansion and improvement of our service in the postwar period.

As you see, this is simply a co-operative plan which benefits all participants as outlined above. We know you will enjoy your activities as an associate, but we have no desire to ask you to commit yourself unless you feel that you can participate wholeheartedly in making it possible for others to receive greater benefits from our service in the saving of time, energy, and money, thus making our purchasing program more worth while and a benefit to every client. Yet, do not delay in sending in the attached form if this plan interests you. If your application is acceptable, we will advise you of the method of completing the transaction.

Remember us as your needs arise, and thank you.

Sincerely yours,
EMMONS-DANE COMPANY

January 10, 1942

and eliminated the expenses of credit investigation and bad debts. Manufacturers often gave preference to Mr. Emmons in allocating merchandise because of his policy of prompt payment. A limited inventory was carried to comply with the franchise requirements of certain manufacturers. During the first two years of business the inventory had never amounted to more than $5,000.

The company did no advertising; customer lists were expanded only through personal contacts and occasional direct mailing. This policy prevented a cloud of complaints from other retailers regarding unfair competition. There were a few instances of such complaints, but the company's prompt payment of bills and the excellent relationships between the partners and the manufacturers' salesmen were sufficient to offset them. Difficulties occasionally arose when a customer obtained a price quotation from the Emmons-Dane Company and then tried to get another dealer to offer a still lower price, but Mr. Emmons found that by close attention to customer relationships he was able to screen out this type of buyer.

In late 1941 Mr. Emmons and Dr. Dane realized that their business would decline drastically as war production cut off their regular supplies. They had to increase their inventory while merchandise was still available; and, further, they were anxious to accumulate a supply of ready cash which would enable them to take quick advantage of postwar merchandise opportunities. Because most of their assets were in the form of franchises, customer goodwill, and contacts with suppliers, they did not believe they could get a bank loan on satisfactory terms. Consequently, they decided to sell the remaining 498 shares of common stock. A letter was mailed to a thousand customers who had been among the company's most active clients, inviting them to purchase from 5 to 20 shares of stock at $50 per share (see Exhibit 1, pp. 342–43). The limits on the size of an investor's holdings had been set in order to insure retention of the business by the founders, while at the same time excluding those whose financial status was not sound enough to permit them to be of real help to the company. Within two months, all the stock had been sold. Sixty customers had become investors, subscribing an average of slightly over $100 each. The new stockholders were given three types of return on their investment:

1. An annual cash dividend of $2.50 per share plus additional distribution in case of higher profits.
2. A commission on business obtained by a stockholder for the company. (This commission was set at 5 per cent of retail price or one third of the company's gross profit on the item, whichever was less.)
3. A special discount on personal purchases. (Stockholders were allowed to buy merchandise from the company at cost plus 10 per cent of cost.)

Sales in 1942 totaled $150,000. Many additional franchises had been secured, and fourteen employees had been hired to aid in selling, storing, and delivering equipment and keeping records. The two founders continued to work from ten to twelve hours a day and made all major business decisions. At the end of 1942, supplies were running out and very few orders could be filled. Mr. Emmons and Mr. Dane therefore dismissed most of their staff and went to work as expediters and sales agents for a newly organized concern of engineers which was producing war materials.

Earnings from this source, plus a small revenue obtained from continued merchandise sales, were sufficient to pay the $2.50 dividend to minority stockholders during the war. There was no certainty that the dividend provision was legally enforceable when earnings from the brokerage business were not sufficient to cover it, and, furthermore, it was not a deductible expense for tax purposes. The partners, however, regarded this dividend as a cost of doing business equivalent to interest. Mr. Emmons and Mr. Dane paid no dividends to themselves on their own stock, although all the shares were similar. Gross revenues for the corporation, including the earnings of the expediting work, totaled about $80,000 annually from 1943 to 1945. No dividends above the $2.50 per share were paid during this period.

At the end of the war, Mr. Emmons concentrated his efforts on rebuilding the brokerage business, while Mr. Dane devoted his time to organizing a sales corporation to find peacetime markets for the products of the engineering firm. Mr. Emmons decided to extend operations of the Emmons-Dane Company into new merchandising fields. He called special stockholders' meetings to secure approval of his expansion plans. Several of the stockholders had long been interested in participating more actively in the business, and Mr. Emmons believed that several of these men could be used as managers of new sales divisions. Six new merchandising undertakings were begun in 1946, of which the most ambitious was a retail appliance store.

A primary factor in the management's decision to enter the retail appliance business was the changed situation in regard to franchises. For instance, the manufacturer of a leading automatic washing machine told Mr. Emmons that his 300 prewar dealers in the San Francisco area would be reduced to 100, since the production of machines during 1946 would not be sufficient to keep 300 dealers adequately supplied. To qualify for a postwar franchise, a dealer had to agree to the following provisions:

1. To buy a sample machine and keep it in operation, which involved providing a constant supply of hot water.
2. To buy and install a $300 electric sign.
3. To carry a share of local advertising.
4. To employ a maintenance man and a woman to demonstrate the machine.

The brokerage office could not very well accommodate a setup of this nature, but Mr. Emmons did not want to lose his franchise privilege. He believed that there were enough potential customers in the area to enable his company to operate a retail store and comply with these new requirements while at the same time continuing to sell merchandise at a discount to a limited number of customers. Therefore, in December, 1945, he signed a long-term lease on a store building two blocks from the Emmons-Dane Company office and employed two stockholders on a salary plus commission basis to manage the new appliance store. Four thousand dollars were spent on renovating and equipping the new store to enable it to compete with the best retailers in the vicinity.

During 1946 the retail store lost $7,000, although some $2,000 of this loss came from writing off building renovating costs. In December, 1946, Mr. Emmons decided to close the store and transfer the remaining inventory to a warehouse. The store was sublet for six months to a surplus-war-goods dealer. Mr. Emmons felt that after another year or two the time would be ripe for re-entry into the retail appliance line.

The failure of the retail store was largely due to the inability of the manufacturers to meet their commitments. For instance, the washing-machine manufacturer, who had promised 160 machines to the Emmons-Dane Company in 1946, delivered only 12. In most cases the poor deliveries were caused by strikes and raw-material shortages beyond the control of suppliers, so that the Emmons-Dane Company could not claim damages for defaulted contracts. Mr. Emmons believed, however, that the store could have been successful in spite of these conditions if the managers had been more experienced. He felt that they had not been sufficiently aggressive in trying to obtain a fair share of what merchandise was available; in some cases, they had stocked up on inferior goods which did not sell well even in the prevailing market. He stated that, if he re-entered the business, he would either retain the direct management of the retail line himself or hire a man with a long background in appliance selling.

Several other merchandising side lines were opened up by the company in 1946. Two other stockholders took on the task of buying and selling at wholesale a line of canned foods. They built up a clientele of 210 retail stores but lost $4,800 during 1946 and ended the year with $12,000 worth of slow-moving inventory. Here, again, the loss was attributed partly to inexperienced personnel in charge and partly to sudden shifts in supply and price conditions which brought about cancellation of many orders and inability to fill others at a profit. At the end of the year, the food business was dropped and the two salesmen released. Efforts were still being made in early 1947 to dispose of the remaining inventory.

A wholesale hardware supply agency with five employees under the direction of another stockholder was also dropped in the fall of 1946, after it had operated for six months and lost $200.

A former employee of the Emmons-Dane Company persuaded Mr. Emmons to open a wholesale office-supply business. The employee solicited sales in his spare time on a commission basis. After a few months he decided that he would like to run the enterprise on his own, and Mr. Emmons sold the inventory to him at cost.

Two retail ventures were still in operation in March, 1947. One of these, a marine-equipment agency, had accounted for $20,000 worth of sales in 1946, although Mr. Emmons believed that it had barely broken even after being charged with its proper share of expenses. This sales division was also being managed by a stockholder. He had secured franchise agreements for Higgins motorboats, Evinrude outboard motors, Whizzer motor bicycles, and a line of rowboats and sailboats. Mr. Emmons believed that all these products were basically sound and had bright futures. He did not expect to open a separate retail outlet for these goods for several months; in the meantime, sales were being handled from the brokerage office. Early in 1947 the marine merchandise was still being sold as fast as delivered; inventory parts stocks and showroom space were not yet problems. Stockholders and regular customers of the Emmons-Dane Company were given the usual discounts on these items, but the bulk of the sales was being made through such methods as exhibitions at sporting goods shows and newspaper advertising. Full retail prices were charged on all such sales.

The other subsidiary enterprise which still gave promise of making money was a photographic agency. Mr. Cable, who was retained in 1946 to help Mr. Emmons with purchasing, was an accomplished amateur photographer. Mr. Emmons decided to back him in a part-time photography business, the proceeds of which would be divided between the company and Mr. Cable. The company financed the purchase of additional equipment; Mr. Cable did the work in his home and received 10 per cent on sales. Mr. Cable also obtained some orders for photographic work from sources not connected with the Emmons-Dane Company, but the company did not share in these earnings.

The customer list of the Emmons-Dane Company had grown to 10,000 by the end of 1946; 2,000 of these were considered regular customers. Total sales for the year were $180,000, of which $100,000 were merchandise brokerage sales. The net loss for the year was $14,000, including $1,250 paid as dividends to stockholders other than Mr. Emmons and Mr. Dane. At the end of the year, net worth was estimated at $25,000, about half consisting of tangible assets. Mr. Emmons attributed the 1946 loss to the secondary enterprises, each of which had been charged a proportionate share of overhead expenses. He expected the brokerage business to do better in 1947, particularly if general business conditions declined and the price differential offered by the Emmons-Dane Company consequently became more important to customers. Suppliers had modified their franchise requirements so that the Emmons-Dane Company could again represent leading manufacturers without carrying a heavy inventory or hiring special salesmen. In March, 1947, the company had 700 franchise agreements.

In 1946, manufacturers had been able to narrow the percentage discounts offered to retailers. This condition developed because dealers were competing strenuously in buying merchandise and would accept lower discounts and also because the level of retail prices had increased. The Emmons-Dane Company had, in turn, reduced the percentage discount offered to customers. The company's price policy during 1946 may be summarized by the following example:

Normal retail price	$100	
Cost to company	70	
Price to stockholder	77	(cost plus 10 per cent of cost)
Price to customer	90	(10 per cent discount from normal retail)
Prewar price to customer	80	(cost plus 10 per cent of retail)

In a few cases the company had to pay more than 80 per cent of the retail price for the merchandise, and Mr. Emmons therefore reduced the discounts to customers. Under these conditons, customers were given a discount equal to half the company's gross profit on the item. For instance, if the company paid $85 for an item retailing at $100, customers paid $92.50 for their merchandise.

During the first few months of business in 1940, Mr. Emmons and his partner limited themselves to $15 a week each in salary. In 1941, when the company had become established, they each received $100 a week. These salaries were continued through 1946. In view of the loss in that year, Mr. Emmons reduced his salary to $50 a week as of January 1, 1947, and Mr. Dane withdrew completely from the management and payroll of the brokerage concern. Mr. Emmons intended to take over Mr. Dane's stock in the Emmons-Dane Company, with Mr. Dane taking over sole ownership of the engineering sales company. This shift was not the result of personal friction; each man felt that he had acquired enough experience to run a business independently and that the need for pooled energies and abilities, which had brought them together in 1940, no longer existed.

In March, 1947, Mr. Emmons stated that his immediate objective was reduction of overhead expenses. He was trying to dispose of the $45,000 worth of accumulated inventory left over from the unsuccessful ventures of the previous year and to return to the prewar policy of buying goods only on customers' orders. He had already reduced his staff to six employees, who received salaries totaling $235 weekly. These included: a purchasing agent (Mr. Cable); a sales-promotion director, who also handled marine sales; a bookkeeper, who prepared all financial statements and tax returns; a warehouseman; a secretary; and an office boy. No outside auditors were employed, nor were written reports issued to stockholders; but company affairs were thoroughly explained at annual meetings. In addition to the permanent staff, Mr. Emmons hired a mechanic by the hour to install equipment in customers' homes and employed a job trucking company to deliver merchandise.

The Von Hoff Research Company

In June of 1952, Mr. Lewis Endicott, a buying supervisor in the procurement department of the Sturgis Engine Corporation, was considering the justification for supplying funds to a subcontractor, the Von Hoff Research Company, over and above the amount required by the terms of the contract. If the payment were not made, the supplier faced real risk of bankruptcy. Von Hoff was the Sturgis Engine Corporation's sole source of hydraulic servo units.

Slow delivery of servo units used in the gunfire control system on the new M-99 medium tank had been one important cause of the critical shortage of such vehicles in the late summer of 1950. The Vectra Company, a major supplier of the servo units, had been producing them in limited quantities before the Korean war. A few weeks after the outbreak of hostilities, this supplier had been swamped with orders from all the armed services. Mr. Endicott realized then that it would be impossible to obtain additional units from this source; accordingly, he decided to develop a new source of supply.

Fortunately, the Von Hoff Research Company, a small firm employing about thirty-five people, was available as an alternate source for the Servo units. Its president, Dr. Sigfried Von Hoff, was considered one of the most brilliant men in his field by the members of the research, engineering, and purchasing departments of the Sturgis Engine Corporation. The Von Hoff Company had successfully completed a number of development contracts for the Sturgis Engine Corporation. Although it had also undertaken some small production orders in the past, the Von Hoff organization was better qualified for experimental work.

The pressure from increasing military requirements for the M-99 tank, coupled with the inadequate supply of servo units, did not give Mr. Endicott much time to consider the question of alternate sources. He reviewed the problem with his superior, Mr. Fred Reardon, the director of material; both men agreed on developing the Von Hoff Research Corporation as a production source for the servo unit. They reached this decision after considering all known producers of similar units. Mr. Endicott reported that all companies in the servo field were heavily loaded with defense contracts. He also found that all of these companies were falling behind in deliveries and that several of them were experiencing design and production difficulties.

The earlier design and development work which Dr. Von Hoff and his company had performed for the Sturgis Engine Corporation had been most satisfactory. The small production quantities of servo units that Von Hoff had delivered in the past had been rated as excellent in quality by the prime contractor's inspection and engineering departments. Von Hoff's only defense subcontracts at the time were with the Sturgis Engine Corporation.

Initially, Mr. Endicott's decision to develop the Von Hoff Company as a major source appeared to be advantageous on all counts. The Von Hoff Research Company plunged wholeheartedly into the new program. As Mr. Endicott had anticipated, the servomechanisms produced by Dr. Von Hoff were found to be of high quality. Deliveries were on time, and the Sturgis Engine found itself one of the few prime contractors not beset with shortages of this particular type of servomechanism. In addition, Von Hoff's price was considerably lower than any of his competitors. By the fall of 1951, nearly all of Sturgis Engine servo procurement was being placed with Von Hoff. In turn, the Von Hoff Research Company had more than doubled its payroll and was delivering about $75,000 worth of equipment to Sturgis Engine each month. This production accounted for almost the entire Von Hoff output.

This favorable picture continued until March, 1952. At that time, Dr. Von Hoff visited Mr. Endicott and after a few moments of conversation admitted that, unless drastic action was taken immediately, the Von Hoff Research Company would in all probability be forced into bankruptcy within the next month. Mr. Endicott had had no warning of the difficulty. To further complicate the matter, Dr. Von Hoff could offer no adequate explanation as to why his company had reached this precarious financial position except to say: "I just seemed to run out of money all at once."

Mr. Endicott had realized that his buyers were awarding contract after contract to the Von Hoff Research Company on a fixed-price basis. Price has never been an important point of negotiation in these contracts, since the Von Hoff bid was invariably the low one. There had been no indication that anything out of the ordinary was happening to the supplier. The flow of servo units into the Sturgis Engine plant had been regular and on schedule. The inspection department seldom had to reject any of the units. The engineering department had maintained close liaison with Dr. Von Hoff and were currently working on new models with him. Thus, it was with real surprise that Mr. Endicott received Dr. Von Hoff's announcement of severe financial difficulty.

Since the Von Hoff Research Company had become virtually the sole supplier for the turret-control servo units, financial failure on its part would soon shut down the entire M-99 production line. Realizing the seriousness of the situation, Mr. Endicott immediately arranged a conference on the matter with the director of material, Mr. Reardon. During the conference which followed, the Von Hoff's Company was found to be approximately $210,000 in debt to its suppliers and subcontractors. A sizable portion of this amount had been due for over sixty days. Von Hoff had not only been threatened with legal action, but necessary supplies of materials and parts to continue production of the servo units were being cut off.

The financial vice-president for the Sturgis Engine Corporation was asked to recommend the best way to remedy the situation. His advice, backed by the other officers of the Sturgis Engine Corporation, was that the Von Hoff Research Company should attempt to obtain a V-loan. As the prime contractor, Sturgis Engine would support this loan in every way possible. It soon became apparent, however, that no bank known to either party would grant such a loan.

Unfortunately, the extent of Dr. Von Hoff's financial difficulties could not be accurately determined. He employed only one part-time accountant, who visited the plant once a week to keep the minimum records required for tax purposes. Dr. Von Hoff was thus unable to supply adequate financial statements to support an application for a V-loan.

The policy of the Sturgis Engine Corporation on such matters was summarized by a statement that "every vendor stands on his own feet." Financial aid had seldom been granted to a vendor. In this case, however, Mr. Endicott believed that mitigating circumstances might justify some variation from company policy. Dr. Von Hoff's company had produced a high-quality product at a price below average. Performance on deliveries was considered the best in the industry. In Mr. Endicott's opinion, Dr. Von Hoff's own scientific ability was unexcelled by any of his competitors. Moreover, the possible loss of production caused by the refusal of Von Hoff's vendors to make deliveries had created a dangerous situation for Sturgis Engine Corporation.

Faced with this dilemma, the Executive Committee of the Sturgis Engine Corporation authorized an immediate loan of $210,000 to the Von Hoff Research Company. The loan was secured by a chattel mortgage on the work in process. To repay the loan, Von Hoff agreed to let Sturgis Engine deduct 30 per cent from the amount of each month's invoices. Based on the current Von Hoff production figures, this would mean that Sturgis Engine would recover its money at the rate of about $20,000 per month.

Dr. Von Hoff seemed very grateful for this aid. However, both he and the Sturgis Engine purchasing department were warned by the Sturgis Executive Committee that the loan definitely did not set a precedent and that the situation must not happen again.

Since Sturgis Engine had so much at stake, both from the point of view of money invested and dependency upon a single source, Mr. Endicott asked Dr. Von Hoff to permit the prime contractor's accounting and production personnel to determine the cause of the financial trouble. Dr. Von Hoff cordially welcomed this help. Teams from the Sturgis Engine's accounting, production, and quality control departments visited the Von Hoff Research Company to determine the cause of the difficulty. The reason reported back to Mr. Endicott was that Von Hoff's simple accounting records were inadequate and that formal cost records were nonexistent.

One of the first objectives of the Sturgis Engine's accounting team was to determine the cost of the major type of servo unit produced by Von Hoff. The price at which Von Hoff had ben selling the unit to Sturgis Engine was $314.50. The item was found to cost Von Hoff $341.25, exclusive of profit. Other items were also found to be underpriced. Most of the products had too small a factory burden charge levied against them. For example, Von Hoff ordinarily charged about 25 per cent of direct labor for factory burden. The cost accountants found that the appropriate burden figure was nearer 100 per cent of direct labor.

The financial vice-president of Sturgis Engine then suggested that Dr. Von Hoff hire a financial consultant to help install an adequate cost accounting and control system. The vice-president gave Dr. Von Hoff a list of several men with financial experience who might be interested not only in consulting work but also in staying with the Von Hoff Research Company in the position of treasurer.

Dr. Von Hoff interviewed a number of the recommended consultants and hired one whom he felt eventually could become an officer in the firm. In a short time, the new financial man had assigned several new people to accounting functions.

The officers of the Sturgis Engine Corporation were now well aware of the danger of relying on Von Hoff as a sole source on the servo unit. Instead of going back to other established sources, which were still overloaded with orders, Mr. Endicott decided to utilize Dr. Von Hoff's unique scientific ability by having him set up a manufacturing and engineering assistance agreement with at least one other new source. Dr. Von Hoff readily agreed. Thus, in April, 1952, Mr. Endicott believed that the problem had been successfully solved.

A short time later, in June, 1952, Von Hoff's new consultant-treasurer reported to Mr. Endicott that, despite capacity production, Von Hoff would be back in the same financial difficulties within about sixty days. The treasurer believed that continued underpricing of the servo units was the basic trouble. In order to conserve cash, he suggested as a first step that the loan repayment rate be cut from 30 per cent of the monthly invoices to 10 per cent. This reduction was accepted by the Sturgis Engine Corporation. Since both parties concurred that this reduction in monthly payments was not a substitute for solving the price problem, immediate steps were taken to negotiate a new price which would cover all costs plus a fair profit for the servo units.

The Ordnance Department was asked to allow a retroactive price increase on the prime contract held by Sturgis Engine Corporation so that the firm could in turn grant a retroactive increase on the fixed price subcontract between itself and Von Hoff. The matter was discussed in detail with the local contracting officer and eventually with the Ordnance representatives in Washington. The Ordnance Department representatives were at first opposed. They were puzzled as to exactly what consideration the government would receive for permitting the increased price. Mr. Endicott pointed out that, if the Von Hoff Company did not get a price increase, it would soon be in bankruptcy.

The two new sources being developed with Dr. Von Hoff's assistance were still suppliers in name only and would not be producing for some months. An order placed with competing servo manufacturers would require a number of months for delivery and would involve a price increase of at least $100 per unit. For these reasons, Mr. Endicott argued, the government would receive consideration in two ways. First, even with the price increase, servo units would be procured at a lower cost than was attainable elsewhere. Second, the government thereby prevented disruption in the production of M-99 tanks by the Sturgis Engine Corporation.

The Ordnance representatives were satisfied with Mr. Endicott's reasons and agreed on a new negotiated price of $382.00 per unit to replace the old price of $314.50. If this new price were applied to all servo units previously supplied under current contracts, the total increase would amount to approximately $207,000. Von Hoff's new consultant-treasurer further reported that any amount much less than the $207,000 would only postpone bankruptcy rather than solve the financial problem. Mr. Endicott discovered, however, that $97,000 of the $207,000 could not be recovered from the Ordnance Department, since it applied to prime contracts which had already been redetermined and completely closed.

Mr. Endicott was convinced that Von Hoff would have to receive the full amount of $207,000 from the Sturgis Engine Corporation or from some other source in order to continue to meet delivery schedules on servo units essential to production of the M-99 tanks.

PART V

DEVELOPMENT OF THE NEW AND GROWING ORGANIZATION

Electroscale Corporation

Seventeen months after he had graduated from business school, it appeared to Hugh Clark that he was finally ready to place on the market his invention, a laboratory instrument called the "Electroscale." An unsuccessful attempt to establish a team to promote the Electroscale had marked the intervening period. In the late fall of 1952, Mr. Clark had formed a new group which he believed was capable of solving most of the expected problems in a new enterprise. Although Clark felt that this new group was adequate for present needs, he thought it should be augmented with two more people, one to be an expert in the day-to-day financial and accounting problems, and the other with access to a relatively large amount of capital.

Hugh Clark was thirty-six years old. He had graduated from a well-known eastern engineering school in 1938. After receiving his S.B. degree, Clark had continued his study at the same engineering school, working toward an S.M. degree in electrical engineering practice. Although it would have been possible for him to obtain his master's degree in June, 1939, Clark's thesis had not met his own standards of quality and he refused to submit it. He continued to work on the thesis and completed the research for it during the summer of 1939, receiving some support during this period from a major electronics company by whom he was later employed.

In the fall of 1939, he accepted a research fellowship at a Midwestern university to enable him to work on his doctor's degree. Early in 1940, he completed the written work for his master's thesis and received his S.M. degree in June of the same year.

During World War II, Clark served as an officer in the Signal Corps. Immediately after the war, he did further graduate work in his selected field. From 1946 to 1949 he was employed by one of the largest electronics companies in the United States as a technical service engineer. His work required that he review manufacturing operations, study their economics, and suggest improvements. He was also required to study the economics of new plant investment. One of Clark's last projects at this company was a review of the results of a change in a major manufacturing process. The change had come about through Clark's insistence that it be instituted, although it was strongly opposed by several of the technical experts in his division. According to his calculations, this change resulted in savings of more than $500,000 per year. He had also been asked to present a paper on this process at one of the company's semiannual technical committee meetings.

Although Clark was a conscientious employee and devoted full time during working hours to his job, he saw no reason why week ends and evenings should not also contribute to his income. Accordingly, he talked several manufacturers into allowing him to distribute their products. In 1947 he formed the Clark Company, with himself as president and a retired executive as a part-time employee. Scientific instruments were sold by mail, and certain small, specialized, and expensive electronic components by personal selling. Although the enterprise was not particularly successful, Hugh Clark felt that the experience he had gained would be valuable in any future endeavor. It also proved to him that running a business was a complicated affair in which he needed additional background.

In the late spring of 1949, Hugh Clark left the employ of the electronics firm with the intention of entering a two-year graduate business school in the fall of the same year. At the tenth reunion of his engineering school class, in June of 1948, Clark had helped to analyze the salary and other data obtained from his classmates. He found his salary to be under the class median. The desire to increase his earning power by rounding out his engineering background with an administrative training was one of his major reasons for attending the business school. He also felt that this experience was necessary because he eventually hoped to run his own business and knew from past experience that it ordinarily took more than mere will to succeed.

For several years he had been accumulating ideas that might provide the basis for a new enterprise. One of these concerned a new type of electrical control meter for both production and laboratory use. This meter could be used to give continuous recordings of the consistency of any fluid material. It appeared to have tremendous potential advantages, both from a cost and quality control standpoint, over some of the older methods of maintaining control—for example, the analysis of spot samples taken at regular periods. While still working for the major electronics company, Clark was able to sell by mail-order advertising a preliminary model of his instrument. He received orders from three large companies. He also received inquiries about the meter from several instrument companies, one of them the largest in its field.

As soon as he felt that his school work was proceeding smoothly,

Clark visited Peter Sullivan, the grandson of a family friend. Clark hoped to interest Mr. Sullivan in helping him to organize a company to promote at least one of his many ideas. Hugh Clark had met Peter Sullivan while doing graduate engineering work immediately after World War II. Mr. Sullivan was about two years older than Clark. At the time, he held the position of assistant treasurer in a large manufacturing corporation. Shortly after Clark contacted him, he became vice-president in charge of sales for the same company. Hugh Clark understood Mr. Sullivan to be well-to-do in his own right, and he knew that other members of the Sullivan family were wealthy.

Hugh Clark presented to Peter Sullivan seventeen possible ideas for a new enterprise. He described his thinking on each idea and explained that he would like to see at least one of them organized as a business before he graduated from the business school. In particular, he told Sullivan he needed someone with experience to prevent him from making the usual mistakes that a young man would probably make in starting a new enterprise. Clark frankly admitted that he believed he did not know enough about setting up a new enterprise to handle such a project alone.

Hugh Clark's request seemed to intrigue Peter Sullivan and he believed that Clark, as the "idea" man, would make an excellent partner for his own management and financial ability. It became apparent, in their discussions, that the new electronic meter was of real interest to Mr. Sullivan. Clark had progressed further with his thinking about this item than he had with any of the others and, at an earlier date, had contacted an instrument wholesaler who was interested in distributing the electronic meter when and if it were produced.

In the following months, Peter Sullivan introduced Hugh Clark to two other men whom Sullivan believed would make excellent directors for the new company. One was a research engineer, Stevan Petrofsky; and the other, a local lawyer, Walter Guild, who was particularly interested in small business ventures. Dr. Petrofsky had in the past worked as the director of research for the same company in which Mr. Sullivan was an officer. Petrofsky, at this time, was president of a small research and development company. Mr. Sullivan had known Mr. Guild for several years and was acquainted with the latter's activities in several successful small businesses.

During the winter Mr. Sullivan suggested the name of Electroscale for the instrument. It was also decided that Hugh Clark would spend his summer vacation interviewing possible users of the Electroscale. A free-lance industrial designer was hired to translate Clark's preliminary designs into an instrument which would be both functional and appealing to the eye.

Clark's objective in interviewing potential consumers was to determine how an instrument of the type he envisaged should be constructed —i.e., what ranges of variables, conditions of measurement, etc., should be considered. He was convinced that, although the immediate potential market was relatively small and confined exclusively to research laboratories, it would grow as the instrument was tested and as knowledge of its use and availability became well publicized.

Clark considered his instrument to be far in advance of anything he had heard about or seen on his trip. By the end of the summer Clark had traveled 10,000 miles by automobile and had interviewed dozens of prospective users. Many of the people he interviewed during the trip believed that there was a need for the new type of meter. Several were doing research in areas where the proposed instrument would be useful, and a few of them had already constructed special setups or relatively crude instruments to help them in their research. At the same time, many of them were unfamiliar with the field of application and could offer no opinion as to the potential of this product. All seemed interested to learn what Clark was doing. In general, they thought the new ideas brought by Clark were intriguing and worthy of further consideration. Some of the research men told Clark they appreciated the opportunity for cross-fertilization of ideas and would be happy to see him again.

In order to more firmly establish the extent of user interest in the Electroscale, Mr. Petrofsky sent out a letter on his stationery requesting information from a distinguished group of American and foreign industrial and academic scientists. These men were known to be interested in the fields to which the Electroscale was applicable. An 80 per cent return resulted. A top industrial research director, a university department head, and a Nobel prize winner were among the respondents. The overwhelming majority expressed an interest in the instrument.

With this favorable reaction buttressing their decision, Sullivan and Clark decided to incorporate as the Electroscale Corporation. Hugh Clark's mother and Mr. Sullivan's wife each contributed $1,000 apiece. A total of 5,000 shares of common stock were authorized, divided 2,500 shares of Class A voting stock and 2,500 shares of Class B nonvoting stock. Each investor received 100 shares of Class A stock for her $1,000.

As an aftermath of Clark's early sales efforts and his field trip, a large instrument company indicated, through Mr. Sullivan, its desire to fully develop the meter as an item in its product line. The instrument manufacturer, however, would only pay Clark 5 per cent of his cost to manufacture the item. This, Clark did not consider an attractive offer, and he refused it.

After the corporation was formed, Sullivan visited the home offices of the same instrument company. Its research director told Sullivan that he considered the entire United States market potential to be only 1,000 units. Shortly thereafter, Sullivan proposed in a letter to the instrument company that they undertake the manufacture and distribution of the item and pay the Electroscale Corporation a royalty of 10 per cent of the retail list price. The letter was never answered by the instrument company.

The industrial designer's drawings were accepted by the directors. The next job was the task of locating someone to make the engineering drawings and construct the first model. Several small firms, experienced in design and model work, were contacted. Walter Guild, the lawyer, was a director in one of these firms, the Marskill Corporation, a small twenty-five-man manufacturer of electronic components. Both Guild and Hugh Clark considered Marskill to have the best equipped shop and the most impressive group of engineering personnel. Marskill's two owners had graduated from the same engineering school that Hugh Clark had attended.

It was decided shortly thereafter to give Marskill Corporation the contract for building the model. A maximum price of $450 was agreed upon, and a letter contract was given the Marskill Corporation. Since that firm was short of working capital, the Electroscale Corporation agreed to make a 50 per cent cash deposit with the order. Delivery was expected by the first of May, 1951.

A new director, Mr. Eugene Snyder, was appointed to the board at about this time. Mr. Snyder had been employed as manager of the new products division of the large distributor of laboratory and specialized instruments which Mr. Clark had originally contacted. At the time of his appointment, Mr. Snyder was employed by an affiliate of the same company. Eugene Snyder was several years older than Mr. Sullivan. Mr. Clark estimated that Snyder's salary was over $12,000 a year. Snyder expressed considerable interest in the Electroscale and indicated that he would be happy to be associated with the group. Both Sullivan and Clark agreed that Snyder would make an excellent director and might possibly be the man eventually to put in charge of the Electroscale Company.

The contact with Mr. Snyder had come through the much earlier contact that Clark had made with Mr. Freeman, the president of the instrument distributing company. Since Mr. Sullivan knew very little about

Mr. Snyder's background, he asked that a credit check be made on the new director. Somehow Mr. Snyder found out about the credit check and was pleased that Mr. Sullivan felt it had been necessary to make one. Snyder felt that it was a businesslike thing to do and indicated competence.

Soon after Snyder was asked to become a director, he told Sullivan and Clark that Mr. Freeman was somewhat upset by what he considered to be a division of Mr. Snyder's loyalties between the two firms. Mr. Snyder added that he believed Mr. Freeman probably thought that, as president of the wholesale company, he should have been the one to have been asked to serve as a director for Electroscale. Mr. Snyder assured Sullivan and Clark that he felt so strongly about the successful future of Electroscale that, should the president of the distributing firm order him to cease work with the Electroscale company, Snyder would resign from his present position rather than give up the potential he saw in the new product.

With the letter contract signed for the model, Clark and Sullivan became interested in where and how they would finance the manufacture and sale of the instrument. Clark had no large amount of capital of his own, although, if necessary, he could raise between $5,000 and $10,000. Sullivan, on the other hand, did not appear particularly interested in putting additional funds into the new company. Sullivan did suggest that some members of his family might be interested in investing heavily in the company. In addition, both men had previously agreed to issue 125 shares of the Class B stock at 10 cents per share to each of the directors of the company—Dr. Petrofsky, Walter Guild, and Eugene Snyder.

Since a total of 375 shares of the Class B nonvoting stock had been promised to the outside directors, Mr. Sullivan suggested that the remaining 2,125 shares be sold to his family at $8.00 per share, the proceeds to be used as working capital. This amount of money seemed to Hugh Clark to be far too small for the needs he had envisaged. After some consideration of this and other points, Hugh Clark wrote the letter to Mr. Sullivan shown in Exhibit 1.

At the next directors' meeting, Mr. Sullivan took Clark aside for a moment, smiled, and said: "Well, I tell you Hugh, I showed the letter to my wife and we both had a good laugh over it. We decided we would keep the letter for a couple of years and then return it to you. We'll bet you will get as good a laugh from it then as we do now." Clark went home and reread his letter; he saw nothing very humorous about what he had written. Although he hinted to Mr. Sullivan that he would still

Exhibit 1

LETTER TO MR. PETER SULLIVAN

DEAR PETER:

The intricate nature of the financial plan of the Electroscale Corporation has me just a little confused. Perhaps this is because I do not clearly see where we are supposed to be going and why.

The value of having stockholders to share the financial risks is clear to me, but somehow I don't see why we should sell shares at $8.00—except perhaps to our directors. It appears to me that our financing has proceeded as follows:

I. We each contributed $1,000 for 100 shares of common Class A.

II. We promised to issue 375 shares of common Class B to directors. This reduces our equity by about $650 each.

III. We plan to issue 2,125 shares of common Class B to new stockholders at $8.00/share. This, if effected, allows each of us to regain about $350 of our previous loss.

It is hard for me to understand why we, who have taken the biggest risk of all, and expended the greatest efforts in behalf of the corporation, should also have to suffer financial loss in the process. Undoubtedly you know where we are heading and probably, if I knew more about these things, I would see the benefits from this line of action. However, in my present state of ignorance, it is somewhat incomprehensible.

Another consideration of some moment is what happens to the other 2,300 Class A common shares? Are we going to issue these to ourselves at $10/share? If so, it will be some time before I can absorb the costs. Or are these being saved for some purpose?

Of course, it could be that you have already figured out a good method of taking care of us financially for the time, effort, and money that we both have expended in the establishment of this business. And this is probably a good assumption. But please let the poor treasurer in on what's coming off! My business-school courses are confusing enough.

Yours,

H. C.

like a direct answer to the letter, he never received one. In fact, that particular method of financing was never brought before the board of directors. As Clark said, "It just died a natural death."

Meanwhile, the work on the model was not proceeding as smoothly as Clark had originally hoped. In the initial stages there were several conferences between the designer, the Marskill engineers, and the board members of the Electroscale Corporation to define the problem and develop a rough plan. The Marskill project engineer then produced a layout drawing which appeared to fit the Electroscale requirements.

Meanwhile, the Marskill management had decided to subcontract the actual fabrication of the model. From the bids received, Marskill estimated that the instrument would cost about $300 per unit in lots of 25. This was disturbing news to Clark, since he expected to retail the instrument at $500 and felt that the estimated cost would not allow sufficient markup to undertake the expensive sales and promotional work required to sell the instrument.

Clark talked over the problem with the designer, who thought that the high cost estimate from the contractors was probably a result of faulty engineering on the part of the Marskill engineers. Time passed rapidly while the matter was discussed with the Marskill management. Finally Marskill indicated that it had found a small machine shop whose owner claimed he could make a model of an instrument for $600 that would cost about $150 in production quantities. Although it would fill the performance requirements set forth in the Marskill drawings, the design would be different.

Clark realized the dangers inherent in agreeing to this solution, but pointed out to his associates that it would be wise to accept the modifications, since it appeared that Marskill was becoming disinterested in the problem. Legal enforcement of the contract seemed impracticable, and the weeks were slipping by.

Marskill, after much prodding by the Electroscale people, finally produced the model. It did not meet the performance requirements which had been specified, and it was returned to Marskill for reworking.

Matters were at this stage when Clark graduated from business school and began to devote full time to following the progress of the model. After more provoking delays, Clark discovered that the subcontractor was the Machine Specialties Company, and he made direct contact with the small firm. He soon found that engineering liaison between Marskill and the Machine Specialties Company was almost nonexistent.

Clark, in attempting to expedite progress on the reworking of the model, became very friendly with the president of the Machine Specialties Company and even spent considerable time working with the machinists who were manufacturing parts and assembling them. As a result of this close association with the president of the Machine Specialties Company, Clark learned about many of that company's problems and was able to give some help toward solving them. Accordingly, when the work was completed, the president told Clark that he would not think of making any additional charge for reworking the model. Although the extra costs were the responsibility of the Marskill Company, Clark appreciated the gesture.

By this time, it was clear to Clark that the Marskill Company had little, if any, further interest in his product. Furthermore, Marskill had a heavy backlog of defense orders. On the other hand, the Machine Specialties Company evidenced a very active interest in co-operating with Clark and seemed genuinely anxious to see the product placed on the market.

Hugh Clark had also learned that there was an opportunity to buy half of the common stock of the Machine Specialties Company for $5,000. Although Clark was interested, he did not feel it would be a good investment for him because of a defaulted $10,000 second mortgage which the Machine Specialties Company had on all its assets. However, he did believe that a possible merger between the two companies might be advantageous to both.

He suggested to Mr. Sullivan that $5,000 be raised by Clark's supplying $2,500 and the additional $2,500 coming from the Electroscale Corporation. The Electroscale Corporation would sell enough stock so that it would be able to pay $2,500 cash for its interest and advance $20,000 as a loan to the Machine Specialties Company. This loan could be used to effect some sort of compromise with the second mortgage holders. Mr. Sullivan was distinctly not interested. Since his opinions had a strong effect on the other members of the board, there was little chance that the idea would be accepted by the other directors. Accordingly, Hugh Clark decided to drop any attempt to merge the two firms.

By the late fall of 1951, Hugh Clark had come to the decision that his board of directors was not directing. It was apparent to him that at each meeting the directors talked about what Mr. Sullivan wished to talk about, rather than discussing the points which Clark brought up. This, he admitted, was quite natural, since the first two outside directors had been old friends of Mr. Sullivan, and the new director, Mr. Snyder, seemed to look to Mr. Sullivan for guidance. Unfortunately, the meetings always ended with little accomplished. As Hugh Clark put it, "I have read several books on the board of directors. These men just were not acting like the directors in the books."

Cash in the corporate bank account amounted to only $200. Clark had discussed with Sullivan his financial problems and what he could expect in the form of a salary, once the company began to sell its product. Sullivan suggested at one of the board meetings that Clark should receive all of the profits during the first few years in lieu of a salary. Clark rejected this on the basis that, if sales estimates were correct, this would only amount to about $2,500 per year. Hugh Clark had been forced to spend some of his savings to meet business expenses. His wife had returned to work to provide them with additional income for the ordinary household and living expenses. In addition to the original $2,000 put in the company, Clark and Sullivan had each loaned the firm an additional $150. It seemed to Hugh Clark that either he should get out of the company and let the present members of the board run it or he should take over the company and operate it himself.

Clark discussed this problem with Walter Guild, the lawyer, at a number of luncheon meetings. He told him that he was sure that the directors were not going to be of any further help in getting the company started. Although the lawyer sympathized with him, Clark got no real advice as to what his next step should be. However, at the next board meeting, Guild did suggest that it seemed to him a good time to write a prospectus aimed at raising about $25,000.

Clark and Eugene Snyder, the new board member, had also talked about financing the Electroscale Corporation at about the time Snyder had joined the board of directors and just after Sullivan had proposed the sale of stock at $8.00 per share to his family. During this conversation, both men had agreed that a figure of $100,000 to $200,000 would be necessary to launch the new enterprise. Snyder frequently used one of his two automobiles, while Clark was still at the business school, to pick up the latter and drive him to the directors' meetings. The Snyders occasionally entertained Clark and his wife at their home. Whenever the two men got together, Snyder described in glowing terms his feeling that the Electroscale had a large and marvelous potential.

The young president was not the only member of the company to whom Snyder talked. Clark had heard that Mr. Sullivan had met with Mr. Snyder several times for lunch and a discussion of Electroscale plans. As Clark became increasingly restive about the lack of company activity, he naturally turned to Snyder and told him of his dissatisfaction. Snyder was sympathetic and agreed with Clark that something should be done. Finally, in December of 1951, both men went to Mr. Sullivan's home to discuss the possibility of selling Clark's share of the Electroscale Corporation to Mr. Sullivan. Clark would then completely divorce himself from all further activities of the firm.

Hugh Clark estimated that the value of his time plus the cash he had invested in the company amounted to about $19,000. However, he was so disgusted with the state of affairs that he was willing to sell his entire interest for $3,000 to $4,000, an amount approximately the total of his own and his mother's cash investment. He was ready to include the Electroscale patent for this price, although he had not previously signed it over to the company.

Mr. Sullivan stated that it would be a mistake for Mr. Clark to leave the company, and he offered to reduce his equity if that were necessary to keep it going. Clark, for his part, told Sullivan that he thought it important to have someone in the operating end of the company who had proven sales experience. Snyder had already hinted that he was dissatisfied with his own job and would probably leave the instrument distributing company in the near future. Sullivan and Clark had been impressed by Snyder's personally expressed ability to operate a large-scale project. Both agreed that Snyder might be the man for the president's job.

Snyder made it plain that he would expect a salary of $12,000 per year. Clark was in favor of paying Snyder that amount even though it meant that his own salary could not exceed $6,000. This was considerably less than he had been offered by other companies since leaving business school. Clark made it clear, however, that if the other board members thought it would help the future of the Electroscale Corporation to hire Snyder as president, then he was quite willing to give up the presidency.

A board of directors meeting was held shortly thereafter. Mr. Guild estimated that about $25,000 could be raised with the present stock authorization. Although Hugh Clark felt that his series of economic studies showed that the odds against success at this level of capitalization were far too great, he joined with the other directors to develop a prospectus. By the time the prospectus was completed, several weeks later, the concensus of opinion was that $50,000 should be the target. Clark considered that this capitalization gave the company only an even chance for success.

The directors recognized that someone had to spend a considerable amount of time to raise the money. Mr. Sullivan and his family made no further offer to advance the money. Mr. Clark knew that an investment house would not be interested in such a small stock issue. When the discussion reached the point as to how the stock would be sold, Mr. Snyder offered to resign from his present job with the instrument distributors and devote full time to the affairs of the Electroscale Corporation.

Hugh Clark had discussed with his friends and some of the people at the business school the type of man needed to head the Electroscale Corporation. All those contacted felt that, since the company intended initially to subcontract the manufacturing, a salesman would be the logical choice. Eugene Snyder seemed well fitted for the job. For years he had sold instruments of a like nature to the same type of customers which Electroscale Corporation would be seeking. Even though the immediate plan was to handle the sale of the Electroscale through a distributor for whom Mr. Snyder had worked, Clark knew that a tremendous amount of missionary selling would have to be done by the parent firm. Accordingly, when Snyder told the directors that he would devote full time to the Electroscale Company, Clark agreed to step down as president, retaining his other job as treasurer. Since he had just been appointed president of a medium-sized manufacturing company, Mr. Sullivan indicated his desire to merely retain a position on the board. Thus the Electroscale Corporation evolved with Mr. Snyder as president and Mr. Clark as treasurer, the only two active officers in the firm.

Shortly after the new president was elected, Clark invited Snyder and his wife to a small party in honor of the event. Although both families had been quite friendly outside of office hours, this party was the last real social contact between the Snyders and the Clarks. Mrs. Clark suggested to Mrs. Snyder several times thereafter that they might go to the ballet or the movies together but was always refused.

Clark was asked by the board of directors to design a plan for redistributing the company stock so that approximately a third of the current capital authorization would be available for sale to investors, plus an additional amount to be set aside in the form of options for Mr. Snyder. He consulted both Guild and Sullivan to obtain their views. During one luncheon meeting with Guild, the lawyer suggested that, if Clark really wished the directors to contribute to the new corporation, Clark should give each of them 5 per cent of the total stock. Later Sullivan strongly recommended that 4 per cent of the stock for each of the directors was sufficient and that care should be taken to leave control with Sullivan and Clark.

Guild reviewed the plan when it was presented to him. His comment was that he had never before seen a stock distribution worked out on such a logical basis. The outside investors were to get 32 per cent of the total stock; Snyder 20 per cent, mainly in options; Clark, 25 per cent; Sullivan, 15 per cent; and the remaining 8 per cent would go to the other two directors. The Class A and B shares were so divided that Clark and Sullivan still maintained voting control. Clark continued to work on economic studies of the different amounts of capital that might be required and the varying methods of financing that might be used. The range of capitalization considered was between $25,000 and $200,000. The results of these studies indicated to Clark that about $200,000 was needed initially to make the venture relatively certain of success. Clark felt strongly that the one instrument on which the company was basing much of its hopes, the Electroscale, would not support the firm forever. He considered it absolutely necessary for a company manufacturing and selling highly scientific, complex instruments to engage in a large amount of research and development if it expected to stay in existence for any period of time. His own experience plus study showed that research and development expense for companies in this field ran as high as 10 to 15 per cent of sales. The $200,000 capital would allow the new company to engage in immediate research. He had ideas for complementary instrumentation which, he estimated, would require about two years' time and $80,000 to develop.

Before Snyder spent much time searching for capital, he took Clark's economic studies to a business executive and well-known management consultant. The consultant looked over the studies made by Clark and finally stated that the Electroscale Corporation was completely underestimating the size of its field. Furthermore, with the amount of research development and sales expense necessary to get into this field, he felt that it would be foolish to start with a capitalization of less than $250,-000.

Both Clark and Snyder tried to bring Sullivan actively into the financing work, but they found him not interested in talking about a sum larger than $50,000. They did generate interest in Guild, who began actively to help with the development of the prospectus. Sullivan gave Snyder several leads to possible investors. When these proved to be valueless, Sullivan stated that he did not think he could be of any further help in this direction. Clark was able to pass along to Snyder a lead which finally led him to two men in the investment business. One of these said that, based on his experience, he would invest in a venture of this sort only if it were worth placing at least $200,000 in it.

Sullivan's attitude began to annoy Clark. Not only did the former control discussions when the directors got together, and effectively thus block any of Clark's ideas, but also he was failing to co-operate in the efforts to line up capital.

Hugh Clark often wondered if he were wise in attempting to organize his own company. He was particularly disappointed that Mr. Sullivan did not actively participate in the capital-raising effort. It was while his spirits were at this low ebb that a management consultant friend told him the results of a psychological test Clark had taken while still at business school. The test purported to give insight into a person's management ability. The results of the test showed that Clark was well qualified to be an executive in a business such as the Electroscale Corporation. The friend suggested, however, that Clark should associate himself with a "detail" man, since Clark's pattern indicated some of the aspects of the "big operator" who did not particularly care for handling petty matters. The consultant, after hearing Clark describe Snyder, suggested that the latter might be the "big-operator" type.

The consultant went on to say that Clark seemed to be the type of person who got things done. While it was possible that the Electroscale Corporation might fail, Clark should not be discouraged, since he eventually would most likely be successful. The consultant mentioned that his group might be interested in putting up $50,000 capital if some other capital could be brought into the company to get it established. Clark was not sure that everything his friend said was completely on the surface—or that the latter was telling him everything he knew.

Clark was much encouraged by this report. He told Snyder that he would definitely see the project through, although he was willing that those who had no confidence in the company should get out. For anyone who did leave, Clark would guarantee that their initial investment would be returned. Snyder applauded this statement and indicated that he definitely intended to continue to work alongside of Clark.

Clark continued to work closely with Snyder and Guild. His contacts with Sullivan became more infrequent as time passed. Dr. Petrofsky begged out of discussions about the prospectus on the basis that he was not financially inclined. Both Clark and Snyder were somewhat upset at Sullivan's lack of help. Clark felt, however, that Sullivan was acting consistently with his own ideas and not doing anything that he considered unethical.

Before Snyder had actively started to work for the company, Sullivan suggested that it would be wise to supplement the Electroscale with other products as a means of spreading sales costs, particularly during the early stages of the company's development. When Snyder became president, he quickly arranged sales franchises from a few established companies in parallel fields. He presented no specific evidence that he had actually obtained more than a promise. A close analysis of the economics of selling these lines based on Snyder's data indicated to Clark that little or no profit, and possibly some loss, might result because of the low margins involved. However, Clark was told by Snyder and the possible underwriters that they were using the idea of the wide product line as a wedge to get more money. Clark suspected that one of the reasons Sullivan had originally backed Snyder as a director, and later as president, was because the latter could obtain the additional products necessary to carry out Sullivan's idea.

As time passed, Clark began to feel that Snyder, although perfectly willing to make use of Clark's economic studies (Exhibits *2a, 2b,* and *2c*),[1] wished to handle the financing job alone. Snyder indicated the last two potential investors with whom he had made contact were interested in the product. Clark learned that these two investors had met several times with Snyder and Walter Guild. Clark had not been asked to attend.

Exhibit 2a

ELECTROSCALE CORPORATION
ESTIMATED EARNINGS STATEMENTS
(LOW-RANGE SALES)

Wholesale

	1953	*1954*	*1955*	*1956*	*1957*
Sales	$ 4,500	$10,500	$30,000	$45,000	$60,000
Cost of sales	2,700	6,300	18,000	27,000	36,000
Gross margin	1,800	4,200	12,000	18,000	24,000
Expenses:					
Product development	2,000	2,100	2,400	3,200	5,200
Selling	13,800	16,200	16,500	16,600	14,100
General and administrative	2,300	2,900	3,700	4,100	4,300
Total	$18,100	$21,200	$22,600	$23,900	$23,600
Net before tax	(16,300)	(17,000)	(10,600)	(5,900)	400
Eliminating salaries—$7,500:					
Net before tax	($ 8,600)	($ 9,500)	($ 3,100)	$ 1,600	$ 7,900

Retail

	1953	*1954*	*1955*	*1956*	*1957*
Sales	$ 7,500	$17,500	$50,000	$75,000	$100,000
Cost of sales	2,700	6,300	18,000	27,000	36,000
Gross margin	4,800	11,200	32,000	48,000	64,000
Expenses:					
Product development	2,000	2,100	2,400	3,200	5,200
Selling	13,600	16,200	16,500	16,600	22,100
General and administrative	2,500	2,900	3,700	4,100	6,300
Total	$18,100	$21,200	$22,600	$23,900	$33,600
Net before tax	(13,300)	(10,000)	9,400	24,100	30,400
Eliminating salaries—$7,500 first two years:					
Net before tax	($ 5,800)	($ 2,500)			

The next meeting of the board of directors was held at Mr. Snyder's home. Mr. Snyder discussed the great amount of time and effort he had spent in arranging capital for the new company. He believed that he now could raise $150,000. For this sum the Electroscale Corporation would give 40 per cent of its common stock to the investors plus another 6 per cent of the stock and about $12,500 cash to the outside promoters. Snyder also felt that an additional $100,000 could simulta-

[1] Exhibits *2a, 2b,* and *2c* are only three of the several dozen detailed charts and tables compiled by Clark to show the economic potential of the product.

neously be raised in the form of convertible debenture bonds. The remainder of the common was to be used as incentive stock for future consultants and management.

Snyder also pointed out that the potential investors were interested in having only common voting stock in the company. Clark supported this viewpoint, since he believed it only fair that all stockholders should

Exhibit 2b

ELECTROSCALE CORPORATION
ESTIMATED EARNINGS STATEMENTS
(HIGH-RANGE SALES)

Wholesale

	1953	*1954*	*1955*	*1956*	*1957*
Sales	$ 7,500	$22,500	$ 60,000	$ 90,000	$120,000
Cost of sales	4,500	13,500	36,000	54,000	72,000
Gross margin	3,000	9,000	24,000	36,000	48,000
Expenses:					
Product development	2,000	2,100	2,400	3,200	5,200
Selling	13,800	16,200	16,500	16,600	14,100
General and administrative	2,300	2,900	3,700	4,100	4,300
Total	$18,100	$21,200	$ 22,600	$ 23,900	$ 23,600
Net before tax	(15,100)	(12,200)	1,400	12,100	24,400
Eliminating salaries—$7,500 first two years:					
Net before tax	($ 7,600)	($ 4,700)			

Retail

	1953	*1954*	*1955*	*1956*	*1957*
Sales	$12,500	$37,300	$100,000	$150,000	$200,000
Cost of sales	4,500	13,500	36,000	54,000	72,000
Gross margin	8,000	24,000	54,000	96,000	128,000
Expenses:					
Product development	2,000	2,100	2,400	3,200	5,200
Selling	13,800	16,200	24,500	24,600	30,100
General and administrative	2,300	2,900	5,700	6,100	8,300
Total	$18,100	$21,200	$ 32,600	$ 33,900	$ 43,600
Net before tax	(10,100)	2,800	31,400	62,100	84,400
Eliminating salaries—$7,500 first year:					
Net before tax	($ 2,600)				

have a vote. Furthermore, he did not think it a healthy situation where one individual could provide an effective block on the rest of the stockholders. At the same time, Clark was becoming more and more concerned with who was going to control the destiny of the new corporation. He had already given some thought to the idea of setting up a voting trust to insure that management control would remain vested in the hands of himself and his present associates.

With these new developments, it became clearly evident that a new stock distribution and financial plan should be made. Clark set out to provide this. In the period which followed, he worked even more closely with Snyder. These meetings culminated one evening at Clark's home with Clark showing Snyder about fifteen different plans for the distribution of 51 per cent of the common stock among the present board members.

Exhibit 2c

ELECTROSCALE CORPORATION

SALES ESTIMATES

1. Mr. Freeman of Freeman Instrument Co.:

   "First-year sales of a new instrument are usually quite small in our experience. If you sell 25, you will be lucky."

2. Mr. Jones of Freeman Associates:

1st year	12–25
2d year	50–100
3d year	100–200

   "If this is a good basic instrument, and I think it is, sales will probably increase rapidly after the third year."

3. Electronic Measuring Service Co.:

   "U.S. market potential is about 1,000 units" (given verbally to a former director in 1951).

4. Eugene Snyder estimates for economic studies:

1st year	39–72
2d year	72–144
3d year	108–216
4th year	144–288
5th year	211–482

CONCLUSION

	Units	$500 Retail Value	$300 Wholesale Value
1953	15–25	$ 7,500–$ 12,500	$ 4,500–$ 7,500
1954	35–75	17,500– 57,500	10,500– 22,500
1955	100–200	50,000– 100,000	30,000– 60,000
1956	150–300	75,000– 150,000	45,000– 90,000
1957	200–400	100,000– 200,000	60,000– 120,000
Total	500–1000	$250,000–$500,000	$150,000–$300,000

Just before he left, Snyder suddenly proposed that Guild's share should be increased above Sullivan's share and that Snyder and Clark should receive the same number of shares each. Although surprised by this recommendation, Clark thought about it for a few moments and then stated that he did not consider it a fair distribution. However, he intended to discuss it with people with experience greater than his, and he would be guided by their judgment. Clark did agree that Guild should get a larger share than Dr. Petrofsky, since the lawyer seemed to have already contributed more to the enterprise.

A few days later, Clark had occasion to talk with Walter Guild on the telephone. Guild told him that he appreciated the fact that Clark felt his contribution was worthy of a larger share of the corporation. This indicated to Clark that Snyder had probably visited the lawyer with his plan to give Guild a larger share of the stock as well as for Snyder and Clark to hold equal shares. Clark also recognized that Snyder, in going to Guild with the promise of a larger share of the company, put

Exhibit 3

ELECTROSCALE CORPORATION

ROUGH NOTES ON THE PROPOSED STOCK DIVISION

H[1]	P[2]	Ge[3]	S[4]	G[5]		
~~7~~ 6	~~3~~ 4	..	..	..	(10)	Initial investment
2	2	2	2	2	(10)	Directors' promotional work
~~8~~ 9	~~2~~ 1	15	..	6	(31)	Promoting corporation
17%	7%	17%	2%	8%	(51%)	Total to promoters and Clark
					(49%)	Sale to public

	A No Par	*B No Par*		*A No Par*	*Projected Shares*	*Per Cent*	*Total*		*Common $1 Par Value (20 for 1)*
H.	100	. . .	=	100	+325	17	425	=	8,500
P.	100	. . .	=	100	+75	7	175	=	3,500
Ge		125	=	50	+375	17	425	=	8,500
G.	. . .	125	=	50	+150	8	200	=	4,000
S.	. . .	125	=	50	None	2	50	=	1,000
Paid in	200A	375B		350A			1275A		25,500 sh.
Value				$2,037.50					$?
For sale									24,500 shares $250,000+

[1] Hugh Clark.
[2] Peter Sullivan.
[3] Eugene Snyder.
[4] Stevan Petrofsky.
[5] Walter Guild.

Clark in the position of agreeing to a bad bargain or taking something away from Guild. As Clark said, "I admired the technique but deplored the ethics."

Snyder and Guild had been working on the prospectus. The lawyer had all the papers at his home when he was suddenly called out of town. Guild asked Clark to relay this information to Snyder and request the latter to pick up the prospectus at Guild's home on the following morning. Clark forgot about this request until he happened to be in the vicinity of Guild's home the next day. Thinking to save Snyder a trip, he picked up the prospectus himself instead of asking the president to do so. In checking to make sure that everything was included in the folder, he found the rough notes on a stock distribution plan shown in Exhibit 3. They confirmed his feeling that Snyder and Guild had been developing a new financial plan without informing him about it.

After Clark talked with his friends, he called Snyder on the telephone and told him quite frankly that he would not support his plan for the division of stock, but would definitely oppose it. He realized that Snyder had been doing a great deal of work toward financing the company and would bear major responsibilities as the president. On the other hand, Clark pointed out that he had originated the idea, had been responsible for getting the company started, had done all the preliminary work with the model, had provided all of the economic studies and forecasts used by Snyder, and actually had put some money into the company to support it in the lean days after its birth.

It was apparent, as the discussion progressed, that Snyder completely disagreed with this viewpoint. Snyder finally asked just what Clark did propose as a stock distribution. Clark answered that he had, at this point, reached no decision. Snyder hung up his receiver without saying goodnight. It was apparent that it would be difficult, in the future, for Clark to talk to the president of the Electroscale Corporation about any matter.

The day following the abruptly terminated telephone conversation, Clark attempted to call Snyder twice. Mrs. Snyder answered each time with the statement that her husband was not at home. Snyder did not call back. The next day, Clark talked to Mrs. Snyder but could not reach her husband. Clark felt that he might be able to smooth things out by pointing out to Snyder that their differences of opinion should not obscure the fact that their most important task was to get funds so as to develop a company that would be worth dividing.

After these several attempts to talk to Snyder, Clark concluded that he was not going to reach the president easily. He called Sullivan and apprised him of the situation in detail. A few days later, he learned that Snyder had also called Sullivan and related his version of the break with Clark. Snyder asked that Sullivan keep his call a secret.

With all this lack of co-ordination and friction in the management group, Clark thought it wise to become better acquainted with one of the potential investors whom he considered would be a major influence on whatever financial plan was adopted. Clark arranged a meeting and brought with him his personal résumé and letters from businessmen and technical associates. Clark did not mention his falling-out with Snyder.

Toward the close of the conversation the investor told Clark several things which, as treasurer, Clark felt he should have known previously. In addition, the man stated them in such a manner that Clark was sure that the investor realized that he had not previously known about them. This irritated Clark, since he thought Snyder should have kept him informed. Of greater import to Clark was the fact that the circumstances clearly indicated that Snyder had disclosed his breakdown in communication with Clark to an outsider.

As an aftermath to this meeting with the potential investor, Clark discovered information, which, although circumstantial, indicated that this man had come to the meeting with Clark directly after having had luncheon with Snyder and Guild. Clark was not pleased at this confirmation of his suspicions that Snyder and Guild were now operating as a team which excluded him.

He also visited the lawyer, Walter Guild, to present his viewpoint. Mr. Guild pointed out that it was very difficult to obtain a man with Snyder's ability to raise money for a small firm. Clark stated that he still controlled the patent and that without the patent he considered the company to be inoperable. The lawyer felt, however, that the corporation, founded on the basis of the knowledge and know-how which Clark possessed, did have certain vested rights in the patent and that a lawsuit could probably be brought against Clark should he try to deprive the company of the use of his patent. Both men agreed that the situation was very unfortunate.

Meanwhile, Clark continued unsuccessfully to try to contact Snyder. He also spent some time in individually meeting with each of the other directors of the company, telling them his story and explaining how communication with Snyder had broken down. In turn, they advised him to keep trying to meet with Snyder so as to, once and for all, settle the problem which seemed to be growing between them.

Several weeks later, Clark finally reached Snyder by telephone at his home. He pointed out that, since both sides were at somewhat of an impasse, there should be a meeting to talk the situation over. Snyder agreed, and Clark suggested the following day. Snyder had a previous appointment and stated that he was extremely busy and would be for several days. He suggested it might be better to arrange the meeting by telephone at some later date. Although Clark tried several times after that to telephone Snyder, he was never successful in doing so.

When Clark found that he was unable to get in touch with Snyder, he thought his next best move was to work through an intermediary. He believed that Mr. Sullivan would be the man most able to act as an umpire between Snyder and himself.

Hugh Clark visited Mr. Sullivan and told him the entire story. Mr. Sullivan agreed that something would have to be done immediately and stated that he would get in touch with Mr. Snyder. Mr. Sullivan was quite hopeful that a sensible solution could be found that was agreeable to both parties. He called Clark shortly thereafter to tell him that he had arranged a luncheon meeting with Mr. Snyder to discuss the problem. The luncheon meeting was never held.

However, Clark did receive a proposal from Mr. Snyder through Mr. Sullivan. The proposal was that Mr. Clark would turn over his patent rights and all rights in the company for 10 per cent of the capital stock, and a 5 per cent royalty on wholesale sales of the Electroscale and accessories covered under the patent application for the life of the patent if granted. The same terms were offered for two years if the patent was refused, less cost of developing accessory equipment covered by the patent.

It was Sullivan's opinion that Clark could obtain 20 per cent of the stock of the company. Clark pointed out he was perfectly willing to leave the company if he could get some cash, a fair royalty agreement, and a stock interest. In balance, he would rather be heavy on the cash and light on the stock interest, since he no longer had any real trust in Mr. Snyder and his financial friends.

At about the same time, Mr. Clark made a trip to New York to talk with several people about a possible position. One company in which he became interested was an investment firm in the new enterprise field. Its management agreed with him that the Snyder offer was not very attractive.

Upon Mr. Clark's return, he made a counterproposal to Mr. Guild as an answer to Mr. Snyder's offer. The latter indicated that he thought the offer would be unacceptable to the financial people. Clark suggested that he be given $5,000 cash; $14,000 in secured notes for the time he had devoted to the company; royalties of 6 per cent of gross sales of Electroscale material for the term of the patent if granted, or 6 per cent for two years and 3 per cent thereafter for fifteen years if a patent was not granted; 10 per cent of the common stock protected against dilution for ten years; the right to elect a director; and the right to inspect and audit the books. He did not present the detailed basis for agreement shown as Exhibit 4 (p. 380)—this was for his own information. Actually, he did not expect to get all that he requested. He presented it as a basis for bargaining with the idea, unexpressed, that he would take less.

The matter continued to drag along for a number of weeks. Finally Mr. Sullivan was able to get all the directors together in a meeting at his office. Mr. Snyder reported his progress to date and stated that the two investors with whom he had been working had done considerable investigation into the electronics field for which the meter would be most applicable. They had also checked the patent situation. It was the opinion of their patent lawyer that, although the Clark patent was worth while, it would only reach its full value if it were backed by a financially strong company. Clark felt that Snyder was suggesting that, unless he had sizable financial resources behind him, the patent would be of little use to the inventor.

Exhibit 4

ELECTROSCALE CORPORATION

PROPOSED BASIS FOR AGREEMENT

Cash		$ 5,000
Notes—6%—secured:		
1 year	$2,000	
2 years	3,000	
3 years	4,000	
4 years	5,000	
		14,000
Royalties—6% on gross sales Electroscale material for term of patent if granted—minimum royalties payable in advance:		
1st year	$1,500	
2d year	3,000	
3d year	4,500	
4th year	6,000	
5th year and after	8,000	
		23,000
Royalties—6% on gross sales Electroscale material for 2 years, 3% thereafter for 15 years if patent is not granted—minimum royalties payable in advance:		
1st year	$1,500	
2d year	3,000	
3d year	2,250	
4th year	3,000	
5th year and after	4,000	
		13,750
Common stock—10% of authorized protected against dilution for 10 years		
Right to elect a director		
Right to inspect and audit books		

Mr. Snyder again offered Clark 10 per cent of the stock and a 5 per cent royalty on the wholesale price of all instruments and accessories sold which were covered by the patent. Clark saw no use in carrying the discussion further. He repeated that his offer still stood as shown in detail in Exhibit 4. If the other people wished to bargain, Clark suggested they visit his new lawyer.

Clark had met this lawyer as a result of a chance contact with an old teacher friend from his engineering school. He had told the professor his problems with the present company organization. The professor had suggested that Clark contact a friend of his, a former assistant county prosecutor. Clark found the lawyer to be an extremely likeable person who was very much interested in new enterprise. The lawyer agreed to represent Clark, without fee, in his future dealings with the Electroscale Corporation.

This statement by Clark was a verbal bombshell which stopped the meeting. It was decided that, in view of Clark's position, it would no longer be sensible for Snyder to go ahead with his capital-raising program. Accordingly, it was agreed that Clark would buy out the other stockholders. He offered to pay $1,500 to Sullivan for his share of the company's stock and other expenses which the latter had incurred for the company. Payment would be in the form of a 5 per cent interest-bearing note to be due on demand after January 1, 1953. He also agreed to return to the directors $12.50 apiece, the price which they had each paid for their shares of Class B nonvoting stock.

Snyder felt that he should also receive something for the expenses he had incurred in the capital-raising program to date. Mr. Sullivan suggested that he be given a note for $1,250 in lieu of the proposed $1,500 note and that a note for $250 be issued to Snyder by Clark. Clark readily agreed to the compromise.

Several days later, Dr. Petrofsky mailed his stock with a friendly memorandum to the effect that there was no need for Clark to return the $12.50. However, Clark sent a check to the doctor immediately. Several days later, Clark arranged a meeting in Sullivan's office at which transfer of the latter's voting common for the demand note was accomplished. Mr. Guild did not forward his stock in the next few days, and eventually Clark personally collected it.

Mr. Snyder's stock also did not arrive, and Clark called to ask the reason. Snyder stated that he had forgotten all about the matter and would attend to it as soon as he returned from a business trip. Three weeks went by and still no word was received by Clark from Snyder. Eventually, he took the note and the check for $12.50 to Mr. Snyder's house, after first calling the latter to make sure that the latter would be available at a set time. However, even though Snyder had agreed to the meeting place, the stock certificates were still in his safe-deposit box at the bank. Snyder promised to send them to Clark by registered mail.

Clark was upset over the treatment he was receiving from Snyder. He checked with his lawyer to see if something could be done to force Snyder into quicker action. The lawyer advised him to wait to see what Snyder's next move would be. A short time later, Clark received a call from Snyder suggesting a personal meeting. At this meeting, Clark obtained Snyder's stock and Snyder received a check and a note. The meeting ended on a friendly key, with both parties wishing each other luck in their future activities. By the end of July, 1952, Clark heard that Snyder had received some capital from the two investors who had originally been interested in the Electroscale Corporation. It was Clark's understanding that Snyder intended to form a new company to sell a general line of laboratory instruments.

Clark's first move, now that he was starting with a clean slate, was to construct a new model of the Electroscale. He contacted the designer who had done the first work on the unit in November, 1950. Even before the final meeting of the board, Clark had told the designer that he was probably going on without his former group. He pointed out that the present model operated so poorly that a new one with improved characteristics was required. He asked the designer's help in producing the new improved model; and he pointed out that, while his funds were limited, he thought they would be adequate for the job. Ordinarily the designer received a large fee for this type of work. However, he was quite willing to help without reimbursement. As he put it, "When you are successful and driving around in a Cadillac, perhaps you will be able to throw some additional business my way."

Clark also contacted the president of the Machine Specialty Company, the manufacturer of the previous model. He told him about the situation and asked whether he would care to do the model making. The president agreed to go ahead in his home workshop at a cost to Clark of about $3.00 per hour. He also told Clark that he would arrange for two draftsmen to make the drawings at the same rate of $3.00 per hour.

Hugh Clark believed that he should form a new group for the company. A few weeks before, he had visited his engineering school during alumni day. Clark told one of his classmates about his problems. The classmate was a competent physicist and the research director for a well-known instrument company. Clark asked if he would be interested in helping to form the new Electroscale Company. The classmate agreed to help whenever Hugh Clark was ready to call upon him.

Clark also visited Mr. Freeman, the president of the instrument distributing company for whom Snyder had once worked. At this time, both parties believed that the Electroscale should be sold by a wholesaler. Mr. Freeman indicated that he was still willing to aid Clark in his attempt to form a new company, even after closer economic studies indicated that wholesale distribution during early years was impractical.

As a means to provide himself with a laboratory for further experimental work on the model, Clark took another course at his engineering school. During this period he met a man with whom he had gone to business school. The latter, a research assistant at the engineering school, was extremely interested in working on the Electroscale. The scope of his present job, he believed, confined his thinking and gave him little exercise for his abilities. He agreed to help Clark on the production and planning problems involved in checking the drawings and expediting the work.

After several meetings of the new group, it assembled to discuss the first set of layout drawings. This happened to be the first meeting the research assistant attended. He suggested major design changes which would require a complete new set of layout drawings. These changes involved considerable simplification and would undoubtedly reduce manufacturing costs, but Clark opposed them on the basis that they would set the group back at least two to three weeks. However, after he presented his objections, he asked each member individually to express his reaction. All were in favor of the new design. Clark agreed to scrap the old design, which increased his total design cost by $300. Although Clark knew more about the field of application for the Electroscale than anyone in the group, he believed that the individual members of his group were probably more expert than he in the various phases of mechanical and electrical design.

Clark had been introduced to a sales manager employed by a firm in the electronics field. The sales manager agreed to devote some time to setting up a proper sales program for the new company. At about the same time, the research director from the instrument company introduced Clark to another man who had considerable experience in instrument sales, although the gentleman now was working in the research and development field.

In addition to the foregoing, Clark had added two other members to his team. Both were professors at the engineering school. One specialized in history, although his original field had been mathematics. He was about forty-six years old and had been associated with the Office of Naval Research during World War II. He also had done considerable work in organizing Navy schools during the war.

The other professor was a doctor of electronic engineering and was considered an expert in the field to which the Electroscale would be applied. With these men behind him, Clark felt that, with the exception of financial problems, he would be able to handle any of the questions which might come up in the establishment of his new company. He felt that in assembling this new team he had taken into consideration three primary points. They were: (1) members should have an interest in his success; (2) members should be competent and intelligent; and (3) members should be ready, willing, and able to add to the value of the venture.

By October, 1952, the new Electroscale Company had held several meetings with those people who were helping to establish it (Exhibit 5). None of them as yet had been appointed to the board of directors.

Exhibit 5

ELECTROSCALE CORPORATION

THE NEW TEAM

Participating Members:

1. Stephen Argo—Research director—graduate engineer—thirty-seven years old.
2. John Freeman—President, Instrument Distributing Company—no technical education—sixty years old.
3. Clarence Nolan—Research assistant—civil engineer—business-school graduate—thirty years old.
4. Professor Johnson—History of science—mathematician—experience with ONR—forty-six years old.
5. Jackson Smith—Sales manager for electronic firm—thirty-five years old.
6. William Lentner—Electronic-instrument salesman and research technician.
7. Dr. James Adams—Expert in electronic instrument field.

Unofficial Members:

1. Mark O'Brien—Loan officer, City Commercial Bank—sixty-five years old.
2. Hiram Land, Jonas White —Draftsmen for an electronic firm.
3. Vincent Cleve—Industrial designer—forty-five years old.
4. Sandy MacNabb—Attorney.

Clark felt that it was entirely too early to find out whether they would make good directors, able to actually contribute to his enterprise. The completely redesigned model had been built, parts plated and painted, although they had not as yet been assembled. As soon as they were assembled and the model tested, Clark intended to take a field trip to get user response to the new piece of equipment. Upon his return from the field trip, he expected to discuss with the members of his group further plans for marketing the Electroscale and later financing and setting the new company in operation.

The Eckdahl Manufacturing Company

Lief Eckdahl, the president and sole owner of the Eckdahl Manufacturing Company, was proud of the fact that his firm had been in existence for nearly twenty-five years. To Frank Cummings, who was considering a position as Mr. Eckdahl's assistant, the past history of the company and its longevity were not nearly so important as the change in company policy from passive existence to the aggressive competitive attitude which seemed to have currently replaced it. It appeared to Cummings that the steady growth of the company during the past two years and the president's desire for further expansion offered an excellent personal opportunity for a young man.

Frank Cummings had taken a combination engineering and business course at a small college. After graduation in 1949, he worked for a year in a small machine shop. The proprietor of the machine shop had hired Frank with the stated plan of eventually making him the manager. However, he warned Cummings that the manager's job would be available only after Cummings had thoroughly learned the business from the ground up. In June, 1950, having progressed only to the $40 per week rung of the success ladder, orders to active duty reminded Cummings that he held a reserve commission in the U.S. Army Engineers.

Training, a year in Korea, and the best part of another year in the United States completed the period to June, 1952, when Frank Cummings again became a civilian seeking employment. In the Army, Cummings had spent the last nine months in staff work determining requirements for engineering equipment. He enjoyed this work and said that, if it had not been for his family and if he could have been assured of continuing in that type of work, he might have stayed in the service.

After a few days' vacation, Cummings set about locating a new job. He had no desire to return to his old position in the machine shop, since he believed that the proprietor never intended him to become other than a handy combination machinist–bookkeeper–truck driver–assistant.

Jobs were not too difficult to find. Although Cummings had managed to save about $2,000 since getting out of school, he did not feel that with a wife and one child he could spend too much time analyzing or selecting his position.

The experience in the machine shop had not dimmed his desire to work in a small company. He liked the close personal relations in the smaller firms and hoped to find a company in which he could buy or earn some equity. On the other hand, he was well aware that working for a large corporation had certain advantages. At the end of three weeks, he had narrowed his choice between a large electronics firm and the Eckdahl Manufacturing Company.

The position in the electronics firm seemed to offer real challenge and an opportunity to get ahead. Two of Cummings' relatives held minor executive positions in another plant of the Electronics Company located in a nearby city. They had described to Frank the excellent opportunities in the firm. In particular, they pointed out that its organization, separated into small divisions, in effect created a series of small businesses.

Cummings had interviewed a number of people in the central offices of the corporation. He had been considered for two different positions in the controller's department. Each of the jobs required a considerable amount of experience. He had received the impression that he had been refused by the controller in each case for lack of that experience. After these first interviews, the personnel office asked him to report to the division of the corporation located in his home town.

After a pleasant interview with the executive assistant to the vice-president in charge, he was offered a position as executive trainee. The vice-president of this division hired approximately a half-dozen young men each year for this purpose. They were placed directly under the executive assistant to the vice-president for a period of six to nine months, during which they were exposed to all phases of the division operations. At the end of that period, they were given junior executive positions in the department for which they were most qualified. The other young men in the group had a few weeks' start on Cummings. In fact, the position would not have been available except that one of the original group had suddenly decided to accept a regular commission in the Air Force.

Cummings was given an opportunity to look at some of the individual reports made by the members of the group and, by chance, to hear one of the young men being chastised for lack of initiative in handling a problem to which he had been assigned. The executive assistant to the vice-president had greeted the trainee as he entered the office with: "What the devil was the matter with you on the Osborne deal? I go out of town for twenty-four hours and find the production manager on my neck when I come back because you didn't carry out orders. I've told you not to let the brass around here frighten you. Giving in to Osborne as you did just because he is sales manager made us all look foolish to the rest of the division. Now get out to your desk and get the report in on the florescent light problem by tomorrow!"

The salary offered to Cummings was $275 a month with a raise promised at the end of the first six months. It was sufficient, he felt, to get by on. In general, Cummings was quite satisfied with the opportunity presented. He was requested to give his decision by the following Monday.

LIEF ECKDAHL, OWNER

During the period Cummings had been contacting the electronics firm, he had also been discussing the possibilities of a job with the Eckdahl Manufacturing Company. He was especially fortunate in having available to him a great deal of information and background about Lief Eckdahl and his firm. Mr. Sven Eckdahl, Lief's father, had been a well-known and respected citizen from a nearby town. He had retired as general manager of a large contracting business after World War II. Thereafter, he occasionally did some consulting work for large contractors, although his primary interest had been in the Eckdahl Manufacturing Company. Mr. Cummings' family was well acquainted with Mr. Eckdahl Sr.; and eventually, through a mutual interest in community activities, Frank Cummings also became acquainted with Mr. Eckdahl Sr. From him he often heard of the trials and tribulations of the pre-1950 Eckdahl Company. Cummings never knew what the Senior Eckdahl's interest in the company actually was, although he suspected that the father had provided most of the original capital.

Sven Eckdahl had died a few months before the outbreak of the Korean hostilities. Although Cummings never learned the complete details, he knew that Lief's numerous brothers and sisters had claimed a share of the company as their part of the father's inheritance. Apparently, Lief Eckdahl had plunged heavily into debt, borrowing every possible cent from all sources he could locate in order to buy out the other heirs' share of the business.

During his several conversations with Cummings, Eckdahl spoke freely of his earlier problems and of the history of the company. Shortly after graduating from high school, he had accepted a job as an apprentice lockmaker. As soon as he felt he had acquired sufficient experience, he opened a little one-man locksmith shop. Initially he tried to get by on a hand-to-mouth basis, but after a few years he found that his expanding business required additional capital. Mr. Eckdahl Sr. provided the necessary money on what Lief Eckdahl claimed was a strictly loan basis. However, from the day his father turned over the first money to him, Mr. Eckdahl Sr. considered himself a part of the management of the business and insisted upon receiving $25 a week remuneration for the time he spent in the shop. Actually, the father was able to provide a good many valuable contacts to the new business among the many contractors and associated firms that he knew.

The depression of the 1930's hit the small company very hard. At that time, production was in four fields: manufacture of special hardware for individual buildings; a special marine hardware line; the production of a cheap line of wrought-iron hardware which was distributed and sold by another company under its own trade name; and a certain amount of subcontract general machine work for larger companies. Many of Lief Eckdahl's competitors were forced into bankruptcy during this period. He not only managed to survive, but in some cases actually was able to purchase certain items of their equipment to supplement his own.

Eckdahl attributed his success in surviving the depression to several things. As pointed out above, his line of products was somewhat wider than the lines of his similar-sized competitors. At the same time, he incurred the absolute minimum of overhead expense, since he had no office and only a part-time accountant who came in every two weeks to check the books. He poured every cent that he could possibly raise into the business. He pared his personal expenses to the bone by sleeping on a bench in the shop for some months at the height of the depression and by eating nothing more substantial than coffee and sandwiches for his meals. He even postponed his marriage for several years because of his strong desire to establish the business upon a firm foundation.

Mr. Eckdahl also admitted that survival during this period had consisted of a large element of good luck, as well as sacrifice on his part. For example, at one time, when it seemed that nothing could prevent several of his creditors from forcing him into bankruptcy, he won $500 on a lottery ticket with which to pay off their claims.

Mr. Eckdahl pointed out to Cummings that his father's death, although unfortunate from a personal viewpoint, actually removed much of the conservative pressure which had previously tied down the business and had prevented any real expansion during World War II. He stated that he had been under no legal compulsion to pay the family for his father's supposed share of the business, since in fact the $25 a week drawing by Mr. Eckdahl Sr. had actually been repayment on the loan. The balance which had been left was, at the time of the father's death, a relatively minor sum. However, Mr. Eckdahl Sr. had always spoken of it as "my business"; and Lief knew that the family considered that he and his father were equal partners, even though he had legal proof to the contrary. He considered it much happier for all, both from a business and family standpoint, to go heavily into debt in order to, once and for all, make the business wholly his own. The fact that his brothers and sisters had been most demanding in their terms and put considerable pressure upon him to make a 100 per cent cash payment had caused him many a sleepless night and a great deal of financial embarrassment.

During the two years between the death of his father and the summer of 1952, Lief Eckdahl had been able to expand his company from twenty-five people to about seventy-five people. He had also moved from a small second-floor shop to a five-story building of his own, with more than adequate office, storage, and manufacturing space. Eckdahl had rented one floor of the building to a small woodworking firm; another floor was used as storage space by a wholesaler; and the large store on the street floor was occupied by a hardware dealer.

Eckdahl had also expanded the types of products which he manufactured. In addition to the items previously mentioned, Eckdahl had become heavily engaged in subcontract work for two large electronic manufacturers. Some of his new working force were skilled tool and die makers, and he now produced jigs, fixtures, and small dies for other companies as well as those used in his own shop. Prime contract work had also been obtained from the Navy and Ordnance Department.

Frank Cummings believed that Eckdahl's story adequately presented the facts of the company's history. One of his best friends had known Eckdahl for years and generally confirmed everything that Eckdahl had told Cummings.

ANTHONY MARHILL, COMPANY ENGINEER

In addition, a relative of Cummings' by marriage, Anthony Marhill, had been employed as engineer by Eckdahl for about nine months. Tony Marhill was enthusiastic about the future of the Eckdahl Manufacturing Company. Initially he had not known that Cummings was interested in working for the same firm; but when the latter broached the subject to him, Marhill encouraged Cummings to accept the position.

Tony Marhill was in his early fifties at the time. He had about thirty years of varied experience in the engineering field. His first position, after graduation as a civil engineer, had been with a large construction firm. After a number of years, he had left this company to become assistant to the chief engineer of a large manufacturing plant. After about five years in this position, he had moved on to become chief engineer and general manager of a small company producing materials-handling equipment. This job had only lasted for a year; and although Cummings had never known the details, he had heard from other members of his family that Marhill and the president of the firm could not agree upon basic policy with regard to the purchase of new equipment.

Marhill had also been a sales engineer and consultant. His last position before coming to Eckdahl had been that of a design engineer for the same electronics company in which Cummings had just been offered a job. Marhill had a small independent income left him by his mother on which he and his family could have lived if they so desired.

Tony Marhill's reaction to the fact that Cummings was considering a position with the electronics firm was summed up in the following advice: "You don't want to work for the Electronics Company. I know, for I speak from experience. You'll either work hard and someone else will get the credit, or your work will be pushed aside for another man's idea which is only half as good. Lief Eckdahl is going places; he has all sorts of contacts and makes use of them. He wants to expand, and I think those of us who are on the ground floor will go up with him."

Tony Marhill went farther than merely giving advice; he invited Lief Eckdahl, Cummings, and their respective wives to dinner one evening. After dinner the men discussed the possibilities for growth in the small company. Both Eckdahl and Marhill emphasized that the president needed a young assistant and that they believed Cummings seemed to have an excellent background for that job. Eckdahl pointed out that eventually he wished to divorce himself completely from the production phase of business and devote himself almost exclusively to sales. He felt that, with Marhill handling production and Cummings handling the purchasing and control end, he would have an excellent team. If the firm continued to expand, Eckdahl mentioned that he would also be interested in disposing of some of his equity to the two men.

Cummings was much impressed by what he learned that evening. When he told his father about Marhill's enthusiasm for the company, Mr. Cummings Sr. reacted adversely, which did not surprise Frank Cummings. Most of the Cummings family were skilled craftsmen and tended to consider Marhill something of a theorist.

"You can't take a craftsman trained as thoroughly as was Eckdahl and ever expect him to let go of the production end of the business," said Mr. Cummings. "Mark my words, Marhill and Eckdahl will be at each other's throats inside of another year. So far as you are concerned, I can't ever see Eckdahl really giving up his responsibility for handling any part of an order which involves big money. You'd better forget about Eckdahl and take that good offer from the Electronics Company."

Cummings felt that his father was somewhat biased in his view. He recognized the basic truth in some of his father's statements; but he felt that the history of the company for the last two years, including the fact that Marhill and Eckdahl had gotten along well together for nine months, indicated the opposite from his father's forecast.

Eckdahl had introduced Cummings to the other people in his office. The Eckdahl Manufacturing Company offices took up about half the space on the second floor of the factory building owned by the firm. The remainder of the floor was devoted to a finished-parts stockroom and shipping room. The office space was divided into Mr. Eckdahl's private office, an office for Tony Marhill which also contained a drafting bench and the dead-storage files, and the main office space in which there were six desks. The main office was separated from the shipping area and finished-parts stockroom by a low open railing. The accountant James O'Brien, an elderly man in his late sixties, occupied a desk in Mr. Eckdahl's private office. Mrs. Katherine Reilly, the bookkeeper and private secretary to Mr. Eckdahl, occupied the desk just outside the door to the proprietor's office. Lucy Eckdahl, Lief Eckdahl's younger sister, acted as stenographer and also sat in the main office. The other regular inhabitant of the main office was elderly John Murphy, a man who had been in the hardware manufacturing business all his life. Mr. Murphy was responsible for the hardware division of the business. The other desks were reserved for the future assistant to the president, the outside salesman Mr. Levi Cohen, and one of Mr. Eckdahl's brothers, Eric, who was a combination expediter and outside-contact man.

MR. JAMES O'BRIEN, ACCOUNTANT

In appearance, James O'Brien resembled the story-book type of accountant. His clothes were always of the most conservative cut, although seldom pressed. His spare angular frame drooped naturally over the extra large ledger books which always seemed to be opened on his desk. Mr. O'Brien had been employed on a part-time basis by Eckdahl during the early days of the company. At that time, Mr. O'Brien kept the books and made out the tax returns for a number of small companies. As he grew older, he lost most of these accounts to his more aggressive competitors. The increase in the amount of work in the Eckdahl Manufacturing Company fortunately made up for the lost accounts, so that Mr. O'Brien's income did not appreciably suffer. He eventually spent most of his time at the Eckdahl Manufacturing Company. Finally, Mr. O'Brien suggested to Lief Eckdahl that he be employed on a full-time basis. Shortly thereafter, Lief Eckdahl agreed to hire Mr. O'Brien.

During one of his trips to the office, Mr. Eckdahl took Cummings out into the stockroom to discuss the details of his job offer. He prefaced his conversation with: "Sometime I would like to have a private office. I pay O'Brien $85 a week, and all he does is sit there and turn pages while listening to everything I say. I have hinted to him a dozen times and in a dozen different ways that I would like to have a private office which is actually private. I wouldn't mind so much if he really were a top accountant, but he has gotten me into trouble with the bank several times by not having statements ready or by forgetting to remind me to sign a check when a loan payment was due."

Cummings had talked with O'Brien several times and had found him very congenial. Unlike the other members of the firm, he generally refused to discuss either the company or the personalities in it. One afternoon, however, he did point out that it was not often that you found a bookkeeper like Mrs. Reilly, who had not studied double-entry accounting until after she had been hired for the bookkeeping job.

MRS. REILLY, PRIVATE SECRETARY

Mrs. Reilly was an attractive widow about forty years old. She was an old friend of Mrs. Eckdahl and had been hired shortly after her husband's death, on Mrs. Eckdahl's recommendation. She had definite ideas about her work and the way the office should be run. Twice in Cummings' presence, she had disagreed strongly with something Mr. O'Brien had asked her to do.

In addition to her bookkeeping duties, Mrs. Reilly was also Mr. Eckdahl's private secretary. Although she normally took all telephone calls for Mr. Eckdahl, made appointments for him, and typed his general business letters, during one interview Cummings noticed that Mr. Eckdahl had been typing out some sales invoices prior to his arrival. Between Mrs. Reilly and Tony Marhill there existed only an armed truce. Marhill apparently considered her an utter egotist, interested only in herself and so narrow in her business views that she was of little worth to the company. "She is getting $50 per week as Eckdahl's secretary and can't even take dictation. If I ask her to type a letter, she is always too busy with the payroll or something O'Brien should be handling. You know what some of the fellows in the shop call her, the 'Queen of Sheba.'" Cummings was easily able to ascertain, both by the tone of voice in which Mrs. Reilly addressed Marhill and the way she looked at him, that she in turn had little liking and respect for the company engineer.

Cummings wondered why a full-time accountant and at least a part-time bookkeeper were needed in the Eckdahl Manufacturing Company. Since it appeared that Mrs. Reilly made out the payroll and did at least some of the ledger posting, he wondered just what the duties of Mr. O'Brien were.

MR. JOHN MURPHY, MANAGER OF THE HARDWARE DIVISION

John Murphy, who had charge of the hardware end of the business, a spry, ruddy-faced man of seventy-two years, lived in the next town to Cummings' home. One evening as he left the office after one of his visits, Cummings offered to drop Mr. Murphy at his home. Mr. Murphy accepted the offer, and during the twenty-five-minute drive the two men exchanged the usual anecdotes and information. Mr. Murphy discovered that he and his wife had been very friendly with one of Cummings' aunts. Further conversation disclosed that Mr. Murphy, until a few years before, had lived on the next street to Cummings' and knew several of his neighbors. With these common denominators established, Mr. Murphy began to speak about the problems of the Eckdahl Manufacturing Company. He was caustic at the way Lief Eckdahl seemed to be forever alienating the hardware customers. "You know, Cummings, I've been in the hardware business for over forty years. I have customers who have been coming to me for almost that long. They don't ask prices. They know what I sell them will be right. Despite this, Lief is forever interfering with these accounts. If I happen to be out and one of my friends comes in to buy something, Lief won't take the order and place it on my desk; no, he will push it through the plant himself. Sometimes I don't hear about it for weeks after the articles have been delivered.

"That's not all either. In turn we often buy certain stock items from these same customers. Invariably these accounts are the ones which, whenever our cash position is tight, O'Brien takes his time in sending them a check."

THE TWO ECKDAHL BROTHERS

Murphy was noncommital about Marhill, but expressed his opinion of the two younger Eckdahl brothers who worked for the company. One of them, Tom Eckdahl, was employed as a machinist. According to

Murphy, he was a good workman but utterly undependable. He would take time off without warning, and sometimes his productivity suffered from a previous night's entertainment. He was unco-operative with the other workmen and often insubordinate to the foreman. Murphy felt strongly, and he also believed that most of the men agreed with him that all of what went on in the shop reached Lief Eckdahl's ears through his brother's lips.

John Murphy admitted that he was never sure whether or not Lief welcomed this tale carrying. Sometimes the owner seemed to make decisions about the shop on the basis of such information. It was also a well-known fact among the workmen that Tom Eckdahl was always paid for at least forty hours' work, regardless of how often he had been late or how many days he had been absent during the week.

Whereas Tom Eckdahl was somewhat surly and likely to make a very poor impression on strangers, his brother Eric was gregarious and well liked by most people on first contact. Eric's job in the company was somewhat vague. He was seldom at his desk in the main office. Sometimes he was assigned as foreman for an outside installation job. At other times, he acted as a salesman or outside contact man for small orders. If any of the employees wished to buy a company product, he often purchased it through Eric.

Tom Eckdahl would occasionally dissipate his week's earnings by gambling. Several times after this happened, Tom Eckdahl's wife lost no time in personally appearing at the office to ask for a "loan," which Lief always granted. Other members of the Eckdahl family also were not hesitant about asking for financial aid whenever they needed it.

Lief Eckdahl seldom could resist "a good buy." Several times he had obtained large quantities of scarce raw materials at below-market prices by merely investigating rumors he had heard in the trade that someone was going out of business or needed some immediate cash. In other cases, the material which he purchased was in the nature of finished goods and was not always pertinent to his business. Quite often the task of disposing of this merchandise fell on John Murphy's unwilling shoulders.

Eric Eckdahl often represented his brother at these transactions. When it came time to pick up the material, Eric, his brother Tom, and one of Tom's cronies often did the work with the company truck.

John Murphy, who had charge of the petty-cash account, had spoken several times to Lief Eckdahl about certain discrepancies in the two Eckdahl brothers' expense slips, as well as the price they claimed they had paid for some of the items. Lief Eckdahl had received the information the first time with "I know they have their faults, but Tommy is the best machinist in the shop and Eric puts in longer hours than any man in the plant. In addition, neither man ever complains about any job I give him." Mr. Murphy had pointed out that, even so, it might be cheaper to hire some outsider to perform their work. Lief Eckdahl retorted: "If I didn't keep them working, their wives would visit the office with their hands out for a loan. I know that, in that case, if I refused the women, their kids would go hungry. It's better to get even a limited amount of work out of them than to support their families without any return to me."

The second time Mr. Murphy had brought the inefficiency of the brothers to the proprietor's attention, Lief Eckdahl indicated he had heard enough about the subject. "So help me," John Murphy told Cummings, "I'll never mention it again."

As Murphy left the car in front of his home, he added: "Don't get me wrong, Cummings, Lief Eckdahl is a good boss for which to work. You couldn't ask for nicer people than he and his sister; but those two brothers of his, well you should be able to draw your own conclusions as to what they are."

MR. LEVI COHEN, SALESMAN

Frank Cummings had not been formally introduced to the outside salesman, Levi Cohen. Apparently the latter came into the office only once or twice a week. In appearance he was a stocky, aggressive-looking man in his fifties. Although he and Mr. Murphy had been in the hardware business for many years and knew the same people, Cummings noticed that there seemed to be a studied politeness between the two men whenever they talked to one another.

Cummings asked Tony Marhill about Mr. Cohen and his position in the firm. Marhill admitted that he had little personal contact with Cohen but stated that he was sure the latter was paid on a straight commission basis. Mr. Cohen knew a number of people in the various government agencies, and Marhill believed it was for this reason that Eckdahl had initially given him office space.

"You know, Frank," said Marhill, "Lief has one of the biggest hearts you will ever find in the business. I don't know how much Levi Cohen has sold in the last three months, but I have kept pretty close check on the orders going into production. Not one of them was sold by Cohen. Yet I've seen him draw money every week from Lief. It irks me a little bit, since I know he uses this office to transact some of his other sales work. If it was up to me, I'd fire him out of here in a minute, for all the good he is to us."

Cummings had promised to let both companies know his decision by a certain date. He spent the evening before the deadline reviewing what he had learned about both companies. He vividly recalled his last meeting with Lief Eckdahl, when the question of salary had been discussed. Cummings had indicated that an amount of $75 per week would be satisfactory. Eckdahl seemed to be visibly relieved that the younger man had not suggested a larger amount. Eckdahl admitted that he might have agreed to a slightly higher starting salary, since he felt that Cummings was the man for the job. However, the $75 figure would allow him to give Cummings a raise at the end of six months without causing some unhappiness among his present management group.

They had discussed Cummings' first job assignment. Eckdahl was a little vague as to what would be immediately expected of Cummings. He did describe a new $120,000 order for radio parts which would be received at the end of the month and for which Cummings would be made responsible. The proprietor indicated that at present Eckdahl, Marhill, and Murphy, as well as himself, were each responsible for certain job orders as they were processed through the plant. Cummings would be expected to relieve Eckdahl of those job orders for which he would normally be responsible and also generally assist Marhill in his work.

"You know, Frank," said Lief Eckdahl, "Marhill needs someone to give him a hand. Like all engineers, he is sometimes too full of theory. You know him, however, and should be able to be a real help in obtaining cost data on his jobs and to see to it that he obtains the necessary raw materials. Our finished-parts stockroom needs to be reorganized, and I intend to assign you that job also."

"Another thing, John Murphy is getting old. You probably know that he had his own business, which failed during the depression. When I hired him, he brought many of his old customers with him. John has never let any one of us really get to know those customers. I'll probably have you spend more time with him so that we won't get caught short when he passes along or is forced to retire because of old age."

Frank Cummings felt that he had a much clearer picture of what would be expected of him in the Electronics Company. He would have been more satisfied, however, if his knowledge of the individuals in the Electronics Company for whom he would be working was more complete.

A few days before the deadline, he and Mrs. Cummings visited some old friends. During the course of conversation their hostess spoke of her experience, after graduation from college, as a member of the personnel department of the Electronics Company. "You know in 1946 I spent eight months at the bench before I was allowed to work in the personnel office. If you are expecting the Electronics Company to be the sort of an organization that has a real interest in you, forget it. It's every man for himself in that firm. During my two years there, it always seemed to me that the fellow who knew the most people and played up to them was the first man to get ahead."

Frank Cummings had heard from other people that the Electronics Company's personnel policies left something to be desired. Yet both his relatives had only the highest praise for the way the company had treated them. "Sure," said his father, "I've heard all that bunk about our poor personnel policies. The fact remains that we get along well with the union and pay the highest wages in the area. Our division has never had a strike. I'll admit that in the thirties we were paying about as low wages as we could, and right after the war we had our reorganization troubles. However, that's all water under the bridge."

With his decision only a few hours away, Frank Cummings admitted to his wife that he still had no idea for which company he wished to work. He felt strongly that, if he survived the training course, he would eventually find himself with a good position in the Electronics Company. He was somewhat confused by the sense of loyalty the Electronics Company seemed to have inspired in two of the men he knew very well; at the same time it had created a feeling of frustration in Marhill.

The wide range of problems in the Eckdahl Company seemed to present a real challenge. Furthermore, it appeared that in only a few weeks' time he would be given the real responsibility of handling a large production order through the plant. Although nothing definite had been said by Lief Eckdahl, he had intimated that, if Cummings worked well with him, they would discuss methods of compensation other than a salary at the end of the first year.

Plastiglass Corporation

The Plastiglass Corporation was established in September, 1945, in Pittsburgh, Pennsylvania. Mr. Frank Snow, president and majority stockholder, had graduated from Massachusetts Institute of Technology in 1937 and had been employed as a civil employee on the Manhattan Project. He had previously owned and operated a small welding and engineering shop in Pittsburgh. While working on the bomb, Mr. Snow became interested in the development of new applications for Fiberglas, the versatile raw material first brought on the market in 1939 by the Owens-Corning Fiberglas Corporation. Fiberglas was manufactured in Newark, Ohio, and sold in sheets to fabricators; the Owens-Corning management had adopted a policy of making only the basic material rather than producing finished goods.

Mr. Snow was convinced that a resourceful engineer could build a business around a product consisting of sheets of plastic resins reinforced or laminated with Fiberglas. After being released from government service, he worked with a management consulting firm for several months, but at the same time he experimented in his basement with various laminated plastic processes. Two other young engineers, Louis Snyder and Allan Starr, joined Mr. Snow in this spare-time developmental work. By late 1945 they were ready to begin commercial production of laminated-plastic sheets, which they called "Plastiglass." They had built some crude presses for the nucleus of their production equipment. Originally, all three men had hoped to devote full time to the project, but it was decided that the future was too uncertain to warrant more than one manager. Accordingly, Mr. Snyder and Mr. Starr remained in their engineering positions, while Mr. Snow left the management consulting firm and became president and treasurer of the Plastiglass Corporation.

Mr. Snow invested $15,000 in the new venture, including the cost of the preliminary developmental work which he had paid for personally. Mr. Snyder put up $3,000; Mr. Starr, $300; and five other friends and relatives of Mr. Snow, a total of $4,800. Common stock was distributed in proportion to the sums invested. Each stockholder agreed to offer his shares to the corporation before trying to sell them to outside interests.

Mr. Snow turned over to the Plastiglass Corporation the processes and equipment which he had developed in his basement.

Production was started in a corner of a local machinery plant. Mr. Snow obtained this space, about 2,000 square feet, at a nominal rental from a friend who was an executive of the machinery company. The original production equipment was valued at about $3,500 and included a press, a steam boiler, ovens, dies, and small tools. The basic process involved the impregnation of sheets of glass cloth with liquid plastic. Impregnated sheets were subjected to moderate pressure and then baked or "cured" in ovens.

The following excerpts from an article written by Mr. Snow for a technical magazine, indicates some of the characteristics of the product:

Stronger than steel, lighter than aluminum, more impact resistant than either: these are the reasons why the newly developed, Fiberglas-reinforced plastics were used for such critical military jobs as flak suits for airmen and landing skids for gliders toward the end of the war. Designers of peacetime products are now beginning to utilize the unique properties of this new material in many important ways.

In addition to its remarkable physical properties, this material has another unique characteristic which should be well understood by product designers. It can be less expensive than sheet metal on many short-run applications. This is possible because it can normally be formed into rounded or streamlined contours with very inexpensive tools costing only a fraction of the cost of the drawing and blanketing dies needed for contour shaping of steel, aluminum, or brass.

Fiberglas as a reinforcing agent for plastics has been an intriguing idea to material engineers ever since they first appreciated the exceedingly high strength and moisture resistance of fine glass fibers. Individual Fiberglas fibers show a tensile strength of over 300,000 p.s.i. [pounds per square inch], which is to be compared with values generally under 10,000 p.s.i. for most plastic resins. The value of a Fiberglas reinforcement in plastics materials is obvious, even though the full strength of individual fibers is not attained in the final product.

During the war, under the stimulus of military demands, intensive research revealed that two major difficulties had to be overcome in order to attain the benefits of Fiberglas properties in plastics. First, it was found that a good bond was not being obtained between the plastic matrix and the surfaces of the individual glass fibers. Second, the high pressure used during the cure of these resins was crimping and crushing the fine glass fibers. Technicians of Owens-Corning Fiberglas Corporation developed treatments for the Fiberglas reinforcement to overcome bonding problems; resin manufacturers who had been working for years on resins that could be cured at low pressure developed the first "polyester" resins that can be cured under no pressure at all, if necessary.

With these problems overcome, fabricators went to work on the problems of producing critical military items from such new-found Fiberglas-plastic combinations. Early arrivals in actual military use were flak suits that were tough enough to stop flying shell fragments and at the same time light enough for combat troops to wear while in action, and shells and sheets for self-sealing gas tanks which, in addition to being light and strong, would not tear into a big flowering hole when pierced by a bullet. These developments were soon followed by a variety of air-duct applications where the Fiberglas-plastic laminates were adopted because of their extreme toughness and fatigue strength in very thin sections, their resistance to high temperature and to vibration, and because of the ease with which they can be fabricated into the contorted shapes needed in such duct work.

By the war's end, this spectacular material had attracted so much military attention that its possibilities were being explored for a wide variety of other troublesome jobs, such as submarine storage-battery cases, small seacraft hulls, seaplane pontoons, salt-water and acid pumps, electrical panel boards and instrument covers, lighting fixtures and reflectors, and for many other applications where existing materials were not satisfactory.

The urgency of military applications allowed no time to consider the potentialities of this new material for industrial uses during the war; but in the short time since the war, many of these have begun to appear. [The Plastiglass Corporation of Pittsburgh, Pennsylvania] has been applying its efforts almost exclusively toward this end since the war.

One of the outstanding advantages of this material is the simplicity of the tooling required to fabricate it into a wide range of curved and dished shapes. It is highly suited to the production of rounded contours such as streamlined covers, baffles, pans, or guards. Because the uncured material is limp and soft, it can be drawn into these shapes over the very simplest of forms without high pressures or heavy presses. In some instances, only wood blocks or plaster forms are needed to mold the required shapes. Obviously, such molds are infinitely cheaper and can be obtained much more quickly than the drawing dies needed to press and form sheet-metal parts. Furthermore, the use of such inexpensive tools relieves the designer of the tremendous risk involved in proceeding with high-cost tooling on a new and untested product. If design changes are found necessary after making pilot pieces, the cost of retooling is not prohibitive.

If a relatively low sales volume is anticipated at first on a new product or a new model, this low tooling cost may become a very important factor. In some instances, tooling charges of $5,000 to $15,000 may be reduced to only a few hundred dollars. When this saving is applied to quantities of a thousand pieces or less, the saving far outweighs the higher cost of the Fiberglas-plastic material.

Such a laminate is essentially a sheet material and should be applied where the required part can be made primarily in uniform wall thickness, although some variation can be accommodated without serious complications.

This new material offers great promise to designers of all manner of new equipment. Here is a material that offers complete freedom of design because curves do not have to be confined to a single plane and sharp corners are not a prerequisite to reasonable cost. Tools are so inexpensive that trial runs can be made on difficult parts before determining final design specifications. Short-run items can be designed for the same streamlined contours that were formerly reserved exclusively for high production items. The combination of high physical properties and low tooling costs is creating many new applications for this material.

The trade-mark "Plastiglass" was registered with the U.S. Patent Office. No basic patent could be obtained by the corporation because Plastiglass was not a new invention or discovery but only the combination of two existing materials. Mr. Snow was advised that he might be able to obtain narrow patents on the exact formula which he was using and on the press which he had built, but he learned that other small companies throughout the United States were experimenting with similar processes and concluded that patent protection would not be practical because equal results could probably be obtained by using formulas and machinery of a slightly different nature. Instead, Mr. Snow expected to rely on technical competence and a head start. Only one other firm in the Pittsburgh area had begun research in laminated plastics, and it had not yet reached the stage of presenting finished products to the market.

Mr. Snow and his associates believed that their best chance for success lay in finished products rather than as suppliers of a semifabricated material. Their first contract, to build fixtures for labeling machines, was obtained in December, 1945, through a scientific associate of Mr. Snow who was connected with a company which produced automatic labeling machinery. Whenever a customer designed a new label, the label-machinery manufacturer would receive an order for label-holding fixtures shaped to the new specifications. Labels were stacked in these fixtures and picked up automatically by the feeding mechanism. The label holders had formerly been made of stamped steel in the label machinery plant. Mr. Snow demonstrated that Plastiglass would last as long as steel and could be shaped just as accurately. Fixtures were made by heating sheets of Plastiglass and pressing them into shape in handmade dies; they were then drilled and threaded for attachment to the labeling machines.

The original order for label fixtures amounted to $2,500. Additional orders continued to come in during the next eighteen months, but the job-order nature of the product precluded long production runs and substantial volume. Mr. Snow charged a flat price in the vicinity of $8.00 for each fixture, rather than bidding separately on each new shape. At this price, the Plastiglass Corporation was able to show a small profit on a majority of the orders. By June, 1947, total sales to this customer had reached $25,000.

A Pittsburgh businessman had developed a device for opening garage doors by means of an "electric eye." He asked Mr. Snow to design a

Plastiglass sphere about the size of a bowling ball which would serve as a housing for his mechanism. The product was to be sold to relatively prosperous home owners and therefore had to be smooth and attractive in appearancc. Mr. Snow built several models but found that, when the cost of new dies and press modifications were included in the selling price, the result was out of line with competitive materials. Furthermore, air bubbles marred the surface of the spheres; Mr. Snow believed that the only way to eliminate them would be to devise a vacuum-casting system, which would boost cost prohibitively. He was therefore unable to bid on the order.

A similar problem arose in the construction of belt and flywheel housings for large electrical motors. Mr. Starr's employer, a leading manufacturer of these motors, expressed interest in reinforced plastic housings, but the Plastiglass Corporation's price could not be kept low enough to permit effective competition. A few orders were obtained from this source, but Mr. Snow did not believe that they had yielded any profits for his company.

Another Pittsburgh manufacturer thought that Plastiglass might replace rubber in the construction of racks used in plating bronze bearings. Racks loaded with bearings were dipped in tanks of chromatic acids during the plating process; rubber racks wore out quickly under continual immersion in acid. After several weeks of experimentation, however, Mr. Snow decided that Plastiglass could not meet the performance requirements for this job.

Mr. Snow gradually spent more and more time away from the plant in missionary selling. The sales task was particularly difficult because he had to talk to designers and production engineers rather than purchasing agents, and it was necessary to point out specific cost or performance advantages of Plastiglass. Many potential customers were still skeptical of plastics in general because of the multitude of conflicting claims and unproven products which were being put on the market.

Mr. Snow hired a plant superintendent at $300 per month to supervise production when he was away. Mrs. Snow served as secretary and bookkeeper. The plant labor force varied between two and five semiskilled workers. An independent accountant prepared monthly income statements and balance sheets and supervised the accounting system. Mr. Snow's salary was $800 a month, but he drew only $500 in cash and permitted the remainder to accrue. The operating statistics of the Plastiglass Corporation for the first ten months of 1946 are given in Exhibit 1.

In the fall of 1946, Mr. Snow conceived the idea of making Plasti-

Exhibit 1

PLASTIGLASS CORPORATION

OPERATING STATEMENTS, OCTOBER, 1946

	Current Month	*Previous Month*	*Year to Date*
Gross sales	$3,652.65	$2,508.95	$25,096.03
Less: Returns and allowances	15.50	103.14	380.96
Net sales	$3,637.15	$2,405.81	$24,715.07
Cost of sales:			
Production material consumed	376.27	458.88	2,545.05
Wages—direct labor	531.44	433.59	4,926.42
Job tools	402.28	203.60	2,325.36
Total cost of sales	$1,309.99	$1,096.07	$ 9,796.83
Gross profit	$2,327.16	$1,309.74	$14,918.24
Manufacturing expense:			
Wages—indirect labor	500.00	500.00	4,412.50
Maintenance of equipment	......	......	56.53
Manufacturing supplies	441.74	319.40	3,864.78
Small tools	6.06	18.10	212.87
Outside processing	......	......	143.61
Depreciation of equipment	69.65	68.49	508.51
Total manufacturing expense	$1,017.45	$ 905.99	$ 9,198.80
Administrative and general expense:			
Officers' salaries	800.00	800.00	8,000.00
Clerical salaries	100.00	100.00	1,005.00
Telephone and telegraph	81.36	135.17	895.86
Postage and express	51.86	35.39	303.81
Office supplies and printing	43.75	28.91	426.20
Memberships, dues, and subscriptions	......	......	44.00
Traveling and entertaining	225.98	8.27	934.81
Rent	200.00	200.00	2,000.00
Professional services	51.00	53.00	606.50
Miscellaneous expense	58.30	132.14	446.86
Insurance on officers	24.10	23.32	91.75
Social security tax	7.56	8.58	128.04
Unemployment insurance	20.42	40.73	388.43
Federal excise tax	......	4.53	40.89
Personal property tax	4.47	4.47	44.77
Domestic franchise tax	2.12	2.12	10.60
Workmen's compensation insurance	20.88	19.61	146.10
Total administrative and general expense	$1,691.80	$1,596.24	$15,513.62
Other income and expense:			
Cash discounts allowed	24.15	12.39	203.13
Less: Discounts earned	2.19	2.89	24.74
	$ 21.96	$ 9.50	$ 178.39
Total all expenses	$2,731.21	$2,511.73	$24,890.81
Net loss	$ 404.05	$1,201.99	$ 9,972.57

Source: Company records.

glass lamp shades which would compete with the higher-priced mica and cloth shades. The basic ingredient for the lamp shades was a different type of Fiberglas in which the fibers were spun or whirled into a closely matted wooly sheet. This "glass wool" was considerably cheaper than the smoother "glass textile" which the company had been using.

After a few weeks of research, Mr. Snow found that a low-price chemical added to the Plastiglass would cause the glass fibers to stand out in relief and produce a novel and brilliant effect. Colored dyes could also be added to make lamp shades of any desired hue.

Mr. Snow consulted a manufacturers' register and learned that the Radcliff Company, one of the nation's largest lamp-shade manufacturers, was located near Pittsburgh. He visited its office and convinced the executives that Plastiglass shades would be a valuable supplement to their line. He demonstrated the durability of Plastiglass shades by kicking one across the room several times and showing that it remained undamaged. After some negotiation, the Radcliff Company ordered $10,000 worth of Plastiglass shades at a price that would provide a very satisfactory profit margin for the Plastiglass Corporation. It was understood that additional orders would be forthcoming at somewhat lower prices. Plastiglass shades would be retailed at about three times the price of the cheapest paper shades. The contract provided that delivery would begin in sixty days.

Mr. Snow was now faced with the problem of financing this new business. He was reluctant to borrow money; he had gone to local bankers when the corporation was being organized and had found that he could not obtain credit because of the experimental nature of his product and his highly specialized and largely homemade machinery. Mr. Snow and his directors, who included his attorney and Messrs. Snyder and Starr, discussed factoring of receivables but rejected this financing method because of the relatively small number of customers. Finally they decided to proceed with the Radcliff contract by delaying payment of bills for sixty days. The original plant space was given up, and 3,000 square feet in an automobile agency was leased at $210 a month; six new women workers were hired, another $3,000 press built, and sizable quantities of resins and glass wool ordered. The Radcliff Company agreed to pay for shades immediately upon delivery.

In January, 1947, as the first sheets of lamp-shade material were rolled off the presses, the vice-president of the Radcliff Company notified Mr. Snow that the contract would have to be suspended indefinitely. After Christmas the lamp-shade market, in common with other household furnishings, had taken a tremendous drop. Inventories had accumulated on retailers' and manufacturers' shelves; and only the cheapest shades, with which Plastiglass could not compete, were moving at all. Mr. Snow and his attorney went to the Radcliff Company at once and laid their cards on the table. They pointed out that large amounts of liquid resins were piled up in the Plastiglass Corporation plant and that these substances had to be processed at once, since they could not be kept in liquid form for more than a few weeks. They also pointed out that the debts incurred by the Plastiglass Corporation in connection with the lamp-shade contract had to be paid promptly or the company would become insolvent.

The Radcliff Company executives became quite sympathetic and indicated that they were vitally interested in keeping the Plastiglass Corporation as a future supplier. They agreed to fulfill the original contract but to spread their purchases out over the next three months. Furthermore, they voluntarily canceled the exclusive franchise which Mr. Snow had given them and put Mr. Snow in touch with a large Chicago broker of household furnishings. These arrangements, combined with a continuing volume of small orders for other products, enabled the Plastiglass Corporation to remain in business and even to show a profit of $725 for the first quarter of 1947. Monthly sales during February and March rose just above the $6,000 mark, which Mr. Snow considered his break-even point. Exhibits 2 and 3 (pp. 406–7) indicate the company's financial status as of March 31, 1947.

Mr. Snow continued to investigate all possible leads for new products. Among the items he was considering were factory windows, panels for trains and bus seats, awning strips, washing-machine tubs, and electrical insulating materials. A manufacturer of aluminum awnings agreed to give the Plastiglass Corporation an experimental order if Plastiglass awnings would stand up under a six months' weather and exposure test. This stipulation forced Mr. Snow to reject the order because he could not afford to start production on items which could not possibly bring in revenue for at least six months.

By the end of April the Radcliff Company had fulfilled its original commitment with the Plastiglass Corporation and had ceased all Plastiglass lamp-shade purchases. No substantial orders had been obtained from the Chicago broker. During May the company's sales dropped back to $3,500.

Early in June, 1947, Mr. Snow signed a tentative contract to furnish molded arm-end sections made of Plastiglass to the National Car Corporation, builders of railway coaches. The Plastiglass sections replaced metal and wooden seat construction and increased the total cost of one railway seat by about 10 per cent. The primary selling point for Plastiglass seats was appearance, although greater durability was stressed. The initial order, on which production was begun in mid-June, called for $4,000 worth of sections. Mr. Snow stated that, if results were satisfactory, the Plastiglass Corporation was assured of monthly sales of $4,000

Exhibit 2

PLASTIGLASS CORPORATION

OPERATING STATEMENTS, MARCH, 1947

	Current Month	*Previous Month*	*Year to Date*
Gross sales	$6,737.04	$6,795.85	$17,667.04
Less: Returns	......	......	49.50
Net sales	$6,737.04	$6,795.85	$17,617.54
Cost of sales:			
Production material	1,915.47	1,759.23	3,757.37
Wages—direct labor	1,216.60	1,074.27	3,428.20
Job tools	80.07	37.00	195.02
Outside processing	46.25[cr]	53.17	111.57
Total cost of sales	$3,165.89	$2,923.67	$ 7,492.16
Gross profit	$3,571.15	$3,872.18	$10,125.38
Manufacturing expense:			
Wages—indirect labor	625.00	450.00	1,350.00
Maintenance of equipment	21.94	50.00	90.44
Manufacturing supplies	592.00	319.38	1,383.49
Power	14.46	35.00	87.44
Small tools	26.15	35.09	61.24
Depreciation of equipment	69.28	64.80	197.88
Total manufacturing expense	$1,348.83	$ 954.27	$ 3,170.49
Manufacturing profit	$2,222.32	$2,917.91	$ 6,954.89
Administrative and general expense:			
Officers' salaries	800.00	800.00	2,400.00
Clerical salaries	100.00	100.00	300.00
Sales salaries	50.00	......	50.00
Telephone and telegraph	115.03	91.87	299.49
Postage and express	154.77	53.48	301.94
Office supplies and printing	32.84	25.48	166.08
Memberships, dues, and subscriptions	18.00	39.50	57.50
Traveling and entertaining	111.69	361.71	573.40
Trade-mark expense	......	10.00	10.00
Advertising	3.58	......	3.58
Heat and light	10.00	10.00	30.00
Rent	247.50	212.50	670.00
Professional services	82.50	60.00	402.50
Miscellaneous expense	......	120.33	191.33
Insurance—Officers	24.10	21.77	69.97
—Auto	......	3.96[cr]	98.72
Social security tax	22.80	21.24	66.28
Unemployment insurance	83.75	63.73	207.85
Personal property tax	20.71	4.47	29.65
Domestic franchise tax	2.12	2.12	6.36
Workmen's compensation insurance	36.29	27.62	90.97
Depreciation—furniture, fixtures, and lease improvements	17.47	17.47	52.14
	$1,933.15	$2,039.33	$ 6,078.03
Operating profit	$ 289.17	$ 878.58	$ 876.86
Other expense: discount allowed	$ 63.76	$ 33.71	$ 151.73
Net profit	$ 225.41	$ 844.87	$ 725.13

[cr] Credit.

Source: Company records.

Exhibit 3

PLASTIGLASS CORPORATION
BALANCE SHEET AS OF MARCH 31, 1947

ASSETS

Current:			
Cash on Deposit—Regular Account	$ 6,870.46		
—Payroll Account	660.16		
Petty Cash	50.00	$ 7,580.62	
Accounts Receivable—Customers		4,184.62	
Inventory—Raw Material	$ 2,090.44		
—In Process	500.00		
—Small Tools	160.00		
—Laboratory Supplies	615.00		
—Production Tools	940.82		
—Office Supplies	41.44	4,347.70	$16,112.94
Fixed:			
Manufacturing and Laboratory Equipment	$ 6,674.89		
Office Furniture and Fixtures	96.51		
Leasehold Improvements	485.70	$ 7,257.10	
Less: Depreciation		418.05	6,839.05
Deferred:			
Prepaid Workmen's Compensation		$ 39.28	
Prepaid Personal Property Tax		88.93	
Prepaid Life Insurance		74.66	
Prepaid Rent		162.50	
Hospitalization		6.45	
Cash Held by Officer		1,000.00	1,371.82
Total Assets			$24,323.81

LIABILITIES

Accounts Payable:			
Purchases and Expense	$ 4,345.27		
Adjusted Compensation	5,053.80	$ 9,399.07	
Accrued Tax:			
Social Security—Employees	$ 63.56		
—Employers	66.28		
Unemployment	207.85		
Domestic Franchise	6.36	344.05	
Accrued—Payroll	$ 285.74		
—Telephone	70.00	355.74	10,098.86
Net Assets			$14,224.95
Investment:			
Capital Stock:			
Authorized	$50,000.00		
Unissued	26,900.00	$23,100.00	
Surplus, December 31, 1946	$ 9,600.18[d]		
Net Profit, Year to Date	725.13	8,875.05[d]	$14,224.95

[d] Deficit.
Source: Company records.

to $20,000 for the next twelve months to the National Car Corporation.

The use of Plastiglass sheets for electrical insulation represented per-

Exhibit 4

PLASTIGLASS CORPORATION

PLASTIGLASS ELECTRICAL INSULATION

During the war great new strides were made in the field of glass-reinforced plastics as applied to military requirements. Since the war, Plastiglass Corporation has been working on the extension of this new knowledge to industrial applications, especially in the field of insulating materials.

We are proud to announce a new electrical insulating plastic panel stock known as PLASTIGLASS. This stock contains 100% inorganic Fiberglas filler, similar to the most expensive Navy panel stock, but with non-condensing thermosetting, polyester resins in place of the usual high-pressure phenolic or melamine resins. PLASTIGLASS is produced in flat sheets from 1/16″ to 1″ thicknesses in sizes up to 30″ × 36″.

This unique material has all the normal attributes of a good, Fiberglas-filled, thermosetting plastic, including the exceptional strength, rigidity, and dimensional stability found only in glass-reinforced plastic materials. In addition, it has punching and machining properties which are superior to the glass phenolics and far superior to the glass melamines. Its heat resistance and nontracking properties are notably superior to the phenolics. Its moisture absorption is lower than that of either phenolics or melamines. Its resistance to acids and many solvents is far superior to that of phenolics. In short, PLASTIGLASS is admirably suited for heavy duty electrical service.

PLASTIGLASS will stand considerably more severe exposure to high temperatures without embrittlement than phenolic laminates. For instance, a high-quality glass phenolic laminate will become brittle after exposure to 150° C for one hundred hours. PLASTIGLASS shows no change in toughness and shows slightly improved surface gloss after the same treatment.

PLASTIGLASS will not "track" in the manner so familiar with phenolic laminates. For instance, a 1,000-volt arc drawn over the surface of a high-grade glass or canvas-base phenolic laminate will carbonize the plastic in a thin line which can be extended into a freely conducting "track" approximately 6″ long in 10 seconds. A similar test on PLASTIGLASS will produce only a very small carbonized area about 1/8″ across, and this area conducts current only very poorly and without following any definite track. If current is continued through the carbonized track in the phenolic, a flame will be started along its entire length, whereas a flame can be started in the PLASTIGLASS only by persistent burning of an arc through the air *over* the material. The small current which will be carried *through* the charred area referred to above will not set fire to the material.

PLASTIGLASS can easily be punched to intricate shapes in thicknesses not practical with the usual melamine Navy panel and with much less abuse to tools. It can be machined without the fraying so common in cut-

Exhibit 4—Continued

ting glass melamines and phenolics and with much less frequent tool sharpening. These comments are particularly true of grade MF PLASTIGLASS, which is designed to facilitate machining, but also apply to other grades.

PLASTIGLASS has excellent resistance to almost all acids, salts, and hydrocarbons. Although it should not be subjected to continued immersion in strong alkalis, ketones, and certain chlorinated solvents, it will not be affected by exposures of short duration. Its performance when immersed in chromic, nitric, sulphuric, and hydrochloric acid solutions for extended periods of time has been completely satisfactory.

PLASTIGLASS is lower in cost than other glass-filled insulating panel stock; and yet it possesses the highest values of heat resistance, dimensional stability, dielectric strength, tensile strength, impact strength, rigidity, and moisture and chemical resistance.

Sheet stock is available for immediate delivery.

haps the most promising long-term prospect for the company. Mr. Snow had carried out sufficient research to be convinced that Plastiglass would outperform the conventional materials used to insulate motors, transformers, and other electric power equipment. Mr. Snow prepared a printed letter (Exhibit 4) outlining the qualities of Plastiglass insulations.

The development of the electrical insulation market was particularly difficult because canvas-base phenolic insulation was cheaper than Plastiglass. Motor manufacturers were reluctant to make a change unless their current products were not giving satisfactory performance. Mr. Snow believed that many designers of new power machinery could be persuaded to specify Plastiglass insulation but pointed out that many months generally elapsed between the origin of a motor design and the beginning of commercial production. He estimated that a competent sales engineer, working full time on Plastiglass insulation sales, might be able to attain a volume of $1,000 per month after six months, $3,000 per month after a year, with an ultimate potential of as high as $25,000 monthly. Such a man, Mr. Snow thought, would have to be paid $500 to $600 per month. In June, 1947, Mr. Snow was trying to build a wide range of potential insulation customers through sales letters and personal contacts.

Inquiries on possible uses for Plastiglass were beginning to arrive at Mr. Snow's office from different manufacturers who had talked with him in the past or had heard of the firm's activities through the Owens-

Corning organization. The National Car Corporation contract, for instance, had stemmed from discussions between executives of National Car and Owens-Corning. Mr. Snow found that he did not have time to follow up all these letters. Every proposed product required a certain amount of research work to determine whether Plastiglass could fill the need adequately and at a profit to the corporation. This research was costly and time consuming and often did not result in contracts for production. The Plastiglass Corporation did no advertising because Mr. Snow believed that 98 per cent of the inquiries which he would receive from advertising would probably be beyond the company's present scope.

Mr. Snow was handling all the company's selling activities and all the technical research. In addition, he had to perform other management functions, such as purchasing, hiring and firing, setting wages, estimating costs, and handling insurance and leases. He thought that it would take a year for him to train a young graduate engineer as a project man to handle technical development and research.

Another problem which the company was facing in 1947 involved the use of the trade-mark "Plastiglass" by competitors. A company on the West Coast was advertising "Plastiglass" fishing rods for $30, and a New England firm which manufactured coffins had incorporated the word "Plastiglass" into its title. Mr. Snow was uncertain whether to bring suit against these companies because he did not know if their activities were actually harmful to his business or if they were sound enough financially to make legal action worth while.

Acme Textile Service Company

In 1946 the Acme Textile Service Company, located in a small town near Philadelphia, was completing its fifth successful year. The company's service consisted of doing one important function of manufacturing cloth. Although all textile mills maintained their own shops, doing the same work as the Acme Textile Service Company, they sent to small independents difficult and overflow work. Unfinished work was received from the mills, processed, and then returned to the mills.

Mr. Tasmin, sixty-one-year-old sole proprietor of the business, stated that the company was wholly a service operation dependent on surplus work from the textile mills. He hoped that the business would have a continued existence and that his son William, a twenty-five-year-old recently discharged veteran, would succeed him as owner-manager. In addition to Mr. Tasmin and his son, Mr. Twilford, the foreman, acted in a supervisory capacity over all the shop force and maintenance men. Besides his duties as foreman, Mr. Twilford advised in the establishment of piece rates.

The company was originally started in 1941 in a small shop, but the business soon expanded; and a larger building, about a half mile away, was purchased to house the storerooms, offices, and 80 per cent of the personnel. The company employed an average of 50 employees; approximately 30 were piece-rate workers and the remainder, office help, indirect workers, and overhead personnel.

HISTORY

Mr. Tasmin had grown up in the textile business and had a wide acquaintanceship both in the trade and in the town. His father had owned and operated a small textile mill of his own and had taught his sons the business while the boys were still in school. Mr. Tasmin had worked in his father's mill during the summer while attending high school and college, and upon graduation from college had attended a well-known textile school. Upon the death of his father, Mr. Tasmin, jointly with a brother, had operated his father's mill, as well as a textile service business. In 1913, however, Mr. Tasmin decided to dispose of his interests in the textile business and for the next twenty-eight years was out of the textile field entirely.

During this period Mr. Tasmin served for three years as a member of a well-known research and statistical organization and then became a paid executive secretary and manager for several national trade associations of manufacturers. Through his work with these trade associations Mr. Tasmin became very concerned about monopolistic and concentration tendencies in certain business areas and became a strong advocate of independent, competitive small business. In 1941 Mr. Tasmin became dissatisfied with trade-association work, since he believed most trade associations were becoming dominated by one or two large corporations in each line. So he decided to leave that work to establish his own textile service business, for which his earlier technical training had fitted him. He returned to his boyhood town and rented a small shop, started a school to train the highly skilled workers needed, hired several experienced workers, and was ready for operation. The business was not incorporated.

With the war boom in textiles the business expanded rapidly, and Mr. Tasmin hired more workers and rented more space to take care of the increased work. Mr. Tasmin stated that highly skilled workers were the heart of his business and that his own contribution was management skill and knowledge of fabric construction. He contracted for the business, established piece rates for the workers, handled billing, established the charges, and supervised all phases of the work. Title to the goods was retained by the mills, who paid all transportation and insurance costs. The work was contracted for on a commission basis.

SERVICE

The wartime increase in demand for textile goods was so great that many textile companies found it advantageous to concentrate on volume production and to send out much of their work for partial processing, such as was done by the Acme company.

When first received at the plant, the goods were examined and a piece-work rate set. This required considerable knowledge because the types of goods were exceedingly varied. The goods were then sent in two-wheeled carts to the pieceworkers.

The most skilled work was done by women. The wide variation in goods required great skill. Because the work was done at piece rates, skillful workers frequently made twice the wages of less skilled workers.

The two basic types of textiles handled were woolens and worsteds.

Woolens, a loosely woven cloth with sometimes as few as 15 strands to the inch, was the type often used in sport coats. Worsted, comprising about 75 per cent of the cloth processed, was more tightly woven, with 50 to 60 strands to the inch. Worsteds were used principally for busi-

Exhibit 1

WOOLEN MACHINERY ACTIVITY

(In Millions)

Year	Active Hours—Average All Shifts	
	Woolen	Worsted
1921	86.2	96.2
1922	106.0	96.3
1923	113.3	115.9
1924	103.9	88.6
1925	102.7	89.0
1926	90.4	92.5
1927	93.0	88.5
1928	92.8	79.0
1929	91.5	84.5
1930	63.3	67.2
1931	63.4	75.3
1932	53.3	58.1
1933	73.0	73.5
1934	68.4	46.2
1935	90.5	82.0
1936	89.6	75.4
1937	80.3	72.1
1938	56.3	58.3
1939	71.6	83.5
1940	74.1	77.2
1941	106.3	120.3
1942	123.1	114.4
1943	124.9	112.3
1944	116.4	104.9
1945	107.5	93.5
January to July, 1946	(116.2)	(109.4)

Source: *Standard & Poor's*, Vol. 97, No. 10 (October, 1942), p. 169 (from U.S. Department of Commerce, Bureau of Census).

ness suits and uniforms. Because woolens could be processed more rapidly, the piece rate on such jobs was approximately one-third cheaper.

Mr. Twilford supervised the workers, directing the flow of work and assigning the work to the individual workers. Mr. Tasmin believed that Mr. Twilford was excellently suited for his job, not only because of his long experience in the textile business, but also because of his equable temperament, which enabled him diplomatically to direct women workers.

At one end of a large room the finished work was checked by women skilled in technical know-how, paid on a day rate. These final checkers made minor corrections but sent back to the workers any work which was not up to standard. This job of final checking was rotated among the skilled pieceworkers. Mr. Twilford spot-checked the work.

Previously the final checkers had not been rotated, and Mr. Tasmin believed that some unsatisfactory work had been allowed to pass. By rotating the checking job, he believed that the workers were more careful of their own work because they could not count on having their work checked by a personal friend. Because the day rate of final checkers was lower than the average piece-rate wage, rotating the checkers tended to equalize the pay and promote morale.

PIECE RATES

Piece rates were established by Mr. Tasmin and Mr. Twilford, with William Tasmin sitting in on the discussions. Over the five-year period the company had accumulated records of the average time required to process the various types of goods. New orders were studied with reference to previous charges, condition of the sample lot, and current labor costs. Because of the wide variations in types and qualities of the goods, Mr. Tasmin insisted on initial sample lots before charges to customers on large orders were stated.

The actual components which made up the piece rates varied with the goods. Some worsteds had as many as fifteen factors which were considered before establishing the yardage rate, while woolens had as few as five factors.

Although there was no union, Mr. Tasmin believed that several employees held union cards taken out while they had worked for other textile companies. He was careful to meet and better all terms demanded by unions in comparable shops in his area. He quoted one of his workers, who had said that "Mr. Tasmin never gives us a chance to object." Because his skilled workers were the most important element in his business, as he saw it, Mr. Tasmin was anxious to give prompt and serious attention to all complaints about piece rates. Workers were always free to take up grievances directly with Mr. Tasmin, although most questions involving the shop were first talked over with Mr. Twilford. Mr. Tasmin was careful at all times to support Mr. Twilford and to work through him.

Exhibit 2

ACME TEXTILE SERVICE COMPANY
MONTHLY SALES

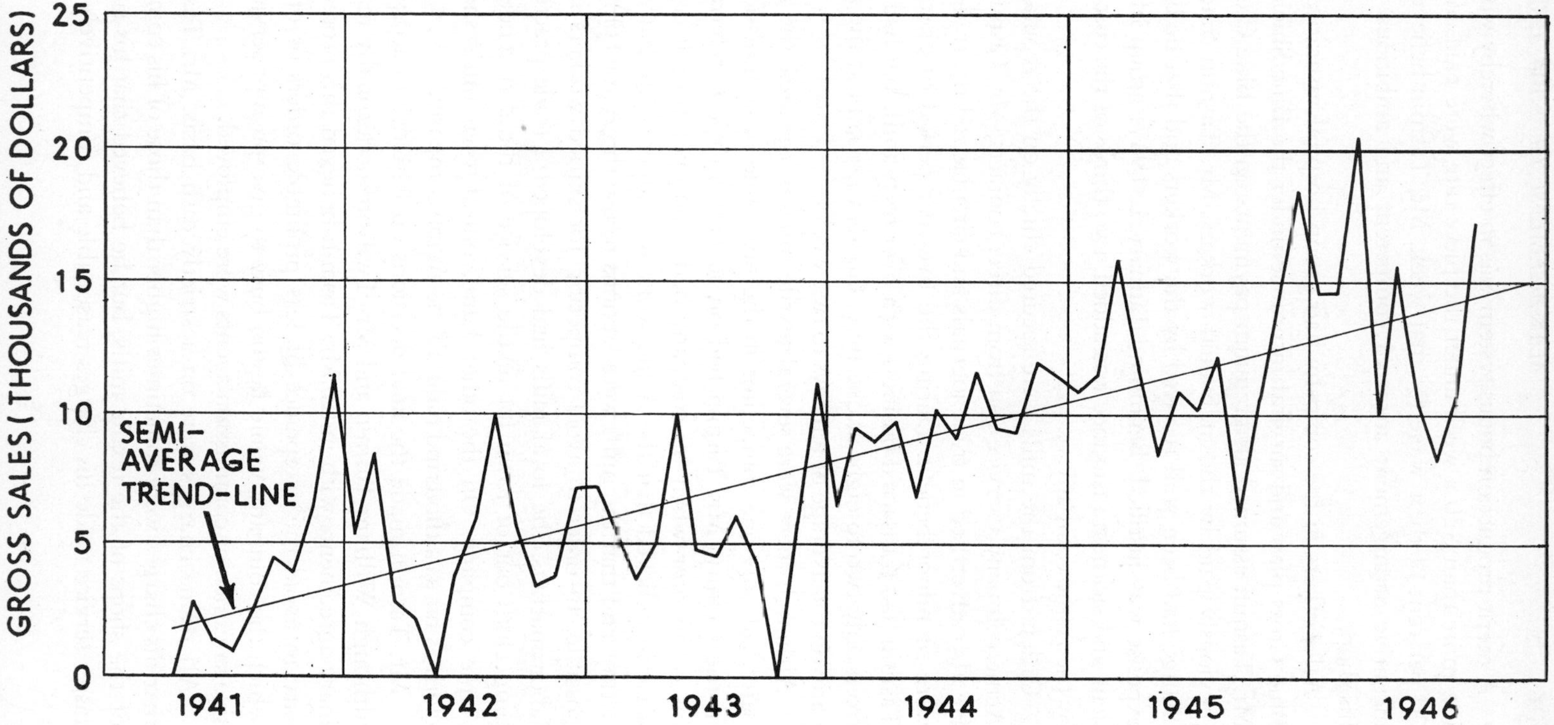

A merit production bonus system was in effect whereby workers earning more than $20 a week under the piece rate were paid an additional 20 per cent of their wage for that week. Mr. Tasmin believed that this incentive arrangement attracted competent and ambitious workers to his shop.

All workers in the company had group hospital insurance under the Blue Cross plan and surgical insurance under the Blue Shield. In 1946 Mr. Tasmin assumed all premium payments on the Blue Cross policies, previously paid by the individual workers. Mr. Tasmin stated that the change had been well received by the workers and that he believed the expense was justified. Beginning January 1, 1947, group life and accident and sickness insurance was added, two thirds of the cost being paid by the Acme company.

Orders from the mills were secured chiefly on the reputation of the Acme company's service and from direct contacts, Mr. Tasmin believed. He also advertised in trade journals and circularized the trade, but these were of minor benefit. During the five-year period of operations, Mr. Tasmin had transacted business with over forty mills but had had orders from only two to eight at one time. Goods were kept at the Acme company on the average of ten days to two weeks.

Although there were several textile mills in the area, the Acme company had only one competitor in the same line of commission business in the vicinity. Mr. Tasmin had on several occasions referred mills to his competitor when his company had been operating at capacity. Mr. Tasmin believed that the Acme work was superior to that of his competitor and that the mills were anxious to use the Acme company when possible. In order to avoid competing for skilled workers in the local labor markets, the local mills had developed a trade practice of shipping cloth out of town for textile service of the sort rendered by the Acme company. On the other hand, out-of-town mills shipped their cloth as far as a thousand miles to the Acme company.

Mr. Tasmin made the final decisions on whether to accept an order, although William Tasmin and Mr. Twilford occasionally made preliminary agreements with mills. Mr. Tasmin believed this procedure necessary to avoid the acceptance of less profitable orders or of orders on which the company would be too busy to give prompt service. No outside salesmen or commission agents were employed.

All Acme charges were on a strictly cash basis. Mr. Tasmin stated that his charges were sometimes higher than those of his competitor and of the shops of the textile mills, but he believed that his superior and faster service made his charges reasonable and competitively sound. Because of his wage system and the personal attention he gave to labor relations, he was able to get better workers.

All work was charged by means of a formula covering direct labor costs, a percentage of wages paid to indirect labor as overhead, a reserve for "intermittency," and a flat profit of 10 per cent. Occasionally, when billings had appeared too high, the mills had requested additional information about the basis of Acme charges. Mr. Tasmin had then indicated that there was a reserve for "intermittency" and had vigorously defended the economic soundness of this reserve for slack periods. This item was accepted as a real cost factor by mills which knew their own costs and which were not "trading" or even "chiseling." Relations with customer mills were on a continuing basis of mutual satisfaction, with the better mills repeating orders again and again. Mr. Tasmin reasoned that his business was a service to the mills which could be, and was, dropped by them whenever the shops of the mills could handle all their own work. Therefore he believed that the mills should pay as a regular charge a premium which would carry him over the low periods of work. Mr. Tasmin hoped to create a reserve large enough to maintain a skeleton force for a year during recessions or depressions and yet meet all expenses.

Mr. Tasmin stated that one of his guiding principles was to avoid pressing his advantages or "getting customers over a barrel." In one instance he had sent a rebate of several hundred dollars to a customer when he learned indirectly that his charges had been substantially higher than those of his competitors. Mr. Tasmin explained the success of his business by continuous adherence to high-quality work, prompt service, his close attention to management problems, and the incentive wage bonuses paid to the workers. "Large companies waste too much time in conferences; it takes too many people and too long to make decisions in large companies." "In that respect, many large companies are as 'bureaucratic' as are political systems." These were cardinal beliefs of Mr. Tasmin. Mr. Tasmin believed that the Acme company had not yet had the real test of its existence, which would come when the postwar backlog of mill orders had been filled. Only the future would tell whether the reserve was adequate for a possible slump in the textile industry.

Mr. Tasmin hoped to retire within five years and gradually sell his control of the business to his son through a sharing of profits. William Tasmin had graduated from high school in 1936 and had held various temporary jobs, including office work in a bakery, until he joined the Army Air Forces in 1942. For two years before entering the service he had gone to accounting school at night, and he had resumed this schooling after four and a half years in the Army. While in the service, he had been a bomber pilot in the Southwest Pacific and had thoroughly enjoyed flying. Since his discharge in the spring of 1946, he had done a variety of jobs in the shop and office of the Acme company and was becoming familiar with all phases of its operations. He was quiet and unassuming and well liked by the workers. Mr. Tasmin believed that William could succeed him immediately, and he stated that William's main problems would be in getting ample experience in human relations and not in the technical phases of the business.

Killingsworth Corporation

The Killingsworth Corporation, located in a large Midwestern city, was organized in February, 1952, by Mr. J. L. Killingsworth, a civil and mechanical engineer, for the purpose of manufacturing new and experimental equipment for the Armed Forces. The corporation operated a woodworking and metalworking machine shop and took on small orders from larger manufacturers and from certain laboratories which were engaged in government research projects. The function of the Killingswoth Corporation was to develop a workable product from the designs of research engineers. These designs might consist of a detailed blueprint or a rough sketch with a few over-all dimensions. The company was managed by Mr. J. L. Killingsworth, who also owned a majority of the common stock of the corporation.

Mr. Killingsworth had considerable practical experience in the field of engineering. He was employed by a power company for a total of twelve years. He spent seven of these years as a topographical surveyor and five years as a designer and draftsman in structural engineering for this company. In addition, he was engaged for five years in mechanical and electrical design for a refrigeration company. During World War II he worked for the power company, supervising the engineering aspects of a civil engineering project.

In 1950 Mr. Killingsworth heard of a small furniture company, the Carleton Company, which had undertaken government contract work and was in urgent need of a man with engineering experience. The company had a small woodworking and metalworking machine shop and up until this time had produced furniture for civilian use. Its Korean war contract work consisted mainly of parts for technical military equipment of a large manufacturer. The owner of this shop offered Mr. Killingsworth a position as production engineer with supervision over the engineering aspects of its contract work. This work involved certain types of engineering which were entirely new to the Carleton Company. The owner of the shop offered Mr. Killingsworth a salary of $5,000 annually and a 25 per cent share in the ownership of the new company in return for the technical assistance which the company so urgently needed. Mr. Killingsworth accepted the offer because he wanted to work in a small company and was attracted by the type of engineering problems which he was likely to encounter. The company was not incorporated, and no common stock was issued. Mr. Killingsworth's 25 per cent share was based solely on a verbal agreement between himself and the owner. Mr. Killingsworth's duties were to contact the laboratory or manufacturer for whom the work was being done, to work out practical engineering problems with these parties, and to secure exact specifications on the product to be made. He would then follow up on the production of the product within the company's own shop, to solve further engineering difficulties and to see that specifications were accurately carried out. Mr. Killingsworth found that the proper performance of these duties required an extremely long working day. On some days he would start work with the company at eight o'clock in the morning, would visit a manufacturer in the afternoon to work over the engineering problems of a new product, and would sometimes work through the second shift with the company engineers until past midnight. The following morning he would be back at the shop attempting to put the new product into production. Every order was a rush order and usually had to be expedited personally by Mr. Killingsworth. No one else in the company had sufficient technical training to do this work.

After working about one year with the Carleton Company, Mr. Killingsworth began to feel dissatisfied with a number of its practices. He felt that production within the shop was inefficient and costly. In the fall of 1951 the company was incorporated; and, contrary to the previous verbal agreement, Mr. Killingsworth was given no share in the ownership. Mr. Killingsworth felt that, in spite of his unsatisfactory position in the company, he should continue to work for the company in the interest of the war effort, although he started to look actively for a better opportunity elsewhere.

About this time the company received an order to produce 400 units of an important piece of military equipment. Objecting to the size of the investment required in material and equipment, the Carleton Company refused the order. At this point Mr. Killingsworth saw an opportunity to go into business for himself. He believed he was in a position to set up his own shop and to carry out not only this order but other similar orders.

Two men in the company, Mr. Curwen and Mr. Thorne, agreed to leave the company to assist Mr. Killingsworth in his new enterprise. These men were the two most skilled craftsmen in the shop. Mr. Curwen had considerable experience as a machinist. Mr. Thorne was an expert welder.

The manufacturer whose order had been refused by the Carleton Company and other manufacturers of similar type were anxious to help Mr. Killingsworth in the organization of a new company for the purpose of completing this and other orders. Accordingly, an order to produce $2,000 worth of equipment was made out personally in the name of Mr. Killingsworth, and a promise was made verbally to place other orders with a total value of about $60,000 as soon as the new shop was set up. Materials were to be supplied by this same company, and Mr. Killingsworth was given two months to complete the first $2,000 order. Relations between this manufacturer and Mr. Killingsworth had always been cordial; and this fact, combined with the help promised above, were the factors which caused Mr. Killingsworth to decide to go into business for himself.

Early in 1952 the three men began to locate the necessary plant and equipment to undertake the first contract. An option was given to them on an unused warehouse for which they would pay a monthly rent of $40 until such time as they could purchase it outright. They were also given, by a friend, the use of about $200 worth of machine-shop equipment free of charge until they were in a position to purchase their own.

Mr. Killingsworth believed that with the help of his wife, Mr. Curwen, and Mr. Thorne he was in a position to organize and finance the company. It was estimated that the following cash expenditures would be required to operate the company for the first three months: $2,000 was allowed for payroll in case additional men were needed, although the three men planned to do the majority of the work themselves. Rent for the first three months would be $120. Two hundred seventy-five dollars was estimated to cover organizing expenses. Additional machinery and equipment was estimated at $1,200, and office furniture and equipment at $250. The metal warehouse, which was about 40 by 60 feet, contained a small office and washroom in one corner and a sizable attic. There were only three electrical drops for overhead lights. Four hundred dollars was the estimated cost of alterations to the building, including $200 in rewiring for power and light.

Mr. Killingsworth believed that, before the new company was organized, the advice of a lawyer should be obtained. The ensuing legal consultation resulted in the decision of Mr. Killingsworth to incorporate the new company. A corporation was formed with Mr. Killingsworth as president, Mr. Curwen as vice-president, Mr. Thorne as treasurer, and Mr. Killingsworth's wife as clerk. Six thousand dollars in cash was invested in the corporation by the three men, $4,000 by Mr. Killingsworth; two cars valued at $800 and additional machinery valued at

$200 were also invested personally by Mr. Killingsworth. The total assets of the corporation, including goodwill on the initial contracts, valued at $3,000, were $10,000. Common stock with a par value of $10,000 was issued, of which $6,000 was issued to Mr. Killingsworth.

After conversing with the lawyer, Mr. Killingsworth was in favor of a corporate organization for the company, mainly on account of the personal risk factor of other forms. The stockholders expected that their income would be mainly in the form of the salaries which they would receive as active officers of the company and would not be subject to the corporate taxes on income from dividend payments. Mr. Killingsworth believed further that the company would derive prestige value from being incorporated which would be helpful in its relations with other manufacturers.

In February, 1952, the Killingsworth Corporation began production on the first order. Mr. Killingsworth, Mr. Curwen, and Mr. Thorne had already done some work on the order before the company was incorporated, and they were the only men in the shop at the outset. Two additional men with experience as machinists were hired in the first month. Mr. Curwen and Mr. Thorne and these two men were in the shop continuously and worked out production problems jointly. They usually referred engineering problems, such as changes in design or errors on blueprints, to Mr. Killingsworth. He also assisted them in laying out work on each new part. During the first four months, while Mrs. Killingsworth was recovering from an operation, a girl who had some bookkeeping experience was hired to keep the company's books, answer the telephone, and handle the company's correspondence.

Mr. Killingsworth found it necessary to spend more and more time outside the shop, although there were many engineering problems in the shop which required his help. He was continuously shopping around for additional tools and equipment. When the company received a new order, Mr. Killingsworth usually made at least one trip to the manufacturer to go over blueprints. The first unit of each order was delivered personally by him, so that both parties were satisfied with the product before the order went into production.

Although he had no training in accounting, Mr. Killingsworth believed that the Carleton Company had done many jobs at a loss because the accounting system was inadequate and costs were not known. He decided that some sort of formal accounting system should be established at the outset. At this time, Mr. Killingsworth believed that the corporation could not afford to pay for the services of a certified public accountant. The assistance of a friend with training and experience in book-

Exhibit 1

KILLINGSWORTH CORPORATION

COST CONTROL SHEET

No.________

CUSTOMER____________________________________**Their Order No.**____________

Job____**Date**____________________

Quantity______________**Their Drawing No.**__________**Our Drawing No.**__________

Finish

MATERIALS	ESTIMATED	ACTUAL	LABOR	ESTIMATED	ACTUAL
Purchased Parts or Services			ENGINEERING		
			SUB TOTAL		
			Factory Burden + %		
TOTAL MATERIAL			TOTAL		
TOTAL LABOR			DESIGN		
SUB TOTAL			DRAFTING		
Gen. and Adm. Overhead + %			PATTERNS		
TOTAL COST OR			TOOLS		
COST EACH			JIGS		
PROFIT + %					
TOTAL					
			PLATING		
QUOTED			ANODIZING		
			PAINTING		

NOTE: Within a few weeks the item "Engineering" was removed from the direct labor category and included in "Design," "Drafting," and "Patterns."

keeping was obtained; and an accounting system was set up which, except for some changes made eight months later, remained the basic system employed by the Killingsworth Corporation during the first year of its operation.

The original accounting system soon proved to be inadequate for the purposes of the company. The first basic failure of the system was found to be its inability to keep separate the costs of each contract. For example, a General Supplies account was set up. Whenever supplies were purchased, they were charged to this account, although at the time of purchase they were invariably "earmarked" for one particular order. Since the company was paid for its work on a cost basis, it was imperative to keep the costs of each work order separate. On experimental orders the company was given a maximum cost which it could not exceed and which it attempted to better, if possible. On production orders a cost plus 10 per cent or cost plus 15 per cent basis was used. From past experience with the Carleton Company, Mr. Killingsworth had developed a cost estimate sheet which he had used to quote prices to the manufacturer. A copy of the cost estimate sheet is shown in Exhibit 1 (p. 423). Since the company's books could not furnish the desired figures soon enough for control purposes, Mr. Killingsworth came to rely more and more upon this sheet and used it as the basis for an informal cost accounting system of his own. Each sheet was given a contract number, and all purchase orders in connection with the particular contract were kept with it in a single folder. Time cards showing direct labor for the job also assigned contract numbers.

Mr. Killingsworth stated that his estimates on contract prices were usually correct within 5 per cent. Factory burden and general and administrative expense were calculated as a percentage of direct labor. Initially, the Killingsworth Corporation estimated factory burden at 70 per cent and general and administrative expense at 30 per cent. On the basis of four months of operation, those figures were changed to 104 per cent and 57 per cent, respectively. Minor revisions were subsequently made about every three months to allow for overtime rates, hiring of new men at different wage rates, and any substantial changes in overhead expenses.

Another of Mr. Killingsworth's accounting problems during the first few months of operation was to determine the cash position of the company. During the first contract, bills were paid as the cash balance would permit according to the length of time that Mr. Killingsworth felt he could delay on each particular payment. The cash balance averaged between $3,000 and $5,000. Since he could not determine accurately the company's cash position from its books of accounts, he made his own estimates from time to time by referring directly to accounts receivable, bills payable, payrolls due, and cash on hand and in the bank.

With the departure of Mr. Killingsworth from the Carleton Company, that company discontinued its subcontract work. Manufacturers and laboratories which previously had placed contracts with this company, now placed them with the Killingsworth Corporation. Within three months the Killingsworth Corporation received a total of twelve orders from several manufacturers, with estimated receipts of $50,000. To carry out this work, five additional men were employed and considerable material had to be purchased. The first payment of $500 for completed work was received three months after the incorporation of the company.

Late in the summer of 1952 the corporation was faced with the problem of having to purchase $3,000 worth of materials in a single order for one contract. Mr. Killingsworth decided to purchase the materials in two equal installments. In order to make this initial $1,500 purchase and to meet other current obligations, the Killingsworth Corporation requested a loan from the commercial bank where its checking account was deposited. A balance sheet was prepared from the company's books. Believing the current asset and current liability figures to be incorrect, Mr. Killingsworth checked back over the company's books and found that the hired girl had made a number of clerical errors in the bookkeeping. These errors were corrected; and the balance sheet, shown in Exhibit 2 (p. 426), was submitted to the bank. A ninety-day loan of $3,000 was obtained at 5 per cent interest. The corporation's contract was assigned as security. Two thousand dollars was paid off in ninety days, and an extension of thirty days was granted on the remaining $1,000, which was paid at maturity. When the contract was one-half completed, the original government order was reduced, so that it never became necessary to purchase the entire $3,000 worth of materials. The second $1,500 installment was therefore not purchased.

By the fall of 1952 there were twelve men on the payroll of the Killingsworth Corporation. Mr. Killingsworth solicited the services of only two men; the rest applied for employment at the advice of others already employed at the shop. Mr. Killingsworth was particularly careful in his hiring policies. He believed that the shop required not only skilled but also creative craftsmen. Every man was given a one-month trial period, and in most instances received 90 cents an hour as an initial wage. A higher wage was paid in the case of men with previous training or experience for the job. The older men in the company were receiving about $1.75 an hour. Only two men were released after the trial period. One, a veteran, had experience as a machine-shop supervisor and claimed knowledge of drafting. His drafting skill turned out below the expectation of Mr. Killingsworth, who felt the corporation was not in a position to pay the higher wage which the man demanded. The second

Exhibit 2

KILLINGSWORTH CORPORATION

BALANCE SHEET, AUGUST 13, 1952

ASSETS		
Cash	$ 996.85	
Accounts Receivable	3,272.00	
Materials and Supplies	2,124.24	
Work in Process	2,200.00	
Total Current Assets		$ 8,593.09
Prepaid Insurance	$ 303.52	
Unamortized Organization Expense	325.03	
Goodwill	3,000.00	
Fixed Assets:		
Machinery and Equipment	1,196.92	
Office Furniture and Fixtures	373.64	
Motor Vehicles	800.00	
Alterations to Property	660.52	
Small Tools	510.92	
Total Assets		15,763.64

LIABILITIES		
Accounts Payable	$ 2,773.47	
Payroll and Withholding Tax	219.18	
Accrued Payroll	285.91	
Total Current Liabilities		$ 3,278.56
Common Stock, No-Par Value, Ascribed Value, $20 per Share; 500 Shares Issued and Outstanding	$10,000.00	
Surplus	2,485.08	
Total Liabilities		15,763.64

Note: Goodwill from initial contracts, valued at $3,000, was listed as an asset on the company balance sheet at its incorporation. It was written off the books at the end of the fiscal year. The small-tools account, consisting mainly of expendable items, was later listed as an operating expense.

man was also one who claimed drafting experience and was given design and drafting problems to work out by himself. Mr. Killingsworth found that it was necessary for him to supervise this work personally; and he felt that, as in the first case, the corporation could not afford to pay for such unproductive work. By the end of the first fiscal year, most of the men had earnings considerably above their hourly base rates, not only from overtime rates but also from bonuses. Mr. Killingsworth intended, when the corporation was formed, to include employee profit sharing as a basic policy of the company. In December, 1945, he estimated from the company books that the company would show a net profit for its first fiscal year. A small Christmas bonus was accordingly issued to all employees. At the end of the fiscal year an additional bonus was issued of 5 per cent of the employees' total wages from the company to date. In May, 1953, Mr. Killingsworth stated that all members of the organization, including five recently discharged veterans, were "solidly behind him."

In about one half of the contracts undertaken, the Killingsworth Corporation found it necessary to have part of the work done outside. Several orders ran into hundreds of units. Some of the parts for these units could be produced more easily by shops with production machinery. One of the largest orders, with a unit cost of $240, required about $64 worth of the work to be done outside. In every case a price was obtained from the factory doing the work and was incorporated in the original cost estimate for the contract. Mr. Killingsworth personally undertook all contacts with these companies and found it necessary in many cases to check on their work to see that specifications were being properly followed.

Procurement of materials was one of the most pressing problems of the Killingsworth Corporation and one of the most time-consuming duties of Mr. Killingsworth. Before submitting cost estimates to the manufacturers and laboratories for whom the company was working, Mr. Killingsworth went over all blueprints for the job with the engineers and research men of these organizations to advise them on the availability of materials, to recommend substitutions when necessary, and to appraise the workability of their designs. The Killingsworth shop worked mainly with wood, brass, and light metals, including aluminum and magnesium. Mr. Killingsworth was familiar with the local sources of these materials, but each contract presented a separate problem dependent upon the quantities and stock sizes required in the order. Procurement, moreover, was a continuous problem. Changes in the original government order were frequent, as were changes in design, particularly in the early stages of production. Unexpected shortages of materials sometimes developed halfway through a contract.

Mr. Killingsworth spent much of his time with a large research laboratory which was engaged in the development of technical equipment. The Killingsworth Corporation was not itself engaged in laboratory research but was concerned with the workability of the designs put out by these laboratories. Mr. Killingsworth found that physicists and engineers of this laboratory were entirely co-operative, and his relations with them were at all times cordial. In the fall of 1952 the Killingsworth Corporation received a letter of commendation from this laboratory for assisting them in the successful completion of several government projects.

In early 1953, Mr. Killingsworth was anxious to go into production of civilian goods. He had always kept a backlog of new ideas for civilian products, which the men in the shop worked upon whenever opportunity permitted. Continuous contract orders prevented substantial accomplishment in this field. A novel device to be installed in private homes had been designed and produced experimentally. About a dozen pieces of plywood furniture had also been made, which a furniture store retailer was anxious to distribute as soon as a sufficient quantity had been produced. Plans had also been drawn up and blueprints completed on a revolutionary method of erecting private homes. Mr. Killingsworth planned to erect a sample house at an initial cost of about $8,000 as soon as the corporation had sufficient working capital. He believed that eventually these houses, suitable for a family of four, could be sold for $8,000.

In February, 1953, the Killingsworth Corporation received an order to construct a new type of antenna for amateur radio stations. An order for only one was received initially, but the customer expected that a great many would be ordered as soon as the new product was advertised as planned in a radio magazine. The customer pointed out that there were thousands of amateur radio operators in the United States and that there was a large unsatisfied demand for these antennae.

In early 1953, Mr. Killingsworth believed that the company was in urgent need of a man to assist Mrs. Killingsworth in the management of the office. He was anxious to relieve Mrs. Killingsworth of her bookkeeping duties and wanted someone who had some technical knowledge of the work in the shop to answer the telephone calls of customers. Mr. Hillman, a man with bookkeeping experience, agreed to a trial period as office manager for the company. His first job was to bring inventory records up to date and prepare income-tax returns for the fiscal year. At first he had frequently to refer to Mr. Killingsworth for the necessary figures. Mrs. Killingsworth continued to keep the day-to-day records of the company.

February was a busy month for Mr. Killingsworth. He spent about half his time on calls outside the shop. He also spent considerable time straightening out the records with Mr. Hillman. Telephone calls to the

Exhibit 3

KILLINGSWORTH CORPORATION

OPERATING STATEMENT FOR THE FISCAL YEAR ENDING FEBRUARY 25, 1953

Gross sales	$43,517.23		
Less: Returns and allowances	42.16		
Net sales		$43,475.07	
Deduct: Cost of goods sold:			
Gross purchases	$19,739.00		
Less: Returns and allowances	362.63		
Net purchases	$19,376.37		
Add: Freight and express inward	123.54		
Total cost of goods purchased	$19,499.91		
Deduct: Inventory	9,599.83		
Cost of goods sold		9,900.08	
Gross profit on sales		$33,574.99	
Deduct: Operating expenses:			
Advertising	$ 346.67		
Depreciation	405.93		
Direct labor	11,600.22		
Heat, light, and power	372.57		
Insurance	302.71		
Maintenance and repairs	1,088.54		
Miscellaneous	76.23		
Office salaries	1,699.74		
Professional services	750.00		
Printing and stationery	465.54		
Rent	240.00		
Supervision	12,862.38		
Social security taxes	715.58		
Supplies used	1,946.21		
Telephone	542.22		
Travel	641.05		
Total operating expenses		34,055.59	
Net loss from operations		$ 480.60	
Deduct: Sundry income		210.80	
		$ 269.80	
Add: Interest paid		49.14	
Net loss			$318.94

office were frequent. The men in the shop, with the assistance of Mr. Curwen and Mr. Thorne, worked out production problems on their own initiative as far as possible; but changes in design or errors in blueprints were frequently referred to Mr. Killingsworth. Often he would refer their joint solutions of these problems to the company concerned for its approval.

The filing of tax returns, both state and federal, was a particularly time-consuming operation for Mr. Killingsworth. He stated that he had to devote all his time to this one subject for a period of two weeks. As a result, there were unavoidable holdups on production in the shop. Ac-

Exhibit 4

KILLINGSWORTH CORPORATION

BALANCE SHEET, FEBRUARY 25, 1953

ASSETS			
Current Assets:			
Cash	$2,554.22		
Petty Cash	100.00	$2,654.22	
Accounts Receivable		5,902.01	
Total Current Assets			$ 8,556.23
Fixed Assets:			
Machinery and Equipment	$1,726.39		
Reserve for Depreciation	86.32	$1,640.07	
Motor Vehicles	$ 800.00		
Reserve for Depreciation	133.33	666.67	
Office Furniture and Fixtures	$ 134.13		
Reserve for Depreciation	3.35	130.78	
Office Equipment	$ 296.23		
Reserve for Depreciation	37.03	259.20	
Total Fixed Assets			2,696.72
Alterations to Leased Property	$1,459.00		
Less: Reserve for Depreciation	145.90		1,313.10
Prepaid Insurance			163.01
Prepaid Rent			60.00
Inventory:			
Raw Materials	$ 753.50		
Work in Process	8,846.33		
Total Inventory			9,599.83
Deficit			3,643.97
Total Assets and Deficit			$26,032.86
LIABILITIES			
Current Liabilities:			
Accounts Payable	$6,693.80		
Employees' Deductions Accrued	55.70		
Salaries Accrued	8,588.75		
Income Taxes Withheld	370.00		
Federal O.A.B. Accrued	129.84		
State Unemployment Taxes Accrued	194.77		
Total Current Liabilities			$16,032.86
Capital Stock			10,000.00
Total Liabilities and Capital			$26,032.86

counting procedures for tax-return purposes differed from the procedures ordinarily followed in maintaining the company's accounting records. Much time was spent in consultation with a lawyer and an accountant who presented alternative methods of handling the accounts.

During March the books were turned over to an accountant, who prepared an operating statement and a balance sheet for the close of the fiscal year (shown in Exhibits 3 and 4) and established a new accounting system for the company. Mr. Killingsworth believed that the new system could be operated with little outside help. He expected that the company would spend about $150 for accounting services during its second year, whereas during the first year $750 was spent for the services of outside bookkeepers and accountants.

The Killingsworth Corporation continued to produce equipment for the Armed Forces through April, 1953. At this time, work on all contracts was almost completed. No further orders were received. The long-range prospects of this business, moreover, were uncertain. Orders were received always at short notice and were subject to frequent changes. Over one half of the company's work was with a single large manufacturer of technical equipment. Mr. Killingsworth had never received any estimates from any of these manufacturers or laboratories on the long-range prospects of their projects.

During the month of May the company was engaged primarily in civilian production. The company's own experimental products were further developed, and a few outside orders were also undertaken. Bids were submitted on unusual types of equipments which larger companies would not want to take on. One of the bids was on a large order of radio parts. If the company received the order, it would have to purchase a few hundred dollars' worth of additional equipment and could devote all its time to the order for several months. The Killingsworth Corporation also sent circulars to various organizations emphasizing the versatility of its shop and stating that it specialized in "the unusual and difficult."

The company by this time had a versatile metalworking and woodworking machine shop. Machines, which had been loaned free of charge to the company, were partially replaced by new company-purchased machines. About $1,500 worth of additional machinery was on order but undelivered. Equipment already in the shop included the following: two band saws, one 12-inch and one 14-inch; two circular saws; one swing saw; one tilting arbor saw; one steel layout table; two lathes; three drill presses; one milling machine; one grinder; one arc welding and one torch welding set; one arbor press; an air compressor with several hand tools, including a rivet gun; and one shaper for woodwork.

Fountain Metals, Inc.

During the summer of 1951, Mr. William Haden was considering the purchase of an interest in a small business, Fountain Metals, Inc. Fountain Metals employed nine workmen and a full-time bookkeeper, and manufactured metal counter and beer-dispensing equipment for restaurants, bars, and grills, as well as a line of walk-in type refrigerators and coolers. The greatest part of the company's sales in 1951, however, resulted from subcontracts for precision sheet-metal work from three or four large electronics manufacturers. This field was new to the company and came about when the start of the Korean conflict in June of 1950 made it difficult to produce a satisfactory volume of the regular products.

Haden had graduated from Massachusetts Institute of Technology in 1938, and in 1940 obtained his master's degree in chemical engineering. During World War II he served with the Ordnance Department, and he returned again to MIT at the end of the war for additional graduate work. He then accepted a position with a major petroleum company and remained with that company until going to business school in 1949.

While at the petroleum company, he had established the Haden Products Company, which sold scientific instruments by mail and special high-priced chemicals through personal selling. It was strictly, a one-man, part-time business. One of his fellow employees described Haden at this time as being "one of the very few men who could take tax deductions for his hobby."

During his first year at the graduate business school, he interested an experienced business executive in the idea of further devloping an analytical instrument he had invented. The following summer Haden spent in market research on this instrument. This involved about 10,000 miles of travel. In September, 1950, he and his friend each invested $1,000 to provide funds for the design and manufacture of a working model. All vacation periods and whatever time he could spare from his studies were spent by Haden in design conferences and negotiations with a potential distributor. Before graduation the basic design was complete, a patent applied for, and a distribution agreement awaited the production of a satisfactory model.

Unfortunately, the production model was not complete when Haden graduated in the spring of 1951. The actual fabrication of the model had been contracted to Fountain Metals, Inc. In the process of expediting the work on his model, Haden gradually became familiar with the many problems facing Fountain Metals. In turn, the two owners leaned heavily on Haden for business advice. By the end of the summer, this relationship had progressed to the point where Haden was considering buying into the business and participating in its affairs on a part ownership basis.

Haden had a definite long-term aim for his career in business. His general background and interests covered a wide range of subjects. Since he intended to work in the area of small business, he believed that the only way to fully utilize both his experience and education was to be interested in several small organizations. He was still vitally interested in his own company, having already invested approximately $5,000 in the work to date; but he felt that it was likely to develop slowly and consequently would require his participation only on a part-time basis.

HOW FOUNTAIN METALS WAS STARTED

The two owners of the Fountain Metals, Mr. Sanford Bellows and Mr. John Middlebury, had been employed during World War II by a large electronics company. Mr. Bellows had been model-shop superintendent; Mr. Middlebury had worked for Mr. Bellows as foreman of the sheet-metal shop. In the drastic reorganization which followed the war, both men had been dismissed from the company.

Middlebury and Bellows both wanted to go into business for themselves. Middlebury expected to use his knowledge of sheet-metal work in that type of manufacturing enterprise; and Bellows preferred some type of distributorship, such as an automobile agency. After two futile attempts to secure such an agency, Bellows learned, through a newspaper ad, of a sheet-metal business which was for sale. He brought the ad to Middlebury's attention, and after some discussion the two men decided to pool resources to procure the company.

Bellows was about forty-five years old. His career had been varied and included experience as an automobile mechanic and superintendent of a machine shop, a radio-model shop, and an electronics-model shop. He was stockily built, with a shock of grey hair which set off his ruddy complexion and ready smile.

Middlebury was about ten years younger than his partner. His experience was almost entirely confined to the metalworking trades, much of it in a foreman's position. Although his training was primarily technical, he was familiar with ordinary accounting procedures and had demonstrated several times in the past a shrewd dollar evaluation of a particular situation.

Fountain Metals, Inc., was located in a medium-sized city adjacent to a large eastern center of population. It owned a single-story brick building built in 1897, located in a manufacturing area. The building contained about 4,000 square feet; there was ample room for enlargement, if necessary. The company's equipment at the time of the purchase consisted of a bench lathe, several sheet-metal bending and shearing machines, and the usual assortment of small hand and power tools necessary to keep the half-dozen workers equipped. Some miscellaneous inventory was also included. The company name, its trade name "Alaska," its good will, and the customer list were also part of the purchase. There were no accounts receivable, and the seller guaranteed all previous debts. The asking price was $33,000.

By checking with several of the company's customers the partners found that Fountain Metals' products apparently enjoyed a good reputation, and there seemed to be some evidence that good will existed. After a period of bargaining, a price of $28,000 was agreed upon by both parties. In order to meet the purchase price, each man contributed $3,000 in cash; and the seller took a $22,000, 4½ per cent first mortgage on the building and all machinery and equipment of the company. This note provided for a six months' period before payments commenced. Each quarter thereafter, $2,000 was due until the note was paid in full.

The payment of $6,000 had left the partners without working capital. Bellows, however, had been able to convince a friend that the new enterprise had excellent prospects and had obtained from him $5,000 on a 6 per cent note. No definite date had been set for repayment; but it was understood by both parties that, should the lender require his money, Fountain Metals would pay it back on demand.

Mr. Bellows became the new company's president and sales manager. In addition, he was to supervise any die or machine work. Mr. Middlebury assumed the duties of treasurer and shop superintendent.

INITIAL OPERATING PROBLEMS

The major products of the company were beer-cooling and dispensing systems. It also manufactured stainless-steel restaurant equipment and walk-in type refrigerators, fabricated both from metal and wood. During the spring and summer of 1947, the company sold all it could make. The major problem at this time was the large volume of customer complaints about defective products and faulty installation. Correction of these mistakes took considerable time and reduced profits. Since neither Bellows nor Middlebury had had any experience in the refrigeration business, they had to rely heavily on the knowledge of their workmen. In particular, they placed considerable confidence in their foreman, who was able to design, as well as to direct fabrication and installation.

In an attempt to increase their knowledge of refrigeration, as well as to make the most use of their scarce working capital, both of the partners often did some of the installation work themselves. Despite this practical knowledge, both men realized that they knew little about the theoretical and design end of refrigeration. To overcome this, they attended night school and graduated as qualified refrigeration repair and installation men. In the course of their education they discovered that their foreman, on whom they had depended as the company's refrigeration expert, knew nothing about the subject. With his dismissal, the quality of the company's work took a decided upward turn.

In these early months the two partners also had to overcome the handicap of the poor reputation built up by their predecessor. Apparently, the few customers they had interviewed were the only ones who had been satisfied with Fountain Metals' earlier work; the great majority of customers in the restaurant business had some fault to find with the company's earlier products. Furthermore, there were no drawings, books, records, or descriptive material of any type about the company's products. Although Bellows knew little about refrigeration during those months of getting under way, he tried to make up for it by exhibiting a spirit of confidence to his customers and by coming up with original ideas even though he was not sure they would work. For example, he designed a new beer system with plastic tubing placed under illuminated glass panels so that the customer could watch the beer flow as the bartender drew it off. Although the mechanism had sales appeal, it turned out that it did not refrigerate beer. Despite these problems, sales increased through the summer and fall of 1947. Sales for 1947 were $93,000. Many of the workmen who had been inherited from the old owner had been replaced by ex-GI's anxious to learn the sheet-metal trade. The volume of complaints had been reduced to a minimum.

SALES TROUBLES

Neither man had realized the extent to which the seasonal influence would affect sales. Sales fell off sharply during the winter of 1948. In order to bolster sales, Bellows studied various beer-dispensing systems and developed one which had distinct advantages over other systems. When sales did not pick up, the partners decided to manufacture for inventory. By spring the company had produced a $9,000 inventory of beer-dispensing equipment. To their chagrin the partners found that competitors had used the winter months to develop new styles of dispensers which made Fountain Metals' obsolete. Sales were very slow, and the company did not dispose of its inventory for two years. Although the company neither made nor lost money on the experiment, it had tied up badly needed capital.

During the first year of operation, Bellows did the selling work. In the second year a salesman was hired and was given an exclusive franchise for their products on a straight 10 per cent commission. Although he built up sales considerably during his first year, his orders gradually declined during the first six months of the second year. As conditions were extremely competitive at that time, his declining sales volume was not considered unusual. Sometime later he announced he was starting his own business to manufacture and sell exactly the same type of product. It was apparent to Bellows and Middlebury that the salesman had been building up his own future volume rather than trying to sell the Fountain Metals line.

Two new salesmen were hired to replace him. They also were paid a 10 per cent commission but were allowed a $50 a week drawing account against future income. Although they were hard workers, they were unable to sell. After thirteen months of effort they were each overdrawn about $800. The company was forced to let them go. Bellows believed the advertising and contacts they had accomplished for the company would eventually prove to be worth more than the $1,600 spent for them.

Shortly thereafter, in February, 1951, a sales representative for a restaurant-equipment wholesaler asked permission to handle the Fountain Metals line for the same 10 per cent commission but without the drawing account. Since it appeared to Bellows and Middlebury that their products tied in naturally with the standard fixtures he sold and were noncompetitive, they granted him the franchise. In the brief period of six months before he was fired, he had misrepresented the company's products, made impossible promises to the buyers, and, in several instances, personally borrowed money from customers on the strength of his company connection. He had made no attempt to check the financial status of his accounts, at least one of which was uncollectible.

In an attempt to bolster the sagging sales by developing a new product, Bellows spent many evenings in his cellar workshop trying to invent an item which would be radically different from those of his competitors. He finally produced a new cooling manifold which could be used to convert the older ice systems to mechanical refrigeration at a lower price than previously had been possible. Although this device did give an added stimulus to sales, it still failed to halt their downward trend.

FINANCING CUSTOMERS

The capital to procure such equipment as was made by Fountain Metals was always a problem with a small bar or grill, and the company that could offer the best credit usually made the sale. Fountain Metals' major competitor was owned by a wealthy man whose strong financial position made it possible for him to offer liberal credit terms. He sold equipment with no down payment, no monthly payments for four months, and then monthly payments for three years at 6 per cent. At first, Fountain Metals could offer nothing that matched these terms.

Bellows and Middlebury were able to find a partial answer to the problem by adopting the trade custom of using automatic coin boxes on all dispensing installations that were sold on time payments. The coin box was merely a device which required a certain number of quarters to be deposited within a twenty-four-hour period. If the management neglected to deposit the necessary number of coins, the electric current was automatically shut off and no beer could be drawn. The bank agreed to discount 6 per cent notes without a down payment on equipment with the automatic coin boxes, although they refused to go along with the four months' initial period without payment. Fountain Metals made all collections from the boxes and were responsible to the bank for any shortages that might occur. As a matter of fact, in Fountain Metals' experience with this financing method a shortage had never occurred. Unfortunately, such a device could not be used to finance the sale of Fountain Metals' other products—principally stainless steel restaurant equipment.

FINANCIAL TROUBLES

In the spring of 1949 the friend who had loaned the company $5,000 called for immediate repayment of the entire amount. To raise the money, Bellows placed a mortgage of $4,000 on his own home. At the same time, payment came due for a new Chicago 8-foot power brake (bending machine), an important piece of equipment. Bellows raised this money by placing a second mortgage on his father's house for $3,000.

Despite these attempts to solve current financial problems and increase long-term earnings by the installation of new equipment, the final statement for 1949 showed a loss for the year's operation of $1,150.12. Sales continued to drop during the winter of 1950.

THE DECISION TO SUBCONTRACT

The start of the Korean conflict in June, 1950, added one more problem to the long list faced by the management of Fountain Metals: the impending shortage of sheet metals and tubing, the company's basic raw materials. Both men recalled the difficulty that electronic manufacturers had during World War II in obtaining suppliers for precision sheet-metal work, and they decided that the immediate answer to their problems of sales and materials was high-priority subcontracting work from large electronic companies.

Carrying out this decision proved difficult. The primary requirements for restaurant equipment were that it be strongly constructed and work well. Tolerances seldom were less than 1/32nd of an inch and greater tolerances were common. Much of the subcontracted work would be radio and radar chassis, which often contain hundreds of punched holes with location distances bearing tolerances of only a few thousandths of an inch. The only way Fountain Metals could do this work with existing equipment was to lay out each hole and punch it separately with a hand machine. Material used for restaurant equipment was primarily steel, stainless steel, and copper. Much of the new work would be fabricated from aluminum or aluminum alloys. Existing welding equipment could not produce an aluminum weld satisfactory in either strength or appearance.

In an effort to be recognized as a supplier for this type of work, bids were entered, even though it was realized that the company probably could not produce some of the items at a profit. Next, Bellows turned to what he considered the company's most immediate problem—raising enough money to purchase equipment which could handle the subcontracted work.

MORE FINANCIAL PROBLEMS

Mr. Bellows spent several months of fruitless effort attempting to raise $20,000. One afternoon in a cocktail lounge he mentioned to a chance acquaintance, a lawyer, that he wished he knew where he could obtain a $20,000 loan for his business. The lawyer introduced him to Messrs. McArdle and Byrd, two small businessmen who owned a profitable fat-rendering plant which was a headquarters for their multiple enterprises. They became interested in Fountain Metals and agreed to lend the money. In addition, they introduced Bellows to their banker, a vice-president of the Community National Bank. This latter contact resulted in Fountain Metals being able to refinance its notes payable on more favorable terms.

In return for $16,500 in cash, McArdle and Byrd received a three-year note for $22,440, repayable $50 a week for the first thirty-eight weeks and $100 per week for the remainder of the period. The balance of the note, $8,740, would be due and payable at the end of the three years. The note was secured by a second mortgage on the building, land, and all equipment; and by its terms the second mortgage holders would be able to vote the common stock should any payments on the note be in arrears.

These payments were, of course, in addition to those being made on the first mortgage. The initial terms of $2,000 each quarter had been modified, since the company found it increasingly difficult to meet them; and in June, 1951, the company was paying $100 a month plus interest charges of approximately $30. In addition, Fountain Metals had to meet monthly payments of about $100 on the two house mortgages.

With the funds made available by the second mortgage, Bellows bought a new Wales-Strippit precision power punch, power shears, a special welding machine for aluminum, a spot welder, two drill presses, a metal-cutting band saw, and miscellaneous other small tools and machines.

Working capital to carry accounts receivable and inventory became more and more critical during 1950–51, although it was offset to some degree by discounting receivables at the bank and borrowing against purchase orders from large customer companies. The year 1950 showed an operating loss of $5,743.79. Bellows attributed the loss to low bidding on the first subcontract orders, the handwork required before the new machines were set up, and the poor sales record of the first six months of 1950. The repayment provisions of the various mortgages siphoned off cash as fast as it was generated. Life was a constant struggle to get sufficient funds to meet the payroll or procure material.

Payments were kept up on the first mortgage, but by the spring of 1951 were being passed on the second. Checks began to be returned for lack of funds. As the strain told on Bellows and Middlebury, arguments occurred over trivial incidents. Finally, in the summer of 1951, Bellows asked Middlebury what he would take for his half of the business. Middlebury's price was $5,000, and Bellows considered this a fair one.

The second mortgage holders, McArdle and Byrd, had not pressed the company for their payments, nor had they exercised their right to take over control. Since they appeared so co-operative, Bellows asked

Exhibit 1a

FOUNTAIN METALS, INC.
BALANCE SHEET, JULY 31, 1951

ASSETS

Current Assets:			
Cash in Bank		$ 340.43	
Notes Receivable		757.03	
Accounts Receivable		9,158.16	
Inventory, July 31, 1951		26,903.02	$37,158.64
Capital Assets:			
Land and Building	$16,822.70		
Less: Reserve for Depreciation	2,229.30	$14,593.40	
Machinery and Equipment	$18,690.45		
Less: Reserve for Depreciation	1,810.73	16,879.72	31,473.12
Other Assets:			
Dealer Cash Reserve		$ 1,376.39	
Robin Hood—Charge Back		461.30	
Prepaid Interest		3,960.00	5,797.69
Total Assets			$74,429.45

LIABILITIES, CAPITAL STOCK, AND SURPLUS

Current Liabilities:			
Notes Payable—Community National Bank		$24,901.49	
Accounts Payable		9,803.60	
Accrued Taxes:			
Real Estate and Excise	$ 1,001.46		
Unemployment Compensation	592.35		
Social Security	651.41		
Withholding	1,481.59	3,726.81	
Accrued Interest		119.54	
Due to Officers:			
Sanford Bellows	$ 4,861.54		
John Middlebury	910.53	5,772.07	$44,323.51
Capital Liabilities:			
First Mortgage		$ 9,542.50	
Second Mortgage		20,360.00	29,902.50
Capital Stock and Surplus:			
Capital Stock—Common		9,197.56	
Surplus:			
January 1, 1951, Balance Deficit	$ 5,676.88		
Add: Net Loss for Seven Months Ending July 31, 1951	3,317.24		
July 31, 1951, Balance Deficit		8,994.12	
Net Worth			203.44
Total Liabilities, Capital Stock, and Surplus			$74,429.45

if they would be interested either in lending him $5,000 to buy out Middlebury's interest or buying all or part of it themselves. Although McArdle and Byrd were not enthusiastic, they instructed their accountant to draw up reports showing the financial condition of Fountain Metals (Exhibits 1*a* and 1*b*). Both Middlebury and Bellows protested that the completed statements did not present a true financial picture of the company. They pointed out that the sales figure was too low

Exhibit 1b

FOUNTAIN METALS, INC.

STATEMENT OF INCOME AND PROFIT AND LOSS FOR SEVEN-MONTH PERIOD ENDING JULY 31, 1951

Sales		$54,795.29	100%
Deduct: Cost of goods made and sold:			
Inventory, January 1, 1951	$12,430.00		
Purchases	30,993.13		
Direct labor	14,264.50		
Outside contractors	5,187.94		
Total	$62,875.57		
Less: Inventory, July 31, 1951	26,903.02	35,972.55	66%
Gross profit		$18,822.74	34%
Deduct: Operating Expense:			
Salaries—Officers	$ 7,106.00		
—Office help	1,100.00		
Advertising	39.56		
Auto expense and travel	1,899.56		
Bad debts	1,185.58		
Bank charges	77.86		
Building repairs	77.00		
Commissions, sales contracts	1,339.76		
Depreciation	1,352.81		
Dues and subscriptions	41.25		
Expendable tools	517.68		
Express	92.61		
Heat and light	520.48		
Insurance	796.93		
Interest paid	2,220.32		
Legal expense	121.00		
Miscellaneous expense	210.23		
Office expense	290.83		
Rent	70.40		
Taxes	2,398.72		
Telephone	846.64	22,295.22	
Operating loss		$ 3,472.48	
Other income		155.24	
Net loss		$ 3,317.24	

and that other figures required adjustment. The accountant was asked to draw up another report as of the same date to contain additional information they would give him.

HADEN'S OPPORTUNITY TO BUY IN

During the early summer of 1951 Haden became a regular visitor at Fountain Metals. He worked closely with Bellows in an effort to expedite the completion of his model. The two men became friendly, and Bellows took Haden into his confidence and asked his advice on various financial and company problems. As Haden participated in the affairs of the firm, he also gained the confidence of Middlebury. In this favor-

Exhibit 2a

August 24, 1951

To the Board of Directors of
Fountain Metals, Inc.

GENTLEMEN:

In accordance with the instructions of Mr. McArdle, the Second Mortgagee, and with your permission, I have audited the books and records of your company for the seven months' period ending July 31, 1951, and submit the following:

Exhibits:

1. Balance sheet, July 31, 1951.
2. Income statement for seven months' period ending July 31, 1951.
3. Letter from the Community National Bank certifying cash in bank, notes payable, contingent liabilities, and pledged accounts receivable.
4. Various supporting schedules to reconcile adjustments from cash basis to accrual basis.

Since you have carried on your operations on a cash basis, it was necessary to bring on unrecorded sales, based on your open accounts receivable and unrecorded expenses, both actual and accrued, based on your open accounts payable, and by construction based on information available in your files.

Cash in Bank—$340.43: This amount was verified by certificate from the Community Trust Company. See letter dated August 15, 1951.

Notes Receivable—$757.03: This amount was verified from the notes on hand. These are as follows:

Commercial Lunch, Inc.	$695.40
Joseph's Grille	61.63
Total	$757.03

The following notes were considered bad, since they were long past due:

Grasselli's Market	$185.68
Town Cafe	210.10
Total	$395.78

These were written off and charged to bad debts. I recommend legal action for their collection.

Accounts Receivable—$3,741.43: These are verified by the balances of the open accounts supporting this total. They are aged as follows and do not include the accounts receivable pledged to the bank.

Over 60 days	$ 983.69
Under 60 days	1,232.92
Current	1,524.82
Total	$3,741.43

Exhibit 2a—Continued

These accounts were adjudged bad, written off, and charged to Bad Debts:

P. Auriello	$137.50
Circle Cafe	9.90
Mattrix Machine	6.60
Jim's Place	3.30
Fred Plenty	103.95
B. Bellows	55.22
ABC Delicatessen	78.56
J. Franck	20.90
Dwarf Eatery	34.93
Hotel Garcon	134.62
Z. N. Jones	4.95
Myrtle's Cafe	192.50
Ye Olde Tavern	2.47
Canal Cafe	4.40
Total	$789.80

Inventory—$26,903.02: This total is the result of the physical count at July 31, 1951, made by you. This figure is verified by your costs and book inventories, and you have certified it to me as representing the correct amount of merchandise and supplies on hand valued at the lower of cost or market. I have checked additions and tested extensions and prices.

Land and Buildings—$14,593.40: This value is based on that reported in the federal tax returns, since there was no formal record of evidence.

Original values as of May, 1948, per federal tax return		$16,822.70
Prior depreciation	$1,818.64	
Allowed this year	410.66	2,229.30
Total		$14,593.40

Machinery and Equipment—$16,879.72: This account showed an increase of $3,386.99 during the period under audit. I examined voucher supporting additions to this account, all of which appear proper charges thereto. Again the original value was taken from your federal tax returns, and the above amount was arrived at as follows:

Original values as of January 1 per 1950 federal tax returns		$15,303.46
Addition during this period		3,386.99
		$18,690.45
Prior depreciation for return	$868.58	
Allowed this year	942.15	1,810.73
Total		$16,879.72

Notes Payable—$8,696.04: This amount was verified from certificate from Community National Bank to whom these notes are payable. See letter dated August 15, 1951.

This account was reduced by pledged accounts receivable as follows:

Notes Payable, Community Trust Co.	$24,901.49
Less: Accounts Receivable discounted	16,205.45
Notes Payable Net	$ 8,696.04

Exhibit 2a—Continued

Accounts Payable—$9,803.60: This account is verified by open balances of the various accounts supporting. This account is aged as follows:

Over 60 days	$2,926.23
Under 60 days	3,084.73
Current	3,792.64
Total	$9,803.60

I examined transactions subsequent to July 31, 1951, to satisfy myself that all liabilities of the company at that date had been entered upon the books, and you have certified to me that all the known liabilities at July 31, 1951, were recorded upon the books prior to that date or made known to me.

Due to Officers—Sanford P. Bellows: $4,861.54: Due Mr. Bellows for money advanced.

First Mortgage—$9,542.50: Direct reduction mortgage at 4 per cent interest. I have verified there are no past due payments of either principal or interest.

Second Mortgage—$20,360.00: An examination of this mortgage shows that principal and interest are in arrears in the amount of $1,760.00. Under the terms of the mortgage the whole amount is now due and payable.

Capital Stock Common—$8,832.60: This value was calculated as follows:

Total assets	$69,158.22
Less: Total liabilities	55,982.22
	$13,176.00
Less: Surplus	4,341.41
Value of capital stock	$ 8,834.59

Surplus—$4,341.41: This amount is made up as follows:

Per federal tax returns:	
Balance 12/31/48	$ 1,217.03
Balance 12/31/49 (Loss)	−1,150.12
Balance 12/31/50 (Loss)	−5,743.79
Balance deficit	$−5,676.88
Net profit for 7 months ending July 31, 1951	10,018.29
Surplus	$ 4,341.41

Subject to the foregoing comments, I affirm that the attached Balance Sheet and Statement of Income and Profit and Loss correctly present the financial condition of Fountain Metals, Inc., at July 31, 1951, and the result of operations for the seven months' period then ended, respectively.

Very truly yours,

SAMUEL J. ROUNDER
Accountant

Exhibit 2a—Continued

DEAR MR. ROUNDER:

At the request of the Fountain Metals Company, Inc., we give you the following information.

1. Balance in checking account as of July 31, 1951: $340.43.
2. Notes payable to the Community National Bank as of July 31, 1951, as follows:

Date	*Amounts*	*Due Date*	*Rate*
7/25/51	$ 2,200.00	8/24/51	5%
7/16/51	4,950.00	10/5/51	5%
7/11/51	4,681.60	10/5/51	5%
7/23/51	2,200.00	10/5/51	5%
6/5/51	3,300.00	10/5/51	5%
7/23/51	1,392.12	9/21/51	5%
7/19/51	2,132.62	8/20/51	5%
5/4/51	3,045.15	8/2/51	5%
	$24,901.49		

3. Leases totaling $12,460.46, covering seven accounts, were discounted with us as of the above date.
4. The balance of Dealer Cash Reserve as of the above date was $1,-376.39.
5. Pledged accounts receivable as collateral for loans listed in item (2) were as follows:

Purchase order—World Wide Electronics Co.	$44,000.00
Assigned Accounts:	
World Wide Electronics Co.	$ 2,640.00
World Wide Electronics Co.	5,948.25
World Wide Electronics Co.	2,200.46
Visual Electronics	1,134.52
Radarscope	2,647.72
Various small accounts	4,282.22
Total	$62,853.17

Very sincerely yours,
Community National Bank
Vice President

(Note) While this letter shows $18,853.17 as assigned accounts, Mr. Middlebury pointed out that the amount of $2,647.72 against Radarscope, Inc., had been paid prior to July 31, 1951, and the proceeds applied against a prior note not listed.

able position, Haden took every opportunity to ease the friction between Bellows and Middlebury. Eventually both men turned to Haden and offered him a chance to buy in and become an active part of the management.

This offer appeared to be in line with Haden's aim to find a small

Exhibit 2b

FOUNTAIN METALS, INC.

BALANCE SHEET, JULY 31, 1951

ASSETS

Current Assets:			
Cash in Bank		$ 340.43	
Notes Receivable		757.03	
Accounts Receivable		3,741.43	
Inventory, July 31, 1951		26,903.02	$31,741.91
Capital Assets:			
Land and Building	$16,822.70		
Less: Reserve for Depreciation	2,229.30	$14,593.40	
Machinery and Equipment	$18,690.45		
Less: Reserve for Depreciation	1,810.73	16,879.72	31,473.12
Other Assets:			
Prepaid Real Estate Tax		$ 145.50	
Prepaid Interest		3,960.00	
Robin Hood—Charge Back		461.30	
Dealer Cash Reserve		1,376.39	5,943.19
Total Assets			$69,158.22

LIABILITIES, CAPITAL STOCK, AND SURPLUS

Current Liabilities:			
Notes Payable—Community National Bank	$24,901.49		
Less: Accounts Receivable Discounted	16,205.45	$ 8,696.04	
Accounts Payable		9,803.60	
Accrued Taxes:			
Unemployment Compensation	$ 563.71		
Social Security	628.53		
Withholding	1,481.59		
Real Estate and Excise	1,001.46	3,675.29	
Accrued Interest		119.54	
Due to Officers—Sanford Bellows		3,785.25	$26,079.77
Capital Liabilities:			
First Mortgage		$ 9,542.50	
Second Mortgage		20,360.00	29,902.50
Capital Stock and Surplus:			
Capital Stock—Common		$ 8,834.59	
Surplus—January 1, 1951, Deficit	$ 5,676.88		
Net Profit for Seven Months Ending August 31, 1951	10,018.29	4,341.41	
Net Worth			13,076.00
Total Liabilities, Capital Stock, and Surplus			$69,158.22

business in which he could share the management and profits. He felt that the greater part of Fountain Metals' difficulties arose from the lack of a competent financial man in the company. Sales were no problem, the company had a backlog of orders; the plant was operating on a forty-eight-hour week, and additional subcontract work was being received at regular intervals. The shop was nonunion; and wage rates averaged only $1.40 per hour, against the union rate of $2.25 in a city forty miles away.

Exhibit 2c

FOUNTAIN METALS, INC.

STATEMENT OF INCOME AND PROFIT AND LOSS FOR SEVEN-MONTH PERIOD ENDING JULY 31, 1951

Sales		$66,220.74	100%
Deduct: Cost of goods made and sold:			
Inventory, January 1, 1951	$12,430.00		
Purchases	30,993.13		
Direct labor	14,264.50		
Outside contractors	5,187.94		
Total	$62,875.57		
Less: Inventory, July 31, 1951	26,903.02	35,972.55	54.3%
Gross profit		$30,248.19	45.7%
Deduct: Operating expenses			
Salaries—Officers	$ 5,610.00		
—Office help	1,100.00		
Advertising	39.56		
Auto expense and travel	1,633.80		
Bad debts	1,185.58		
Bank charges	77.86		
Building repairs	77.60		
Commissions, sales contracts	1,339.76		
Depreciation	1,352.81		
Dues and subscriptions	41.25		
Expendable tools	517.68		
Express	92.61		
Heat and light	520.48		
Insurance	796.93		
Interest paid	2,220.32		
Legal expense	11.00		
Miscellaneous expense	210.23		
Office expense	290.83		
Rent	70.40		
Taxes	1,234.28		
Telephone	846.64	19,269.02	
Net operating profit		$10,979.17	
Add: Other income: sale of equipment		165.34	
Total profit		$11,144.51	
Deduct: Other charges:			
Real estate taxes, 1949–50	$ 647.13		
State unemployment tax, 1950	479.09	1,126.22	
Net profit for seven months 1951		$10,018.29	

Haden was not impressed by either set of financial statements submitted by McArdle and Byrd's accountant, although the second reports (Exhibits 2*a*, 2*b*, and 2*c*) presented a far happier picture than the first statement. He was fairly sure that the current financial problem could be traced in large part to the substantial capital required to process the defense orders—in particular, one $40,000 contract which could not be shipped or billed until all work was completed. He believed, however, that the potential profit on that one order might well establish the company on a firm financial footing.

The future action of McArdle and Byrd would, of course, be crucial. Haden summed up the possibilities in this way:

Liquidate the Company

Since the second mortgage holders have also guaranteed all notes held by the bank, liquidation would probably result in a serious loss to the former.

Exercise Voting Rights and Keep Present Management

There is little chance that present management will remain to take orders from the second mortgage holders. I believe that both men are too independent to remain working for someone else in a business which they feel is, by right of work and effort, theirs, especially when they could be earning half again as much in some other company.

Exercise Voting Rights and Bring in New Management

Installation of a new management would in effect be starting a new business under the most adverse circumstances. They would be losing the two best operating assets of the company, the present owners, with, in all probability, the new man earning a much higher rate.

Add Money in Exchange for Stock

Adding more money would aid in solving the company problems. However, the second mortgage holders have stated that they want to recover what they have in the company, not put more in it.

Sell the Notes

There is little likelihood that an outside buyer can be found to purchase the notes from them at any price except as possible liquidation value, which I believe will be very low. Moreover, present company management has no way that it can raise sufficient money to procure them.

Reduce Note Payments

Since the major desire of the second mortgage holders is to get their money out of the company, they may well listen to a financial reorganization which will allow them to do so, even though with a longer time lapse than they had originally planned. This might be in the form of a longer period with correspondingly smaller payments to repay the note, or substituting stock for part of the face value of the note.

Haden thought he could probably get a one-third interest in the company for an investment of $3,500, although he was reasonably certain that a total investment of at least $10,000 would be required in order to provide a minimum working capital. He admitted that, from the financial point of view, Fountain Metals, Inc., did not make an overly attractive picture; but he felt that he could work well with Bellows and Middlebury and that the three together would constitute a strong management team. Haden was especially impressed by the fact that the company had refused to be downed during the three years of adversity.

American Multicraft Company

In June of 1952, Mr. Brooks joined the American Multicraft Company as an active partner. Since there were at that time four partners in the business, it was felt that the business must expand in order to produce sufficient returns for all partners. Before joining the American Multicraft Company, Mr. Brooks felt that he might be able to obtain work with some large firm. His feelings on the future of going into a small self-owned business, however, were crystallized in the following letter from Mr. Bard, one of the partners:

> The possibilities of making large sums of money go along with ownership, and I think that we are on the right track by going into American Multicraft even though we may eventually wind up in something altogether different from what we are manufacturing now. If we can line up a different product with good future possibilities and then set ourselves up, even though we may not have complete knowledge of the industry, by careful management and application of common sense, I think we can get by. I have known a number of people who have gone into a business altogether strange to them and have made successes of it. Of course, the easy way out is to work for some large corporation, but to me that would be like being in the Navy again, and the only answer is to be your own boss even though temporarily the returns may be small. American Multicraft has been established for two years, and numerous contacts have been developed that will be an asset no matter what product we produce.

The American Multicraft Company was organized in July, 1950, by Mrs. Brooks and Mrs. Bard. At that time their husbands were overseas. One day, while shopping, Mrs. Bard was about to buy a set of ornamental combs when Mrs. Brooks restrained her from making the purchase, with the statement: "A simple item like that can be duplicated by hand at one quarter of the price." Whereupon Mrs. Brooks proceeded to purchase the necessary materials and make the combs. Mrs. Bard suggested that they make a few similar and original styles as samples and see if they would be acceptable to one of the buyers of a leading department store in the city. The buyer was pleased and placed an initial order which encouraged the women to go ahead with their idea.

Mrs. Brooks and Mrs. Bard had had little business experience. Mrs. Bard had majored in journalism in college and afterward had taught kindergarten. Mrs. Brooks had majored in art at college and had attended a costume-designing school. She had also spent two weeks with a women's sportswear company, three months with the designing department of a moviet studio, and nine months as a bond-house secretary.

Realizing that the business must have a name, the women chose "American Multicraft Company," thinking that, if the business were a success, such a name would cover the marketing of a multitude of specialty products. They then filed a "Certificate of Doing Business under an Assumed Name." Other legal permits secured were: a city license, called a "peddler's license," and a "Sales Tax Exemption" certificate. No partnership agreement was written.

PRODUCTION

For the first two months of operations, all work was done in Mrs. Bard's home. Upon applying for a license, however, it was discovered that manufacturing must be done at an address within the manufacturing zone. The company was then installed in a dentist's office which was located in that zone. Rather than employ a secretary, the firm employed a phone-answering service. All manufacturing was carried out at the office between sales calls by Mrs. Brooks and Mrs. Bard. Soon, however, the partners hired a full-time secretary, who also aided in manufacturing. With defense activity at its peak in this area, the women soon found it difficult to find and hold competent full-time help. Therefore, several college girls, preferably art students, as well as a part-time bookkeeper who also helped in manufacturing, were hired for part-time work.

Manufacturing as carried out by the company was broken down into two parts: design and assembly. Since the success of the company's products depended on adapting or originating a fashion or fad, the partners spent a small part of each week designing new products or original variations of products already on the market. As each new item was produced, it was rushed to a buying office for approval or rejection. If an item was accepted and orders were received, materials for manufacturing twice the amount required for such orders were usually purchased. Occasionally, after a sample had been produced and orders received, the materials required for production of that item were no longer available; but since none of the materials used were considered essential to the defense effort, no great difficulty was experienced in locating a source of supply.

Assembly was relatively simple; but since all work was done by hand, a close check had to be kept on quality. The first five dozen of a new item might have up to 25 per cent rejects; but as production gathered momentum, rejects usually dropped to less than 3 per cent. Since the company was selling to higher-quality stores which expected the best possible workmanship, all shipments were inspected personally by one of the partners.

The principal materials used were made of plastic. The manufacture of an item from plastics required a large investment in machinery, but many small plastic manufacturers in the area were willing to subcontract for small items to fill in slack production. Therefore, all molding and some dyeing work was subcontracted, and the company's actual manufacturing processes were limited to special dyeing and assembly.

PRICING POLICY

The partners found from experience that, in marketing plastic specialties, at least three items failed for every item that was successful. Stores retailing this type of item expected at least a 50 per cent markup. Therefore, in pricing a given item, the retail price was determined according to what the market would bear; the company's price to the retailer was one half of that amount. The costs of production were not expected to be more than one half of the company's price, i.e., one quarter of selling price. No product was produced for the market that did not meet this rule-of-thumb. Costs of designing failures and proprietorship drawings were charged against gross profits, but all other expenses were charged against overhead. Overhead was estimated roughly and then charged arbitrarily to each product in a rather foggy relationship to the selling price.

SALES

American Multicraft was located in an area known throughout the United States as a manufacturing center of high-style goods. Most large stores in the country either subscribed to a buying-office service in that area or sent their buyers to the area once or twice a year. By developing contacts with these buying offices the company succeeded in getting distribution in over 150 of the larger stores in the United States.

Whenever one of the partners traveled to another area, she would stop in to see the accounts there; but no regular selling trips were made, since the line was too small to support the costs of such trips. Local stores were contacted at least once each month, and always when a new item was produced. Mrs. Brooks and Mrs. Bard usually called on stores together and became known to the buyers in the home area as the "Powderpuff Twins." Initially, the novelty of having two young inexperienced women develop a business made conversation in local buying circles; this word-of-mouth advertising became the source of many unsolicited local orders. When certain buyers were observed to be partial to one of the partners, however, these accounts were called on by that partner alone.

Sales agents were used in a few territories but were not deemed successful, since orders solicited from a few such accounts had not been good credit risks. On occasions, relatives of the partners living in differ-

Exhibit 1

AMERICAN MULTICRAFT COMPANY

COMPARATIVE BALANCE SHEET FOR THE FISCAL YEAR ENDING APRIL 30, 1951, AND AS OF MARCH 31, 1952

ASSETS	*April 30, 1951*		*March 31, 1952*	
Current Assets:				
Cash in Bank	$3,341.14		$1,256.02	
Inventory	932.35		600.00*	
Total Current Assets		$4,273.49		$1,856.02
Fixed Assets:				
Furniture, Fixtures, and Equipment	$ 63.37		$ 98.19	
Less: Reserve for Depreciation	11.02		11.02	
	$ 52.35		$ 87.17	
Sales Tax Deposit	10.00		10.00	
Total Fixed Assets		62.35		97.17
Total Assets		$4,335.84		$1,953.19
LIABILITIES				
Current Liabilities:				
Federal and State Old Age and Unemployment Insurance Withheld—Employees	$ 18.76		$ 9.73	
Federal Income Tax Withheld	9.30		21.10	
Sales Tax	......		0.98	
Total Current Liabilities		$ 28.06		$ 31.81
Net Worth:				
Jack and Gloria Nard, Partners' Capital	$2,153.89		$ 971.92	
Merle and Leta Brooks, Partners' Capital	2,153.89		949.46	
Total Net Worth		4,307.78		1,921.38
Total Liabilities and Net Worth		$4,335.84		$1,953.19

* Estimated.

ent areas were sent sample lines to sell, but the business from this source was small.

No advertising program had been developed, but at times the company sent out brochures and single-sheet "fliers" announcing new products. The buying offices sent bulletins to their clients, and in this way many American Multicraft products had been nationally advertised. At a customer's request, showcase placards and newspaper layouts were made up.

In November, 1951, Mr. Bard had been released from the Navy and had spent that and the following month working with the company on

Christmas business. During January and February, 1952, he investigated the possibilities of employment in his pre-Korea occupation (the accounting field). Despite the limited financial structure of the company as shown by Exhibits 1, 2, and 3, Mr. Bard decided to join American Multicraft as an active full-time partner. Mrs. Brooks had gone east with

Exhibit 2

AMERICAN MULTICRAFT COMPANY

COMPARATIVE PROFIT AND LOSS STATEMENT FOR THE FISCAL YEAR MAY 1, 1950—APRIL 30, 1951, AND FOR THE PERIOD MAY 1, 1951—MARCH 31, 1952

	Fiscal Year Ended April 30, 1951		*Period May 1, 1951, to March 31, 1952*	
Sales (net)		$25,341.83		$16,823.45
Cost of goods sold:				
Purchases	$9,253.44		$4,558.58	
Beginning inventory	......		932.35	
	$9,253.44		$5,490.93	
Less: Ending inventory	932.35		600.00*	
	$8,321.09		$4,890.93	
Salaries—labor	2,441.92		1,736.33	
Total cost of goods sold		10,763.01		6,627.26
Gross profit on sales		$14,578.82		$10,196.19
Less: Expenses:				
Sales tax expense	$ 0.72		......	
Advertising expense	261.97		$ 225.04	
Delivery and auto expense	920.00		960.00	
Traveling expense	552.00		......	
Freight expense	32.72		76.49	
Bank charges	8.54		5.59	
Auditing and legal expenses	115.00		223.50	
Insurance expenses	84.50		86.50	
Miscellaneous expenses	128.89		96.08	
Office supplies	59.56		74.76	
Postage	23.50		22.92	
Telephone and telegraph	204.95		263.27	
Federal old age and unemployment insurance	7.46		3.67	
Rent	267.50		405.67	
Taxes and licenses	23.08		7.00	
Depreciation—equipment	11.02		......	
Total expenses		2,701.41		2,450.49
Net profit on sales		$11,877.41		$ 7,745.70
Add: Other income:				
Miscellaneous income		....		265.37
Net profit		$11,877.41		$ 8,011.07

* Estimated.

her husband; so the active management of the company was in the hands of the Bards until Mr. and Mrs. Brooks returned in June, 1952.

Upon their return to the company, the Brookses spent the first two weeks calling on various accounts, establishing personal contacts, and selling some hand-painted beach bags and ornamental sunglasses.

Mr. Brooks's first project was a "wonderful idea"—the sale of plastic containers for holding conical paper cups in the home. The holders were to be highly colored and put up in packages of 8 holders complete with 100 paper cups. The Lily-Tulip Co. offered the company a distributorship for its conical paper cups, which were sold almost entirely to the soda fountain and restaurant trade. The Lily-Tulip Co. said, however, that, if the idea gained favor, it would give away the holders themselves in order to sell its cups. After the partners estimated the costs and potential sales, they did not feel justified in putting the required money into a cup die to make the holders.

***Exhibit** 3*

AMERICAN MULTICRAFT COMPANY
ANALYSIS OF CAPITAL ACCOUNTS

		Total	*The Bards*	*The Brookses*
Contributions or balance		$ 530.37	$ 265.18	$ 265.19
Profit for period—year to 4/30/51		11,877.41	5,938.71	5,938.70
		$12,407.78	$6,203.89	$6,203.89
Less: Drawings		8,100.00	4,050.00	4,050.00
		$ 4,307.78	$2,153.89	$2,153.89
Profits—11 months to 3/31/52		8,011.07	4,005.53	4,005.54
		$12,318.85	$6,159.42	$6,159.43
Drawings		8,522.47	4,250.00	4,272.47
		$ 3,796.38	$1,909.42	$1,886.96
Less: Drawings and salaries:				
Leta M. Brooks	$700			
Jack G. Bard	875			
Gloria Bard	300			
		1,875.00	937.50	937.50
Capital account as of 3/31/52		$ 1,921.38	$ 971.92	$ 949.46

For the fall trade a cigarette case was redesigned, a line of novelty sweaters was developed, and the hand-painted beach bags were stocked for the winter resort trade. Although the items were sold in a few stores in every section of the country, they were only moderately successful.

As Mr. Brooks summed up the situation at the end of January, 1953: "At the present time the buyers seem to have the jitters and have instructions to buy only what they need to fill in. Where they used to look over a line with an order pad, they now look it over with a memo pad . . . with the promise that should things pick up they will send you an order."

In that both women partners were pregnant, their future activity would be limited to product design, while the active management of the business would lie in the hands of Mr. Bard and Mr. Brooks as equal partners.

Yankee Assemblers, Inc.

Second Lieutenant Timothy Canning, at Air Materiel Command Headquarters, United States Air Force, was somewhat puzzled by his new assignment in the spring of 1952. He had been given the task of investigating the circumstances surrounding a request by a small company, Yankee Assemblers, Inc., for financial relief under Public Law 921. Although he had collected a sizable amount of information about the case, he still had been unable to reach a firm decision as to whether the Air Force should grant the additional $165,000 requested by the general manager of Yankee Assemblers, Inc.

Lieutenant Canning had spent some time in familiarizing himself with the background against which the Air Force buyer and contracting officer operated and the way Public Law 921 affected their work. He knew, as a basic fact, that the General Accounting Office checked to see that finance officers expend appropriated funds only within the limits of the appropriation and for legal purposes. He was also aware that no officer has any authority to give away the nation's money or gratuitously deprive the nation of any vested right and that no contracting officer has the authority to amend a contract to the monetary detriment of the government without the government's receiving something in return. However, when a contract, as drawn, fails to express the intent of the parties because of a mutual mistake, an appeal to the Comptroller General, who heads the General Accounting Office, will usually result in the contract's being reformed in accordance with such intention.

During World War II the limitations on the power of contracting officers and the uncertainty and delay involved in submitting claims to the General Accounting Office tended to hamper the defense effort. The First War Powers Act contained, among other things, provisions to remedy this situation. With the outbreak of the Korean conflict, the services were faced with the same problem once again. Congress consequently enacted legislation (Public Law 921, 81st Congress) in January, 1951, amending and extending certain provisions of the First War Powers Act. This law allowed the President to authorize the military departments to amend and modify contracts without regard to previously existing provisions of law. The Air Force, by virtue of Defense Department regulations, was permitted in certain cases to amend contracts without consideration, to correct mistakes in contracts, and to formalize informal commitments for material and services made by contracting agencies.

All contract amendments, however, made under the authority of Public Law 921 and the Executive Order and Regulations thereunder, had to include a finding that the national defense was thereby facilitated. There was no fixed formula for determining whether or not the national defense would be facilitated in a particular case. Such a determination, Lieutenant Canning realized, was a matter of judgment; and he understood that it was the intent of the Air Force and the other armed services to use the authority described with great caution.

Yankee Assemblers, Inc., a small company located in New England, specialized in research, development, and fabrication of special electronic test equipment. Eighty per cent of its manufacturing process was the assembly of the more or less standard components produced by well-known firms in the electronic industry. With the advent of the Korean conflict, Yankee Assemblers received prime contracts from all three military services and from the Civil Defense Agency. In addition, the company had subcontracts under military prime contracts held by several large corporations.

The letter from the general manager of Yankee Assemblers requesting aid stated its case as follows:

Commanding General Air Materiel Command

DEAR GENERAL:

We at Yankee Assemblers, Inc., are making a request for relief under the authority of Title II, First War Powers Act, 1941, as amended by Executive Order 10210, in the amount of $165,427.89.

We believe we should have this relief because the following four fixed-priced contracts were negotiated prior to the Korean conflict, when we had absolutely no way of knowing or forecasting the tremendous jump that would take place in all our costs before the contract could be completed.

Contract I. Bids opened July, 1949. Yankee Assemblers low bidder at $205,000. Next low bidder $210,000. Preproduction model submitted January, 1950. Preproduction model approved May, 1950. First shipment September, 1950.

Contract II. Bids opened May, 1950. Elmira Company low bidder, $240 per unit. Yankee Assemblers bid, $280 per unit. Yankee awarded contract 15 June 1950 at $280 per unit. Preproduction model submitted July, 1950. Preproduction model approved November, 1950.

Contracts III and IV. Negotiated contracts awarded August, 1950. No preproduction samples required. First unit shipped April, 1951.

When these contracts were entered into, we anticipated a reasonable profit. All were negotiated, however, before the weight of inflation resulting from Korea was known. Our costs were increased because of the following: (*a*) substantial increase in material costs, (*b*) approximately a 20 per cent increase in labor rates, (*c*) shortage of parts from suppliers resulting in increased labor costs as production line stood idle, (*d*) increase in indirect labor and overhead cost, and (*e*) increased labor turnover as workers shifted to other defense jobs.

All the above factors were beyond our control and certainly could not have been anticipated at the time we entered the contract. Our losses to date on these four contracts have caused us considerable financial difficulty, which even at the present time is a factor in the delivery schedule of current production. It is a definitely serious factor in any future contracts for national defense work.

We feel that in our minor capacity we are important to the national defense effort, self-evident from the following prime and subcontracts that we have: (1) Sole source for a special controlling unit used by several companies. (2) Prime contract for Navy Bureau of Ships, which called for the design of an off-beat simulator, prototype run in production. Will be adopted as standard by the Navy. (3) First subcontractor to be set up by Pile-A-Tron Corporation to manufacture their new guide meter, for which they have the prime contract. (4) Secret research project for the Bureau of Standards. (5) Research and development contract for guided rockets, Bureau of Ships. (6) Research and development contract and sole source of production of sonic sounder for Navy Bureau of Ships. (7) Confidential sole source contract for Air Force. (8) Radio transmitter for Army, currently producing 40 per month. (9) Confidential research and development contract for Air Force.

To date, no equipment submitted under the above contracts has been rejected after delivery. We have endeavored to keep down our overhead. No dividends or money other than the following salaries has been paid to our officers. President no salary, General Manager $8,000, Director of Research $9,000, Chief Engineer $7,000, Treasurer $5,000.

During World War II, we produced more than $12,000,000 worth of equipment for the services. We were awarded the Army-Navy E, one of the few small companies to receive it. We asked for no financial relief during that period. It is only the pressure of the present economic situation that regretfully forces us to do so as allowed under Executive Order 10210.

In the event this request for relief is denied, it will seriously impair the ability of the company to deliver on present and future prime and subcontracts with the United States Government.

(*Signed*) GEORGE DAYMON, General Manager

Lieutenant Canning set to work methodically to build up an analysis procedure. After studying Public Law 921 and related regulations, he acquainted himself with the four contracts in question. He then studied in detail the claims and statements made in the letter. With this background assimilated, he felt himself ready to determine whether the government should amend its contract upward by $165,000.

Exhibit 1

YANKEE ASSEMBLERS, INC.
BALANCE SHEET, JUNE 30, 1951

ASSETS		
Current Assets:		
Cash	$ 28,000	
Net Accounts Receivable	75,000	
Inventory	400.000	
Total Current Assets		$503,000
Fixed Assets:		
Machinery	$ 10,000	
Less: Reserve for Depreciation	8,000	
Net Machinery		2,000
Office Equipment	$ 12,000	
Less: Reserve for Depreciation	9,000	
Net Office Equipment		3,000
Motor Vehicles	$ 10,000	
Less: Reserve for Depreciation	4,000	
Net Motor Vehicles		6,000
Total Assets		$514,000
LIABILITIES AND NET WORTH		
Current Liabilities:		
Notes Payable	$385,000	
Accounts Payable	60,000	
Accrued Expense	10,000	
Total Current Liabilities		$455,000
Capital:		
First Preferred Stock	$180,000	
Second Preferred Stock	10,000	
Common	15,000	
(Deficit)	−149,000	
Profit for Preceding Six Months	3,000	
		59,000
Total Liabilities and Net Worth		$514,000

The file on Yankee Assemblers contained the current balance sheet and profit and loss statement shown in Exhibits 1 and 2. In addition, there were letters of praise for Yankee Assemblers from two major electronics manufacturers, excerpts of which read as follows:

[*Manufacturer A:*] We believe they are operating at least possible cost consistent with their excellent-quality work. The co-operation of this subcontractor has been very good and the administration of their job excellent.

[*Manufacturer B:*] Our experience with Yankee Assemblers has extended over a period of years and has been wholly satisfactory as to quality of workmanship, conformance to contractual agreement, and co-operation in administration of subcontracts.

A copy of a nine-month-old report from an Army group that had received 25 of one of the Yankee Assemblers' new items was not so complimentary. Although none of these items were returned for factory repair, all required several alterations and repairs at the Army depot before they could be placed in service. Some of these repairs were necessitated by defects which the Army personnel called "careless workmanship."

Exhibit 2

YANKEE ASSEMBLERS, INC.

PROFIT AND LOSS STATEMENT, JANUARY 1, 1951—JUNE 30, 1951

Net sales to commercial customers	$115,000		
Net sales to government		$260,000	
Cost of sales to commercial customers	90,000		
Cost of sales to government		245,000	
Gross profit commercial sales	$ 25,000		
Gross profit government sales		$ 15,000	
Total gross profit			$40,000
Administrative expense			38,000
Operating profit			$ 2,000
Other income			1,000
Net Profit first six months of 1951			$ 3,000

A six-month-old letter from the Chief of the Bureau of Aeronautics was more favorable. It read in part: "Performance under this contract is highly commended. It is considered that the continued contribution of Yankee Assemblers, Inc., is highly essential to the over-all defense effort."

Lieutenant Canning's next step was to contact the other armed services. He sent a letter to each Navy bureau and Army organization which had given contracts to Yankee Assemblers. In the letter he requested information as to whether there were other suppliers capable of producing the item which Yankee Assemblers had manufactured for the particular service and whether such sources had present available capacity, and a definite statement as to whether Yankee Assemblers was considered a source essential to national defense. Despite the fact that there was already a letter in the files from the Bureau of Aeronautics, Lieutenant Canning requested more current information from that Bureau.

With action started in the other services, Lieutenant Canning visited the contracting officers and buyers at Air Materiel Command who had dealt with Yankee Assemblers, Inc. He found a general feeling that Yankee Assemblers was not necessary to the defense effort. As summed up in the words of one contracting officer, "Anyone can make those black boxes. Don't give them a red cent."

Lieutenant Canning was not satisfied with generalities. With the aid of the Procurement Sources Section, he compiled a specific list, by product name, of the equipment manufactured by Yankee Assemblers, Inc. Then, item by item, he checked to find out who would make it if Yankee did not. This changed the picture to the extent that one contracting officer admitted that, at the particular time when the original contracts were awarded, there was no other firm better qualified than Yankee Assemblers to do this type of work. On the other hand, the buyers felt that some of the company's increased cost of material and delay in receipt of material had resulted from not placing their orders with suppliers as soon as they should. Lieutenant Canning also discovered that George Daymon, general manager of Yankee Assemblers, and the chief contracting officer in one buying section had engaged in several wordy altercations in the past.

The amount of information contained in the letter from George Daymon was far too scanty to satisfy the lieutenant. He arranged a trip to the plant of Yankee Assemblers as well as one to the plant of a competing company which had just been low bidder on a contract for an item which previously had been produced by Yankee. He spent a day at the competitor's plant familiarizing himself with the manufacturing processes necessary to perform that type of work.

The following day, Lieutenant Canning met with Mr. Daymon at the Yankee Assemblers' plant. After looking over the production operations, the two men adjourned to the general manager's office. Mr. Daymon spent some time explaining the industry position of his company. He pointed out that the president, Mr. Palonis, drew no salary because he was independently wealthy and took a great deal of pride in the fact that his company had such a fine record in defense work. Mr. Daymon showed a backlog of $3,000,000 in orders and stated that in the last nine weeks they had been offered orders in the amount of $15,000,000. He proudly declared that the company had enough faith in the future so that management currently was planning a $100,000 plant expansion.

Lieutenant Canning asked why a competing company had been able to underbid Mr. Daymon on a product which Yankee had previously made. The general manager pointed out that the competitor had not known what he was getting into and had already run into production problems. In fact, the competitor had been to Yankee Assemblers three times since receiving the contract to obtain engineering help. The Air Force regional office had, in fact, suggested that they go to Yankee Assemblers for this help. Mr. Daymon went on to state that his firm had a Munitions Board availability rating and that not more than 10 per cent of his competitors had been given such a rating. Lieutenant Canning, upon further investigation, discovered that a Munitions Board rating was of little consequence in times of less than full-scale mobilization, and thus he tended to discount its value as a meritorious attainment of Yankee Assemblers, Inc.

Lieutenant Canning believed that he still required more specific evidence. He asked Mr. Daymon to submit additional information in support of his basic letter. In particular, he asked Mr. Daymon to describe the extra costs for which relief was requested under these separate headings: (1) Those costs over which the company normally had some control. For example, those costs caused by delay in receipt of material, defective work, etc. (2) Those costs over which the company had no control and which were believed to have been caused by the government, such as delay in testing the first article, failure to notify when first article accepted, etc. (3) Those costs over which the company and the government had no control, such as lack of critical material, rising prices, labor shortages, etc.

As further supporting evidence, Lieutenant Canning asked for the dates of all purchase orders that Yankee Assemblers had placed to support the four contracts in question. Mr. Daymon agreed to obtain all this information immediately. The lieutenant left the same evening with the feeling that he would receive all co-operation possible from Yankee Assemblers.

His next step was to arrange a meeting with six representatives from the regional office. He discovered that, in general, they were favorably disposed to granting aid to the company. It seemed to them that the case should be decided, not in terms of whether the company was necessary to national defense at the moment, but rather whether Yankee Assemblers was essential at the time the contract was granted to it. The fact that the company received negotiated contracts appeared to be some evidence to them of its essentiality at that time. They also pointed out, as an offsetting factor, that the president of Yankee Assemblers, who was also the major stockholder, had sufficient outside resources so that it was improbable he would let the company get into any serious financial difficulty even if the government did not come to his aid.

One of the men stated that he found the company to be unco-operative in furnishing information. He believed that some of the difficulty had been caused by slow placement of purchase orders. Another conferee quickly retorted that everyone had material troubles at this time.

Still another man pointed out that many of the major electronics manufacturers in the area had only high praise for Yankee Assemblers' work as a subcontractor. He wondered if the company might be found essential to national defense as a subcontractor, even though determined to be nonessential as a prime contractor.

Before leaving the area, Lieutenant Canning checked with the quality-control people at the district office. He found that the company was in the process of changing over its quality-control system and expected to have the new control operating in two months. In the past, the company had been short of inspection personnel, and those available had not been properly trained. Management, however, had co-operated with the Air Force inspectors and had the new system installed as soon as possible.

Back at his desk in AMC, Lieutenant Canning found a letter from the Bureau of Aeronautics. It listed ten contractors with equal or better facilities capable of manufacturing the entire range of Yankee Assemblers products. Eight of these companies had current open capacity. Five additional companies were listed with mobilization capacity.

The letter went on to state that the Bureau of Aeronautics' last experience with Yankee had been in 1947. In 1952, Yankee had not been low bidder on any Bureau of Aeronautics contracts. They considered that the plant was located outside of any possible enemy action and had an outstanding no-strike labor record. Despite this, the Bureau of Aeronautics did not consider Yankee Assemblers an essential source for the products it manufactured. The letter was signed by a different officer from the one who signed the previous letter.

Another letter from the Bureau of Ships, Navy Department, stated in part:

> 1. The loss of Yankee Assemblers, Inc., services to the Bureau would result in a delay of approximately 18 months in delivery of the equipment under contract. New procurements would have to be initiated and production models tested prior to establishment of new production lines. In such event, present test equipment would, of necessity, be used during the period of delay.
>
> 2. In spite of the foregoing, the Bureau of Ships cannot support a finding that Yankee Assemblers, Inc., as a supplier of defense items, is essential to National Defense in so far as this Bureau is concerned.

A final letter from the Signal Corps, Department of the Army, substantiated the view that Yankee Assemblers, Inc., was not essential to National Defense, and went on to say that no procurements had been placed with the company in recent months due to high bids.

With the mass of information available, Lieutenant Canning tried to sum up his progress to date. He had discovered that the over-all performance of Yankee Assemblers was excellent. There had been some delays in delivery, but on investigation he believed that these were largely due to slow processing of contract charge notices by Air Materiel Command. Moreover, Lieutenant Canning, as a result of his investigation, was convinced that the company had placed all of its purchase

Exhibit 3

YANKEE ASSEMBLERS, INC.

REGULATIONS GOVERNING THE EXERCISE OF CERTAIN AUTHORITY GRANTED BY TITLE II OF THE FIRST WAR POWERS ACT, AS AMENDED, AND EXECUTIVE ORDER NO. 10210, ISSUED THEREUNDER

PART I. GENERAL CONSIDERATIONS

. . . .

3. The authority granted by the Act and the Executive Order as described herein is an extraordinary one and its exercise must be carefully administered. Carelessness and laxity on the part of contractors should not be encouraged by the practice of granting relief to such contractors even though denial of relief in a particular case may result in some lack of cooperation on the part of a contractor.

PART II. STANDARDS GOVERNING EXERCISE OF AUTHORITY

1. Any action taken under this Part II must be based on a finding that the national defense will be facilitated thereby.

2. The determination of whether in a particular case a contract amendment to be entered into without consideration, or the correction of a mistake or ambiguity in a contract, or the formalization of an informal commitment will facilitate the national defense is a matter of sound judgment to be made on the basis of all of the facts of such case. Although it is obviously impossible to predict or enumerate all the types of cases with respect to which relief may appropriately be granted, examples of certain cases or types of cases where relief may be proper are set forth below. Such enumeration is not intended to exclude other cases where the circumstances are such as to warrant the granting of relief, and even in the enumerated cases other factors may result in a denial of relief.

a. Amendments without consideration

(1) Where an actual or threatened loss on a defense contract, however caused, will impair the productive ability of a contractor whose continued operation as a source of supply is found to be essential to the national defense, the contract will generally be equitably adjusted to the extent necessary to avoid such impairment of the contractor's productive ability.

(2) Where a contractor suffers a loss (not merely diminution of anticipated profits) on a defense contract as a result of Government action, the character of the Government action will generally determine whether any adjustment in the contract will be made and its extent.

(*a*) Where the Government action is directed primarily at the contractor

Exhibit 3—Continued

and is taken by the Government in its capacity as the other contracting party, the contract may be equitably adjusted if fairness so requires. Thus, where such Government action, although not creating any liability on its part, increases the cost of performance, considerations of fairness may make appropriate some equitable adjustment in the contract.

(*b*) When the action is not taken by the Government in its capacity as the other contracting party, but in its sovereign capacity, relief will generally not be granted. However, exceptional cases, depending on the nature of the action, the circumstances, and the effect on the contractor, may require an equitable adjustment in the contract when necessary to insure maximum cooperation and production in the national defense effort.

Exhibit 4

YANKEE ASSEMBLERS, INC.

AIR FORCE CONTRACT ADJUSTMENT BOARD PROCEDURE NO. 1
(Incl. to DOI 70–65)

PART I

Requests for Amendments without Consideration

Amendments without consideration require approval of the Board. Requests therefore, which are favorably recommended, shall be submitted to the Board for decision. Requests which are unfavorably considered by contracting officers or high authority concerned may be denied by such persons and in such event need not be submitted to the Board.

1. Each request forwarded to the Board for action will be accompanied by a full statement of the circumstances surrounding the relief requested, including, but not limited to, the following information. Affidavits of parties concerned should be obtained where deemed necessary or advisable.

a. Provisions and status of contract

(1) A copy of the contract, as amended, will be furnished.

(2) Brief description of contract indicating date executed, items being procured, price, delivery schedule, and special clauses, such as, price adjustment, progress payment and advance payment clauses.

(3) Extent of completion of performance and amounts paid (including advance payments and progress payments), indicating whether final payment has been made on the contract as theretofore amended.

(4) A statement showing whether a claim or dispute with respect to the subject matter of the request has been referred to the General Accounting Office or other Government agency, and the status thereof.

b. Factors creating need for relief

(1) Nature of items being procured (standard, new or experimental).

(2) Previous experience of contractor with similar production.

(3) Changes in conditions or Government action affecting contractor's costs.

(4) Cost experience of the contractor under the contract, and relation to original estimates.

Exhibit 4—Continued

(5) Reserves or allowances included in original price for the particular contingency out of which the request for relief arises. Nature and amount of reserves or allowances for other contingencies included in original price and an analysis of the extent, if any, to which such other reserves or allowances have been exhausted or utilized.

(6) An explanation should be given as to why the matter cannot be, or has not been, handled under the terms of the contract itself.

c. *Importance of contract or contractor to national defense*

(1) Size of contract and need for item.

(2) Available sources of supply other than the contractor.

(3) Quality of performance by contractor (rate of production, delays, rejections).

(4) Probable future orders to contractor for such item, or for other national defense work.

d. *Extent of relief needed*

(1) Analysis of financial position of contractor, with certified balance sheets and certified profit and loss statements, together with such supporting schedules, to the extent practicable, as are necessary to a full understanding of the financial condition of the contractor immediately prior to the execution of the subject contract, throughout the contract period, and as near the date the request is forwarded to the Board as may be practicable.

(2) Estimates of future costs under the contract accompanied by an analysis of all variances from costs as originally estimated by the contractor, together with an explanation of the cause or causes for any such variances.

(3) Other defense contracts and brief summary of other government and nongovernment business of contractor, indicating to the extent possible the estimated profits anticipated under such contracts.

(4) Statement of responsible officer of contractor setting forth the exact relief needed.

(5) Effect of granting relief on profits before federal income taxes.

(6) Comparison with prices of other contractors within the same industry.

(7) Effect of refusing relief.

(8) There should be indicated whether the costs involved, if any, which would be reimbursed to the contractor, were considered as part of the contractor's gross costs in statutory renegotiation proceedings, the amount of refund of excessive profits, and to what extent, if any, the probability of obtaining the relief now proposed was considered.

(9) The exact relief recommended.

orders for supplies with the least amount of delay. As he thought about the problem, and reviewed excerpts relating to Public Law 921 (see Exhibits 3 and 4), he believed that the following determinations were sound:

1. So far as he could determine, this case involved more money than any theretofore processed under Public Law 921. Any decision must be considered in the context of the amount involved.

2. If any other military department or branch thereof stated that Yankee Assemblers, Inc., was essential to its particular defense program, then he would recommend that the Air Force grant the necessary relief under Public Law 921.

3. Essentiality for National Defense, so far as Public Law 921 was concerned, rested upon "continued operation" of the facilities in question; or, to put it another way, essentiality had to be in terms of future or present requirements, not past needs, for relief to be obtainable under the regulations.

Lieutenant Canning recommended in a report to his immediate superior, Major White, that the company's request for relief under Public Law 921 be denied. His report became the basis for formal denial of the company's request. The letter so advising the company gave no details as to the Air Force findings and reasons, nor were any alternatives suggested.

Avtex Engineering, Inc.

Early in 1953, Mr. Robert Evans, president of the Avtex Engineering company in Texas, was seeking to re-establish a recently canceled Air Force order for electronic-controlled navigation units. He believed that he had adequate data to substantiate both the technical superiority and the lower cost of his company's product, in contrast to that of the supplier whose contract had been continued.

Mr. Evans also recognized his own relative inexperience on the complex problem of military contract negotiations. He took seriously the warnings given to him by business associates regarding the extreme danger of permanent impairment of his ability to do business with the military services. In particular, he had been cautioned against aggressive sales efforts which might seem straightforward and logical from the business viewpoint but which might violate the unwritten military codes.

Mr. Evans, at the age of thirty-six, was relatively young in executive experience as well as in years. He had graduated as an electronic engineer in 1938, and he started his business career in the sales department of a major automobile company. In 1948 the automobile company transferred him to a newly organized electronic division as a project engineer. In mid-1950 the company transferred him to a sales engineering position in the electronic division, with compensation appreciably above that ordinarily paid to engineers of his age and experience.

While employed by the electronic division during the early part of 1949, Mr. Evans had joined with another engineer in the same company to back a new business idea which had evolved from a series of informal discussions. The two men had decided that a need existed for an electronics engineering firm which would supply the functions of an engineering department for a number of small businesses in the Southwest and which could also handle overflow assignments for larger firms whose need periodically exceeded the capacity of their own technical staff.

Accordingly, on May 26, 1949, the two men—Mr. Evans and his associate, Mr. Carl Allen—incorporated Avtex Engineering, Inc. Carl Allen resigned from his position with the automobile company in order to devote full time to the new business. Except for a few hundred dollars required to cover incorporation proceedings, the men put no capital into the organization. For the first year, the firm consisted of Mr. Allen, two younger engineers, and one secretary.

By mid-1950, business was expanding at such a rate that Carl Allen urged Mr. Evans to join Avtex on a full-time basis. Finally, late in September of 1950, Evans resigned from his position with the automobile company and joined the new firm. Just three weeks later, Carl Allen died of a heart attack and Robert Evans became president of the organization. Under Evans' management, the firm continued to expand. By the end of 1952 it had over 200 employees and an annual revenue of approximately $2,500,000. The margin of profit on this work, before taxes, averaged about 12 per cent.

The business problem that was giving Mr. Evans particular concern in the early part of 1953 involved a contract similar to one which Avtex had been instrumental in developing for one of their clients, the Master Control Company. Peacetime sales of the Master Control Company consisted largely of electrical equipment for automotive plants. By the beginning of 1951, restrictions on the use of critical materials forced a shrinkage from 300 employees to 75. At that time, Mr. Evans suggested that he might make his firm's experience with electronic navigation systems available to the Master Control Company in order to develop a military contract proposal for that company.

The relationship thus developed between the two companies provided that Avtex would do all the engineering and would prepare the proposal, with both companies sharing equally in the expense. Thereafter, Avtex would have the engineering assignment in the event that the Master Control Company received a contract award.

Early in 1951 the Master Control Company first received a contract totaling $2,300,000 for development and for an initial production quantity of electronic-controlled navigation units to be used on long-range intercontinental bombers. An additional $12,500,000 contract was issued early in 1952, bringing the total to $14,800,000. Out of that total, the Avtex Engineering organization was allocated $197,000 for engineering services.

During this period, Avtex Engineering, Inc., had developed a widely recognized position of technical leadership in the development of electronic navigation systems. Four other clients of the Avtex organization had also received contract awards for similar electronic systems designed by Evans and his associates. These companies had a backlog of orders totaling approximately $68,000,000, which was estimated to be around 25 per cent of all such items produced for Air Force use.

Early in 1952 the Avtex Engineering company received a request from the Air Materiel Command for a quotation on the design and manufacture of another new electronic navigation system especially designed for use on one of the newer-type intercontinental bombers. Mr. Evans found that only three such requests for bids had been circulated, the other two going to large long-established companies. Since the contract might involve close to $20,000,000, Evans knew that the Avtex Engineering company itself did not have either the facilities or the financial qualifications to handle the contract. Moreover, their currently active clients, such as the Master Control Company, were unable to handle any more work.

In view of the fact that one of the other two companies that had been invited by the Air Force to bid on the pending contract had had a most unsatisfactory experience recently on similar work, Mr. Evans was confident that this company would either not submit any bid or would submit one which was intentionally noncompetitive. Thus, the only real competition was expected to come from the second company, a major producer of electrical equipment. That company was already receiving a price of $27,000 for a functionally identical unit. This price, moreover, did not include that company's developmental expenses or tooling costs, which had already been amortized. Based upon published contract information, Mr. Evans was able to determine that the total cost per unit of the units being secured from this other supplier, including engineering and tooling charges, was approximately $60,000 per unit. Evans was thoroughly convinced that a technically superior unit could be developed, tooled, and produced for less than half the $27,000 "production price" that the existing contractor was obtaining.

Accordingly, Evans selected a company, the Union Electro Corporation, which he believed was well qualified to handle the work. Although the Union Electro Corporation was only a medium-sized company employing about 600 workers, it was widely recognized throughout the automotive industry as a reliable producer of high-quality electrical equipment. The company had an excellent credit standing and strong financial reserves. Union Electro had handled an appreciable volume of military contracts since World War II and had a good record of military production during the 1940–45 period.

Avtex accordingly proposed an arrangement with Union Electro similar to the one that had worked satisfactorily with the Master Control Company. The two firms agreed to work on that basis. Avtex Engineering accordingly prepared a proposal which was submitted to the Air Materiel Command. This proposal resulted in the Union Electro

Corporation's obtaining a contract for 1,500 units at a price of $17,300 each. This price included development and tooling. The contract form employed was the so-called "Form No. 4 contract," which included provision for price redetermination up or down to a maximum of 10 per cent at the end of the developmental period. The contract price included a provision for $400,000 to cover the engineering, construction, and testing of nine prototypes which were allocated to Avtex as a subcontract. Avtex received its subcontract order to proceed on this work during the first week of June, 1952.

By early October, Avtex Engineering had completed an estimated 55 per cent of the work, including all developmental engineering and fabrication of the first three prototypes. At this point, the Air Force reduced their estimated requirements for these electronic navigation units and canceled the contract with the Union Electro Corporation.

When the contract was canceled, Avtex Engineering submitted its costs to Union Electro for payment, showing that a little over 55 per cent of the $400,000 job had already been completed. The costs that Avtex had incurred amounted to more than $200,000. The Air Force auditor ruled, however, that since the subcontract called for the delivery of nine prototypes and only three had been fabricated, Avtex was entitled to only 33⅓ per cent rather than 55 per cent of the total amount of their subcontract. By early 1953, this question had still not been resolved, and Mr. Evans had to decide whether to appeal to higher authority or to relinquish in the event that the contracting officer continued to support the ruling of the Air Force auditor.

Whether or not he succeeded in obtaining the difference between the amount Avtex had billed to Union Electro and the amount recommended by the Air Force auditor had not, however, concerned Mr. Evans nearly so much as had the problem of obtaining either reinstatement of the original contract or else issuance of a new prime contract to Avtex for completion of the engineering and developmental work. He believed completion of the work to be completely justifiable on every consideration of technical and financial merit.

Mr. Evans was unable to determine at the Air Materiel Command headquarters at Wright Field exactly why and on what basis the decision to reduce the requirements for these navigational units had been reached. He then went to the Strategic Air Command base at which the intercontinental bomber equipment was being tested; and he found that the reduction in Air Force requirements had been based upon a partial test during one flight, which he considered too short for adequate measurements, and upon certain engineering assumptions that had been originated by a committee of officers. These officers were experienced combat pilots; but, as far as he could determine, they had had little training in electrical engineering. Upon the basis of such data, which appeared totally inadequate and inconclusive to Mr. Evans, this committee of officers had decided that the new electronic system would not produce the intended results in service. They had accordingly decided to cut back that part of the budget in order to use the funds on an item in which at least one member of the committee expressed more interest and confidence.

Mr. Evans was, however, advised by the senior colonel in charge of the total intercontinental navigation project that in this officer's opinion the recent partial tests were inconclusive and that the full requirements, as originally determined for the electronic navigation system, still existed. Evans discovered, in fact, that sharp differences of opinion were to be found in various Air Force offices as to whether or not the contract with Union Electro should have been canceled. He concluded that most of those officers who were actually in senior positions and who were best equipped to pass judgment were in favor of continuing the original procurement.

The particular contract with which Mr. Evans was concerned had been issued by the Air Materiel Command but was "audited" by the Wright Air Development Center (WADC) in Ohio, which was a branch of the recently created Air Research and Development Command (ARDC) with headquarters in Baltimore. Evans reported to his associates that the officers exercising authority at the WADC were frank in their admission to him that they had recently been directed to proceed with the full original program by the ARDC headquarters in Baltimore, but that they were not bound to do as directed by the Baltimore headquarters and had decided at WADC to curtail the program to an extent that no longer necessitated maintenance of Union Electro as a source. The other contractor, although charging a higher price, they explained, was an experienced supplier with known capacities and a long record of outstanding performance; consequently, when the reduced Air Force requirements permitted continuing only one source, the better-established facility had been selected.

Mr. Evans next proceeded to the ARDC headquarters in Baltimore. While there, he was advised by a colonel in the commanding general's office that a favorable decision had been made by the general regarding retention of the original full requirements for the electronic navigation units. The favorable decision, he was told, had been based on a report by the colonel responsible for such decisions at the Strategic Air Command (SAC); and this report had advised the commanding general of ARDC as to the need to have the full program continued, in order to fulfill SAC operational requirements.

While Evans was at the ARDC headquarters in Baltimore, he was unable to locate the ARDC lieutenant colonel in charge of the electronic navigational project. The same officer handled the liaison work between ARDC and Wright Field. Evidently, this lieutenant colonel was not in his office during the period of several days that Evans was in Baltimore. Neither was Evans able to determine precisely when he would be accessible. He thus had to return to Texas without seeing the responsible ARDC officer.

Evans believed that he had found sufficient evidence with respect to the continuing requirements for the navigation units so that he could go to the commanding general of ARDC and demonstrate to him that the WADC group was acting independently and contrary to official determinations through proper command channels. He believed that he could make a convincing case to prove that the negative action by the WADC officers was unjustified.

Mr. Evans believed, also, that he could demonstrate the technical superiority, as well as the lower cost, of the unit that his firm had designed. Units meeting identical specifications that were being secured from the large established company were still costing the government over $27,000 each. He was prepared to demonstrate that the Union Electro Corporation, using the Avtex design, could produce the same quantity for less than half that price. Moreover, the newer unit designed by Avtex was about 11 per cent lighter. Although the new Avtex unit had not completed all of the actual service and flight tests, Mr. Evans believed that the results of tests to date had been sufficient to merit completion of the developmental work so that the Air Force would have the superior item, proved and available on the shelf when needed. He pointed out that the war reserve funds had been set up for just such purposes.

At this point, a business associate introduced Mr. Evans to a firm of "contractor representatives" who specialized in handling negotiations with Air Force officers. The top man in this firm of contract negotiators stressed the importance of the close personal relationships with influential officers that had been built up by lavish entertainment and special considerations. Mr. Evans had, in fact, recently been included in a party given in a suite at one of Washington's finest hotels by the contractor representative, a party providing costly entertainment for high-rank military officers.

This contractor representative also introduced Evans to another client, who explained how, with the representative's help, he had succeeded in avoiding price renegotiation proceedings on an exceedingly profitable item. This example and others led Mr. Evans to believe that the representative could indeed exercise a strong influence over the decisions of a small but powerful group of officers. Evans advised his associates that he believed this man could probably get the contract in question reinstated.

Evans also pointed out to his associates that the higher price charged by the large electrical company whose contract had been more profitable and secure included a liberal allowance for a highly paid staff engaged in a number of evidently expensive activities in Washington and at Wright Field. Since that staff consisted in part of former military officers who had little engineering or business experience, Evans considered their functions to be related to sales rather than to engineering or production.

After review of the evidence at their disposal, Evans and his associates had concluded that the difficulty they faced was "a special kind of a sales problem." They were unable to find any engineering, production, or financial aspect upon which the units they had designed did not seem, to them, to equal or excel those of the higher-cost producer.

Halt Metal Company

In October, 1946, the Halt Metal Company of Louisville, Kentucky, manufactured metal tubing and metal parts for furniture manufacturers and toy companies and was developing a few finished metal products which they hoped to expand into a full line as the demand for raw tubing and parts declined. The company manufactured tubular metal chair parts and table legs for chrome dinette sets. In 1946 it also made parts for 50,000 bar stools and manufactured about 10,000 chrome bathroom clothes racks, which it sold under its own brand name.

Originally organized as the Division Electric Company of Louisville, it operated both a vacuum-cleaner business and as, a part thereof, a small shop for bending and plating metal tubes. Inasmuch as the Division Electric Company had never made more than nominal profits during its first eight years, the president, Mr. Miller, decided in 1941 to sell the assets to satisfy creditors' claims. Not only was the business not up to a profitable sales level, but defense activities had limited the amount of aluminum castings available for vacuum cleaners.

All the vacuum-cleaner manufacturing equipment of the Division Electric Company was to have been sold at an auction sale in 1941. But Mr. Miller, having in mind the operation of a tubular metal company, segregated all the tube-handling equipment with the chrome and nickel plating tanks in one room of the basement of the Division Electric plant. On the day of the auction he took the auctioneer down to the room and asked for an estimate on the value of the machinery. The auctioneer said the equipment and inventory were worth approximately $16,000. Mr. Miller, subtracting the amount of the auctioneer's fees and the cost of advertising the sale, paid the Division Electric Company $15,000 for the equipment and inventory. This material was used to set up the Halt Metal Company.

The new company was located in the basement of the building which had housed the Division Electric Company. The initial capital of $15,000 was supplied by Mr. Miller ($10,000) and Mr. Hedden ($5,000), former general manager of the Division Electric Company. The company began operations on June 10, 1941, and during the remainder of the first year earned a net income of $2,173.

Exhibit 1

HALT METAL COMPANY

Statement of Profit and Loss

	% of Net Sales	1941	% of Net Sales	1942	% of Net Sales	1943	% of Net Sales	1944	% of Net Sales	1945
Net sales	100.00	$83,322.55	100.00	$111,636.68	100.00	$235,229.93	100.00	$522,197.15	100.00	$690,934.52
Cost of goods sold	88.54	73,776.41	76.82	85,754.85	76.29	179,445.91	75.99	396,807.46	74.60	515,408.34
Gross profit	11.46	$ 9,546.14	23.13	$ 25,881.83	23.71	$ 55,784.02	24.01	$125,389.69	25.40	$175,526.18
General expense	8.36	6,964.38	15.80	17,639.96	10.06	23,661.39	7.10	37,051.76	6.07	41,961.47
Operating profit	3.10	$ 2,581.76	7.33	$ 8,241.87	13.66	$ 32,122.63	16.91	$ 88,337.93	19.34	$133,564.71
Add: Other income	0.20	169.73	0.51	569.51	0.005	1,075.47	0.41	2,175.12	0.005	4,089.30
Less: Other deductions	.....	....	.....	....	0.005	1,069.25	0.68	3,609.25	0.005	4,006.63
Net income (before federal taxes)	3.30	$ 2,751.49	7.89	$ 8,811.38	13.66	$ 32,128.85	16.64	$ 86,903.80	19.34	$133,647.38
Provision for federal income tax	0.69	577.81	3.22	3,599.51	9.37	22,032.50*	12.20	63,716.62†	14.08	97,324.67
Net income	2.61	$22,173.68	4.67	$ 5,211.87	4.29	$ 10,096.35	4.44	$ 23,187.18	5.26	$ 36,322.71

* $6,715.42 excess profits tax refund has been deducted from this total.
† $2,139.39 excess profits tax refund has been deducted from this total.
Source: Company records, 1941–45.

Exhibit 2

HALT METAL COMPANY
COMPARATIVE BALANCE SHE

	Original Statement June 10, 1941	*Dec. 31, 1941*	*Dec. 31, 19*
ASSETS			
Current Assets:			
Cash	......	$ 1,918.29	$ 7,423.6
United States Bonds	......	......	......
Accounts Receivable	......	6,529.72	8,359.6
Inventory—Materials and Supplies	$ 8,446.21	6,624.23	5,266.4
Postwar Tax Refund	......	......	......
Total Current Assets	$ 8,446.21	$15,072.24	$21,049.7
Prepaid Insurance	......	......	......
Fixed Assets:			
Buildings (on leased ground)	......	......	......
Machinery and Equipment	6,306.79	7,055.81	10,109.0
Furniture and Fixtures	247.00	247.00	247.0
Trucks	2,790.81	2,790.81	835.0
Less: Depreciation Reserve	......	811.55	1,199.8
Total Fixed Assets	$ 9,344.60	$ 9,282.07	$ 9,991.1
Total Assets	$17,790.81	$24,354.31	$31,040.9
LIABILITIES AND CAPITAL			
Liabilities:			
Accounts Payable	$ 2,790.81	$ 3,991.61	$ 2,127.3
Notes Payable	......	......	166.0
Accrued Wages	......	1,342.73	1,304.1
Accrued Social Security Taxes	......	1,093.23	868.6
Accrued Federal and State Taxes	......	753.06	4,189.2
Total Current Liabilities	$ 2,790.81	$ 7,180.63	$ 8,655.3
Capital Stock	15,000.00	15,000.00	15,000.0
2,000 Shares, Common	......	......	......
Par Value $10	......	......	......
Authorized—Issued 1,500 Shares	......	......	......
Surplus	......	2,173.68	7,385.5
Total Liabilities and Capital Stock	$17,790.81	$24,354.31	$31,040.9

By 1946 the company had ceased taking job orders from other manufacturers to utilize their equipment. Dinette parts constituted 70 per cent of Halt's output of bent and plated parts; 5 per cent were bar-stool parts; 14 per cent, velocipede handle bars and rear frames; and 11 per cent, clothes racks.

Mr. Miller, president of the old vacuum-cleaner company, became president of the Halt Metal Company when it was first formed. Mr. Hedden became the treasurer of the new company in charge of production, payrolls, and records. Mr. Miller, in his early fifties, was in poor health but had an extensive background in promoting and managing business ventures. He had a striking personality and supplied many of

	Dec. 31, 1943	*Dec. 31, 1944*	*Dec. 31, 1945*	*August, 1946*
ASSETS				
Current Assets:				
Cash	$29,528.70	$ 48,082.06	$ 19,965.54	$ 20,810.43
United States Bonds	5,000.00	15,000.00	30,000.00	39,083.80
Accounts Receivable	14,138.44	4,061.14	14,698.88	21,905.56
Inventory—Materials and Supplies	1,448.46	36,828.22	19,019.34	36,140.17
Postwar Tax Refund	2,139.38	8,854.80	2,139.38	....
Total Current Assets	$52,254.98	$112,826.22	$ 85,823.14	$117,939.96
Prepaid Insurance	....	342.75	316.69	316.69
Fixed Assets:				
Buildings (on leased ground)	....	....	15,936.22	15,936.22
Machinery and Equipment	16,329.02	20,376.28	63,402.87	70,193.93
Furniture and Fixtures	431.40	1,401.40	1,401.40	1,401.40
Truck	2,006.00	2,006.00	3,765.38	3,765.38
Less: Depreciation Reserve	2,812.01	5,187.25	9,065.71	14,497.11
Total Fixed Assets	$15,954.41	$ 18,596.43	$ 75,440.16	$ 76,799.82
Total Assets	$68,209.39	$131,765.40	$161,579.99	$195,056.47
LIABILITIES AND CAPITAL				
Liabilities:				
Accounts Payable	$11,764.77	$ 31,359.82	$ 7,113.23	$ 7,154.04
Notes Payable				....
Accrued Wages	1,954.91	3,051.81	2,202.24	5,153.16
Accrued Social Security Taxes	1,148.16	2,050.16	1,487.19	1,759.90
Accrued Federal and State Taxes	21,021.23	46,733.61	73,482.77	70,443.52
Total Current Liabilities	$35,889.07	$ 83,195.40	$ 84,285.43	$ 84,510.62
Capital Stock	15,000.00	15,000.00	15,000.00	15,000.00
2,000 Shares, Common	....	....	....	....
Par Value $10	....	....	....	....
Authorized—Issued 1,500 Shares	....	....	....	....
Surplus	17,320.32	33,570.00	62,294.56	95,545.85
Total Liabilities and Capital Stock	$68,209.39	$131,765.40	$161,579.99	$195,056.47

* $1,017.13 pledged to secure notes payable.
Note: $6,000 common-stock dividends paid 1944; $6,000 dividends on common stock paid 1945.
Source: Company records, 1941–46.

the ideas which the Halt company adopted. Because of his health, he did not desire to work long or regular hours.

Mr. Hedden was about fifty years of age. He had business background in the production field, having worked for some time for the American Telephone and Telegraph Company and having taught engineering in a college for five years.

Shortly after the company was formed in 1941, Mr. Miller left the Halt company to work with the War Production Board in Louisville. Mr. Hedden was made president and directed the company until Mr.

Miller returned early in 1945. When Mr. Miller left the company in 1941, he told Mr. Hedden that he was not sure that the company could be made profitable but urged him to salvage the company if possible.

The company had no organization chart. Mr. Hedden stated that titles were not important in the company and that Mr. Miller, as the majority stockholder, was the real boss of the business. "I never make any major management decisions without consulting Mr. Miller," said Mr. Hedden.

Mr. Miller left the War Production Board after one year because of differences with WPB officials, who, he said, did not understand business problems. After leaving the War Production Board, he did some independent consulting work for other manufacturers in the area. In 1943 he took a year's leave of absence because of illness. Mr. Miller customarily took two months off every summer and two months off every winter. Other top personnel were a superintendent and three foremen in the plants and a woman office head.

The board of directors was composed of Mr. Miller; Mr. Hedden; the head of the office force; and Mr. Miller's son-in-law, who had no other connection with the business. Mr. Miller said: "Of course, the board can be nothing but a rubber stamp for Mr. Hedden and myself, inasmuch as we own and operate the company."

Mr. Miller said his general policy was to reinvest as much of the company's earnings as possible in the business and to finance expansion only out of earnings. Although the company was short of working capital, surplus amounted to $62,000 at the end of 1945 and to $95,000 by September, 1946.

During the war years the company, because of metal shortages, switched to subcontracting and prime contracting work for the government. One of the first war contracts received by the company was to build emergency stretchers for the Red Cross, initially of metal and later of wood. The company also accepted subcontracts from various machinery firms and utilized their existing equipment. Mr. Hedden stated, however, that this policy was not completely successful because it was a jobbing business rather than manufacturing.

Mr. Hedden stated that he took a list of the company's machinery to a prospective client; but initially the clients would toss up their hands, saying that they could not use the Halt equipment. "I finally got smart," said Mr. Hedden, "and did not take a list of all the equipment with me. Someone would ask me if we could make a certain product; I would agree, take the contract, rush back to Louisville, and then go around to secondhand machinery dealers and buy the necessary used equipment to handle the contract." Such policies enabled the company to secure a substantial volume of subcontract work in 1942, 1943, and 1944. When machines were no longer needed, they were sold or scrapped. In 1944 a small nearby shop was leased to expand production. Beginning in 1945, the company negotiated prime contracts with the United States government for the manufacture and assembly of bomb-holding adapters. This contract work was possible because Mr. Miller had secured certification from the Smaller War Plants Corporation authorizing the company to handle prime contracts. All this work stopped upon cessation of hostilities.

Exhibit 3

YODER TUBE WELDING MILL

The new Tube Welding Mill, built by the Yoder Co. of Cleveland, Ohio, is housed in a spacious and modern addition to the main plant of the Halt Metal Company. This mill can produce high-finish tubular steel at the rate of up to 100 feet per minute.

Mr. Miller was convinced that no company could be profitable by merely buying tubing and then bending and plating it. He believed the bending and plating functions were too limited to support a profitable business. There were three competing firms in the area doing bending and plating work. In 1944, therefore, to make its own tubing the company had ordered a Yoder tube mill (Exhibit 3), which was capable of taking strip steel, curving it into tubes, welding it, and cutting it into desired lengths. This machinery, costing approximately $47,000, was delivered in October of 1945 and was put into immediate operation. To finance this machine the company was forced to use the reserve set aside for the federal income tax payment. In 1944, Mr. Miller also placed orders for large quantities of strip steel, which the Yoder machine could make into tubing. Difficulty was experienced in securing steel deliveries until arrangements were made with the Ashby Steel Company of Ashby, West Virginia, which was able to supply approximately 200 tons of strip steel a month.

A building approximately 40 by 100 feet was built on land adjoining the Halt Metal Company plant to house the Yoder machine. The building was built largely by chosen employees, retained after termination of prime contracts. This means of construction enabled the Halt company to maintain low capital investment. In 1946 the company was working two shifts, five days a week, except in the plating department, which worked three shifts, six days a week. During the coal-strike crisis in December, 1946, there was insufficient steel for two-shift operation. Rather than discharge the employees before the Christmas holidays, Mr. Miller put all night-shift employees on the job of painting and cleaning the plant and doing necessary repairs.

PRODUCTION

The work flow of the Halt company was inherently simple: (1) The Yoder tube-forming machine took the raw strip steel and processed it into tubes. These tubes were then buffed to remove the welded spots. (2) Raw tube was cut into desired lengths. (3) The cut tube lengths were bent into the desired shape. For example, to make a chair frame, eighteen bending operations were accomplished in thirty-one seconds by use of modern equipment. (4) The formed pieces of the tube were pierced in desired locations and buffed to eliminate any surface irregularities. (5) The pieces were nickel- and chrome-plated. (6) Finally, the pieces were wrapped and shipped.

The equipment of the Halt company varied from the most modern tube-forming equipment to handmade pieces of machinery which were used on some minor operations (see Exhibit 4). Four full-time skilled machine-tool repairmen maintained and rebuilt equipment. Mr. Hedden and Mr. Miller were satisfied with all operations except the plating room. Because of the great expense involved in buying automatic plating equipment—about $100,000 completely installed—plating was done entirely by hand, a laborious operation performed under the most undesirable working conditions. Workers in the plating room were paid on an hourly basis after experience had shown that piece-rate workers tended to give inadequate soaking to parts in the solution pits.

The company employed approximately 90 workers, most of whom were unskilled and semiskilled. Twelve of the employees were women, ased chiefly in wrapping and packaging operations. The company was not unionized, and Mr. Miller did not believe that the employees were dissatisfied with the present arrangement and therefore did not believe that there was a threat of unionization. Wage rates were reviewed every six months by Mr. Miller and Mr. Hedden to insure that the company's rates were as high as, or higher than, other rates in the community.

Mr. Hedden said the company used four incentives to secure higher production volume and lower labor costs. The first incentive was a

Exhibit 4

HALT METAL COMPANY
LIST OF PRINCIPAL EQUIPMENT

1	Yoder tube mill
1	Radiac abrasive cutoff
3	Automatic tube-bending machines (another on order)
4	Air compressors
8	Drilling machines—automatic feed
1	Shaper
1	Miller
3	Lathes
1	Planer
1	Surface grinder
1	Tool and cutter grinder
1	Electric hardening furnace—automatic heat controls
3	Buffing machines, new, individual drive
8	Buffing machines, rebuilt, individual drive
9	Power punch presses, 10 to 40 tons
6	Plating tanks—homemade
1	Hoop-rolling machine
1	Tube hoop-rolling machine, homemade
1	8-ton truck with winch
1	Plymouth sedan
	Gauges, micrometers, and measuring instruments
	Arch, torch, spot, and butt welding equipment
	Conveyor and hand trucks
	Office equipment, including an adding machine, comptometer, and calculator

piece-rate incentive plan, which allowed the worker to make from 30 per cent to 50 per cent above the day rate by voluntarily going on a piece-rate plan. The company, furthermore, had the policy of never reducing a piece rate, which meant that employees, by devising short cuts and improved methods of handling material, could increase their production and consequently increase their wages. The second incentive used by the company was a group incentive plan. If the company as a whole succeeded in reaching a certain work productivity goal for a monthly period, every employee, both direct labor and overhead, was given a 5 per cent bonus on his monthly salary. The third incentive plan was to give two company parties each year. At one of these parties the laborers had each been given $5.00 for every six months of service with the Halt company. The fourth incentive policy was a paid vacation plan.

Mr. Hedden said that he consciously patterned his wage and incentive programs after those of Mr. James L. Lincoln of the Lincoln Electric Company of Cleveland, Ohio. Mr. Hedden had had numerous conversations with Mr. Lincoln and hoped that the Lincoln practices would help make the Halt Metal Company as successful as the Lincoln company.

As an example of the importance of his labor philosophy, Mr. Hedden cited the condition existing when he assumed direction of the company in 1941. The company had no money, and its only assets consisted of inventories. Realizing the precarious situation with which the company was faced, Mr. Hedden spoke to the employees, told them of the serious financial condition, and said he wanted to be fair with them. To show that he did mean business, he had told the workers that he would raise the hourly wage from 60 cents to 70 cents an hour and the piece rates by a comparable amount. "Production of the company jumped from 900 units a week to 3,000 units a week as a result of this policy," stated Mr. Hedden.

Under the rulings of the Office of Price Administration an 11 per cent price increase was granted makers of tube steel in September, 1945, and Mr. Miller estimated that 50 per cent net profit could be made on all strip steel sold as raw tubing. The Yoder machine had a maximum capacity of approximately 1,000,000 feet a month. Two-shift operation was producing about 700,000 feet a month, which used all the strip steel obtainable. Between 200,000 and 300,000 feet of tubing were sold monthly as raw tubing to other manufacturers. Mr. Miller recognized, however, that this condition was temporary and that it was necessary to develop outlets currently for future tube production.

SALES

Throughout its experience, all sales were handled by Mr. Hedden and Mr. Miller, and no other sales personnel was employed. In 1941, over half of the company's sales were made to the Imperial Company, a group of five furniture manufacturers. A total of $55,492 out of the Halt Metal Company gross sales of $87,215 were made to the Imperial chain. The Allet Company purchased $31,234 worth of parts in 1941.

In 1942 the company's primary manufacturing operations were job contracting for miscellaneous firms. Out of gross sales of $113,733 the Imperial chain purchased $17,474 worth of products, and the Allet Company $9,963. The company's first war contract for emergency stretchers totaled approximately $35,000. The company also did some war work for the Boston Ordnance Depot on ejector pins. In 1942 the company was beginning to do work for the Barker Company, prime contractors on fire extinguishers for the Navy.

In 1943 the company sales totaled $235,230. Sales to the Barker Company amounted to $179,065. A higher percentage of sales for the year again were made up of job-contracting work.

Total sales in 1944 amounted to $522,197. Work for the Barker Company on applicators, ball shafts, and tool work amounted to $193,-770. The remainder of the sales were on a job-contract basis.

The primary source of orders in 1945 was the Boston Ordnance Depot. The company manufactured adapter clusters M12 and other small parts for the U.S. Army Air Force. Sales to the Boston Ordnance Depot alone amounted to over one-half million dollars.

In 1946 the Imperial Company purchased roughly 70 per cent of Halt's output. Less than 10 per cent was sold as finished products, and the remaining 20 per cent of sales consisted of miscellaneous parts chiefly bar-stool parts. The market for tubular metal furniture fluctuated sharply and in the fall of 1946 was depressed by the oversupply of metal parts manufactured by "war-baby" firms entering the field. The Halt company had a long-standing verbal agreement with the Imperial chain built up through mutual confidence to sell dinette parts only to Imperial, in return for which Imperial agreed to take the Halt company's entire output. This agreement enabled the Halt company to have a constant market at peak production and protected Imperial against Halt, as a low-cost producer, selling parts to competing furniture assemblers. The Imperial management desired to put this agreement in the form of a written contract, but Mr. Hedden believed that a written contract was unnecessary and a source of potential conflict.

During 1946, therefore, the Imperial chain continued to purchase all Halt dinette parts but immediately placed them in inventory, awaiting a more favorable market. Also, in 1946, $166,000 worth of bar-stool parts were sold to the Allet Company.

The company had had some merchandising experience while it was selling vacuum cleaners. When Mr. Hedden prepared to merchandise his new clothes rack (Exhibit 5, p. 484), he gave exclusive selling rights to Mr. Wardwell, a commission agent in New York. The Halt company sold the rack to him for approximately $2.50. Mr. Miller stated that it retailed for around $5.50. Mr. Wardwell was extremely enthusiastic about the sales possibilities of this item. During their original conversation, Mr. Hedden said, Mr. Wardwell had commented that a large department store would take 100,000 racks during 1946 if it was given exclusive sales rights and a reduction from 20 to 10 per cent in the broker's fees. Mr. Hedden said, however, that Mr. Wardwell did not

Exhibit 5

ADVERTISEMENT FOR CLOTHES RACK

want to fulfill this agreement. "Sales of the item are trickling in," said Mr. Hedden, "and we have several thousand racks in inventory. If Mr. Wardwell had given us all the business that he said he could, we would have had neither the metals nor the manufacturing experience to handle the item." Mr. Hedden also pointed out that Sears, Roebuck and Company had remarked that the product had very little sales potential, approximately three per store per year. In the latter part of 1946, Mr. Hedden and Mr. Miller became dissatisfied with Mr. Wardwell's performance and withdrew his franchise for the southeastern states. Mr. Miller's subsequent sales efforts in the Southeast more than doubled former sales. He also was handling export sales of the clothes rack, although he believed it was priced too high for extensive export. Mr. Wardwell remained in charge of sales in other geographic areas.

Since steel tubing was critically short in 1946, the Halt company had the opportunity to sell virtually its entire output of raw metal tubing directly to other manufacturers of metal-tubing products. It decided to process as much tubing as possible and to find markets for its fabricated products rather than depend on selling tubing directly. Mr. Miller estimated that the potential profits of the company would be the same if no processing of metal tubing was performed.

By expanding the operations of the Halt Metal Company to include forming the tubes and completing the fabrication of several products, the management believed the company had greatly increased its possibilities of continued profitability. By the time the postwar demands for steel and metal tubes had been met, the management hoped the company would have established itself in the market for metal parts and would have developed its line of brand products.

The company was contemplating the purchase of complete automatic plating equipment. Mr. Hedden believed that the equipment would pay for itself in two years and would permit about five times as much work with one fifth of the current personnel. Automatic plating equipment would give the Halt company the third of the three production elements the management believed essential for successful operation in its field: an efficient tube mill, good bending equipment, and automatic plating equipment.

The market for welded tubular metal was believed to be almost unlimited, and the Halt management hoped in time to do an annual business of $1,000,000. The management had considered, but not developed, many ideas for its product: trailers for boats, folding wheel chairs, frames for ironing boards and for machine-tool stands, and parts in the fuselage of aircraft.

INDEX OF CASES

Index of Cases

This book has been set on the Linotype in 12 and 10 point Garamond No. 3, leaded 1 point. Case titles are in 24 point Garamont italics. The size of the type page is 27 by 46½ picas.